IN LIFE AND DEATH:
ARCHAEOLOGICAL EXCAVATIONS AT THE QUEEN'S
CHAPEL OF THE SAVOY, LONDON

Spoilheap Monograph Series

1   A Neolithic ring ditch and later features at Staines Road Farm
Phil Jones
ISBN 978-0-9558846-0-3

2   Roman and Medieval Staines: the development of the town
Phil Jones with Rob Poulton
ISBN 978-0-9558846-1-0

3   Excavations at Oatlands Palace
Rob Poulton with Alan Cook and Simon Thurley
ISBN 978-0-9558846-2-7

4   Settlement sites and sacred offerings: prehistoric and later archaeology in the Thames Valley, near Chertsey
Graham Hayman, Phil Jones and Rob Poulton
ISBN 978-0-9558846-4-1

5   Upper Palaeolithic sites in the lower courses of the rivers Colne and Wey: excavations at Church Lammas and Wey Manor Farm
Phil Jones
ISBN 978-0-9558846-7-2

6   Living by the sword: the archaeology of Brisley Farm, Ashford, Kent
Jim Stevenson
ISBN 978-0-9558846-8-9

7   Alien cities: consumption and the origins of urbanism in Roman Britain
Dominic Perring and Martin Pitts
ISBN 978-0-9558846-9-6

8   A Mesolithic 'Persistent Place' at North Park Farm, Bletchingley, Surrey
Phil Jones
ISBN 978-0-9576509-0-9

9   Flavian and later buildings at Snodland Roman villa: excavations at Cantium Way, Snodland, Kent
Giles Dawkes
ISBN 978-0-9576509-3-0

10   Around the ancient track: archaeological excavations for the Brighton & Hove Waste Water Treatment Works and adjacent housing at Peacehaven, East Sussex
Diccon Hart
ISBN 978-0-9576509-4-7

11   Excavations on St Anne's Hill: A Middle/Late Iron Age site and Anglo-Saxon cemetery at St Anne's Road, Eastbourne, East Sussex
Anna Doherty and Christopher Greatorex
ISBN 978-0-9576509-8-5

12   Foragers and farmers: 10,000 years of history at Hengrove Farm, Staines. Excavations between 1997 and 2012
Rob Poulton, Graham Hayman and Nick Marples
ISBN 978-0-9576509-9-2

13   Between Thames and Medway: archaeological excavations on the Hoo peninsula and its environs
Giles Dawkes
ISBN 978-1-912331-00-0

14   Beside the River Trent: archaeological investigations at Shardlow Quarry, Derbysire
K Krawiec, A J Howard, and B R Gearey
ISBN 978-1-912331-01-7

15   The Boxgrove wider area project: Mapping the Early Middle Pleistocene deposits of the Slindon Formation across the coastal plain of West Sussex and Eastern Hampshire
M B Roberts and M I Pope
ISBN 978-1-912331-02-4

16   The moated medieval manor and Tudor royal residence at Woking Palace. Excavations between 2009 and 2015
Rob Poulton
ISBN 978-1-912331-03-1

17   In life and death: Archaeological excavations at the Queen's Chapel of the Savoy, London
Lucy Sibun and Paola Ponce
ISBN 978-1-912331-04-8

IN LIFE AND DEATH:
EXCAVATIONS AT THE QUEEN'S CHAPEL OF THE SAVOY, LONDON

by
Lucy Sibun and Paola Ponce

with contributions by

Michelle Alexander, Enid Allison, Luke Barber, Madeleine Bleasdale, Trista Clifford,

Susan Chandler, Patrick Daley, Jenna Dittmar, Hayley Forsyth, Rob Janaway

Susan Pringle, Elke Raemen, Justin Russell, Mark Samuel and Andrew Wilson

Illustrations by Fiona Griffin and Antonio Reis

Monograph 17

SpoilHeap Publications

A joint venture of Archaeology South-East (UCL Institute of Archaeology)
and Surrey County Archaeological Unit (Surrrey County Council)
2018

Produced by SpoilHeap Publications
a joint venture of Archaeology South-East (UCL) and Surrey County Archaeological Unit (Surrey County Council)
intended to provide a publication outlet for the results of archaeological investigation
and research from across south-east England

© Archaeology South-East, Centre for Applied Archaeology, UCL Institute of Archaeology and the authors 2018
2 Chapel Place, Portslade, East Sussex, BN41 1DR

All rights reserved. No part of this publication may be reproduced, stored in a retrieval system, or transmitted in any form or by any means, electronic, mechanical, photocopying, recording, or otherwise, without the prior permission of the publisher.

Modern map bases and outlines used in this volume are reproduced based on Ordnance Survey data © crown copyright and database right 2016.

Edited by Louise Rayner
Copy editing by Anne Marriott
Designed and typeset by Fiona Griffin

Front cover: Lead breast plate of Mr Francis Wadbrook [1430], died 14th February 1838 aged 54 years
Back cover: (clockwise from top) The eastern facade of the Queen's Chapel of the Savoy today; excavating the charnel pit [1237] looking west; painting of the fire that engulfed the Queen's Chapel of the Savoy 17th September 1860 ©Duchy of Lancaster; Poet George Wither (1588–1667) who is buried within the Queen's Chapel of the Savoy (©WL, V0006334 used under CC BY 4.0)

Printed by Lavenham Press, Suffolk, CO10 9RN

As for the trees and grass in the old churchyard (Chapel Garden) – they thrive wondrously for London Vegetation, and gather no smoke – they can scarcely be said to be green at early morn. The leaves and herbage seem chameleon-hued. You shall find maize and primrose in their lights, blue and purple in their shadows. Laminae of silver play on blades and veins; and upon my word, I think that on summer nights the dew falls here – the only dew that is shed in all London, beyond the tears of the homeless.

—Dickens, C. 1860 All the Year Round; A weekly Journal. Vol III (May 12th) 119

CONTENTS

CONTENTS vii
LIST OF FIGURES ix
LIST OF TABLES xiii
SUMMARY xvi
RÉSUMÉ xvii
ZUSAMMENFASSUNG xviii
ACKNOWLEDGEMENTS xix

1 INTRODUCTION AND BACKGROUND 1
1.1 Introduction 1
1.2 Archaeological background 1
1.3 Previous works and archaeological excavations 3
1.4 Structure of the book 3

2 LONDON AND THE SAVOY PRECINCT 5
2.1 Historical background 5
2.2 The Savoy Precinct 14

3 HISTORY OF THE SITE 19
3.1 Savoy Hospital 19
3.2 Savoy Barracks 28
3.3 Savoy Chapel and burial ground 40
3.4 Savoy improvements 47

4 BURIAL REGISTERS 49
4.1 The registers 49
4.2 Death and burial 61
4.3 Population studies 65

5 THE HUMAN REMAINS 67
5.1 Introduction 67
5.2 Demography 67
5.3 Stature 70
5.4 Preliminary isotopic analysis on bone collagen 71
5.5 Preliminary isotopic analysis on hair 72
5.6 Palaeopathology 73

6 ARCHAEOLOGICAL RESULTS 139
6.1 Introduction 139
6.2 Spatial analysis 139
6.3 Tombs and memorial stones 147
6.4 Identification of named individuals 150
6.5 Charnel 160
6.6 Burial-related finds 160
6.7 Non-burial features 172

6.8 Discussion 176

7 SPECIALIST REPORTS 179
7.1 Architectural stone 179
7.2 Miscellaneous stone..181
7.3 Pottery 181
7.4 Ceramic building material..185
7.5 Clay tobacco pipe..187
7.6 Coins 188
7.7 Musket ball 189
7.8 Other objects 190
7.9 Glass 191
7.10 Discussion...191

8 CONCLUDING COMMENTS 193

BIBLIOGRAPHY...197
INDEX 203

LIST OF FIGURES

Fig 1.1 Site location 2

Fig 1.2 Location of previous archaeological work 4

Fig 2.1 The Strand, 1560, from a map of Ralph Agas 6

Fig 2.2 Sir John Evelyn's plan for rebuilding London after the fire of 1666 8

Fig 2.3 Wood engraving depicting cramped and squalid housing conditions, Grey's Inn Lane 9

Fig 2.4 *The Gin Shop*, by George Cruikshank, 1829 10

Fig 2.5 George ('Graveyard') Walker 13

Fig 2.6 Hearth Tax data: Duchy of Lancaster/Savoy ward, 1666 15

Fig 2.7 Total population of the Savoy Precinct, 1801–1921 15

Fig 2.8 Total number of deaths as recorded in the London Bills of Mortality, 1657–1758 17

Fig 3.1 The church and hospital of Savoy, London, by George Virtue, 1750; Hospital of Santa Maria Nuova, Florence, Italy, etching, by B S Sgrilli after G Zocchi 20

Fig 3.2 Plan of the Savoy Hospital 21

Fig 3.3 Portrait of John Evelyn, by Nanteuil after himself 25

Fig 3.4 A copy of John French's *Art of Distillation*, London, 1651 27

Fig 3.5 Eighteenth-century military uniform 29

Fig 3.6 Hannah Snell, mezzotint, by J Young after R Phelps, 1789 31

Fig 3.7 Plan of the Savoy Barracks, 1736 32

Fig 3.8 Stephen Hales, mezzotint, by J McArdell after T Hudson 37

Fig 3.9 Image of ventilation apparatus devised by the Revd Stephen Hales, 1758 38

Fig 3.10 Savoy Chapel and Prison, by George Virtue, 1753 41

Fig 3.11 George Wither, line engraving, by T S Engelheart after J Payne, 1669 42

Fig 3.12 Anne Killigrew (self-portrait) 42

Fig 3.13 Dr Cameron being drawn on a sledge to Tyburn to be executed for high treason 44

Fig 3.14 Savoy Chapel and Prison, 1791 45

Fig 3.15 The fire of 1860: a – the outside of the chapel; b – the inside 46

Fig 4.1 Total number of deaths per decade 50

Fig 4.2 Sex distribution, 1720–1820 51

Fig 4.3 Sex distribution, 1680–1850 51

Fig 4.4 Total deaths per decade: males, females and soldiers 51

Fig 4.5 Living and dead population, 1800–59 52

Fig 4.6 Census data: population of the Savoy Precinct, 1801–51 52

Fig 4.7 Male and female distribution in the buried population, 1740–9 53

Fig 4.8 Male, female and soldier distribution in the buried population, 1790–9 53

Fig 4.9 Proportion of males, females and subadults, 1754–1854 54

Fig 4.10 Total burials per decade, 1790–1859: young adult 55

Fig 4.11 Total burials per decade, 1790–1859: prime adult 55

Fig 4.12 Total burials per decade, 1790–1859: mature adult 55

Fig 4.13 Total burials per decade, 1754–1854: subadults 56

Fig 4.14 Total burials per decade, 1750–1859: infant, child, juvenile 56

ix

Fig 4.15 Total burials by decade, 1780–1819, and age category: soldiers 57

Fig 4.16 Map showing the number of deceased from each parish buried in the Savoy burial ground 66

Fig 5.1 Location of skeletons referred to in Chapter 5 68

Fig 5.2 Distribution of the population by age..69

Fig 5.3 Comparison of stature estimation across cemeteries analysed 71

Fig 5.4 Mean $\delta^{15}N$ and $\delta^{13}C$ of human bone collagen and individuals with pathologies 72

Fig 5.5 Hair sample from skeleton [1716] 73

Fig 5.6 Incremental isotope analysis ($\delta^{13}C$) 73

Fig 5.7 Incremental isotope analysis ($\delta^{15}N$)..73

Fig 5.8 Skeleton [1807] showing: a – healing fracture of the right maxilla; b – healing fracture of the nasal bones 75

Fig 5.9 Skeleton [300] showing a healed spiral fracture of the left humerus 76

Fig 5.10 Skeleton [1719] showing anterior and lateral views of an oblique fracture of the right tibia and fibula 77

Fig 5.11 Radiography of disarticulated left femur showing an oblique and displaced fracture 78

Fig 5.12 Number of metacarpals fractured within the population...78

Fig 5.13 Number of metatarsals fractured within the population 79

Fig 5.14 Skeleton [643] showing views of a well-healed Bennett's fracture: a – lateral; b – medial 79

Fig 5.15 Skeleton [857] showing calcanei with ossification of the Achilles tendon: a – left; b – right...81

Fig 5.16 Comparison of Schmorl's nodes distribution among all individuals buried at the Savoy Chapel 82

Fig 5.17 Skeleton [996] showing cavitations on L1, L2 and L5 vertebral bodies and a slight anterior curvature of the spine following a wedge-shape and collapse of L1 83

Fig 5.18 Skeleton [589] showing extensive degeneration and exuberant marginal osteophytes on the left shoulder joint thought to relate to a dislocation; radiography showing sclerotic areas resulting from bone-to-bone contact 85

Fig 5.19 The endocranial and ectocranial views of a gun shot 86

Fig 5.20 The endocranial and ectocranial views of a gun shot 86

Fig 5.21 Comparison of spinal osteoarthritis among the adults from the Savoy Chapel 88

Fig 5.22 Skeleton [1498] showing palmar aspects of: a – left metacarpals; b – right metacarpals. Erosive lesions have partially destroyed the distal articular facets of the 2nd, 3rd and 5th right bones and the 2nd left 91

Fig 5.23 Skeleton [448] showing medial–lateral bending (scoliosis) of the thoracic spine (T2–T8) 93

Fig 5.24 Skeleton [208] showing superior and dorsal views of merged 1st and 2nd right ribs 95

Fig 5.25 Skeleton [1667] showing an ad hoc formed acetabulum for a dislocated left femur 96

Fig 5.26 Skeleton [679] showing views of an example of symphalangism of the 2nd digit from the left hand: a – palmar; b – dorsal; c – lateral 97

Fig 5.27 Skeleton [1369] showing a synostosis of the right tibia and fibula..98

Fig 5.28 Skeleton [1319] showing: a – the left os trigonum detached and missing from the talus; b – the right os trigonum partially fused to the parent bone; c – a healing stage of osteochondritis dissecans on the left talus with a partially reattached loose ossicle; d – a non-healed lesion on the right talus..98

Fig 5.29 Skeleton [1767] showing bilateral os navicular 99

Fig 5.30 Skeleton [1178] showing division of the os cuneiform: a – incomplete; b – complete...99

Fig 5.31 Skeleton [652] showing reactive woven bone (periostitis) on the visceral aspect of right-side ribs................................101

Fig 5.32 Skeleton [566] showing new bone formation on the left maxillary sinus, thought to relate to maxillary sinusitis 101

Fig 5.33 Skeleton [1074] showing a large focal periosteal reaction on the left tibia, thought to relate to a skin ulcer................102

Fig 5.34 Skeleton [525] showing endocranial lesions on the occipital bone 103

Fig 5.35 Skeleton [1518] showing views of the left maxillary sinus: a – superior; b – anterior; c – lateral....................................104

Fig 5.36 Skeleton [1360] showing the lateral views of T1–L1 and the collapse of T1–T11 owing to the destruction of their vertebral bodies. Note the wedge-shape of T10..105

Fig 5.37 Skeleton [939] showing: a – healing caries sicca lesions on the frontal bone; b – newly formed lesions on the left parietal. Close-up images show periosteal reaction on proximal, distal and diaphyseal areas of long bones 108

Fig 5.38 Views of a disarticulated right femur with typical snail-track pattern of gummatous periostitis, thought to relate to tertiary syphilis: a – anterior; b – medial; c – posterior 111

Fig 5.39 Skeleton [1719] showing maxillary teeth with circular and semicircular grooves, thought to result from clenching clay tobacco pipes: a – medial–lateral right; b – medial–lateral left 118

Fig 5.40 Skeleton [1770] showing anterior–posterior and medial–lateral bending of the lower limb bones, thought to relate to rickets 121

Fig 5.41 Distribution of rachitic subadults according to age 122

Fig 5.42 Distribution of scurvy in subadults according to age 123

Fig 5.43 Skeleton [731] showing views of T4 to T11 with the so-called 'candle wax' flowing ossification of the anterior longitudinal ligament, thought to relate to DISH: a – left; b – anterior; c – right 125

Fig 5.44 Skeleton [1090] showing: a – the flattened, mushroom-shaped, right femoral head; b – the normal left femoral head 126

Fig 5.45 Skeleton [1077] showing a typical 'punched-out' lesion on the anterior right side of the mandible, extending from the right 1st mandible to the left 1st incisor 128

Fig 5.46 Skeleton [490] showing: a – a cluster of lytic lesions on the inner table of the right parietal; b – scattered clusters of lytic lesions on the right ilium; radiograph showing multiple 'punched-out' holes; c – lytic lesions penetrating the right scapula; d – destructive lytic lesions affecting the vertebral bodies and apophyseal joints of C4–C5 129

Fig 5.47 Skeleton [1826] showing hypertrophy of the right inferior turbinate 131

Fig 5.48 Skeleton [1525] showing rib deformations thought to relate to the prolonged wearing of corsets 131

Fig 5.49 Skeleton [1304] showing abnormal lateral deviation of the big toes, thought to relate to the prolonged use of pointed shoes: a – left; b – right 132

Fig 5.50 Skeleton [445] showing views of a dissected skull: a – posterior; b – anterior; c – lateral right 135

Fig 5.51 Skeleton [1508]: SEM image of a kerf mark showing the diameter of a single pass with the saw blade vs multiple passes 137

Fig 6.1 Plan of excavation area showing all recorded skeletons 140

Fig 6.2 Excavation area within the burial ground 141

Fig 6.3 Phase plan 141

Fig 6.4 Examples of skeletons: a – truncated skeleton [147]; b – complete skeleton [1077] 142

Fig 6.5a Plan of adult burials located below 6.49m OD 143

Fig 6.6 Memorials and associated dates 144

Fig 6.7 Variations in the orientation of burials 146

Fig 6.8 Plan showing the location of tombs 147

Fig 6.9 Photograph of tomb [107] 148

Fig 6.10 Tomb ashlar with iron fittings 148

Fig 6.11 Mortar keying with jadd pick or racer 148

Fig 6.12 Finlay and kin memorial stone: a – photograph; b – transcription 149

Fig 6.13 Richard Lemon Lander 150

Fig 6.14 Excavation plan and superimposed 1930s burial ground survey 151

Fig 6.15 Identification of individuals by matching survey, archaeological and osteological data 154

Fig 6.16 Named individuals: a – skeleton [1473]; b – coffin plate for burial [597]; c – transcription of coffin plate 157

Fig 6.17 Coffin plaque for burial [1215] 157

Fig 6.18 Location of possible burial stacks/family graves 159

Fig 6.19 Photograph of burials [427] and [445] 160

Fig 6.20 Burial plan showing location of charnel pits 161

Fig 6.21 Charnel pit [1237] 161

Fig 6.22 Example of poor survival of wooden coffins on site – skeleton [1810] 162

Fig 6.23 Location of burials with coffins or evidence for coffins 163

Fig 6.24 Copper-alloy upholstery nails: a – with fabric remains; b – with black coating; c – triangular patterns; d – nails on the lid and sides; e – possible ovoid/eye-shaped nails with round examples in coffin wood as found 164

Fig 6.25 Lead coffin [1215] showing staining remains from wooden outer coffin 165

Fig 6.26 Inscription plate for Francis Wadbrook, [1430], and transcription 166

Fig 6.27 Grips: type 1, type 2a, type 4 166

Fig 6.28 Kingston-type grip and plate 167

Fig 6.29 Location of grips, grip plates and breast plates mentioned in the text 167

Fig 6.30 Location of burials containing burial goods 169

Fig 6.31 Shroud pins 170

Fig 6.32 Buttons 171

Fig 6.33 Dress accessories: a – buckle; b – tortoiseshell comb 172

Fig 6.34 Jewellery: a – pale blue glass bead; b – gold fitting; c – colourless glass bead 172

Fig 6.35 Non-burial-related features 173

Fig 6.36 Photograph of drain [1955] 173

Fig 6.37 Paths: a – of brick fragments, [1927]; b – of reused brick and tile, [1890]–[1893]; c – of reused tile and limestone fragments, [1973] 174

Fig 6.38 Paths: a – herringbone pattern, [110]; b – photograph of burial ground showing perimeter path, taken in 1937 174

Fig 6.39 Walls: a – photograph of walls [1858]/[1859], [2000] and sandstone blocks [2004]; b – watercolour of the Savoy Chapel, 1787 175

Fig 7.1 Location of burials referenced in Chapter 7 179

Fig 7.2 Window plan detail showing stones a and b 180

Fig 7.3 Coping stone c (composite reconstruction) 180

Fig 7.4 Coping stone d with lead plug (composite reconstruction) 180

Fig 7.5 Coping stone e (wall-set) 181

Fig 7.6 Drip mould f 181

Fig 7.7 ?Coade architrave stone g 181

Fig 7.8 Decorated clay pipes 188

Fig 7.9 Selected coins 189

Fig 7.10 Finds from graveyard soil [117]: a – lead weight; b – 17th-century thimble 190

Fig 7.11 Dagger chape from [117] 190

Fig 7.12 Wig curlers 191

Fig 8.1 Savoy Chapel and burial ground, *c* 1800 195

LIST OF TABLES

Table 2.1 Households with the largest number of hearths 15
Table 2.2 Nineteenth- and 20th-century population of the Savoy Precinct and total number of houses recorded 15
Table 2.3 Total number of deaths as recorded in the London Bills of Mortality, 1657–1758 16
Table 2.4 Total number of deaths as recorded in the London Bills of Mortality, 1603, 1625 and 1636 16

Table 3.1 Hospital accounts, 1526–7 22
Table 3.2 A nurse's expenses 23
Table 3.3 Record of prisoners in the Savoy Prison, 1776–88 39

Table 4.1 Summary of information recorded in the burial registers 49
Table 4.2 Causes of death as recorded in the burial registers 57-58
Table 4.3 Definition of selected medical terms 58
Table 4.4 Causes of death recorded for soldiers 58
Table 4.5 Prevalence of consumption by sex, 1754–1819 60
Table 4.6 Prevalence of consumption by age, 1754–1819 60
Table 4.7 Prevalence of fever by sex, 1754–1819 60
Table 4.8 Prevalence of fever by age, 1754–1819 60
Table 4.9 Prevalence of convulsions by sex, 1754–1819 61
Table 4.10 Prevalence of convulsions by age, 1754–1819 61
Table 4.11 Prevalence of smallpox by sex, 1754–1819 61
Table 4.12 Prevalence of smallpox by age, 1754–1819 61
Table 4.13 Time delay between death and burial, 1751–1854 62-64
Table 4.14 Average time delay between death and burial by decade, 1800–60 64
Table 4.15 Parishes of the deceased as recorded in the burial registers, 1813–48 65

Table 5.1 Age categories and distribution of the population by age 69
Table 5.2 Composition of the adult population 70
Table 5.3 Stature estimations 70
Table 5.4 Comparison of stature estimation 71
Table 5.5 Crude prevalence rates of all pathologies found within the total population 74
Table 5.6 Number of fractured bones according to the number of individuals 74
Table 5.7 Crude prevalence rates of facial fractures (nasal + maxilla) within the total population 75
Table 5.8 Crude prevalence rates of rib fractures within the population 76
Table 5.9 Crude prevalence rates of long-bone fractures within the total population 76
Table 5.10 Crude prevalence rates of hand and foot fractures within the total population 78
Table 5.11 Crude prevalence rates of enthesopathies by location within the adult population 81
Table 5.12 Crude and true prevalence rates of Schmorl's nodes within the total population 82
Table 5.13 Crude and true prevalence rates of spondylolysis within the population 83
Table 5.14 Comparison of spondylolysis in cemeteries from the London area 83
Table 5.15 Crude and true prevalence rates of os acromiale within the total population 84
Table 5.16 Crude and true prevalence rates of spinal joint disease within the adult population 88
Table 5.17 Crude prevalence rates of extra-spinal joint disease within the adult population 89

Table 5.18 True prevalence rates of extra-spinal joint disease within the adult population	89
Table 5.19 Crude prevalence rates of congenital anomalies within the total population	92
Table 5.20 Different types of spinal disarrangement	94
Table 5.21 Crude prevalence rates of periostitis within the total population	100
Table 5.22 Comparison of tuberculosis in cemeteries from the London area	106
Table 5.23 Comparison of syphilis in cemeteries from the London area	110
Table 5.24 Crude prevalence rates of dental pathology within the total population	110
Table 5.25 True prevalence rates of dental pathology within the population	112
Table 5.26 True prevalence rates of dental pathologies in the adult population according to teeth	113
Table 5.27 True prevalence rates of dental pathologies in the subadult population	114
Table 5.28 Comparison of ante-mortem tooth loss in cemeteries from the London area	115
Table 5.29 Comparison of dental enamel hypoplasia in cemeteries from the London area	116
Table 5.30 Crude prevalence rates of dental trauma within the total population	117
Table 5.31 Comparison of clay-pipe smokers within the adult population	118
Table 5.32 Crude prevalence rates of dental anomalies within the total population	119
Table 5.33 Crude and true prevalence rates of cribra orbitalia within the total population	120
Table 5.34 Crude prevalence rates of rickets within the total population	121
Table 5.35 Comparison of rickets in cemeteries from the London area	122
Table 5.36 Comparison of scurvy in cemeteries from the London area	123
Table 5.37 Comparison of DISH in cemeteries from the London area	125
Table 5.38 Crude prevalence rates of osteochondritis dissecans within the total population	127
Table 5.39 Comparison of cranial dissections in cemeteries from the London area	137
Table 6.1 Number of burials by depth and sex	145
Table 6.2 Retained worked stones from memorials and monuments	149
Table 6.3 Identification of individuals by matching survey and archaeological data	152-153
Table 6.4 Insect sample details	168
Table 6.5 Catalogue of textile materials examined	171
Table 7.1 Retained 'worked stones'	180
Table 7.2 Pottery assemblage by period	182
Table 7.3 Summary of the early post-medieval pottery assemblage	183
Table 7.4 Summary of early post-medieval pottery assemblage by vessel type	184
Table 7.5 Summary of building materials	185
Table 7.6 Broad date ranges of contexts containing ceramic building material	185
Table 7.7 Brick dimensions by context and Museum of London fabric type	186
Table 7.8 Overview of makers' marks	187

LIST OF CONTRIBUTORS

Principal authors	Lucy Sibun and Paola Ponce
Architectural stone	Mark Samuel
Burial registers	Hayley Forsyth, Lucy Sibun
Ceramic building material	Susan Pringle
Clay tobacco pipes	Elke Raeman
Coffin furniture	Susan Chandler
Coins, other objects	Trista Clifford, Lucy Sibun
Craniotomies	Jenna Dittmar, Paola Ponce, Lucy Sibun
Insects	Enid Allison
Isotopic analysis on bone	Michelle Alexander, Madeleine Bleasdale
Isotopic analysis on hair	Andrew Wilson, Patrick Daley
Musket ball	Justin Russell
Post Roman Pottery	Luke Barber
Textiles	Rob Janaway
Illustrations	Fiona Griffin (publication), Antonio Reis (finds and human remains photography), Justin Russell (post-excavation)
Editor	Louise Rayner

SUMMARY

Archaeological excavations were carried out within the burial ground of the Queen's Chapel of the Savoy in 2011, before the redevelopment of this part of the site into a sunken garden and robing room for the chapel. The site, which sits at approximately 9.0m OD, is situated on Savoy Street, City of Westminster, London, with the Strand to the north and Victoria Embankment, close to Waterloo Bridge, to the south. The excavation area measured 180m^2 and was reduced by up to 3m in depth during the works.

In medieval times the land was occupied by the Savoy Palace, destroyed in the 14th century during the Peasants' Revolt. From the ruined remains of the medieval palace, the Savoy Precinct was developed by Henry VII as a hospital for the poor; it was opened in 1517, after his death. In 1642 the hospital buildings were converted into a military hospital, the first of its kind, designed to cater for the parliamentary soldiers of the English Civil War. The final transformation came at the beginning of the 18th century, when the Foot Guards took over completely, establishing the Savoy Barracks and Prison within the existing buildings. The Savoy Precinct reverted to civilian occupation in the 19th century as the military moved out and the area underwent significant redevelopment.

The Queen's Chapel of the Savoy (formerly St John's Chapel) was constructed as part of the original hospital and is still in active use. The associated burial ground was utilised throughout the life of the precinct buildings and beyond, until the final burial in 1854. The 2011 excavation area, which constituted approximately 17% of the original burial ground, contained the remains of 612 individuals, 609 of which were recovered for osteological analysis. Owing to the density of graves and level of truncation, it was not possible to phase the burials closely but the majority probably dated to the later stages of the burial ground's use by the barracks and prison as well as by the 19th-century civilian population.

While confident phasing could not be applied to the site, possible patterns were identified among the burials with the help of GIS analysis and interpreted with the help of historical records. Clear rows were visible in the layout of the graves, indicating some degree of organisation, but, as a result of the constant reuse of the burial ground over 300 years, there was no obvious chronological development. Clues to burial practice were supplied by the coffin furniture assemblage, although limited by poor preservation, evidence of burial clothing and a few personal accessories. These exemplified mostly poor and simple burials, in shrouds and wooden coffins, as might be expected from this population. Only two lead coffins were uncovered, both dating to the 19th century.

The excavations uncovered a number of non-burial features, among them a 17th-century drain and several paths. Some of the surviving paving was constructed from reused bricks and floor tiles that date from the 13th to the 17th century, including some tiles that could have originated from the hospital. The base of a medieval buttress was uncovered on the southern border of the excavation area, consistent with buttresses that originally lined the northern wall of the hospital dormitory.

The buried population itself was dominated by younger males, and osteological analysis revealed a range of a diseases typical of post-medieval London and afflictions consistent with a military lifestyle. Traumatic conditions were the most prevalent pathological manifestations recorded followed by joint diseases, congenital anomalies, infections, dental and metabolic diseases as well as some evidence for post-mortem examination and surgical intervention. The majority of pathologies evident accurately reflected the status of the population, some being consistent with the poorer elements of society and fewer associated with wealth and dietary excesses.

The survival of associated historical records – which included three volumes of burial registers detailing nearly 11,000 burials and dating from 1680 to 1854 – greatly enhanced the archaeological results. They enabled the osteologically and historically recorded populations to be compared in a study that examined their demographic profiles as well as their general health status and the prevalence of specific diseases. In some cases it was possible to identify specific individuals through a combination of the historical and archaeological data. Additional historical records provided insight into the general functioning and lifestyle of the hospitals and military institutions and some of the individuals associated with them. The 19th-century civilian burials were detailed in two surveys undertaken in the 1930s that recorded any upstanding memorial stones prior to their removal. The data generated were instrumental in the interpretation of the burial ground and in the identification of a number of individuals.

RÉSUMÉ

Des fouilles archéologiques ont été effectuées dans le cimetière de la Chapelle de Savoie en 2011, avant le réaménagement de cette partie du site en un jardin à contrebas et un vestiaire. Le site, qui se trouve à une altitude d'environ 9 m OD (Ordonance Datum), est situé dans la rue Savoy, dans la cité de Westminster à Londres, avec le Strand au nord et Victoria Embankment, près de Waterloo Bridge au sud. La zone d'excavation mesurait 180m^2 et a été réduite jusqu'à 3m de profondeur pendant les travaux.

A l'époque médiévale le terrain était occupé par le Palais de Savoie, détruit au 14ème siècle pendant la révolte paysanne. Des ruines du palais médiéval, le Savoie a été développé par Henry VII comme hospice pour les pauvres, l'hôpital étant fondé après sa mort en 1517. En 1642, les bâtiments hospitaliers sont transformés en hôpital militaire, le premier en son genre, conçu pour assister les soldats parlementaires de la Première révolution anglaise. La transformation finale a lieu au début du 18ème siècle, lorsque l'infanterie prend entièrement la relève, établissant les casernes et la prison de Savoie dans les bâtiments existants. Le quartier revient sous l'occupation civile au 19ème siècle, lorsque les militaires se retirent et le secteur subit un réaménagement intense.

La Chapelle de Savoie (anciennement la Chapelle de St Jean) a été construite dans le cadre de l'hôpital d'origine et est toujours utilisée aujourd'hui. Le cimetière, qui lui est associé, a été occupé tout au long de la vie des bâtiments de l'hospice, et au-delà, jusqu'au dernier enterrement en 1854. La zone d'excavation de 2011, qui représente environ 17% du cimetière d'origine, contenait les ossements de 612 personnes, dont 609 étaient exhumés à des fins ostéologiques. En raison de la densité des tombes et des troncatures, il était impossible de mettre précisément en phase les inhumations mais dans la majorité des cas elles correspondent probablement aux derniers stades de l'utilisation du cimetière par les casernes et la prison ainsi que par la population civile du 19ème siècle.

Bien que la chronologie du site ne pouvait pas être reconstituée avec certitude, des modèles possibles ont été identifiés parmi les sépultures avec l'aide de l'analyse des données SIG et interprétés avec l'aide de documents historiques. Des rangées ordonnées étaient visibles parmi les tombes, indiquant un certain degré d'organisation, mais en raison de la réutilisation constante du cimetière pendant plus de 300 ans, il n'y avait pas de développement chronologique évident. Les indices concernant les pratiques d'inhumation ont été fournis par les vestiges de cercueils, bienque limités par une mauvaise conservation, par les vêtements d'enterrement et par quelques effets personels. Ceux-ci illustrent principalement des enterrements simples en linceuls et cercueils de bois, comme on pouvait s'y attendre de cette population. Seulement deux cercueils en plomb ont été découverts, tous deux datant du 19ème siècle.

Les fouilles ont également révélé d'autres structures non funéraires dont une canalisation du 17ème siècle et plusieurs chemins. Certains des revêtements survivants ont été construits à partir de briques et de carreaux de sol réutilisés qui datent du 13ème au 17ème siècle, y compris des carreaux qui auraient pu provenir de l'hôpital. La base d'un contrefort medieval a également été découverte à la limite sud de la zone d'excavation, compatible avec les contreforts qui à l'origine bordaient le mur nord du dortoir de l'hôpital.

En ce qui concerne la population enterrée elle-même, elle était dominée par des jeunes hommes et l'analyse ostéologique a révélé une série de maladies typiques du Londres post-mediéval et des maladies compatibles avec un style de vie militaire. Les conditions traumatiques constituaient les manifestations pathologiques les plus répandues suivies de maladies articulaires, congénitales, infectieuses, dentaires, métaboliques, circulatoires et néoplastiques, ainsi que des preuves d'autopsies et d'interventions chirurgicales. La majorité des pathologies évidentes reflètent correctement le statut de la population, avec certaines consistantes avec les éléments les plus pauvres de la société et un plus petit nombre associé à l'abondance et aux excès alimentaires.

La survie de documents historiques a considérablement amélioré les résultats archéologiques, y compris trois volumes de registres funéraires, détaillants près de 11 000 sépultures datant de 1680-1854. Cela a permis de comparer les populations enregistrées à partir des ossements et historiquement dans une étude qui a examiné leurs profils démographiques ainsi que leur état sanitaire général et la prévalence de certaines maladies. Dans certains cas, il était possible d'identifier certains individus en particulier grâce à une combinaison de données historiques et archéologiques. Des documents historiques supplémentaires ont fourni des renseignements sur le fonctionnement général et le mode de vie des hôpitaux et des institutions militaires et sur certains individus qui leur sont associés. Les enterrements civils du 19ème siècle ont été détaillés dans deux relevés des années 1930 qui ont enregistré toutes les pierres commémoratives avant leur retrait. Les données générées ont contribué à l'interprétation du cimetière et à l'identification d'un certain nombre d'individus.

ZUSAMMENFASSUNG

Im Jahre 2011 wurde ein Teil des Friedhofes der Queen's Chapel of the Savoy archäologisch untersucht bevor er in eine speziell bepflanzte Gartenanlage (einen sogennanten ‚tiefergelegten Garten') und eine Sakristei umgebaut werden konnte. Das Gelände liegt ca. 9m über NN an der Savoy Street in der City of Westminster, London. Die Straße ‚The Strand' liegt nördlich der Queen's Chapel of the Savoy und das Victoria Embankment (nahe der Waterloo Bridge) südlich davon. Die Grabungsfläche betrug ca. 180m^2 und das Gelände wurde während der Grabungen ca. 3m tiefer gelegt.

Im Mittelalter stand hier der Savoy Palast, welcher im 14. Jahrhundert während der Bauernrevolte zerstört wurde. Aus den Ruinen dieser mittelalterlichen Anlage wurde der Savoy Bezirk unter Heinrich VII zu einem Armenhospital weiterentwickelt, welches aber erst nach seinem Tode im Jahre 1517 seine Tore öffnete. 1642 wurden die Gebäude dann in ein Miliärkrankenhaus umgewandelt. Dieses Krankenhaus war das erste seiner Art: es war mit dem Gedanken errichtet worden, während des englischen Bürgerkrieges die Soldaten der Parlamentarier aufzunehmen und zu behandeln. Die letzte Weiterentwicklung fand zu Beginn des 18. Jahrhunders statt, nachdem die ‚Foot Soldiers' (Regimente der Infanterie) den Bau vollständig übernommen und die Savoy Barracken und das Militaergefängis innerhalb der bereits vorhandenen Gebäude eingerichtet hatten. Der Savoy Bezirk wurde erst im 19. Jahrhundert wieder zivil besetzt, nachdem das Militär ausgezogen und das Areal einer beachtlichen Sanierung unterzogen worden war.

Die Queen's Chapel of the Savoy (zuvor unter dem Namen ‚St John's Chapel' bekannt) war als Teil des ursprünglichen Spitals gebaut worden und wird noch bis heute benutzt. In dem der Kapelle angeschlossenen Friedhof fanden bis in das Jahr 1854 Beisetzungen statt. Bei der Grabung, die 2011 durchgeführt wurde, wurden 17% des Friedhofes erfaßt, d.h. Gräber von 612 Individuen. Von diesen konnten 609 osteologisch untersucht werden. Wegen der generell hohen Gräberdichte und der hohen Anzahl der sich ueberschneidenden Beisetzungen war es oftmals nicht möglich die Gräber in genaue Phasen einzuteilen. Die Großzahl der Bestattungen wird jedoch sowohl in die spätere militärische Belegphase, als auch in das 19. Jahrhundert datieren, als der Friedhof von der hier ansässigen Zivilbevölkerung genutzt wurde.

Obwohl es nicht möglich war, die Gräber genau zu datieren und in gesicherte Phasen einzuteilen, konnten mit Hilfe der GIS Analyse doch einige mögliche Schlußfolgerungen gezogen und dank der historischen Aufzeichnungen verifiziert werden. Die Einteilung der Gräber in klare Reihen läßt auf einen gewissen Grad von Organisation schließen, aber eine Folge der fast 300-Jahre-langen ununterbrochenen Benutzung des Friedhofens zeigt dass es keine deutliche chronologische Abfolge gab. Hinweise auf die Art und Weise der Bestattungen gab es durch die Särge, Leichentücher und Leichenkleidung und die wenigen persönlichen Beigaben der Verstorbenen. All diese zeugen von zumeist armen oder einfachen Bestattungen in Leichentüchern und Holzsärgen, wie es von einer Bevölkerung wie dieser auch zu vermuten gewesen wäre. Es wurden nur zwei Bleisärge geborgen und beide datierten ins 19. Jahrhundert.

Neben den Bestattungen kamen auch andere Befunde zutage, zum Beispiel ein Abwassergraben aus dem 17. Jahrhundert und mehrere gepflasterte Fußwege. Wo die Pflasterung der Wege noch erhalten war, da bestand sie aus wierderverwerteten Ziegeln, Mauersteinen und Fliesen, die aus dem 13.-17. Jahrhundert stammten. Einige dieser Pflastersteine datieren vermutlich sogar in die Zeit des ersten Spitals. Auf der südlichen Seite der Grabungsfläche wurde außerdem der untere Teil eines mittelalterlichen Stützpfeilers geborgen. Dieser gehörte vermutlich zu den Pfeilern der nördlichen Mauer des Spitalsschlafsaales.

Bei den Friedhofsbestattungen handelt es sich zumeist um jüngere Männer und osteologische Analysen weisen auf eine Reihe von Erkrankungen hin, die für das frühneuzeitliche London und den Militärdienst typisch waren. Die häufigsten Verletzungen wurden durch äußere Gewalteinwirking verursacht, gefolgt von Gelenkerkrankungen, Geburtsfehlern, Infekten, Zahn- und Stoffwechselerkrankungen. Außerdem gab es Hinweise auf Post-Mortem Untersuchungen und operative Eingriffe. Der Großteil der Erkrankungen stimmt mit dem überein was wir über die damalige Bevölkerung wissen, insbesondere dem ärmeren Teil der hiesigen Bevölkerung. Nur sehr wenige Bestattungen lassen Reichtum oder kulinarische Extravaganz vermuten.

Die historischen Aufzeichnungen und vor allem das dreibändige Sterberegister von 1680-1854, in dem fast 11,000 Bestattungen verzeichnet sind, bestätigen diese Grabungsergebnisse. Sowohl diese Sterberegister als auch die osteologisch untersuchten Grabungsfunde ermöglichen den direkten Vergleich zwischen einer bekannten Bevölkerungsgruppe, ihrer allgemeinen Gesundheit und die Verbreitung von bestimmten Erkrankungen. In einigen Fällen war es sogar möglich durch die Aufzeichnungen von bestimmten Verletzungen oder Erkrankungen Individuen in den Gräbern wiederzuerkennen. Weitere Aufzeichnungen ermöglichten es, sowohl einen generellen Einblick in das Spitals- und Militärleben, als auch einen direkten Eindruck vom Leben und Sterben gewisser Individuen zu bekommen.

Die Bestattungen aus dem 19. Jahrhundert wurden in zwei Studien bereits in den 1930er Jahren zusammengefasst. Diese Untersuchungen befassten sich mit dem Inschriften auf den jeweiligen Grabsteinen bevor sie entfernt wurden. Die Daten, die dabei aufgenommen wurden waren extrem hilfreich bei der Interpretation des Friedhofes und der Bestimmung der Anzahl der hier zur Ruhe gelegten Individuen.

ACKNOWLEDGEMENTS

Archaeology South-East would like to thank The Chancellor and Council of the Duchy of Lancaster for funding the project and Crowther Overton-Hart for commissioning the work on behalf of their client the Duchy of Lancaster, particularly Patrick Crowther for his support throughout the project. The advice and guidance of Diane Abrams of the Greater London Archaeology Advisory Service (GLAAS) is also gratefully acknowledged.

Lucy Sibun wishes to thank Katie Roberts, Assistant Keeper of the Records, Duchy of Lancaster, for her assistance and time; Saul David, Professor of Military History at the University of Buckingham and Programme Director for the university's London-based MA in Military History by Research, for his comments and expertise; and Alistair Massie, National Army Museum, for his help and advice.

Paola Ponce would like to thank Dr Keith Manchester from the Biological Anthropology Research Centre, University of Bradford and Professor Chris Raine from the Bradford Royal Infirmary, Bradford for their help regarding the diagnosis of skeleton 208. Special thanks should also be given to Dr Eric Whites and Fiona Ball from King's College London Institute, Guy's Hospital, London for their time and expertise in conducting computed tomography (CT) images and helping with the pathological diagnosis of skeleton 1077.

Andy Wilson and and Patrick Daley would like to thank Marise Gorton at the Bradford Stable Isotope Laboratory, University of Bradford. Madeleine Bleasdale and Michelle Alexander would like to thank Matthew Von Tersch at the BioArCh laboratories, University of York. Jenna Dittmar would like to thank Dr Piers Mitchell from the University of Cambridge for providing invaluable expertise on post-mortem medical examination.

Thanks are also due to Dr Jane Sidell, Inspector of Ancient Monuments for Historic England, and Natasha Powers, Senior Manager at Allen Archaeology, for their comments and suggestions on earlier drafts, all of which were extremely useful.

Alice Thorne supervised the excavation and completed some preliminary post-excavation work and was assisted on site by Gary Webster. The project was managed in the field by Andrew Leonard and in post-excavation by Louise Rayner. Illustrations were prepared by Fiona Griffin and Justin Russell and photographs by Antonio Reis. Members of the excavation team were: Kary Bower, Ian Cipin, Brenton Culshaw, Cormac Duffy, Tara Fidler, Lauren Figg, Cat Gibbs, Jasmine Hall, Ceilidh Hamill, Yvonne Heath, John Joyce, Rupert Lotherington, Roddy Mattison, Claire McGlenn, Dennis Morgan, Tomasz Moskal, Becky Peacock, Antonio Reis and Andy Tynan.

The summary was translated into French by Karine Le Hégarat and German by Dot Bruns. The index was compiled by Francesca Hillier.

CHAPTER 1 INTRODUCTION AND BACKGROUND
Lucy Sibun

> … For labour yields me true content,
> Though few the same do see;
> And when my toiling hours are spent
> The sweeter sleep shall be …
> … It makes our bread more sweet than theirs
> Who idly spend their wealth;
> We seldom have so many cares,
> And live in better health.
> If we at night begin to tire,
> Next morning fresh we grow;
> And for our meat, or for our hire,
> To work again we go …
> … Lord! grant me health and strength to bear
> The labours laid on me;
> And those works to persevere
> Whereto I call'd shall be.
>
> —George Wither,
> Hymn IX When we are at our Labour
> (Farr 1857, 11–12)

1.1 INTRODUCTION

During 2011 and 2012 an archaeological excavation was carried out within the burial ground of the Queen's Chapel of the Savoy (hereafter the Savoy Chapel), Savoy Street, City of Westminster, London (NGR: TQ 3058 8074; Fig 1.1). The excavation was prompted by an application to extend the chapel to include a robing room and sunken garden, both of which were to involve ground reduction of approximately 3.0m. As previous archaeological investigations on site had identified human remains at a depth of approximately 1.6m below the existing surface, this work offered an opportunity to investigate the archaeology of a site with a rich and well-documented history.

The site is located approximately 150m to the north-west of Waterloo Bridge, with Savoy Row to the north, Savoy Street to the east and Savoy Hill to the south. The Savoy Chapel itself forms the western boundary, adjacent to Savoy Steps. The site, which at approximately 9.0m OD is considerably higher than the surrounding area, is on a steeply sloping embankment that leads down to the Thames to the south. The southern end of the site has been artificially raised and it is possible that the northern end has been terraced into the natural slope. According to data from the British Geological Survey (BGS 2012), the geology of the site comprises Alluvial Fan Deposits of gravel, sand, silt and clay over London Clay formation.

1.2 ARCHAEOLOGICAL BACKGROUND

Archaeological evidence for the area before the medieval period is sparse. Only a single prehistoric spearhead has been found in the area and the focus of Roman activity was located further to the east, in the present-day City of London. After the Roman abandonment, a Middle Saxon trading centre known as Ludenwic developed to the north of the site but no Saxon remains have been found in the immediate vicinity.

From the medieval period onwards the Savoy site is well documented. The most comprehensive history of the area was written by Robert Somerville (1960), formerly Clerk of the Council, Duchy of Lancaster. This work has been used to provide the summary that follows but interested readers are recommended to his book for greater detail. However, the first history of the area was produced by the Revd William John Loftie in 1878, when he wrote his *Memorials of the Savoy. The Palace: The Hospital: The Chapel*, while he was assistant chaplain of the Savoy. This work has also been referred to throughout.

SAVOY PALACE

In the 13th century the land, described as scattered houses and gardens on the Thames in 'La Straunde', belonged to Brian de L'Isle, a counsellor to King John until his death in 1233 (Somerville 1960, 3). The earl of Leicester, Simon de Montfort, built on the land in 1245, but in 1246 it was passed by Henry III to Peter, count of Savoy, who was the uncle of Henry III's queen, Eleanor, and brother to the archbishop of Canterbury. With further gifts of land and acquisitions, Peter possessed the entire area, which was to become the Manor of the Savoy.

Loftie notes that at this time the area was extensively occupied by the 'villas of great Nobles' (1878, 7). However, he also records that 'the situation was too insecure to tempt many who could not, like the religious houses, or the bishops, defy, with the terrors of the supernatural, predatory bands

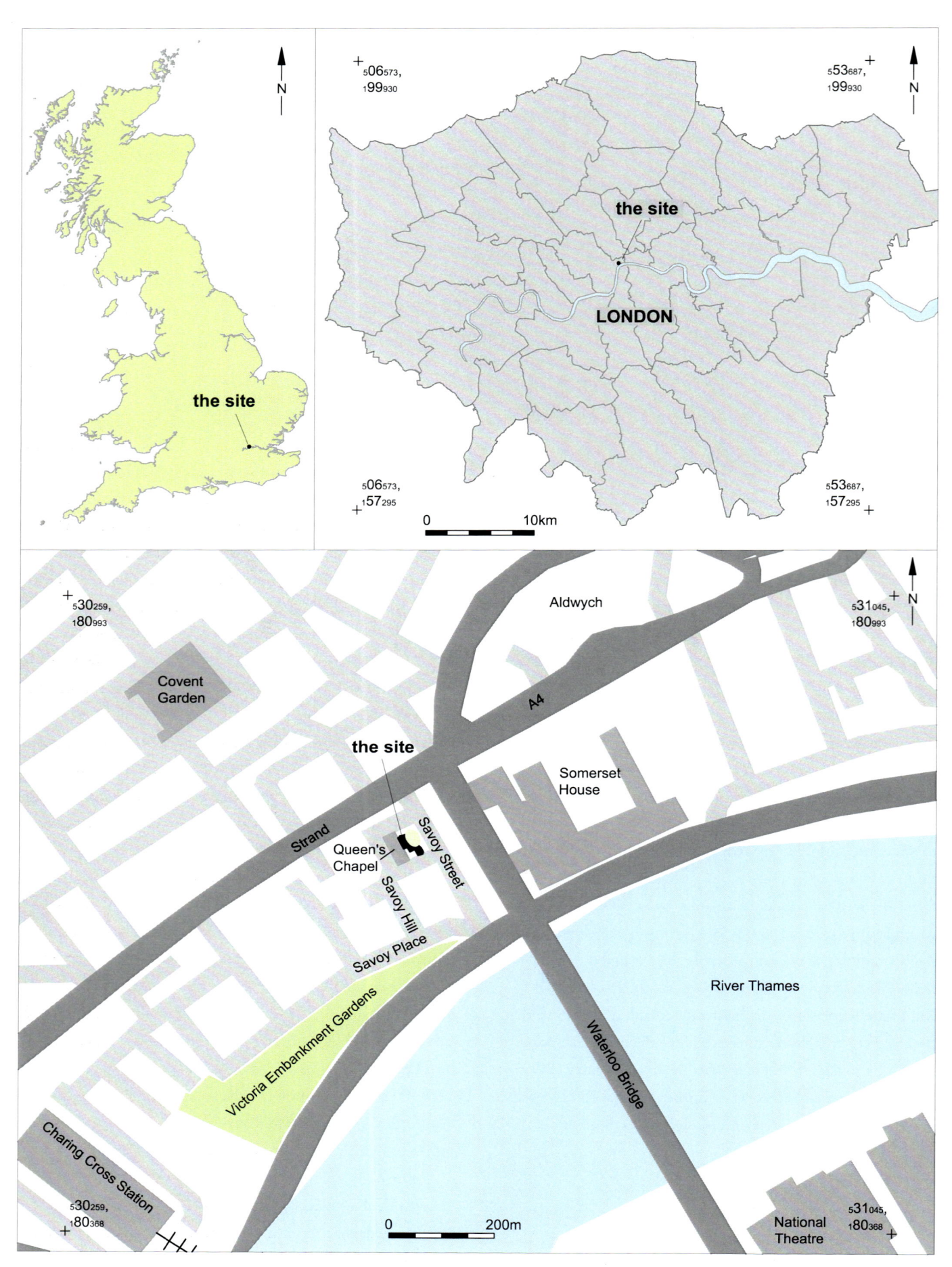

Fig 1.1 Site location

and riotous soldiery'. He adds a final comment: 'As the event proved, the caution was not unfounded.' Although this undoubtedly refers to the precarious situation of the nobles in 13th-century England, it seems to encapsulate the entire history of the Savoy, which was continually troubled.

It appears that Peter was rarely in England after 1263 and after his death in 1268 (Vincent 2008) the lands were bequeathed to the hospice of Great St Bernard, Monjoux, Savoie (Somerville 1960, 3). Two years later the land was bought by Queen Eleanor for 300 marks and passed to her son Edmund, brother of Edward I. In 1293 Edward I granted his brother permission to strengthen his manor of 'Sauvoye', providing the first evidence of the name that was to be associated with it (ibid, 4). From Edmund the manor was passed to his two sons Thomas and Henry. Henry's son, also Henry, a great military commander, used the booty from a successful campaign in France in 1345 to rebuild the Savoy Manor, spending nearly £35,000. The building contained a cloister, a chapel and a productive hedged garden as well as stables, fishpond and bakehouse. The manor was partially walled with stone, with great gates giving on to the street as well as a riverside watergate (ibid, 5).

When one of Henry's heirs, Blanche, married John of Gaunt (fourth son of Edward III) the manor became his to use. It is said that John of Gaunt had at least 150 knights in his service all lodged with the duke (ibid, 6). According to Loftie, John of Gaunt could be considered the equivalent of a present-day prime minister but unfortunately his 'adherents' misgoverned the country (1878, 71). Consequently, resentment against the House of Lancaster grew. During the Peasants' Revolt and the disturbances of 1381 the duke's palace was attacked and the buildings and contents set on fire. While it could not subsequently be used as a noble residence, some buildings and the gardens remained. Simeon's Tower, on the western side, is thought to have survived into the 16th century (Somerville 1960, 7).

In 1399, following John's death, Henry IV annexed the Savoy Manor and all estates of the House of Lancaster to the Crown (Cowie 1974, 175). Although the Crown did little with the lands, a new stone wall was constructed along the Strand in 1404 and some of the buildings were put to use as the lord of the manor's prison. Produce was sold from the gardens and new houses were built in the grounds along the riverside (ibid). However, it was not until the early 16th century that plans for the redevelopment of the partially derelict site were considered, and the area converted into the 'Hospital of Henry late King of England of the Savoy' (discussed in detail in Chapter 3). Buildings associated with the hospital remained on the site until the early 19th century. The only structure that still survives of the original hospital is the Savoy Chapel and the associated burial ground. The last interment in the burial ground was in 1854.

1.3 PREVIOUS WORKS AND ARCHAEOLOGICAL EXCAVATIONS

The Duchy of Lancaster archives contain information and documents relevant to the excavations, kindly made available for use in this study. A document referenced as 'Plan No. 2867 – Savoy Chapel Burial Ground', contains a survey of the burial ground carried out in the 1930s, which records that the site was largely covered in headstones dating to the first half of the 19th century. A further survey of the burial ground undertaken by the Duchy itself in 1934 details the memorials present.

Changes were made in 1938 to lay the burial ground out as a garden. It was not anticipated that this would disturb human remains as it mostly involved the removal of headstones to a new position. However, when further excavation work was carried out in the 1950s, previously disturbed remains were uncovered and disturbed for a second time. It is unclear whether the disturbed remains uncovered in the 1950s dated to the work of the 1930s or to a time when the burial ground was in active use.

During 2010 and 2011, various exploratory archaeological works were carried out on the site (Fig 1.2). Disarticulated human bone and artefacts were recovered down to 1.60m below ground level at the southern end of the site, at which depth *in situ* burials were encountered (Oxford Archaeology 2010; ASE 2011). At the start of this stage of works, the hand excavation of a 1.0m² test pit through the articulated horizon to formation depth (3.0m below ground level) identified five articulated skeletons. No coffin furniture was identified and grave cuts and fills were not discernible. In summary, the archaeological work established that a horizon of burial soil containing disarticulated human bone was present across the development area to a depth of approximately 2.20m below ground level.

1.4 STRUCTURE OF THE BOOK

Almost without exception, each chapter in this volume makes use of, or reference to, information contained in other chapters. The structure of this book has therefore been designed to make the progression through each chapter as logical as possible. Thus, before the post-medieval site history is discussed in

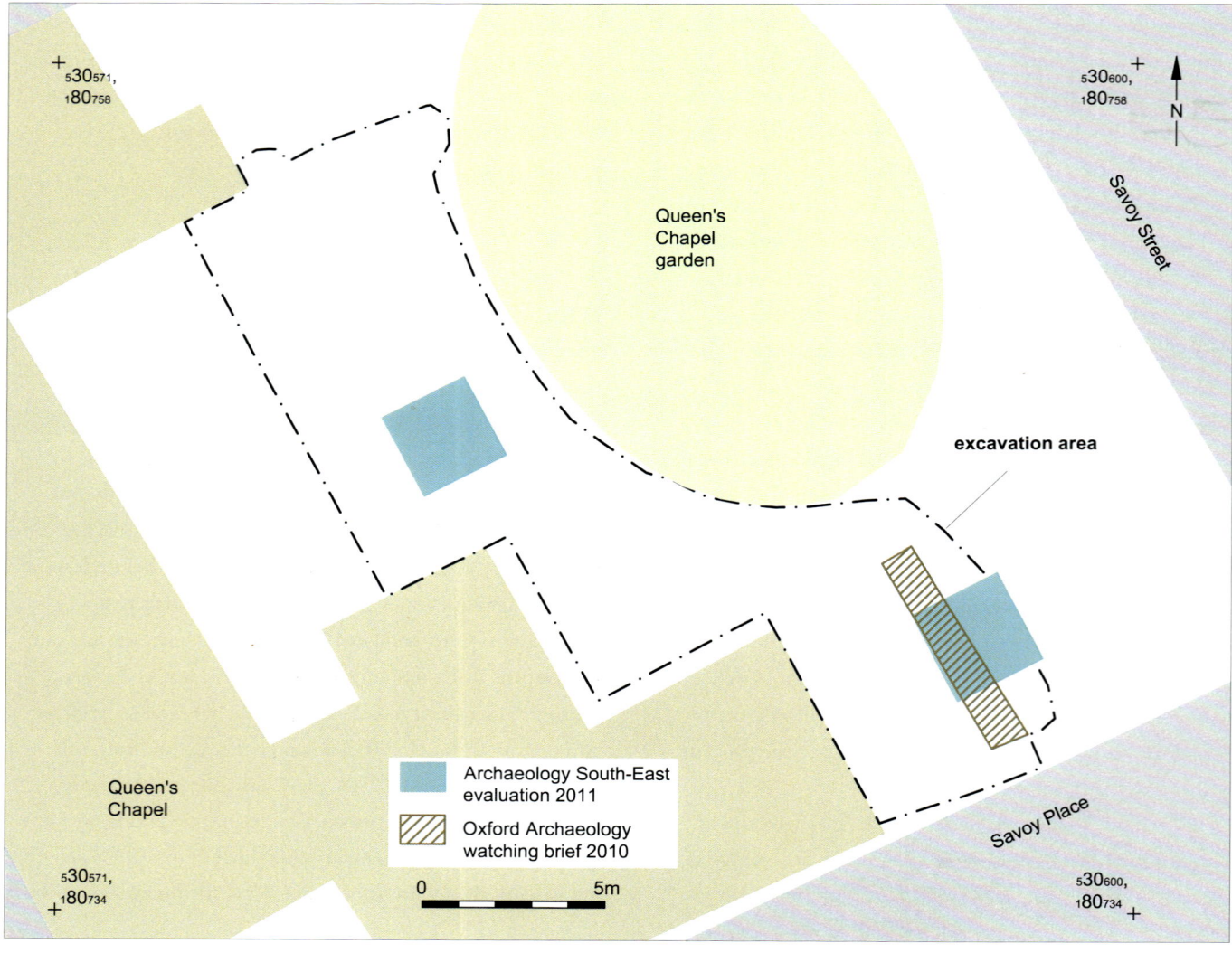

Fig 1.2 Location of previous archaeological work

detail, 16th- to 19th-century London society is considered so that the Savoy Precinct can be seen in context. The description of the archaeological results has been left until later in the publication so that the information in the preceding chapters can be used to help understand their interpretation.

During the excavation context numbers were assigned to all features. Each burial was assigned at least three numbers: grave cut, skeleton and grave fill. Additional numbers were used when necessary – if a coffin was present, for example. Context numbers are shown in square brackets, thus: [0000]. As far as possible, an integrated approach to the text has been taken. Environmental samples are shown in angled brackets, thus: <0>. In Chapters 6 and 7 finds have been given their associated skeleton numbers rather than grave fill numbers so that they may be easily located on figures.

HISTORICAL DOCUMENTARY SOURCES

A variety of historical sources has been used in the production of this report. Abbreviations of those sources referenced in the report are summarised here:

London Metropolitan Archives	LMA
National Archives	NA
National Army Museum	NAM
National Portrait Gallery	NPG
Old Bailey online	OB
Wellcome Library, London	WL
Westminster City Archives	WCA

The poetry extracts cited in this publication are by George Wither (1588–1667) and Anne Killigrew (1660–85), both of whom were buried in the Savoy Chapel burial ground.

CHAPTER 2 LONDON AND THE SAVOY PRECINCT

Lucy Sibun

*From Satan's bait, from folly's lures,
From ev'ry cause of ill,
Preserve me clean whilst life endures,
In action and in will.
At least when I shall tempted be,
Protect Thy servant so,
That evil overcome not me,
But victor let me grow.*

*Veil, Lord, mine eyes till she be past,
When Folly tempts my sight;
Keep Thou my palate and my taste
From gluttonous delight.
Stop thou mine ear from sirens' songs,
My tongue from lies restrain;
Withhold my hands from doing wrongs,
My feet from courses vain.*

—George Wither
Hymn LXXXI For Deliverance from Temptation
(Farr 1857, 126)

The following chapter is divided into two parts. The first looks at aspects of development of society in 16th- to 18th-century London so that the Savoy Precinct can be placed within a wider setting. By examining different elements of London society at this time it is possible to gain a greater understanding of the living Savoy population and to what extent the buried population might reflect it. The elements discussed have been chosen for their relevance to the story of the Savoy. The second part looks at the Savoy Precinct in more detail through a range of historical sources.

2.1 HISTORICAL BACKGROUND

In 1550 London was covered by a haze of smoke from domestic wood fires, a haze that was only to get worse with the introduction of coal over the next two centuries, impacting the city's development. With the smoke cloud drifting eastwards and sewage carried eastwards by the river, east London became a poorer, less desirable area. The area's dockyards grew with increasing trade and the district attracted more industrial activities such as carpentry, brewing, tanning, brickmaking. This was in sharp contrast to west London, which was attracting the wealthier Londoners, who moved partly to avoid the east but also in their desire to be closer to Whitehall and the Court at Westminster (Bucholz & Ward 2012, 34–5, 56). Little changed through the period and east London remained an industrial area with narrow streets and slums (Olsen 1999, 64).

In the 16th century the Savoy Precinct was located among a line of riverside palaces. To the north was the Strand which, although essentially a muddy track, was paved by 1532 and beginning to attract craftsmen keen to follow the westwards migration of wealth. Beyond it, however, to the north the area was still largely undeveloped open land (Bucholz & Ward 2012, 55) (Fig 2.1).

It was during the first half of the 17th century that prestigious traders began to move to the west from Cheapside, previously London's main shopping area (ibid, 47; Sharpe 2000, 201–2). The Strand was considered the most fashionable street in London (Loftie 1878, 130) and it was here that the first cabstand was introduced in 1634 (Hemstreet & Hemstreet 1910, 114). The whole area was inhabited by aristocrats and high-end businesses and shops, taverns, printers, exhibitions and an increasing trade in luxury goods (Olsen 1999, 65–7; Bucholz & Ward 2012, 99). The westwards movement of retailers was encouraged by the Great Fire in 1666, which destroyed so much of the east (Porter 2009b, 129; Russell 2014, 1). One of the direct consequences of the disaster was a dramatic growth in the West End, with numerous people seeking refuge there, many of whom became permanent residents (Coupland 1997, 37).

By the middle of the 18th century the Strand had developed into a shopping metropolis, packed with traffic and coffee houses alongside existing taverns and shops. The elite wished to be situated closer to Whitehall and the Court at Westminster, and away from the noise and smells of the city. In contrast, the area around Covent Garden and Drury Lane, just to the north-east of the Savoy, had become notorious for illicit pleasures, 'infested with prostitutes, bawds and pimps' (Durston 2012, 57). It was this environment that enveloped the Savoy Precinct.

POPULATION AND SOCIETY

The 16th to 18th centuries saw rapid population increases in London, faster than in the rest of England. From a population of approximately 120,000 in 1550, by the end of the 17th century London was the largest city in Europe with more than 500,000 inhabitants (Rappaport 2002, 62). With the population increasing to 675,000 by 1750 London accounted for approximately 10% of the entire English population

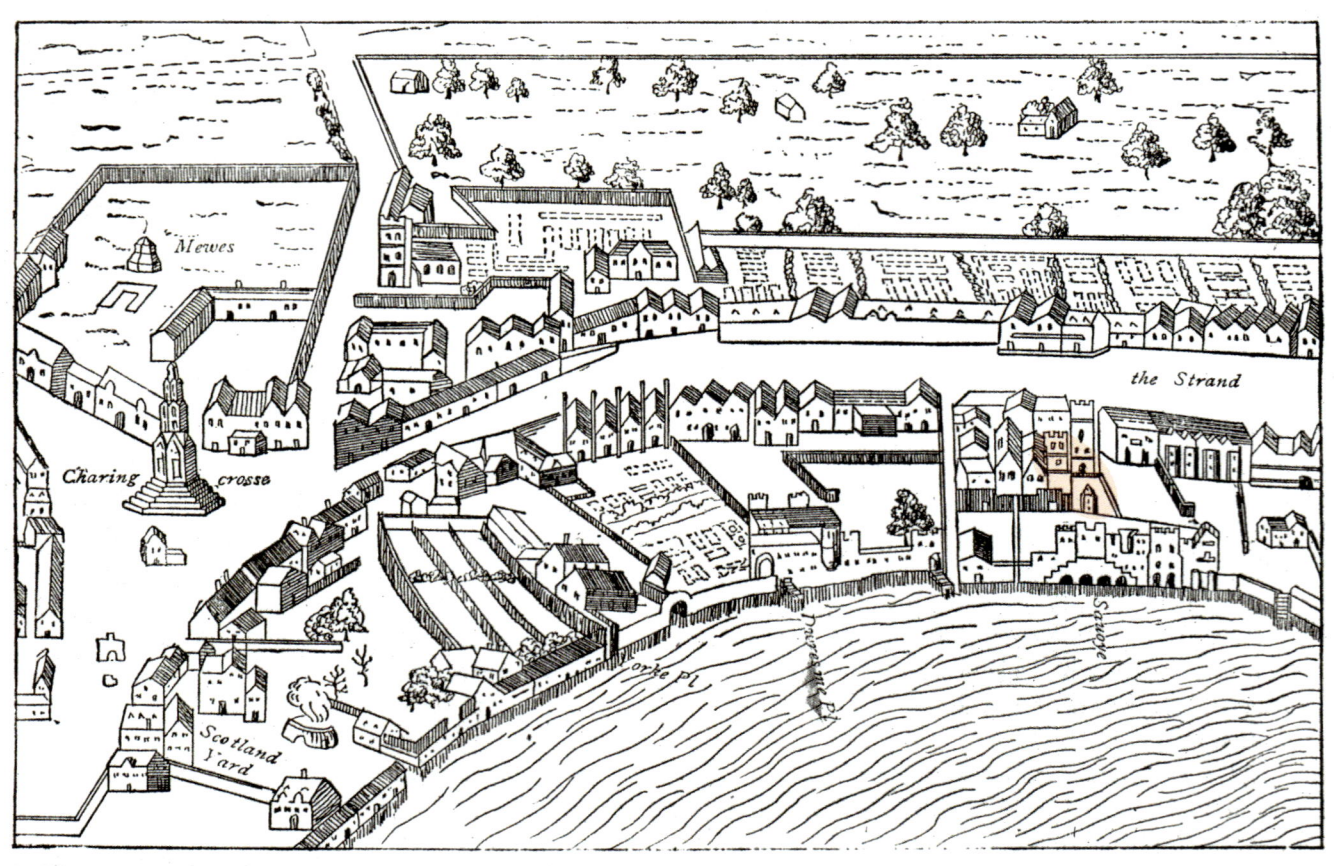

Fig 2.1 The Strand, 1560, from a map of Ralph Agas (©WL, M0003590 used under CC BY 4.0)

throughout the 18th century (McLynn 2002, 1–2). This was despite the fact that the death rate was still higher than the birth rate. High infant mortality rates were one of the main problems. Between 1700 and 1750, 40% of deaths recorded in the Bills of Mortality were of infants under 2 years of age. In some areas less than 60% of children survived to 15 years. There was severe overcrowding and a large number of dilapidated properties, which contributed to disease rates as well as to crime and structural collapse (Bucholz & Ward 2012, 64–5). Several outbreaks of plague as well as bouts of cholera, diphtheria, smallpox, typhus and tuberculosis, among other conditions, added to the problems (Durston 2012, 45).

Population growth is affected by external factors. In the case of London it was migration, with people flocking there from all over the country as well as from abroad (Rappaport 2002, 68–9; Durston 2012, 46). Europeans and Africans were arriving as merchants but this was also at a time of an increasing slave trade; the first black slave arrived in London in 1555. London also attracted the younger generation eager to find apprenticeships and employment among the 'largest concentration of jobs in northern Europe'. The economic situation in the rest of the country was exacerbating the problem, as many agricultural labourers were forced to leave the countryside after a succession of bad harvests (Newman & Brown 1997, 10; McLynn 2002, 2). For those who could not afford an apprenticeship the answer was to go into service and even the less wealthy families employed one or two servants if they could (Bucholz & Ward 2012, 66–75).

THE PLAGUE

In the 16th and 17th centuries Londoners regularly faced the threat of the plague, one of the most feared diseases in medieval and post-medieval Europe because of its contagiousness, the large numbers affected, the high mortality rate, the speed at which it spread, and significantly, an apparent inability to slow or cure it (Porter 2009a, 7–8). During the 1577 epidemic the Savoy Liberty was seen as a safe place. A bailiff was appointed to keep the district closed with a threat of 'plucking the coat from his back' if he failed to do so. Constables patrolled back and forth to ensure the houses were shut in (MacKenzie 1953, 19). The plague was becoming more persistent towards the end of the 16th century, leading to three major epidemics in the 17th century (Scott & Duncan 2001, 192).

With no real understanding of the cause of the disease, the fact that the outbreaks in 1603 and 1625 coincided with changes in monarchy led to a belief that the epidemics were a warning, sent to purge the sins of the last reign (Porter 2009a, 11). Other possible causes under consideration at this time included foul air and a lack of cleanliness, so preventative measures were taken such as cleaning the streets, the expulsion of vagrants, the prohibition of public gatherings and the killing of stray cats and dogs, who were thought to carry the disease (ibid, 18–20). Another preventative approach involved the isolation of the sick, putting an entire household in quarantine for up to 40 days from the last plague death inside (Moote & Moote 2004, 53). This placed additional pressure on communities, testing family loyalties with a great temptation to conceal suspected cases (Porter 2009a, 16–19). It appears this was the case with the death of the first victim of the 1665 epidemic, the young daughter of a society physician from St Paul's, Covent Garden – worryingly close to Westminster (Moote and Moote 2004, 52).

Funeral traditions also came under attack as families were expected to comply with new regulations, which included the banning of public funerals and the burying of plague victims at night (ibid, 123). Customary processions and gatherings were thought dangerous for fear of spreading the disease and the corpse itself was considered a source of contagion (Hays 2005, 127).

THE GREAT FIRE

Londoners did not have to wait long before facing their next challenge: the Great Fire of September 1666. Having started in Pudding Lane, the fire spread rapidly through the timber buildings and nearby wharves, stacked with timber and coal. High winds made the situation worse, as did the narrow lanes, which allowed the fire to jump across gaps. After a slow response, many people tried to salvage their possessions and head to the Thames for transport. The diarist John Evelyn describes boats filled with belongings and other goods floating on the river (Porter 2009b, 27–30). He also describes how he witnessed the scene, recording his increasing apprehension for the maimed seamen under his charge at the Savoy Hospital (Rideal 2016, 173).

As the fire spread, concern also grew over the safety of Whitehall and Westminster. When the natural firebreak across the River Fleet failed to curb the advance of the flames the decision was made to establish new breaks by demolishing or unroofing houses at suitable points along the predicted route of the fire. Finally, however, it was a change in wind direction that brought some relief and the fire eventually died down (Porter 2009b, 37–40).

Many Londoners lost their homes, either as a result of the fire itself or because they lay in the path of one of the strategically placed firebreaks. Although ultimately the fire stopped some 400m away from the area around the Savoy, houses in the parish of St Mary Savoy had been destroyed as a preventative measure. As well as the obvious and immediate difficulties this would cause the inhabitants, there were knock-on effects – for example, the sheer number of Londoners who had been displaced. Many were forced to retreat to the suburbs; Covent Garden, close to the Savoy, became extremely crowded (ibid, 41). There was also a detrimental effect on rental incomes, with many landlords having to reduce or forget rents until their properties could be restored (ibid, 58).

In the aftermath of the fire John Evelyn and Christopher Wren, among others, presented the king with plans for a redesigned London (Fig 2.2). The plans of both these well-travelled men displayed Continental influences: a basic grid pattern with wider roads, on which were superimposed squares and piazzas with radiating streets (Porter 2009b, 80; Rideal 2016, 206). Their plans also included measures to improve the city by moving the more pollutive industries and the cemeteries to the suburbs (Bédoyère 2004, 10).

HEALTH
SANITATION

As discussed above London suffered from frequent outbreaks of disease, poor living conditions, overcrowding and poor water quality being just some of the contributing factors (Cherryson et al 2012, 15). Dustmen would often refuse to go into the poorest areas to collect rubbish, and communal latrines, where they existed, were often left uncleaned by landlords. Any run-off from sewerage and rubbish dumped in the streets filled the gullies and emptied into streams such as the Fleet and from there into the Thames (Jackson 2014, 53–7). Some improvements had been made by 1750 but these sometimes caused further difficulties. Cellar cesspits were introduced in many houses, for example, but were often dug too deep, with the result that they could come into contact with groundwater and be a problem in times of flooding (ibid, 58).

By 1767 the Chelsea Waterworks Company was pumping Thames water into wealthy houses but there was no attempt at purification (Bucholz & Ward 2012, 336). Still, as general improvements in sanitation and drainage were carried out the health of Londoners improved. The death rate had started to fall after 1750 and fell at an increased rate after 1780 (McLynn 2002, 13). Although much improved, the problems did not go away and for much of the 19th century London was reported as having 'the dirtiest streets of any city in the civilised world' (Jackson 2014, 27). It was not until this time that London's first 'modern' underground sewerage system was developed (Mims et al 2006, 53).

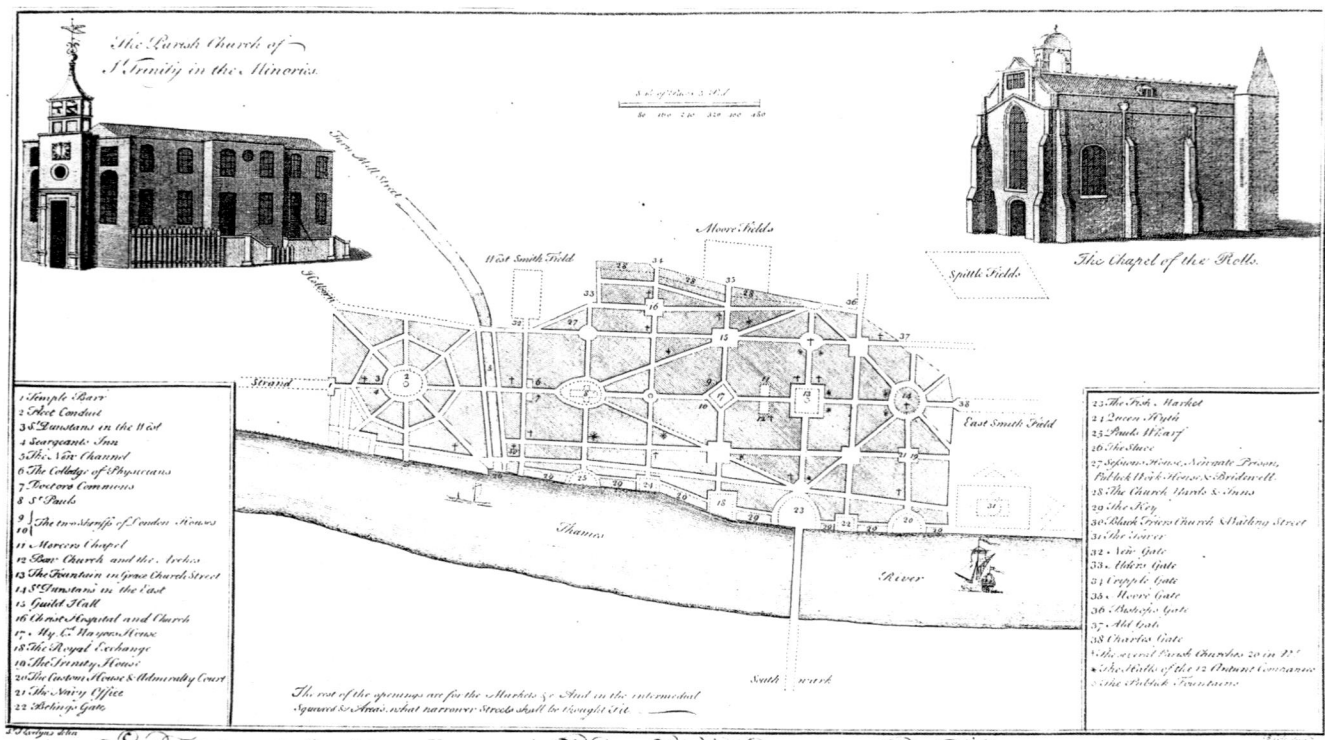

Fig 2.2 Sir John Evelyn's plan for rebuilding London after the fire of 1666 (©WL, M0003249 used under CC BY 4.0)

CHOLERA

During the first half of the 19th century the Savoy population, like the rest of London and elsewhere, would have felt the effects of the cholera outbreaks, the first in 1831 and the second in 1849 (Arnold 2006, 111). These outbreaks caused anxiety and fear among the populace for several reasons, not least because cholera was associated with a quick and painful death but also because both the cause and cure were uncertain. Doctors believed that the cause was a miasma, impure air polluted with waste (Arnold 2006, 112; Thomas 2015, 22). However, the fact that those who were worst affected lived in the slums led to the belief that cholera was a disease of the poor, linked to unsanitary living conditions (Jackson 2014, 61); if nothing else, the outbreaks highlighted the situation of the poor to the rich (Fig 2.3). The City of London Board identified precautionary measures, such as keeping the streets clean, particularly in poor areas, as well as the regular draining of sluices, drains and ditches (Thomas 2015, 42) but, as already mentioned, this was not always easy. The concern over poor living conditions was short-lived and once the immediate threat was over the plight of the poor was soon forgotten (Jackson 2014, 59).

By studying the outbreaks in London, a connection was seen between those areas affected and those areas supplied by water from the Thames. Some individuals, for example Dr Gavin, were convinced by the link, stating to the General Board of Health on the Supply of Water to the Metropolis in 1850 that 'the connection between foul water and cholera was established by *irrefragable evidence*' (Parkin 1859, 54). However, the evidence was not seen as 'irrefragable' by everyone. While acknowledging that the Thames contained decomposing organic materials, sewerage and industrial waste from manufacturing industries, Dr Parkin, a member of the Royal College of Surgeons, did not think the concentrations of pollutants were sufficient to cause such a problem, nor the statistics persuasive enough to prove the case. He concluded that, however bad the Thames water was, it had no influence on the production or spread of epidemic cholera (ibid, 55–61).

Once again, in a response similar to that made during the plague epidemics of the 17th century, it was recommended that victims should be burnt straight after death. According to an angry Charles Greville, the 19th-century diarist, this caused 'scenes of uproar, violence, and brutal ignorance … and this on the part of the lower orders, for whose especial benefit all the precautions are taken, and for whose relief large sums of money have been raised and all resources of charity called into activity in every part of the town' (Lewis 2010, 205). It seems that many victims were buried in the already overcrowded burial grounds, giving rise once more to the arguments for moving cemeteries to the outskirts of London (see below).

Fig 2.3 Wood engraving depicting cramped and squalid housing conditions, Grey's Inn Lane (©WL, L0073462 used under CC BY 4.0)

FOOD AND DRINK

Food and drink were an increasingly important part of London culture during the 16th to 18th centuries, with coffee houses and clubs springing up alongside pre-existing taverns and inns. By 1620 there were 100 taverns located along the Strand alone and over 400 in London as a whole by 1638. The late 17th century saw the introduction of gin, and the rapid increase in its consumption resulted in more than 8000 spirit houses in London by 1739 (Bucholz & Ward 2012, 191, 194). The health risks associated with drinking water were partly to blame for the increasing popularity of ale and spirits, which caused health problems of their own (Fig 2.4). Gin was seen as the 'source of most evils' and blamed for crime, a falling birth rate, a rising infant mortality rate (due to 'spoiled women's nurse milk') as well as for destroying the health of the military (White 2012, 330).

Gin houses were spreading and if the figures are correct, when combined with alehouses and taverns, the number of houses selling alcohol in London ranged by area from one in fifteen to one in four. In 1750, as much as 50% of the wheat sold in London markets every week was used to produce alcohol (McLynn 2002, 12; White 2012, 330). By the second half of the century the problem was subsiding but a large number of gin houses remained (Durston 2012, 66). Drinking had become a pastime for all classes of the 18th-century London population and, although heavily regulated, it led to drunkenness, which was another cause of criminality (McLynn 2002, 12; White 2012, 327).

While the alehouse or public house sold drink alone, and usually to the lower classes, food could be found in inns and taverns, with the first restaurants or 'ordinaries' appearing in the early 17th century. A fixed-price meal could be bought, while those on a lower budget could buy food at the market and take it to a tavern for cooking (Bucholz & Ward 2012, 191–2).

LAW AND ORDER

A culture of heavy drinking, bawdy houses, illiteracy and low life expectancy bred an ephemeral, gambler's attitude to 'law and order'
—McLynn 2002, 4.

A particular problem faced by the Savoy Precinct was the existence of criminal sanctuaries. A church was considered immune from civil and royal law and could grant the rights of sanctuary to any criminal or person seeking protection (Fritze & Robison 2002, 486). There were 24 such sanctuaries in Tudor times, of which the Savoy Precinct was one. These

Fig 2.4 *The Gin Shop*, by George Cruikshank, 1829 (©WL,V0049130 used under CC BY 4.0)

privileges in the Savoy led the Recorder of London to complain that the area was the 'chief nursery for rogues and masterless men' (Locking 1889, 661). The privileges of sanctuary were finally abolished in the Savoy in 1697 (Weinreb et al 2008, 825) and throughout London by 1712 (McLynn 2002, 3).

Looking more generally, the volume of crime experienced in London was due partly to problems of overcrowding and poverty but was also a consequence of London's developing topography, with dark lanes, alleyways and hidden courts (ibid). Before the late 17th century most London streets were exceptionally dark at night, with additional problems caused by poor paving and piles of street rubbish (ibid, 130). London experienced a short reprise following the installation of revolutionary convex-glassed lanterns devised by John Vernatti and Edward Hemming in the 1680s but the system fell into disuse after Hemming lost his patent in 1717. This made crimes easier to commit and catching criminals even harder in the dark streets (McLynn 2002, 13). Crime was certainly rife in London, with a much higher crime rate than the rest of the country: while the Old Bailey recorded 500–600 crimes between 1725 and 1750, the county of Sussex dealt with just 30 (Bucholz & Ward 2012, 241).

During the second half of the 18th century commissions were set up that were specifically designed to take responsibility for street lighting, pavements, cleaning and drainage but these schemes were initially limited to the City rather than London as a whole. The decades that followed saw improvements on a wider scale with oil lamps, stone pavements, deeper gutters and clearance of street obstructions as well as house and shop numbering (Bucholz & Ward 2012, 130–1).

With regard to the crimes themselves, the 17th century saw an increase in the number of crimes punishable by death, largely as a consequence of the hard times being felt by the population, which led to such crimes as petty theft, shoplifting and pickpocketing (Bucholz & Ward 2012, 241). Pickpockets were a particular concern in the 18th century, with those in London more skilled than elsewhere. Congregating around Convent Garden and the Strand, both areas close to the Savoy, pickpockets, who were often armed, targeted theatregoers (McLynn 2002, 6). Footpad robberies were also common up until the second half of the 18th century, frequently involving violence and shooting in an attempt to steal anything of value (McLynn 2002, 6; White 2012, 394). After 1750, however, the situation seems to have changed: fewer crimes of violence were taking place, but burglaries became more frequent (McLynn 2002, 13).

Before the introduction of the first recognisable police force in London in 1829 the job of upholding the law fell to watchmen, organised and paid for by the ratepayers in each parish. They patrolled the streets in pairs, carrying staffs and lanterns (Bucholz & Ward 2012, 194; White 2012, 444); by the middle of the 18th century there were as many as 900 of them (ibid, 439). There were also constables, elected from among the taxpayers, who had the power to interrogate and decide whether the case should be brought before the magistrate. In times of real civil disorder, which were not uncommon, peace officers and magistrates had to be rescued by the military (ibid, 444) and Foot Guards from the Savoy Barracks were often called upon (See Chapter 3, 'Military life').

DUCHY OF LANCASTER: THE SAVOY LIBERTY

It is unclear when the area around the Savoy became a liberty (an area outside the jurisdiction of Westminster) but the first mention of it as such is in 1393, in a report on the tenants residing in the Savoy Liberty (Somerville 1960, 149–51). As early as 1585 an act of parliament enabled the Duchy of Lancaster to introduce a form of government within the Savoy Liberty under the chancellor or steward of the Duchy and his appointed burgesses. This would work alongside the court system that had been in existence since the end of the 14th century (ibid, 150–6). The year 1619 witnessed the introduction of a parliamentary statute listing the orders and ordinances for the liberty, 'provided for the good of the said Liberty' (Somerville 1960, 252). These can be found in full in Somerville (ibid, Appendix II, 252–61) but are worthy of summary here as they outline the laws governing life within the precinct and the behaviour expected of its inhabitants. Although 32 in number and each quite specific in content, the ordinances can be grouped into three main themes: trade within the liberty; cleanliness for the general wellbeing of all; and regulations governing the nature of inhabitants and tenants. Punishment for breaking the rules usually involved imprisonment or paying fines (sometimes both) with fines payable used for the poor of the liberty.

With regard to trading, if any person was found to be using false weights and measures to buy or sell or to otherwise misrepresent or falsify the goods in question, they were imprisoned and fined according to the severity of the crime. Bakers, brewers, colliers, and woodmongers were singled out with separate ordinances for each. Licences were needed for selling ale and the number of alehouses dedicated to that purpose was to be limited to 20, each having to provide two guest beds for 'wayfaring people'.

Ordinances concerned with cleanliness and wellbeing cover the cleaning of chimneys to avoid fire as well as regulating the timing of controlled fires in the street. Also listed were the daily cleaning of gutters, rules concerned with soil and sweepings from the house and the prohibition of hogs wandering in the streets. In addition, victuallers were to light candles in their windows at night unless the moon rendered it unnecessary.

Finally, the inhabitants themselves appeared to be strictly regulated. Any tenant, servant or apprentice living within the liberty had to be accounted for, providing testimonials that had to be approved. Sick and infected people could only be taken in on approval. Any incontinency of behaviour or attempt to resist officers would be punished according to the crime; one such punishment could be banishment from the liberty. If you dared to return following banishment you would be 'whipped naked at the cart's tail throughout the said Liberty' (ibid, 256). Fines were also payable by constables who failed to apprehend rogues or beggars in the street.

In the first of the regular court books, introduced in 1683, four constables are recorded along with occasional deputies, four scavengers, four aleconners and two flesh-tasters (Somerville 1960, 171). The duty of the Savoy constables was to maintain peace within the liberty, a role that was distinct and additional to that of the parish constables. They were also responsible for appointing watchmen, paid for by the householders, in an area that was 'in great need of policing', while they themselves would become more concerned with identifying 'suspicious persons and disorderly houses or brothels' (ibid, 178–80). As elsewhere in London, the constables and watchmen were ineffective in their duty in a system that persisted until the beginning of the 19th century and the introduction of a recognisable police force (ibid, 185).

VIOLENCE IN SOCIETY

Violent crime was not uncommon in the 17th and 18th centuries, with rape and sexual assault being regularly reported. Based upon trials at the Old Bailey, covering London between 1674 and 1797, the statistics suggest that almost all rape and sexual assault cases involved victims and offenders of similar social standing. In 76% of such cases children aged between 7 and 12 years were involved (Toulalan 2013, 27). The victims tended to belong to the working classes – servants, daughters of artisans, craftsmen or tradesmen – and the offenders appear to have been men of the same social class, with whom the girls would have unaccompanied contact during their everyday lives, making them vulnerable. Such assaults might take place within the home or the workplace, and occasionally on the street as girls ran errands (ibid, 27–44).

Assault was also commonplace, between men, between women and between men and women. Some of these assaults may have been associated with domestic violence, used to assert authority between men and women as well as over children. This behaviour has been described as 'an enduring undercurrent of life in London' (White 2012, 414–15) Of course, with social structure the way it was, servants and apprentices would also be likely to suffer.

In the 18th century violence was also creeping into several pastimes and pleasures. In the first half of the century cockfighting, bear-baiting and goose-throwing were popular entertainments, as well as bare-knuckle fist-fighting (McLynn 2002, 4). Bare-knuckle fist-fighting, a precursor to boxing, consisted largely of bare fists and head butts and, although illegal, was becoming a popular sport among gentlemen (Olsen 1999, 168). Fighting was also used by the lower ranks of society to resolve their differences, whereas the upper classes might use a duel to find a resolution to a disagreement (White 2012, 414–15).

PROSTITUTION

For those girls who struggled to find a job in service once they had migrated to London, prostitution offered a solution and it became one of the main sources of employment for young women (Olsen 1999, 49; Bucholz & Ward 2012, 76–7; White 2012, 347). Although they could be found throughout the city, most street women were centred around the Strand, Covent Garden, Drury Lane, Fleet Street and Charing Cross (Olsen 1999, 49; White 2012, 347). The most notorious area, which was frequently referred to, was Catherine Street, opposite Somerset House and leading north to Drury Lane. In other words the Savoy would have been in the heart of the busiest area. It is recorded that in the Savoy Hospital, which served the regiments of Foot Guards in the 17th century (see Chapter 3), head nurses were required to keep their eyes open for 'idle or loose women that frequent or lie in the hospital' soliciting for business. This became so much of a problem that hospital staff petitioned for action to be taken against 'layabouts and lewd persons' in their grounds (Gruber-von-Arni 2006, 56).

As well as the street walkers, numerous bawdy houses or brothels were recorded: over 100 bawdy houses existed in London by the late 1580s (Bucholz & Ward 2012, 205). By the late 17th century there was a concentration around Covent Garden and Drury Lane, attracted by the male theatregoers, at least 30 active in the adjacent parish to the Savoy, Mary-le-Strand. Added to this was the increasing number of clubs and bawdy houses that served the 'underground' gay community. Covent Garden also contained a large number of 'molly' houses or homosexual brothels (ibid, 347). 'Molly' life was a recognised way for the poorly paid soldier to make some extra money in times of need (White 2012, 374). With particular regard to the Savoy, the Savoy bog-house, or public toilets, was well known as somewhere to frequent if you wished to show an interest in such activity (Trumbach 1999, 99; Holland 2004, 448). Of course, such behaviour was much condemned and it opened up the possibilities of blackmail. A soldier in one of the regiments of Foot Guards, Richard Cope, was sentenced to five years' imprisonment in 1785 for locking away an eminent gentleman and, upon his release, accusing him of an unnatural crime (White 2012, 374).

LONDON CEMETERIES

The potential problems associated with overcrowded burials grounds were recognised as early as the 17th century. The architect Christopher Wren commented on the worrying rise in ground level in churchyards and the detrimental effect this would have on the fabric of the church buildings. In a similar vein John Evelyn, the famous diarist and courtier during the reign of Charles II, describes how churches appeared to have been built in pits, with bodies stacked up around them (Arnold 2006, 69). In the aftermath of the Great Fire in 1666 both men took the opportunity to present plans for the redesigning of London, one of the key elements being the establishment of suburban cemeteries (ibid). Evelyn wanted to build a 'universal cemetery to all parishes' beyond the city walls. Whether or not he saw the existing cemeteries as a health problem, he likened the smell that arose from them to gutters, lay-stalls and kennels (Jackson 2014, 106).

The subject was highlighted again at the beginning of the 19th century when George Frederick Carden began a campaign to build public cemeteries in 'places where they would be less prejudicial to the health of the inhabitants' (Weinreb et al 2008, 138). Despite insisting that public health was his main concern, his financial motivation was evident as he attempted to establish companies to provide funerals and burial plots across London at fixed prices. Unfortunately, his first attempts,

The Economic Funeral Company and the General Burial Grounds Association, were unsuccessful. He finally made a breakthrough in 1830 with the establishment of the General Cemetery Company and the subsequent consecration of the Kensal Green cemetery in 1833 (Jackson 2014, 112–13). By 1841 there were seven commercial cemeteries in the areas surrounding the residential suburbs (Weinreb et al 2008, 138) but as they charged considerably more than parish burial grounds they were not an option for the poorest of London, who continued to struggle with the overcrowded parish and small, privately owned burial grounds (Jackson 2014, 114–15).

At the end of the 1830s George Walker (Fig 2.5), a surgeon practising on Drury Lane where the problems were particularly noticeable, embarked on a campaign to end 'intramural interment' once and for all (ibid, 115–16). While acknowledging persistently poor living conditions associated with such things as the sewers, slaughterhouses and narrow streets without circulating air, he put the cause of many diseases down to 'exhalations arising from the putrefaction of dead bodies on the very surface of the earth' (Walker 1839, 2–3).

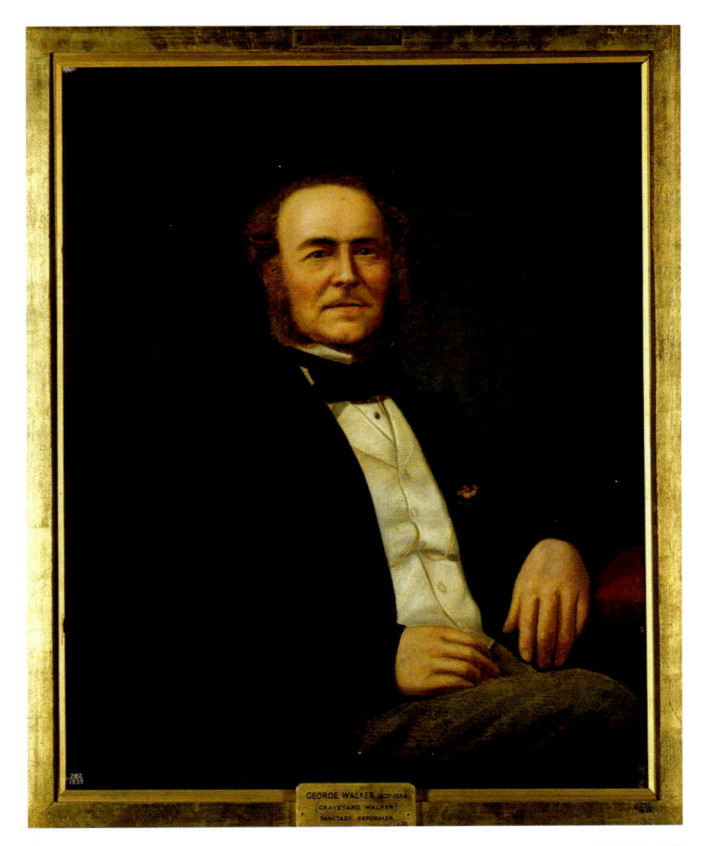

Fig 2.5 George ('Graveyard') Walker (©WL, V0018099 used under CC BY 4.0)

Walker toured the capital's cemeteries gathering new information, which was summarised in his leaflet entitled *Gatherings from Grave Yards* (1839). He gives a good description of a disturbing situation but it does at times read like propaganda.

While his arguments were very similar to those of Carden, he was careful not to associate himself with the commercial interests of the cemetery companies (Jackson 2014, 116).

> They [ie, human remains] are exhumed by shovelfuls, and disgustingly exposed to the pensive observations of the passer-by ... The grave digger's pick is often forced through the lid of a coffin when least expected, from which so dreadful an effluvium is emitted, as to occasion immediate annoyance; most of the graves are very shallow, – some entire coffins, indeed, are to be found within a foot and a half of the surface (Walker 1839, 168).

One particular cemetery, Portugal Street in the adjacent parish of St Clement Danes, appears to offer a good example of the problem as he saw it:

> The soil of this ground is saturated, absolutely saturated, with human putrescence ... Several bones were lying on the surface of the grave nearest to us – a large heap of coffin wood was placed in readiness for removal, and, at a small distance, a heap covered with coarse sacking ... proved also to be long pieces of coffin wood, evidently not in a decayed state (ibid, 150).

Walker goes on to recount the sorry experience of a poor mourner when visiting a graveyard in Southwark: 'In making a grave, a body, partly decomposed, was dug up, and placed on the surface, at the side, slightly covered with earth; a mourner stepped upon it, - the loosened skin peeled off, he slipped forward, and had nearly fallen into the grave' (ibid, 202).

It seems Walker had many examples to support his argument, including one from the Savoy Chapel burial ground.

> William Jackson, aged 29, a strong, robust man, was employed in digging a grave in the 'Savoy'; he struck his spade into a coffin, from which an extremely disgusting odour arose; he reached his home, in Clement's Lane, with difficulty; complained to his wife that he had 'had a turn; the steam which issued from the coffin had made him very ill' (ibid, 134).

It appears poor William suffered 'pain in the head, heaviness, extreme debility, lachrymation, violent palpitations of the heart, universal trembling, with vomiting'. When poverty forced him to return to gravedigging after a few days' recovery he was unlucky enough to experience the same thing, this time collapsing, and dying within 36 hours. His death was attributed to cholera, caught as result of his work (ibid, 135).

The practices of the resurrectionists, or bodysnatchers, are well known but even after the passing of the Anatomy Act in 1832, when laws were put in place to prevent the unlawful removal of a corpse, the grave does not appear to have been sacred, its commercial value extending beyond the body placed in it. Walker describes the value in coffin furniture – nails, for example – to certain trades, such as marine stores (Walker 1839, 199). He also suggests that coffin wood was being used for fuelling domestic fires in poorer neighbourhoods, hastily pointing out the likely health problems that might result from such a practice (ibid, 200). He recognises that 'warmth constitutes one of the most essential necessaries of life' and blames the excessive price of coal in the capital (upwards of 30 shillings per ton as opposed to 11 shillings elsewhere), stating that even faced with using 'wood frequently saturated with human putrescence, – their poverty, and not their will consents' (ibid, 201).

The removal of bulky coffin wood is also described as a necessity, with the constant requirement to clear graveyards and to make room for more burials. While the wood was given away or sold, the bodies, being 'more easily destructible', were 'got rid of in various ways' (ibid, 201). It seems unlikely and perhaps surprising that such practices were allowed to continue but, while Walker's description is probably embellished, the worst practices were overlooked by the clergy as burial fees formed a significant part of their income (Jackson 2014, 105).

At the beginning of the 1840s Walker was joined in his campaign by the barrister and radical journalist Sir Edwin Chadwick. They made their case before the House of Commons in 1842, using the vast number of deaths from the cholera epidemics to emphasise the problem (Arnold 2006, 100, 114). Eventually a new Burial Act was introduced in 1853 (UK Public General Acts nd), enabling the closure of many London cemeteries on health grounds and the establishment of new, suburban ones.

2.2 THE SAVOY PRECINCT

Several further historical sources serve to shed light on the population living and dying in the Savoy Precinct.

LIVING POPULATION

A list of householders in the precinct is available for 1662 (WCA, 0012/002). At this time there appear to have been 46 householders, providing lodgings for an additional 43 people. Of course this total of 89 would be living in private households and therefore not encompass the entire precinct population, which would be considerably inflated by the presence of the military hospital within it (see Chapter 3). This figure stands against the 74 deaths recorded for this year, bearing in mind that the St Mary-le Strand parishioners are included in this total.

HEARTH TAX

The Hearth Tax was designed to grade houses based upon the number of fireplaces in each and was introduced in 1662 as a source of revenue for Charles II. The information recorded at the time can now be used to make comparisons and assessments of relative wealth between neighbourhoods. The 437 records available for the Duchy of the Savoy provide a useful insight into the Savoy population at the time of the survey in 1666 (Hearth Tax Online nd; Centre for Metropolitan History 2011).

According to the maps that have been produced from the data the Savoy was, in 1666, one of the wealthiest neighbourhoods, immediately surrounded by others of similar wealth, with an average of six hearths per household (Centre for Hearth Tax Research, University of Roehampton, https://www.roehampton.ac.uk/research-centres/centre-for-hearth-tax-research/). Of these, tax was paid for an average of five hearths per household. The only parish with a higher average was nearby St Paul's, Covent Garden, which had 7–10 hearths per household, with all taxes paid.

The number of hearths in the Savoy ward ranged from one (15 households) to 59 (1 household), with the greatest number of households (75) having four hearths (Fig 2.6). While a large number of households have between 1 and 13 hearths, once the number of hearths reaches 14 the number of households reduces to between one and four. Those householders with the largest numbers of hearths are listed (Table 2.1).

Additional sources are available for the Savoy Precinct from the 19th century. The following data have been taken from the Great Britain Historical GIS Project (2017), using historical material which is copyright of the Great Britain Historical GIS Project and the University of Portsmouth.

The population of the precinct has been recorded over several decades – every decade for the first half of the 19th century and intermittently until 1921 (Table 2.2; Fig 2.7).

To understand the population pattern the site history must be taken into account and while relevant facts are outlined here, the details are given in Chapter 3. The data suggest an overall decline in numbers within the precinct through the 19th century (Page 1911a). There was a decrease in population

CHAPTER 2 LONDON AND THE SAVOY PRECINCT

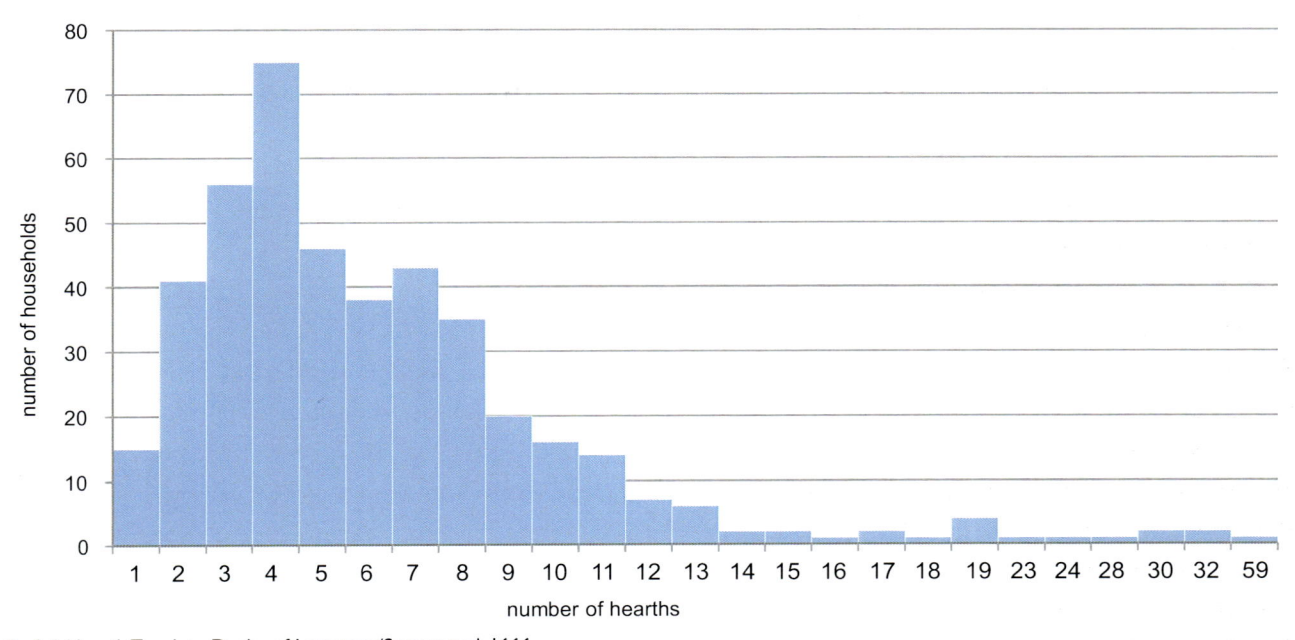

Fig 2.6 Hearth Tax data: Duchy of Lancaster/Savoy ward, 1666

Householder	No of hearths
Esqr Elnigsby	15
Mrs Coney	15
Xpofer Hill	16
Widd Newton	17
Thomas Springall	17
Thomas Spence	18
Widd Woodcock	19
Francis Alking	19
Lord Ashley	19
Lord Bridgman	23
Henry Crosse	24
The Lady Wimblton	28
The Honourable Henry Howard	30
Earl of Salisbury	32 (unpaid)
Capt. Richard Black	32
Dutchey Countess of Somerset	59

Table 2.1 Households with the largest number of hearths

Year	Population	Total no of houses
1801	320	
1811	287	
1821	222	
1831	431	
1841	372	64
1851	245	58
1881	201	55
1901	166	35
1911	104	
1921	33	10

Table 2.2 Nineteenth- and 20th-century population of the Savoy Precinct and total number of houses recorded

Fig 2.7 Total population of the Savoy Precinct, 1801–1921

size at the beginning of the century after the removal of the military, which had been in residence throughout the 18th century. The increase seen from the 1820s to the 1840s followed completion of the improvement works undertaken in the area, which rendered the Savoy a more respectable place to live. From 1841 onwards the number of houses recorded in the precinct is also available and both data sets suggest a continuation of the gradual population decrease throughout the 19th century and into the beginning of the 20th century (Table 2.2)

In 1860 Charles Dickens noted that in his opinion the population of the Savoy were 'quiet folks, dwelling peaceably in the little houses, with white door-steps and the green blinds, which nestle round the church'. With regard to the occupations of the inhabitants, Dickens observes that 'from their smooth bald heads and subdued whiskers, I take them to be mainly

Year	No of deaths	Year	No of deaths	Year	No of deaths
1657	60	1691	145	1725	130
1658	72	1692	141	1726	102
1659	82	1693	130	1727	117
1660	91	1694	160	1728	73
1661	102	1695	128	1729	99
1662	74	1696	120	1730	83
1663	71	1697	124	1731	66
1664	80	1698	82	1732	76
1665	303	1699	114	1733	118
1666	72	1700	104	1734	90
1667	89	1701	126	1735	92
1668	88	1702	104	1736	96
1669	104	1703	112	1737	116
1670	104	1704	130	1738	121
1671	75	1705	120	1739	83
1672	74	1706	141	1740	156
1673	83	1707	132	1741	185
1674	99	1708	124	1742	83
1675	63	1709	157	1743	90
1676	62	1710	156	1744	117
1677	95	1711	168	1745	126
1678	108	1712	125	1746	191
1679	103	1713	113	1747	151
1680	121	1714	145	1748	179
1681	147	1715	113	1749	94
1682	111	1716	118	1750	68
1683	123	1717	113	1751	60
1684	135	1718	162	1752	71
1685	143	1719	110	1753	55
1686	140	1720	146	1754	68
1687	116	1721	141	1755	83
1688	99	1722	171	1756	79
1689	124	1723	177	1757	135
1690	100	1724	161	1758	92

Table 2.3 Total number of deaths as recorded in the London Bills of Mortality, 1657–1758

accountants, clerks, retired tradesmen, commission-agents, and employés, interested in pale ale, in pickles, and Wallsend coals' (Dickens 1860, 120).

The occupations listed for the precinct in 1881 also reflect the changes: whereas in the previous century it had been largely occupied by soldiers housed in the Savoy Barracks, by the end of the century only two people were recorded as working in 'Defence of the Country'. By contrast 49 or 28% (9 male, 40 female) were working in domestic service or offices and 21 or 12% (20 male, 1 female) were professionals. A total of 54 (31%) are recorded either as without specific occupations or unknown.

LONDON BILLS OF MORTALITY

The London Bills of Mortality are another valuable source of information. These weekly bills were first published in the 16th century to record and monitor the death rate due to plague, but by the beginning of the 17th century had been expanded to include all causes of death (Ross 2014, 4). Their completeness and accuracy has been questioned, especially those for the early years (Wrigley & Schofield 2002, 77) but they are still considered an invaluable source of information.

The recorded numbers of deaths in the Savoy parish for 100 years from 1657 to 1758 are shown in Table 2.3 and Fig 2.8. The numbers before 1727 are inflated because the parishioners of St Mary-le-Strand were also included, having shared the Savoy Chapel and burial ground until their own new church was consecrated in 1727. During this time the Savoy Chapel temporarily became known as St Mary-le-Savoy (Loftie 1878, 179). In the Bills of Mortality the entries for the Savoy were recorded as 'Savoy' or 'Savoy Parish' from 1657 to 1660, when the name switched to St Mary Savoy. Between 1700 and 1727 the parish was known as St Mary Savoy in the Strand and the parish of St Mary-le-Strand appeared as a separate entity in 1726. The last change was in 1727, when the Savoy parish finally became the Precinct of the Savoy.

Three additional entries have been found in the bills, showing the effect of the plague within the precinct (Postlethwayt et al 1759) (Table 2.4).

Year	Total no of deaths	Deaths due to plague
1603 (1 June – 10 Nov)	199	187
1625	250	176
1636	106	54

Table 2.4 Total number of deaths as recorded in the London Bills of Mortality, 1603, 1625 and 1636

Overall there was a very slight rise in the numbers of deaths in the parish between 1657 and 1757. The only dramatic change to the pattern is a single peak when numbers increased from 80 in 1664 to 303 in 1665. This was the year of the plague epidemic in London and of the 303 deaths in the precinct, the plague accounted for 198.

The fall in numbers after 1727 can be explained by the separation of the St Mary-le-Strand parish. For the remaining 31 years the number of deaths ranges from 55 to 191, with an average of 96 per year. Numbers over 100 appear in 13 separate years over the three decades with more significant increases

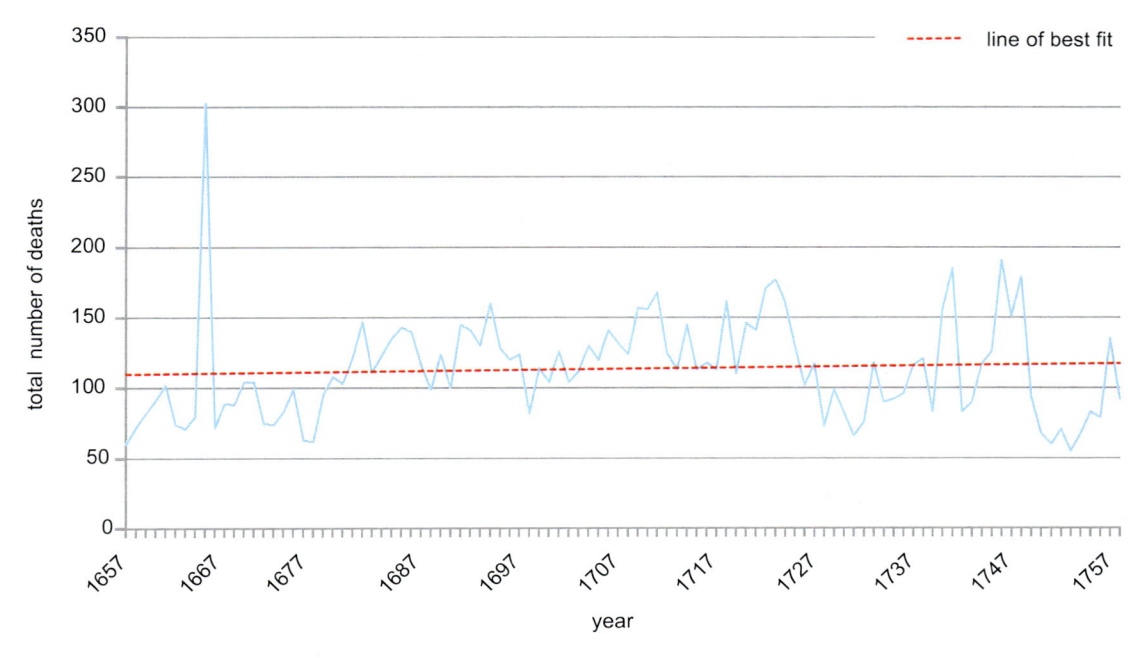

Fig 2.8 Total number of deaths as recorded in the London Bills of Mortality, 1657–1758

occurring between 1739 and 1742, when the numbers almost double from 83 deaths in 1739 to 156 in 1740, rise again to 185 in 1741, then drop back to 83 in 1742. This particular peak mirrors the overall pattern for London at the time but this is not the case for the sustained peak in the number of deaths between 1744 and 1748, with an average number of deaths at 152.8 for the five years. While there was a sharp increase in the numbers of burials from 1744 and 1745, the overall figures for London show a decrease in numbers for the next two years.

Possible reasons for these fluctuations are discussed in later chapters but death within the parish is best examined in the burial registers. For the Savoy Chapel, these cover the period from 1680 to 1854 and are examined in detail in Chapter 4.

CHAPTER 3 HISTORY OF THE SITE

Lucy Sibun

> Inexorable Death, Lean Poverty,
> Pale Sickness, ever sad Captivity.
> Can I, alas, the sev'ral Parties name,
> Which, muster'd up, the Dreadful Army frame?
> And sometimes in One Body all Unite,
> Sometimes again do separately fight:
> While sure Success on either Way does waite,
> Either a Swift, or else a Ling'ring Fate.
> But why 'gainst thee, O Death! should I inveigh,
> That to our Quiet art the only way?
> —Anne Killigrew, The Miseries of Man (Morton 1967, 33)

3.1 SAVOY HOSPITAL

At the beginning of the 16th century Henry VII proposed the construction of a new hospital where:

> nedie pouer people bee lodged, visited in their siknesses, refreshed with mete and drinke, and if nede be, with clothe and also buried yf thei fourtune to die withine the same
> (extract from the will of Henry VII; Loftie 1878, 87).

In 1508 Henry made three payments of £333 6s 8d, £6666 13s 4d, and £200 for the new building of the hospital (Somerville 1960, 9). Unfortunately, he died in 1509 before much work had been undertaken. It was not until July 1512 that the executors of the will received their licence to found the 'Hospital of Henry late King of England of the Savoy' on the site of the old ruined palace (ibid, 11). Instructions for the continued works were outlined in Henry's will, including payments in instalments to the priest William Holgill, who had been appointed surveyor and master of the works (ibid, 10). Executors transmitted 67 sealed bags of coins to be held at Westminster Abbey (500 marks) and a further 100 marks later for the construction and fitting of the hospital (Sanders et al 2007, 115). It is recorded that 165 labourers worked on the project, under candlelight in winter, and these included masons, joiners, carpenters, sawyers, bricklayers, plasterers and labourers. The total paid out in wages between 1513 and 1515 was £2734 10s 7d.

It is thought that the hospital design was based upon the 16th-century Ospedale di Santa Maria Nuova in Florence (Park & Henderson 1991, 167), with the cruciform ground plan of a church (Fig 3.1).

The large building measured approximately 320ft long with walls that were 3ft thick (Fig 3.2). Between the nave, north and south transepts there were beds for 100 poor, thought likely to have been in cubicles (Somerville 1960, 13–14). The smaller transept on the north is likely to have contained the poor man's hall, with three floors and a staircase on the east. The other small transept contained the two floors of the sisters' hall. The sisters, as the female hospital staff were known, also had a separate kitchen. The Lady Chapel was at the east end of the dormitory but the largest chapel was that of St John (discussed in detail below), linked to the west end of the dormitory by a block of rooms. A 75ft-high tower, also recorded as the steeple or belfry, lay in the angle between this block and the eastern wall of St John's Chapel and housed three small rooms, with the bell rope descending through a chamber into the lower chapel (ibid, 13–16).

To the south-west of the chapel was a range of buildings running south to the Thames. A paved court at the northern end ran along the west of the chapel to the hospital's main entrance in the Strand. This consisted of a three-storey tower that contained the hospital records, jewels and plate, the exchequer and counting house. On the south side of the court was the master's hall, with a further court to the south of this. The master's chambers included a kitchen, study and gallery. On the waterfront were buildings that had probably been there before the hospital. The water stairs, used by people to bathe in the Thames, lay at the western end and next to them came a hall, kitchen, buttery, larder and cellar. The hospital bath house and 'hothouse' came next, connected to the sisters' hall and kitchen. The easternmost part consisted of a house and garden occupied by the Duchy of Lancaster. Duchy Lane ran down the eastern side of the hospital with the Strand along the north. The great gate of the Hospital was at its western end (ibid, 17–22).

The hospital, complete and formally founded in 1517, soon became one of the sights of 16th-century London (ibid, 24; Cowie 1974, 177). William Holgill was officially appointed master of the hospital in March of the same year (Somerville 1960, 236) and received four statute books, governing

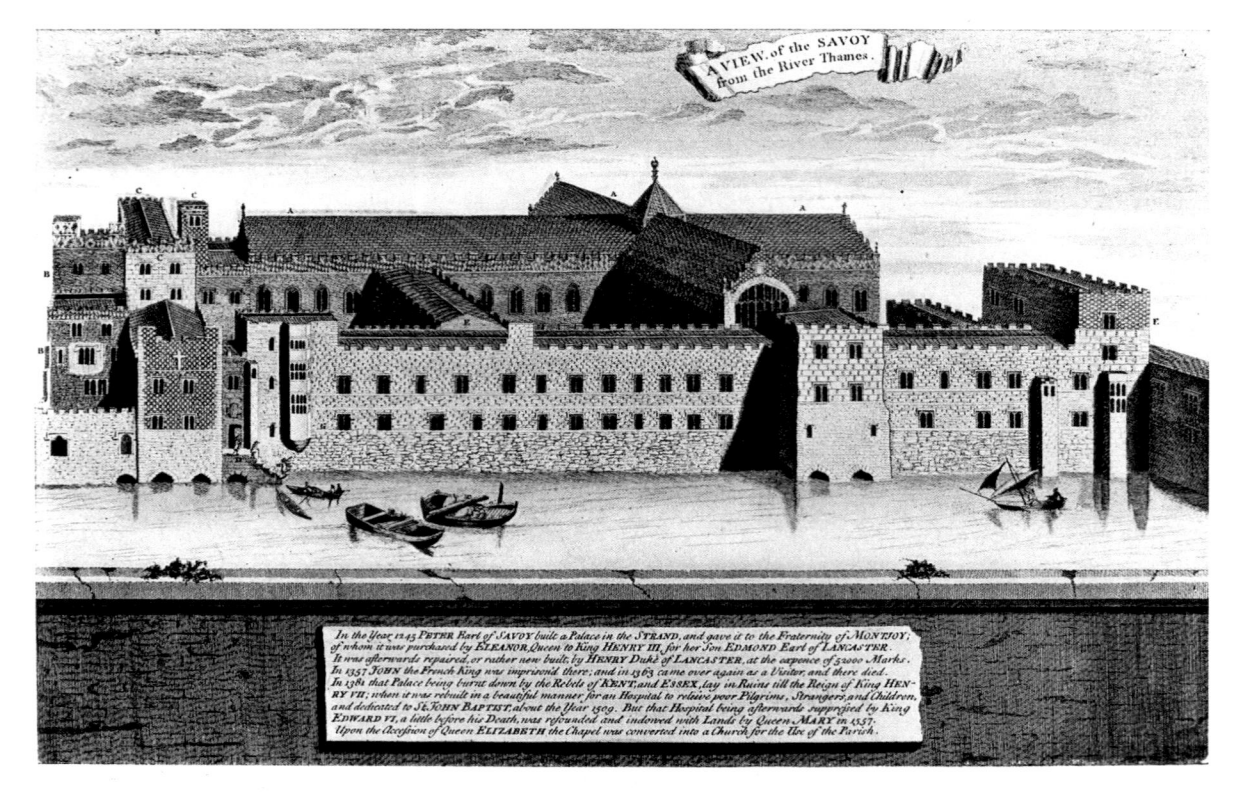

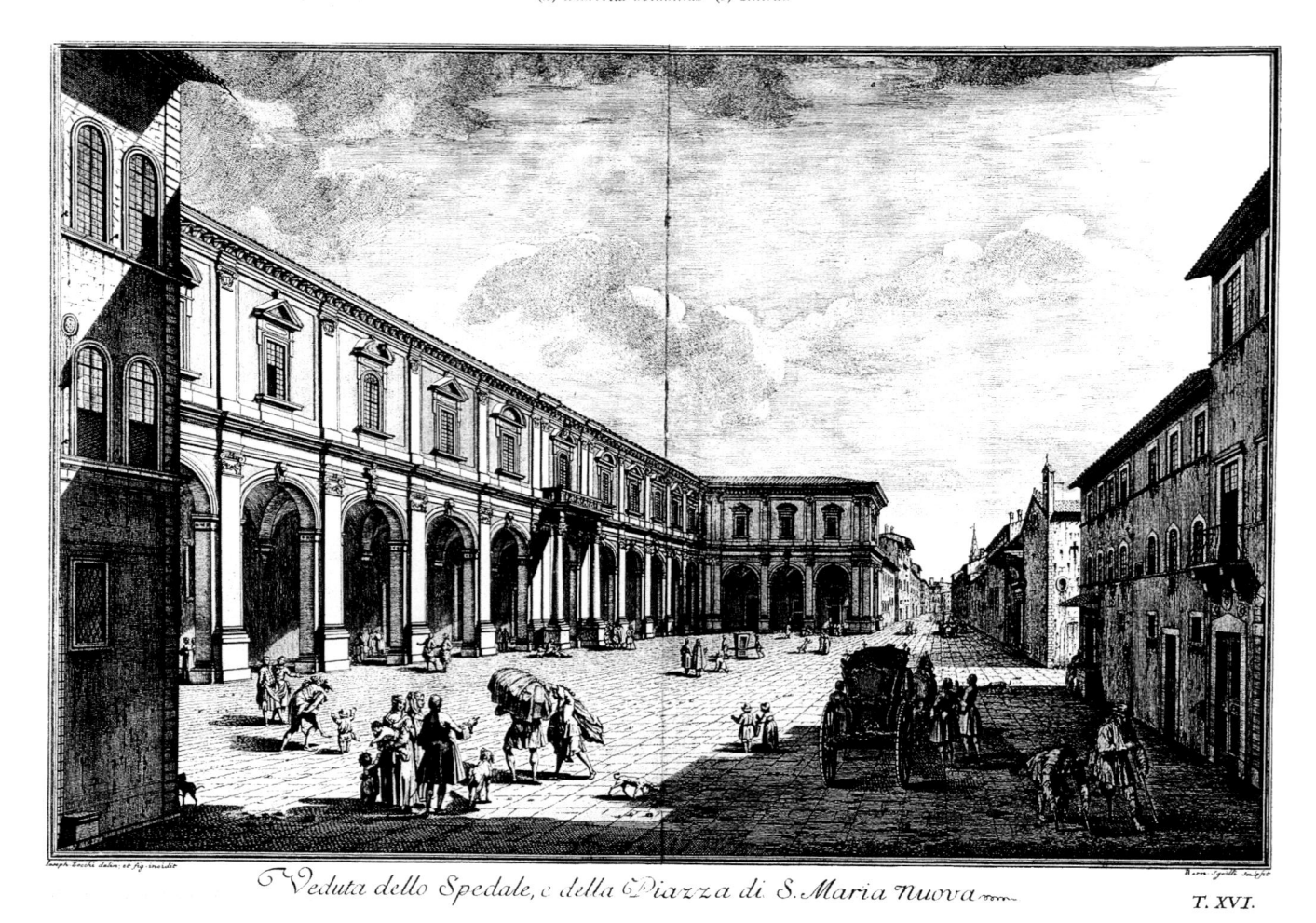

Fig 3.1 The church and hospital of Savoy, London, by George Virtue, 1750 (WL, M000798); Hospital of Santa Maria Nuova, Florence, Italy, etching, by B S Sgrilli after G Zocchi (©WL, V0014712 used under CC BY 4.0)

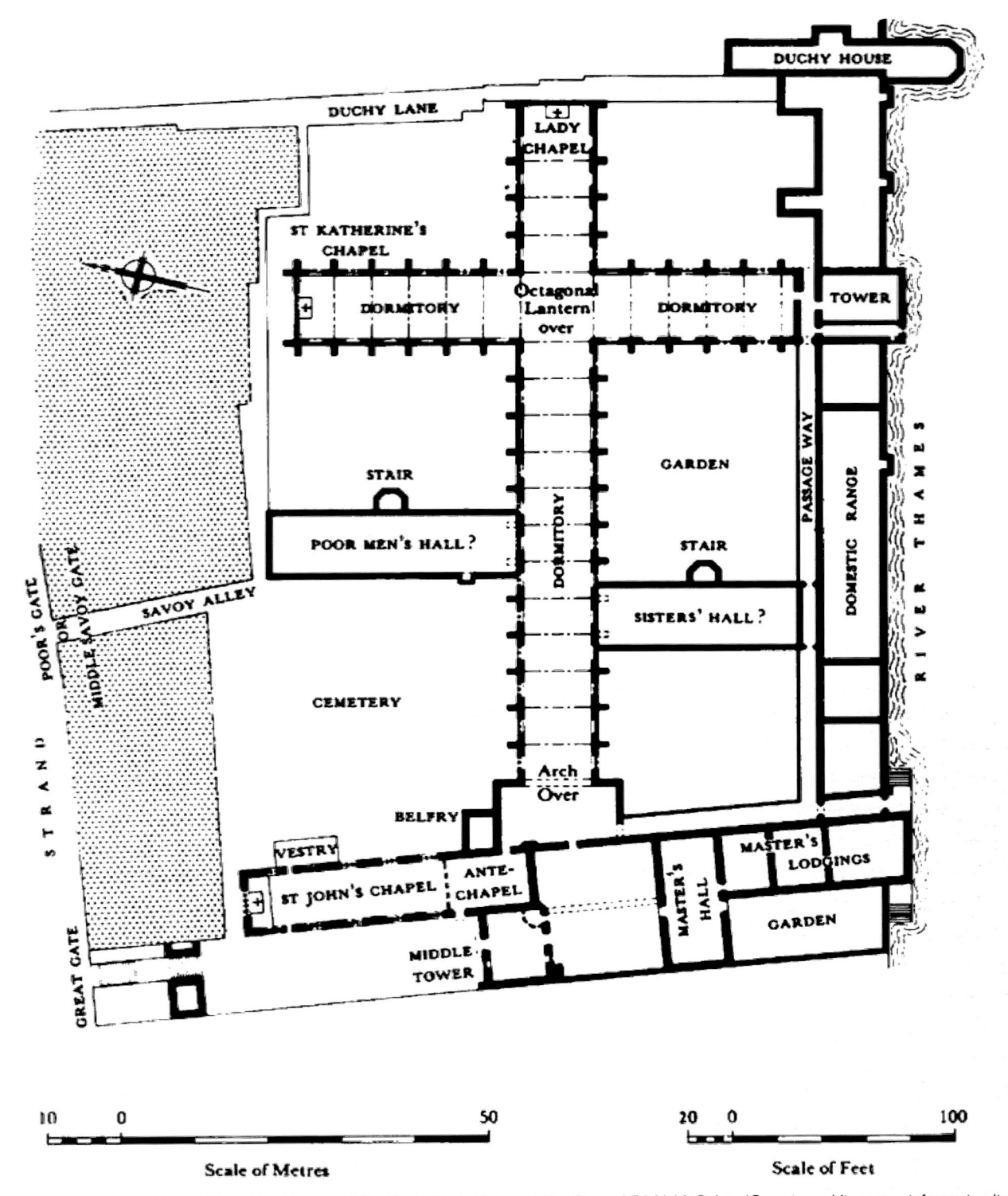

Fig 3.2 Plan of the Savoy Hospital from The History of the King's Works Volume III by General Ed. H. M. Colvin (Contains public sector information licensed under the Open Government Licence v3.0)

its operation (Sanders et al 2007, 115). The statutes were astonishingly detailed, outlining not only the appointments of hospital staff but even the number of sheets and blankets to be placed on the beds (Somerville 1960, 27).

As well as the design of the hospital, the hospital statutes shared common features with those of the Ospedale di Santa Maria Nuova in Florence, such as the requirement for inmates to attend the chapel daily (ibid, 73; Henderson 2006, 192).

There were also, however, marked differences – the Ospedale di Santa Maria Nuova accepted both males and females, for example (ibid, 272), and the organisation at the Savoy was more hierarchical in nature (Park & Henderson 1991, 168). There were appointments for male members of staff including a master, four chaplains (all with assistants), a porter, gardener and domestic staff – butler, cook, under-cook and under-porter – as well as two part-time posts for a physician and surgeon

(Somerville 1960, 29). The master or rector, who would be over 40 years old, would make a tour of the hospital twice or three times a week. The chaplains, all academically qualified, would take confession in the hospital ward and mass in the chapel, loud enough for all to hear (Swift 2014, 16). Female staff would work under the matron, who received £4 6s 4d for her yearly allowance. There were 12 sisters with their own quarters, kitchen and hall. They needed to be at least 36 years old, unmarried and a virgin, if possible (Somerville 1960, 30). All staff should wear simple, coarse, grey habits displaying the hospital seal (Swift 2014, 16)

Every night the matron, one of her women and the porter would stand at the door to welcome the poor. The Florentine hospital was designed to care solely for the sick poor, but at the Savoy, although preference was given to the sick, they also took in 'the crippled, blind or infirm', 'shamefaced poor beggars' and 'all others' (Park & Henderson 1991, 168). The statutes did, however, bar the admittance of lepers (Somerville 1960, 3), who would have been cared for at one of the ten leper hospitals in existence at the time of the Reformation in the early 16th century (Richardson 2000, 89).

Once inside the men could expect a hot bath, their clothes cleaned and conversation in front of a fire. The beds in the dormitory would have comprised feather beds or flock mattresses, feather pillows and bolsters, and coverlets in Tudor white and green, decorated with, among other things, a Tudor rose. Similarly coloured and decorated curtains could have been drawn to separate each bed (Somerville 1960, 31). Having been woken by the loud and repeated chiming of the chapel bell, the inmates would have to be out by seven o'clock (summer) or eight o'clock (winter). The sick could, however, remain in bed for visits by the physician and surgeon (ibid, 32). The hospital was designed to provide overnight accommodation for the poor folk. However, many returned night after night, spending their days lying in the surrounding field and hedgerows (ibid, 30; Cowie 1974, 177).

Henry VII had endowed 500 marks (£334) a year annual value in land. The lands owned by the hospital included the various buildings in the precinct as well as others over London and further afield (Somerville 1960, 33). In 1535 the hospital's net income was recorded as £529 15s 7¾d and in 1550, a year in which the hospital received 8399 sick and impotent, the expenses for the poor amounted to £133 7s 4½d.

Surviving hospital accounts from the year 1526–7 detail the payments made to staff as well as expenses for supplies, including expenses for the church, the poor, the physician, food, repairs and basic supplies (Table 3.1). To supplement the diet, the Savoy Hospital had been built with a large, well-stocked garden, which could have supplied food as well as medicinal herbs (Hudson 2007, 140). Indeed, with no evidence for a pharmacist, the gardens herbs may well have been relied upon (Park & Henderson 1991, 168).

Payment made	Payment details	£	s	d
Master of the Hospital	annual annuity	40		
Clerk of the kitchen	stipend	3	6	8
Head cook/butler/head porter	stipends	2		
Gardener/under porter/women to wash linen		1	6	8
Church expenses	7000 breads for masses		5	4
	wine	1	14	0
Expenses for poor	linen cloth for burying (2 × 92 yards)	1	2	0
	candles (3 dozen)		3	0
	sackcloth for bags for the ashes		1	0
	straw for beds		11	8
Physician	fees	4	0	0
Surgeon	fees	2	0	0
Apothecary	fees/medicines	3	7	6
Supplies	bakers	11	14	4
	butchers, fishmongers	87	5	1¼
	brewers	34	12	0

Table 3.1 Hospital accounts, 1526–7
(information reproduced from Tatchell 1961, 151–9)

The Savoy Precinct began to attract its fair share of less welcome inhabitants almost from its foundation. The problems were blamed on the behavioural habits of the poor, who were spending their daytimes lounging in the surrounding fields before returning to the hospital before sunset (see above). In his survey of London, John Stow describes how the hospital had become a 'lodging for Loyterers, Vagabonds, and Stumpets, that lay all day in the fields and at night were harboured there, the which was rather the maintenance of beggary, than any relief to the poor' (Stow 1598, 638). The recorder for London, William Fleetwood, also steward of the Savoy, described the Savoy as 'the chief nursery for rogues and masterless men' (Locking 1889, 661). Consequently, the hospital itself drew unwanted comments and attention. Even under the first master, Holgill, the statutes were not being adhered to and there was perhaps even discrimination against the most sore and diseased in favour of the 'most clene of the poore'. While trying to fulfil several posts, Holgill struggled to maintain the hospital and by the time he died in 1548 the money had run out and the number of sisters had been reduced to seven (Somerville 1960, 34–5).

Reports that followed highlighted the true debts of the hospital and it was duly dissolved in 1553. The hospital lands, valued at £450, as well as household furnishings and fittings were given for use at Bridewell Prison and Hospital, established in a former royal palace in 1553 (Hitchcock et al 2012). The hospital's debts were paid by the Corporation of London and the mayor and Bridewell took over responsibility for lodging the poor (Somerville 1960, 39). The number of London's poor continued to increase, however. In 1552 there were 2100 Londoners in need of help: 300 orphans, 600 sick or elderly, 350 poor men struggling to keep their children, 650 'decayed householders' and 200 vagrants (Bucholz & Ward 2012, 222), and so the closure of the hospital was short-lived. Refounded by Queen Mary in 1556, it was completely refurbished and orders were given that the statutes were to be vigorously observed (Somerville 1960, 40).

Unfortunately, the hospital's troubles were not over. Thomas Thurland, appointed master of the hospital in November 1559, had financial difficulties of his own and used and abused his position at the hospital for his own needs. Although supposedly deposed as master in 1570 he continued in his role until officially reinstated in April 1574. After his death in October that year an investigation uncovered a list of his misdemeanours including affairs with hospital staff and gambling, as well as his debt to the hospital, which amounted to £2500 (ibid, 44, 238).

Queen Mary's orders were soon forgotten. A continued disregard for the statutes was evident in 1582, when William Fleetwood, the recorder, sent constables to the hospital who were able to throw out several able-bodied brewers' draymen who, not classified as poor, should not have been admitted (ibid, 66). Somehow, the hospital struggled on with a reduced staff but it was in a poor state of repair by 1595 (ibid, 46). It did however, continue to provide refuge for the poor until 1642, when it was taken over by the parliamentary army (Cowie 1974, 177). This was the end of the hospital as a charitable institution (Somerville 1960, 71).

At the beginning of the 17th century there was an almost unbroken line of mansions along the Strand, among them those of Lord Burleigh, Lord Southampton and Lord Buckingham. On the other side of the Savoy was Somerset House, occupied by the court of Queen Anne. The Savoy was thus advantageously situated in the most fashionable quarter of London (Loftie 1878, 130). With continued financial difficulties within the hospital, other forms of income had to be sought and by the early 17th century some of the hospital's buildings were let to noblemen and gentlemen (Cowie 1974, 178). These buildings, situated along the Strand, the riverside and Duchy Lane, formed the Savoy rents and were on long-term lets. Lodgers included eminent clergy and noblemen, as part of a wider trend which saw many gentlemen looking to rent lodgings on short- or long-term leases in order to be closer to the court and fashionable areas (Bucholz & Ward 2012, 65).

The precinct's problems were not so easily solved, however, and the hospital was only a part of the problem. The troubles were exacerbated by the fact that the precinct had been given the right of sanctuary, and thus lay outside the normal legal jurisdiction (Somerville 1960, 66). With such a status the Savoy was a magnet for 'rogues, thieves, idle and drunken persons' (Cowie 1974, 177).

The character of the place changed dramatically in the second half of the 17th century: the nobility left and tradesmen, such as glove makers, printers, clockmakers and wigmakers, moved in (Somerville 1960, 65); the king's printing press was established here in 1669 (Loftie 1878, 155). It is also here that Ravenscroft established his glasshouse in 1673, where his experimentation led to the invention of lead crystal glass (Davison 2003, 40; Dodsworth 2003, 10; Campbell 2006, 255). It is perhaps no coincidence that the nobility left as the soldiers and seamen arrived, first in the hospital and later in the prison and barracks (see below).

MILITARY HOSPITAL

In 1627 the Privy Council ordered that the hospital be prepared for the reception of wounded parliamentary soldiers. It could initially provide accommodation for 200 men and, once established, it provided a dozen nurses for every 100 wounded servicemen, the nurses often being soldiers' widows (Stewart 1950, 175; Somerville 1960, 72; Webster 2002, 296). This required the removal of the poor and needy, who were consequently asked to leave. Although the hospital seems to have reverted to helping the poor, the precedent had been set and its reconversion to military use in times of war meant that the hospital served a dual purpose over the decades until 1672, when the military took over completely (Somerville 1960, 72; Cook 1990, 6).

The Barber-Surgeons (later to become the Royal College of Surgeons) refused to run the hospital, so parliament ordered the Committee for Maimed Soldiers to run it with a physician and some surgeons, although the salaries assigned to the physician and apothecary would suggest that initially, at least, both roles were part-time (Stewart 1950, 176). Nevertheless, the medical staff were chosen because of their competence and their interest in the experimental sciences (Webster 2002, 296). The 200 beds were soon full and the overflow found themselves in civilian hospitals. The hospital was not exempt from financial pressures and as early as 1647 the wounded soldiers were close to starvation and there was no wood to warm them (Donagan 1998, 122).

To begin with the soldiers occupied the beds in the dormitory. As the numbers of wounded soldiers and seamen increased they took over what could be described as the nave, transepts and chancel and these became known as the Long, Newbury, Reading and Chapel wards (Somerville 1960, 73). Accounts from 1649 record the continued employment of four sisters to oversee the four main hospital wards and at least 12 nurses staffed them (Gruber-von-Arni 2007a, 124). It seems that military nurses were afforded a higher status than their contemporaries in civilian hospitals; at the Savoy nurses were paid 5s a week, compared with the 3s 6d paid to their contemporaries elsewhere. Although nurses may have been responsible for day-to-day patient care, medical care and administration of treatments were overseen by the physician and surgeon on their daily rounds (Gruber-von-Arni 2007a, 124). At a time when a holistic approach was taken to medicine, treating body and soul together (Burkhardt & Nagai-Jacobson 2002, 39), the wounded were also required to attend the chapel as part of their routine (Somerville 1960, 73).

The head nurse would have been responsible for preparing daily food but, unlike civilian nurses, military nurses were not expected to wash linen, which became the task of specifically employed washerwomen. Sheets and towels were laundered weekly along with two changes of underwear. Cleanliness was an important part of the routine. Bed frames were regularly whitewashed and beds were removed from wards for airing while the wards were cleaned (Gruber-von-Arni 2007a, 127–8, 137–42).

Nurses also had the authority to make small-scale purchases for necessary equipment. In April 1654, for instance, Nurse Bedwyn claimed expenses for a number of items (Table 3.2)

Item	£	s	d
One kettle		8	
One small kettle		3	
One plain skillet		3	
One small skillet		2	
One small iron pot		2	
Two washing tubs		3	
Two iron candlesticks			8
For mending kettles		1	2
Exchanging kettles and skillets		8	
Total expenses	1	10	10

Table 3.2 A nurse's expenses (data reproduced from Gruber-von-Arni 2007a, 129; source NA, SP24 n.f.)

Soldiers, once admitted, were still entitled to their 4s pension with which they could supplement their diet with beer or tobacco (ibid, 139). Webster notes the unusually comfortable conditions at the hospital, with the provision of clay pipes and good food and beer (2002, 53, 298). While the tobacco smoke may have contributed to breathing problems, another major factor in this was the burning of pitch, which was used to fumigate the wards. This was at a time when a belief that nocturnal air was harmful meant that windows would have been closed in already inadequately ventilated rooms (Gruber-von-Arni 2007a, 139). The financial difficulties facing both the Protectorate and the hospital continued after Cromwell's death in 1658. Funding failed completely in the first six months of 1659 and even with some emergency payments and a more aggressive policy of discharging patients, the final payment was made in November of the same year. The situation did not improve and on 1 March 1660 a statement was produced outlining the condition of the inpatients and pensioners of the hospital. It was reported that the numbers of wounded had greatly increased and there were now large numbers of poverty-stricken injured who could not fend for themselves (Gruber-von-Arni 2006, 3). Two days after Charles II was proclaimed king on 29 May 1660 and after a petition by 2500 inpatients and pensioners, as well as 3000 widows, parliament sanctioned a fast day to collect donations for the sick and wounded of the hospitals at the Savoy and Ely House. Further money was also released from the exchequer (Gruber-von-Arni 2006, 3).

The diarist and scholar John Evelyn (Fig 3.3) was appointed a commissioner for sick and wounded seamen and, seeing that most sick and injured were being boarded in private houses and inns, something which necessitated far more nursing staff, he requested the reopening of the Savoy as a military hospital (Gruber-von-Arni 2006, 34). During the Dutch Wars of the 1650s and 1660s the hospital was mainly occupied by wounded seamen. In 1666, Evelyn described the 'miserably dismembered and wounded men being dressed' (Somerville 1960, 72). According to the accounts of the treasurers for sick and maimed soldiers, in October 1648 the Savoy Hospital was accommodating between 200 and 213 soldier patients a week (NA, SP28/141B) – more than the three main London hospitals at that time: Ely House, St Thomas' and St Bartholomew's (Gruber-von-Arni 2007a, 126). This large patient turnover is illustrated by the hospital accounts for the three-month period between December 1653 and March 1654, which record that a total of 280 shirts were brought for inpatients as well as 35 shrouds (Gruber-von-Arni 2007a, 128).

Fig 3.3 Portrait of John Evelyn, by Nanteuil after himself
(©WL, L000966 used under CC BY 4.0)

Although a promise had been made to restore the hospital to its original purpose of providing care and lodgings for the poor, this was not kept and more and more buildings were given alternative uses. The Reading Ward was given over to the royal Wardrobe, the chaplains' quarters had disappeared and the sisters' and porters' lodgings had been leased. In 1679, these lodgings as well as the great dormitory were given over to the company of Foot Guards, and the barracks remained there throughout the next century (Somerville 1960, 74).

The conversion of the hospital to military use did nothing for the precinct as a whole, which was still offering sanctuary. After an incident in 1696 a newspaper article commented that 'The Bog of Allen, the passes of the Grampians, were not more unsafe than this small knot of lanes, surrounded by the mansions of the greatest nobles of a flourishing and enlightened kingdom' (ibid, 67). The privileges of sanctuary were finally abolished in 1697 (Loftie 1878, 155; Weinreb et al 2008, 825).

By the turn of the 17th century all the buildings, with the exception of the main 'cross' had been leased out and only the master's house and chapel were 'devoted to their original purpose' (Loftie 1878, 157). The final dissolution of the hospital did not take place until 1702, after the death of the last master of the hospital, Dr Henry Killigrew, in 1700 (ibid, 159; Somerville 1960, 85). A complex series of visitations and commissioners' reports followed. These are best discussed by Somerville (1960, 85–90) but, in summary, over the next two decades the hospital debts were paid and the depleted staff given a living elsewhere.

MILITARY MEDICINE

In the 17th century military medicine was seen as inferior to and more sordid than private practice. A London surgeon described it as no place for a 'man of superior merit' and considered that those employed in it would soon abandon it for more respectable work in private practice (Holmes 2001, 96). Even in the 18th century a medical man working in the Georgian army described it as 'the lowest step of professional drudgery and degradation' (Alsop 2007, 33). For this reason it attracted young, less experienced medical men, who often learned on the job after cursory training (Cook 1990, 15).

It seems that the ideas and philosophies associated with military medicine were fundamentally different to those of private practice: combining medicine and surgery, it was oriented towards large numbers rather than to individual patients. The military medical practitioner would have to learn to react quickly to a situation or problem, not having time to exercise medical judgement (ibid, 2, 15). The theory, based upon a belief in 'specific disease entities rather than unique physiological imbalances' (ibid, 2–3), was that diseases were identified and classified according to symptoms, which made it easier to standardise diagnosis and treatment as well as to teach others. Any medical practitioner who could offer new and effective treatments was actively encouraged (ibid, 16).

Bleeding was seen almost as a first response to all problems. It was a preventative measure against fever and used to dry the moisture around the wound (David 2013, 75). Amputations, when necessary, were undertaken quickly and without anaesthetic (Holmes 2001, 254). Other recognised treatments included the use of spirit vinegar for cleansing, and of salt and onion juice for burns (David 2013, 75).

Suturing techniques were standardised but methods for dressing wounds, including the type of dressing, material and style, were variable, designed to enable successful wound closure. Bandages were generally made from strong, evenly woven, white cloth without seams or hems but at the Savoy red flannel was used. Bandage widths ranged between 1in for fingers and toes to 6in for shoulders (Gruber-von-Arni 2007a, 131). The most difficult patients to treat were gunshot victims, because of the ragged opening of the wound, likely widespread tissue damage and the likelihood of clothing or other foreign materials being carried into the wound by the missile (Donagan 1998, 117; Gruber-von-Arni 2007a, 131). It was recognised that time was of the essence in these cases and bullet extraction would be quickly followed by wound cleansing and dressing, soft-tissue removal, or amputation to give the patient the best chance of survival (ibid).

In the 17th century, the French physician Ambroise Paré was a great influence on military surgeons (ibid, 130). Paré was employed as an army surgeon in 1637 and became surgeon to four French monarchs. He is perhaps best known for revolutionising the treatment for gunshot wounds: when he ran out of oil, which in the past had been boiled and poured over such wounds, he used a combination of egg yolk, rose oil and turpentine, only to find that it was more effective (Packard 1921, 26–7). Paré is also known for his innovative surgical instruments and the use of prosthetic limbs. His ideas and techniques spread across Europe, and helped to raise the status of the Barber-Surgeons in England (Editors of Encyclopaedia Britannica 1998a; Science Museum nd a). The use of prosthetics at the Savoy and Ely House hospitals is evidenced by the bills submitted by the hospital carpenter, William Bradley, who charged for the supply of legs and straps and buckles for Thomas Swaine in May 1654 as well as adjusting the legs of seven residents (Gruber-von-Arni 2007a, 139).

After an operation, a patient could expect a normal diet unless blood loss had weakened them or the wound was inflamed, in which case a light diet of broth and jellies was recommended. Richard Wiseman, surgeon to Charles II, also recommended vulnerary drinks, including comfrey, lady's mantle or red roses boiled in white wine and honey, to help the wound to heal (ibid, 131). The apothecaries at Ely House were responsible for making the drugs, which were dispensed by Mr Kirk Bond, who received a salary of £30 a year (WL, RAMC/341). The specific ingredients were a trade secret and the apothecaries' bill listed pills, cordials, liquorice juice, sweating potions and gargles as well as styptics and precipitators for the surgeon (Gruber-von-Arni 2007a, 133).

After the development of muskets from the flintlock to the long land pattern musket (Brown Bess) at the beginning of the 18th century the number of injured increased but even so soldiers were less likely to die from wounding, maiming or death in battle than they were from disease (Cook 1990, 3; David 2013, 42). However, musketry was responsible for more than 60% of casualties. A musket ball to the head or abdomen was likely to result in death but damage in other areas might not be life-threatening unless infection was allowed to set in (Holmes 2001, 252–4).

Regimental surgeons for the Foot Guards were allowed to hold a small stock of external applications, valued at less than 40 shillings; internal medicines, provided by the Apothecary General Richard White, were limited to 40 pounds a year, which was considerably more than other regiments (Gruber-von-Arni 2006, 34). The situation and reputation of the military medical personnel seems to have improved: by 1797 a military surgeon could be a Captain and allocated quarters. Both the surgeon and their assistants (Lieutenants) would be paid regularly and provided with medicines but not equipment. By 1798, military surgeons had to be qualified and assistants had to pass an examination. Still, the death of many sick and injured was being blamed on the lack of sufficient resources (Holmes 2001, 97).

SURGEONS AT THE SAVOY
JOHN FRENCH

John French was born in Oxfordshire and studied medicine at New Hall Inn in Oxford, obtaining his BA in 1637 and MA in 1640 (Linden 2003, 208). He joined the parliamentary army under General Fairfax as a physician and after the Civil War became the physician of the Savoy Hospital, with a salary of £200 per year (Webster 2002, 297; Haeffner 2004, 123). He was awarded his MD in 1648 while already at the Savoy (Webster 2002, 297).

French was an advocate of spa water treatments for maimed soldiers and between 1647 and 1654 frequent applications were made to take wounded soldiers from both the Savoy and Ely House hospitals to the waters at Bath. The hospital treasurers, not always willingly, spent over £1500 financing such trips (Webster 2002, 299; Gruber-von-Arni 2007a, 134). As well as spa treatments and anatomical dissection, French had some more radical ideas and his work has been described as both mystical and millenarian (Moran 2014, 73). A Paracelsian physician, he was part of the Hartlib Circle, who worked on the borderline of chemistry and alchemy (Haeffner 2004, 134).

The Parcelsians followed the beliefs and ideals of the German physician and alchemist Paracelsus (1493–1541). Paracelsus travelled the world as a military surgeon and believed that the body was a chemical system that needed to be balanced and in harmony with the environment. He believed that metals, controlled by God, were the key elements in the universe and that learning would be most effective through experimentation (Goodrick-Clarke 1999, 30; Science Museum nd b) He tried applying chemistry to medicine, finding new remedies that utilised, for example, mercury, sulphur, iron and copper sulphate.

Paracelsians also advocated the use of mummies and human-derived materials for medicinal purposes. German Paracelsian physician Oswald Croll described the ideal corpse as 'a red man, whole, clear without blemish, of the age of twenty-four years that hath been hanged, broke upon a wheel, or thrust-through, having been for one day and night exposed to the open air, in a serene time'. The corpse would be diced, 'seasoned with powder of myrrh and aloes, and repeatedly macerated in spirit of wine'. This mixture was used to treat multiple ailments (Moran 2014, 73).

Flesh was commonly used to treat external bruising and bleeding. It could be administered externally as plaster or internally as a liquid. It could also be used for gout, inflammations or poison. Powdered skull was useful in cases of epilepsy or other head diseases. Another cure for epilepsy was to 'take the brains of a young man that hath died a violent death, together with the membranes, arteries, veins, nerves, all the pith of the back, bruise these in a stone mortar til they become a kind of pap'. Spirit of wine was added, and the whole allowed to digest in horse dung before distillation (Sugg 2011, 46). For cases of gout, wounds, breast cancer and melancholy, oil of human fat might be applied. In his treatment of the military wounded John French would perhaps have administered powdered moss from a skull, which was of most use when inserted into wounds caused in accidents or warfare (ibid, 15).

In his 1651 book *The Art of Distillation* (Fig 3.4) French describes a method for preparing oil and water of blood. It would be 'taken inwardly and applied outwardly, cureth most diseases, and easeth pain' (Sugg 2011, 44; Moran 2014, 73). Rather than just using cured human flesh he believed in distilling it: 'cut small, four onces', add spirit of wine and set the two in a large glazed vessel in horse dung for one month. What remained in the vessel would be an oil-like substance, 'which is the true elixir of mummy' and 'a wonderful preservative against all infections' (Sugg 2011, 44).

One of the most useful commodities was the human skull and in 1678, Gideon Harvey, the Royal Surgeon, placed the value of a human skull as between 8 shillings and 11 shillings (ibid, 94). There were two ways of making skull into spirit. The first method stated that after breaking the skull into small pieces and putting it into a glass, it should be heated in a fire until yielding 'a yellowish spirit, a red oil, and a volatile salt'; after further processing for a couple of months a 'most excellent spirit' would be produced. This was designed for the treatment

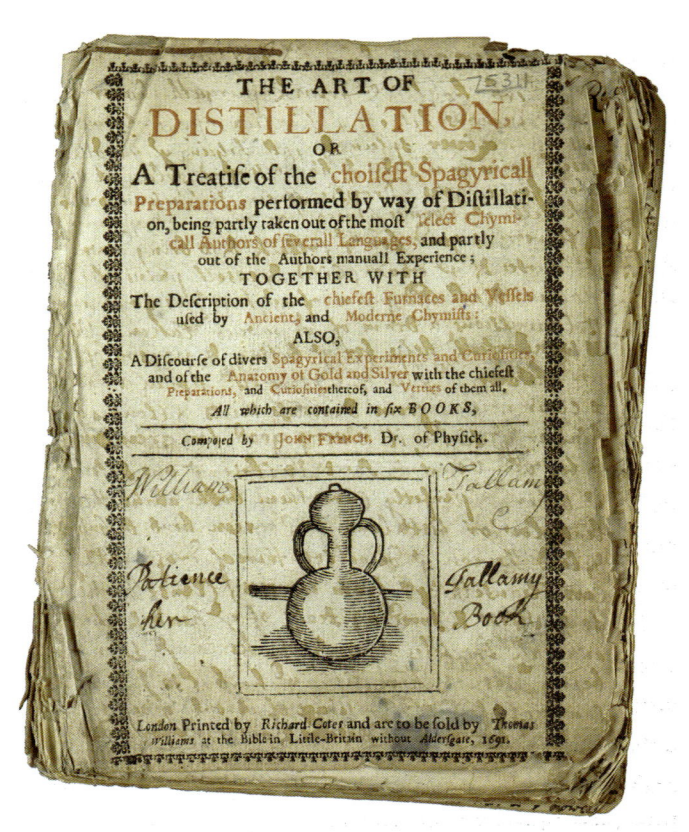

Fig 3.4 A copy of John French's *Art of Distillation*, London, 1651, R Cotes for T Williams (©WL, L0051469 used under CC BY 4.0)

of gout, dropsy and infirm stomachs. Alternatively, pieces of skull could be boiled with hartshorn and ivory in a mesh, until the consistency of soft cheese was achieved; it should then be pounded with spirit of wine into a paste ready for distillation. The final spirit would treat epilepsy, convulsions and fevers among other things (ibid, 45).

French would have had access to a supply of corpses ready for dissection, particularly during the 1640s and 1650s when the hospital was treating both poor civilian and military patients; records indicate that dissections were routinely undertaken by French at the hospital (Webster 2002, 299; Sugg 2011, 46). In fact, both French and Trapham (see below) were singled out and thanked for allowing access to dissections at the hospital (Webster 2002, 299).

THOMAS TRAPHAM

Thomas Trapham qualified in medicine from Oxford in March 1633 (Wadd 1827, 212). In 1642 he offered his services to the parliamentary army, gaining notoriety in 1649 by embalming the decapitated Charles I and commenting that 'I sewed on the head of a goose' (Lane Furdell 2001, 148). He served as sergeant-surgeon to Cromwell, the Lord Protector, after Charles' execution despite being described as a 'rascally quack physician' by a fellow physician. Trapham was appointed as surgeon to the General of the parliamentary army in 1649 (ibid) and in this role became surgeon at the Savoy in 1653 (Webster 2002, 297; Gruber-von-Arni 2007b, 331). State papers for the Savoy and Ely House hospitals from 1658 record the annual salary for Trapham and his surgeons' mates as £264 5s (WL, RAMC/341).

He found it difficult to free himself from his political leanings and retired after the Restoration to practice medicine in Abingdon, dying in 1683 (Lane Furdell 2001, 148).

CHARLES HALES

Charles Hales was a surgeon appointed to the Savoy Hospital in the late 18th century. Having been called for by General Car, Lieutenant-Colonel of the 1st Foot Guards, following a 'fit of stone', he and the general began discussing the prevalence of venereal disease among soldiers. According to Charles Hales, the usual treatment of salivation was frequently unsuccessful, often resulting in patients dying from consumption or in too 'feeble' and 'sickly' a state to carry out normal duty (Hales 1770, 12). They came to an agreement that Charles would treat 10–20 soldiers of the 1st Foot Guards, deemed incurable by salivation, by his own undisclosed methods. By 1758 he was treating 150 cases from all regiments, several of whom successfully returned to duty (ibid, 14–17).

Most of the population would not have been able to afford to see a medical physician, so there was a trend for self-medication (Bucholz & Ward 2012, 176) with advertisements and advice often found in newspapers. In one such advertisement, placed by Mrs Hales, self-proclaimed widow of the late surgeon Mr Charles Hales, in the *World and Fashionable Advertiser* (London, England) published on Tuesday 15 May 1787 (issue 116), Mrs Hales offered to continue her husband's treatment for venereal disease, scurvy and leprosy, boasting that her late husband had 'perfectly cured 750 men … all deemed incurable' through his revolutionary techniques.

SUMMARY AND DISCUSSION

It is perhaps unfortunate that Henry VII never saw his hospital for 'nedie pouer people', which, with its progressive design, would at the beginning have been an enviable institution. However, any attractiveness was soon limited to purely visual qualities as financial problems and continued misuse ruined its reputation. The hospital was given a new lease of life at the beginning of the 17th century when, once again at the forefront of medical infrastructure, it was established as the first designated military hospital. During this period of its history, however, in addition to continued financial pressures, problems were exacerbated by the overuse, rather than the misuse, of the hospital.

Attempts were made to resolve the financial problems by gradually relinquishing the use of many of the hospital buildings, leasing them for other purposes, but it was not until the dissolution of the hospital at beginning of the 18th century that the debts were finally cleared. This, combined with the abolition of the privileges of sanctuary within the Savoy Precinct at the end of the 17th century gave the Savoy a fresh start, enabling it to enter a new phase in its history.

3.2 SAVOY BARRACKS

> To My Lady Berkeley, Afflicted upon her Son, My Lord Berkeley's Early Engaging in the Sea-Service (extract)
>
> Alas, he was not born to live in Peace,
> Souls of his Temper were not made for Ease,
> Th' Ignoble only live secure from Harms,
> The Generous tempt, and seek out fierce Alarms…
>
> Two French Campagnes he boldly courted Fame,
> While his Face more the Maid, than Youth became
> Add then to these a Soul so truly Mild,
> Though more than Man, Obedient as a Child.
> And (ah) should one Small Isle all these confine,
> Vertues created through the World to shine?
> Heaven that forbids, and Madam so should you;
> Remember he but bravely does pursue
> His Noble Fathers steps; with your own Hand
> Then Gird his Armour on, like him he'll stand,
> His Countries Champion, and Worthy be
> Of your High Vertue, and his Memory.
> —Anne Killigrew (Morten 1967, 25–6)

In 1679 three regiments of Foot Guards, the 1st (subsequently the Grenadier Guards), the 2nd (later the Coldstream Guards) and the 3rd (to become the Scots Guards), turned the hospital buildings into the Savoy Barracks. In rotation, these regiments would be in residence at the barracks until the late 18th century. The 1st Foot Guards were established as part of the 4000-strong Royal Body Guards to Charles II. This was the first time that a British monarch had kept regiments during peace time (David 2013, 11–12).

RECRUITMENT

It was common practice for ensigns to buy commissions, so these posts usually went to the sons of nobility and landed gentry (David 2013, 14). Many of the officers who had bought commissions spent much time at court or parliament and almost half of the officers in the Guards Regiments had seats in the House of Commons (ibid, 15). These officers would then be sent on recruiting trips to enlist ordinary soldiers. A recruiting officer would take advantage of economic difficulties, favouring out-of-work labourers and workers, as well as seeking recruits from the poor and homeless teenaged and adult male population (Bucholz & Ward 2012, 232). It was then within his charge to offer the potential recruit a bounty of several pounds as an enticement. Following possible negotiations and haggling, the new recruit would accept the position (Reid & Hook 1996, 3–6). Once a man had accepted the 'king's shilling' he was effectively signing up for life. Problems for the recruiting officer occurred if the recruit deserted before he reached headquarters or if he should subsequently be rejected by a commanding officer; in such circumstances the officer was responsible for all costs incurred (Reid 2002, 21, 28).

There were strict guidelines surrounding recruitment and by 1760, the ideal 16- to 20-year-old soldier should be at least 5ft 5in tall, or thought likely to grow to that size; if aged between 25 and 35, they should be 5ft 6in tall. These guidelines could be relaxed according to need – in other words, in desperate times of war. In 1797 13- to 18-year-olds were being recruited into Foot Regiments (Holmes 2011, 272). It was logical to favour younger recruits; by 1839 only 5% of 40-year-olds were fit for service. Other requirements were that they had to be able-bodied, free from any remarkable deformity, ulcerous sores or ruptures and free from fits, all supported by a surgeon's certificate (ibid, 270). Recruits also needed to swear in front of a magistrate that they were Protestant and not affected by anything that would inhibit their enlistment (Reid & Hook 1996, 5).

Certain professions were less welcome than others – for example, vagabonds and tinkers, also chimney sweeps, colliers and sailors (Holmes 2011, 270), as it was considered that these would be more likely to be bringing with them inherent breathing or health problems (Reid & Hook 1996, 5). A typical soldier would be unemployed, a journeyman or a criminal, for enlisting was an effective way of avoiding arrest (David 2013, 15–16). He would be unmarried, could not be a householder or run a tavern, would have no permanent home and few possessions (ibid). Although most recruits were trying to escape from something, some were also attracted by the promise of an easy life and military glory (Reid & Hook 1996, 5).

Once enlisted, it was not easy to end a military career. If a soldier was discharged he had to be classed as disabled in order to be eligible for a pension. Support would come from the Committee for Maimed Soldiers, who were responsible for the role of ministry of pensions, providing financial and supervisory support for incapacitated soldiers (Stewart 1950, 172). Severe wounding in battle or being crippled by disease while in the king's service was enough to merit a discharge and pension but venereal disease and alcoholism did not count. If a soldier was still fit and healthy when dismissed there was no reason to provide him with a pension. Certainly in the first half of the 18th century a soldier did not qualify for a pension on the grounds of long service, unless classed as 'worn out' (David 2013, 16; Reid & Hook 1996, 21–2). Instead, the more able of the wounded might be employed in garrison duties, as night watchmen, for instance (ibid, 21).

UNIFORM

The Foot Guards were dressed in hats, red coats, breeches and stockings and waist sashes (Fig 3.5). The colour facings on the coat and breeches and stockings varied according to regiment. By the late 1680s the influence of French fashion had caused the introduction of long coats, baggy breeches and wigs. An officer would wear a broad-brimmed hat, a white linen shirt and a cravat. Breeches ended just below the knee and shoes were high-heeled and buckled (David 2013, 18). The uniform changed little into the 18th century but now included a tricorne hat. Although admired by some (Olsen 1999, 131) the uniform was uncomfortable and ill-fitting (David 2013, 207).

Fig 3.5 Eighteenth-century military uniform (http://www.britishempire.co.uk/forces/armyuniforms/britishinfantry/1stfootuniform.htm)

During the second half of the 17th century a soldier was expected to have shoulder-length hair, worn either loose or in a short ponytail, whereas an officer might sport an elaborate peruque-style wig. From the beginning of the 18th century the ordinary soldiers would wear their hair, which could be up to a foot long, greased with tallow or lard and tied in a ponytail, doubled up and held with leather straps (Holmes 2011, 466–7; David 2013, 207). It would then be generously powdered, often with flour. These preparations were seen by some as time-wasting and the procedure could not be undertaken by a soldier on his own – the task would be carried out in pairs or by soldiers' wives. As wigs went out of fashion in the second half of the 18th century officers' own hair was 'pomaded and powdered' even after the hair powder tax was introduced by Pitt in 1795 (Holmes 2011, 466).

WEAPONS

> And now, methinks, I present do behold
> The Bloudy Fields that are in Fame enroll'd,
> I see, I see thousands in Battle slain,
> The Dead and Dying cover all the Plain,
> Confused Noises hear, each way sent out,
> The Vanquisht Cries joyn'd with the Victors shout;
> Their Sighs and Groans who draw a painful Breath,
> And feel the Pangs of slow approaching Death:
> Yet happier these, far happier are the Dead,
> Than who into Captivity are led:
> What by their Chains, and by the Victors Pride,
> We pity these, and envy those that dy'd.
> And who can say, when Thousands are betray'd,
> To Widdowhood, Orphants or Childless made.
> —Anne Killigrew, The Miseries of Man (extract)
> (Morton 1967, 37)

The standard weapon of the Foot Guards was the musket. During the reign of Charles II, this had been a matchlock musket but this slow, clumsy weapon was replaced by the flintlock musket in the 1670s. The musket was now fired by a spark igniting the powder in the pan, caused by a flint striking against a coarse steel surface. This was found to be much more efficient, and further improvements were made by changes to the loading mechanism. Early muskets were loaded with powder poured into the pan, followed by a round metal ball, then wadding to secure it, rammed home with a ramrod. In the 17th century the correct quantity of charge and the ball came pre-wrapped as a cartridge. Firing routine now involved the soldier tearing the end of the paper with his teeth before pouring a little of the powder into the flintlock pan, then adding the remains of the cartridge and ramming it home. The rammer was then replaced and the lock would be cocked. It was now ready to fire (Gascoigne 2001; David 2013, 42). An improvement on the flintlock musket was the long land pattern musket or 'Brown Bess', which was in use from the early 18th century until the late 19th century (Alex 2014). Frequent drills were needed to improve both loading time and aim.

While the musket could be used over a distance of approximately 100 yards, close fighting would involve the bayonet, which was the final improvement to the weapon (David 2013, 41–2). The bayonet was a 17in fluted iron spike with a potentially lethal point and was attached to the muzzle of the musket (Reid & Hook 1996, 32; Holmes 2001, 201). Having been used as a defensive weapon, held at shoulder height, it became an offensive weapon held at the waist (David 2013, 132) as it could be thrust towards the enemy.

Throughout the 17th to 19th centuries the three Regiments of Foot Guards fought in almost every major campaign of the British Army, including the Dutch Wars (1665–7), the War of the Spanish Succession (1702–15), the War of American Independence (1775–83), the French Revolutionary Wars (1793–1802) and the Battle of Waterloo (1815) (Luscombe & Griffin nd; Coldstream Guards nd)

WOMEN

The military was a male-dominated environment but females did have a part to play in barrack life and the influence of women was seen as civilising. Soldiers were permitted to marry with the permission of the commanding officer but this was usually restricted to six wives per company. The numbers of women were increased by unofficial wives and girlfriends, but these had to fend for themselves (David 2013, 20). James Collins and James Whem, soldiers from the Savoy, were recorded in the Proceedings of the Old Bailey (OB, OA17621013) as both having wives big with child (as well as two small children in the case of Whem) at the time of their arrest and subsequent execution for robbery in 1762 (see further below). Wives and children could sleep in quarters and were entitled to a share of the company rations. In return, they carried out certain duties such as cleaning, washing linens and fuelling the fires.

Of course, it was not unheard of for women, who became known as women drummers, to try to pass themselves off as men for the sake of enlisting. In the middle of the 18th century Hannah Snell (Fig 3.6) spent four and a half years undetected in the Royal Marines before her discharge in 1750. With the overcrowded nature of barracks, privacy would have been a problem and would have made it harder for an ordinary female soldier to keep up the disguise. Thus one of the most successful was James Miranda Barry, a medical officer, who between 1813 and 1858 rose from being a hospital assistant to the rank of Inspector General of the Army Medical Department and would have had her own quarters. The fact that she was a woman was discovered upon her death in 1865 (Holmes 2001, 98–9).

Somewhat surprisingly, the Savoy registers record the burial of two women described as soldiers, both in 1767: Elizabeth Johnston on 1 May and Mary Woodward on 10 December. Though not impossible, it seems unlikely that both women were enlisted as soldiers in the Savoy at the same time. The Savoy Barracks seem to have accommodated married couples and there are a few instances within the records where the status of 'soldier's wife' is recorded so perhaps Elizabeth Johnston and Mary Woodward were soldiers' wives.

Fig 3.6 Hannah Snell, mezzotint, by J Young after R Phelps, 1789 (©WL,V0007232 used under CC BY 4.0)

Alternatively, it is possible that they worked in the barracks, like the wife of retired soldier Robert Damsell (see below). There are a number of discrepancies within the records so the entries could simply be errors. Mary was the third of three burials on the same day, with the first recorded as a soldier and the two below, of which Mary was the second, simply recorded with 'ditto'. Mary's entry could therefore be a mistake due to repetition. In the case of Elizabeth Johnson, however, such a mistake seems less likely. Elizabeth's was the only burial on 1 May and her entry is made at the top of a new page, so clearly 'soldier' was not written out of repetitious habit.

BARRACKS

At the beginning of the 18th century the recruits were normally held in the Savoy Barracks or Tilbury fort, both described as prison-like and unpleasant (Reid & Hook 1996, 50). Because of the constraints of space, a great many soldiers were billeted in private households and few purpose-built barracks were in existence (David 2013, 16). The Savoy Barracks are likely to have been at variance to the norm. A soldier's life was likely to follow the same rules, regulations and routine wherever he was but the design of the barracks was in this case largely dictated by the already existing buildings – converted from the military hospital, which in turn had been converted from the original medieval hospital. The overall layout can be seen in Fig 3.7.

There is possible evidence for a second floor, which has been attributed to the conversion from hospital to barracks to enable the accommodation of the 600 men quartered there, against the walls of the nave and transepts (Somerville 1960, 15). It seems that the eastern range of buildings on the Thames was converted for use as a laboratory by the military apothecaries and two additional houses were rebuilt after 1728 as a three-storey building that was used as an infirmary and, after 1736, was partly occupied by officers' quarters (ibid, 92).

MILITARY LIFE

Life in barracks was far from comfortable. Soldiers slept in wooden cribs or straw-filled palliasses. There would be a communal table that ran down the centre of the room, often with only 5in between the table and the end of the beds. Until the end of the 19th century, everything but drilling was carried out in the barracks (Holmes 2011, 522). Recruits were often housed there for considerable periods of time awaiting transportation, which, although it did nothing for their health and morale, was a problem that had at least been identified. According to the *Daily Journal* (London, England) published on Tuesday 18 October 1729 (issue 2748):

> The Officers who from time to time recruit for the several regiments in Gibraltar, are come to a Resolution not to raise any more Volunteers for those troops, till an opportunity for their Transportation offers. Doctors Bills have run high, and burials been very frequent, thro' tedious Detentions in the Savoy Barracks, which Inconveniency will, for the future be avoided, to the great encouragement of such as shall enlist for the said Garrison.

This would suggest that however fit and healthy the men were upon recruitment, too much time in spent in the barracks was likely to render them less so. In 1748 it was reported that the barracks were to be 'cleaned and made more commodious' (Somerville 1960, 94). Overcrowding was a recognised problem in the Savoy Barracks, not helped by the fire of 1776, which resulted in many soldiers being moved to Somerset House and nearby public houses (*Bath Chronicle and Weekly Gazette*, Thursday 7 March 1776). The fire had broken out in the buildings of an adjacent printer as a consequence of an unfortunate servant making too large a fire in the Dutch stove, which spread to papers hanging nearby. The barracks were destroyed 'down to the stonework' but thankfully the soldiers managed to remove the gunpowder before the flames reached it (*Ipswich Journal*, Saturday 9 March 1776). The problem of overcrowding in barracks seems to have been a perpetual one.

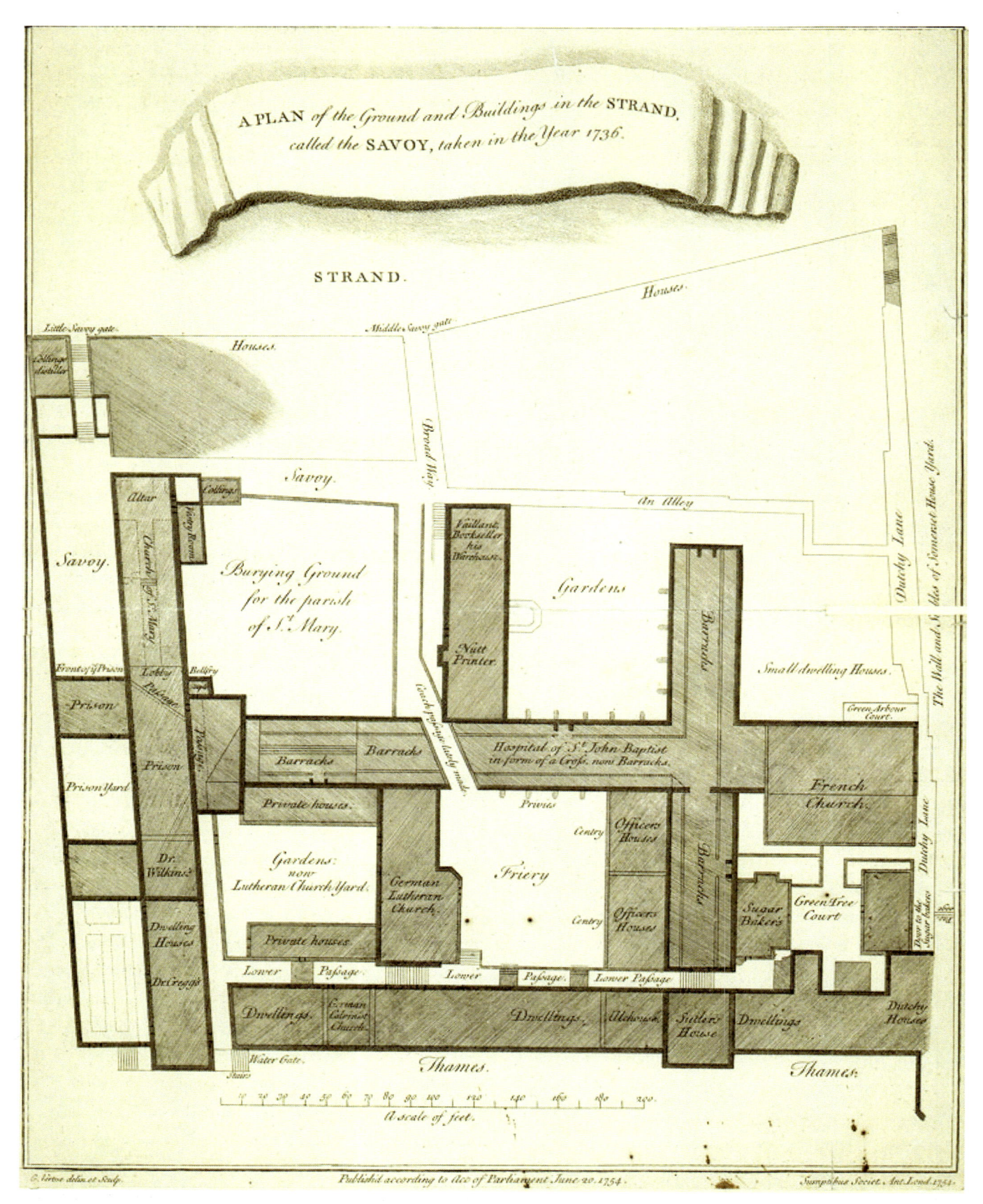

Fig 3.7 Plan of the Savoy Barracks, 1736 © British Library Board, Shelf mark Maps Crace Port. 13.52

In 1858 it was stated in the House of Lords that the average air allowance for a convict was 1000 cubic feet, but only 400 for a soldier, with some barracks and military hospitals only managing 300 (Holmes 2011, 522). Although not applicable to the Savoy as these barracks had by been demolished by this time, it does highlight a situation that is likely to have existed for decades.

Foot Guards were paid approximately eight pence (8d) a day, most of which covered their subsistence and clothing (Reid & Hook 1996, 7; David 2013, 15). What little remained was often spent on strong drink (Reid & Hook 1996, 11). With subsistence taken out there was very little left for everyday living. Being based in London would have had a great influence on the roles and daily life of a Foot Guard. They also had a close relationship with the Royal Household (David 2013, 103). Situated in central London, they had access to facilities such as Hyde Park, the largest open area adjacent to London and one that could be used for training and drilling (Bucholz & Ward 2012, 355). On Saturday 16 April 1788 the duke of York's regiment of guards left the Savoy Barracks to gather in Hyde Park. On a word of command from his Royal Highness 'several evolutions and firings were executed with the most minute exactness' (*Hereford Journal*, Thursday 1 May 1788). Other regiments without that luxury rarely got together enough men for practice (Reid & Hook 1996, 27).

The Savoy regiments were often called upon to attend and disperse public disorders and quell riots. This included preventing or stopping looting during fires and guarding against rescues from execution (White 2012, 444). After a fire in Mr Peck's grocers, no 106 in the Strand, a party of Guards were called out simply to prevent the sufferers from being robbed (*Kentish Gazette*, Saturday 5 August 1780). The presence of the soldiers readied for action served as deterrent; in 1771, after disturbances from a riotous mob, the Guards from the Savoy Barracks were ordered to be in readiness to march in case of further disturbances (*Caledonian Mercury*, Wednesday 3 April 1771). In 1775 all the guards in the Savoy Barracks were ordered under arms along with four horse troops for the preservation of peace. As a result, 'the laws were infringed only by the numerous tribe of pickpockets' (ibid, Wednesday 1 May 1775).

The nature of rioting began to change from the early 18th century. At this time rioters were usually armed only with stones and only the soldiers and authorities carried weapons but by the second half of the 18th century, and particularly during the industrial riots of the 1760s, more weaponry was in general use (Shoemaker 2007, 142). In 1769 the rioters were the silk weavers or 'cutters' centred round the Spitalfield area and unhappy at the increasing and apparently uncontrolled smuggling of foreign silks into England. After failed attempts to change the situation by petitioning parliament, the breaking of the windows of merchants dealing in French silks escalated to full scale riots (Page 1911b, 132–7).

On one night in September 1769 there was a meeting of the committee for the 'cutters' at the Dolphin Alehouse in Spitalfields. When peace officers, untrained constables and a detachment of soldiers arrived requesting that the committee surrender, they instead opened fire, resulting in the death of the soldier Adam McCoy. According to Thomas Yates, a sergeant in the 3rd Regiment of Foot Guards, McCoy was 'shot through the head and died instantly without speaking a word' (LMA, MJ/SP/1769/10/061). His burial in the Savoy Chapel cemetery (recorded in the burial registers on 3 October 1769) was described in a London publication, providing a wonderful insight into the way that military funerals might be conducted.

> Yesterday the Body of the Soldier who was shot on Saturday Night by the Cutters, at the Dolphin in Hog-Lane, Spitalfields, was carried from thence in Military Funeral Procession through the city to the Burial Ground in the Savoy for interment. The Corpse was preceded by a File of Musketeers, a Drum beating and Fifes playing a solemn March; the Coffin was covered with a Velvet Pall; a white Plume of Feathers and two Swords were placed on it; and a great Number of Soldiers unarmed followed the Coffin two and two; the whole making a very decent and mournful Appearance. Three Vollies of Small Arms were discharged over his Grave. He was a well-behaved young Man, and much respected by the Corps he belonged to'
> (*Derby Mercury*, Friday 13 October 1769).

Whether the nature of his death gave cause for such a procession to accompany his funeral and burial is unclear but the fact that this detailed description was printed suggests that it may not have been a regular occurrence. The traditional firing of volleys over the grave originated from the same practice used by the military in the 18th and 19th centuries to announce that the battlefield had been cleared of the dead (Bryant & Peck 2009, 490).

Unfortunately, soldiers were not always so 'well-behaved'. Their behaviour was more often far from exemplary and their appearance in the Savoy did not improve its condition or reputation, with offence caused by their 'violent and licentious habits' (Somerville 1960, 92). This would not have been helped by the immediate environment, exposing the soldiers to numerous temptations (see Chapter 2).

A book entry from the period October 1746 to July 1747 records the activities of the Foot Guards under Major General Alexander Duty. It details how the 2nd Battalion of the 1st Regiment of Foot Guards, many of them drunk, marched from the Savoy Barracks to Dartford in January 1747, to join the 2nd Battalion of the 3rd Regiment of Foot Guards, 'who were very riotous and fired in the street' (NAM, 1986–12–38–120). Drunkenness was considered an offence but this did not seem to deter soldiers from drinking (Holmes 2001, 315). The influence of drink might lead to absenteeism, and in turn to desertion (David 2013, 315), a crime that could be severely punished.

In his commentary on the medical treatment of military patients, Richard Wiseman, as a prominent royalist surgeon during the Civil War, recognised that drink played such an important part in the lives of some soldiers and sailors that during illness and treatment they would have a better chance of survival if they were allowed the 'hair of the dog' rather than being completely deprived of alcohol (Hudson 2007, 130). Of course, with the ever-present risk of contaminated water, and with tea and coffee still rare, particularly on campaign, beer was often the drink of choice (Reid & Hook 1996, 11). After a successful display of arms in Hyde Park in 1788, the duke of York ordered that the soldiers from the Savoy Barracks should have a pint of porter 'to clear their mouths from the powder' (*Hereford Journal*, Thursday 1 May 1788).

MILITARY CRIME AND DISCIPLINE

Desertion was one of the main problems facing the standing army when recruits realised that a soldier's life might not be all it had promised to be; desertion accounted for an annual average of approximately 33% of military crimes between 1796 and 1825 (Holmes 2011, 511). Although it might be considered easier to desert from an army on the move, being resident in secure barracks did not seem to deter potential deserters. The recruitment system also had a part to play. Soldiers would enlist and be given the bounty payable to them only to desert and try to enlist again under a different name, receiving a new payment each time until they were caught. Repeated desertion was a crime worthy of the death penalty (David 2013, 316), designed to act as a deterrent to fellow soldiers.

In 1739 a court martial ordered that Colonel Meyrick, of the 3rd Regiment of Foot Guards, was to accompany 500 soldiers from all three regiments to Hyde Park to supervise the execution of a deserter from the 1st Regiment (*London Weekly Magazine*, Friday 7 September 1739). Deserters could be shot rather than hung, which was considered the more honourable way to go (David 2013, 318). The prisoner, who would have spent days in the company of the chaplain preparing him for his ordeal, as reported by the *London Weekly Magazine* (Somerville 1960, 139), would be blindfolded for the execution. The inaccuracies of the weapons meant that a second firing squad was often in attendance in case the first failed to complete the job (David 2013, 316). The Savoy registers record the burial of Samuel Jackson on 13 February 1752, shot for desertion.

It appears that not all deserters were treated equally. On 8 April 8 1777 a deserter from the same regiment was taken to St James' Park, surrounded by a circle formed from men of his regiment, to hear that he had been sentenced to 1000 lashes, to be received in four sittings. This unenviable punishment would be carried out by the three regiments of Foot Guards to make his punishment exemplary. After his punishment he was cut from the halberds (three tied together to form a triangular frame) and carried by two men to the orderly room, to be attended by the surgeon before being handcuffed and returned to the Savoy Prison (*Universal Magazine of Knowledge and Pleasure*, Vol. 60, April 1777). The lucky soldier might receive a reprieve, and instead be sent for transportation. This was not an uncommon outcome and of the 76 death penalties given out in 1835, 35 resulted in transportation (Holmes 2011, 319).

In an attempt to catch the deserters announcements were made in the *London Gazette* giving particulars of name and rank as well as detailed description. Pardons were often offered if the deserter returned within a set time frame, or rewards offered to anyone who could apprehend the offender. The *Gazette* records rewards of £5 on offer from each relevant regiment, together with the 'king's bounty money' of 20s a head, by application to Captain Edison, regimental agent, from his house in the Savoy, Strand (Holmes 2012, 510). Despite repeated offers to pardon deserters if they returned to re-enlist, few returned voluntarily and desertion remained a problem throughout the 18th and into the 19th century (Holmes 2011, 511). In 1800 there was a report of a deserter named Conjuror, who found himself arrested by a disbanded sergeant who happened to notice him 'performing his *Hocus Pocus* dexterity' on stage. The incident apparently caused disappointment in the watching crowd but astonishment to the Conjuror (*Sussex Advertiser*, Monday 31 March 1800).

The year 1718 saw the introduction of updated Articles of War and as a result more crimes such as treachery, mutiny and desertion became court-martial offences even during times of peace. Punishments could range from flogging or whipping to the death penalty (David 2013, 103). Of course a number of 'civilian' crimes were also punishable by death. It was not uncommon for soldiers to turn their hand to robbery. They were poorly paid and often large numbers would be demobilised between wars. In the 17th century there were many occasions when this became a problem – for example, after Buckingham's wars (1620s), the Civil War (1660s) and the Dutch Wars (1650,

1670) (Bucholz & Ward 2012, 232) – and this continued to be the case into the 18th century. A connection between war and crime rates has been noted by both contemporary and modern writers, with the outbreak of war coinciding with a marked decrease in recorded crime (Durston 2012, 123). Conversely, records would certainly suggest that the number of footpad robberies increased in periods of post-war demobilisation (McLynn 2002, 6). There were two reasons for this link. First, a large number of criminals were being recruited into the military, thus removing them from the street (but at the same time polluting military stock). Second, as outlined above, the large numbers of soldiers demobilised between wars had little else with which to occupy themselves. Disabled soldiers would turn to begging and fit men to crime (Olsen 1999, 132). Highway robbery was largely taken up by cavalrymen, who, allowed after demobilisation to keep their horses, would put horse and skills to an alternative use. The problem was so apparent that a line of guardhouses was built on the road from Kensington to the city to protect travellers from soldiers (David 2013, 53).

The conduct of serving soldiers would be influenced by their officers but unfortunately they often set a bad example with regard to drink, women and violence (Holmes 2001, 155). Soldiers' unruly behaviour did not go unnoticed. In 1744 the officers of the three regiments of Foot Guards were given orders to 'make a proper enquiry into the conduct and character of every private man in their several regiments'. Any who could not give a good account of themselves would be 'secured'. These orders seem to have stemmed from the discovery that 'many Robberies were, and still are, committed by Soldiers in disguis'd Dresses' (*Derby Mercury*, Friday 26 October 1744).

Certainly the temptations of London must have been influential in the matter of behaviour but they cannot be wholly to blame. While on campaign in 1815 and after a number of fist fights between officers and French civilians, Wellington had to remind his officers that 'striking individuals with fists' was quite inconsistent with their duty, and with their character as British officers (Holmes 2001, 155). In 1826, when discussing the relative merits of billeting soldiers in private quarters versus barracks, their being in private quarters was considered by some as a contributing factor to their behaviour. The objections were not to the problems of distance and the scattered nature of the regiments but rather, the 'ill effect on exposing soldiers in private quarters to the danger of being mixed up with the worst members of society' (*The Examiner*, Sunday 12 March 1826).

Although minor disagreements and arguments might result in fist fights in the barracks between officers, soldiers and, sometimes, even women (David 2013, 296), more serious arguments might be resolved in a duel. There are numerous accounts of duels taking place in the London parks, involving both officers and soldiers, as both ranks were equally expected to resolve their differences 'with cold steel' despite military regulations against the practice (Olsen 1999, 252; Holmes 2001, 155). The readily available sword might be used by the young and healthy but pistols were frequently the weapon of choice. One such duel between officers is described in the *London Chronicle* or *Universal Evening Post* (Vol. 13, 1763). The argument began by one Captain calling the other a coward and, having already fought with sword and cane until they were separated, the officers met with pistols the next morning in Hyde Park. The result was the loss of three fingers and left-side damage to one of the officers.

> Hymn for a soldier (extract)
> It is not loss of limbs or breath
> Which hath me so dismay'd
> Nor mortal wounds nor groans of death
> Have made me thus array'd:
> I start no more
> Than mountains from their place,
> Nor feel I fears,
> Though swords and spears
> Are darted at my face …
> … The rapes, the spoils, and acts unjust
> Which are in soldiers rife,
> Their damned oaths, their brutish lust,
> Their cursed course of life,
> More dreadful are,
> When death draws near
> Than death itself can be;
> The fear of those,
> The mouth of hell doth see.
> —George Wither (Farr 1857, xvi)

EXECUTIONS: SOLDIERS FROM THE SAVOY

The dubious behaviour of soldiers is further exemplified by seven entries in the burial registers for executed soldiers; missing details have been filled in by reference to newspaper reports and court proceedings. All seven soldiers were found guilty of crimes other than desertion.

ROBBERY (INCLUDING HIGHWAY ROBBERY)

The first execution of a soldier recorded in the burial registers was that of Robert Damsell, executed at Tyburn for highway robbery in 1751 at the age of 39 (OB, A17510617). Although at the time of his crime and subsequent conviction he had an alehouse near the Savoy, he had been a Foot Guard for many years. Once leaving the Guards his income could not compensate for his idleness and extravagance, so he turned his hand to robbery, successfully for a while. Robert perhaps exemplifies the 18th-century recruit, spending years in idle pursuits until forced into enlisting as a last resort. The details of this case highlight one further point of interest – in addition to his income from the alehouse in the Savoy his wife worked at 'a sort of hospital there'. The military hospital was officially dissolved in 1702 but records indicate the rebuilding of an infirmary in 1728 (Somerville 1960, 92), and when John Howard made his prison visitations in the 1770s (below, 'Savoy Prison') he recorded the presence of an infirmary over the large hall (Howard 1792, 240).

Just 11 years later, in 1762, two more soldiers were executed for robbery: James Whem, aged 33, and James Collins, aged 20 (OB, OA17621013, t17620917–7). The robbery took place in Pancras Fields and involved the assault of a woman and use of a sword to injure her male companion. Unfortunately for the soldiers, Pancras Fields had a history of such crimes and were consequently being patrolled by a High Constable from the parish with a number of assistants. The soldiers and the stolen property were discovered in a ditch, covered with mud and brambles. Their defence was that they were 'in liquor' at the time of the crime but both soldiers were keen to repent and regularly attended the chapel in the preparations for their day of execution. When the day of their execution finally arrived on 13 October 1762 the spectacle was witnessed by a large crowd; 'a considerable number of the foot-guards being present, behaved decently, were much affected, and some wept' (OB, OA17621013).

On 12 July 1797, soldier Patrick Keough, aged 25, and his accomplice Henry Ives, aged 24 (recorded in the burial registers as 'William' Ives) were convicted of highway robbery and sentenced to death (OB, t17970712–1). The court reports that they 'on the 14th May, in a certain field and open place near the Kings highway, in and upon John Shepherd, did make an assault, putting him in fear, and taking from his person two iron keys, value 4d. part of a steel watch chain, value 1d. a metal watch key, value 1d. a cornelian seal set in gold, value 10s. and ten copper half-pence, value 5d. the property of the said John'. According to the Newgate Calendars, Keough and Ives 'behaved with a decency becoming of their unhappy situation, and were launched into eternity about a quarter past eight o'clock' (Jackson nd, 494).

RIOTING

In the case of 20-year-old John Lewis, it was a lack of drink rather than drink itself that caused his downfall. He was a soldier with the 3rd Foot Guards who, along with 'divers other persons' incited a riot at Charing Cross on 16 September 1795. Having been told by the inhabitants of the King's Arms, Charing Cross that since their licence had been removed they were unable to provide him and his companion with drink, Lewis proceeded to assault several members of the house before going outside and, with a fanciful story, managing to incite a mob of at least 12 people into rioting. This figure is significant as, according to the Riot Act (1 Geo. I, c.5) enforced in 1715, a riot was classified as any assemblage of 12 or more people who 'unlawfully, riotously, and tumultuously remain or continue together', refusing to disperse within an hour of being asked to do so by someone in authority (Gregory & Stevenson 2007, 172; Bucholz & Ward 2012, 271). This particular riot resulted in the destruction of the inside of the house, with all the furniture destroyed or carried off. The rioting continued in a similar vein for some days after his arrest, with windows broken at the Downing Street residence of Mr Pitt, the prime minister, and a subsequent attack on a recruiting house in Lambeth and the Royal George, St George's Field. In both cases the furniture was dragged outside and burnt in the streets. Although Lewis was recommended for mercy as a result of his good character, the recommendation was refused and he was executed at Newgate on 11 November 1795 (*The New Annual Register* 1796, 61; OB, t17950916–50). He was buried in the Savoy Chapel burial ground on 16 November 1795.

RAPE

The registers in 1796 record the burial of a soldier of the 1st Foot Guards – Thomas Davenport, executed. According to the Proceedings of the Old Bailey (OB, t17960217–37) Thomas, who was 26 years old, was charged with the assault and rape of Ann Thacker, who was only 11 years old. Davenport had been quartered with another soldier in the Thackers' house for a couple of months and took advantage of the situation. Unfortunately for Ann, Thomas had been suffering from a venereal disease, like so many soldiers at that time. Ann, now also infected, was consequently put on a course of mercurial treatment. Thomas was found guilty, sentenced to death and executed on 20 April 1796 (Jackson nd, 466). He was buried two days later.

SAVOY PRISON

Extract from 'A Prisoner's Lay'
These iron chains, these bolts of steel,
Which often poor offenders grind;
The wants and cares which they do feel
May bring some greater things to mind.
For by their grief thou shalt do well
To think upon the pains of Hell

Again, when he that feared to die
(Past hope) doth see his pardon brought,
Read but the Joy that's in his eye,
And then convey it to thy thought;
Then think between thy heart and thee,
How glad will 'Come ye blessed' be!
—George Wither (Willmott 1839, 110)

During the last decade of the 17th century the Savoy was used to house Irish prisoners from the campaign of William III, leading to the establishment of a regular military prison within the Savoy at the start of the 18th century (Somerville

1960, 92). This occupied the northern part of the old master's lodgings but changes at the western end of the great dormitory and the addition of a new passage suggest that proposals by Wren, when asked to look for a suitable spot to have a prison, may also have been implemented. The prison was used to house military offenders from England, Scotland and Ireland as well as new recruits for the Guard Regiments (Somerville 1960, 93).

A description of the Savoy Prison can be found in Howard's report (1777, 192), which highlighted the conditions of prisons in England and Wales (discussed in more detail below). The prison had two guard rooms for confining offenders. The hall was found on the other side of the court down five steps. On the left-hand side of the court was another smaller hall, leading to barrack rooms described as 'very close and unhealthy'. More 'airy' barracks rooms are located above these. In addition to these rooms were the 'black-hole', the 'condemn'd hole' and the 'cock pit'.

Just as the hospital suffered from the neglect and malpractice of the masters, so the prison suffered at the hands of the appointed marshals. In 1708, deputy marshal Terence MacMahan managed to cause the death of a number of soldiers by selling them an unwholesome beer and ale, having overcharged them for it and prevented their buying beer from anywhere else. Then in 1721, 1725 and 1730 fines were issued for not providing the prisoners with adequate bedding, keeping them in a very poor state and for selling short-weight bread (Somerville 1960, 94).

The Savoy Prison had an evil reputation for gaol distemper, otherwise known as typhus or gaol fever (Clark-Kennedy 1929, 190). This was a widespread problem that did not affect just the Savoy. A severe typhus outbreak in 1750 is known to have spread to the courts, killing among others the Lord Major and two judges (Bucholz & Ward 2012, 260). Typhus was louse-borne and associated with unhygienic and closed living quarters; although it was not necessarily fatal, the poor conditions found in the barracks and prison would have been conducive to the worst type, in which patients could suffer delirium, raving, unbearable pains in the head and livid spots on the skin (Creighton 1894, 99). Those most likely to be worst affected may have experienced a sudden change in living conditions or have found themselves unexpectedly in contact with those infected, such as criminals newly thrown in jail, soldiers returning from campaign to confined conditions, the family of a discharged prisoner or soldier – all parts of society that would have formed part of the Savoy population (ibid).

In the early 18th century the Revd Dr Stephen Hales, 1677–1761 (Fig 3.8), not a scientific or medical man by trade, realised that clean air was necessary for the health of living things and recognised that this was not readily accessible in many

Fig 3.8 Stephen Hales, mezzotint, by J McArdell after T Hudson (©WL, L0008639 used under CC BY 4.0)

situations (Harris 1916, 441). Some of the most notorious places were prisons, including military prisons, full of men pressed into service and awaiting transportation. The situation was such that recruits from the Savoy were feared by recruits in service as they often brought infection with them (Clark-Kennedy 1929, 190). Without fully understanding the process of respiration (the exhalation of carbon dioxide by animals was not discovered until 1754 and oxygen was not discovered until 1774), Hales began to develop an apparatus for removing foul air from one location so that it could be changed (Harris 1916, 442). The result was the invention of the ventilator (Fig 3.9).

Following on from the success of this apparatus on slave ships, convict ships and in Winchester prison, and at the request of the Secretary of State for War, Dr Hales visited the Savoy Prison in order to assess its suitability for ventilation (Clark-Kennedy 1929, 190). As reported in *The Gentleman's Magazine and Historical Review* (Thursday 29 June 1749) the ventilators were considered extremely advantageous to 'the health of those whose hard lot obliges them to breathe the putrid air of a prison or other close place' (Urban 1749, 282).

A letter written by Dr Hales in 1750 (LMA, CLA/035/02/049) outlines his observations after visiting the

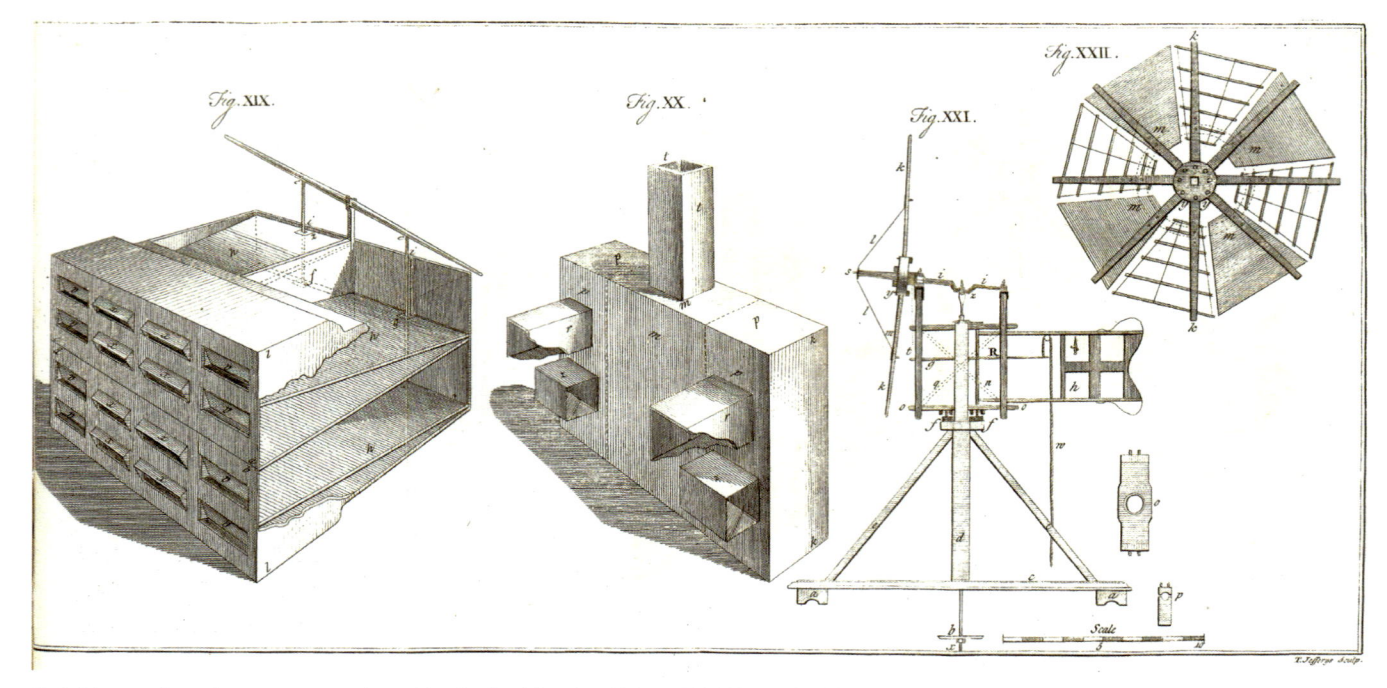

Fig 3.9 Image of ventilation apparatus devised by the Revd Stephen Hales, 1758 (©WL, L0040397 used under CC BY 4.0)

prison once the ventilators had been installed. He recalls that before their installation 50 to 100 prisoners were dying from gaol fever each year but in the years immediately after their installation the situation had dramatically changed. Of the 200 imprisoned in 1749 only one died of smallpox, and in 1750 two died out of 240 prisoners. There were no deaths in 1751 and a single death in 1752 – a prisoner described by Hales as 'a great glutton'. Dr Hales also compliments the Master of the Prison, Mr Hayward, on his continued efforts to keep it clean, burning 2lb of brimstone in the large wards every 6 weeks and 1lb in the smaller wards. He describes the whitewashed walls, which not only helped to lighten the gloomy and dark rooms but also to 'cure in some measure, the nasty infectious matter, which has for many years been settling on the walls from foul putrid air'. Dr Hales suggests that individual cells could be ventilated by placing a single ventilator on the ceiling of the common passage with a pendulum-like handle operating like a pump to move the air through the cells. However, his next comment sheds further light on the general management of the prison, observing that 'it is suspected' that such a device, if working, 'would be much neglected.' Whitewashing or liming seems to have continued for a number of decades as it is also described by Howard (1777, 192), who saw it as 'salutary' for the prisoners.

A report from 1788 details the overcrowded nature of the prison, resulting from a fire the previous year (see below). The prison was described as dirty, with prisoners being left nearly naked without shirts, shoes or stockings, and a great number of deaths. Consequently, a new prison yard was planned to improve the health of the prisoners (Howard 1792, 240; Somerville 1960, 94). However, things do not seem to have improved, and in 1795 further fines were made to the prison-keeper for gross neglect. The bedding straw had not been changed for at least six months and the sick were left largely unattended (Somerville 1960, 95). Unsurprisingly, considering the poor and unaltering condition of the prison, the 18th-century newspapers were full of reports of rebellions and escape attempts.

As early as 1707, the broadsheets report escape attempts by prisoners unhappy with their lot, having been confined for more than 25 weeks in Canterbury and the Savoy for refusing to fight the French at sea (ibid, 93). In 1763, several Savoy prisoners enlisted to the service of the East India Company, knocked down the turnkey and sentinels and, taking their keys and muskets, fired upon and wounded the line of waiting musketeers. Three of the unfortunate prisoners were killed by return fire and several more were 'desperately wounded' (*London Magazine* or *Gentleman's Monthly Intelligencer*, January 1763). Several years later a prisoner made his escape 'by means of a Rope-Ladder, conveyed to him from the Wharf adjoining the place where he was confined' (*Oracle and Daily Advertiser* (London, England) Monday 11 November 1779 (issue 22139)).

Prisoners would have been keen to take advantage of any situation. When the fire of 1776 was spreading through the barracks, several men made their escape (*Bath Chronicle and Weekly Gazette*, Thursday 7 March 1776). Then again in 1778 several prisoners were successful in their escape, having broken through the wall dividing the prison and the minister's house (Somerville 1960, 93). In 1788, the prison was 'wilfully set on fire by the prisoners confined for desertion', something that apparently left the inside of the prison completely destroyed. At the time 89 prisoners were recorded as being held there, most of whom had been there less than five months and none more than 15 months (*World* 1788 (London, England), Tuesday 15 April 1788 (issue 404) and Monday 28 April 28 1788 (issue 415)).

Later the same year approximately 50 prisoners attempted, but failed, to escape. Having locked themselves in a room inside the prison for a couple of days they surrendered, only to find themselves put in irons, with some placed in the dungeon (*World and Fashionable Advertiser* (London, England), Monday 29 October 1788 (issue 247)).

In 1773, John Howard was made High Sheriff of Bedfordshire, which had attached to it the responsibility for the county gaol. He was so disgusted by what he saw when he visited the gaol that he felt obliged to visit other penal institutions in England, Wales and Europe to assess them in the hope of finding examples of more humane conditions (Howard League nd). He produced an extensive report (Howard 1777), which was subsequently updated, detailing each prison visited. The reports detail the number of prisoners confined in the Savoy. This and additional information taken from his reports (1777; 1791; 1792) has been summarised below (Table 3.3).

The information recorded highlights some of the common problems encountered in the prisons at that time, and a set of prison reforms were set in place (for example, the 1779 Penitentiary Act) as a result of Howard's work. An article from the beginning of the 19th century paints a slightly better picture. When the Leet Jury for the Duchy of Lancaster visited the prison in 1811 it was described as clean, though ill ventilated, with healthy prisoners. The cleanliness no doubt had a dramatic effect on their health but diet may also have been influential. Prisoners were provided with bread, meat, cheese, potatoes and beer, 'all good of the kind' and in the same portions as the soldiers in barracks were receiving.

SUMMARY AND DISCUSSION

The barracks and prison dominated the Savoy Precinct throughout the 18th century. Although the number of Foot Guards would have fluctuated, the barracks and prison would have received a constant supply of new recruits, either for involvement in battle itself or to take the place of those fighting. Their other duties, such as peace-keeping, kept them in the public eye, as did their often dubious behaviour. This conduct, although undesirable, was largely a result of the military system: for many soldiers drinking was a popular distraction and for those discharged and unsupported in times of peace, crime was a viable and easy option.

Date	Total no of prisoners	Detail	Other information
15 March 1776	119	49 transports	many sick and dying, distemper
25 May 1776	37		many sick; gaol distemper Keeper, Capt. Jackson (salary £50, 4d daily for provisions)
14 August 1779	98	64 deserters 21 impressed men 13 Guards	better health, rooms more airy 3 rooms over the hall set up as infirmary
20 December 1782	92	3 Guards	clean rooms except infirmary, 3 Guards in close confinement on bread and water for 48 hours 1 sick in prison and 2 in the infirmary close rooms, 1 transport lay dead Keeper, Capt. Osbourne
29 August 1783	56	14 Guards	10 Guards in the black hole, bread and water for 24 or 48 hours; some deserters been there for 7–16 months clean rooms, lime-whited twice a year, washed every day, none sick in two months
13 September 1788	45 (deserters)		crowded in 2 rooms at night; very dirty, not whitewashed for 2 years, prisoners almost naked 6 Guards in black hole for drunkenness or neglect of duty

Table 3.3 Record of prisoners in the Savoy Prison, 1776–88

Historical records suggest that the Foot Guards were very much integrated into London society, not only indulging in the cultural experiences surrounding them but in some cases billeted in civilian houses. For the majority accommodated in the barracks and prison, their employed status did not protect them from some of the unenviable conditions being felt by the poorest in London, namely overcrowding and uncleanliness, both factors detrimental to health. It seems probable that during this time of cultural change many of the influences from the surrounding environment would have affected the soldiers in residence; equally, it can be assumed that the presence of the soldiers would have greatly influenced life within the precinct and, in all likelihood, in the surrounding areas.

3.3 SAVOY CHAPEL AND BURIAL GROUND

Among the precinct buildings and associated with the hospital were three chapels, the most significant of which was St John's Chapel, later the Queen's Chapel of the Savoy. This, together with its attached burial ground, is the only part of the original hospital to survive to the present day (Fig 3.10).

There has been some debate about the origins of the chapel. It has been argued that it contains remnants of the original 14th-century chapel associated with John of Gaunt's palace, or at least stands on the same spot (Somerville 1960, 19–20). The two pieces of evidence supporting this are that the present chapel, dating from the time of the hospital, is oriented north–south rather than the customary east–west, and the earliest burial commemorated in the chapel dates to 1510, suggesting that there was a burial place there before the hospital chapel was built (Loftie 1878, 64–5). In consideration of these arguments Somerville points out that the 1510 inscription does not definitively state that the burial took place in the chapel at this time, also that the north–south orientation of the chapel was necessary because of the sloping ground and position of the other hospital buildings (Somerville 1960, 19). More conclusively, excavation works in the 1950s demonstrated that the foundations are of Tudor brickwork, making the chapel contemporary with the hospital (ibid, 20). Nevertheless, without contrary evidence for the site of the original 14th-chapel the possibility remains that St John's Chapel was built in the same location as its predecessor.

Between 1564 and 1717 the parishioners from St Mary-le-Strand also used the Savoy Chapel, theirs having been pulled down by Lord Somerset so that his new palace could be built in its place. From this the chapel became temporarily and mistakenly known as 'St Mary-le-Savoy' (Loftie 1878, 179). The body of the chapel was covered in 8ft-high oak panelling but in the chancel it was 3ft high, and the decorative style, carved branches, leaves and fruit indicate a 17th-century date. Earthenware pots were built in under the desks to improve acoustics (Somerville 1960, 17). The main entrance was towards the northern end on the western side, with a further door leading from the chapel to the vestry (since repositioned) on the eastern side. The ceiling was the chapel's focal point, with 138 carved panels (ibid, 18).

The chapel building had been neglected throughout the hospital's life and the desperately needed repairs were carried out in 1721 (ibid, 123). This included the construction of a new brick wall around the north and eastern side of the burial ground. In 1723 the burial ground was completely enclosed and levelled, with access now through iron gates on the northern side. Given the number of fires that are known to have taken place in the barracks and prison throughout the 18th century it seems probable that the chapel would have been affected. At least one such incident is recorded in 1762, when two soldiers convicted of robbery were visited in their cells, 'the chapel not being as yet put in order since the late dreadful fire' (OB, OA17621013).

Although an accompaniment to the hospital, the burial ground was used also for other burials. The first recorded were of hung and dissected criminals in 1552 (Somerville 1960, 124). When the parishioners of St Mary-le-Strand were without a church (before 1727) they too were buried in the Savoy burial ground. Burials also took place in the chapel itself, perhaps as early as 1550, and a number of memorials are still present. Among those buried were the poet George Wither (1588–1667; Fig 3.11), Anne Killigrew (1660–85; Fig 3.12), poet and daughter of Dr Henry Killigrew, master of the hospital (see below), Dr Archibald Cameron of Lochiel (1707–53; see below) and the painter Peter de Wint (1784–89).

DR HENRY KILLIGREW (1613–1700), THE LAST APPOINTED MASTER OF THE SAVOY HOSPITAL

Henry Killigrew was born in 1613 to a family who were royalist courtiers through the 16th and 17th centuries (The Twickenham Museum nd; Partington 1838, 99–100). The Killigrews had struggled to keep lands in the family since Henry VIII but in 1674 the original settlement granting the manors to the family reached the end of its term and so they became more dependent upon court for their income (Barash 2001, 162). The family also possessed literary talent: Henry's brothers William and Thomas became playwrights, and Henry himself published *The Conspiracy* in 1638 (later *Palantus and Eudora*, 1653) as well as volumes of sermons (Loftie 1878, 153). In 1642 he was appointed as chaplain to the king's army. Henry's other posts included almoner to the duke of York and canon of Westminster (Hammond & Hopkins 2007, 357). Following the Restoration in 1663 Dr Henry Killigrew was appointed as the last of the masters of the hospital, and served for 37 years until his death in 1700 (Loftie 1889, 152; Somerville 1960, 71).

His work as master has received mixed reviews. Some describe him as 'a man of generous and publick spirit' while others such as Loftie accuse him of being the ruin of the hospital 'by his improvidence, greed and other bad qualities' (Loftie 1878, 152; Somerville 1960, 71). As already seen, the hospital was in a poor state of affairs. Dr Killigrew tried to restore it, returning the dormitory and beds to their intended

CHAPTER 3 HISTORY OF THE SITE

The SAVOY HOSPITAL *in the* STRAND.

AN *historical account of the Savoy, so called from* Peter *earl of* Savoy, *who built a palace there; has been given already in* Plate V *of this* Volume. *But that palace being destroyed by the rebels of* Kent *and* Essex, *this hospital was erected there by* K. Henry VII. *In memory whereof the date of its foundation, with the two following Latin verses written in the manner of those times, were placed over the gate towards the street.*

1505
HOSPITIVM HOC INOPI TVRBE SAVOIA VOCATVM
SEPTIMVS HENRICVS FVNDAVIT AB IMO SOLO.

That inscription remained till the building was burnt down, not long after the great fire of London *in 1666, as* Newcourt *relates,* Repertor. Vol. I. pag. 696.

The CHAPEL *of the* HOSPITAL.

THIS *chapel now serveth as a parish church to the tenements near adjoining, and others in the neighbourhood; and is reckoned in the bills of mortality, as one of the seven parishes in the city and liberties of* Westminster, *by the name of* St. Mary Savoy.

G. Vertue delin. et sculp.   *Published according to Act of Parliament,* Nov. 29. 1753.   Sumptu Societ. Ant. Lond. 1753.

Fig 3.10 Savoy Chapel and Prison, by George Virtue, 1753 (©WL, V0013828 used under CC BY 4.0)

Fig 3.11 George Wither, line engraving, by T S Engelheart after J Payne, 1669 (©WL, V0006334 used under CC BY 4.0)

Fig 3.12 Anne Killigrew (self-portrait) (©National Portrait Gallery, D3420)

use and using some of the income for charitable gifts. However, as many of his predecessors had, Dr Killigrew took more from the hospital than he was entitled to. Rather than the £30 stipend as outlined in the statutes, he was taking £200 a year as well as claiming any fines from leases (Somerville 1960, 71). After his death in 1700 the hospital was finally dissolved. Perhaps Dr Killigrew's most lasting legacy is his daughter Anne, whose reputation exceeds his own.

ANNE KILLIGREW (1660–85)

> Her superior genius being improved by a polite education, she made a great proficiency in the arts of Poetry and Painting: and had it pleased Providence to have prolonged her life, she might probably have rivalled the greatest masters in each
>
> —Barber & Thornton 1755, 2

Anne, an accomplished poet and artist, was the daughter of Dr Henry Killigrew. Her aunts, as well as her father, were involved in courtly life. One was paid £10–15 a year to dress the young princes and princesses, and another was a royal mistress. Anne's uncle, Thomas Killigrew, vice chamberlain to Queen Henrietta Maria, became groom of the bedchamber to Charles II (Barash 2001, 163), a powerful position that allowed him to control access to the monarch (Bucholz & Ward 2012, 118).

Once reaching adulthood Anne herself was appointed maid of honour to Mary of Modena, duchess of York and future queen of England (Hager 2004, 187). This entitled her to £200 a year plus room and board (Barash 2001, 152). The two main influences in Anne's short life were her family and her court experiences. Her father Dr Killigrew was a dramatist but Anne also had two playwright uncles, one of whom, Thomas, received a Charles II patent to open a theatre in 1662 (ibid, 163). Consequently Anne grew up in an environment that would encourage her artistic talents (Brackett 2008, 244).

During this period women were expected not to concern themselves with politics or divinity but rather to concentrate on household duties. They were not supposed to travel alone, practise law or enter the Church (Hager 2004, 187). However, Mary of Modena was greatly influential, providing a sense of female community and a patronage of women artists, where women exchanged writings and performed in plays and masques. It was a world 'where women's education and women's imagination were taken seriously' (Barash 2001, 150).

Anne's poetry would have been influenced by the upper-class women surrounding her (Hager 2004, 188) and life at the court of Charles II would have provided a wealth of subject matter and life experiences that could be used as material in her works. Indeed, her poems are thought to be largely autobiographical (Brackett 2008, 245), a sad fact when considering that many of her poems have a depressing theme (Hager 2004, 188). They are said to reflect 'the sparkle of

Restoration court life, but more of the sorrow produced by Mary of Modena's consistent unpopularity' (Morton 1967, 2). Anne would soon have realised that at court, women were thought to exist for the pleasure of men (Hager 2004, 188). Much of her poetry seems to highlight the complications of life at court and how women servants to the royal family had to define and separate the role of friendship, which cut through class differences, and the apparent reality that servants' individual lives were inconsequential (Barash 2001, 162).

Also renowned as a talented artist, Anne is known to have painted the Duchess Mary of Modena and the duke of York (later James II) as well as two self-portraits (see for example Fig 3.12). In common with many female artists of the time, she also depicted religious themes in her *St John in the Wilderness*, *Herodias with the Head of St John* and *Diana's Nymph* (Gray 2009, 159).

Anne began to make her poems public in 1680 but they were published posthumously as a memorial edition by her father Dr Killigrew just three months after her death (September 1685). Aged only 25, Anne died of smallpox in her father's quarters in Westminster and was buried in the Savoy Chapel on 15 June 1685 (Hager 2004, 188; WCA, system ID 2599).

> When I am Dead, few Friends attend my Hearse,
> And for a Monument, I leave my VERSE
> —Anne Killigrew, An Epitaph On Her Self
> (Morton 1967, 82)

DR ARCHIBALD CAMERON OF LOCHIEL

The youngest son of a Highland family, Archibald Cameron studied and qualified as a doctor in Edinburgh, Paris and Holland before returning and settling to married life in the Highlands (Knapp & Baldwin 1825, 179). Such was his life when the Jacobite rebellion unfolded in 1745. When Bonnie Prince Charlie landed in August 1745 it was to Archibald's elder brother Donald Lochiel that he turned for support in his uprising, having received only a tepid welcome from the other clans who were loyal to the cause but with either insufficient power to raise support or no stomach for another campaign (Chambers 1869, 24–6, 42–3; Macpherson 1995; Harmsworth 2015).

Archibald Cameron, having failed to dissuade his elder brother from taking up arms, agreed to join him as his physician, but refused to take a position in the rebel army (Henderson 1753, 25). The Jacobites faced the government forces for a decisive battle in Culloden on 16 April 1746, where the Jacobites were outnumbered and suffered heavy losses (Education Scotland nd; Chambers 1869, 296–7). Cameron was noted for his humanity, treating all battle casualties equally, whether they came from the royal or the rebel army (Knapp & Baldwin 1825, 179). While government forces were hunting down anyone who took part in the rebellion, Cameron and his brother managed to escape to France. Cameron made several furtive visits to Scotland after 1746, staying after his final visit in 1751. When he was discovered in 1753 the government were determined to make an example of him (Chambers 1869, 514). He was returned to London and committed to the Tower. When finally he admitted his true identity at the king's bench in May, he received the following sentence:

> You, Archibald Cameron, of Lochiel, in that part of Great Britain called Scotland, must be removed from hence to his majesty's prison of the Tower of London, from whence you came, and on Thursday the 7th June next, your body to be drawn on a sledge to the place of execution; there be hanged, but not till you are dead; your bowels, to be taken out, your body quartered, your head cut off, and affixed at the king's disposal; and the Lord have mercy on your soul!
> Knapp & Baldwin 1825, 180.

The severity of the punishment was seen as unnecessary but the government sought to use his death as a deterrent against further plots to seize the British throne (Chambers 1869, 514). His voyage to Tyburn on 7 June 1753 drew a large crowd (Fig 3.13). Keeping a cheerful composure till the end he told the waiting clergyman, 'I have now done with this world, and am ready to leave it.' After being hung for 20 minutes his heart was removed and burnt before his remains were interred in a large vault at the Savoy Chapel on Sunday 9 June 1753. Dr Archibald Cameron Lochiel was the last Jacobite to be executed for the 1745 uprising (Knapp & Baldwin 1825, 182).

His great-grandson erected a memorial in his name in 1846:

> To the Memory of
> DR ARCHIBALD CAMERON,
> Whose remains, after his execution, were deposited in the vault beneath, this monument,
> With the gracious permission of Her Majesty the Queen Victoria,
> Is erected by his great-grandson, A.D 1846,
> One hundred years after the Battle of Culloden
> *To soothe the sufferer then was all thy thought;*
> *Whatever the banner under which he fought,*
> *Thy hand would stanch the blood of him that bled,*
> *Were it for Brunswick or Stewart shed*
> (WCA, Box 22 18b)

Sadly, this sculpted memorial plaque was destroyed in the fire in 1864. In 1870 it was replaced by a window, dedicated to his memory (Loftie 1878, 245–6). This in turn was destroyed during the Blitz, along with several other stained glass windows, and a final memorial plaque was dedicated at a service of commemoration in 1993 (Topliss nd).

Fig 3.13 Dr Cameron being drawn on a sledge to Tyburn to be executed for high treason (©WL, L0040867 used under CC BY 4.0)

LATER REPAIRS

The buildings were still in a state of disrepair in the later 18th century, and further works were carried out between 1775 and 1800 (Fig 3.14). These included roof repairs and internal and external painting. In 1820, as part of the overall precinct improvement works, Robert Smirke was called upon to make necessary alterations. The tower was dismantled and moved to its present position and the wooden south wall was replaced with brick. In an attempt to cure the damp brought on by the high ground levels in the burial ground, the soil was cut back and iron gratings were inserted above floor level. These works, completed in 1821, resulted in the shortening of the chapel to interior dimensions of 90 × 23ft (Somerville 1960, 129).

It seems that at this time it was not uncommon for struggling parsons to allow livestock to graze in burial grounds in exchange for a few pounds a year and the Savoy was no exception. This was, however, considered by some to have a detrimental effect on the livestock as they could be 'killed by swallowing with the grass the poisonous products of the overfilled ground' (Holmes 1896, 268). The burial ground was becoming increasingly overcrowded and in an attempt to ease the situation in 1849 the burial fees for people not resident in the precinct were increased from twice to four times that of residents (Somerville 1960, 125). Finally, on 24 October 1853 an act was introduced 'to amend the Laws concerning the Burial of the Dead in England beyond the Limits of the Metropolis and to amend the Act concerning the Burial of the Dead in the Metropolis'. This stated that burials in any part of the metropolis were to be wholly discontinued for the protection of public health, on and after 1 May 1855 (WCA, SMGLC/0090/20). At the Savoy, the final burial recorded is that of 57-year-old Anne Turner on 1 July 1854. There appears to have been only one burial in the previous year, that of 64-year-old Mary Watkins, who was buried on 10 April. In fact, of the 10,926 burials recorded, the 1840s and 1850s account for only 198, or 1.8%.

Unfortunately, the newly restored chapel had almost outlived its usefulness. As a result of the general Savoy improvements it was the only remaining hospital building and there were hardly any residents left in the precinct. Despite continued financial difficulties (the money received from burial fees and pew rents did not cover maintenance costs) the chapel continued in use until 1843, when considerable damage was caused by a fire (Somerville 1960, 132). Sydney Smirke, younger brother to Robert, who had undertaken the previous works, was employed to undertake the renovation. The main eastern doorway was enlarged and the steps down to it widened. Tudor-style decoration was reintroduced to the interior and the 16th-century ceiling reproduced. For a further £762, Smirke undertook interior alterations again in 1859–60. The internal gallery was removed, the aisle widened and a new mortuary (bone house) was built outside.

Astonishingly, two more fires befell the chapel: one in 1860 and one, the most devastating, in 1864 (Fig 3.15). After this only the walls were left standing (ibid, 134). The chapel reopened in 1865 and remained unchanged until 1877, when the vestry was rebuilt and a new entrance on the eastern side was constructed. It is recorded as the first church to have electricity, installed in 1890 (ibid, 136).

Fig 3.14 Savoy Chapel and Prison, 1791 (©WL,V0013829 used under CC BY 4.0)

THE CHAPEL MINISTERS

After the dissolution of the hospital in 1702, the chapel remained in use and still, therefore, required chaplains to administer it. One of the most infamous was John Wilkinson, minister for 30 years from 1728. His roles included preaching twice on Sundays, prayer readings on Wednesdays, Fridays and holy days as well as acting as chaplain to the three regiments of Foot Guards, attending the sick in the Savoy Barracks and accompanying prisoners to their executions when necessary. When he took the position he had been receiving approximately £40 a year, but by 1737 this had been increased to £100, in light of his arguments and in view of his apparently needing an assistant (Somerville 1960, 139–40).

Still feeling financial pressure, however, Wilkinson is known to have removed and sold two marble tombstones from the chancel. He was also accused of selling a bell for his own profit (ibid, 140). As a consequence, his stipend was stopped in 1749. The 1750s saw his introduction of clandestine marriages: unregistered marriages that took place without parental consent, licence or banns, away from the home parish of the spouses, and often bigamous (Relationships: the law of marriage nd; Probert 2009, 203). These marriages provided him with an extra income, but defied the Marriage Act of 1753. In fact, it seems that all the clandestine marriages took place after the act (Loftie 1878, 209).

After Wilkinson placed an advertisement in the *Public Advertiser* (January 1754) the marriage rate in the chapel increased from 19 in 1753 to 1190 in 1755 (Somerville 1960, 141). He believed that he was entitled to grant such licences as the Savoy was considered extra-parochial (Loftie 1878, 209), or, in other words, outside the normal jurisdiction of any parish. When officers finally came for him in 1755, he escaped through a private door to the prison kitchen, through the gardens and out along the foreshore and up Strand Lane. Of the marriages he had licensed 1400 were declared null and void (White 2012, 498). When he surrendered in 1756 he was convicted and sentenced to 14 years' transportation but in the event he died of gout in 1757, before his ship had been able to leave British waters (Somerville 1960, 142).

The chapel continued with a series of less noteworthy ministers for the next 100 years. Its fortunes finally improved in 1859 with the appointment of Henry White. Thanks to his amiable personality and improvements to the choir and choral practices, the Savoy congregation increased from fewer

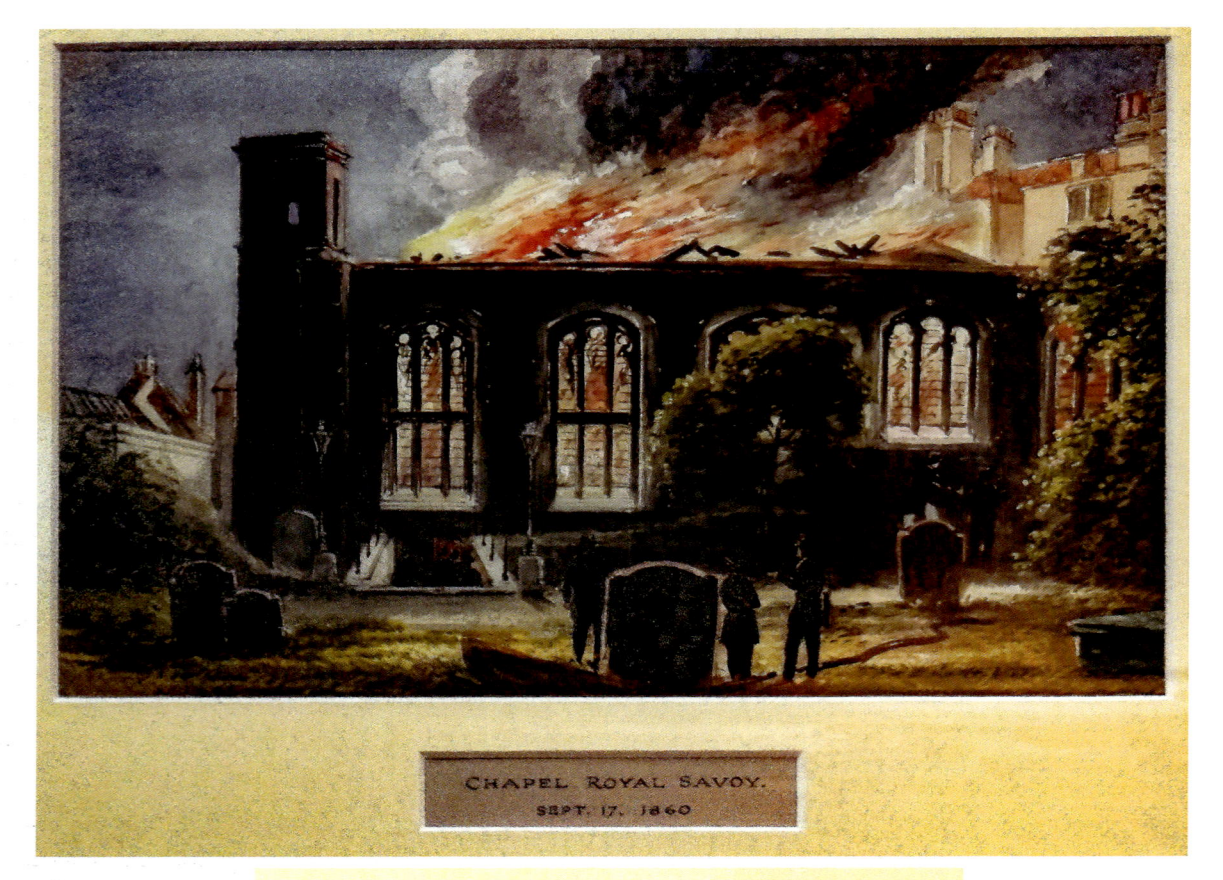

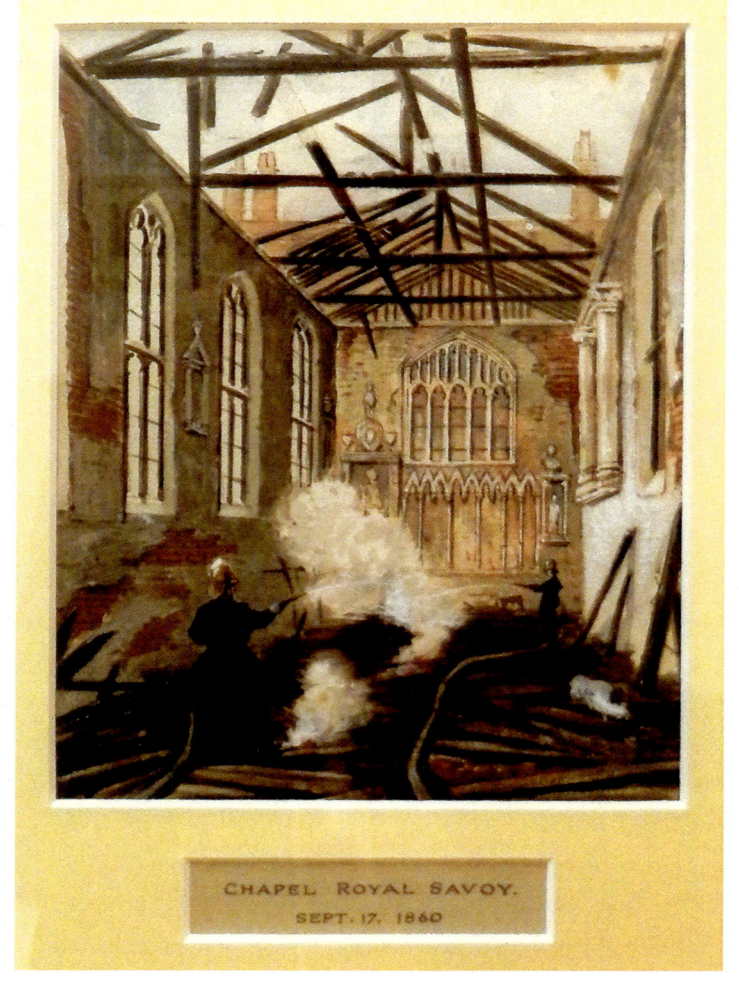

Fig 3.15 The fire of 1860: a – the outside of the chapel; b – the inside. Displayed in Queen's Chapel of the Savoy. Reproduced by kind permission of Her Majesty in Right of Her Duchy of Lancaster

than 30 to a stage where the Duchy needed to make special arrangements to ensure that all residents could get in. The Savoy Chapel became the only full church in the Strand district (ibid, 143). In 1937 it was established as the chapel of the Royal Victorian Order by George VI and as a private royal chapel it remains extra-parochial, exempt from episcopal jurisdiction (Queen's Chapel of the Savoy nd).

SUMMARY AND DISCUSSION

Throughout the various permutations of the precinct, the one constant was the chapel of St John. Constructed as part of the original 'Hospital of Henry late King of England of the Savoy' it would have been an integral part of the lives of both staff and patients. Later, just as the hospital buildings were given a new purpose in the 18th century, transformed into the military barracks and prison, the chapel was given a new lease of life with some much-needed repairs. It continued as a chapel for the Foot Guards, surviving the many turmoils that took place in the surrounding buildings. Records suggest that the most substantial damage befell the chapel in the 19th century during a series of fires, the most devastating of which left just the four walls standing.

Unfortunately, the problems faced by the chapel challenged both its structural and its moral fabric and it was not until the mid 19th century that its luck changed and it became a fashionable place to worship. The burial ground itself was in use from the hospital's origin and, although originally intended for use only by the hospital, interments continued until 1854. Despite only serving a relatively small parish, the burial ground did not escape the overcrowding issues experienced by burial grounds throughout the capital and it was closed as a result of the 1853 Burial Act (UK Public General Acts nd).

3.4 SAVOY IMPROVEMENTS

In 1772 the ownership of the Savoy Precinct was split between the Crown and the exchequer, who now owned the interior, or the buildings of the hospital (except the chapel), and the Duchy, who were responsible for the rest – the outer buildings and the chapel (Somerville 1960, 103). The hospital buildings were in a very poor state of repair and the river frontage was no better. The site thus had significant development potential but the dual ownership proved to be an obstacle in the development plans.

It was proposed that the barracks and riverside buildings be demolished and that new riverside buildings and wharves be constructed in their place, along with a new embankment. While various detailed plans and proposals were drawn up, the fire in the barracks in 1776 left them a 'roofless ruin' (ibid, 106–7). The buildings became more dilapidated and once again 'a receptacle for vagabonds'. Among other things, the slaughtering of pigs, hanging of dogs and cats and beating of carpets took place among the ruins of the hospital buildings (ibid, 108). The site had also become a quarry for stone and brick. Every day one or two industrious individuals could be seen 'sitting on the ruins and cutting the stone with knives into squares, which they sell as a proper material to clean hearthstones and the steps before doors' (Hughson 1817, 185).

Finally, after 40 years of deliberations and setbacks, the first brick of the new development was laid in 1811. Somewhat changed in form from the original proposals, this now involved the construction of a new bridge over the Thames: Waterloo Bridge, so named in 1816 (Somerville 1960, 110).

With the exception of the chapel, the hospital was comprehensively demolished in the 19th century. The *Morning Post* records the near completion of the Savoy prison ship, which was to be a replacement for the Savoy Prison. It had been fitted out with guard room, dungeons, kitchen, water closets, offices etc. Once it had been painted, it was to be moored near Waterloo Bridge and the prisoners transferred, allowing the demolition of the prison, which was the last building to go, in 1820 (*Morning Post*, Friday 28 May 1819 (issue 15087); Somerville 1960, 112). Despite the dilapidated state of the buildings the demolition was a hard task as some walls were reportedly 8–10ft thick. The works appear to have been a novelty, attracting crowds to watch the activity daily (Somerville 1960, 112).

Perhaps true to form, given its controversial history, even in its dying moments the hospital managed to attract unwanted attention. The *Morning Chronicle* on Thursday 30 March 1820 reported a dreadful accident in which three workmen, while trying to demolish the walls of the prison, 'which are of great thickness', were 'crushed dreadfully' when the wall collapsed on them. The wife of one of the unfortunate men, Mr Fred Windemude of Horseferry Road, watched as her husband's body, which 'presented an awful spectacle' was removed from the rubble. When she had finished screaming, however, she was able to remove '4l. in bank notes, and his watch, not at all damaged' from his pocket (*Morning Chronicle*, 30 March 1820 (issue 15887)).

The final works followed the design of the architect Robert Smirke. He proposed the wide approach to Waterloo Bridge but as the road was considered too close to the Navy Houses on the west of Somerset House only one side was built up. The new riverside development and embankment became the Savoy Wharf and Duchy Wharf, with buildings above. The Strand was linked to the new embankment by the newly constructed Savoy Street. The Savoy pump, halfway down the road, was adapted from a well, thought to date to the time of the hospital (Somerville 1960, 111–13). The last of the works were complete by 1823 and the area once again became a respectable place to live.

Development and improvement works continued in the area throughout the 19th century. New embankment works had rendered the Savoy wharves useless so the Duchy looked at the whole area between the Savoy Chapel and the Embankment. Both Savoy Street and Savoy Hill were extended southwards to the Embankment. Various buildings within the precinct were redeveloped for different purposes such as Turkish baths (1884–1923), the Royal College of Surgeons (1885–1909) and a public elementary school (1883–1914). The Savoy theatre and hotel appeared at the turn of the century. Road widening schemes also continued and, after 120 years, Waterloo Bridge was replaced in 1944 (ibid, 117–20).

CHAPTER 4 BURIAL REGISTERS

Lucy Sibun and Hayley Forsyth

Tell me thou safest End of all our Woe
Why wreched Mortals do avoid thee so:
Thou gentle drier o'th' afflicteds Tears,
Thou noble ender of the Cowards Fears;
Thou sweet Repose to Lovers sad dispaire,
Thou Calm t'Ambitions rough Tempestuous Care.
If in regard of Bliss thou wert a Curse,
And then the Joys of Paradise art worse;

Yet after Man from his first Station fell,
And God from Eden Adam did expel,
Thou wert no more an Evil, but Relief;
The Balm and Cure to ev'ry Humane Grief:
Through thee (what Man had forfeited before)
He now enjoys, and ne'r can loose it more.
—Anne Killigrew, On Death (extract)
(Morten 1967, 14)

4.1 THE REGISTERS

Three volumes of the Savoy Chapel burial registers are held at the Westminster City Archives (WCA, system ID 2599). They date from 1680 to 1854 and record nearly 11,000 burials. It should be noted that they do not include the earliest period of the history of the Savoy Precinct, when the burial ground was used by the medieval hospital. Instead, the available registers correspond to the use of the buildings as a military hospital, barracks and prison and to their later use by the civilian population of this and the surrounding parishes. In addition to these data, the London Bills of Mortality (Chapter 2.2, 'London Bills of Mortality') record the total number of deaths in the Savoy Precinct for the years from 1625 to 1758.

The level of detail recorded routinely within the registers varies through the decades. The name of the deceased was always recorded when known, as was the day and month of the burial. Before the English Civil War there was little formality to record-keeping, which was undertaken by the clergy. For a brief period responsibility was passed to a lay officer, but was then returned to the clergy after the Restoration. It was not until 1812 that registers were standardised and burial entries set at eight to a page, with columns for date, name, abode, age at death and the name of the clergy who presided (Raymond 2014, 135–7). The level of detail recorded in the Savoy registers is tabulated and described in Table 4.1.

Minimal information is recorded between 1680 and 1754. Each page is split into two columns and the date of the burial and a name is all that is provided. On rare occasions, if the death was considered to be of particular significance, the entry might include additional information, for example the burial of Richard Harabin in 1686, who:

> Died on the 10 Day of July 1686 and was Buried the 14th day of the said Month: after he had been Clarke & Registrer of the Parish and Precinct of St Mary le Strand also Savoy; nine Years and five Months.

A memorandum written on a page in March 1714 notes that between March 1714 and January 1722 the burials were mistakenly recorded in the St Mary-le-Strand parish registers. From 1754 until 1756 the registers are more informative and each entry includes the date, name, age and cause of death as well as the presence of soldiers. However, each entry flows somewhat illegibly along a single line. From 1757 the format changes again and the registers now include a margin, making them easier to read. There are distinct columns on each page for month, day of the month, name and 'other', which tends to have been used to record the presence of an 'infant', 'child' or 'soldier'. The occasional entry includes details of parish or place of residence – for example, 'of St Andrews Holborn' or 'of Somersett House'. The next change in entries comes midway through 1789, when the 'other' column records individuals as 'W', 'Woman', 'M', 'Man' 'C', 'Child' or 'soldier'. By 1791 this column has been simplified to 'Soldier', 'Grown' or 'Child', and occasionally 'Pauper'.

Ages at death are not recorded again until 10 November 1793, but this detail then stays until the last entry in 1854. Cause of death information is reintroduced somewhat randomly on the same date, midway down a page of the register. The final change comes in 1813, when the data are

Years covered in registers	Age at death		Cause of death	Abode	Other (eg soldier/pauper)
	years/months	infant/child/grown			
1680–1754				occasional	occasional
1754–6	✓		✓		occasional
1757–92		✓		occasional	✓
1793–1813	✓		✓		
1813–54	✓			✓	

Table 4.1 Summary of information recorded in the burial registers

recorded in a table format, with column headings of 'Name', 'Abode', 'when Buried', 'Age' and 'by whom the ceremony was performed'. Unfortunately, despite the apparent improvement in the layout and organisation of the registers, these final stages are not always as easy to read as the previous 20 years.

It is worth noting that in the process of the research into the burial registers several discrepancies have been found between the details in the registers and other historical sources, such as the Proceedings of the Old Bailey and the data recorded from the memorial stones surveyed in the 1930s. Examples include the occasional misspelling of a name, different first names or slight differences in the age at death. Furthermore, archaeological evidence indicates that not all burials were in fact recorded, with no record entries for the burials of individuals with surviving nameplates (Chapter 6). It does not seem unreasonable that such errors should have occurred but for the purposes of the analysis outlined below, the registers have been taken at face value.

Because of the large number of entries within the registers it has not been possible to fully explore every possible avenue of analysis for this current project. The work has focused on those areas considered to be the most useful and informative in light of the excavation results. Consequently, the analysis has examined the basic demographics of the buried population (sex and age) as well as cause of death and, given the history of the site, the presence of soldiers. An Excel spreadsheet was used to record the data per year and each entry has been recorded as male, female, soldier, infant or child. The cause of death was also recorded for those years when this was available. Any other information deemed to be significant or unusual was also noted.

DATA ANALYSIS

The total number of entries recorded is 10,926. The data have been analysed for all years of the burial ground's use; owing to the volume of entries the data have been combined into decades (Fig 4.1)

According to the graph the burial ground was most active from 1720 through to 1810, at a time when the barracks and prison were both operational. Two significant peaks exist in 1740–9 and 1790–9, which are examined in more detail below. Given that the adult population living within the precinct during the burial ground's busiest century would have been dominated by males associated with the barracks and prison, it is no surprise that the ratio of males to females was significantly high, as demonstrated by Fig 4.2, which shows the sex distribution for the population from 1720 to 1820: approximately 71% of the adult individuals buried in the cemetery between these years were male. However, when the population is examined over the entire span of the burial ground's active life this disparity is still evident (Fig 4.3).

The presence of soldiers within the burial ground is noted from 1750 onwards. Although this might suggest that soldiers are routinely recorded after this date, this does not mean that every soldier was recorded as such. There are at least three entries that by their nature must refer to soldiers, but where that status has not been recorded: Samuel Jackson 'Shot for Desertion' in 1752 and John Rouse and Edward Hughes, both 'Wounded by the French' in 1793. From this date until 1820, when the barracks and prison buildings had been demolished and the last of the prisoners had left for the Savoy

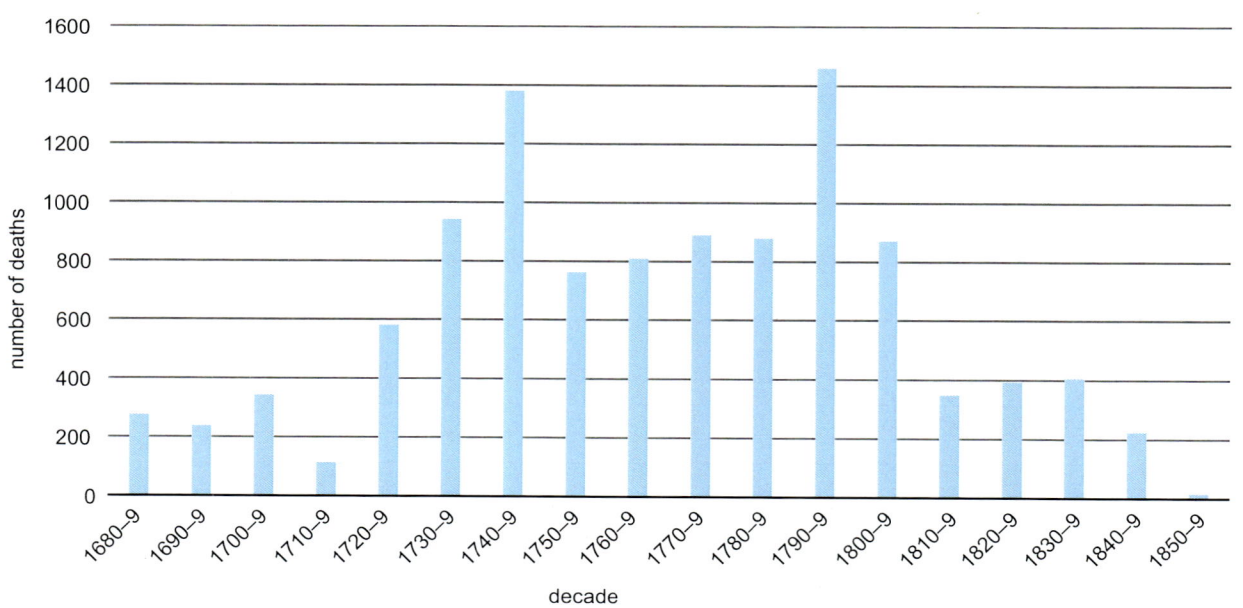

Fig 4.1 Total number of deaths per decade

CHAPTER 4 BURIAL REGISTERS

prison ship, the adult population can be separated into males, females and soldiers (Fig 4.4)

Given the military associations and the history of the site it is surprising that soldiers do not dominate more convincingly between 1750 and 1809 but this can probably be seen as confirmation of the fact that not every soldier was recorded as such. With no requirement to record it, it might have been seen as unnecessary when the majority of burials were in fact soldiers. Before the 1750s the only evidence for the known military associations of the burial ground are in the rare entries recorded as 'Captain' or 'Sergeant'. Perhaps the ordinary and more plentiful lower-ranking soldiers were not consistently considered worthy of mention.

Soldiers are most numerous in the next three decades but surprisingly few are recorded in the 1790s. It was 1793 that saw the burial of two individuals not recorded as soldiers but as 'Wounded by the French' at a time when the Foot Guards were involved in the French Revolutionary Wars. The reasons for the inconsistencies can only be guessed at but it is possible that during busy periods only basic information was considered necessary. What is apparent in the graph (Fig 4.4) is the closer correlation between the total numbers of males and females for the first and last few decades, particularly so after 1810 when the soldiers and prisoners had finally left the precinct.

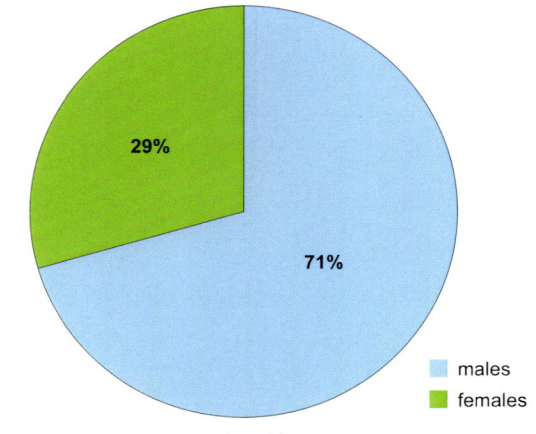

Fig 4.2 Sex distribution, 1720–1820

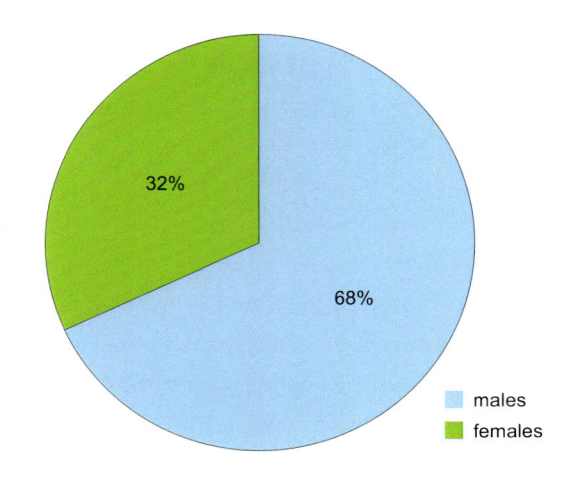

Fig 4.3 Sex distribution, 1680–1850

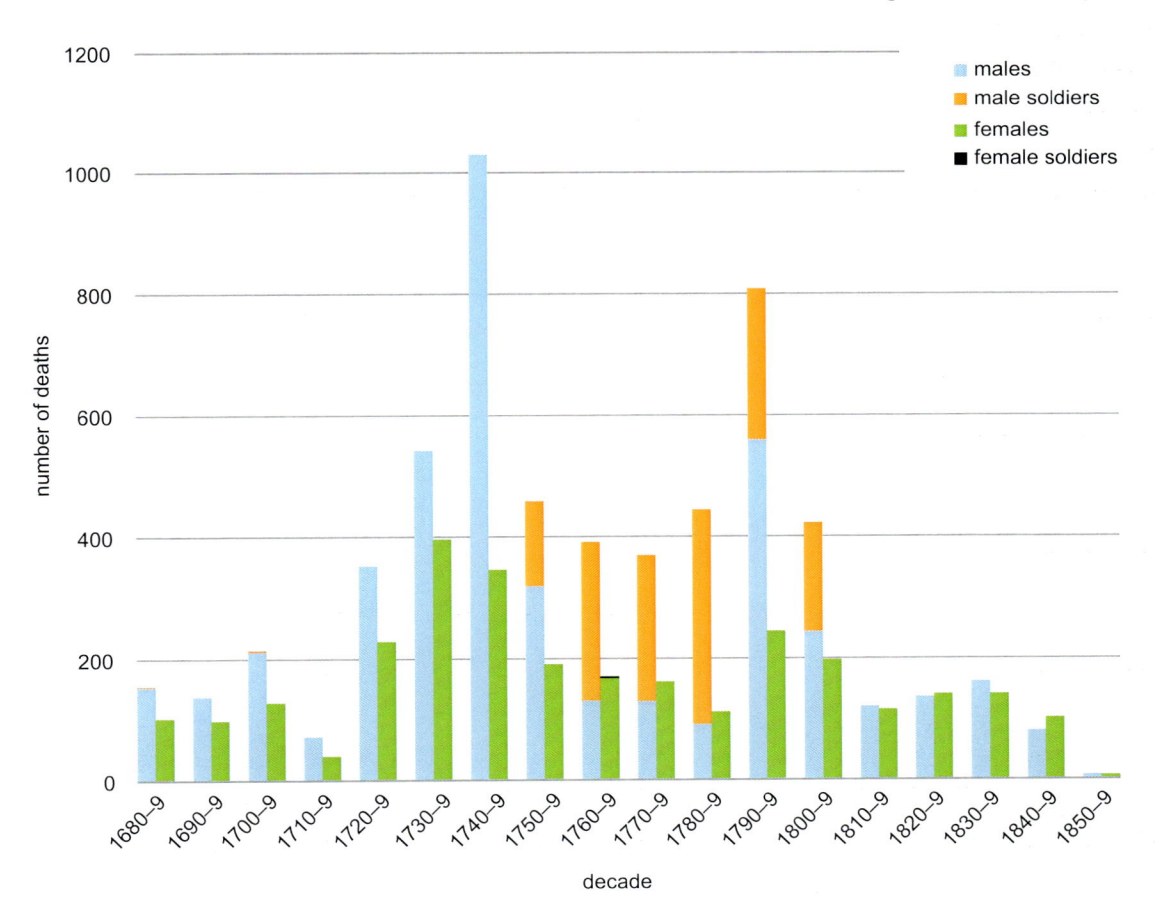

Fig 4.4 Total deaths per decade: males, females and soldiers

CENSUS DATA

Between 1801 and 1851 population census data are also available for the Savoy Precinct. The following data have been taken from the Great Britain Historical GIS Project (2017), using historical material which is copyright of the Great Britain Historical GIS Project and the University of Portsmouth.

The two data sets have been combined in Fig 4.5; census data alone, divided by sex, is shown in Fig 4.6.

From 1800 to 1829 the burials outnumber the living, significantly so between 1800 and 1809. There were still a large number of soldiers or prisoners in the precinct during this decade and it is probable that they formed the majority of the burials. Furthermore, it was not until 1841 that the 'modern' census came into effect and attempted to record every person in the land; before this date only households were recorded, so the Savoy prisoners, for example, would not be included. The years between 1810 and 1829 witnessed many changes, with the removal of the military and large-scale design and construction improvements to the area. These improvements were not complete until the 1820s, which might explain why the population does not seem to increase until the 1830s. With regard to the burial numbers, after an initial drop the numbers increase again from 1810 to 1839 but, as detailed and discussed below (4.3, 'Population studies'), from 1810 onwards (the period for which this information is available) burial numbers were being augmented by outsiders to the parish. The decline in burial numbers from 1840 onwards is not surprising given the overcrowded nature of the burial ground. As mentioned in Chapter 3 ('Savoy Chapel and burial ground'), in 1849 the burial fees for outsiders were increased to four times that of precinct residents. The last interment took place in 1854. While this explains the low levels of burials in the final decades, the census data would also suggest that the size of the living population was in a gradual decline at this time.

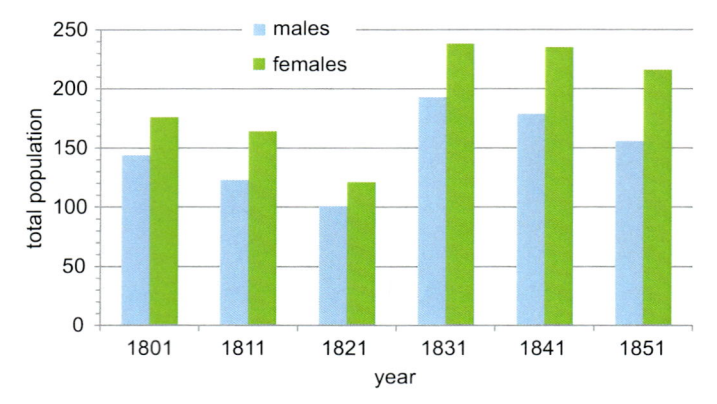

Fig 4.6 Census data: population of the Savoy Precinct, 1801–51

The census data highlight something else of interest – a much more evenly proportioned population with less discrepancy between the numbers of males and females, more typical of a residential community. Of further interest is the fact that the female population living in the precinct is consistently greater than the male population during the first half of the 19th century, probably for the first time in 200 years.

HIGHLIGHTED DECADES

Within the decades illustrated above, two peaks in the total numbers of burials are particularly noticeable: 1740–9 and 1790–9. These decades have been examined in greater detail in the charts below (Figs 4.7 and 4.8). Unfortunately, there are limited data available for the first of these decades, when just name and date were recorded. The second decade is much more informative, with age and cause of death recorded (these factors are discussed separately, in more detail below).

The male over female dominance in the buried population is evident in both graphs, as is a greater degree of fluctuation in the number of male burials recorded. Between 1740 and 1749 the most significant feature is a 'trough' between 1742 and 1744 when the total number of both female and male deaths drops, although more noticeably for males. However, rather than the apparent drop in the number of

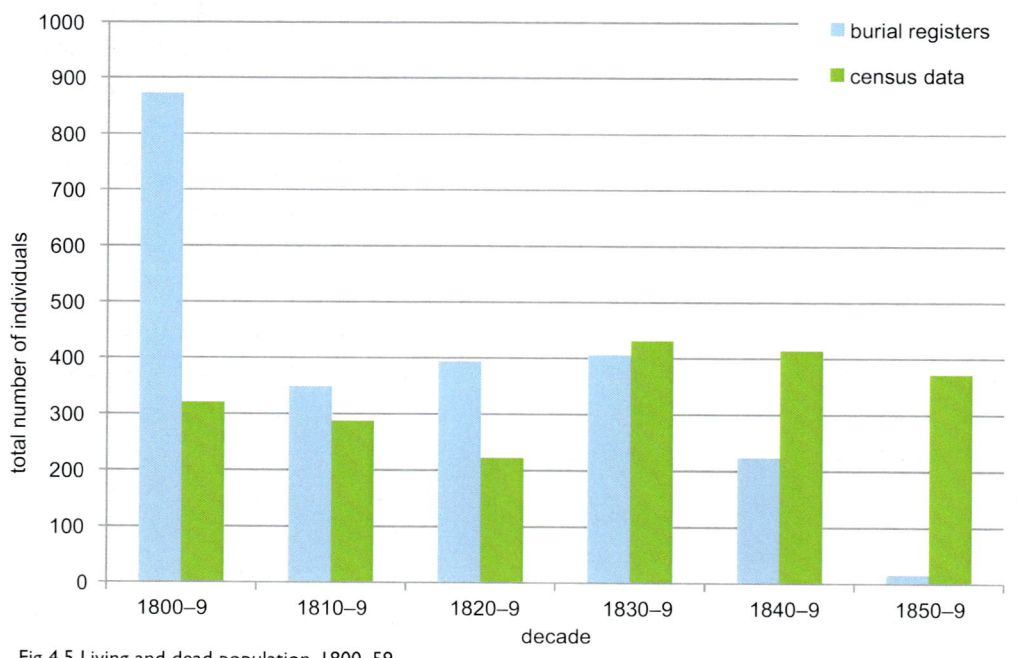

Fig 4.5 Living and dead population, 1800–59

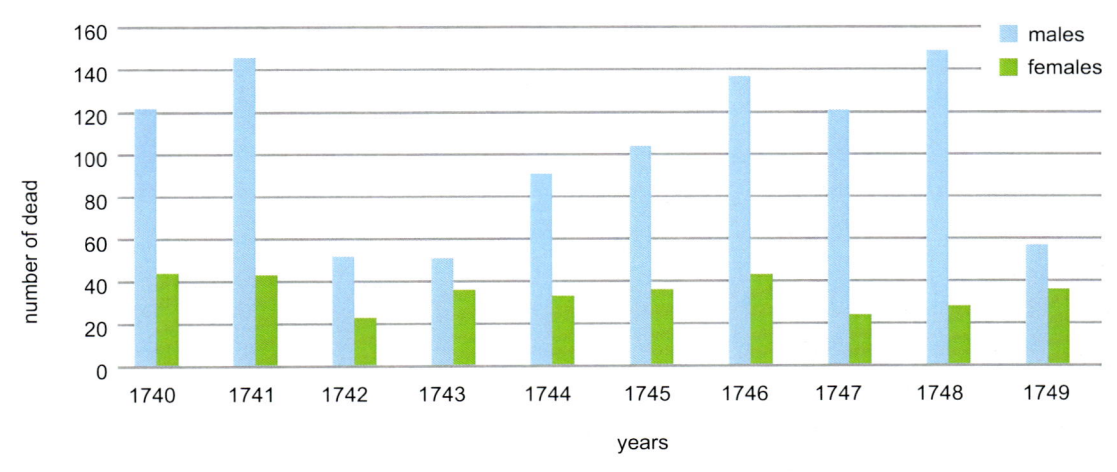

Fig 4.7 Male and female distribution in the buried population, 1740–9

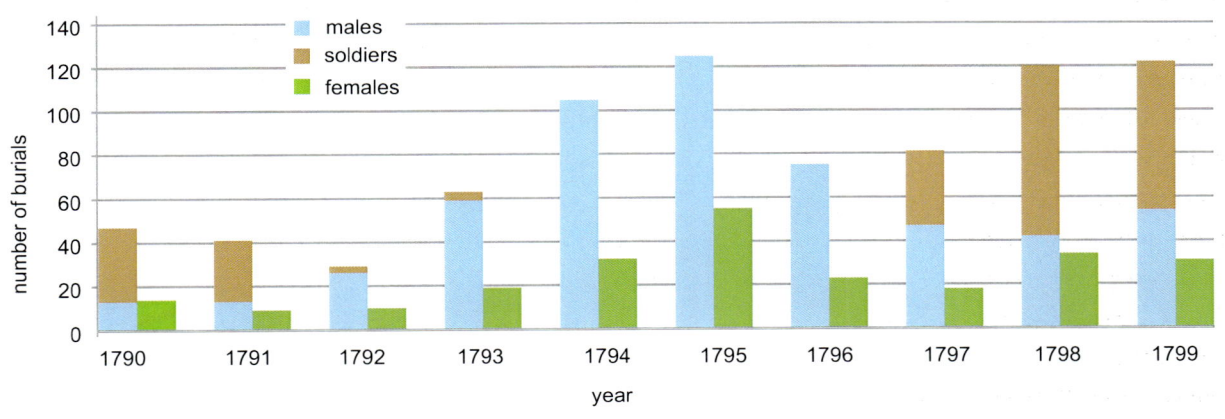

Fig 4.8 Male, female and soldier distribution in the buried population, 1790–9

deaths between 1742 and 1744, the figures for these years are actually very similar to 'the norm' and the anomaly is in fact the high numbers of deaths in 1740–1 at the start of the decade as well as the rising toll from 1743 onwards. Between 1790 and 1799, when soldiers are also recorded, both male and female burials increase between 1794 and 1796. The possible reasons for the low number of soldier burials recorded are discussed above but it can be assumed that they are included, at least partially, in the male population.

The notably harsh winter of 1739/40 caused 'much want and distress' in London (Creighton 1894, 78). Ice on the Thames prevented the delivery of coal, which increased the price, and snow made many streets impassable. This was followed by a very dry spring and summer. Mortality rates in London rose considerably during these years, which were plagued with fever epidemics. The mortality problems experienced were also blamed on the drunkenness of the population, also seen as an epidemic and one that had weakened the populace, who were found to be in bad physical and moral condition (Creighton 1894, 78–84). The death rate rose again from 1743 to the end of the decade. One possible cause of this rise is the problem of typhus or 'gaol' fever, something known to have badly affected the Savoy Prison. The letter from Stephen Hales (Chapter 3.2, 'Savoy Prison') that discusses the success of the ventilators put in place to tackle the problem is dated 1750. According to Hales, the positive effect that his ventilators had on the number of typhus-related deaths could be seen by 1749. This suggests that the situation had been worsening for the years leading up to this date and significantly improved from 1749 onwards. It therefore seems probable that the 1740–9 peak reflects the grim conditions facing the prisoners before the ventilators were installed.

The activities of the Foot Guards also have to be considered. During both decades all three Regiments of Foot Guards were involved in wars: the War of the Austrian Succession (1740–8) and the French Revolutionary Wars (1793–1802). This might have had a negative effect on the number of burials at the Savoy, with the population of the precinct reduced when the soldiers were away fighting. However, in times of war extra recruits would be enlisted, and at least at the beginning of the century, new recruits were often held in the Savoy Barracks. So the increase in numbers might instead reflect a general increase in the overall population. Greater numbers of recruits on standby would also increase overcrowding, which itself would increase the likelihood of poor conditions and health deterioration, both of which could lead to disease spreading rapidly through the population.

AGE AT DEATH

With the addition of age-at-death information from 1754 onwards it becomes possible to look at the adult population in more detail, as well as at the number of infant and child deaths in the registers. However, as described above, the way this information is recorded varies over time. Ages in years and months are recorded from 1754 to 1756 and then again from 1813 onwards. In the intervening years the entries are limited to 'infant', 'child' or 'grown'. In order to be able to use this information effectively over the widest time frame, data on those individuals under the age of 18 years have been combined into an all-encompassing subadult category. The numbers of subadults within the population can then be examined over the century from 1754 to 1854 (Fig 4.9).

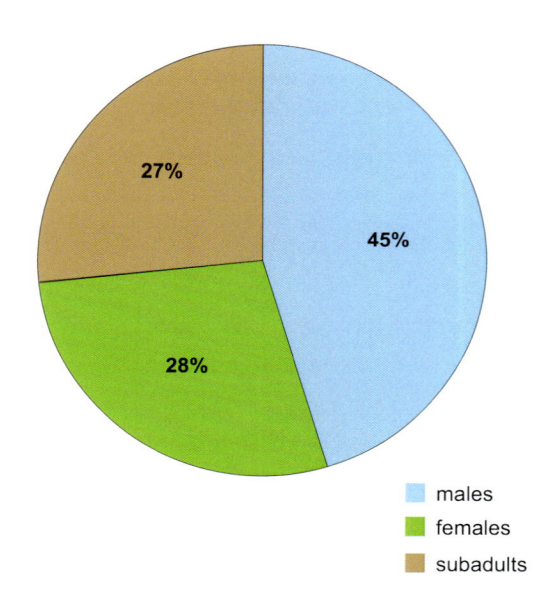

Fig 4.9 Proportion of males, females and subadults, 1754–1854

Although the dominance of males is still evident at 45% of the total, subadults are well represented, making up 27% of the buried population. The data from the London Bills of Mortality indicate that in the 18th century over 30% of the total recorded deaths were of infants under 2 years of age, approximately 10% were aged from 2 to 10 years and overall throughout the 18th and 19th centuries approximately 50% died before the age of 20 (Cherryson et al 2012, 14). The proportion of subadults at the Savoy therefore seems slightly below average, but this is not surprising given that this is not a typical 'civilian' community.

ADULT POPULATION

Age of death has also been examined across the entire adult population between 1790 and 1854 for young, prime and mature adults (Figs 4.10–4.12). The three adult age categories employed are based upon those used in the osteological analysis: young (18–30 years), prime (30–45 years) and mature (45+ years) (Chapter 5) in order that the two data sets may be compared.

These three graphs seem to be an accurate reflection of the population composition through the decades. Both the young and prime adult graphs demonstrate the dominance of males and/or soldiers until the 1810s, when the barracks and prison were finally demolished. Once the Savoy had become a residential area after this date, the male to female ratio appears more evenly balanced in all age categories and individuals of mature age dominate the burial registers.

For the periods in which age at death was recorded (1754–6 and 1793–1854), of the 1071 adults that fit in the osteologically mature category 299 were aged over 60. Between 1798 and 1850, ten were in their 90s and two were over 100: James Cri*tie, St Martin-in-the-Fields, 16 April 1795, aged 101; Thomas Britton, 2, Savoy Hill, 17 November 1839, aged 101.

SUBADULTS

The subadult population (<18 years) has been quantified (Fig 4.13). Looked at in isolation, the number of subadult burials over time seems to mirror that of the whole population (Fig 4.1). The highest numbers of subadult deaths occurred between 1760 and 1810 and in common with the overall burial distribution the highest single peak of subadult deaths occurred between 1790 and 1799.

In his comprehensive history of the Savoy, Somerville noted an apparent connection between the increase in soldiers and an increase in subadults, commenting on the number of births recorded in the Savoy registers as having taken place in the hospital, barracks and prison (1960, 95). In consideration of the information discussed in Chapter 3, perhaps the relatively large numbers of infant births and deaths recorded in the Savoy registers related not only to the soldiers' wives but also to the women 'hangers on' and even perhaps the 'idle' and 'loose' women known to have frequented the area (Gruber-von-Arni 2006, 56). The 1790–9 peak does also support the idea of an overall increase in the living population at this time.

CHAPTER 4 BURIAL REGISTERS

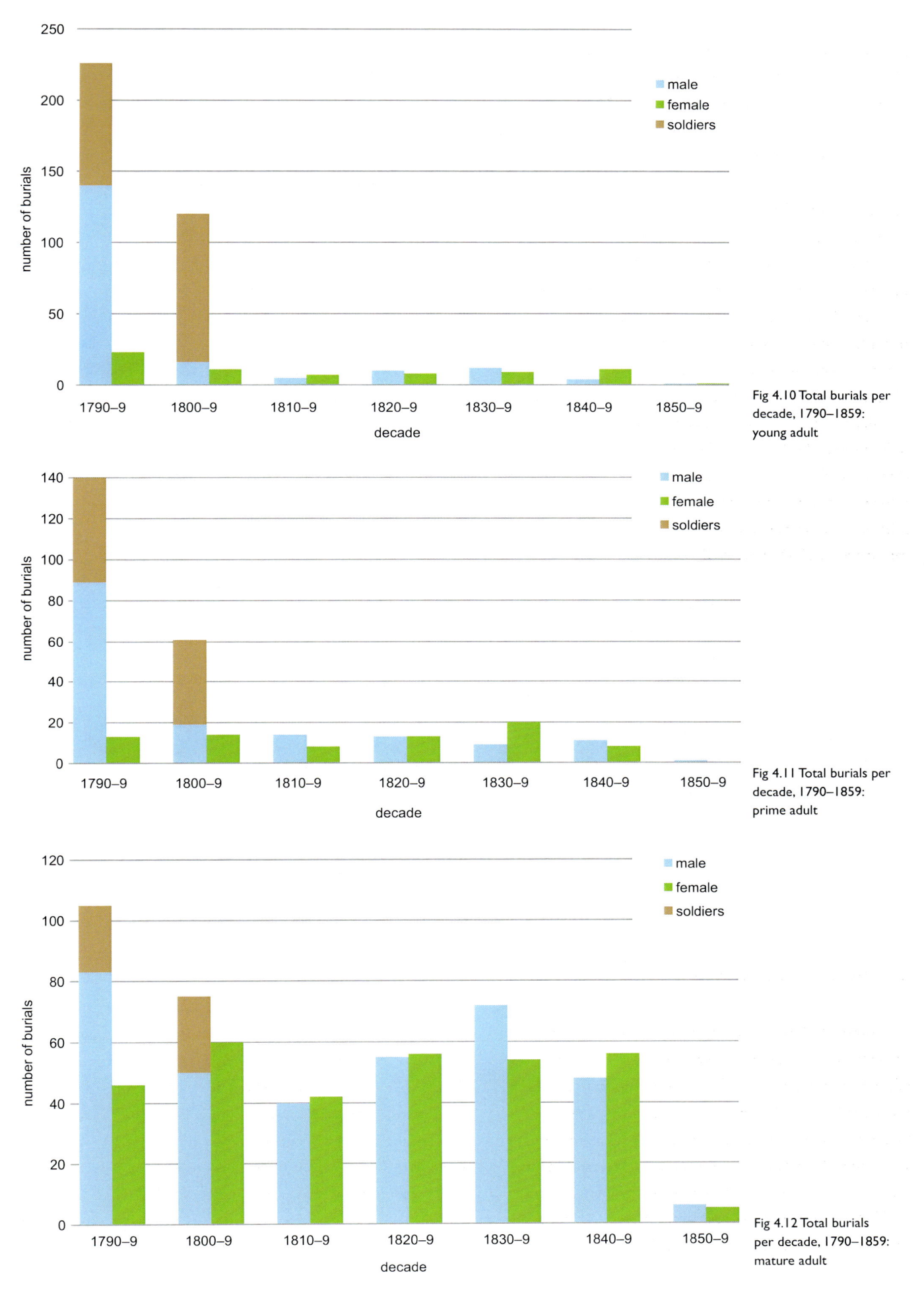

Fig 4.10 Total burials per decade, 1790–1859: young adult

Fig 4.11 Total burials per decade, 1790–1859: prime adult

Fig 4.12 Total burials per decade, 1790–1859: mature adult

55

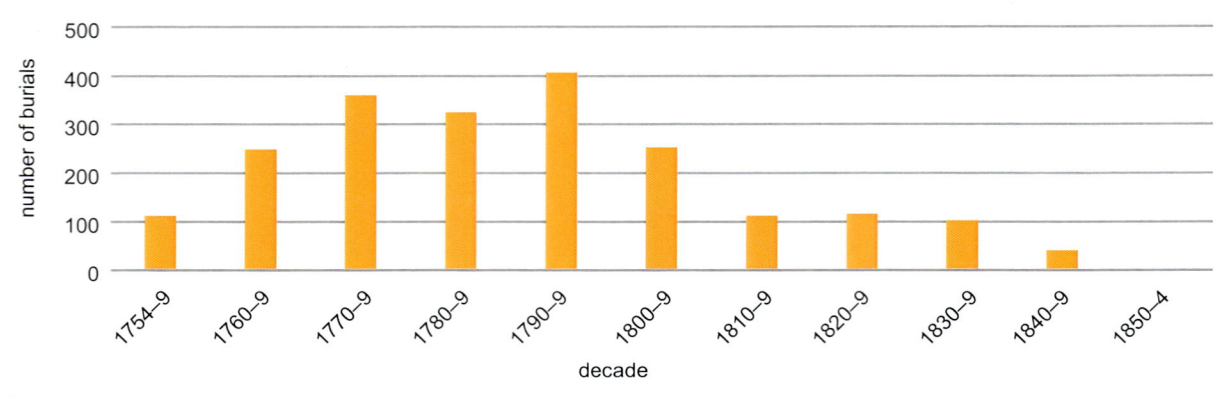

Fig 4.13 Total burials per decade, 1754–1854: subadults

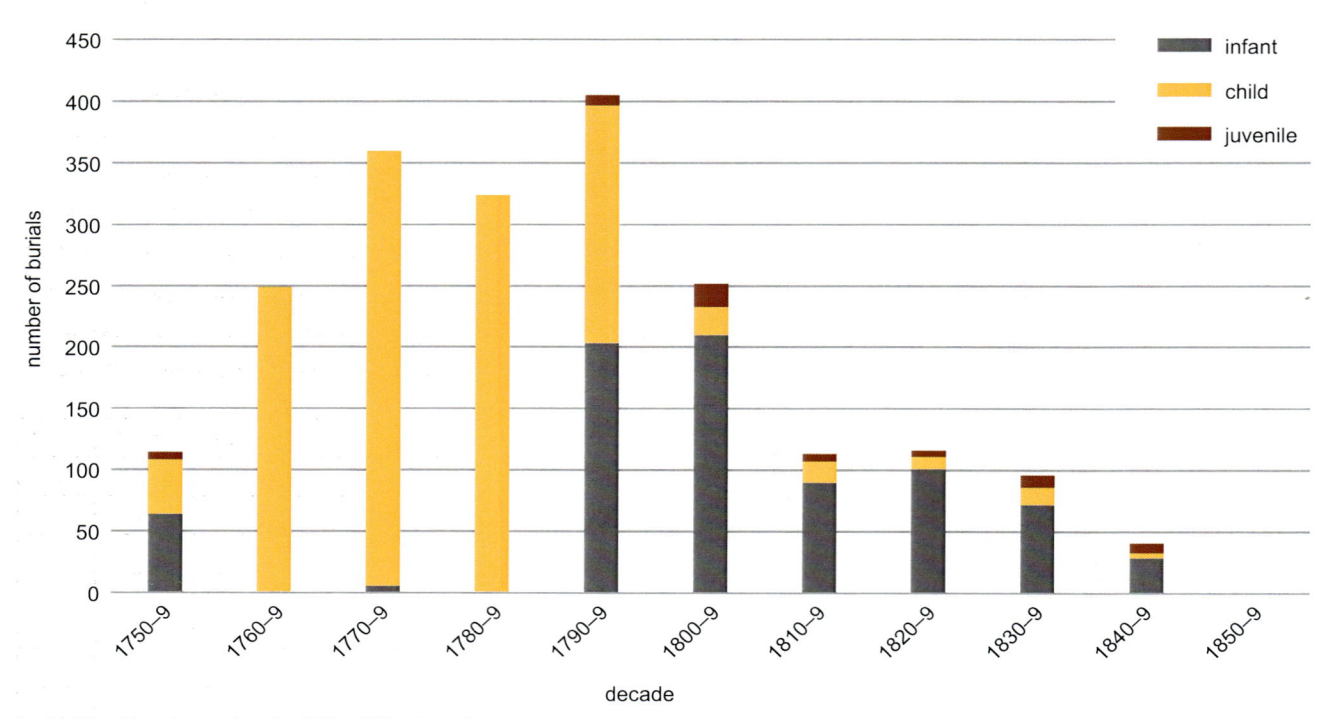

Fig 4.14 Total burials per decade, 1750–1859: infant, child, juvenile

It is unfortunate that the recording of subadult age categories was not consistent and at times when 'infant' or 'child' was recorded cannot necessarily be considered accurate. However, the division of subadult burials into categories was attempted with what data were available (Fig 4.14). As with the adult categories, these are based where possible upon osteological divisions: foetal and neonate (before birth to 11 months); infant (12 months to 6 years); child (7–12 years); and juvenile (13–17 years).

The most noticeable feature is the dominance of the 'child' category between 1760 and 1789. It is possible that 'child' was used as a generic term during this time (although some infants are also recorded) but it is interesting if taken at face value. It suggests that perhaps those diseases likely to affect the most vulnerable in the population (infants) were not as prevalent. In the 1750s infants do outnumber children. Perhaps the consequences of the typhus epidemic were still being felt by the youngest. Nevertheless, this increased number of infants does come after a decade of increased military presence in the precinct. The dramatic reappearance of infants occurs in 1790–9, the decade that saw an overall increase in the population, probably as a result of the boosted military population (see above). After this date, the subadult population does appear to be dominated by infants. Juvenile burials are less numerous in all decades; it would have been the healthiest infants that made it to childhood and on into juvenile years. It should, however, be noted that in 1797, the time of the French Revolutionary Wars, the Foot Regiments were recruiting 13- to 18-year-olds (Holmes 2011, 272). It is therefore possible that the juvenile population might reflect these young recruits. Indeed, of the 27 juveniles buried between 1790 and 1809, only two were female.

CHAPTER 4 BURIAL REGISTERS

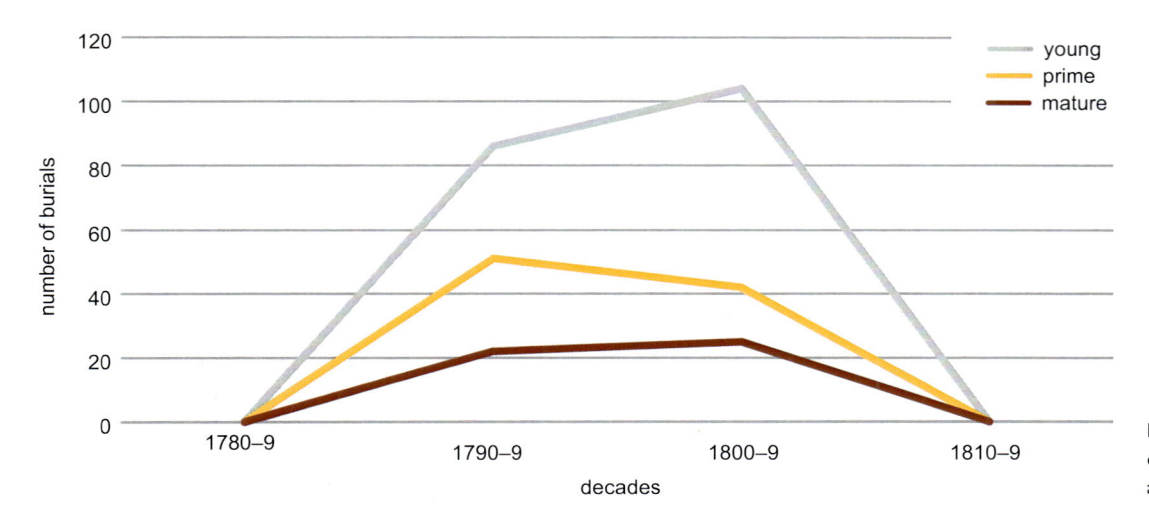

Fig 4.15 Total burials by decade, 1780–1819, and age category: soldiers

SOLDIER POPULATION

Given the military history of the site, the soldier population was considered worthy of further investigation. This has been done, dividing the population into the three age groups: young, prime, mature (Fig 4.15).

Between 1750 and 1769 there are only seven soldiers with age at death recorded – two young adults, two prime adults and three mature adults – but between 1780 and 1820 an interesting pattern emerges. A definite peak exists for all categories between 1790 and 1809, with the largest number of burials being young soldiers, followed by prime-aged soldiers and lastly those of mature age. This peak coincides with the Guards' involvement in the French Revolutionary Wars (1793–1802). As discussed above, this would mean extra recruits, young if possible (Holmes 2011, 272). The dominance of young soldiers in the buried population is therefore probably an accurate reflection of the composition of the living population. In the case of the battles themselves, the majority of soldiers' lives lost in the wars would not have impacted the Savoy burial ground as their deaths would have occurred on foreign land. Nevertheless, it is possible that the Savoy Precinct saw the return of battle-injured, who survived to reach home. The fact that the burial registers for 1793 record the cause of death for two soldiers as 'Wounded by the French' is testament to the fact that at least some of the war-wounded managed to return. All age categories decrease greatly again by 1819, at which time the Savoy Barracks and Prison were no longer in use.

CAUSE OF DEATH

Information about cause of death is routinely available for two periods, 1754–6 and 1793–1813. While this is valuable information the possible inaccuracies and inconsistencies in diagnosis and recording at this time are worth noting in order to allow for changes in disease classifications as medical knowledge and understanding improved as well as for miscommunications between the certifier of death and the record-keeper (Berridge et al 2011, 31). All recorded causes between these dates have been tabulated in alphabetical order for each time period, with the total number of each (Table 4.2). Definitions for a selection of the more obscure medical terms included in the registers are provided in Table 4.3. These have been found and combined from a number of sources (Copland

Cause of death	1754–6	1790–9	1800–9	1810–19	Total
Accident		1	2		3
Age	4	15	10	4	33
Ague	1				1
Apoplexy/Apoplex fits	1	2	1		4
Asthma	3	17	9		29
Bilious complex		1			1
Fracture (broken back, limbs)		2	1		3
Burnt		1	3	1	5
Cancer		1	1		2
Child bed/birth	1	3	2	1	7
Cold			2		2
Concussion break			1		1
Consumption	45	103	99	16	263
Convulsions	20	73	76	12	181
Cough			1		1
Croup		2			2
Decay				2	2
Decline		96		5	101
Decline of health			1		1
Dropsy	4	9		1	14
Drowned	2	3	1	1	7
Excessive drinking	1				1
Executed	1	3			4

Table 4.2 Causes of death as recorded in the burial registers

57

Cause of death	1754–6	1790–9	1800–9	1810–19	Total
Fall				3	3
Fever	29	145	22	2	198
Fits	3	4	3	1	11
Flux		1			1
Gout		1	2		3
Gravel		1	1		2
Whooping cough	3	20	9	3	35
Hung			1		1
Hung/lunacy	1				1
Inflammation + inflammation in bowels	2	12	26	1	41
Jaundice	1	2	1		4
Killed			1		1
Lunacy	2	2	1		5
Measles	2	7	8	3	20
Melancholy	1				1
Mortification	2	3	2		7
Palsey	1	1		1	3
Parelitic				1	1
Plurisy		1	1		2
Ptisick (cough)	1				1
Rupture		1		1	2
Shot	2				2
Small pox	26	55	57	2	140
Spotted fever	3				3
Sudden	1	4			5
Teeth	3	12	10	1	26
Thrush	2	3	1		6
Tumour		1			1
Twisting of gut		1			1
Violent		5			5
Water head		1	3		4
White swelling	1				1
Wounded by the French		2			2
Yellow jaundice	2				2
Total	**145**	**611**	**360**	**59**	**1175**

Table 4.2 *continued*

Ague	malarial or intermittent fever; characterised by paroxysms consisting of chill, fever, and sweating, at regularly recurring times
Apoplexy	nervous disease, paralysis caused by stroke
Bilious complex	bilious fever – fever caused by liver disorder
Consumption	any wasting away of the body, formerly applied especially to pulmonary tuberculosis
Convulsions	severe contortion of the body caused by violent, involuntary muscular contractions of the extremities, trunk and head
Decline	a gradual sinking and wasting away of the physical faculties; any wasting disease, esp. pulmonary consumption; as, to die of a decline (Porter 1913)
Dropsy	a swelling caused by accumulation of abnormally large amounts of fluid; caused by kidney disease or congestive heart failure
Flux	an excessive flow or discharge of fluid like haemorrhage or diarrhoea
Gravel	kidney stones: a disease characterised by multiple small calculi (stones or concretions of mineral salts) which are formed in the kidneys, passed along the ureters to the bladder, and expelled with the urine; synonym = kidney stone
Mortification	death or decay of one part of a living body; gangrene or necrosis
Palsy	palsy is a loss or diminution of sense or motion, or of both, in one or more parts of the body; paralysis or uncontrolled movement of controlled muscles; loss of muscle control
Pleurisy	inflammation of the pleura (membrane enveloping the lungs), usually occurring as a complication of a disease such as pneumonia, accompanied by accumulation of fluid in the pleural cavity, chills, fever, and painful breathing and coughing
Rupture	a hernia, especially of the groin or intestines
Spotted fever	a febrile disease typically characterised by a skin eruption, such as typhus gravior, epidemic cerebral meningitis, and the infections caused by tick-borne rickettsiae
Water head	Hydrocephalus? an accumulation of fluid within the ventricles or subarachnoid spaces of the brain; in the congenital form, the head is noticed to be unusually large at birth, or very soon develops after coming into the world (Thomas 1907)
White swelling	tuberculosis of bones and joints, producing strumous arthritis, or white swelling, and cold abscess

Table 4.3 Definition of selected medical terms

Cause of death	1755–98
Ague	1
Apoplexy	1
Consumption	10
Convulsions	1
Dropsey	2
Drowned	2
Executed	4
Fever	1
Suicide (hanging)	1
Small pox	3
Total	**26**

Table 4.4 Causes of death recorded for soldiers

1858; Thornber 2013; Willetts 2003–17; Rudy's List nd). As has been noted elsewhere, cause-of-death information was occasionally recorded at other times on a random, individual basis, throughout the registers. Some of these (for example, military executions) have been discussed in Chapter 3.

The information was going to be divided into males, females and soldiers but it became apparent that cause of death had been recorded for only 26 soldiers. It seems unlikely, given the overcrowded nature of the barracks and prison, that the soldiers were immune from the diseases encountered, and more likely that the information simply was not recorded and occupation was given instead. Whatever the reason, the separation of soldiers in the overall study seemed fruitless so they have been included in the male category totals. The causes of death recorded for the 26 soldiers are, however, tabulated separately below (Table 4.4).

Burning is listed as the cause of death for five individuals: one woman and four children, aged from newborn to 16 years. While it is assumed that these were accidents, burning was a form of execution for both women and men up until the late 18th century, although later restricted to women and relatively rare by this date (Webb 2011, 64; Cherryson et al 2012, 128). However, given the fact that the majority of victims were children, and that all other executions are recorded as such in the burial registers, it seems more likely that these were accidental deaths and could even have resulted from the numerous fires known to have befallen the barracks.

In the case of drowning, victims washed up in an advanced state of decomposition could be rapidly buried outside burial grounds if necessary and foreigners might be buried on the shoreline. The presence of seven victims of drowning in the Savoy population therefore suggests that they were probably locals (Cherryson et al 2012, 115).

As mentioned above, cause of death was recorded for certain individuals outside these time intervals, presumably when the death was considered significant. An additional four individuals are recorded as drowned, at times when cause of death was not routinely recorded: a man in 1731 and three boys in 1749. Of all these deaths, the identity of only one, the man in 1731, was unknown. The three boys who drowned in 1749 died in a single accident and were all buried on 11 September. Two of them appear to have been brothers, Joseph and William Judkins; the third was named as James Tomlinson. Also considered significant were two mothers and their sons, buried in November 1742, 'killed by the face of a knife'. A further five boys or men are simply recorded as 'killed' and buried in April 1763. Lastly, 24-year-old Timothy Reaby was 'killed' in 1806.

For the two men who 'hung', this was in fact suicide, blamed on lunacy in the case of John in 1756. The other man was a soldier, William Gregory, who hung himself in 1800, at the age of 30 years. Suicide was considered an unforgivable sin, and up until the end of the 17th century those who committed suicide were often not buried in consecrated ground. Attitudes began to change in the 18th century and if an underlying explanation for the suicide could be found, such as insanity or youthful age, the blame could be shifted away from the victim and the normal penalties would not apply (Maris et al 2000, 481). Suicide victims were then more frequently buried in consecrated ground, often on the north, less favourable side of the church (Cherryson et al 2012, 120). Given the position of the Savoy Chapel, the only available burial space was on the eastern side so if the suicides were to be included they would have to be in the main body of the burial ground. Even after the relaxation of the regulations suicide burials were often still distinguished from other burials, and throughout the lifespan of the Savoy burial ground any such interments should have been carried out between the hours of 9pm and midnight (Cherryson et al 2012, 121).

In addition to the executions of soldiers discussed in Chapter 3, one further individual suffered the same fate: Thomas Clifton, buried on 3 June 1798. In April that year Thomas Clifton, with one other, was indicted for 'breaking and entering the dwelling-house of John Nicholson, about the hour of five in the night of the 10th of February, and stealing a gold watch, value 10l. a watch gilt, with an enamelled case, value 4l. three other watches with gold cases, value 18l. a watch in a silver case gilt with gold, value 4l. another watch with a silver case, value 4l. six gold ear-rings set with pearls, value 6l. 27 leather ring-cases, value 12s. 24 cornelian stone seals set in gold, value 20l. Three crystal seals set in gold, value 2l. 66 gold rings, value 18l. a pair of gold sleeve buttons, value 1l ...', and the list continues (OB, t17980418–105).

For the population as a whole, the most common causes of death were consumption (263 deaths), fever (198), convulsions (181) and smallpox (140). These have been examined in more detail below, looking at sex and age distribution. Prevalence rates were calculated to aid interpretation of the results. These calculations were made per decade by dividing the total number of individuals dying in each category (age or sex) from each disease by the total number of deaths for the same category; for example, the total number of males dying from fever between 1754 and 1756, divided by the total number of males dying between 1754 and 1756. This figure is then turned into a percentage.

CONSUMPTION

The worst decade for consumption was 1790–9, when it was responsible for 103 deaths. Although a greater number of males died of consumption than females, statistically a greater percentage of the female population died from it than males in all but the final decade: approximately 24% of female deaths were attributable to consumption between 1754 and 1756 and between 1800 and 1809, as opposed to a maximum of 20% for males between 1754 and 1756 (Table 4.5). In percentage terms,

Years	Male	Male %	Female	Female %	Total	Total %
1754–6	29/141	20.56	16/63	25.39	45/204	22.05
1790–9	67/808	8.29	36/245	14.69	103/1053	9.78
1800–9	51/422	12.08	48/198	24.44	99/620	15.96
1810–19	9/121	7.43	7/116	6.03	16/237	6.75
Total	156/1492	10.45	107/622	17.20	263/2114	12.44

Table 4.5 Prevalence of consumption by sex, 1754–1819

Years	Subadult	Subadult %	Young	Young %	Prime	Prime %	Mature	Mature %
1754–6	7/53	13.21	18/51	35.29	5/12	41.66	17/39	43.58
1790–9	28/405	6.91	17/249	6.83	23/153	15.03	40/151	26.49
1800–9	25/352	7.10	13/131	9.92	12/75	16.00	55/135	40.74
1810–19	3/113	2.65	0/12	0.00	4/22	18.18	13/82	15.85
Total	63/923	6.83	48/443	10.84	44/262	16.79	125/407	30.71

Table 4.6 Prevalence of consumption by age, 1754–1819

from 1790 to 1809 consumption affected almost twice as many women as men. With regard to age, the data suggest that the chances of dying from consumption increased with maturity: between 2.7% and 13.0% of subadults were affected as opposed to between 15.9% and 43.6% of mature adults (Table 4.6).

It is likely that the spread of consumption was mainly a result of the overcrowding in the precinct, for the disease, spread through respiration, would be hard to isolate. Indeed, the risk was higher in poorly ventilated environments and among people in prolonged proximity to those infected (Bates 1992, 8). Both prison and barracks could be classified as such environments. Given this background, the male population might be more greatly affected than the females. However, once infected, females were more likely to suffer to a greater degree, perhaps explaining the discrepancy in the numbers of deaths (Bynum 2012, xviii).

FEVER

Fever seems to have been most prevalent during the 1790s, causing 145 deaths in the decade, the majority of which (126) were of males. The prevalence rates confirm this male dominance, with 15.6% of male deaths attributable to fever during this decade as opposed to only 7.8% of women. Although all ages seem to have suffered, the prevalence rates suggest that young and prime adults were most affected, with fever accounting for 25% of deaths for both age categories in this decade (Tables 4.7 and 4.8). After 1800 females were more susceptible than males and prime and mature adults suffered more than the young. These figures support the idea that the spread of fever was directly linked to the presence of closely confined younger men (soldiers) until this date. The number of deaths caused by fever dropped significantly following their departure from the precinct.

Closely confined areas and poor ventilation would have been conducive to the spread of conditions such as fever. Changes to the window tax, which had been introduced in the 17th century, were brought in by George II in the middle of the 18th century. More windows were boarded up as the laws became more stringent, adding to ventilation problems (Creighton 1894, 89). Looking at the Savoy data and combining all the information, it seems extremely likely that the young and prime adults affected were males. The history of the site would suggest that these were soldiers who suffered as fever spread through the overcrowded barracks and prison. A fever epidemic is known to have swept through London in 1799 (ibid, 88).

Years	Male	Male %	Female	Female %	Total	Total %
1754–6	26/141	18.44	3/63	4.76	29/204	14.22
1790–9	126/808	15.59	19/245	7.75	145/1053	13.77
1800–9	10/422	2.36	12/198	6.06	22/620	3.55
1810–19	1/121	0.83	1/116	0.86	2/237	0.84
Total	163/1492	10.92	35/622	5.62	198/2114	9.36

Table 4.7 Prevalence of fever by sex, 1754–1819

Years	Subadult	Subadult %	Young	Young %	Prime	Prime %	Mature	Mature %
1754–6	6/53	11.32	13/51	25.49	3/12	25.00	6/39	15.38
1790–9	16/405	3.95	67/249	26.91	35/153	22.87	25/151	16.55
1800–9	9/352	2.55	3/131	2.29	3/75	4.00	7/135	5.18
1810–19	0/113	0.00	0/12	0.00	1/22	4.55	1/82	1.21
Total	31/923	3.35	83/443	18.73	42/262	16.03	39/407	9.58

Table 4.8 Prevalence of fever by age, 1754–1819

CONVULSIONS

Convulsions are the recorded cause of death for 181 individuals, being most prevalent between 1790 and 1809, with similar numbers of both males and females affected. However, as with consumption, the prevalence rates indicate that females were far more greatly affected than males: between 6.0% and 15.2% of female deaths were attributed to convulsions as opposed to between 4.1% and 10.9% of male deaths (Table 4.9). The age-related figures show a distinct pattern, with subadults most affected (Table 4.10). Between 1754 and 1756, 28.3% of subadult deaths were caused by convulsions. For the other age categories, however, taken as an average across the decades less than 1% of young and prime adult deaths were caused by convulsions and only 2.7% of mature deaths.

Years	Male	Male %	Female	Female %	Total	Total %
1754–6	12/141	8.5	8/63	12.69	20/204	9.8
1790–9	40/808	4.95	33/245	13.46	73/1053	6.9
1800–9	46/422	10.9	30/198	15.15	76/620	12.25
1810–19	5/121	4.13	7/116	6.03	12/237	5.06
Total	103/1492	6.90	78/622	12.54	181/2114	8.56

Table 4.9 Prevalence of convulsions by sex, 1754–1819

Years	Male	Male %	Female	Female %	Total	Total %
1754–6	20/141	14.18	6/63	9.52	26/204	12.75
1790–9	38/808	4.70	17/245	6.93	55/1053	5.22
1800–9	35/422	8.29	22/198	11.11	57/620	9.19
1810–19	0/121	0.00	2/116	1.72	2/237	0.84
Total	93/1492	2.21	47/622	7.55	140/2114	6.62

Table 4.11 Prevalence of smallpox by sex, 1754–1819

Years	Subadult	Subadult %	Young	Young %	Prime	Prime %	Mature	Mature %
1754–6	15/53	28.30	0/51	0.00	0/12	0.00	2/39	5.13
1790–9	60/405	14.81	2/249	0.80	1/153	0.65	4/151	2.65
1800–9	55/352	15.62	0/131	0.00	1/75	1.33	5/135	3.70
1810–19	10/113	8.84	0/12	0.00	0/22	0.00	0/82	0.00
Total	140/923	15.16	2/443	0.45	2/262	0.76	11/407	2.70

Table 4.10 Prevalence of convulsions by age, 1754–1819

Years	Subadult	Subadult %	Young	Young %	Prime	Prime %	Mature	Mature %
1754–6	11/53	20.75	10/51	19.61	1/12	8.33	4/39	10.25
1790–9	31/405	7.65	19/249	7.63	2/153	1.31	0/151	0.00
1800–9	57/352	16.19	0/131	0.00	0/75	0.00	0/135	0.00
1810–19	2/923	0.22	0/12	0.00	0/22	0.00	0/82	0.00
Total	101/923	10.94	29/443	6.55	3/262	1.15	4/407	0.98

Table 4.12 Prevalence of smallpox by age, 1754–1819

Convulsions seem to have replaced 'infantile diarrhoea' in the London Bills of Mortality (Creighton 1894, 751) and for the first few decades of the 18th century it was used as a generic term for all deaths of those under 2 years of age (ibid, 699). This explains the prevalence of convulsions among the subadult population but at the same time implies that the numbers recorded as dying from the condition might be inflated. Convulsions are noted as a disease of the autumn, often aggravated by hot summers. It is also noted that the disease would be more widespread in highly populated cities such as London, with the associated problems of sanitation – effluvia rising from cellar cesspits and from overcrowded burial grounds. This would be combined with a general lack of fresh air in tightly packed housing and alleyways (ibid, 764).

SMALLPOX

Smallpox was responsible for 140 deaths between 1754 and 1819, with 1790–1809 being the most troubled years. Between 1754 and 1756, 14.2% of male deaths were caused by smallpox as opposed to 9.5% of females. From 1790 onwards the female population was more adversely affected, with between 1.7% and 11.1% of deaths caused by smallpox as opposed to between 0% and 8.3% of male deaths (Table 4.11). The data suggest that the subadult and young adult population was most adversely affected: between 1754 and 1756 approximately 20% of subadult and young adult deaths were due to smallpox, approximately twice that of prime and mature adult deaths (Table 4.12). All the figures are much lower for the remaining decades, apart from 1800–9, when 16.2% of subadult deaths were caused by the disease – and indeed they were the only part of the population affected.

In agreement with the results from the Savoy, statistics suggest that infants and the young were most adversely affected by smallpox and 'Most born in London have smallpox before they are seven' (Creighton 1894, 443, 533), although adults were far from immune. There were many years of smallpox epidemics in London, but during the 18th and early 19th centuries smallpox accounted for fewer deaths per capita in London than in other cities (ibid, 434–70, 529–56). Possible reasons for the relatively small numbers of smallpox deaths include the fact that many infant deaths may well have been recorded under the all-encompassing term 'convulsions'. Also, although a smallpox diagnosis would not be missed in the later stages, it is possible that many may have died from complications earlier on. In a similar vein, in London there was a greater chance of infants dying from other disease or ailments before smallpox had a chance to afflict them (ibid, 534). In London and at odds with many other cities there was a constant influx of immigrants to the capital including young, serving classes. These individuals, who may have come from areas where there were few or no cases of the disease, only to be struck down with it in the capital, could be included in the Savoy subadult category, which was not restricted to infants.

4.2 DEATH AND BURIAL

Through a combination of the excavation results, the burial registers and the surveys undertaken in the 1930s on behalf of the Duchy, it has been possible to look at the time delay between death and burial. Information from all available sources has been combined (Table 4.13). Only individuals for whom both dates have been confidently determined are included.

Name	Year	Date of death (according to gravestones)	Date of burial (according to burial registers)	Time between death and burial (days)	Age according to memorial stone (or to burial register)	Other information
Robert Damsell	1751	17 June 1751	18 June 1751	1	39	executed
Archibald Cameron de Lochiel	1753	7 June 1753	9 June 1753	2	46	executed
James Whem	1762	13 October 1762	15 October 1762	2	33	executed
James Collins	1762	13 October 1762	15 October 1762	2	20	executed
Mary Martha Wilton	1789	21 January 1789	23 January 1789	2	3	
Robert Menzies	1792	12 February 1792	17 February 1792	5	39	
Thomas Wilton	1792	6 June 1792	10 June 1792	4	2	
John Lewis	1795	11 November 1795	16 November 1795	5	21	executed
Thomas Davenport	1796	20 April 1796	22 April 1796	2	26 (30)	executed
Robert Menzies	1796	16 October 1796	21 October 1796	5	9	Sergeants Inn
Patrick Keogh	1797	2 August 1797	3 August 1797	1	25 (40)	executed
Henry Ives	1797	2 August 1797	3 August 1797	1	24 (35)	executed
Thomas Clifton	1798	30 May 1798	3 June 1798	4	25	executed
Henry Menzies	1799	19 June 1799	24 June 1799	5	10	
Sarah Pratt	1800	16 January 1800	23 January 1800	7	58	performer at Theatre Royal, Drury Lane, Haymarket and Covent Garden
Catherine Susannah Pesey	1800	30 March 1800	3 April 1800	1	54	
Archibald Menzies	1802	24 December 1802	29 December 1802	5	28	Walworth, Parish of St James
Elizabeth Edmonds	1810	1 August 1810	7 August 1810	6	70	
James Wilton	1813	8 July 1813	12 July 1813	4	16	Christ Church, Surrey
Charles Herring	1815	18 February 1815	23 February 1815	5	53	St Martins Street, Leicester Square
Thomas Prosser	1816	25 March 1816	28 March 1816	3	68	Little King Street, St James
Sarah Charlotte McFarlane	1817	4 March 1817	10 March 1817	6	3 (5)	Denmark Court - trand???
George Buckmaster	1817	13 June 1817	20 June 1817	7	8 (7)	Adelphi
Thomas Robert McFarlane	1818	19 January 1818	25 January 1818	6	2	St Paul, Covent Garden
William Craig McFarlane	1819	20 July 1819	23 July 1819	3	19 mths	St Paul, Covent Garden
William Ion	1819	14 November 1819	23 November 1819	9	8	St George's, Hanover Square
Thomas William Prosser	1821	20 May 1821	25 May 1821	5	10 mths	St George's, Hanover Square
Susannah Ion	1823	18 April 1823	2 May 1823	14	30	St George's, Hanover Square
William Childs Treadgold (Prosser)	1824	1 January 1824	7 January 1824	6	1	St George's, Hanover Square
Mary Edmonds	1824	27 April 1824	3 May 1824	6	53	Change Court, Exeter Change
John Bittleston	1826	1 August 1826	10 August 1826	9	32	St Martin-in-the-Fields,
Thomas Burgess	1829	19 May 1829	26 May 1829	6	63	Artist. Hammersmith Hamlet
William Willoughby Esq	1830	28 January 1830	5 February 1830	5	71	Sergeants Inn, Fleet Street
Elizabeth Burgess	1830	14 February 1830	19 February 1830	5	54	Wimbledon (Surrey)
Sarah Edmonds	1830	4 April 1830	9 April 1830	5	51	Covent Garden
John Mitchell MD	1830	17 June 1830	23 June 1830	6	50	Savoy Precinct
Emma Matilda Spillman	1830	29 October 1830	7 November 1830	9	1	St Clement Danes, Strand
Charles Gibert Esq	1831	30 May 1831	4 June 1831	5	62	author of Gilbert's Historical Survey of the County of Cornwall, St Clement Danes
Elizabeth Macfarlane	1831	6 September 1831	10 September 1831	4	59	Cecil Street, St Martin-in-the-Fields
Ann Elizabeth Finlay	1833	19 January 1833	28 January 1833	9	26	St Martin-in-the-Fields

Table 4.13 Time delay between death and burial, 1751–1854

CHAPTER 4 BURIAL REGISTERS

Name	Year	Date of death (according to gravestones)	Date of burial (according to burial registers)	Time between death and burial (days)	Age according to memorial stone (or to burial register)	Other information
Diana Buckmaster	1833	05 March 1833	16 March 1833	11	58	St Paul, Covent Garden
Anna Marion Lees	1833	17 April 1833	24 April 1833	9	30	surgeon, Camberwell
Eliza Cochran	1833	4 May 1833	12 May 1833	8	37	St Mary-le-Strand
Joseph Whitaker	1833	26 June 1833	4 July 1833	8	42	Thatched House, the Strand, St Martin in the Fields
Charles Byrne Esq	1833	8 August 1833	9 August 1833	1	25	Lancaster Place
Anna Marion Lees	1833	29 August 1833	5 September 1833	7	63	Camberwell
Elizabeth (Mary) Jaggers	1833	21 November 1833	1 December 1833	10	55	St Martin-in-the-Fields
Richard Lander	1834	29 January 1834	12 February 1834	14	13 mths	St Martin-in-the-Fields
William Finlay	1834	4 February 1834	12 February 1834	8	15 mths	St Martin-in-the-Fields
Sarah McFarlane	1834	27 November 1834	7 December 1834	10	45	St Paul, Covent Garden
Charlotte Matilda Jaggers	1835	28 January 1835	4 February 1835	7	17	St Martin-in-the-Fields
Ann Brown	1835	14 February 1835	22 February 1835	8	34	St Clement Danes
William Jaggers	1835	17 February 1835	24 February 1835	7	21	St Martin-in-the-Fields
Mary Hinton	1835	12 April 1835	17 April 1835	5	76	St Pancras
Justine Hinton	1835	8 October 1835	15 October 1835	7	34 (36)	Royal Academy
James Smith	1835	15 December 1835	22 December 1835	7	36 (37)	surgeon, Lancaster Place
Elenor Spirin	1835	27 December 1835	19 January 1836	23	74	St Clement Danes
Mary Appleyard	1836	13 May 1836	19 May 1836	6	49 (50)	St Martin-in-the-Fields
Henry Perlee Parker	1836	17 August 1836	20 August 1836	3	16	St John Wapping
William West Fenton	1836	17 August 1836	22 August 1836	7	24	St Clement Danes
Charles Biddley	1836	24 November 1836	1 December 1836	7	69	Wellington Street
John Jaggers	1837	9 January 1837	15 January 1837	6	60	victualler, asylum Camberwell
Eve Mitchell	1837	11 April 1837	27 April 1837	16	13 (15)	St George the Martyr
Francis Wadbrook	1838	14 February 1838	22 February 1838	8	54	Lambeth
James Lowe	1838	18 November 1838	24 November 1838	6	45	Duke Street, Adelphi or Northumberland Street, Strand
Ellen Spillman	1839	12 March 1839	24 March 1839	12	4	St Clement Danes
Thomas Britton	1839	12 November 1839	17 November 1839	5	101	2, Savoy Hill
William Hinton Esq	1839	30 December 1839	7 January 1840	8	53	Keeper of the Royal Academy, Trafalgar Sq
Susannah (Landifield)	1840	29 February 1840	08 March 1840	8	92	St Clement Danes
William Appleyard	1840	27 June 1840	5 July 1840	9	23 (35)	Duke Street, Adelphi
Alfred Albertus Joseph (Prosser)	1840	20 August 1840	3 September 1840	14	17	drowned in London Dock; St George's, Hanover Square
Rebecca Sommers	1841	1 March 1841	14 March 1841	13	86 (88)	Limehouse
Robert Willoughby Esq	1841	15 April 1841	22 April 1841	7	49 (50)	St Pancras
William Pettit Esq	1841	25 April 1841	30 April 1841	5	65	10, Lancaster Place, Savoy
Clare Fanny Spillman	1841	3 October 1841	16 October 1841	13	1	St Clement Danes
Susannah Elliott	1842	14 January 1842	20 January 1842	6	78 (71)	St George's Pimlico
Elizabeth Ellis	1843	1 June 1843	8 June 1843	7	34	St Martin-in-the-Fields
Elizabeth Wright	1843	10 July 1843	16 July 1843	6	42	Catherine Street
Julia Mary Willoughby	1843	26 October 1843	2 November 1843	7	17	4, Lancaster Place
Sarah Appleyard	1843	6 November 1843	16 November 1843	10	61	Duke Street, Adelphi

Table 4.13 continued

Name	Year	Date of death (according to gravestones)	Date of burial (according to burial registers)	Time between death and burial (days)	Age according to memorial stone (or to burial register)	Other information
Marme T (Harriette) Phillips	1844	12 August 1844	20 August 1844	8	29 (33)	St John the Baptist, Margate, Isle of Thanet
George Archibald Turner	1845	27 September 1845	2 October 1845	5	25	St Martin-in-the-Fields
Emily March	1845	18 December 1845	27 December 1845	9	31	St Giles, Camberwell
Sarah Isabella Crowley	1846	22 April 1846	26 April 1846	4	14	St Mary le Strand
Angelica Cochran	1846	15 May 1846	20 May 1846	5	20	St John's Wood, Regents Park, residence of mother-in-law
Francis Calcroft Turner	1846	12 June 1846	15 June 1846	3	63	artist; 11 Cranmer Place, Waterloo Road
Jane Eyre	1847	23 January 1847	31 January 1847	8	31 or 51	John Street, Adelphi
William Lees	1848	26 February 1848	4 March 1848	7	83	St Giles, Camberwell
Sarah Maries	1848	30 July 1848	6 August 1848	7	47	St Clement Danes
Thomas Spillman	1849	25 February 1849	4 March 1849	7	9 mths	St Clement Danes
Emma Bignell	1849	22 April 1849	29 April 1849	7	34	Great Windmill Street, St James, Westminster
Peter de Wint Esq	1849	30 June 1849	7 July 1849	7	65	St Pancras
John Cottingham Esq	1849	31 September 1849	4 August 1849	4	59	barrister at law, police magistrate for Southwark, Fellow of Trinity Hall, Cambridge, Recorder of Chester. Lancaster Place, Savoy
Laura Harriett Willoughby	1852	25 January 1852	31 January 1852	6	18	Blackheath
Ann Turner	1854	27 June 1854	1 July 1854	4	57	209 Piccadilly

Table 4.13 continued

Decade	Total no of days	Total no of deaths	Average time delay
1790–99	32	9	3.5
1800–9	13	3	4.3
1810–19	49	9	5.4
1820–9	46	6	7.7
1830–9	282	36	7.8
1840–9	173	24	7.2
1850–9	10	2	5.0
Total	584	89	6.6

Table 4.14 Average time delay between death and burial by decade, 1800–60

As most decades contain several entries the results have been further analysed to find averages for each (Table 4.14).

The figures indicate a gradual increase in the number of days between death and burial as the decades passed, with an average of 3.5 days between 1790 and 1799, increasing to 7.8 days between 1830 and 1839. The overall average is 6.6 days and of the 89 burials, 30 (approximately 34%) were buried close to this: either six or seven days. The last decade (1850–9) can perhaps be considered as a rogue result as only two deaths were recorded. While in the 18th century some recorded that it was customary for a body to be kept at the family home for two or three days after death so that friends and relatives could pay their respects (Litten 1991, 80), it seems that the time between death and burial was actually quite variable.

Data from the contemporary cemetery at Christ Church, Spitalfields show a time a delay of between one and 21 days (Molleson & Cox 1993, 186), while the maximum time between death and burial at the Quaker burial ground, Kingston-upon-Thames was 14 days in the second half of the 18th century, a marked increase from previous decades (Bashford & Sibun 2007, 42). Reasons for delaying the burial included beliefs concerning the lingering of the soul, as well as fear of being buried alive (Cherryson et al 2012, 39). The complexity of the funeral arrangement would also be a factor; children's funerals were usually less elaborate and therefore quicker to arrange (ibid, 38). With regard to the Savoy, there do not appear to be any obvious differences between child and adult burials. For 11 of the 24 children included in the table (46%), the time delay between death and burial was longer than the average seven days. This percentage increases to 50% if only the 16 youngest children are included (those aged 10 years or less). The longest time delay was 14 days for 13-month-old Richard Lander in 1834, but in this instance a possible reason for the delay has been identified. Richard was buried alongside his cousin, 15-month-old William Finlay, on 12 February 1834. As Richard died only six days before his cousin it seems probable that they were both suffering from the same illness, in which case Richard's burial could have been postponed if it was felt that William would share a similar fate. Of course, unbeknownst to all concerned, Richard's father, the explorer Richard Lemon Lander, died on the West African island of Fernando Po on 6 February of the same year, before his son and nephew had been buried (Chapter 6).

The most significant outlier is 74-year-old Elenor Spirin, whose burial in 1835 apparently took place 23 days after her death. If the inscriptions were uncertain when the memorial survey was carried out, this was made clear in the recorded text but this does not appear to be the case with Elenor, suggesting therefore that the 23-day time delay is accurate. A further 11 burials took place at least ten days after death. The possibility that the burial of executed individuals may have been different was also considered. The seven individuals identified were all buried within five days and five of them within one or two days. Only three non-executed individuals were buried with similar haste: 3-year-old Mary Martha Wilton in 1789; 54-year-old Catherine Susannah Pesey in 1800; and 25-year-old Charles Byrne Esq in 1833. It is tempting therefore to link the hasty burial of execution victims with a possible lack of customary funeral preparations.

One further consideration was the time of year in which the death occurred. It is possible that the increased number of deaths in winter months resulted in individuals having to wait longer for burial, or that the hard ground in winter months made longer time delays inevitable (Jane Sidell, pers comm). The Savoy data would suggest that time of year may have been an influencing factor, with nine of the 11 burials that took place after ten or more days occurring over the winter months between October and March, including that of Elenor Spirin.

4.3 POPULATION STUDIES

From 1813 onwards, as noted above, the abode of the deceased, recorded only sporadically until the 1800s, is routinely recorded in the burial registers. Unfortunately the information recorded is not entirely standardised: sometimes the parish is recorded, sometimes the street name or area. Despite being a small parish surrounded by much larger ones, the Savoy burial ground seems to have attracted a population from far and wide. A list of parishes in which the deceased were living is given in Table 4.15 and shown visually in Fig 4.16. For reasons of scale, this figure does not include the most outlying areas, which are recorded in tabular form only. In order for the table and map to be produced, only the information that was readily accessible was used. Any records for which the place of abode remained questionable were not included. Street names have been subsumed into parishes

Parish no	Area/Parish	No of deceased
	Blackheath	1
1	Camberwell	4
2	Chelsea	6
	Christ Church Surrey	1
3	Clerkenwell (St James)	3
	Croydon	1
	Ealing	1
	Fulham	1
	Hammersmith Hamlet	1
	Isle of Thanet	1
4	Islington	4
5	Kensington	9
6	Lambeth	16
7	Limehouse	1
8	Mary-le-bone	36
9	Newington	7
10	Paddington	3
11	Pimlico	6
12	Precinct of the Savoy	144
	Richmond Green	1
13	Shoreditch	1
14	St Andrew, Holborn	9
15	St Anne, Soho	11
16	St Brides	4
17	St Clement Danes	149
18	St George in the East	5
19	St George the Martyr	5
20	St George, Bloomsbury	10
21	St George's, Hanover Square	7
22	St Giles-in-the-Fields	44
	St Giles, Reading	1
23	St James	8
24	St Luke (Old Street)	2
25	St Martin-in-the-Fields	170
26	St Margaret, Westminster	6
27	St Mary-le-Strand	104
28	St Pancras	19
29	St Paul, Covent Garden	51
	Streatham	1
	Sydenham	1
30	Temple	5
31	Wapping	1
32	Whitechapel	1
	Wimbledon	1

Table 4.15 Parishes of the deceased as recorded in the burial registers, 1813–48

Fig 4.16 Map showing the number of deceased from each parish buried in the Savoy burial ground

wherever possible. As noted above (Chapter 3.3, 'Later repairs') the Savoy Chapel burial fees for non-residents were twice that of the precinct residents prior to 1849, a figure that doubled for the last five years of the burial ground's active life in an attempt to deter people from choosing the overcrowded ground.

The data indicate that people were attracted to the Savoy Chapel burial ground from a wide area, although the Savoy parishioners accounted for 144 burials. The majority of the deceased in the burial ground from outside the precinct appear to have resided in the large neighbouring parishes of St Martin-in-the-Fields (170 burials) and St Clement Danes (149). Smaller adjacent parishes, such as St Mary-le-Strand, also made a significant contribution to the burial ground (104). The remaining contributing parishes generally account for fewer than ten burials. It is likely that at least some of those from parishes further afield were returning to be buried in an existing family grave. Certainly, the presence of numerous repeated surnames was noted throughout the registers suggesting that familial ties were strong and that perhaps many stayed in the family home or parish.

CHAPTER 5 THE HUMAN REMAINS

Paola Ponce, with contributions by Lucy Sibun

> The Grief were Endless, that should all bewaile,
> Against whose sweet Repose thou dost prevail:
> Some freeze with Agues, some with Feavers burn,
> Whose Lives thou half out of their Holds dost turn;
> And of whose Sufferings it may be said,
> They living feel the very State o'th' Dead.
> Thou in a thousand sev'ral Forms are drest,
> And in them all dost Wretched man infest.
> —Anne Killigrew, The Miseries of Man (extract) (Morten 1967, 14)

5.1 INTRODUCTION

With all the available historical documentation that has been outlined and discussed in the previous chapters it has been possible to create a picture of the lives and deaths of the population that is buried in the Savoy Chapel. The excavations themselves recovered the remains of 609 of these individuals and it is their osteological analysis that forms the basis of the following chapter. The osteological analysis of a skeletal population can be used in isolation to establish a demographic profile as well as to provide insights into health, lifestyle and disease, but the addition of historical data adds an extra dimension to the study. This chapter discusses the results of the osteological analysis against the historical background of the Savoy. Unfortunately, some discussions are necessarily limited because of the lack of phasing available for the site (see Chapter 6). The locations of all the individual skeletons mentioned below can be found on Fig 5.1.

The results obtained from this osteological analysis were compared with those from 11 sites scattered across different parts of London: Sheen's burial ground, Bow Baptist Church and St Mary and St Michael's burial ground (Henderson et al 2013), the Royal Hospital Greenwich (Boston et al 2008), St Benet Sherehog (Miles et al 2008a), St Marylebone Church burial ground (Miles et al 2008b), All Saints, Chelsea Old Church (Cowie et al 2008), New Bunhill Fields burial ground (Miles 2012), City Bunhill burial ground (Connell & Miles 2010), the London Hospital (Fowler & Powers 2012) and St Pancras burial ground (Emery & Wooldridge 2011). These sites were chosen for comparison because of their broad contemporaneity with the Savoy Chapel and because they represent a variety of socioeconomic backgrounds that would facilitate comparisons of patterns for health and disease. Particular emphasis was given to the study of Boston et al (2008), which analysed the Royal Navy sailors and marines buried at the Royal Hospital Greenwich, because of the similarities in demography and lifestyle between this population and that of the Savoy Chapel.

DISARTICULATED MATERIAL

As well as the 609 articulated burials recovered, the excavations produced large quantities of disarticulated human remains from the grave soil [117]. The majority were separated for reburial on site but any disarticulated remains that displayed signs of pathology were retained for analysis. While this introduces an element of bias, all pathological specimens were considered an important addition to the data set from what was originally a hospital cemetery. All disarticulated fragments were recorded as fully as possible and the data produced were recorded separately for infants, juveniles and adults. The information on sex was recorded where appropriate and available. Acknowledging the element of bias that would be introduced, the disarticulated fragments were not included in the pathological prevalence calculations carried out on the rest of the skeletal population.

5.2 DEMOGRAPHY

Age and sex estimations form the basis of a demographic profile. Both estimates were carried out using standard osteological techniques, outlined below. Although the excavations covered only a small area of the entire burial ground, recovering only 5% of the individuals recorded in the registers, the excavated sample does seem to be representative when compared to the historically recorded buried population.

AGE ESTIMATION

Multifactorial age-at-death assessments were used as these provide the most accurate results (Lovejoy et al 1985). Methods included morphological changes observed in the pelvis such as the pubic symphysis (Brooks & Suchey 1990) and the auricular surface (Lovejoy et al 1985) as well as the development of the epiphyseal union of long bones (Scheuer & Black 2004), the eruption of teeth and dental development (Gustafson & Koch 1974; Ubelaker 1989) and the measurements of long-bone lengths (Maresh 1970; Scheuer et al 1980). The age categories employed are summarised in Table 5.1.

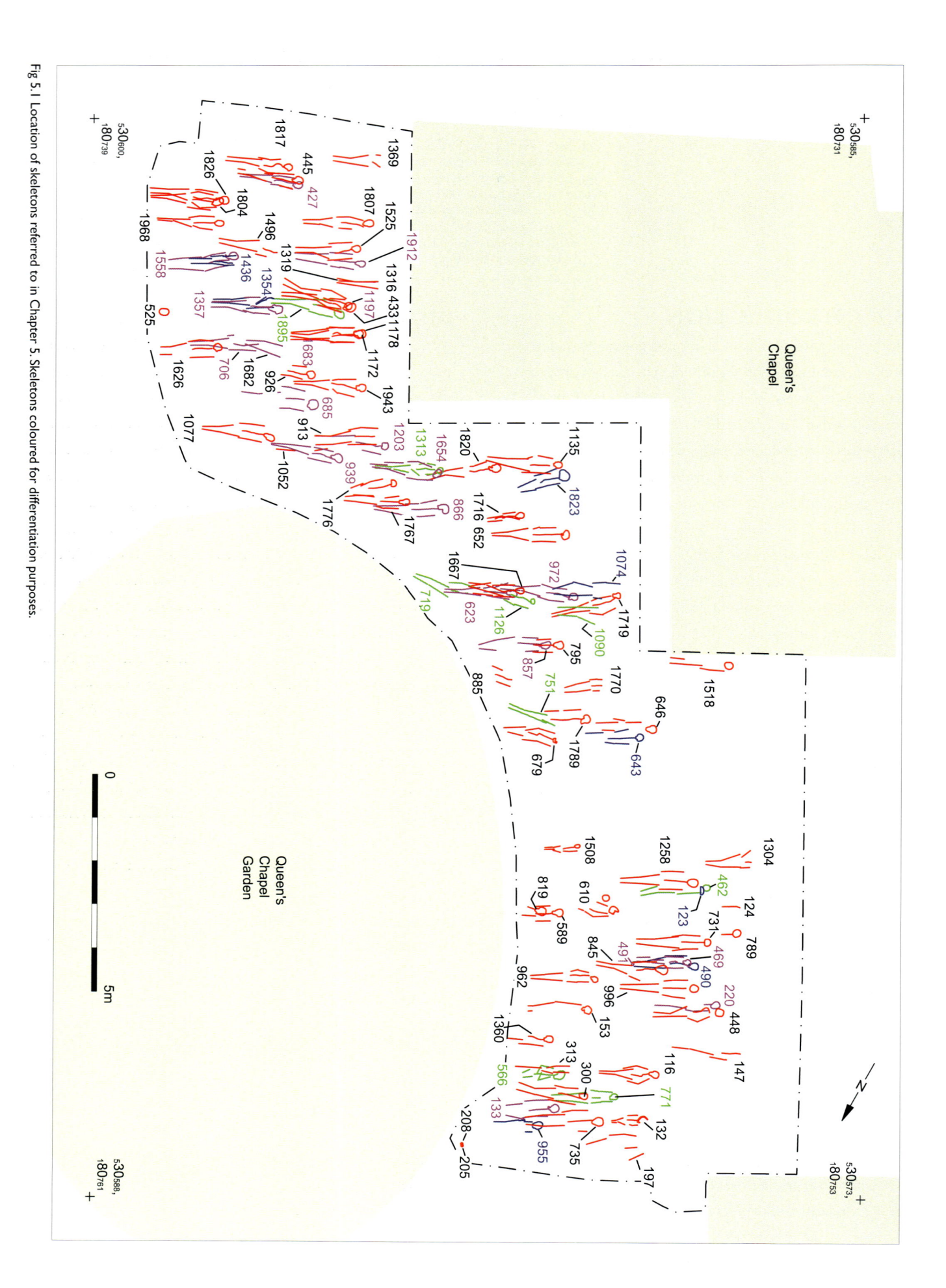

Fig 5.1 Location of skeletons referred to in Chapter 5. Skeletons coloured for differentiation purposes.

CHAPTER 5 THE HUMAN REMAINS

Age category	Age (months/years)	n	%
Foetus and neonate	before birth – 11 months	34	5.5
Infant 1	12 months – 6 years	28	4.5
Infant 2	7–12	13	2.1
Juvenile	13–17	15	2.4
Young adult	18–29	143	23.4
Prime adult	30–44	149	24.4
Mature adult	45+	71	11.6
Adult	18+	156	25.6
Total		609	

Table 5.1 Age categories and distribution of the population by age

The results show that 85.2% of the population (519 individuals) were categorised as adults (18+ years of age) compared with 14.8% (90 individuals) categorised as subadults (foetus to 17 years of age), showing a clear imbalance between the adult and subadult population in this population (Fig 5.2). This imbalance can also be seen in the burial registers, which, although limited to between 1754 and 1854, record 73% of the population as adult and only 27% as subadult. The slight discrepancy between the two sets of figures is discussed further in Chapter 6, but is likely to result either from the poor survival of subadult remains or from the fact that only a small proportion of the burial ground was excavated.

The largest percentage in the subadult category comprised foetuses and neonates (37.7%, 34/90), highlighting the significant period of mortality risk around the time of birth. According to Scheuer and Black (2000) the full-term gestational period is considered to be 40 weeks and although there was no direct evidence of intra-uterine deaths in the buried population, the remains of a 26-week-old foetus, [491], were found located between the ankles of adult female [490], aged 31–45 years (discussed further in Chapter 6). The results from the Savoy Chapel reflect the overall picture in London with the London Bills of Mortality recording over 30% of all deaths for the period up to 1800 as those below 2 years of age (Roberts & Cox 2003). The high percentage of deaths within this age group was probably a result of poor health status, exposure to infectious diseases and poor diets in both infants and their mothers.

Significantly fewer individuals fell into the subsequent subadult age categories, with only 14.4% reaching the age of 7–12 years (infant) and only 16.6% reaching 13–17 years (juvenile). Unfortunately, the inconsistencies in the level of detail recorded in the burial registers mean that a direct comparison of percentages within each subadult age category is not possible (Chapter 4).

When considering life expectancy for the adults, the results suggest that 80.4% of all adult deaths (292/363 individuals) occurred between young adult and prime adult age groups. Only 19.5% of the population (71/363) were categorised as mature adults, living beyond 45 years of age. Unfortunately, the largest group within the adult population were 156 individuals who could not be more closely aged as they were incomplete owing to the extent of truncation in the burial ground.

These results are consistent with the overall picture of post-medieval London populations as indicated in the Bills of Mortality (Roberts & Cox 2003), with individuals in their 30s and 40s representing the highest percentage of adult deaths in London between 1728 and 1850. Although the limited data recorded in the burial registers do not allow for a comparison before the 1790s the dominance of the young and prime adults until the 1810s is evident (Chapter 4). While this is consistent with the general situation in post-medieval London, these figures can also be seen as a reflection of this specialised population. According to the burial registers between 1810 and 1850, it was the mature adults who dominated the population. Once again, this can be explained by aspects specific to the Savoy, with the departure of the military and the return of a civilian population (Chapters 3 and 4).

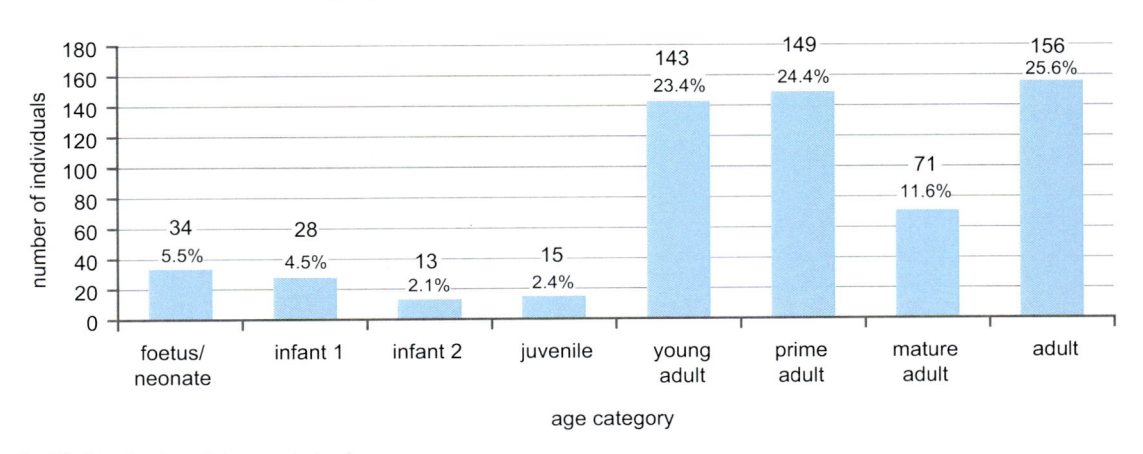

Fig 5.2 Distribution of the population by age

SEX ESTIMATION

The assessment of biological sex was based upon observation of dimorphic traits in the pelvis, sacrum and skull, combined whenever possible with osteometric data used to compare, enhance or clarify results. In the pelvis, the ventral arch, the sciatic notch, the sub-pubic angle, the ischio-pubic ramus, the pre-auricular sulcus, the obturator foramen, the acetabulum and the pelvic inlet were used according to Buikstra & Ubelaker (1994) and Bass (2005). In the sacrum, the sacral ala and the sacrum shape were used according to Bass (2005). In the skull, the supraorbital ridges, the glabellar profile, the mastoid process, the frontal slope, the posterior zigomatic, the nuchal crest, the mental eminence and the gonial flaring of the mandible were used according to Buikstra & Ubelaker (1994) and Bass (2005). The osteometric analysis was based on measurements taken on the humeral, radial and femoral heads, the bicondylar width, the maximum length of the clavicle and the width of the glenoid cavity of the scapula. These were estimated following Stewart (1979).

Adult skeletons were assigned to one of five categories: male (M); possible male (?M); female (F); possible female (?F); and unknown (?), when the degree of incompleteness, poor preservation or ambiguous results prohibited definitive assignments to either sex. To make the data sets statistically viable 'possible males' were grouped with males and 'possible females' with females. The skeletons of subadults (newborn, infant and juvenile individuals) were not assigned to any sex category.

The results show that the ratio of males to females in the population was strongly unbalanced (Table 5.2). Of those adults for whom sex could be estimated, 75.5% were male (325/430) and 24.4% female (105/430) giving an approximate male:female ratio of 3:1. This can, however, be explained by the burial ground's associations with the military hospital, barracks and prison and has been confirmed by a study of the burial registers, which record 68% of the adult population as male between 1680 and 1850 as opposed to 32% female.

Male deaths outnumbered those of the females in all age categories, with deaths among females remaining fairly constant throughout. A large proportion of males and females (16.1%, 84/519) fell in the 18+ adult age group that could not be assigned to a specific age category.

Age category (years)	M+M?	%	F+F?	%	?	%
Young adult (18–29)	106	32.6	27	25.7	10	11.2
Prime adult (30–44)	118	36.3	26	24.7	5	5.6
Mature adult (45+)	40	12.3	29	27.6	2	2.2
Adult (18+)	61	18.7	23	21.9	72	80.8
Total	325	100	105	100	89	100

Table 5.2 Composition of the adult population (note: M+M? are all males and probable males; F+F? are all females and probable females; ? are all adults 18+)

5.3 STATURE

Stature is a reflection of a combination of factors including environment (nutrition, exposure to hazardous materials, quality of air, water supply) and genetics (Roberts & Cox 2003). However, there are several methodological variables that must be considered when comparing the stature of skeletal populations, including the bone/s employed for stature calculation as well as the equation used, the age of individuals included in the sample and the period to which the skeletons belonged. These can all influence the results and, ultimately, the interpretations.

Stature calculations for the Savoy Chapel population were carried out on adult individuals for which sex estimates had been achieved. The left femur was used preferentially (n=200) but tibiae (n=54) and fibulae (n=1) were used instead if the femur was absent, broken or pathological. The humeri (n=74), radii (n=16) or ulnae (n=12) were used if the lower limbs were entirely absent. The maximum length of the bones was measured using an osteometric board following the standards proposed by Buikstra & Ubelaker (1994) and the maximum stature was calculated using the equations of Bennett (1993). Stature estimation was possible for a total of 84.0% (273/325) adult males and 80.0% adult females (84/105).

As shown in Table 5.3, males were taller than females. The average height for all men was 1.73m and that of the females was 1.60m, although the latter group showed more height variation.

Sex	n	Mean (m)	Range (m)	SD (m)
M+M?	273	1.73	1.52–1.91	0.059
F+F?	84	1.60	1.46–1.77	0.063

Table 5.3 Stature estimations

Table 5.4 shows the comparisons between the stature of the Savoy Chapel population and other post-medieval burial grounds from the London area; these are also shown visually in Fig 5.3. If using these data for comparisons with other areas of the country, it should be noted that the individuals buried in London cemeteries are derived from an open population (i.e. one that includes immigrants), which may skew the data.

The mean height among males across all the cemeteries ranged from 1.68m to 1.75m. The figures for the Savoy Chapel males are closer to those of the St Benet Sherehog, which represent the tallest males reported from the London area and are close to modern white British male adults at 1.76m (Freeman et al 1990). On the basis of the evidence from wills, St Benet Sherehog was one of the more affluent and wealthy parishes of the city, which would imply a relationship between socioeconomic status, welfare and stature (Miles et al 2008a). In the case of the Savoy Chapel, male stature might have been related to occupation rather than to

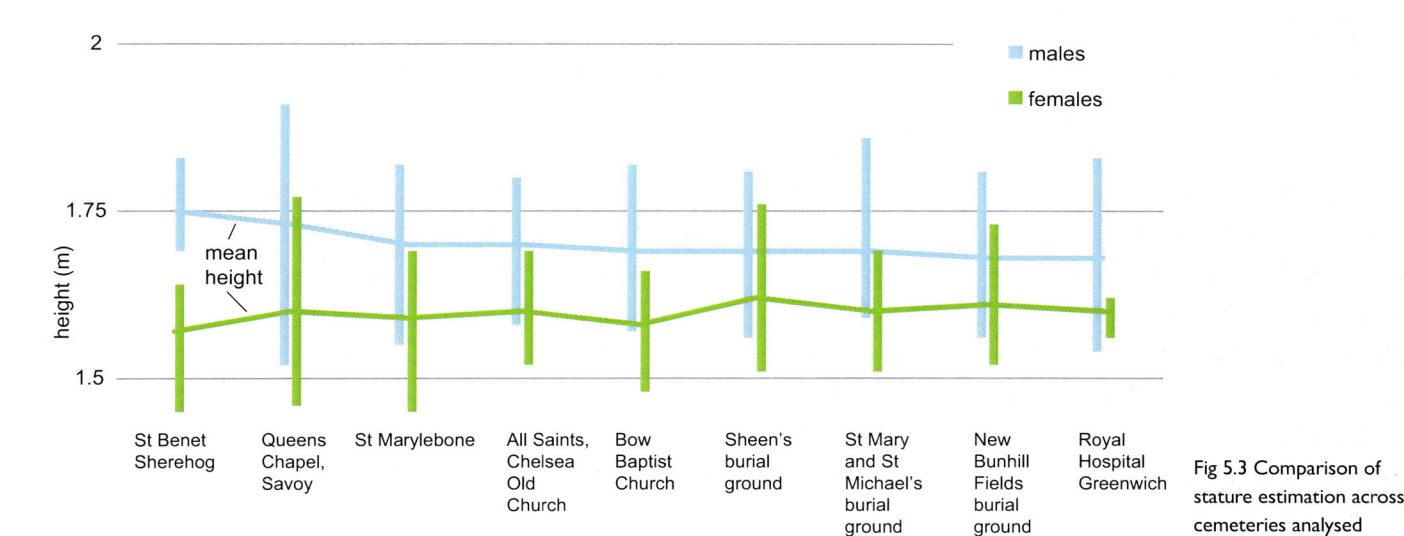

Fig 5.3 Comparison of stature estimation across cemeteries analysed

London-area cemeteries	Males Mean (m)	Males Range (m)	Females Mean (m)	Females Range (m)
St Benet Sherehog	1.75	1.69–1.83	1.57	1.45–1.64
Queen's Chapel Savoy	1.73	1.52–1.91	1.60	1.46–1.77
St Marylebone Church burial ground	1.70	1.55–1.82	1.59	1.45–1.69
All Saints, Chelsea Old Church	1.70	1.58–1.80	1.60	1.52–1.69
Bow Baptist Church	1.69	1.57–1.82	1.58	1.48–1.66
Sheen's burial ground	1.69	1.56–1.81	1.62	1.51–1.76
St Mary and St Michael's burial ground	1.69	1.59–1.86	1.60	1.51–1.69
New Bunhill Fields burial ground	1.68	1.56–1.81	1.61	1.52–1.73
Royal Hospital Greenwich	1.68	1.54–1.83	1.60	1.56–1.62

Table 5.4 Comparison of stature estimation (for references see above, 5.1)

wealth. Recruiting heights for the Foot Guards, although variable, were set at an ideal minimum height of 5ft 6in (1.67m) (Chapter 3). Within the excavated population, the average male height was 1.73m or slightly over 5ft 8in. Although not conclusive evidence, the fact that the males at the Savoy were taller than average supports the idea of a selective or specialised population. Contrary to what might be expected, the Royal Navy soldiers and marines buried at the Royal Hospital Greenwich were comparatively short, interpreted by Boston et al (2008) as reflecting the deprived working-class origins of these individuals.

Comparisons between females show that the mean height ranged from 1.57m to 1.62m. Unlike the Savoy males, the height of the Savoy Chapel females was within the normal range of variation when compared with other contemporaneous females from the London area and slightly shorter than the average modern white adult British female, at 1.63m (Freeman et al 1990).

5.4 PRELIMINARY ISOTOPIC ANALYSIS ON BONE COLLAGEN

Madeleine Bleasdale and Michelle Alexander

To explore dietary variation a select group of human remains from the Savoy Chapel underwent carbon (δ^{13}C) and nitrogen (δ^{15}N) stable isotope analysis. Stable isotope-based dietary reconstructions are well established within archaeology and provide direct insights into spatial, temporal and sociocultural variations in food consumption (eg Richards 2006; Alexander et al 2015; Hemer et al 2017). The analysis took place at BioArCh, University of York Archaeology Department and was carried out by Madeleine Bleasdale under the supervision of Michelle Alexander.

Carbon isotope analysis was used to investigate the contribution of C3 and C4 plants in the diet and to aid the differentiation between animal and marine protein consumption (Schwarcz & Schoeninger 2011). C3 and C4 plant groups are distinguished by their different photosynthetic pathways, which influence carbon uptake and lead to their distinctive carbon stable isotope values (Calvin & Benson 1948). The majority of the plants consumed in Britain in the post-medieval period were C3 plants such as oats, barley and wheat. C4 plants such as the tropical grasses sugarcane and maize were available but maize in particular was only consumed in large quantities in areas such as the Americas. The carbon results could therefore explore the potential inclusion of migrants or military personnel in the Savoy Chapel population. Nitrogen isotopes can be used to trace trophic levels due to step-wise fractionation of δ^{15}N enrichment as the food chain progresses (O'Connell et al 2012: 431). Therefore, nitrogen can be used to explore differences in protein consumption relating to geographic location, such as coastal environments, and socioeconomic status, with enriched nitrogen values usually indicating a high proportion of terrestrial or marine protein in the diet (Schwarcz & Schoeninger 2011; O'Connell et al 2012).

Preliminary observations from 48 individuals (male, female and of unknown sex) corresponded with the expectation for a largely C3-based diet during the post-medieval period in London, with a mean $\delta^{13}C$ value of -19.3±0.5‰ (1σ) and mean $\delta^{15}N$ value of 12.3‰ ±0.9 (1σ) (Fig 5.4). The variability in $\delta^{15}N$ values reflected the use of the cemetery for the burial of a large cross-section of the social classes with values falling between published isotope data from comparable British post-medieval urban sites representing the poor/working classes such as St Martin's, Birmingham and Lukin Street, London (Richards 2006; Beaumont 2013) and higher-class London sites such as Spitalfields and Coventry (Nitsch et al 2011; Trickett 2006).

In post-medieval Britain the wealthier classes would have had greater access to high-trophic-level protein from meat and fish than other groups, but historical documents have demonstrated that the British Army and Royal Navy were also provisioned with greater quantities of animal protein than the civilian population (MacDonald 2014). Therefore, the variation in nitrogen reflects the different diets of the individuals buried at the Savoy Chapel, among whom were wealthy parishioners, the London poor treated at the hospital and military individuals.

The nitrogen signatures of bone collagen in particular can also be influenced by physiological processes, so individuals with specific pathologies are discussed in the osteological summaries for each individual in Chapter 5.6.

5.5 PRELIMINARY ISOTOPIC ANALYSIS ON HAIR

Andrew Wilson and Patrick Daley

Biomolecular analysis of hair samples was applied to a set of human remains from the Savoy Chapel in order to assist with understanding of diet (including seasonal variation in diet), and potentially for information on drug use and exposure to chemical pollutants. At least seven individuals were found with hair adhering to the skull, but bulk measurements for $\delta^{13}C$ and $\delta^{15}N$ ratios of hair keratin were only possible to obtain from one individual, [1716].

Hair is a unique tissue that offers considerable potential in terms of diachronic information, given that hair grows incrementally on average roughly 10mm per month in Caucasoid-type hair (Wilson et al 2007). Hair is largely composed of the sulphur-rich protein keratin and is known to survive over archaeological timescales in favourable depositional environments – ie conditions that limit microbial growth (Wilson 2008). Although keratotics may survive under a variety of conditions they will commonly undergo some degree of alteration, which can be assessed by morphological and biochemical means. Where long lengths of hair are available from archaeological remains they have been used to interpret

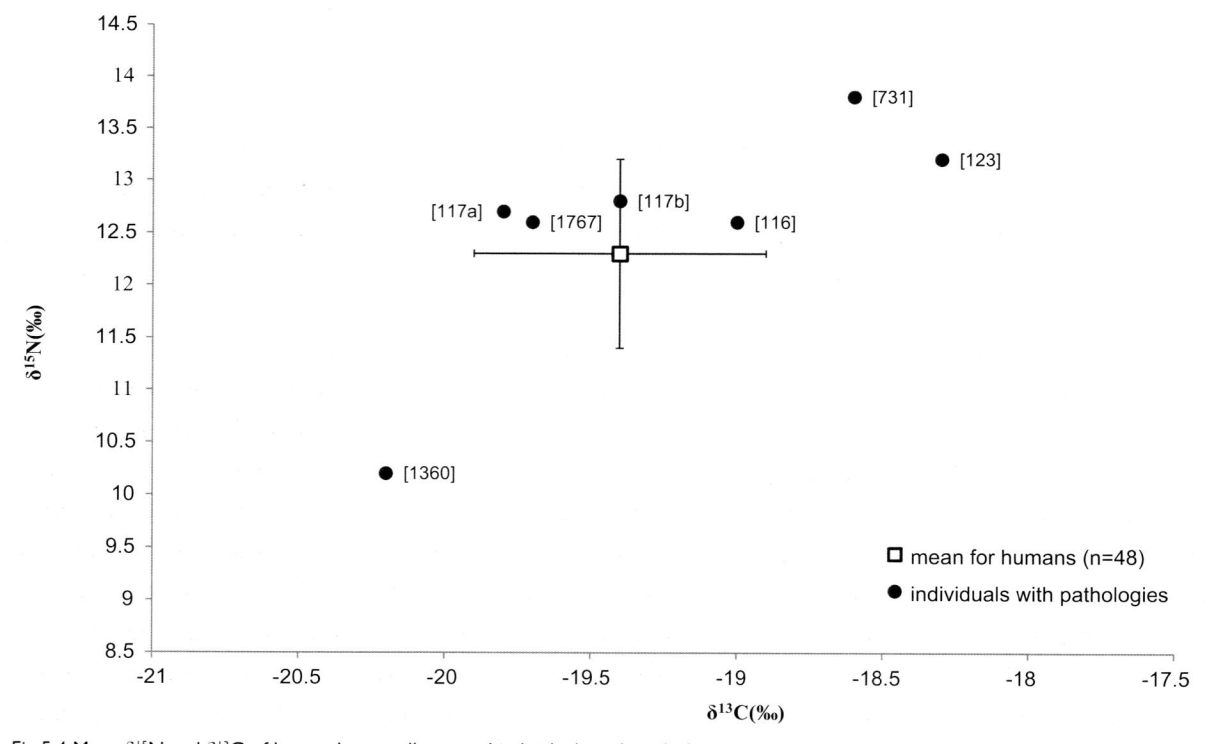

Fig 5.4 Mean $\delta^{15}N$ and $\delta^{13}C$ of human bone collagen and individuals with pathologies

changes in diet, health, and mobility prior to death (Wilson et al 2007; Thompson et al 2014; D'Ortenzio et al 2015). Similar approaches have been used to study metabolic activity in living individuals (Mekota et al 2006). However, hair is largely under-represented in the archaeological record. Within this context, isotopic analysis of human remains can produce information about nutrition and health. By combining multiple measurements of different isotopes and tissues, interpretations of dietary composition (Phillips 2001), weaning practices (Tsutaya & Yoneda 2013; Henderson et al 2014; Tsutaya & Yoneda 2015), nutritional stress (Hobson et al 1993) and disease (Reitsema 2013; Beaumont et al 2015) are possible.

Hair samples from the Savoy population were assessed for surface condition using scanning electron microscopy. Briefly, fibre samples were mounted on aluminium stubs using carbon adhesive tabs. Secondary electron imaging in low vacuum mode was undertaken at the University of Bradford Analytical Centre using an FEI Quanta 400 Environmental Scanning Electron Microscope. Three samples were imaged using scanning electron microscopy. Fig 5.5 shows the hair sample from skeleton [1716] with signs of embrittlement and clear evidence of fungal tunnelling as the likely cause.

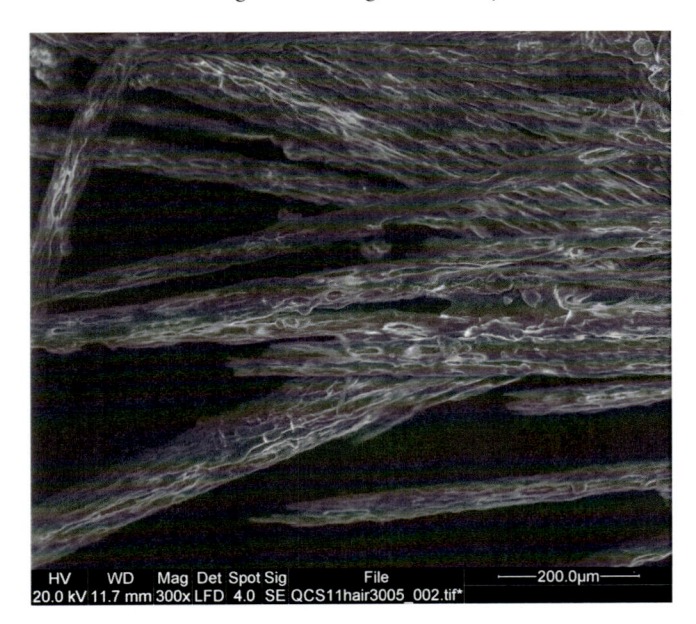

Fig 5.5 Hair sample from skeleton [1716]

The results obtained for skeleton [1716] show that the incremental data represent less than six months' worth of hair growth in the final stages of life. Furthermore, in both Figs 5.6 and 5.7 the changes are of a low order of magnitude and should therefore be interpreted with caution. Incremental carbon data (Fig 5.6) show a sigmoidal curve, the shape of which can often be linked to seasonal effects in foodstuffs. The increasing nitrogen isotope values (Fig 5.7) may be interpreted as increased protein consumption, but in the case of individual [1716] it could be the result of physiological stress; perhaps, as discussed below ('Metabolic disease'), this individual suffered from rickets. In support of the evidence for extended episodes of stress during childhood, this child also displayed dental enamel hypoplasia in the deciduous teeth.

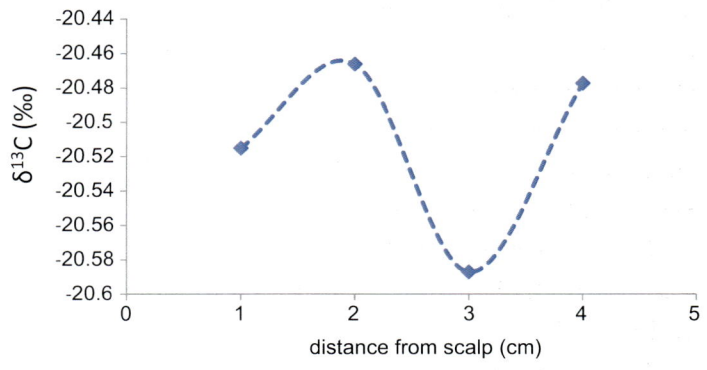

Fig 5.6 Incremental isotope analysis (δ^{13}C)

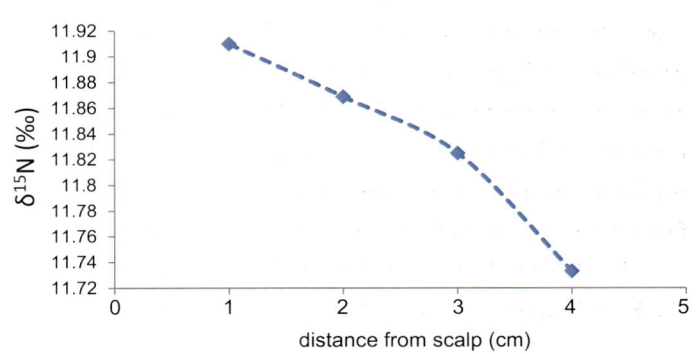

Fig 5.7 Incremental isotope analysis (δ^{15}N)

5.6 PALAEOPATHOLOGY

The following section discusses the diseases, abnormal conditions and pathologies observed in the Savoy Chapel population.

PATHOLOGY QUANTIFICATION

All significant gross pathology was assessed following the diagnostic criteria of Aufderheide and Rodríguez-Martín (1998) and Ortner (2003), with supplementary references as required. To facilitate comparisons with other sites, crude and true prevalence rates were calculated whenever possible for each pathological condition analysed. Following Waldron (2007), crude prevalence rates were calculated by determining the ratio of the total number of individuals affected with the condition (n) and the total number of individuals sampled (N), regardless of preservation of specific bone elements. In the totals tabulated below, individuals that were affected bilaterally by a particular condition were counted only once.

True prevalence rates were calculated by determining the ratio of n/N, 'n' being the numerator resulting from the total number of osseous elements affected with the condition and 'N' the denominator, resulting from the total number of osseous elements present for the particular age and sex category considered. The data were subjected to a series of Pearson Chi-square tests to determine whether or not there was any relationship or association between pathologies and sex. Thus, inter-group comparisons (males vs females) were carried out using true prevalence value rates only and the level of statistical significance was always set at p<0.05.

When discussing pathological conditions affecting the spine, abbreviations C1–C7 were used for the cervical vertebrae, T1–T12 for the thoracic vertebrae and L1–L5 for the lumbar vertebrae. For dentition, the abbreviations I1 and I2 were used to refer to the 1st and 2nd incisors, C for the canines, P1 and P2 for the 1st and 2nd premolars, and M1, M2 and M3 for the 1st, 2nd and 3rd molars.

Of the 609 individuals assessed, 77.9% (475/609) of skeletons showed evidence of being affected by some palaeopathological condition compared with 22.0% (134/609) that did not show any evidence of disease. The conditions found within the Savoy Chapel population were trauma, joint disease, congenital abnormalities, infectious diseases, dental disease, metabolic diseases, circulatory disease, neoplastic conditions and a small number of miscellaneous conditions. The evidence of post-mortem examination is also included at the end of this chapter but as these procedures are not considered pathologies per se, they were not counted in the overall prevalence of pathologies. The results obtained are presented and discussed in the order of prevalence as shown in Table 5.5 starting with trauma, which constituted the most prevalent condition among the population.

Pathology	n	%
Trauma	417	68.4
Joint disease	155	25.4
Congenital	155	25.4
Infection	154	25.2
Dental disease	146	23.9
Metabolic	118	19.3
Circulatory	65	10.6
Neoplastic	6	0.9
Miscellaneous	5	0.8

Table 5.5 Crude prevalence rates of all pathologies found within the total population

TRAUMA

Trauma, which can be defined as any extrinsic mechanism that causes injury to a living tissue of the body (Lovell 1997), was the most prevalent condition encountered among the Savoy Chapel population, affecting 68.4% (417/609) of individuals. This figure is likely to reflect the history of the cemetery and its buried population, which showed a marked preponderance of males over females, particularly soldiers, who were exposed to a risk of injury. However, this prevalence might have been artificially inflated by the inclusion of a number of conditions of ambiguous aetiology such as enthesopathies, recorded by many with joint disease, or os acromiale, and spondylolysis recorded by others with congenital anomalies. They were included here as the general consensus is that they are thought most likely to result from trauma. The traumatic conditions recorded included different types of fracture, trauma to the soft tissues, Schmorl's nodes, Scheuermann's disease, spondylolysis, os acromiale, ankyloses secondary to trauma, joint dislocation, two examples of gunshot wounds and two examples of penetrating trauma from within the disarticulated group.

FRACTURES

A fracture is a break in the integrity and continuity of a bone, whether this is complete or incomplete (ibid). The crude prevalence calculation showed that 15.5% (95/609) of all individuals from the Savoy Chapel suffered from some kind of fracture. Males presented a higher prevalence rate of fractures: 26.1% (85/325) compared with 3.8% (4/105) of females (χ^2=24.1397, df=1, p<0.05). Of adults of unknown sex 1.1% (1/89) were affected; of subadult individuals, 4.4% (4/90) presented at least one fracture. Owing to the nature of the population studied it is not surprising that the number of fractured bones was significantly higher among male individuals and within this context it could be assumed that the majority of these injuries were sustained during service, although accidental fractures cannot be ruled out. In total 176 fractured bones were recorded in 95 individuals. Details may be found in Table 5.6.

No of fractured bones	No of individuals (total = 95)
1	65
2	16
3	2
4	5
5	2
6	1
8	2
9	1
12	1

Table 5.6 Number of fractured bones according to the number of individuals

Healed fractures formed the majority of the examples, accounting for 14.1% (86/609). Unhealed fractures, whether the union failed to unite the broken pieces or fractures in the stage of healing where a callus of woven bone was forming around the site of injury, accounted for 0.9% (6/609) of the total. Finally, perimortem fractures were present in 0.6% (4/609) of the population.

Ribs were the most commonly fractured bone (7.0%, 43/609) but multiple fractures were recorded individually, which may have artificially inflated the figures. Next common were long-bone fractures (5.0%, 31/609), those of the hands and feet (5.5%, 34/609) and lastly those of the skull (0.4%, 3/609).

Skull factures

Skull fractures were the least prevalent of all fractures found in the Savoy Chapel population and all were limited to the facial area with no examples of neurocranial trauma found (Table 5.7). Evidence of trauma to the face was presented by 0.4% (3/609) of all individuals: two adult males [789], [1807] and one female [1968] exhibited examples of well-healed nasal fractures.

M+M? (n/N)	F+F? (n/N)	? (n/N)	Subadults (n/N)	Total (n/N)
0.6% (2/325)	0.9% (1/105)	- (0/89)	- (0/90)	0.4% (3/609)

Table 5.7 Crude prevalence rates of facial fractures (nasal + maxilla) within the total population

Male [789] displayed a depressed fracture on the left nasal bone. Similarly, adult female [1968] presented a well-healed fracture on the left nasal bone. The second male, [1807] (Fig 5.8), displayed fractures of the nasal bones along with the right maxilla, which showed a depressed fracture located just below the right orbit. The nasal fragments had been displaced and had reunited, deviating towards the left side. The fracture of the right maxilla was in the process of healing at the time of death. The reossification led to the production of a 5mm-long spicule of bone protruding medio-laterally from the zygomatic process of the maxilla. Although the association cannot be proved, several teeth appeared to have been lost ante-mortem, possibly as a result of the maxillary trauma. Thus, the upper right P2 and all the molars from that side were absent. However, tooth decay cannot be ruled out as a causative factor, particularly as this has resulted in the loss of P2 to M2 in the left maxilla.

The cause of these facial fractures was difficult to identify but they may have represented interpersonal violence, particularly those occurring on the nasal bones, or they may just have represented accidents such as falling, perhaps common in military action. Nasal fractures have been linked to activities such as boxing if seen in conjunction with other skeletal markers such as lesions on the lesser trochanter of the humerus and metacarpal fractures. The low prevalence of skull fractures may suggest that direct hand-to-hand combat was uncommon among the Savoy soldiers or that hand-to-hand combat did not always result in facial trauma but in rib and metacarpal fractures as described below. It was not until the mid 1880s that boxing was first introduced by the army as a form of military training (Mason & Riedi 2010).

Rib fractures

Rib fractures have often been interpreted as resulting from direct trauma such as a blow (eg while boxing) or a fall against a hard object, but they can also result from interpersonal violence and assault (Brickley & Smith 2006). Rib fractures were the

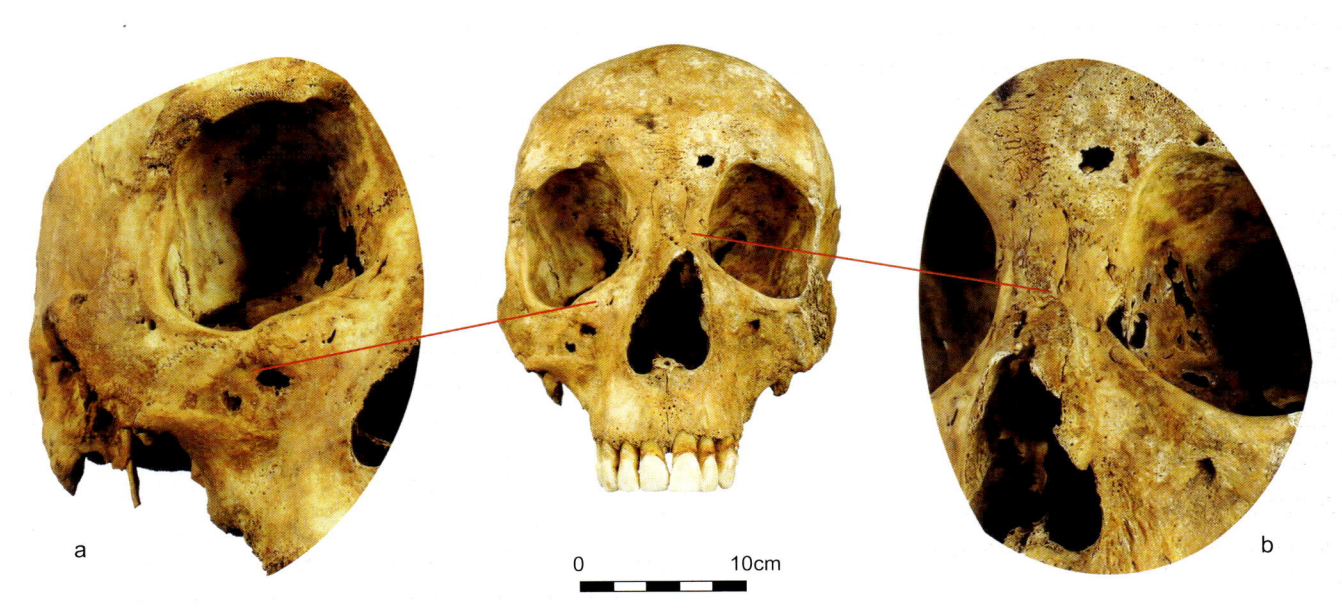

Fig 5.8 Skeleton [1807] showing: a – healing fracture of the right maxilla; b – healing fracture of the nasal bones

most common form of thoracic injury in the Savoy population, affecting 7.0% (43/609) of all individuals (Table 5.8). These were counted only once if the rib was fractured more than once. If multiple ribs were fractured these were counted separately. Both sexes and all ages suffered from rib fractures but males were significantly more affected (12.3%, 40/325) than the females (0.9%, 1/105) (χ^2=11.8633, df=1, p<0.05).

M+M? (n/N)	F+F? (n/N)	? (n/N)	Subadults (n/N)	Total (n/N)
12.3% (40/325)	0.9% (1/105)	1.1% (1/89)	1.1% (1/90)	7.0% (43/609)

Table 5.8 Crude prevalence rates of rib fractures within the population (individuals affected bilaterally were counted once)

The majority of rib fractures were well healed but five examples of unhealed rib fractures or fractures in the process of healing suggest a traumatic event that occurred not long before death. These were observed in two adult males, one adult female, one adult individual of unknown sex and one subadult.

Long-bone fractures

Long-bone fractures were present in 5.2% (32/609) of individuals (Table 5.9). In keeping with the results obtained for the ribs, males appeared to be more frequently affected than females. Long-bone fractures can be the result of both direct and indirect trauma and may therefore be produced by accidents, occupational hazards or assault (Lovell 1997; Browner et al 2014).

Long-bone fractures	M+M? (n/N)	F+F? (n/N)	? (n/N)	Subadults (n/N)	Total (n/N)
Clavicle	4.3% (14/325)	- (0/105)	- (0/89)	- (0/90)	2.2% (14/609)
Humerus	0.3% (1/325)	- (0/105)	- (0/89)	1.1% (1/90)	0.3% (2/609)
Radius	2.1% (7/325)	1.9% (2/105)	- (0/89)	- (0/90)	1.4% (9/609)
Ulna	0.3% (1/325)	- (0/105)	- (0/89)	- (0/90)	0.1% (1/609)
Tibia	0.6% (2/325)	- (0/105)	- (0/89)	- (0/90)	0.3% (2/609)
Fibula	1.2% (4/325)	- (0/105)	- (0/89)	- (0/90)	0.6% (4/609)
Total	8.9% (29/325)	1.9% (2/105)	- (0/89)	1.1% (1/90)	5.2% (32/609)

Table 5.9 Crude prevalence rates of long-bone fractures within the total population

Fractures in the clavicle were present only among the male population. There were ten left-side, well-healed fractured clavicles compared with four from the right side.

Fig 5.9 Skeleton [300] showing a healed spiral fracture of the left humerus

Additionally, an adult male, [300], aged 30–45 years exhibited a spiral fracture at the mid diaphysis of the left humerus (Fig 5.9). Shaft fractures can result from direct or indirect trauma and may present complications such as displacement of both parts (Lovell 1997) as is seen in this individual.

Seven of the nine fractures present in the radius were the so-called Colles' fracture. This can be seen about 20mm above the distal articular surface of the radius and causes the distal fragment to displace posteriorly (Lovell 1997). Both the remaining cases presented a well-healed fracture just below the mid diaphysis: one in the left and one in the right. In the ulna, one adult male displayed a healed fracture of the right trochlear notch. The joint congruity between the three bones of the elbow was affected and new articular surfaces were formed.

Fractures of the tibia were observed in two adult males, [1683] and [1719]. The first exhibited an incomplete fracture on the medial condyle of the right tibia. The condyle appeared to be displaced medially from the normal anatomical position and pushed downwards. The articular surface of this condyle was fragmented and secondary osteoarthritic changes were visible along with eburnation. The medial condyle of the right femur was also affected with secondary osteoarthritis. A large bony excrescence was present on the posterior aspect of the right femoral condyle surrounding the articular surface, which resulted from exuberant osteophytic formation. Fractures of the tibia at the knee joint are rare in the archaeological record but in exceptional observed cases they heal with deformity (Lovell 1997), just as seen in skeleton [1683].

The second male, [1719], had a well-healed oblique fracture present just below the mid diaphysis of both right tibia and fibula (Fig 5.10). Although the bones were not well aligned as they presented a posterior displacement of their diaphysis, there was no sign of infection. This kind of oblique fracture in the shafts of the tibia and fibula can only take place as a result of angular forces (ibid).

Four adult males also suffered fractured fibulae. These were all well healed and located on the proximal epiphysis of the bones in two individuals and on the distal end in one case. Skeleton [1357] had both fibulae fractured, each at opposite ends of the bone.

Finally, two left femora from the disarticulated group of human remains exhibited fractures. As explained above (5.1, 'Disarticulated material'), these cases were not counted in the overall prevalence of long-bone fractures. One of them, belonging to an unsexed adult, was observed as an oblique and severely displaced fracture located on the proximal third of its diaphysis (Fig 5.11). Both fractured portions of the bone overlapped and were sealed by exuberant new bone formation that served as a sheath of healing callus. As a consequence of the mal-aligned union of the two displaced portions, the limb was significantly shortened. Despite this, evidence suggests that the limb was mobile and used until the time of death.

The second example belonged to another unsexed adult individual, who had suffered an oblique fracture on the mid diaphysis. Similar to the example described above, this bone suffered from a displaced fracture that led to a shortening of the bone. The union of both portions were mal-aligned when healed. The distal end had overlapped posteriorly to the proximal end and had also rotated externally. It can be surmised from the considerable callus formation in the affected area that the accident took place a long time before death. The way in which both femoral fragments had united as well as the overall gracile appearance of the bone suggests that the use of the limb for walking was minimal.

Hand and foot fractures

The total crude prevalence rate of fractures in the hands and feet was 5.5% (34/609) (Table 5.10), most of them being located in the metacarpals and metatarsals. Fractures in these locations are suggestive of interpersonal violence or assault (Lovell 1997), representing indirect trauma from punches or kicks.

As observed in Table 5.10, these particular traumatic lesions were typically suffered by men. Crude prevalence rates showed that the most commonly fractured bones were the metacarpals (3.9%, 24/609) followed by the metatarsals (1.1%, 7/609). Metacarpals often suffer from longitudinal compression fractures, which result from impacting the fist when punching in activities such as boxing (Brickley & Smith 2006). The so-called Bennett's fracture (Bennett 1882), occurring at the base of the 1st metacarpal (MC1), was the most common

Fig 5.10 Skeleton [1719] showing anterior and lateral views of an oblique fracture of the right tibia and fibula

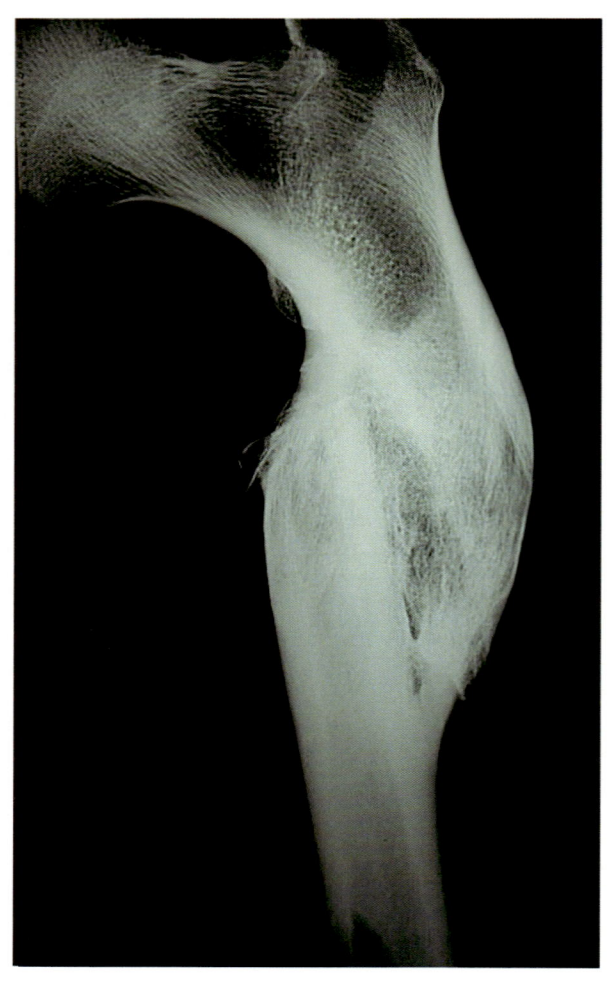

Fig 5.11 Radiography of disarticulated left femur showing an oblique and displaced fracture

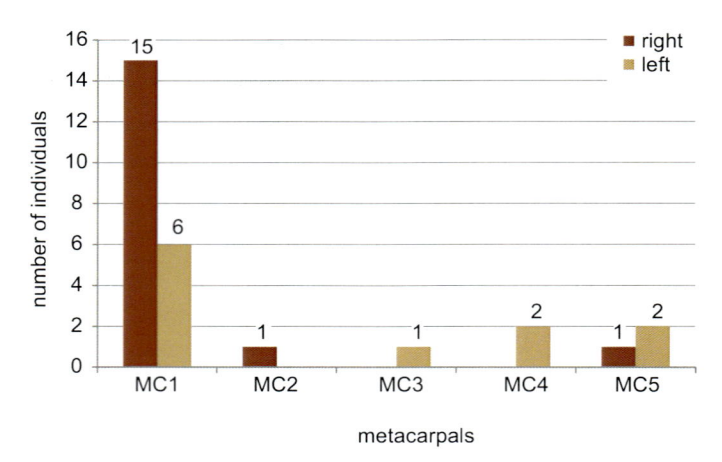

Fig 5.12 Number of metacarpals fractured within the population

Hand/foot fractures	M+M? (n/N)	F+F? (n/N)	? (n/N)	Subadults (n/N)	Total (n/N)
Right metacarpals	4.9% (16/325)	- (0/105)	- (0/89)	- (0/90)	2.6% (16/609)
Left metacarpals	2.4% (8/325)	- (0/105)	- (0/89)	- (0/90)	1.3% (8/609)
Hand phalanges	0.3% (1/325)	- (0/105)	- (0/89)	- (0/90)	0.1% (1/609)
Right metatarsals	0.6% (2/325)	- (0/105)	- (0/89)	2.2% (2/90)	0.6% (4/609)
Left metatarsals	0.9% (3/325)	- (0/105)	- (0/89)	- (0/90)	0.4% (3/609)
Foot phalanges	0.3% (1/325)	- (0/105)	- (0/89)	- (0/90)	0.1% (1/609)
Navicular	0.3% (1/325)	- (0/105)	- (0/89)	- (0/90)	0.1% (1/609)
Total	9.8% (32/325)	- (0/105)	- (0/89)	2.2% (2/90)	5.5% (34/609)

Table 5.10 Crude prevalence rates of hand and foot fractures within the total population

type of metacarpal fracture observed (Fig 5.12). Incomplete fractures were present in the left MC1 of two adult males but in the remaining 19 examples the fracture was complete. It is interesting to note that Bennett's fractures were more prevalent on the right side when compared with the left side, probably reflecting sidedness and hand-use preference.

A number of possible occupational hazards were considered in relation to this injury. The first was the use of the musket, both loading and firing. The musket would be held in the left hand leaving the right hand, and for certain actions, the right thumb, to carry out the loading procedure (Great Britain: Adjutant-General's Office 1776; Reid 2016, 29–32). While this implies that the right thumb may have come under stress from repeated use this is more likely to have caused joint problems than fractures. If soldiers regularly suffered fractures from such a routine military procedure, this surely would have been remedied with a change in weapon design.

Another possibility considered was the use of the bayonet. It was easily attached, placed in the socket and twisted, so this is unlikely to have caused a problem. Its use involved the firearm and bayonet being levelled across the chest at shoulder height, with the right hand holding the butt. The bayonet would then be thrust forward (Reid & Hook 1996, 45). It would not be unreasonable to suggest that when making contact with its target some force would have travelled backwards and through the hand, possibly into the 1st right metacarpal. However, whether this would have been enough to cause a fracture is doubtful, and, in practice, the bayonet was rarely used in anger (Holmes 2001, 201).

It does therefore seem that the most likely cause of the fractures was fist-fighting or boxing, whether as self-defence, acts of aggression or recreational activity. As summarised by Brickley and Smith (2006), fist-fighting was an accepted way of settling interpersonal disputes. Londoners were often associated with public fist-fighting – it was a recognised part of English culture, appearing to foreigners to be 'an inherent part of the national character' (Durston 2012, 84). With their location in the Savoy, soldiers would have encountered this developing cultural pastime and would have mimicked such activity (Saul David, pers comm).

In the feet, the most commonly fractured bones were the 2nd and 3rd metatarsals (Fig 5.13) and this type of fracture may result from kicking (Lovell 1997). One subadult, [132], had unhealed, oblique fractures on the 2nd and 3rd right metatarsals with extensive callus formation taking place around the injury site at the time of death.

Finally, one adult male presented an incomplete fracture of the right navicular on the distal articular facet, passing across the articular facets for the 2nd and 3rd cuneiforms.

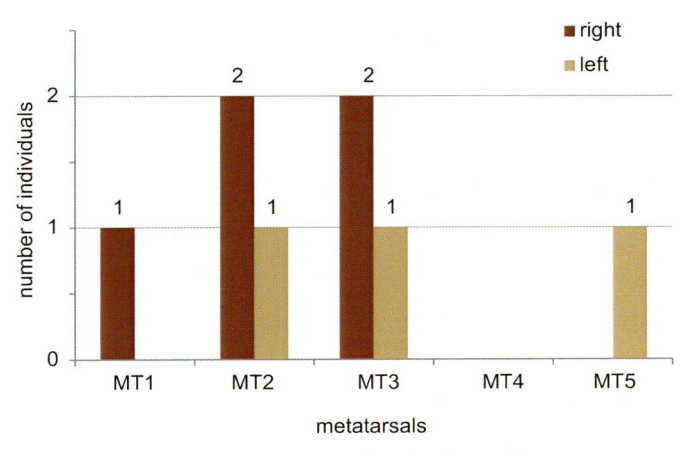

Fig 5.13 Number of metatarsals fractured within the population

Other fracture locations

Other fractures sites included one scapula, one os coxa, one thoracic vertebra and one lumbar vertebra. Adult male [646] had multiple fractures on his right scapula. A healed fracture was present across the infraspinous fossa and at least two other well-healed fractures were present on the lateral border, producing a downward displacement of the glenoid cavity along with exuberant callus formation around the area. Fractures to the scapula are uncommon and comminute fractures as seen in [646] are usually the result of direct trauma (Lovell 1997). Consideration of occupational hazards identified the use of a musket as a possible causative factor. A musket would be levelled at shoulder height and when fired with a well-rammed charge, could give a sharp kick-back (Holmes 2001, 198).

One adult male displayed a fracture of the iliac fossa, near the arcuate line of the right ilium, that was in the process of healing at the time of death. The spine of one adult male appeared to have a possible fracture on the transverse process of L1 and a second adult male had a compression fracture of the end plate of the T7 vertebra. Compression injuries usually result from indirect trauma such as jumping on to the feet or falling (Lovell 1997) but can be caused by other low-energy mechanisms in vulnerable individuals, particularly those affected by osteoporosis or metabolic disease (Browner et al 2014).

Multiple fractures

Some individuals presented multiple fractures that could have resulted from either accidental trauma or physical abuse. For instance, two adult males, [643] and [913], had eight fractured bones. The former had four left-side ribs fractured, two of them on the sternal end, one on the vertebral end and one on the mid diaphysis. He also had three ribs from the right side fractured, one near the head and two on the mid diaphysis. Finally, the base of the right 1st metacarpal exhibited a well-healed Bennett's fracture (Fig 5.14).

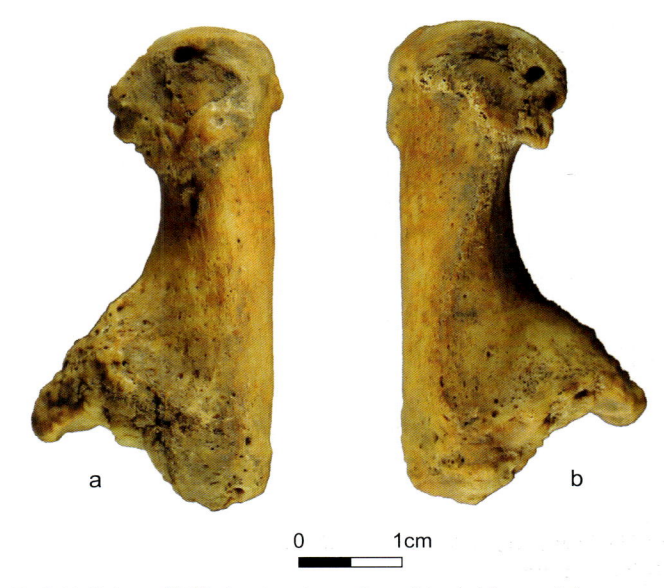

Fig 5.14 Skeleton [643] showing views of a well-healed Bennett's fracture: a – lateral; b – medial

The second male, [913], had well-healed fractures on the mid diaphysis of two right-side and three left-side ribs, along with well-healed oblique fractures at the mid diaphysis of the left 3rd, 4th and 5th metacarpals.

Nine cranial and post-cranial lesions were found in one adult male ([1807]). Those in the skull are described above ('Skull fractures') and consisted of well-healed fractures of both nasal bones and a healing fracture of the right maxilla just below the orbital margin (Fig 5.8). In the post-cranial skeleton the right 2nd metatarsal had suffered an oblique fracture near its base. The left fibula also displayed a well-healed oblique fracture to its proximal epiphysis, and four left ribs displayed well-healed fractures in their diaphyseal areas. It has been suggested that certain fractures of the skull, such as those encountered in the nasal and zygomatic bones and the mandible and also those on the posterior aspect of ribs, vertebral spinous and the metatarsals, are of clinical significance because of their link with assault and interpersonal violence (Lovell 1997).

Finally, the individual with most fractures in the Savoy Chapel was adult male [1943], who had 12 broken bones. Seven right-side ribs and four left-side ribs displayed well-healed fractures at their mid diaphyses and the left clavicle had an oblique fracture on the distal end of its diaphysis. Both broken pieces appeared to have healed with some degree of overlapping and it appeared shortened when compared with the opposite clavicle. This malunion could have caused this individual a number of symptoms which, according to a modern study (Hillen at al 2010), could have included pain, loss of strength in the arm and impairment in daily activities because of the shortening of the trapezius muscle, responsible for moving, rotating and stabilising the scapula.

Multiple fractures with different stages of healing may represent physical abuse in both adults and children whereas multiple but simultaneous fractures may represent accidental trauma (Lovell 1997). In the case of skeleton [1943] all multiple-fractured ribs from the right side displayed a similar stage of healing and the fractures were found symmetrically positioned in relation to each other. The fractured ribs from the opposite side showed a similar pattern. Although it is uncertain whether the 11 ribs were fractured simultaneously, the evidence supports an accidental trauma aetiology and suggests that, at least on each side, they were sustained in a single, accidental event.

A similar situation exists for the above mentioned individuals, [643] and [913], who also exhibited both right- and left-side rib fractures. In both cases it is difficult to confirm whether they occurred simultaneously or not and whether they resulted from accidental trauma. The various stages of healing in the bones of the face, left-side ribs, left leg and right foot suggest that they resulted from more than one traumatic event. Multiple well-healed fractures with different stages of healing could result from physical abuse, a recognised element of 17th- and 18th-century London (see Chapter 2) or perhaps a hazardous occupation.

Perimortem fractures

Perimortem injuries are those that take place near or around the time of death and do not show any evidence of healing. Examples of these affected accounted for 0.6% (4/609) of the total population: two adult males, one adult female and one subadult of unknown sex.

One of the adult males, [433], had an unhealed fracture in the mid diaphysis of one unsided rib and a second male, [735], had an unhealed fracture to the mid diaphysis of the right femur. Female skeleton [1823] exhibited a fracture near the symphysis of her mandible that could have resulted from perimortem trauma, although the poorly preserved bone prevented a more conclusive diagnosis. Finally, subadult [1126] exhibited a 20mm-long injury located across the inter-tubercular groove of the left humeral head, just below the epiphyseal line. As the edges of this linear injury were not sharp, the lesion could have resulted from a crush injury.

SOFT-TISSUE TRAUMA

Soft-tissue trauma affected 13.8% (72/519) of the total adult population. The results show sex-related differences and a similar pattern in the distribution of lesions that included the joints, muscles and tendons involved in ambulatory and manual activities. The results outlined below suggest that, as might be expected with a physically demanding military lifestyle, males were exposed to more soft-tissue trauma, such as contusions, strains or overuse injuries, than females.

Myositis ossificans traumatica

This is a condition that results from local trauma to a muscle or tendon by an external force, which in turn triggers an inflammatory response and the formation of new bone and connective tissue on the affected area (Defoort et al 2012). In the Savoy Chapel population the condition was present in 11 individuals – one of unknown sex and ten males – in other words 2.1% (11/519) of the adult population.

Ossified muscle and ligament tissue was present in five humeri, three tibiae, two fibulae and one femur. In the humerus, the ossified muscles were the brachialis (four individuals) and the deltoid (one individual). The tibia and fibula presented bony projections located in similar areas: the interosseous ligament at the distal end of the tibia (two individuals) and fibula (one individual) and the soleus attachment at the proximal tibia and fibula (one individual each). In the single, right femur, the medial head of the gastrocnemius was ossified just above the medial condyle on the posterior aspect.

Studies of myositis ossificans traumatica in other sites from the London area show that in line with the results found in this study, the arm, thigh and leg appear to be the body parts with most evidence for soft-tissue trauma. Not surprisingly this condition was reported by Boston et al (2008) in the leg of one of the veterans from the Royal Hospital Greenwich. Miles et al (2008b) found myositis ossificans traumatica in the left femur of an adult male from St Marylebone Church, thus giving a crude prevalence of 0.3% (1/301) of the total sample studied. Henderson et al (2013) found the condition in three adult individuals from the St Mary and St Michael's burial ground and in one subadult from the Bow Baptist Church.

The adult individuals were affected on the right distal femur, the left femur (vastus medialis attachment) and on the right inferior tibiofibular ligament. The subadult was affected on the right proximal humerus, resulting in 0.4% (3/705) and 0.2% (1/416) crude prevalence rates respectively.

Enthesopathies

Enthesopathies are anomalies observed at the insertion of muscles and tendons into bone. They can be regarded as a form of soft-tissue trauma resulting from strenuous physical activity, occupation and mechanical factors such as differential strain and biomechanical changes in bone load, although they are highly correlated with age (Ponce 2010).

The bones and the entheses with muscle or ligament involvement most commonly observed in this population are summarised in Table 5.11. It was found that 11.7% (61/519) of all adult individuals presented at least one enthesopathy in one bone; 37 individuals showed it in one location, 24 individuals in more than one. Table 5.11 also shows the number of enthesopathies found by location within the adult population. As expected in a condition associated with age, these lesions were only present in the adult population. Thus the presence of entheseal reactions in the adult population was 20.0% (104/519). A higher prevalence was recorded among males (24.9%, 81/325) compared to the females (16.1%, 17/105). While differences in lifestyle and levels of physical activity may have been responsible for these results, the correlation between the development of enthesophytes and age should not be ignored.

In the upper limb, the humerus displayed most entheseal changes (3.2%, 17/519) followed by the patella in the lower limb (4.4%, 23/519). Fig 5.15 shows an example of enthesophyte at the calcaneal tuberosity, the area of the Achilles tendon insertion, which is mainly linked to walking.

SCHMORL'S NODES

Schmorl's nodes are depressions on the vertebral bodies that result from herniations of the nucleus pulposus material of the intervertebral discs (Aufderheide and Rodríguez-Martín 1998; Ortner 2003). Some authors regard these as being related to joint disease but as they can result from repeated trauma due to exerting compression forces in the spine while bending, lifting weight or twisting motions (Roberts & Cox 2003) they are included here within this section. As shown in Table 5.12, Schmorl's nodes were present in individuals of both sexes and all ages and were the most prevalent of all traumatic lesions encountered in the Savoy Chapel population.

Limb	Bone	M+M? (n/N)	F+F? (n/N)	? (n/N)	Total (n/N)
Upper	clavicle	0.3% (1/325)	0.9% (1/105)	- (0/89)	0.3% (2/519)
	scapula	0.3% (1/325)	- (0/105)	- (0/89)	0.1% (1/519)
	humerus	4.9% (16/325)	- (0/105)	1.1% (1/89)	3.2% (17/519)
	radius	0.6% (2/325)	- (0/105)	- (0/89)	0.3% (2/519)
	ulna	1.8% (6/325)	1.9% (2/105)	- (0/89)	1.5% (8/519)
Spine	vertebrae	1.2% (4/325)	- (0/105)	1.1% (1/89)	0.5% (5/519)
Lower	os coxa	4.6% (15/325)	1.9% (2/105)	- (0/89)	3.2% 17/519
	femur	2.1% (7/325)	0.9% (1/105)	1.1% (1/89)	1.7% (9/519)
	patella	4.9% (16/325)	4.7% (5/105)	2.2% (2/89)	4.4% (23/519)
	tibia	1.2% (4/325)	1.9% (2/105)	1.1% (1/89)	1.3% (7/519)
	fibula	0.3% (1/325)	- (0/105)	- (0/89)	0.1% (1/519)
	calcaneus	2.4% (8/325)	3.8% (4/105)	- (0/89)	2.3% (12/519)
Total		**24.9% (81/325)**	**16.1% (17/105)**	**6.7% (6/89)**	**20.0% (104/519)**

Table 5.11 Crude prevalence rates of enthesopathies by location within the adult population

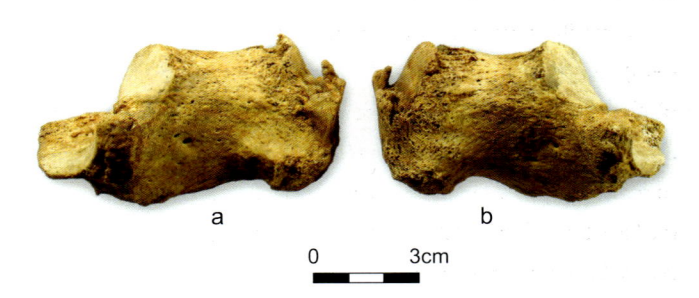

Fig 5.15 Skeleton [857] showing calcanei with ossification of the Achilles tendon: a – left; b – right

Crude prevalence rates showed that Schmorl's nodes were present in 31.8% (194/609) of all individuals studied and nearly half of the male population from the Savoy were affected by the condition. Comparisons between the sexes suggested that on the basis of true prevalence rates, males were more affected than the females in all spinal regions (χ^2=128.37883, df=1, p<0.05). These injuries can result from compression forces and might be sustained by soldiers in their thoracic and lumbar spines as a consequence of carrying heavy loads on their backs. A study by Knapik et al (2004) found that during the Napoleonic Wars of the early 19th century troops carried up to 15kg of load in the form of equipment while they marched. It also records that among modern soldiers exposed to carrying

	M+M? (n/N)	F+F? (n/N)	? (n/N)	Subadults (n/N)	Total (n/N)
Crude prevalence	49.2% (160/325)	20.9% (22/105)	12.3% (11/89)	1.1% (1/90)	**31.8% (194/609)**
True prevalence	17.7% (1007/5665)	6.9% (129/1860)	18.3% (66/359)	0.1% (3/1555)	**12.7% (1205/9439)**

Table 5.12 Crude and true prevalence rates of Schmorl's nodes within the total population

loads over a prolonged period, common injuries include spinal disc trauma and back strain.

True prevalence rates also showed that 12.7% (1205/9439) of all vertebrae available for study from all spinal regions were affected by Schmorl's nodes. As depicted in Fig 5.16 these lesions were absent in the cervical spine but present elsewhere. The highest vertebra affected by the condition was the 4th thoracic, the lowest was the 1st sacral vertebra. In a cranial caudal fashion, the highest peak of the distribution appeared in the lower thoracic spine, between the 8th and the 12th, with the number of vertebrae affected decreasing both cranially and caudally.

Other sites from the London area, such as St Marylebone Church (Miles et al 2008b), St Mary and St Michael's burial ground, Bow Baptist Church and Sheen's burial ground (Henderson et al 2013), showed that in line with this study Schmorl's nodes were present in both the thoracic and lumbar spine. The mid to lower thoracic spine was the area with the highest predilection. Finally, the males always appeared more severely affected than the females, suggesting that they were generally engaged in more weight-bearing activities. At the Savoy Chapel the high percentage of soldiers among the population offers a possible explanation.

SCHEUERMANN'S DISEASE

Scheuermann's disease belongs to the family of the osteochondroses, a group of disorders affecting the joints of children and adolescents, especially males. It is characterised by erosion and necrosis of the anterior aspect of the vertebral endplates leading to loss of anterior height and secondary kyphosis. The condition can affect one or two vertebrae, although the involvement can extend to the entire thoracic spine (Aufderheide and Rodríguez-Martín 1998). Wedge-shaped vertebrae are commonly found, and when present they usually coincide with the apex of the curvature. The condition may be triggered by the presence of underlying Schmorl's nodes so a traumatic aetiology has been widely accepted over that of genetic factors (Ortner 2003).

Three adult males aged 30–35 years from the Savoy Chapel were diagnosed with Scheuermann's disease: a crude prevalence rate of 0.4% (3/609) of the total assemblage, 0.5% (3/519) of the total adult population and 0.9% (3/325) for the adult male group. Skeleton [147] had a wedge-shaped T8 vertebra and displayed erosions on the anterior aspect of the apophyseal rings of T8 and T9, indicative of Scheuermann's disease. Marginal anterior lipping was also present on the anterior rims of these vertebrae. He also presented Schmorl's nodes on T5 down to L4. Similarly, skeleton [885] had a combination of necrotic cavitations along with Schmorl's nodes on the thoracic and lumbar spine. The former were located from T6 to T9 and also T11, and on L1, L3 and L4 vertebrae. Coincidentally, Schmorl's nodes were present from T5 to L2. Lastly, skeleton [996] probably represented the early stages of Scheuermann's disease as cavitations were present on the anterior aspect of the vertebral bodies of L1, L2 and L5 vertebrae (Fig 5.17). Schmorl's nodes were also noted affecting the thoracic and lumbar

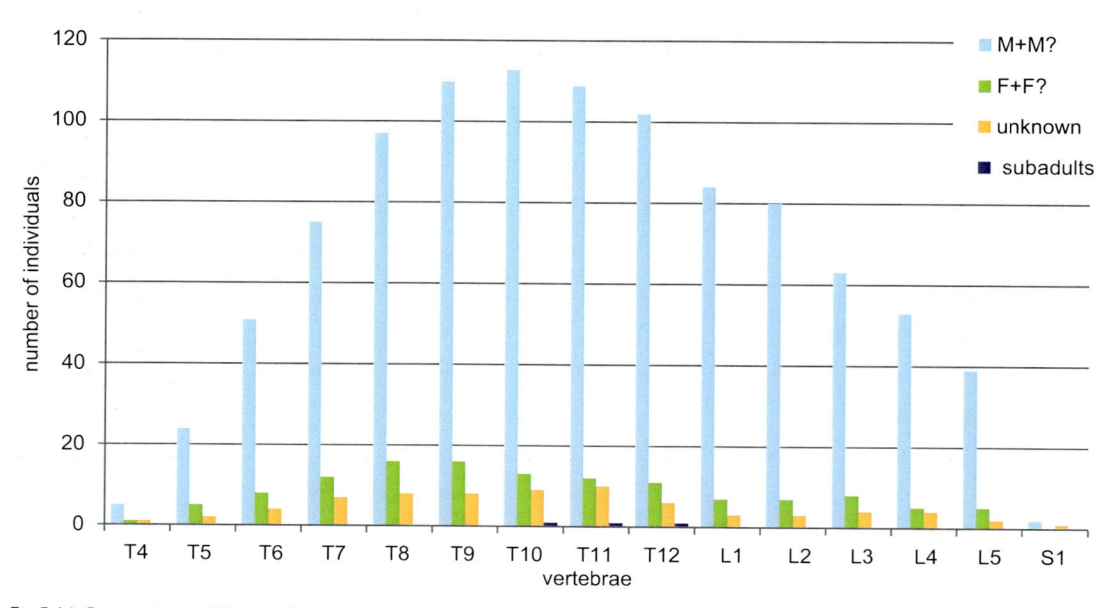

Fig 5.16 Comparison of Schmorl's nodes distribution among all individuals buried at the Savoy Chapel

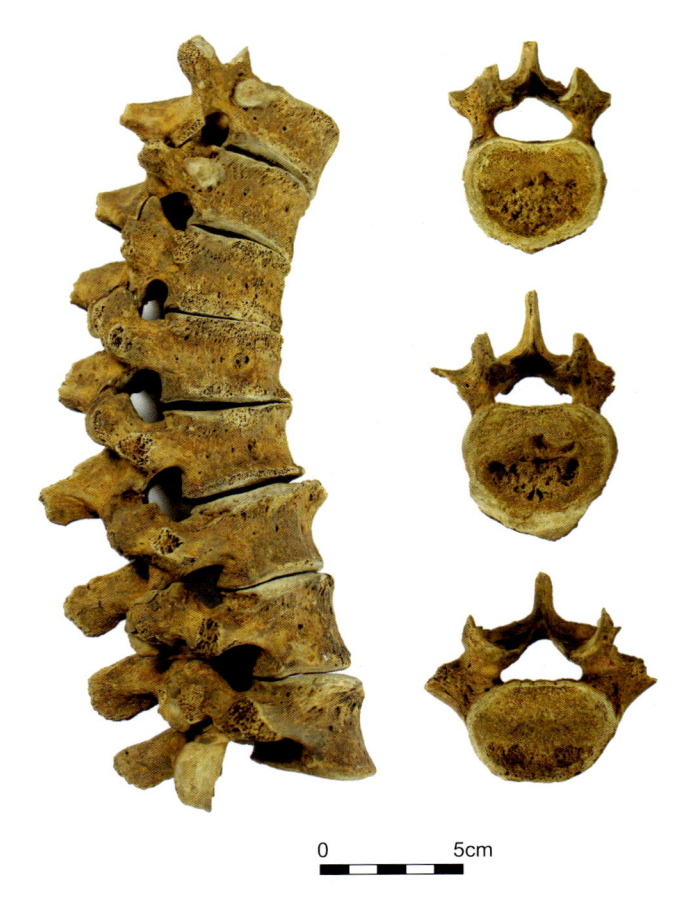

Fig 5.17 Skeleton [996] showing cavitations on L1, L2 and L5 vertebral bodies and a slight anterior curvature of the spine following a wedge-shaped and collapse of L1

spine from T4 to L6 vertebrae. All three examples displayed different degrees of loss of anterior height in the affected vertebrae and a secondary kyphosis with different degrees of involvement.

SPONDYLOLYSIS

Present-day consensus supports the idea that spondylolysis is an acquired traumatic lesion and the consequence of a stress fracture, fatigue fracture or overuse injury occurring during growth. The combination of repeated extension and hyperflexion of the lumbar spine that exceeds the capacity of bone repair results in the separation of the vertebra into two parts, namely the anterior vertebral body and posterior the pars interarticularis (Aufderheide and Rodríguez-Martín 1998).

Fourteen adult individuals from the Savoy Chapel presented spondylolysis and the condition was observed affecting only one of their lumbar vertebrae. It was complete bilateral on the L4 of one adult male, incomplete unilateral on the L4 of one female and on L5 of a male and complete on L5 on the remaining 11 individuals. Crude prevalence rates showed that spondylolysis was present in 2.2% (14/609) of the total population and 2.6% (14/519) of the adult population (Table 5.13). No cases of spondylolysis were recorded among subadults.

Comparisons between the sexes suggested that the condition was not distributed evenly, affecting 12 males (3.6%, 12/325) compared with two females (1.9%, 2/105). In accordance with the results obtained for Schmorl's nodes and Scheuermann's disease, males appeared to have sustained more lower back stress than females. This may have started at a young age before skeletal maturity was attained or could have developed during the years of military service. Indeed, as described in Chapter 3, by 1760, the ideal age for recruiting a soldier was between 16 and 20 years of age, before skeletal maturity.

True prevalence rates (Table 5.13) showed that 1.6% (14/845) of all 4th and 5th lumbar vertebrae of the total adult population was affected by spondylolysis. Statistical analysis showed that the comparison between males and females was not significant ($\chi^2=0.3828$, df=1, $p<0.05$).

	M+M? (n/N)	F+F? (n/N)	? (n/N)	Subadults (n/N)	Total (n/N)
Crude prevalence	3.6% (12/325)	1.9% (2/105)	- (0/89)	- (0/90)	2.2% (14/609)
True prevalence	2.1% (12/551)	1.3% (2/146)	- (0/28)	- (0/120)	1.6% (14/845)

Table 5.13 Crude and true prevalence rates of spondylolysis within the population

Comparison of spondylolysis from other London sites showed that the crude prevalence ranged from 0.6% to 5.0% and the population of the Savoy Chapel was therefore average (Table 5.14). Comparisons between these populations were based on the observation of the condition among all adult individuals, apart from the City Bunhill burial ground (Connell & Miles 2010) where both adults and subadults were counted. As spondylolysis represents an overuse injury occurring during growth, the reason for the high prevalence in other cemeteries would have to be found in the physical activities in which subadults were involved.

London-area cemeteries	Prevalence (n/N)
Sheen's burial ground	0.6% (1/166)
City Bunhill burial ground	0.8% (3/239)
St Marylebone Church burial ground	1.7% (4/223)
Bow Baptist Church	1.8% (4/214)
St Mary and St Michael's burial ground	1.8% (5/268)
Queen's Chapel Savoy	**2.6% (14/519)**
St Benet Sherehog	3.0% (5/165)
Royal Hospital Greenwich	3.8% (4/105)
All Saints, Chelsea Old Church	4.2% (7/165)
New Bunhill Fields burial ground	5.0% (8/157)

Table 5.14 Comparison of spondylolysis in cemeteries from the London area (all adult individuals are pooled; for references see above, 5.1)

OS ACROMIALE

In the scapula, the failure of the distal end of the acromion to fuse with its base is called os acromiale. This failure is believed to result from an overuse injury and indicates persistent motion and repetitive stress on the shoulder starting before skeletal maturity, in other words before the age of 20, which is when the acromial ossification centre fuses with the acromion (Scheuer & Black 2004; Demetracopoulos et al 2006). Sixteen adults from the Savoy Chapel presented os acromiale but none of these exhibited the condition bilaterally; it was recorded on the right acromia of seven individuals and on the left acromia of nine. One of these, [926], was an example of healed os acromiale that showed a visible line of reattachment between the ossicle and the acromion of the scapula.

Crude prevalence rates showed that os acromiale was present in 2.6% (16/609) of the total population and 3.0% (16/519) of the adult population (Table 5.15), females being slightly more commonly affected than males. True prevalence rates showed that 2.4% (16/665) of all acromia present were affected by the condition, in other words, 2.8% (12/557) of the total adult population.

	M+M? (n/N)	F+F? (n/N)	? (n/N)	Subadults (n/N)	Total (n/N)
Crude prevalence	3.3% (11/325)	4.7% (5/105)	- (0/89)	- (0/90)	**2.6% (16/609)**
True prevalence	2.7% (11/405)	3.8% (5/129)	- (0/23)	- (0/108)	**2.4% (16/665)**

Table 5.15 Crude and true prevalence rates of os acromiale within the total population

Although comparisons between males and females suggested that the women buried at the Savoy Chapel were slightly more affected than the males, this was not statistically significant ($\chi^2=0.4529$, df=1, p<0.05). In line with these results, those obtained by Miles et al (2008b) for the females buried at St Marylebone also showed that they were more affected by os acromiale than males (5.7%, 5/87 compared with 3.9%, 4/103) although this difference was not statistically significant.

It will be difficult to pinpoint the traumatic activity that might have triggered the presence of os acromiale in the population in general and among the females in particular, but according to modern clinical literature os acromiale is likely to result from repetitive overhead arm motions combined with abduction and external rotation of the arm (Pećina & Bojanić 1993). With no real difference between the sexes, this particular condition does not appear necessarily to be directly related to the occupational hazards of military life. Perhaps, given that the foot regiments were recruiting 13- to 18-years olds in late 18th century (Chapter 3), an age at which the acromial end of the scapula is not expected to be fused, this is somewhat surprising.

ANKYLOSIS

Twenty-one adult individuals presented fusion between the mid and distal phalanges of the foot. These were fused on 11 phalangeal joints from the right side, five from the left and five bilateral. Eleven of the 21 adults were males (3.3%, 11/325), eight were of unknown sex (8.9%, 8/89) and the remaining two were females (19%, 2/105). As radiography of such small joints will not help to understand what the underlying aetiology is, it is not known if this type of fusion was secondary to trauma or from degenerative conditions of the aged (Ortner 2003). Congenital fusion and failure segmentation of the interphalangeal joint within one digit (or symphalangism) is another possible causative factor (Barnes 2012).

JOINT DISLOCATION

Joint dislocation is a disruption of the normal joint congruity owing to trauma (Ortner 2003). One adult male, [589], aged 45+ years, presented a very interesting case of shoulder dislocation (Fig 5.18) with the left humeral head showing severe bone mass loss, reducing it to half of its normal size. Radiography did not reveal any obvious fracture line so it could be suggested that the traumatic event associated with the dislocation resulted in injury to the blood supply of the humeral head and the consequent avascular necrosis and tissue death. It could also be that the continued use of the dislocated shoulder led to the severe alteration of the joint. Either way the joint continued to function, as is evident in both the glenoid and humeral head articular surfaces. Both the glenoid cavity and the humeral head show extensive eburnation. The humeral head in particular showed extensive degeneration and exuberant marginal osteophytes secondary to the malalignment of the joint.

Other possible interpretations for the lesion include humerus varus deformity (HVD), a disturbance of the ossification of long bones, particularly in the growing plates, owing to multifactorial causes (Molto 2000) including trauma following the use of forceps for difficult birth deliveries. As expected in HVD, individual [589] exhibited the glenohumeral deformity and the absence of the humeral neck but the humerus did not show rotation of its shaft and angulation of its upper diaphysis, which are characteristic of the condition. In addition to the left shoulder trauma, two left-side ribs displayed well-healed fractures, supporting the idea that a traumatic event led to the dislocation of the shoulder.

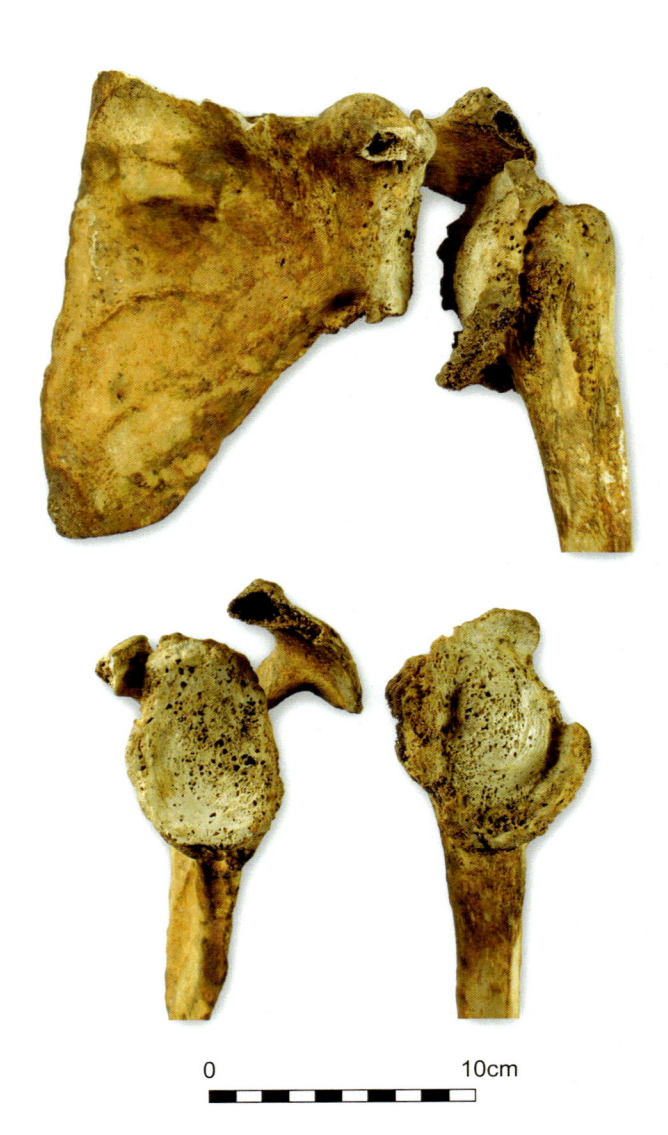

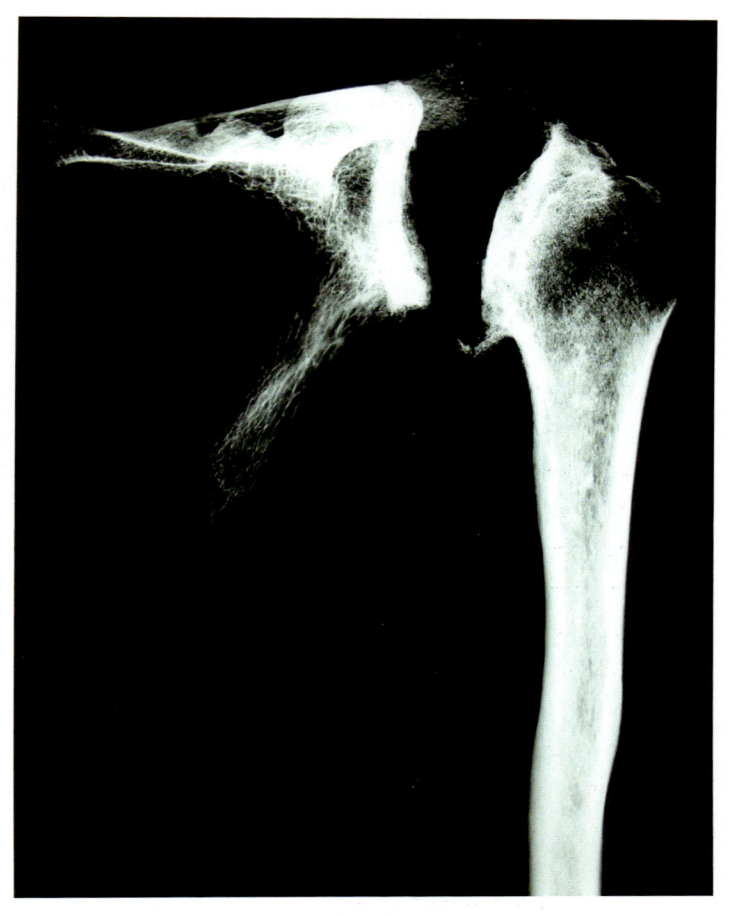

Fig 5.18 Skeleton [589] showing extensive degeneration and exuberant marginal osteophytes on the left shoulder joint thought to relate to a dislocation; radiography showing sclerotic areas resulting from bone-to-bone contact

GUN SHOT

Gunshot injuries were found in two individuals and in both cases the evidence suggests that they proved fatal. Unfortunately, both skulls were disarticulated and/or unstratified so it is not possible to link the crania confidently to the named individuals but with only three historically recorded it is tempting to try.

The first skull belonged to an adult, probably a male, and displayed a circular hole on the right side of the frontal bone close to the coronal suture (Fig 5.19). The perforation was complete and measured 15mm in diameter. It was clean on the outer table of the skull but bevelled on the inner table, suggesting that this was an entrance wound. The wound itself is circular, neat and regular, which suggests that the projectile entered the skull perpendicular to the bone, rather than tangentially, which would have created an irregular or keyhole-shaped wound with possible bevelling on the external surface (Ross 1995; Roberts & Manchester 2012, 2, 105).

The outer margins of the perforation did not look very sharp, probably as the result of taphonomic processes. Only one radiating fracture developed from the margin of the perforation to the coronal suture. However, this section of the skull was subsequently fractured, possibly along pre-existing weak fracture lines. The absence of macroscopic evidence of healing indicates that the individual died as a result of the shot.

It is worth considering that in most cases an entrance wound is likely to correspond to the size of the projectile (Crist 2006, 112). At just 15mm in diameter, the hole was only a fraction larger than the average pistol shot of the time at 13mm (Harding 2012, 187–8) so it seems likely that this individual was shot by a pistol or a weapon of similar size. Its position on the top of the frontal bone of the cranium would be consistent with being shot at from above, and would therefore fit the historical account of the shooting of Adam McCoy (see below) who, according to eyewitness accounts, seems to have been at the bottom of a flight of stairs and fatally shot at by someone at the top (LMA, MJ/SP/1769/061).

The second skull belonged to an adult male and displayed an unhealed circular perforation on the right parietal, measuring 28mm in diameter. The clean appearance of the hole on the inner table of the skull with bevelled margins on

endocranial view

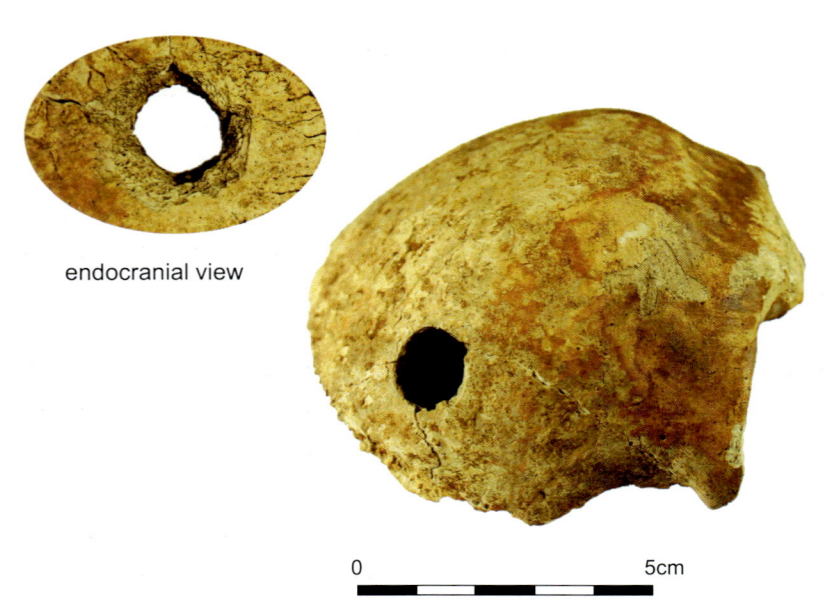

Fig 5.19 The endocranial (entrance) and ectocranial (exit) views of a gun shot

the outer layer, together with four radiating fractures, suggested this was an exit wound (Fig 5.20). Small radiating fractures present in the inner table of the skull were not visible to the naked eye but were identifiable with radiography.

The diameter of 28mm was quite significantly larger than a pistol shot, but in contrast to an entry wound, exit wounds are commonly much larger than the projectile and so a pistol cannot be ruled out. As well as being larger, exit wounds are often more irregular (Crist 2006, 112; Roberts & Manchester 2012, 2, 105). This is due to a number of factors such as the loss of velocity and stability of the projectile as it travels through the new medium, the possible distortion of the projectile on impact and the secondary damage caused by debris such as bone fragments collected as it passes through (Jones nd). On the other hand, the possibility of a larger calibre weapon must be considered. The average size of a musket shot of this date was approximately 0.69 inches or 18mm (Harding 2012; Saul David, pers comm), so still smaller than this exit wound.

Logically, the entrance of the projectile could have been from the opposite side of the skull, perhaps the left side of the mandible or from around the left side of the neck, to travel upwards and diagonally to exit on the right parietal. Unfortunately, the exact place of entry is hard to determine, firstly because the skull was damaged and secondly because projectiles can be deflected by whatever they encounter and leave at an angle as a consequence. The wound was more irregular than the entrance wound in the first cranium but still fairly circular. This may suggest that the projectile left the skull perpendicular to the

endocranial view

Fig 5.20 The endocranial (entrance) and ectocranial (exit) views of a gun shot

bone, although with no entry wound surviving it is not possible to say whether there had been any change in direction.

To put these gunshot wounds in context, the historical records document three individuals who died as a result of shooting in the mid 18th century: Samuel Jackson in 1752, William Knox in 1755 and Adam McCoy in 1769. During the 18th century the two weapons in common use would have been the musket, primarily used by the military, and the pistol (Newman & Brown 1997, 751–3; Justin Russell, pers comm). Samuel Jackson was shot for desertion, which at the time would have involved musket fire (Saul David, pers comm). William Knox on the other hand was shot by persons unknown, which suggests that this may have been a street crime and therefore more likely to have involved a hand gun such as a pistol. The same can be said for Adam McCoy, who was shot while trying to break up a clandestine meeting. The data from the historical records thus suggest that both pistol and musket injuries might be expected. The possibility that the gunshot wound in the second skull resulted from suicide was considered and cannot be ruled out, although the only suicides noted in the burial registers were recorded as 'hung'.

These two gunshot victims were included in the isotopic study (recorded as 117a and 117b) as their injuries could suggest a military association. If these individuals are taken as representing a military diet then their isotopic signals were consistent with expectations (see Fig 5.4). They showed slight nitrogen, possibly due to higher protein intake than the civilian population, and the $\delta^{13}C$ values fell within the range anticipated for a largely C3-based post-medieval diet.

PENETRATING TRAUMA

One disarticulated and incomplete skull from an adult of unknown sex displayed an injury on the left parietal that could have resulted from a sharp and penetrating object. This injury, 18mm long and 8mm wide, generated four radiating fracture lines from the margins of the wound, producing considerable intracranial bevelling. The dimensions of the wound make it plausible to suggest that the object that penetrated the skull reached the soft tissues and probably caused the death of this individual. The absence of any macroscopic healing supports this assumption.

One other disarticulated and very fragmented skull from an adult of unknown sex displayed at least three penetrating injuries in the skull. One of them, a circular injury, was located on the left side of the frontal bone, near the coronal suture. This penetrating injury had an irregular shape and measured approximately 8mm in diameter. The entry showed sharp ectocranial margins and considerable bevelling endocranially. The second injury was located on the anterior portion of the left parietal near to the line of the temporalis insertion. The exact size and shape cannot be fully described as there was considerable post-mortem damage in the area. The surviving margins, which were circular in size and measured approximately 17mm diameter, were remarkably similar to those described above resulting from a gunshot. However, in contrast to those, no radiating fractures were visible and there was less endocranial bevelling. The third injury was located 50mm posteriorly to the circular one described above, but oriented along the coronal plane. It measured approximately 16mm long and 8mm wide and it resembled the size and shape of that observed in the skull described previously. As no macroscopic evidence of healing was observed it is plausible to suggest that these injuries were fatal and almost certainly killed this individual.

Finally, one more disarticulated skull was assessed as belonging to a possible male aged 18+ years. This individual exhibited two penetrating injuries on the right parietal. One of them measured 30mm and was produced along the sagittal plane, on the anterior third portion of the parietal, near the coronal suture. The instrument that produced this injury was sharp and likely to be a blade, penetrating the diploë but not producing an exit endocranially. The second injury was shorter, at 20mm, and was visible on a coronal plane on the anterior right portion of the parietal, close to the squamous suture. There was less force exerted on this injury as it produced only a slight depression on the bone without penetrating it completely. While the severity of these injuries would not necessarily have proved fatal in all circumstances, the absence of evidence of healing in this individual may suggest that they were fatal for him in this case.

It is possible that these three individuals were Foot Guards. In battle a soldier could be injured by sword, dagger or bayonet, and injuries from bladed implements were recorded on two of the skulls. Of most interest was the skull displaying what seemed to be three penetrating injuries, one of which, although damaged, did display the characteristics of a gun shot. If this is the case, it would be logical that the individual was shot and then attacked or 'finished off' at close range by a different weapon. This scene could be imagined in a battle scenario, but fatally wounded soldiers are very unlikely to have reached home, a consideration relevant to all the penetrating injuries described. Historical records, however, also document duels among the soldiers fought with swords and pistols, soldiers using swords in highway robberies, and prisoners shot during escape attempts (Chapter 3).

On the other hand, these injuries could have resulted from a civilian crime carried out as an isolated attack or during one of the notorious riots that took place in 18th-century London. An unattractive part of 17th and 18th century London society was the violence associated with street crime. It is possible that some of the penetrating injuries seen in skulls result from street or civilian crime and, as noted in Chapter 4, at least ten individuals were recorded as killed, four by a knife.

JOINT DISEASE

Joint disease refers to degenerative conditions of the joints and was the second most prevalent pathology encountered, affecting a total of 29.8% (155/519) of adults of both sexes. Osteoarthritis was the most common degenerative condition affecting the joints of the Savoy Chapel population followed by ankyloses secondary to joint disease, gout and rheumatoid arthritis.

OSTEOARTHRITIS

Osteoarthritis (OA) affects the fully movable joints of all major articular surfaces of the body (the diarthrodial joints of the skeleton) by producing an alteration of the normal joint anatomy. In weight-bearing joints, further bone-to-bone contact and friction leads to eburnation (from the Latin 'ebur', ivory), which manifests as polished and sclerotic bone (Bullough 2010). It has been suggested that the presence of eburnation is the only pathognomonic indication of osteoarthritis in human skeletal remains (Jurmain 1999) but in its absence, two other features such as marginal osteophytes and changes in the normal contour shape of the joint or pitting should also be present (Rogers & Waldron 1995). Osteoarthritic symptoms can change from one joint to another depending on the degree of joint mobility and can manifest by complaints of pain, stiffness, abnormal swelling and loss of motion. However, the lack of correlation between symptoms of OA and radiographic features is also widely recognised in the clinical literature.

On the basis of Jurmain's diagnosis of OA, the presence of eburnation was found affecting the joints of 35 individuals, 7.0% of the males (23/325), 7.6% of the females (8/105) and 4.4% of the individuals of unknown sex (4/89). In accordance with Rogers and Waldron (1995) 23.6% of males (77/325), 32.3% of females (34/105) and 13.4% (12/89) of adults of unknown sex had at least one joint affected by osteoarthritis. Within this context, osteoarthritis secondary to trauma or any other pathology was not counted in the final prevalence rate. Only primary OA was considered.

Spinal joint disease

Osteoarthritis was observed at all vertebral levels. Within each spinal segment the vertebrae more frequently affected by OA were C4 to C7 in the neck, T9 to T12 in the thorax and L1 to L3 in the lower spine. The difference between the sexes was more marked from the mid thoracic to the lumbar spine and less pronounced on the cervical spine (Fig 5.21).

True prevalence rates of spinal joint disease (Table 5.16) suggested that 7.1% (679/9439) of all vertebrae analysed among the adult population had OA in at least one of their articular facets. Females had a higher prevalence (11.4%, 213/1860) than males (7.7%, 438/5665), which was statistically significant (χ^2=24.5187, df=1, p<0.05). These results did not reflect those obtained from

	M+M? (n/N)	F+F? (n/N)	? (n/N)	Total (n/N)
Crude prevalence	72.0% (234/325)	72.3% (76/105)	89.8% (80/89)	75.1% (390/519)
True prevalence	7.7% (438/5665)	11.4% (213/1860)	1.4% (28/1914)	7.1% (679/9439)

Table 5.16 Crude and true prevalence rates of spinal joint disease within the adult population

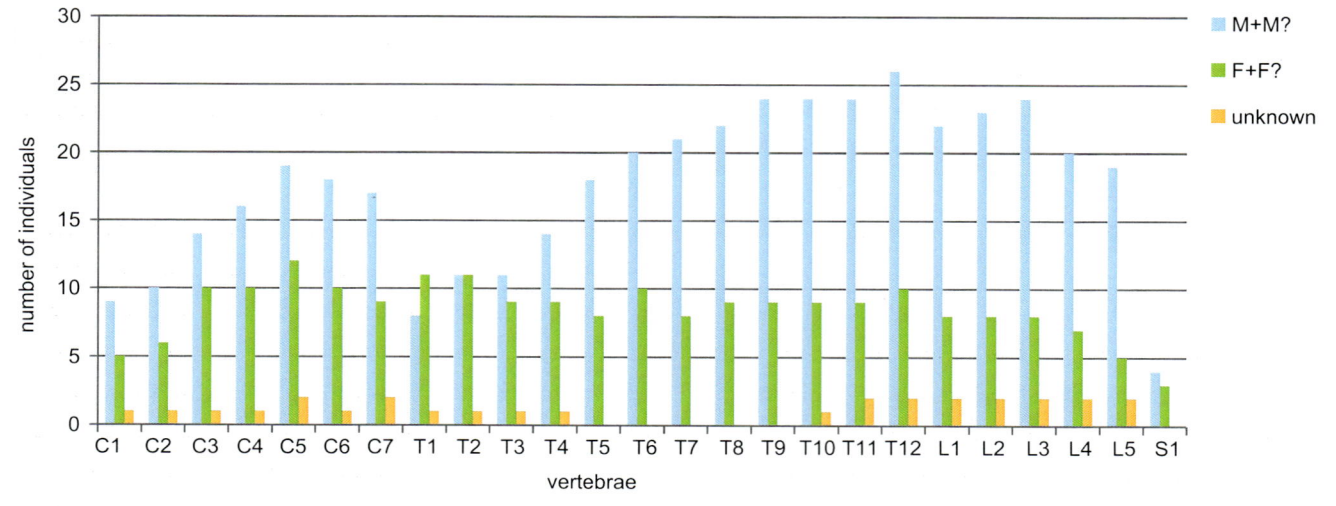

Fig 5.21 Comparison of spinal osteoarthritis among the adults from the Savoy Chapel

Schmorl's nodes, where the males were more affected than the females in all spinal regions. Although Schmorl's nodes do not always induce degenerative joint disease their presence may be related to disc degeneration (Aufderheide and Rodríguez-Martín 1998). In the case of degenerative joint disease among the females, age and hereditary variables could have played a role.

Extra-spinal joint disease

Numerous extra-spinal joints were affected by OA, with differences in their location, prevalence and distribution, but for the convenience of their analysis they were pooled according to distinctive areas within the body. For instance, the temporomandibular joint was recorded, as it represents the only movable joint of the skull. The shoulder included the glenohumeral and the acromioclavicular joints. The elbow included the tripartite joint of the humeroradial, the humeroulnar and the proximal radioulnar. The distal radioulnar joint, the carpal joints and the proximal carpometacarpal joints were included in the wrist and the hand included the metacarpophalangeal and interphalangeal joints. In the thorax were the proximal sternoclavicular joint, the costosternal and the costovertebral joints and the coxofemoral, the iliosacral and the pubic symphysis joints in the hip. The knee joint included the femorotibial and the femoropatellar joints and the distal tibiofibular joint, the tarsal joints and the proximal tarsometatarsal joints were included in the ankle. Finally, the metatarsophalangeal joints and the interphalangeal joints were included in the feet.

Table 5.17 shows crude prevalence rates of extra-spinal joint disease in the adult population from the Savoy Chapel. Osteoarthritis affected the joints of 31.0% (161/519) adults with the highest prevalence rates being 5.9% (31/519) in the feet, followed by 4.8% (25/519) in the hip and 3.8% (20/519) in the shoulder.

The high prevalence rate of OA in the feet may have been due in part to the large number of bones and joints that are included in this area, such as all metatarsophalangeal joints and all the interphalangeal joints. The 1st metatarsophalangeal joint was the most severely affected joint of the foot with 24 out of 31 individuals affected in this location, eight of them on the left side, five on them on the right and 11 bilaterally. At a population level, this represented 4.6% (24/519) of all adults studied.

True prevalence rates of extra-spinal joint disease suggested that 2.4% (161/6523) of all joints analysed among the adult population had OA in at least one of their articular facets (Table 5.18). It was seen in 10% (31/307) of all adult joints in the feet making this the most commonly affected area. Interestingly, the highest prevalence of osteoarthritis among the Royal Navy sailors from the Royal Hospital Greenwich was also

Extra-spinal joint disease	M+M? (n/N)	F+F? (n/N)	? (n/N)	Total (n/N)
Temporo-mandibular	0.3% (1/325)	1.9% (2/105)	- (0/89)	0.5% (3/519)
Shoulder	4.6% (15/325)	3.8% (4/105)	1.1% (1/89)	3.8% (20/519)
Elbow	0.6% (2/325)	3.8% (4/105)	- (0/89)	1.1% (6/519)
Wrist	3.0% (10/325)	3.8% (4/105)	1.1% (1/89)	2.8% (15/519)
Hand	1.5% (5/325)	0.9% (1/105)	- (0/89)	1.1% (6/519)
Thorax	4.3% (14/325)	5.7% (6/105)	1.1% (1/89)	4.0% (21/519)
Hip	4.9% (16/325)	6.6% (7/105)	2.2% (2/89)	4.8% (25/519)
Knee	1.8% (6/325)	7.6% (8/105)	4.4% (4/89)	3.4% (18/519)
Ankle	2.7% (9/325)	0.9% (1/105)	6.7% (6/89)	3.0% (16/519)
Feet	5.5% (18/325)	6.6% (7/105)	6.7% (6/89)	5.9% (31/519)
Total	**29.5% (96/325)**	**41.9% (44/105)**	**23.5% (21/89)**	**31.0% (161/519)**

Table 5.17 Crude prevalence rates of extra-spinal joint disease within the adult population

Extra-spinal joint disease	M+M? (n/N)	F+F? (n/N)	? (n/N)	Total (n/N)
Temporo-mandibular	0.2% (1/356)	1.4% (2/138)	- (0/148)	0.4% (3/642)
Shoulder	3.0% (15/497)	2.4% (4/166)	5.8% (1/17)	2.9% (20/680)
Elbow	0.3% (2/555)	2.1% (4/189)	- (0/41)	0.7% (6/785)
Wrist	1.7% (10/578)	2.3% (4/171)	3.3% (1/30)	1.9% (15/779)
Hand	2.2% (5/226)	1.4% (1/71)	- (0/18)	2.2% (6/297)
Thorax	2.4% (14/571)	3.8% (6/156)	5.0% (1/20)	2.8% (21/747)
Hip	2.7% (16/586)	4.1% (7/170)	11.1% (2/18)	3.2% (25/774)
Knee	1.2% (6/481)	5.8% (8/137)	8.1% (4/49)	2.6% (18/667)
Ankle	1.6% (9/552)	0.5% (1/172)	4.6% (6/130)	1.8% (16/854)
Feet	9.0% (18/198)	11.6% (7/60)	12.2% (6/49)	10.0% (31/307)
Total	**2.0% (96/4600)**	**3.0% (44/1430)**	**4.0% (21/520)**	**2.4% (161/6523)**

Table 5.18 True prevalence rates of extra-spinal joint disease within the adult population

found in the feet and particularly on the 1st metatarsal (Boston et al 2008). The authors explained that the custom of sailors having bare feet and the abnormal weight distribution while maintaining their balance aboard ship could have played a role.

Comparisons between the sexes suggested that females had a higher true prevalence rate (3.0%, 44/1430) than males (2.0%, 96/4600) in all extra-spinal joints studied and this proved to be statistically significant (χ^2=4.7142, df=1, p<0.05).

Modern clinical studies such as that of Rossignol et al (2005), Grotle et al (2008) and Andrianakos et al (2006) have found no consistent results in the analysis of OA according to sex in weight-bearing joints such as the hip and the knee. However, in non-weight-bearing joints such as those of the hand, females were generally more affected than males. The Savoy Chapel data did not support this premise, probably because of differences in methodological assessment of OA between clinicians but also owing to the degree of preservation and completeness of the joints of the hands available for study.

ANKYLOSIS

This section refers only to fusion between two skeletal elements as a result of joint disease and it does not take into consideration skeletal fusion following trauma or congenital disorders. Fusion between vertebrae as a result of joint degeneration occurred in the spine of two adult males, [771] and [845], aged 45+. Two poorly preserved thoracic vertebrae belonging to [771] were fused through their bodies and in [845] it was the bodies and apophyseal joints of C6 and C7.

Fusion between vertebrae also occurred as a result of bridges of osteophyte formation in three adult male skeletons. In skeleton [1077] C4 and C5 were fused through a large bridge of osteophyte and in [197] three segments were ankylosed (C7 to T1). In [1820] two non-identifiable thoracic vertebrae were fused through their bodies via the ossification of the anterior longitudinal ligament. Diffuse idiopathic skeletal hyperostosis (DISH) was rejected as a possible causative factor as this individual did not present extra-spinal manifestation of the disease.

Other forms of fusion were present in the joints of the hands and feet. In the right hand, skeleton [1622] had the mid–distal phalangeal joint of the second finger fused, probably secondary to OA or another related articular arthropathy. Ankylosis of the feet in 21 individuals is described in the trauma section above.

GOUT

Gout is an erosive arthropathy characterised by the destruction of the articular surface owing to the deposits of urate crystals associated with a metabolic imbalance of uric acid in the blood (Aufderheide and Rodríguez-Martín 1998; Roberts & Cox 2003). The aetiology of the condition is still unknown but several contributory factors have been suggested. Hereditary and genetic features seem to play a role, although dietary excesses (consumption of large quantities of meat and alcohol), which seem to be responsible for hyperuricemia, are also listed as contributory factors (Aufderheide and Rodríguez-Martín 1998). Males are more affected than the females in a 6:1 ratio (ibid). The image of middle- and upper-class, overindulgent and obese Englishmen suffering from gout is one often depicted by artists and cartoonists of the post-medieval period.

The most common location for gouty lesions is the metatarsophalangeal joint of the big toe. Lesions are characterised by scooped-out defects located near the margin of the articular surface and often involve both bones of the joint with the exposure of the underlying subchondral bone. To the sufferer, gout can cause needle-like pain in the affected joint and possibly a deformity to the joint that might limit movement.

Two possible cases of gout were found in the adult population of the Savoy Chapel. Possible female [462] exhibited lytic lesions on both 1st metatarsal bones. These were found on the articular margins, the outer cortical area of the distal articular facet of these bones, but no erosive changes were found on the proximal articular facet of the 1st phalanges. Similarly, adult male [1654], aged 45+ years, displayed scoop-like lytic lesions on the distal articular margins of both 1st metatarsals. The preserved 1st left proximal phalanx showed a similar pattern on the margins of the proximal articular facet, but with less involvement.

It could be surmised that the two individuals affected with this condition had differential access to a great diversity and quantity of foodstuffs. Indeed, burial records (see Chapter 4) show that high-ranking individuals were buried at the Savoy Chapel. The burial of Captain Farmery P Epworth, for instance, who commanded the *Nymphe*, is recorded on 25 August 1828. As summarised by Bleasdale (2016) military personnel would have consumed a relatively large amount of protein in comparison with prisoners and other working-class civilians. The differential diet of high-ranking generals and their wives could be represented in these gout cases although the underlying genetic component of gout cannot be dismissed as a possible aetiological explanation.

RHEUMATOID ARTHRITIS

Rheumatoid arthritis (RA) is another erosive arthropathy characterised by polyarticular involvement producing destruction of the joint tissue in a symmetrical fashion (Ortner 2003). It can produce painful, swollen joints that are warm and stiff when at rest and, like gout, movement might be limited by any associated joint deformity. One adult male aged 45+ [1498], displayed multiple articular as well as peri-articular destructive changes in the bones of the hands and feet compatible with RA (Fig 5.22). These erosive lesions are oval and suboval in shape, presenting fairly smooth edges and round margins. These erosions reveal the internal structure of the underlying subchondral bone of the majority

Fig 5.22 Skeleton [1498] showing palmar aspects of: a – left metacarpals; b – right metacarpals. Erosive lesions have partially destroyed the distal articular facets of the 2nd, 3rd and 5th right bones and the 2nd left

of the articular and para-articular areas of the carpal bones, the metacarpophalangeal joints and the interphalangeal joints of the hands as well as the tarsal, tarsometatarsal and metatarsophalangeal joints, with no sign of healing.

The onset age of RA may take place any time between the ages of 20 and 50 years (Aufderheide and Rodríguez-Martín 1998). On this basis it could be suggested that the condition developed not long before the death of [1498] as he was suffering from the early manifestation of the condition. Early stages of RA are apparent when the erosive lesions affect only the bones of the hands and feet (ibid). Later stages should involve the knee, shoulder, elbow, temporomandibular joint and the spine, which were not affected in [1498].

In summary, the prevalence of RA in the total adult population was 0.1% (1/519), which is 0.3% (1/325) of the adult males. It is believed that about 2% of today's adult population is affected by RA (Aufderheide and Rodríguez-Martín 1998). Comparisons with other post-medieval cemeteries from the London area revealed that exceptional cases of RA have been found and reported, such as that of a female aged ≥46 years recovered from the St Mary and St Michael's burial ground (Henderson et al 2013), an adult male recovered from the Royal Hospital Greenwich (Boston et al 2008), and two other cases reported in an adult male and adult female from St Marylebone (Miles et al 2008a).

CONGENITAL ANOMALIES

Congenital anomalies occur during embryological development and affect the normal formation of organs and tissues (Ortner 2003). As most congenital anomalies follow familial genetic linkages (Barnes 2012) the study of congenital anomalies offers potential for inheritance studies within bioarchaeological contexts as demonstrated by the analysis of metopism and spinal abnormalities (discussed in Chapter 6).

The Savoy Chapel population showed great variability in the types of congenital disease present, with 25.4% (155/609) of all skeletons having some form of congenital anomaly: 28.1% (146/519) of adults and 10.0% (9/90) of subadults. Eleven per cent (67/609) of individuals were affected by only one condition and 4.2% (26/609) by multiple anomalies: 20 individuals were affected by two developmental conditions, five by three conditions and one was affected by four. This gives support to the idea that it is not uncommon to see more than one disturbance occurring within the same developmental field. For instance, it is not unusual to find more than one type of developmental disturbance in the same vertebral column. Consequently it is easy to observe how one developmental mistake can affect another developmental field, leaving both with detrimental effects. Although none of the congenital anomalies described below was life-threatening, some would have caused various degrees of disability and could have interfered with normal daily activities.

A summary of all congenital anomalies found in the adult and subadult population is presented in Table 5.19, divided by skeletal areas.

CONGENITAL ANOMALIES OF THE SKULL

The congenital anomalies found in the skull included those observed in the cranial vault and those in the face. This group of anomalies was found only among adult individuals, with a crude prevalence of 3.2% (17/519) – 3.0% (10/325) of males and 6.6% (7/105) of females. Congenital anomalies of the skull included sutural agenesis, metopism and craniosynostosis. Sutural agenesis

Area	M+M? (n/N)	F+F? (n/N)	? (n/N)	Subadults (n/N)	Total (n/N)
Skull	3.0% (10/325)	6.6% (7/105)	- (0/89)	- (0/90)	2.7% (17/609)
Spine	22.4% (73/325)	12.3% (13/105)	2.2% (2/89)	5.5% (5/90)	15.2% (93/609)
Thorax	3.3% (11/325)	2.8% (3/105)	1.1% (1/89)	2.2% (2/90)	2.7% (17/609)
Pelvis	0.3% (1/325)	1.9% (2/105)	- (0/89)	- (0/90)	0.4% (3/609)
Upper limb	0.9% (3/325)	0.9% (1/105)	- (0/89)	1.1% (1/90)	0.8% (5/609)
Lower limb	4.6% (15/325)	2.8% (3/105)	1.1% (1/89)	1.1% (1/90)	3.2% (20/609)
Total	34.7% (113/325)	27.6% (29/105)	4.4% (4/89)	10.0% (9/90)	25.4% (155/609)

Table 5.19 Crude prevalence rates of congenital anomalies within the total population

is a failure of a suture to develop (completely or partially) between opposing cranial bones, as evidenced by 18- to 30-year-old male [1197], whose sagittal suture was entirely absent.

Metopism is the failure of the membranous parts of the two primordial frontal bones to coalesce into one. The obliteration usually begins at the end of the first year and finalises no later than the age of five or six (Mann & Hunt 2012). The retention of infantile metopic suture into adulthood was recorded in five adult males and six adult females. In one female, [1823], the obliteration was incomplete as the metopic line was present only on the anterior third portion of the frontal bone.

Craniosynostosis is a condition in which one or more sutures of a growing skull fuse prematurely, producing a cranial deformity. Scaphocephaly is one of the most common forms of craniosynostosis (ibid) occurring when the sagittal suture closes prematurely and the skull continues to grow in the transverse direction, resulting in a compensatory long-headed and narrow skull (Aufderheide and Rodríguez-Martín 1998). This anomaly was observed in one adult female and two adult males whose skulls showed a bulging on the occipital area which may have resulted from the premature closure of the sagittal suture.

CONGENITAL ANOMALIES OF THE SPINE

Of all the areas analysed the spine had the highest prevalence of congenital abnormalities, affecting 15.2% (93/609) of all skeletons with a variety of spinal disarrays: single and multiple block vertebrae, vertebral hypoplasias, scoliosis and kyphosis, cleft neural arches, cranial–caudal shifts such as sacralisation, lumbarisation and sacrococcygeal coalition. This group of anomalies affected both adults and subadult individuals. It affected 22.4% (73/325) of all males, 12.3% (13/105) of all females, 2.2% (2/89) of adults of unknown sex and 5.5% (5/90) of subadults. A summary of these can be found in Table 5.19.

Single block vertebra

This condition, in which two adjacent vertebral bodies fail to separate during embryology (Barnes 2012), was observed in two adult males. The disturbance took place in the thoracic spine of both individuals, producing a complete union of T2 and T3 in one case and of T9 and T10 in the other. Conditions such as this should not give spinal complications as the malformed block maintains the integrity with the same dimensional separation expected (ibid).

Multiple block vertebrae

This condition occurs when three or more vertebrae fail to separate (ibid). One adult male had four thoracic vertebrae (T8 to T11) fused partially though the anterior aspect of their bodies. However, the apophyseal joints and the mid posterior aspect of the vertebral bodies were normally separated from one another.

Ventral hypoplasia

Ventral hypoplasia is diagnosed when the ventral cartilaginous centres for the vertebral bodies are underdeveloped, leading to a wedge-shaped vertebral body (Barnes 2012). One adult male, [133], presented a possible case of this condition with a wedge-shaped T7 vertebra. According to Barnes (2012) ventral hypoplasias can be confused with compression fractures. Although the underlying trauma-related aetiology cannot be ruled out, the fact that this individual was affected by other congenital conditions such as sacralisation, bipartite patella and rotated teeth (discussed below) means that the spinal defect is more likely to represent a developmental anomaly. Vertebral hypoplasias can produce lower back pain and sciatica and can also lead to abnormal curvature and rotation of the spine (ibid).

Scoliosis and kyphosis

These conditions result from the underdevelopment of cartilaginous centres for the vertebral body leading to laterally wedged vertebral segment (scoliosis) and ventrally or dorsally wedged vertebral segment (kyphosis) and the consequent medial–lateral or anterior–posterior bending of the spine (Barnes 2012). Adult male [1789] suffered from mild ventral hypoplasia on his T8 to T11 vertebrae, which led to a secondary kyphosis of his spine. In addition to this, his spine suffered from segmentation disarray, so that his L1 vertebra did not develop. One adult female, [795], also showed a ventrally oriented T5 to T7, producing a mild kyphotic thoracic spine.

One adult male, [448], suffered from contralateral hypoplasia (Fig 5.23). Two vertebral segments were laterally wedged resulting in the fusion of the C4 to C5, T2 to T3 and T4 to T8 vertebrae. The vertebral bodies had fused in the posteriorly along with the laminae, which in turn caused the spine to adopt an 'S' shape, accompanied by severe, convex scoliosis.

Lateral hypoplasia causes the apophyseal joints to go missing and the laminae to coalesce into a bony mass known as post-lateral bar (ibid). Developing ribs associated with lateral hypoplasia fuse together and do not always form a costovertebral joint. Unfortunately, the ribs in skeleton [448] were too fragmented to be able to reconstruct the deformed rib cage or to observe possible evidence of pulmonary disease. Finally, an example combining lateral and dorsal hypoplasia (kyphoscoliosis) was observed in adult female [1817], who also exhibited contralateral hypoplasia, in which three vertebral segments were affected on both sides of her thoracic and lumbar spine. Lateral wedge-shaped vertebrae (kyphosis) were present in her thoracic spine (T4–T5 and T7–T9 vertebrae) and dorsal hypoplasia (scoliosis) was noted in the lumbar spine (L1–L5 lumbar). In addition to this severe segmentary problem, the right transverse process of the atlas of this individual was incomplete, causing an open transverse foramen.

Cleft neural arches

Cleft neural arches are commonly diagnosed during routine radiological examination (Aufderheide and Rodríguez-Martín 1998), and examples in the Savoy Chapel population ranged from slight bifurcation of the laminae and spinous process to cleft laminae with or without involvement of the spinous process. The sacrum was most commonly affected by cleft neural arches. Also known as 'spina bifida occulta', this condition could be recorded only as possible in five skeletons (one subadult and four adult male) because of poor preservation, but was recorded as present in two subadults, three adult females, 17 males and one adult of undetermined sex. In these cases it is not known how the neural structures might have been affected or if they protruded through the defect.

Cranial–caudal shifts

These conditions, which should not cause any adverse complications, manifest during the segmentation of the spine and result in vertebral disarrangement that can either produce supernumerary vertebrae or shift vertebral segments to take unusual characteristics. The most common spinal disarrangement was observed in 13 individuals, where six lumbar vertebrae were found in 11 adult males, [341], [623],

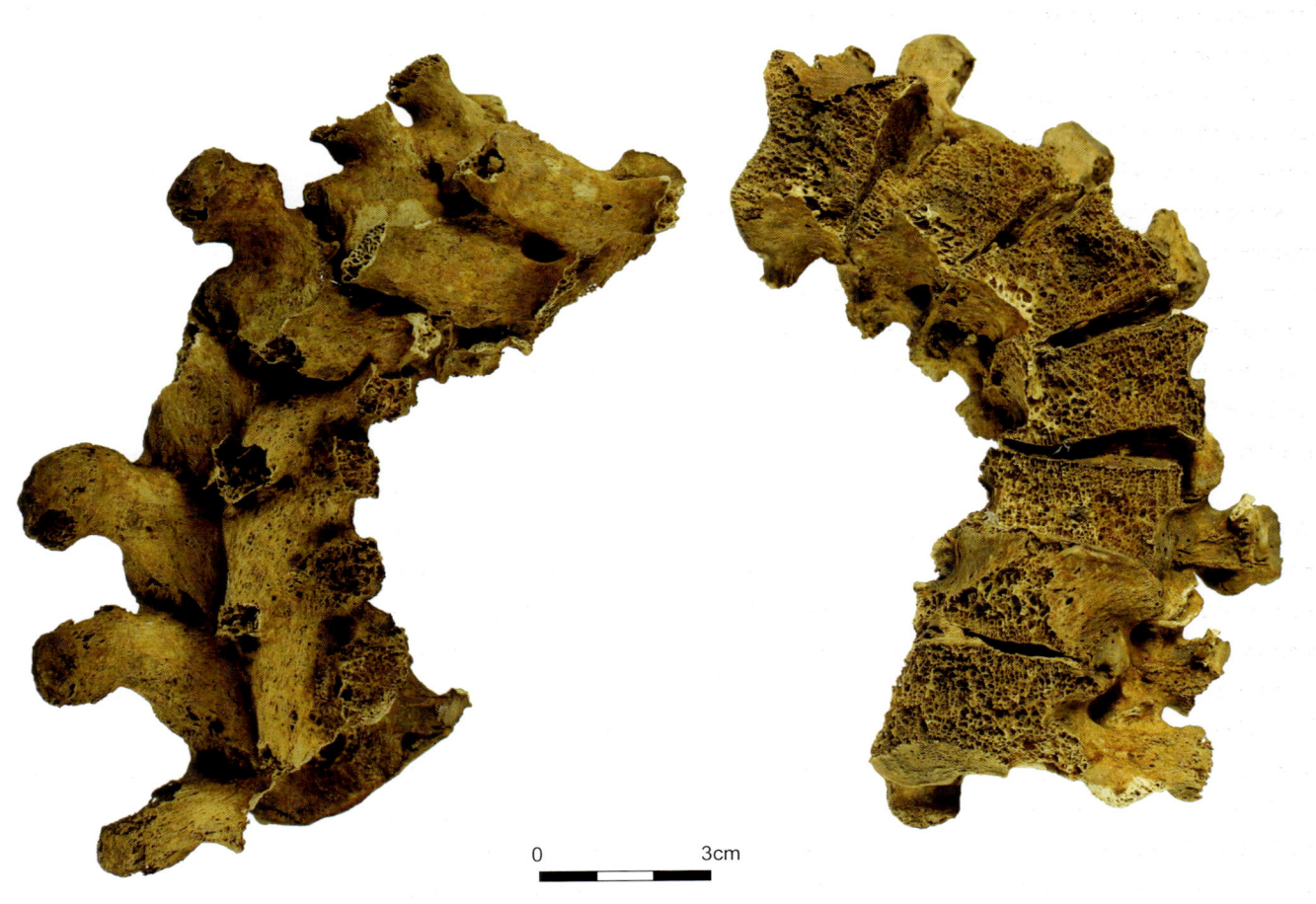

Fig 5.23 Skeleton [448] showing medial–lateral bending (scoliosis) of the thoracic spine (T2–T8)

[706], [719], [866], [913], [972], [1203], [1354], [1558], [1654], one adult female, [1895], and one subadult [685]. Other cranial–caudal shifts are shown in Table 5.20.

Context no	Cervical	Thoracic	Lumbar
[745], [1823], [1898], [2018]	C1–C7	T1–T11	L1–L6
[433], [1647]	C1–C6	T1–T11	L1–L6
[1262]	C1–C7	T1–T12	L1–L4
[576]	C1–C7	T1–T13	L1–L4
[1686]	C1–C7	T1–T13	L1–L6
[1055]	C1–C6	T1–T12	L1–L5
[639]	C1–C5	T1–T11	L1–L6

Table 5.20 Different types of spinal disarrangement

A cranial shift in which the last lumbar vertebra becomes part of the sacrum is called sacralisation and this was seen in ten adult males and two adult females. The condition ranged from complete to incomplete unilateral expressions depending on the degree of transformation of the pedicles and transverse processes into sacral alae. It was incomplete in three, complete in six and difficult to confirm owing to the degree of preservation in another three individuals. Like vertebral hypoplasias, incomplete unilateral expressions of sacralisation can also cause lower back pain (Barnes 2012).

A caudal shift in which the first sacral segment takes on lumbar characteristics is lumbarisation and was found in nine adult males and two adult females. The condition can be complete or incomplete depending on the degree of shifting and degree of transformation from sacral alae into transverse processes. It was incomplete in six, complete in two and unconfirmed in three, owing to the degree of preservation. Other examples of caudal shifts in which the first caudal segment of the coccyx unites with the sacrum were present in seven adult males. The first segment of the coccyx was partially fused to the sacrum in one individual but it was complete in the remaining examples.

CONGENITAL ANOMALIES OF THE THORAX

These were represented by variations in the ribs and the sternum. Rib anomalies generally arise from irregular segmentation of the sternum but can be associated with the rudimentary buds of the vertebrae (Scheuer & Black 2000). They have been reported as either symptomatic or asymptomatic. When symptomatic, patients complained of chest wall mass according to Kaneko et al (2012). When asymptomatic, they have been found in conjunction with other anomalies and syndromes affecting organs such as the heart and kidney that, like the ribs, are mesodermal in origin (Wattanasirichaigoon et al 2003). In the Savoy Chapel population, anomalous ribs were represented by cervical and lumbar ribs, bifurcated ribs, flared ribs and merged ribs.

The congenital abnormalities found in the sternum included a sternal aperture, pectus excavatum and cleft xiphoid process. This group of anomalies was present among adult and subadult individuals with a crude prevalence of 2.7% (17/609). It affected 3.3% (11/325) of adult males, 2.8% (3/105) of adult females, 1.1% (1/89) of adults of unknown sex and 2.2% (2/90) of subadults. A summary can be found in Table 5.19.

Cervical and lumbar ribs

These rudimentary ribs appear as a result of a cervical–thoracic or thoracic–lumbar shifting – in other words, when C7 or L1 create a rib or rib-like extension (Barnes 2012). One adult female had one rib articulating on the left costal facet of C7. Two other individuals, a subadult and an adult male, had six lumbar vertebrae and the 1st presented articular facets for a rib on either side.

Bifurcated ribs

Bifurcated ribs are identified by their single head and a body that divides at the sternal end, adopting a fork-like appearance. According to Mann and Hunt (2012) and Barnes (2012) this anomaly usually affects the ribs located on the superior portion of the thorax, between the 3rd and 5th ribs. In the Savoy, two adults and one subadult displayed four examples of bifurcated ribs with bilateral involvement. In each case, unfortunately, owing to poor preservation and a high degree of fragmentation it was impossible to identify which rib was affected.

Flared ribs

These ribs are characterised by a wider but flattened sternal end compared to the body (Barnes 2012). Examples of these were found in one male in two left-side ribs and one female in a right-side rib.

Merged ribs

Merged ribs, also called bifid or bicipital ribs, result from the fusion of two ribs, usually the 1st and the 2nd (Mann & Hunt 2012). Two adult males, including [208] (Fig 5.24), exhibited this condition on the 1st–2nd right-side ribs and one adult of unknown sex showed it in the 1st–2nd left-side rib.

CHAPTER 5 THE HUMAN REMAINS

superior view

dorsal view

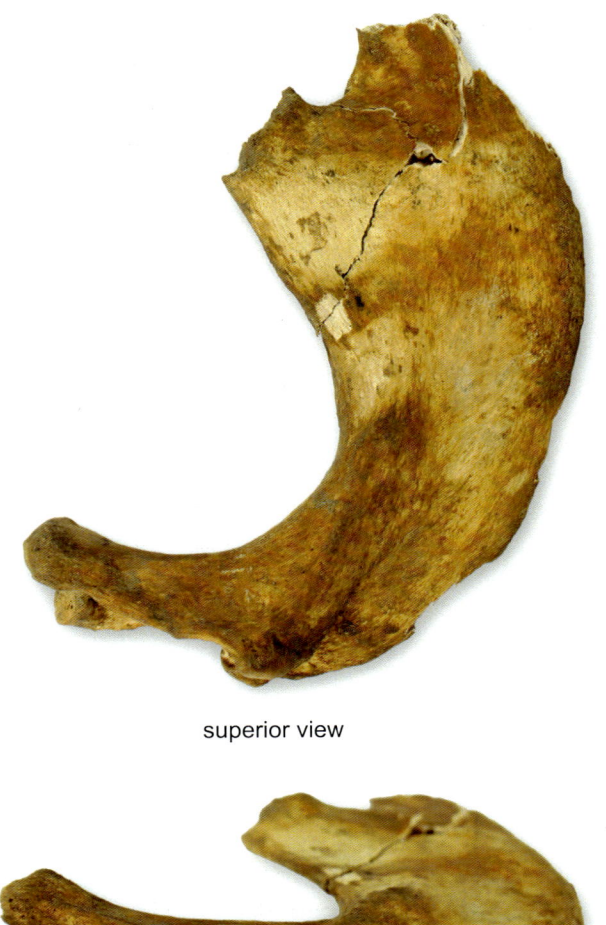

0   5cm

Fig 5.24 Skeleton [208] showing superior and dorsal views of merged 1st and 2nd right ribs

Sternal aperture

With regard to the congenital anomalies of the sternum, the sternal aperture (also called sternal foramen) is a defect that results from a failure of the sternal segments to fuse. Fusion of the sternum begins cranially and progresses caudally ossifying separately from the left and right centres (Mann & Hunt 2012). However, failure to complete the fusion of the lower two or three sternal segments of the sternum results in an oval or circular defect on the sternal body (Barnes 2012). Two adult males exhibited this condition in the distal end of their sterna.

Another congenital condition of the sternum believed to go unnoticed in palaeopathology (ibid) is pectus excavatum (also called funnel chest). The sternum itself is not affected but the direction of its growth is – in other words, the lower portion of the sternum is characterised by an abnormal inward direction. This condition, found in two adult males and one adult female, is known for producing breathing difficulties and the displacement of the underlying organs such as the heart (ibid). Finally, one adult male had a cleft xiphoid process of the sternum, which occurs when the caudal ends of the sternal segments delay in meeting at the midline (ibid).

CONGENITAL ANOMALIES OF THE PELVIC GIRDLE

These were represented by congenital dislocation of the hip and sacroiliac coalition. This group of anomalies was found among adult individuals with a crude prevalence of 0.4% (3/609), affecting one male 0.3% (1/325) and two females 1.9% (2/105). A summary can be found in Table 5.19.

Congenital dislocation of the hip

One female aged 45+ years of age, [1667], presented skeletal changes consistent with congenital dislocation of the left hip (Fig 5.25). The left femoral head appears to have articulated with the lateral margin of a false acetabulum, which was displaced laterally. The acetabulum presented a shallow depression and the femoral head a mushroom shape. As a result both the acetabulum and the femoral head exhibited areas of pitting, marginal osteophytes and eburnation suggestive of secondary long-standing degenerative joint disease of the left hip joint.

Hip dislocation can be very debilitating. Within the spectrum of developmental dysplasia of the hip, this individual suffered from subluxation (Mitchell & Redfern 2011), which occurs in a dysplastic acetabulum where the femoral head is displaced laterally, articulating only with the lateral margin of the acetabulum.

Sacroiliac coalition

This condition, which causes no dysfunction, results from the failure of the sacroiliac joint to separate during bone formation (Barnes 2012). Contrary to fusion that results from degenerative changes, sacroiliac coalition gives a smooth and uninterrupted fusion that can occur unilaterally or bilaterally. The union of the sacrum with the ilium was observed in one male and one female and was unilateral in both examples, affecting the left sacroiliac joints.

CONGENITAL ANOMALIES OF THE UPPER LIMBS

Congenital anomalies of the upper limbs were represented by variations in the ulna, carpal bones and phalanges and included congenital aplasia of the styloid process, examples of hamates with no hamulus and symphalangism. Despite the

Fig 5.25 Skeleton [1667] showing an ad hoc formed acetabulum for a dislocated left femur

anomaly, this group of anomalies may not have produced a manual disability. Both adults and subadult individuals were affected, with a crude prevalence of 0.8% (5/609). Three adult males were affected (0.9%, 3/325), one adult female (0.9%, 1/105) and one subadult individual (1.1%, 1/90). A summary can be found in Table 5.19.

Congenital aplasia of the styloid process
This is the failure of the styloid process of the ulna to develop and was observed in the right ulna of one adult male.

Hamate with no hamulus
In the hand, the hamate with no hamulus is a condition that results from a failure of the ossification centre for the hamulus to unite with the hamate during morphogenesis (Barnes 2012). This condition was seen in one adult female and one subadult, unilaterally affecting the right hamate of both individuals.

Symphalangism
The hands of two adult males exhibited examples of symphalangism, the failure of segmentation of the interphalangeal joint within one digit of the fingers (Aufderheide and Rodríguez-Martín 1998). Although this condition can be confused with union of bones secondary to trauma, in the following examples radiography suggested that this was not the case. The 5th and 4th digits followed by the 3rd and 2nd are the most prevalently affected and in both cases from the Savoy the condition was recorded in the 2nd digit. In one example, the condition was unilateral on the right hand and union was complete on the distal symphalangism. The other example, [679], was unilateral on the left hand (Fig 5.26). The union was complete in the proximal symphalangism but incomplete on the distal symphalangism as the distal interphalangeal joint was united on the dorsal aspect and non-united on the palmar aspect of the hand.

CONGENITAL ANOMALIES OF THE LOWER LIMBS
These conditions were observed as variations in the femur, patella and tibia and included coxa valga, bipartite patella and congenital synostosis of the tibiofibular joints. In the feet, a number of bipartite and separate marginal elements were found in the tarsal bones, including the talus, calcaneus, 1st (medial)

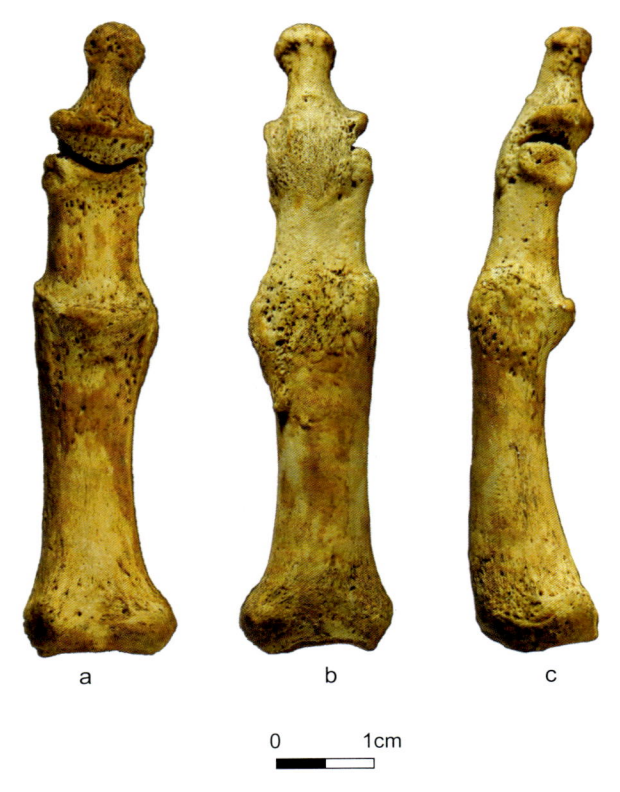

Fig 5.26 Skeleton [679] showing views of an example of symphalangism of the 2nd digit from the left hand: a – palmar; b – dorsal; c – lateral

cuneiform and the navicular. These congenital anomalies do not necessarily cause ambulatory disabilities. They result from ossification centres that fail to unite during the ontogenesis (Barnes 2012). They may later unite completely or partially, or remain separate from the parent bone connected only by fibrocartilaginous tissue.

This group of anomalies was found in adults and subadults, with a crude prevalence of 3.2% (20/609). Fifteen adult males (4.6%, 15/325) were affected, three adult females (2.8%, 3/105), one adult of unknown sex (1.1%, 1/89) and one subadult individual (1.1%, 1/90). A summary can be found in Table 5.19.

Coxa valga

This condition takes place when the femoral neck of the femur grows straight and upwards causing the femoral head to be located high above the greater trochanter and a subsequent greater angle of the femoral neck (Barnes 2012). In some cases it can cause the leg to be stiff and limit abduction, which can lead to ambulatory complications (ibid). Coxa valga was observed in the right femur of one adult female, but the left femur was not present for observation.

Bipartite patella

Bipartite patella, which may result in a vastus notch, is a condition that results from the lack of ossification of one of the osseous centres that make up the patella (Barnes 2012). The condition was observed in five adult males and one subadult individual. It was bilateral in one individual, unilateral in one right and one left patella, and on the right and left of two further individuals, although in both cases the opposite bones were not present.

Tibiofibular synostosis

This anomaly, which is much less common and far less complex than other skeletal synostosis like the radioulnar (Barnes 2012) was present in two individuals and while it may be asymptomatic, it can cause ankle discomfort (O'Dwyer 1991). In adult male [1369] both bones from the right leg were united at their distal third by their interosseous membrane (Fig 5.27).

In the second example, an adult of unknown sex, the separation failure occurred bilaterally at the proximal tibiofibular joint. Despite the fact that these areas were broken post-mortem, which made it difficult to confirm the diagnosis, both proximal articular joints showed increased hyperostosis that would have resulted from the conjoining of these bones in this region.

Os trigonum

The congenital non-fusion of the lateral (posterior) tubercle in the talus is called 'os trigonum' (Barnes 2012) and four adult males were found with this condition. It was bilateral in one example while in another the condition was incomplete on the left talus and normal on the right. In [1319] the left talus presented a void from which the ossicle had detached but the right talus was normal (Fig 5.28). This individual was also affected by osteochondritis dissecans, discussed below ('Circulatory disease'). In the fourth case the condition was present on the left talus but as the right talus was not present, it was impossible to see if the condition was bilateral.

Os calcaneus

Two adult males and one adult female were found with separate elements at the anterior, articular area of the sustentaculum tali of the calcaneus. The unfused ossicles are often called 'os calcaneus' or 'calcaneus secundarius' (Barnes 2012). The condition was bilateral in one male and unilateral on the left calcaneus of the second male and the female [427]. However, none of the unfused ossicles were recovered.

Fig 5.28 Skeleton [1319] showing: a – the left os trigonum detached and missing from the talus; b – the right os trigonum partially fused to the parent bone; c – a healing stage of osteochondritis dissecans on the left talus with a partially reattached loose ossicle; d – a non-healed lesion on the right talus

Fig 5.27 Skeleton [1369] showing a synostosis of the right tibia and fibula

Os navicular

Other tarsal divisions, either complete or partial, are limited to the navicular and 1st (medial) cuneiform (Barnes 2012). A condition called 'os navicular', which results from the non-fusion of the navicular tuberosity to its body, was found bilaterally in one adult possible female, [1767] (Fig 5.29). The margins of the joint in both the naviculars and the ossicles showed osteophytes and porosity indicative of osteoarthritis.

Os cuneiform

Examples of bipartite 1st cuneiform (also called 'os cuneiform') were observed in two possible males of adult age, bilaterally in one and unilaterally in the second (Fig 5.30) as the division was incomplete on the right cuneiform. In line with the results obtained by O'Dwyer (1991) with a large population study, the separation in both individuals took place in a horizontal fashion with the plantar segment being larger than the dorsal.

Os vesalianum

With regard to digital anomalies, an example of 'os vesalianum' was found unilaterally at the base of the right 5th metatarsal of an adult male. This ossicle develops as a separate ossification at the base of the 5th metatarsal tubercle and can remain separate or unite completely or partially with the base (Barnes 2012). The ossicle was not found but evidence of its attachment was present as pitting on the site. Nineteen individuals presented the mid–distal foot phalanx ankylosed to the distal phalanx of the foot. It was present in one of the phalanges of the left foot in five individuals, on the right foot in nine individuals, and bilaterally in five. These cases were not counted in the overall prevalence because it is impossible to know if the fusion resulted from symphalangism or after trauma.

CHAPTER 5 THE HUMAN REMAINS

Fig 5.29 Skeleton [1767] showing bilateral os navicular

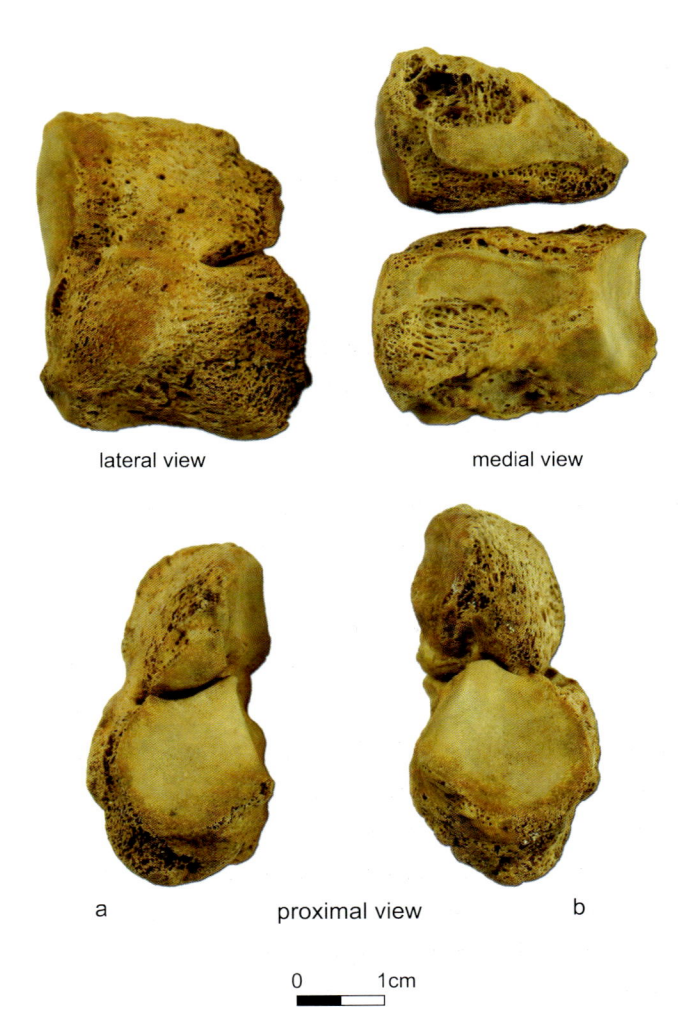

Fig 5.30 Skeleton [1178] showing division of the os cuneiform: a – incomplete; b – complete

INFECTIOUS DISEASES

This group of disorders results from the invasion into the body of agents such as bacteria, viruses, fungi or parasites, producing an inflammatory response in the bone (Aufderheide and Rodríguez-Martín 1998; Ortner 2003).

Before the arrival of modern treatments, infectious diseases were the major cause of mortality and the greatest threat to life (Ortner 2003). At the Savoy, the spread of some infectious conditions would have been exacerbated by the poor, overcrowded and generally squalid conditions known to have existed in the barracks and prison.

Conditions such as syphilis and tuberculosis (or consumption) became significant problems in post-medieval Britain, representing the major causes of death (Roberts & Cox 2003). On the other hand, non-specific infections such as periostitis, which reflect localised infection, are unlikely to produce debilitating or crippling symptoms. The infectious diseases found in the Savoy Chapel population were both non-specific, including periostitis and osteomyelitis, and specific, including tuberculosis and syphilis. The evidence suggests that 25.2% (154/609) of all skeletons analysed had suffered from one or more of the infectious diseases listed above.

Those who suffered from infectious diseases were individuals with sub-acute and chronic conditions that may not necessarily represent the immediate cause of death but the indirect effect of the disease. Sub-acute and chronic infections such as osteomyelitis, syphilis and tuberculosis indicate a high resistance to the organism and, as suggested by the osteological paradox concept (Wood et al

1992), those buried at the Savoy may represent individuals who survived such conditions rather than those that perished.

No cases of leprosy were found at the Savoy Chapel but the Bills of Mortality (Roberts & Cox 2003) recorded only one death owing to this type of infection in post-medieval London and, of course, the Savoy Hospital statutes barred the admittance of lepers (Somerville 1960, 30).

NON-SPECIFIC INFECTION

This type of infection results from various non-specific bacteria and can be produced by several agents such as trauma, circulatory disorders and neoplastic disease (Ortner 2003). Examples of non-specific infection at the Savoy included periostitis in the bones of the limbs, shoulder and pelvic girdles, axial skeleton, as well as rib lesions, maxillary sinusitis, skin ulcers, mastoiditis, endocranial lesions and osteomyelitis. Only periosteal lesions resulting from non-specific infection are discussed in this section and those associated with specific infections are addressed in the following section.

The crude prevalence calculation showed that 23.4% (143/609) of all individuals from the Savoy Chapel suffered from some form of non-specific infection, with males presenting a slightly higher prevalence of infected bones (27.6%, 90/325) compared with the females (22.8%, 24/105), although this was not statistically significant (χ^2=0.9523, df=1, p>0.05). Of adults of unknown sex 16.8% (15/89) were affected compared to 15.5% (14/90) of subadult individuals. As discussed below, the bones of the limbs, shoulder and pelvic girdles, and axial skeleton were most affected by periostitis (15.7%, 96/609) followed by the ribs (5.5%, 34/609).

Periostitis

Periostitis is an inflammation of the periosteum (the outer layer of the bone) manifesting as longitudinal striation and pitting secondary to hypervascularity, producing an irregular bone surface of various degrees of thickness (Roberts & Manchester 2005). In the Savoy population periostitis was recorded in the axial bones, the shoulder and pelvic girdle and the upper and lower limbs, affecting 15.7% (96/609) of all individuals (Table 5.21). Men were more affected than females but no more affected than children.

The tibia, then the femur and the fibula were the bones most commonly affected by periostitis. As the skin surrounding the tibia is thin the bone is close to the surface, making it prone to minor injuries and exposed to invasive agents (Roberts & Manchester 2005). At the Savoy Chapel, this affected 4.7% (29/609) of all individuals.

Rib lesions

An inflammatory response to specific infectious diseases such as tuberculosis or to non-specific infection as seen in certain pulmonary diseases such as bronchitis or pneumonia can lead to the formation of periosteal new bone on the visceral aspect of the ribs (Ortner 2003; Roberts & Manchester 2005). Other rib lesions, also seen as periosteal reactions on the visceral aspect of the ribs, appear secondary to infection of the pleura (membrane that covers the lungs). These can present as porous woven bone (representing an active reaction), as seen in [652] (Fig 5.31), which is sometimes incorporated into the underlying cortex as lamellar bone (representing a stage of healing).

Only rib lesions resulting from non-specific infection are discussed in this section. Crude prevalence rates suggested that at the Savoy 5.5% (34/609) individuals showed non-specific periosteal reactions in the ribs: 7.0%

Area	Bone affected	M+M? (n/N)	F+F? (n/N)	? (n/N)	Subadults (n/N)	Total (n/N)
Axial	skull	0.6% (2/325)	0.9% (1/105)	- (0/89)	2.2% (2/90)	0.8% (5/609)
	sternum	0.3% (1/325)	- (0/105)	- (0/89)	- (0/90)	0.1% (1/609)
Shoulder girdle	scapula	0.3% (1/325)	- (0/105)	1.1% (1/89)	- (0/90)	0.3% (2/609)
	clavicle	0.3% (1/325)	0.9% (1/105)	1.1% (1/89)	- (0/90)	0.4% (3/609)
Upper limb	humerus	0.6% (2/325)	0.9% (1/105)	1.1% (1/89)	1.1% (1/90)	0.8% (5/609)
	radius	0.3% (1/325)	0.9% (1/105)	1.1% (1/89)	1.1% (1/90)	0.6% (4/609)
	ulna	0.6% (2/325)	- (0/105)	1.1% (1/89)	1.1% (1/90)	0.6% (4/609)
	metacarpals	0.3% (1/325)	- (0/105)	- (0/89)	- (0/90)	0.1% (1/609)
Pelvic girdle	os coxa	- (0/325)	0.9% (1/105)	- (0/89)	1.1% (1/90)	0.3% (2/609)
Lower limb	femur	3.3% (11/325)	0.9% (1/105)	- (0/89)	3.3% (3/90)	2.4% (15/609)
	patella	0.3% (1/325)	- (0/105)	- (0/89)	- (0/90)	0.1% (1/609)
	tibia	5.5% (18/325)	3.8% (4/105)	4.4% (4/89)	3.3% (3/90)	4.7% (29/609)
	fibula	4.0% (13/325)	0.9% (1/105)	- (0/89)	1.1% (1/90)	2.4% (15/609)
	calcaneus	0.3% (1/325)	- (0/105)	- (0/89)	- (0/90)	0.1% (1/609)
	metatarsals	1.2% (4/325)	0.9% (1/105)	3.3% (3/89)	- (0/90)	1.3% (8/609)
Total		18.5% (59/325)	11.4% (12/105)	13.4% (12/89)	14.4% (13/90)	15.7% (96/609)

Table 5.21 Crude prevalence rates of periostitis within the total population

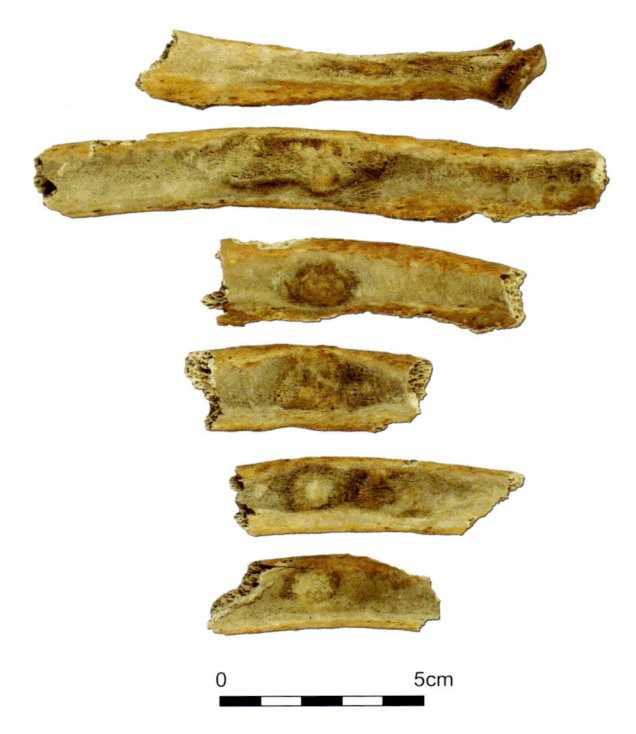

Fig 5.31 Skeleton [652] showing reactive woven bone (periostitis) on the visceral aspect of right-side ribs

(23/325) of males, 6.6% (7/105) of females and 3.3% (3/89) of adults of unknown sex. Only one subadult individual displayed periostitis of the ribs, giving 1.1% (1/90) prevalence.

It would not have been difficult to acquire any of the above-mentioned forms of pulmonary infection in the inadequately ventilated rooms of the Savoy Hospital, a situation made worse by the fact that the soldiers admitted there were entitled to supplies of tobacco and clay pipes (Gruber-von-Arni 2007a, 139; Webster 2002, 53, 298), which undoubtedly contributed to respiratory diseases and predisposed many to develop more serious conditions such as emphysema or lung cancer. The appalling overcrowding in the barracks, as explained in Chapter 3, provided similarly poor conditions and healthy recruits might soon have found themselves struggling after time spent in the barracks breathing the putrid air.

Maxillary sinusitis

The spread of bacteria from a primary source of infection such as the teeth, throat, ear, chest or even as a result of allergies, poor ventilation and air-polluted environments can lead to an infection of the underlying mucosa lining in the maxillary sinuses, which in turn can lead to periosteal new bone formation inside them (Aufderheide and Rodríguez-Martín 1998; Roberts & Manchester 2005). Sinusitis was detected in three adult skeletons with broken maxillae, allowing direct observation of the cavity that otherwise would have needed drilling for inspection. The crude prevalence of the condition was therefore 0.4% (3/609) of the total population but could have been higher for it was not possible to record when the sinuses were well preserved. Female [566], aged 30–45 years, showed new bone formation on the floor and walls of both maxillary sinuses (Fig 5.32). The right sinus in particular was inflamed and the antrum had expanded medially. A small orifice also connected with the upper right canine, probably serving as a draining cloaca. It is possible that the infection of the sinus through this oro-antral fistula (connection between the mouth and the sinus) could have developed secondarily to the dental abscess of the upper jaw.

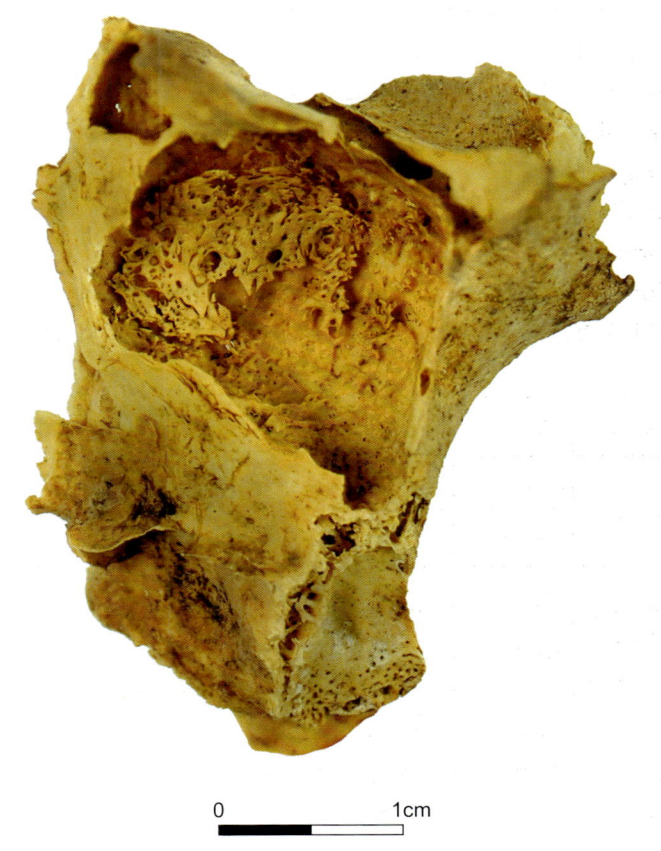

Fig 5.32 Skeleton [566] showing new bone formation on the left maxillary sinus, thought to relate to maxillary sinusitis

One 18- to 30-year-old male presented new bone formation on the floor of both maxillary sinuses. The right side was noticeably more affected than the left side, with a small draining cloaca connecting to the roots of the upper 2nd molar. In this case, and as explained above, the inflammatory reaction on the right sinus could have been produced as a response to the dental disease. The infection seems to have spread to the palatine bones, with the external surfaces showing porotic new bone formation.

Finally, a 30- to 45-year-old female exhibited lesions similar to those described above but on the left maxillary sinus only. However, as the right side was absent it was not possible to determine whether the infection was bilateral. In contrast to the examples above, there was no connection between the maxillary sinus and dental disease, supporting the idea that the inflammation could have resulted from direct environmental pollution.

Maxillary sinusitis has been linked to living in urban areas, poor air quality and indoor pollution resulting from burning fuel for warmth and cooking, which would have favoured the production and secretion of pus within the sinuses (Roberts & Manchester 2005). These environments would have been familiar to the inhabitants of the Savoy Barracks and Prison. Perhaps even the historically documented burning of pitch or brimstone in the hospital and prison could have been a contributing factor (see Chapter 3). Smoking tobacco would have been commonly practised within the hospital and may also have contributed to breathing problems in the wards. In already inadequately ventilated rooms the situation would have been particularly worse at night when windows were closed because of the popular belief that nocturnal air was harmful (Gruber-von-Arni 2007a, 139).

Skin ulcers

Skin infections that spread to the underlying tissues can often reach the bone and manifest as reactive periostitis in areas close to the surface such as the anterior aspect of the tibiae (Aufderheide and Rodríguez-martín 1998; Roberts & Manchester 2005). Trauma to the skin (direct blow or infection) is usually the main causative factor for the development of these periosteal lesions but in other cases they can result from venous stasis, a failure of the blood to flow from the veins of the legs to the heart, as seen in individuals suffering from varicose veins (Ortner 2003; Mann & Hunt 2012). In the Savoy, there were three skeletons with leg ulcers, giving a crude prevalence of 0.4% (3/609) of the total population.

The tibia of one male aged 45+ years exhibited a well-defined raised and patchy periosteal reaction of approximately 110mm in length located on the anterior diaphysis of the left tibia. The focal lesion appeared well healed as there was no sign of active woven new bone formation apart from small pitting present on the margins of the calcified area. Similarly, the left tibia of 18- to 30-year-old male [1074] presented a large focal new bone formation that extended across most of the proximal half of the diaphysis producing extensive remodelling of the bone (Fig 5.33). The local ossified periostitis appears to have been deposited gradually over time and progressively incorporated into the cortex in the form of remodelled lamellar bone. It can be hypothesised that such considerable thickening and deformity of the tibia can only have resulted from long-standing chronic skin ulceration.

Fig 5.33 Skeleton [1074] showing a large focal periosteal reaction on the left tibia, thought to relate to a skin ulcer

The final example was an 18- to 30-year-old possible male presenting a 70mm-long raised area of compact bone on the anterior aspect of the mid diaphysis of the left tibia. This raised focal lesion was covered in porous new bone, suggesting an overlying leg ulcer that was active at the time of death. Striated new bone formation was found in diaphyseal areas of the tibia, on the margins of the plaque-like lesion. Similar changes of striated bone were present directly opposite the tibia, in the mid diaphysis of the fibula.

Mastoiditis

An infection of the middle ear that bursts internally or externally into surrounding bone is called mastoiditis (Roberts & Manchester 2005). Discharge to the interior of the skull is fatal but external discharge generally means a probable recovery with consequences such as induced inflammatory changes to the middle ear bones cavity or deafness if prolonged. Only one adult female, of unknown age, displayed lesions compatible with mastoiditis, giving a crude prevalence of 0.1% (1/609). Destructive lesions were recorded on the superior surface of the petrous portion of both temporal bones, penetrating the middle ear cavity and exposing the right mastoid air cells, which allowed the communication with the internal soft-tissue structures. From the presence of similar destructive lesions with sharp margins on both superior surfaces of the sphenoid alae with a focal destructive area of coalescent foramina located on the greater wings, it can be hypothesised that the middle ear infection spread to the adjacent structures and bones including the sphenoid. On the other hand, the presence of osteolytic lesions in both greater wings with an absence of internal spiculation would favour sphenoid wing meningioma as a possible causative aetiology.

Endocranial lesions

New bone formation in endosteal areas of the skull has long been regarded as evidence for meningitis, an infection of the meninges (the membranes covering the brain and spinal cord). Their presence has also been linked with non-infectious conditions such as metabolic disorders, tumours or haemorrhage resulting from head injuries, especially because questions have been raised regarding how long a person would have to survive meningitis in order to manifest the bone lesion (Roberts & Manchester 2005).

At the Savoy Chapel, endocranial lesions were recorded in one skeleton from the general demographic population and one from the disarticulated skeletal material, thus giving a crude prevalence of 0.1% (1/609). The prevalence could, however, be higher for, as with conditions such as sinusitis where the observation of the infection depends on the presence of broken maxillae, direct observation of the endocranial areas was possible only when the skull was fragmented. Male [525], aged 18–30 years, had endocranial lesions along the sagittal suture and in scattered areas of the frontal and occipital bones (Fig 5.34). Other areas of the skeleton affected by infection were the pleural aspect of several ribs and a dental abscess between the lower central incisors. One disarticulated skull belonging to an 18- to 30-year-old male, also found with a cranial dissection (below, 5.6, 'Craniotomies'), showed scattered endocranial lesions in the frontal and parietal bones.

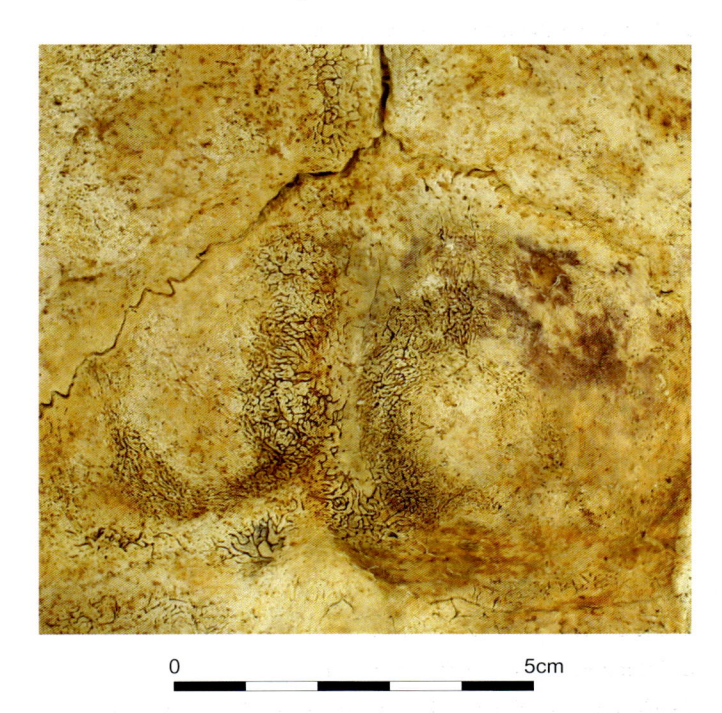

Fig 5.34 Skeleton [525] showing endocranial lesions on the occipital bone

Osteomyelitis

Osteomyelitis is an infection of the bone marrow that results from the introduction of bacteria (usually *Staphylococcus aureus*) into the marrow either by direct contact with infective blood or secondary to adjacent soft-tissue infection, open fractures or wounds (Ortner 2003). Sometimes the infection can spread to the surrounding blood vessels and lead to subsequent necrosis of a bone fragment (sequestrum). Evidence of healing is recognised as reactive new bone formation (involucrum) around the sequestrum. This can sometimes be perforated by a suppurative abscess (cloaca), which allows the pus to drain (Aufderheide and Rodríguez-Martín 1998).

Five adult individuals presented bone changes compatible with osteomyelytis, giving a crude prevalence of 0.8% (5/609). Male [751], aged 30–45 years, presented with a possible case of healed osteomyelitis on the left fibula. The bone shows severe thickening on both proximal and distal ends of the diaphysis, which is mostly formed of sclerotic new bone with little involvement of the mid diaphysis. There are two foci of bone reaction showing a worm-like track pattern on both the proximal and distal epiphyses, which could have worked as draining channels that penetrated the proximal and distal growth plate but subsequently healed. Therefore, the idea of osteomyelitis cannot be rejected.

The left os coxa of male [913], aged 45+ years, presented a round cavity of approximately 15mm diameter located on the superior–anterior margin of the acetabulum. This probably served as an open cloaca, surrounded by reactive periosteal new bone formation. The acetabulum was severely eburnated as the left femoral head had exposed the underlying subchondral bone. A compensatory bony built-up wall had formed near the anterior–superior margin of the acetabulum. The distal end of the affected femur was also affected by periostitis and the left tibia presented a localised periosteal reaction, a possible skin ulcer (as discussed above). Other bones also affected by periostitis included the shaft fragments of three right-side ribs and the pleural surfaces of two left-side ribs.

Adult female [1518] presented a rare example of osteomyelitis on the left maxillary sinus (Fig 5.35), visible as a result of its fragmentary nature. A shell of reactive new bone formation (involucrum) presenting several cloacae of different sizes was present inside the left maxillary sinus occupying most of the antrum. Pus should have drained through the opening of the maxillary sinus, which was not preserved, but also through a small maxillary abscess located above the root of the left 1st molar. This periapical infection might have been responsible for the intra-oral fistula, chronic osteomyelitis of the left maxillary sinus and possibly the ante-mortem loss of all the upper left premolars and molars.

The presence of woven new bone formation on the left side of the palatine process indicated that the reaction was active, but the extent of the infection could not be assessed because of poor preservation. Reactive periosteal formation was also recorded over the diaphyseal areas of both fibulae and the right tibia.

An adult possible female had osteomyelitis in the left fibula recorded as a cloacal orifice of 2mm diameter on the medial aspect of the diaphysis, on a raised area formed of reactive new bone formation. Finally, a 30- to 45-year-old male had osteomyelitis on the left ulna. An orifice of 5mm diameter was present on the anterior aspect of the distal third of the diaphysis and a second smaller one on the posterior aspect of the distal third. These two cloacae, with smooth edges, were surrounded by reactive new bone formation, making this part of the bone appear thickened.

SPECIFIC INFECTION

Specific infection refers to infectious diseases such as leprosy, tuberculosis and treponemal disease for which the specific organism responsible for causing the infection is known (Roberts & Manchester 2005). This type of infection has diffuse boundaries and covers large areas of the skeleton (Ortner 2003). At the Savoy Chapel specific infections included tuberculosis and syphilis and crude prevalence calculations show that they affected 1.8% (11/609) of all individuals: (1.8%, 6/325) males, (2.8%, 3/105) females and (2.2%, 2/90) subadults.

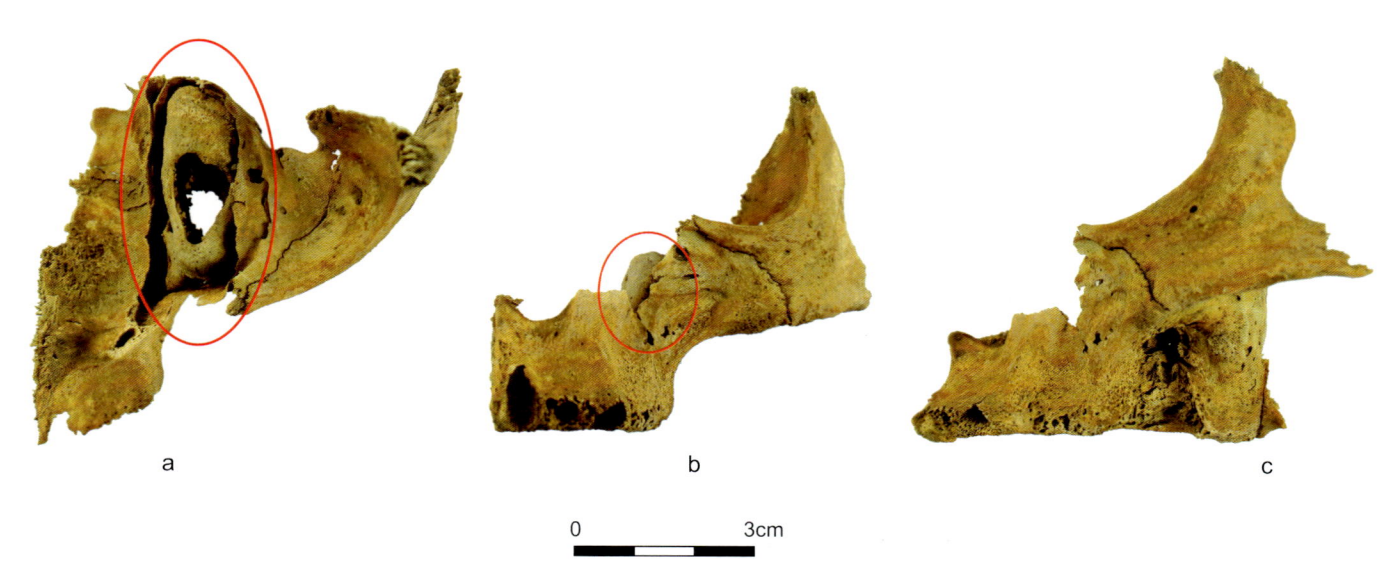

Fig 5.35 Skeleton [1518] showing views of the left maxillary sinus: a – superior; b – anterior; c – lateral; a and b show the involucrum (circled) and cloaca; c shows the maxillary periapical abscess

Tuberculosis

Tuberculosis (TB), also called Pott's disease, is an acute or chronic infection caused either by *Mycobacterium tuberculosis*, in which the infection is transmitted from human to human through respiratory fluids, such as cough, sneeze or spit, leading to a primary focus in the lung, or by *M bovis*, where the infection is transmitted through contaminated dairy product making the intestinal pathway the primary focus (Aufderheide and Rodríguez-Martín 1998; Ortner 2003). Five adults from the Savoy Chapel population showed skeletal lesions compatible with TB, giving a crude prevalence of 0.8% (5/609). These included lytic lesions, local destruction and cavitations with very little bone reaction and were most common in the spine followed by the pelvis. Long bones were also affected by TB, displaying destruction of the metaphyseal or epiphyseal plates.

One skeleton showing clear skeletal changes consistent with TB was that of 18- to 30-year-old female [116]. The spine was bent in on itself as a result of the destruction and collapse of the vertebral bodies of T8 to L3 and although the spinous processes of these vertebrae were present they were not affected. An abscess was observed on what was left of the body of the ankylosed L2, with a very deformed and compressed L3 body. This very pronounced secondary kyphosis of the spine would have certainly posed a neurologic compromise to the spinal cord. Indeed, the upper and lower limbs of this individual as well as the bones of the hands and feet appeared to be very petite and slender. In line with these observations, the ribs corresponding to the affected area of the spine were contorted and deformed.

Male [1052], aged 18–30 years, showed abnormal cavitations and destruction of two adjacent vertebrae, T11 and T12. Both vertebrae exhibited destructive lytic lesions that produced almost total destruction of their bodies, causing T11 to collapse over T12. As less than 25% of the skeleton was present it was not possible to carry out further observation of infectious manifestations with the exception of the right ulna, which was affected by a long-standing infection in its upper third diaphysis.

The vertebral column of 18- to 30-year-old female [1360] had collapsed almost entirely from T1 to T11 (Fig 5.36). These vertebrae were fused together, forming one undifferentiated block. The T10 was wedge-shaped and had been displaced slightly posteriorly by the adjacent collapsed vertebrae. Secondary kyphosis resulted from the sharp and

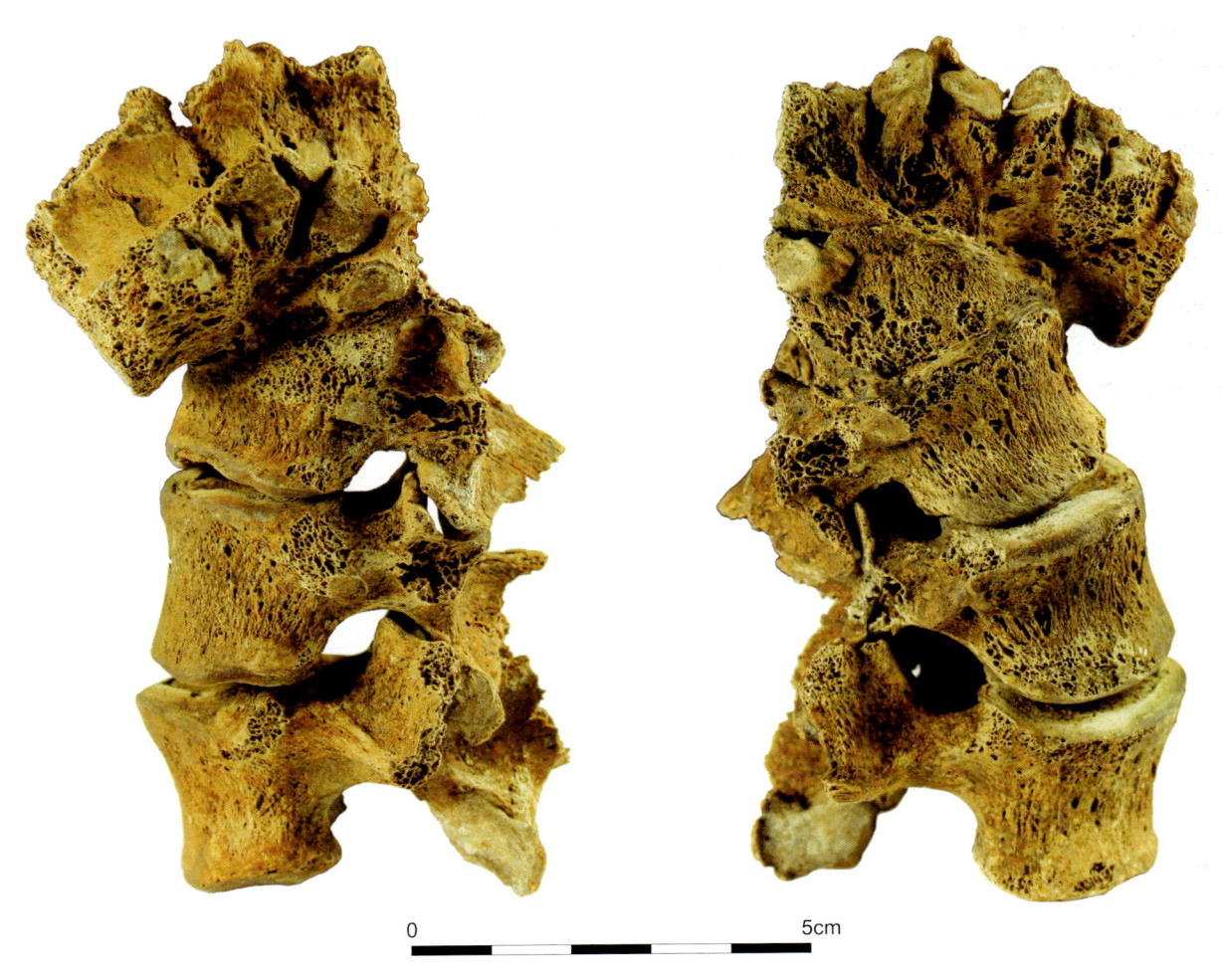

Fig 5.36 Skeleton [1360] showing the lateral views of T1–L1 and the collapse of T1–T11 owing to the destruction of their vertebral bodies. Note the wedge-shape of T10

severe angulation of the thoracic spine but the extent of the neurological complications that may have followed owing to the compromise of the spinal cord is unknown.

Although the surviving bones from the left upper and lower limbs did not show signs of infection the incompleteness of the skeleton hindered examination of any other extra-spinal manifestations of TB. The last abnormality was the ankylosed left iliosacral joint but it is not known if this was a congenital condition or a compensatory response to the kyphosis.

Skeleton [208] was an adult male of unknown age, largely incomplete because of severe truncation. The elements present included the skull, a section of the spine (C7–T9), several fragments of sided and unsided ribs, the sternum, left clavicle, scapula and humerus. The base of the skull exhibited a combination of lytic and blastic lesions on the sphenoid. Lytic lesions were also observed on the wall of the sphenoidal sinus (smooth and remodelled orifice) and on the wall of the medial pterygoid plate (irregular and aggressive orifice). An irregular osteoblastic lesion adjacent to these but located posteriorly was present in the form of spicules of compact bone at the sphenoid–occipital junction. Both lytic and blastic lesions on the sphenoid sinus and pterygoid plate did not appear to be of primary pathogenesis, but secondary to an adjacent chronically progressive inflammatory and infective lesion that emerged from the surrounding soft tissues of the posterior nasopharynx.

A series of endoscopic images were taken of the internal walls of the sphenoid sinus at Bradford Royal Infirmary (West Yorkshire) thanks to Keith Manchester (Biological Anthropology Research Centre, University of Bradford) and Chris Raine, Consultant ENT surgeon (Bradford Royal Infirmary). Their observation revealed a normal appearance, which gives support to the idea that the primary pathogenesis was not in the sphenoid sinus but secondary to nasopharyngeal tuberculous granulomatous lesion. Nasopharyngeal TB is rare today but was significantly higher in post-medieval London (Ponce & Manchester 2015) and can be confused with nasopharyngeal carcinoma (Prasad et al 2008) and acute pyogenic nasopharyngeal abscess. The lesions in skeleton [208] were not compatible with either of these diagnoses.

Finally, in addition to nasopharyngeal TB, skeleton [208] exhibited the right nasal turbinate displaced to the left side along with the vomer that presented a 'dome-like' blastic lesion in the right side located inferior-posteriorly. The lateral deviation of the nasal septum could have resulted from a progressive and expansile polypoidal lesion of idiopathic aetiology arising from the nasal mucosa.

An 8- to 12-year-old child, [955], presented destruction of the left elbow and left hip joints. The distal end of the left humerus was absent but the left ulna showed lytic lesions and necrotic destruction of the olecranon and coronoid process, which exposed some of the underlying subchondral bone, and a new joint surface had been formed as a result. The elbow is the joint most frequently affected by TB in the upper extremity and the majority of the lesions start between 1 and 20 years of age (Ortner 2003), supporting the finding for this young individual. Tuberculosis of the hip joint is the second most frequent skeletal lesion after tuberculous spondylitis and most cases start in childhood (ibid). The left coxofemoral joint of [955] was destroyed and ankylosed so it is plausible that initial destruction was followed by a stage of healing through disorganised, porous new bone formation leading to the fusion of the left hip joint. On the other hand, ankylosis secondary to trauma and localised non-specific infection cannot be ruled out. With regard to the spinal abnormalities, these may only account for 25–60% of all cases of skeletal TB (Roberts & Manchester 2005), but unfortunately in [955] the spine was too fragmentary and incomplete for observation.

Two individuals from this group were analysed using carbon and nitrogen stable isotope analysis. The individuals sampled with TB so far ([116] and [1360]) show no trend in their isotope values, with one elevated and the other depleted in nitrogen (see Fig 5.4). Expansion of the isotopic analysis of TB victims could be used to investigate the likelihood that nitrogen enrichment is attributed to prolonged illness or whether it is more reflective of the low protein diet of the London poor (Fuller et al 2005).

Comparisons of TB with other post-medieval sites from the London area (Table 5.22) revealed that the Savoy population was below the midpoint of the 0.4% to 2.8% range reported.

London-area cemeteries	Prevalence (n/N)
London Hospital	0.4% (3/636)
St Pancras burial ground	0.5% (4/715)
St Mary and St Michael's burial ground	0.7% (5/705)
Sheen's burial ground	0.7% (2/254)
City Bunhill burial ground	0.8% (2/239)
Queen's Chapel Savoy	**0.8% (5/609)**
New Bunhill Fields Burial ground	0.9% (5/514)
All Saints, Chelsea Old Church	1.1% (2/198)
St Benet Sherehog	1.3% (3/230)
St Marylebone Church burial ground	1.3% (4/301)
Bow Baptist Church	1.9% (8/416)
Royal Hospital Greenwich	2.8% (3/107)

Table 5.22 Comparison of tuberculosis in cemeteries from the London area (all adult and subadult individuals are pooled; for references see above, 5.1)

Tuberculosis infection at the Savoy Barracks would easily have been passed through droplet transmission. Historical records (Chapter 3) detail the issues of overcrowding and how this might have posed a threat to the wellbeing and health of the inhabitants. At the prison, the situation would have been equally poor, especially before the installation of ventilators in 1750 (Chapter 3). It is thus possible to hypothesise how these overcrowded spaces would have facilitated the spread of respiratory infections between the soldiers, prisoners, recruits and the general personnel working there. Similar conditions were experienced at the Royal Hospital Greenwich, where lack of ventilation and confined spaces were to be blamed for the spread of TB between seamen (Boston et al 2008).

Syphilis

Syphilis is an infection caused by *Treponema pallidum*. This bacterium enters the body through sexual intercourse (venereal or acquired syphilis) by direct contact with an infected person, or through the skin or mucous membrane or transplacentally in a child born from a syphilitic mother (congenital syphilis). In both cases, the organism reaches the skeleton via the bloodstream (Ortner 2003). Following a period of incubation and the manifestation of primary and secondary syphilis, tertiary syphilis is mostly characterised by progressive involvement of the skeleton. Pathognomonic signs of syphilis involve 'crater-like' lesions of the skull along with post-cranial periosteal manifestations in bone closer to the skin such as the tibia or the nasal cavity (Ortner 2003). There were six possible cases of treponemal disease within the Savoy population providing a crude prevalence of 0.9% (6/609). The condition affected both males and females and one 13- to 19-year-old.

Male [153], aged 30–45 years, showed cranial and post-cranial lesions consistent with syphilis. The skull presented the typical 'caries sicca' lesions which are diagnostic of tertiary syphilis. These lesions were all healed but permanent secondary scars remained in the frontal bones and on the parietals. In certain areas of the skull the scars had destroyed the line of the sagittal suture. Finally, at the base of the skull, the palate showed increased porosity. The surviving proximal third of the left tibia showed reactive bone formation producing the classic 'sabre' tibia in the lateral view. As the bone was fragmented it was possible to see the abnormal periosteal, cortical and endosteal thickening as well as its abnormal density in cross-section. Other bones affected included the right femur, right radius and right ulna, which all appeared affected by long-standing periostitis and the formation of heavily vascularised sclerotic bone in most diaphyseal areas. Unfortunately, the left-side bones were absent.

In 13- to 19-year-old [819] the dentition was severely affected by hypoplastic lesions. The upper and lower 1st molars were the most severely affected teeth: their crowns show enamel defects similar to the so-called 'mulberry' molars where the crowns are smaller than normal and the occlusal surfaces are pitted, poorly formed and very irregular. Other teeth affected were the upper and lower central and lateral incisors as well as both canines, which show multiple lines as well as pitting on the enamel. Other abnormal areas included the palatine bones, which showed periosteal, reactive bone formation. None of the post-cranial bones present (the vertebrae, ribs, left clavicle, humerus, radius and ulna along with the right os coxa) showed periosteal reaction or any other indication of infection. Dental enamel hypoplasia would be an alternative aetiological factor responsible for the severe dental anomalies, especially in the absence of syphilitic lesions outside those described in the teeth.

Adult male [939], of unknown age, showed skeletal changes compatible with venereal syphilis (Fig 5.37) and the different developmental stages of the lesions at the time of death indicate that the infection was still active. The parietals and occipital bones of his skull presented numerous focal and active lesions, recorded as small, isolated, destructive foramina. Other more advanced lytic lesions resulted in larger clusters that uncovered the underlying diploë with or without a sclerotic response surrounding the crater-like lytic focus. These caries sicca lesions were present throughout the skull. In the frontal bone a combination of depressed scars along with nodular sclerotic formation showed a more advanced stage of healing. In the base of the skull, the left palatine bone also presented two small clusters of perforations on the horizontal plate. In the face, the right side of the maxilla showed a depressed scar and the consequent loss of the central and lateral right incisors owing to a possible focal destructive lesion in that area. This individual also suffered from a dental abscess located on the left maxillary 1st premolar. It is not known if this resulted from his poor dental health and caries or secondarily to hematogenous spread due to the syphilis.

Post-cranial lesions included periosteal reaction with different degrees of severity in most of the surviving post-cranial bones from the upper and lower limbs, pelvis and feet. The long bones were affected bilaterally and symmetrically with periostitis. The consistent pattern of syphilitic infection included deposits of woven and striated bone combined with long-standing sclerotic plaquing in diaphyseal areas, although more pronounced on the proximal and distal epiphyses. The long-standing periosteal formation had caused both tibiae to adopt the sabre-like malformation, whereas both femora looked 'fusiform'. Syphilitic

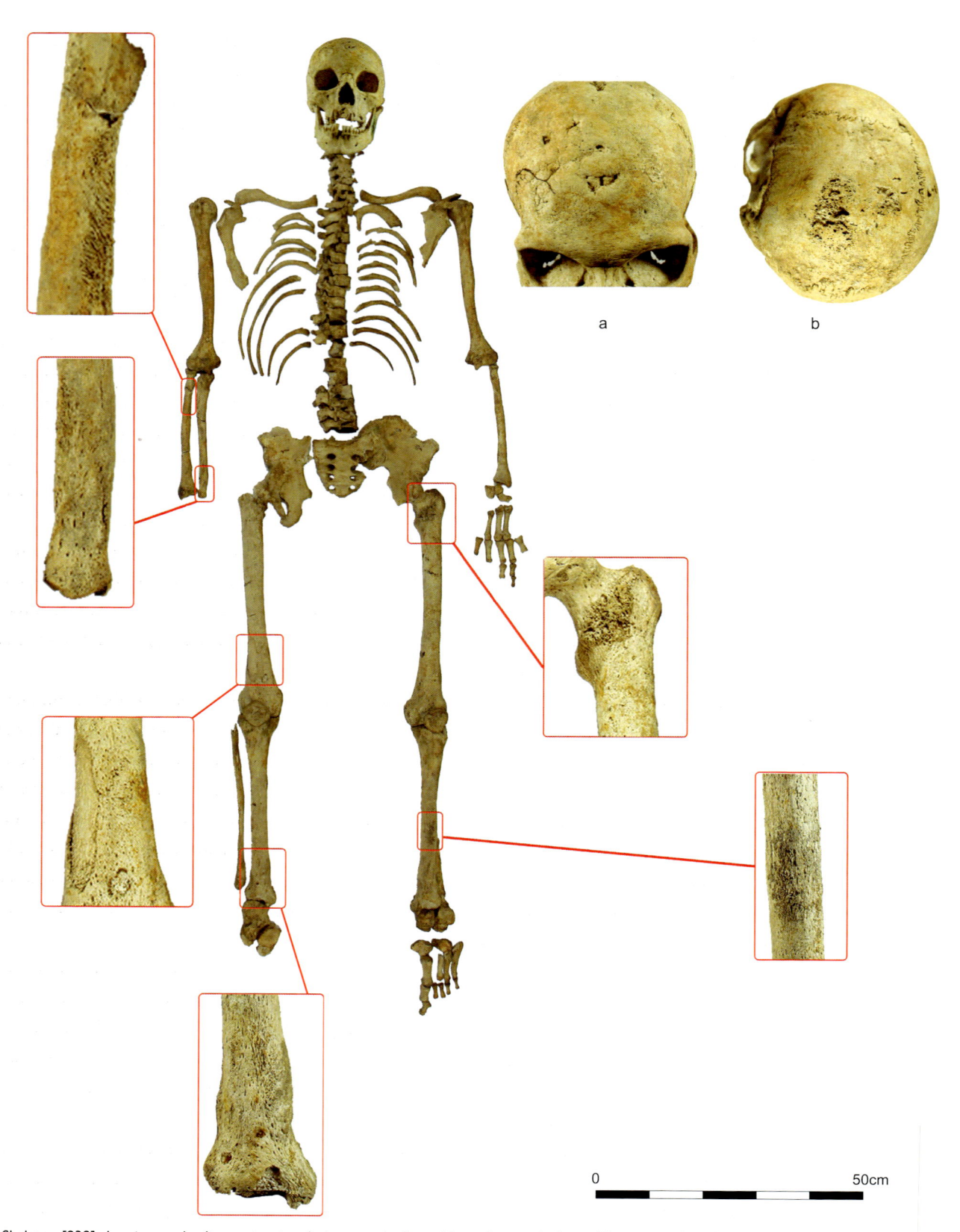

Fig 5.37 Skeleton [939] showing: a – healing caries sicca lesions on the frontal bone; b – newly formed lesions on the left parietal. Close-up images show periosteal reaction on proximal, distal and diaphyseal areas of long bones

changes in the pelvis also included active periostitis, striated new bone combined with sclerotic bone formation in periosteal areas, particularly near the acetabuli. Finally, woven bone was recorded on the diaphyseal areas of several rib fragments

Male skeleton [1077], 30–45 years old, exhibited cranial and post-cranial lesions consistent with venereal syphilis. The skull presented porous new bone formation on the cranial vault, particularly on the anterior right side of the frontal bone and on the entire surface of both parietals. Syphilitic diagnostic features included caries sicca lesions. These were present on the frontal bone and both parietals and the degree of healing suggested that the infection had started a long time before death. The hard palate also presented numerous, isolated, porous lesions. In the post-cranial skeleton both humeri and the left radius were affected with periostitis as well as the left scapula, the manubrium of the sternum, the right clavicle and the hyoid. The right humerus showed localised periosteal reactions on the proximal diaphysis and they were visible on the distal third of the left. Similarly, the radius was affected with periostitis and slight pitting was distributed on its proximal and mid diaphysis. The clavicle exhibited abnormal diaphyseal thickness and focal pitting. Marked hyperostosis was also found on the acromial end of the scapula. The involvement of lower limb bones consisted only of patchy periosteal new bone formation on the distal diaphysis of the right femur. The tibiae were not affected, nor were the spine or the pelvis.

Another skeleton with lesions compatible with venereal syphilis was 30- to 45-year-old male [1135]. The skull was particularly badly affected as patches of concentric caries sicca lesions were distributed across the frontal bone with different stages of development. Endocranial lesions were also present, mostly in the frontal bone. Along with these, considerable porous new bone formation was present on the palatine bones. All long bones of the post-cranial skeleton were affected bilaterally. The consistent pattern was a combination of striated woven bone with sclerotic new bone formation present in diaphyseal areas, sometimes along with the proximal or distal ends of the bones. The midshaft of both femora and both humeri presented bony bridges that developed over blood vessels and undercut periosteal new bone. The sternum and the lamina of the lumbar vertebrae were also affected with periostitis, and the clavicles, the scapulae and a few shaft fragments of ribs from the right side were affected with porous woven bone.

The skull of possible female [1767], over 45 years of age, was greatly thickened and abnormally heavy. The cranial vault was extensively affected with confluent caries sicca lesions that covered most of the frontal, parietal and occipital bones giving the skull a badly remodelled appearance. The cranial sutures show diffused and poorly defined lines, which may have resulted from advanced sclerotic healing. In the post-cranial skeleton syphilitic infection was observed only in the acromial end of both scapulae, which presented a layer of porous reactive bone and the acromial end of the clavicles. Both tibiae show localised periostitis forming slight plaquing near the medial aspect of the proximal end. The right femur appears to be normal but the left shows localised periostitis on the middle of the diaphysis near the linea aspera, which appears as a plaque-like deposition of porous new bone formation.

Rib samples were taken from this individual for nitrogen and carbon isotope analysis. The results indicated an elevated $\delta^{15}N$ (see Fig 5.4). Protein catabolism from a period of illness is reported to result in $\delta^{15}N$ enrichment (Fuller et al 2005), but it is difficult to attribute the elevation to sickness as the enrichment was not significantly higher than others in the population.

Two more skeletons displayed changes possibly consistent with treponemal disease but they were not counted in the general prevalence of the condition because their poor degree of completeness and preservation made a more conclusive diagnosis unachievable. One possible male aged 30–45 years displayed generalised periosteal reactions in diaphyseal areas of the left clavicle, sternal body, acromion and lateral border of the left scapula. One left-side rib also showed porous new bone formation on its diaphysis and a more advanced sclerotic periostitis was present on the upper third diaphysis of the left femur. In the absence of the skull and most of the right-side bones of the body that would allow the assessment of the bilateral distribution of the lesions, syphilis can be considered only as a possible cause.

The last skeleton was an adult individual of unknown sex and very poorly preserved. The surviving left humerus showed extensive reactive and sclerosed new bone formation on all aspects of the distal epiphysis. Fragments of diaphyseal areas of both claviculae, acromial ends of scapulae and unsided ribs also presented reactive periosteal new bone formation. Similarly, in the absence of the skull, spine, pelvis, lower limbs and forearms syphilis cannot be confirmed as the underlying causative condition.

One disarticulated right femur belonging to an adult individual of unknown sex exhibited massive gummatous periostitis (Fig 5.38) that could have resulted from tertiary syphilis. As explained above (5.1, 'Disarticulated material'), disarticulated examples were not counted in the overall prevalence of infectious diseases.

Comparisons of treponemal disease with other contemporary cemeteries from the London area suggested that the prevalence of the condition at the Savoy was slightly higher (Table 5.23).

There is no mention of syphilis in the burial registers but this is perhaps to be expected as it was regarded as a shameful disease and John Graunt notes that officers were often bribed by families to register a different cause of death for the Bill of Mortality (Siena 2004, 32). Certainly the work and records of Charles Hales, a surgeon appointed to the Savoy Hospital in the late 18th century, certainly suggest that sexually transmitted

London-area cemeteries	Prevalence (n/N)
All Saints, Chelsea Old Church	- (0/198)
New Bunhill Fields Burial ground	0.1% (1/514)
Bow Baptist Church	0.2% (1/416)
St Marylebone Church burial ground	0.3% (1/301)
Sheen's burial ground	0.3% (1/254)
St Mary and St Michael's burial ground	0.7% (5/705)
City Bunhill burial ground	0.8% (2/239)
Queen's Chapel Savoy	**0.9% (6/609)**
London Hospital	1.2% (8/636)
St Benet Sherehog	1.7% (4/230)
St Pancras burial ground	1.6% (12/715)
Royal Hospital Greenwich	2.8% (3/107)

Table 5.23 Comparison of syphilis in cemeteries from the London area (all adult and subadult individuals are pooled; for references see above, 5.1)

diseases were all too common among the soldiers (Chapter 3). This is supported by other historical documents, such as the Proceedings of the Old Bailey (t17960217–37) that record Thomas Davenport, a soldier of the First Foot Guards who had been suffering from gonorrhoea, being charged with the assault and rape of an 11-year-old girl, Ann Thacker, who then also contracted the infection. Prostitution is reported as a main source of employment for young women during the 18th century in London (Olsen 1999, 49; White 2012, 347) and the Savoy was favourably located. The unwanted presence of 'lewd and loose' women in and around the hospital and precinct is documented and, in addition to street walkers, the area contained a large number of 'molly' houses or gay brothels, described as a way for the poorly paid soldier to make some extra money (White 2012, 374). These facts certainly offer a possible explanation for the slightly higher prevalence of syphilis among the Savoy population. This situation was also recognised among the sailors buried at the Royal Hospital Greenwich and can only be interpreted as resulting from the lifestyle of seamen and marines that made them particularly vulnerable to contracting sexually transmitted diseases such as syphilis (Boston et al 2008).

DENTAL DISEASE

Dental disease refers to any acquired or congenital pathology of the teeth. In the Savoy Chapel population acquired pathologies included calculus, periodontal disease, ante-mortem tooth loss, dental enamel hypoplasia, caries, abscesses and dental trauma. Congenital anomalies included agenesis, retained teeth, rotated teeth, peg-shaped teeth and a small group of miscellaneous conditions. In contrast to acquired dental pathologies, most congenital anomalies of the teeth would not have posed any serious health complication and would therefore have been more likely to remain asymptomatic. Impacted teeth, however,

dependent upon the tooth involved and the location, produce prolonged headache or jaw ache, difficulty in opening the mouth, pain or tenderness in the gingiva and secondary complications such as infection, malocclusion or abscess (Yavuz et al 2007). Of all the skeletons analysed 23.9% (146/609) appear to have suffered from either acquired or congenital dental disease (Table 5.24).

Dental condition	M+M? (n/N)	F+F? (n/N)	? (n/N)	Subadults (n/N)	Total (n/N)
Caries	37.5% (122/325)	44.7% (47/105)	3.3% (3/89)	13.3% (12/90)	30.2% (184/609)
Calculus	42.7% (139/325)	36.1% (38/105)	- (0/89)	6.6% (6/90)	30.0% (183/609)
Ante-mortem tooth loss	33.8% (110/325)	49.5% (52/105)	2.2% (2/89)	2.2% (2/90)	27.2% (166/609)
Periodontal disease	32.9% (107/325)	37.1% (39/105)	2.2% (2/89)	1.1% (1/90)	24.4% (149/609)
Dental enamel hypoplasia	24.9% (81/325)	21.9% (23/105)	2.2% (2/89)	13.3% (12/90)	19.3% (118/609)
Abscess	12.3% (40/325)	25.7% (27/105)	1.1% (1/89)	1.1% (1/90)	11.3% (69/609)

Table 5.24 Crude prevalence rates of dental pathology within the total population

The results obtained from the Savoy population, as outlined below, and those obtained by others would suggest that tooth-cleaning was not a regularly practised activity during the early to mid post-medieval period. A lack of education/information and the lack of accessible water supply were probably among the factors responsible for this. Indeed, it was not until the early 17th century that the importance of dental hygiene was highlighted, although not necessarily practised (Roberts & Cox 2003). Toothbrushes were either not in existence or not in use until the 18th century so the little attention that was paid to oral hygiene, such as using toothpicks or rubbing teeth with various abrasive whitening products, did nothing other than damage the enamel.

Despite that, barbers in every market town during the 17th century offered dental treatment (Roberts & Cox 2003) but their poor training and reputation for infecting patients with venereal diseases would certainly have discouraged patients from seeking their help. Without doubt, poor dental health impacted on the quality of life. 'Teeth' was listed among the top ten causes of death during the 18th century in the London Bills of Mortality (Roberts & Cox 2003) and it was also listed among the top ten causes of death recorded in the Savoy Chapel burial registers (see Table 4.2). However, this fact should be considered with caution as the term 'teeth' was interchangeable with 'teething' and was used to encompass infantile deaths of various causes that occurred at a time in their life when infants were considered to be more at risk of infection (Lock et al 2001, 461–2).

CHAPTER 5 THE HUMAN REMAINS

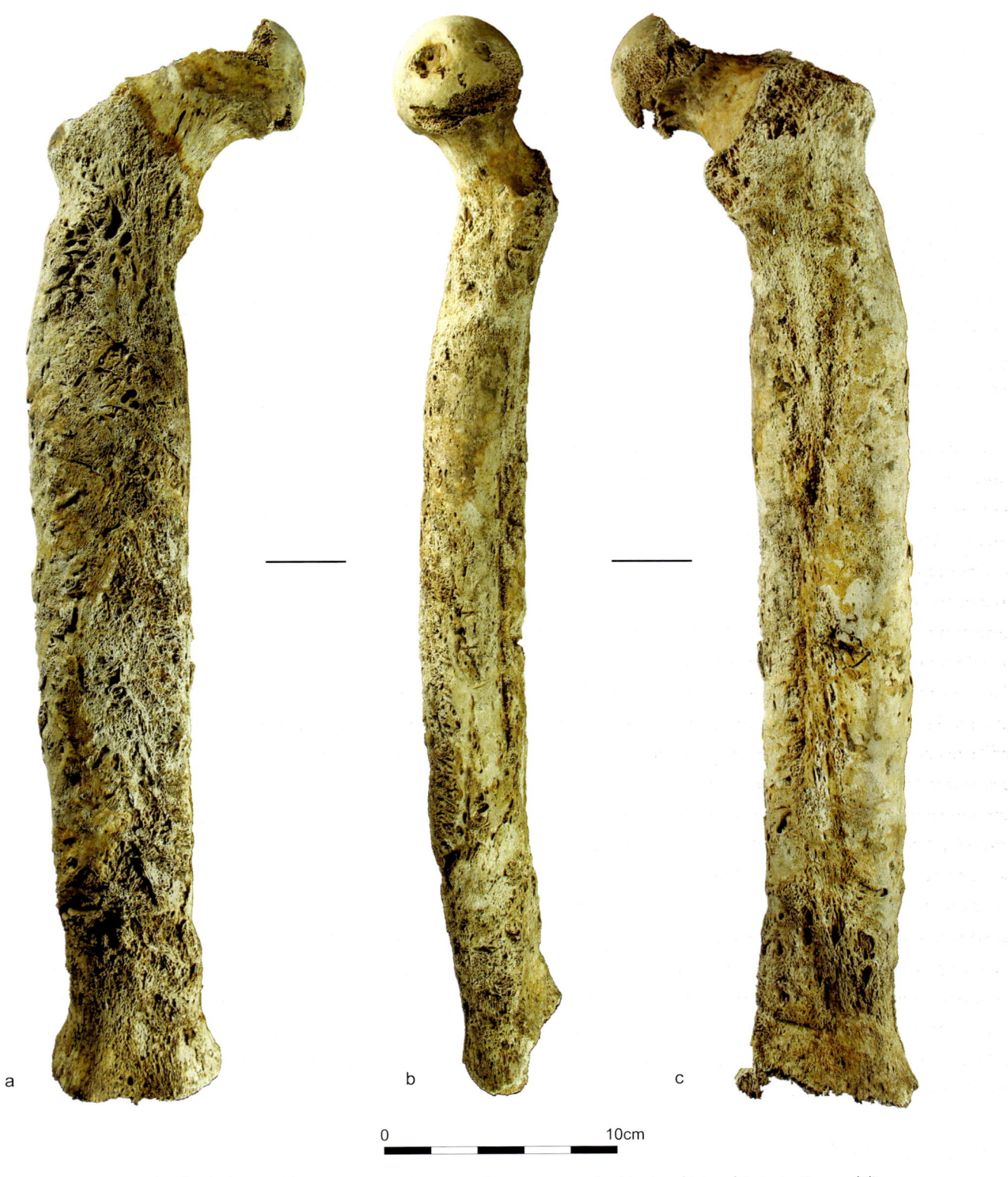

Fig 5.38 Views of a disarticulated right femur with typical snail-track pattern of gummatous periostitis, thought to relate to tertiary syphilis: a – anterior; b – medial; c – posterior

Unlike other contemporaneous sites such as St Marylebone (Miles et al 2008a), St Pancras burial ground (Emery & Wooldridge 2011) and St Mary and St Michael's burial ground, Bow Baptist Church and Sheen's burial ground (Henderson et al 2013), no dentures were recovered from the Savoy Chapel, nor was there evidence of dental treatment or dentistry. In the mid 18th century dentures and false teeth were expensive and regarded as items of high social status (Powers 2006). The fact that no such items were found on site does not necessarily mean that these were unaffordable for the Savoy population. Previous chapters have highlighted the cross section of social classes interred in the burial ground, so although they may have been out of reach for many, they would have been accessible for some, such as the nobility or high-ranking military men.

111

The following abbreviations are used: I1 and I2 for the 1st and 2nd incisors; C for the canines; P1 and P2 for the 1st and 2nd premolars; and M1, M2 and M3 for the 1st, 2nd and 3rd molars.

CALCULUS

Dental calculus or dental plaque is a form of hardened accumulation of micro-organisms on the tooth surfaces and is the most common dental condition affecting teeth (Hillson 1996). Although it is not considered pathology per se, dental calculus is a precursor of dental disease and a manifestation of poor dental hygiene.

Dental calculus was the most prevalent condition affecting adult dentition from the Savoy Chapel, present in 30.0% (183/609) of all individuals studied and found in both maxillae and mandibles (Table 5.24). It was recorded as present when seen as hard concretions on the tooth surface but the surface on which the calculus was deposited was not specified. The fact that similar results were obtained from several contemporaneous populations from the London area suggests that during the post-medieval period little attention was paid to oral hygiene or to preventing the formation of dental calculus. Males were the most severely affected of all individuals analysed and, as expected, subadults the least affected. This is because calculus deposition increases with age (Lu et al 2011) – in other words, subadult individuals would not have lived long enough to show the same hard concretions that were found on the tooth surfaces of adults.

As observed in Table 5.25, true prevalence rates suggested that dental calculus was the most common dental pathology observed in the adult population, present in 33.0% (1981/5992) of all teeth examined. This marked trend appears to be commonly observed in other post-medieval populations from London: St Marylebone Church burial ground (Miles et al 2008b), New Bunhill Fields burial ground (Miles 2012), All Saints, Chelsea Old Church (Cowie et al 2008), the London Hospital (Fowler & Powers 2012), St Mary and St Michael's burial ground, the Bow Baptist Church and Sheen's burial ground (Henderson et al 2013).

Comparisons between the sexes suggest that males were more affected than females and this was confirmed by statistical analysis based on the true prevalence rates (χ^2=11.4821, df=1, p<0.05). The analysis of dental calculus in adults according to tooth (Table 5.26) suggested that this condition affected fewer maxillary teeth (35.1%) compared to mandibular teeth (41.5%), this being of statistical significance (χ^2=21.7564, df=1, p<0.05). Calculus deposition showed a very specific

Dental condition	M+M? (n/N)	F+F? (n/N)	? (n/N)	Subadults (n/N)	Total (n/N)
Calculus	41.2% (1594/3862)	35.3% (341/966)	4.8% (10/208)	3.7% (36/956)	**33.0% (1981/5992)**
Periodontal disease	25.5% (987/3862)	27.9% (270/966)	2.8% (6/208)	0.5% (5/956)	**21.1% (1268/5992)**
Ante-mortem tooth loss	13.6% (526/3862)	53.9% (521/966)	17.3% (36/208)	0.3% (3/956)	**18.1% (1086/5992)**
Dental enamel hypoplasia	13.6% (527/3862)	14.0% (136/966)	11.0% (23/208)	4.4% (43/956)	**12.1% (729/5992)**
Caries	8.7% (337/3862)	17.5% (170/966)	37.0% (77/208)	4.9% (47/956)	**10.5% (631/5992)**
Abscess	2.1% (82/3862)	5.4% (53/966)	0.9% (2/208)	(0.1%) (1/956)	**2.3% (138/5992)**

Table 5.25 True prevalence rates of dental pathology within the population (n = number of teeth affected; N = number of teeth available for study (maxillary + mandibular); subadults' dentition includes permanent + deciduous teeth)

trend, with a predilection in the maxilla for both M1 followed by both M2 but in the mandible for mostly C and left and right I1 and I2.

Calculus forms preferentially on the lingual surface of the lower anterior teeth and the labial aspect of upper molars for several reasons (Dawes 2006). Plaque in these areas is generally thin so any sugary ingested food will clear out more rapidly, helped by the salivary film velocity, which is also highest in these regions. Regardless of the location of calculus deposition, the results from the Savoy support those of Dawes in relation to the teeth affected (maxillary molars and mandibular incisors) and are consistent with those found by Henderson et al (2013) at Bow Baptist Church and Sheen's burial ground and similar to those found at All Saints, Chelsea Old Church (Cowie et al 2008) and New Bunhill Fields burial ground (Miles 2012).

As seen in Tables 5.24 and 5.25, dental calculus was only the third most significant condition affecting the dentition of the subadult group after caries and dental enamel hypoplasia. Given the wide range of ages included in this group (from neonates to 17 years of age), true prevalence rates as shown in Table 5.27 support the idea that calculus deposition increases with age (Lu et al 2011).

PERIODONTAL DISEASE

Periodontal disease (PD) refers to the loss of bone mass around the alveolus or tooth socket owing to inflammation of the gingiva (gum), which ultimately leads to tooth loss (Hillson 1996; Roberts & Manchester 2005). This is usually triggered by bacterial plaque and calculus located adjacent to the inflamed gingiva, which in turn creates an abnormal space between the bone and the cemento-enamel junction (Ortner 2003). For the purpose of this study periodontal disease was

CHAPTER 5 THE HUMAN REMAINS

Dental condition	Maxilla (right) M3 (n/N)	M2 (n/N)	M1 (n/N)	P2 (n/N)	P1 (n/N)	C (n/N)	I2 (n/N)	I1 (n/N)	Maxilla (left) I1 (n/N)	I2 (n/N)	C (n/N)	P1 (n/N)	P2 (n/N)	M1 (n/N)	M2 (n/N)	M3 (n/N)	Total (n/N)
Calculus	30.7% (35/114)	39.8% (65/163)	49.3% (74/150)	35.8% (58/162)	35.5% (58/163)	35.8% (58/162)	33.5% (44/131)	35.4% (44/124)	31.1% (42/135)	29.0% (38/131)	34.1% (59/173)	34.2% (52/152)	30.4% (49/161)	40.7% (57/140)	40.1% (61/152)	21.2% (24/113)	35.1% (818/2326)
Periodontal disease	21.9% (25/114)	23.9% (39/163)	29.3% (44/150)	23.4% (38/162)	21.4% (35/163)	22.8% (37/162)	25.1% (33/131)	24.1% (30/124)	23.7% (32/135)	26.7% (35/131)	27.1% (47/173)	24.3% (37/152)	19.2% (37/161)	30.0% (42/140)	13.8% (21/152)	23.0% (26/113)	23.9% (558/2326)
Ante-mortem tooth loss	28.9% (33/114)	19.6% (32/163)	30.0% (45/150)	17.9% (29/162)	17.1% (28/163)	9.2% (15/162)	13.7% (18/131)	16.9% (21/124)	11.8% (16/135)	6.7% (21/131)	9.2% (16/173)	23.6% (36/152)	22.3% (36/161)	32.1% (45/140)	21.0% (32/152)	31.8% (36/113)	19.8% (461/2326)
Caries	13.1% (15/114)	12.2% (20/163)	18.0% (27/150)	13.5% (22/162)	17.1% (28/163)	4.9% (8/162)	9.9% (13/131)	8.0% (10/124)	10.3% (14/135)	12.2% (16/131)	9.8% (17/173)	15.7% (24/152)	14.9% (24/161)	20.0% (28/140)	16.4% (25/152)	14.1% (16/113)	13.1% (307/2326)
Dental enamel hypoplasia	0.8% (1/114)	1.2% (2/163)	3.3% (5/150)	7.4% (12/162)	12.8% (21/163)	26.5% (43/162)	23.6% (31/131)	29.0% (36/124)	27.4% (37/135)	16.7% (22/131)	27.7% (48/173)	10.5% (16/152)	9.3% (15/161)	7.8% (11/140)	3.2% (5/152)	1.7% (2/113)	13.0% (304/2326)
Abscess	2.6% (3/114)	4.2% (7/163)	7.3% (11/150)	4.9% (8/162)	6.1% (10/163)	2.4% (4/162)	0.7% (1/131)	0.8% 1/124	1.4% (2/135)	1.5% (2/131)	1.1% (2/173)	3.2% (5/152)	3.7% (6/161)	7.8% (11/140)	3.2% (5/152)	4.4% (5/113)	3.5% (83/2326)

Dental condition	Mandible (right) M3 (n/N)	M2 (n/N)	M1 (n/N)	P2 (n/N)	P1 (n/N)	C (n/N)	I2 (n/N)	I1 (n/N)	Mandible (left) I1 (n/N)	I2 (n/N)	C (n/N)	P1 (n/N)	P2 (n/N)	M1 (n/N)	M2 (n/N)	M3 (n/N)	Total (n/N)
Calculus	32.1% (46/143)	40.1% (61/152)	37.2% (48/129)	34.7% (67/193)	37.8% (73/193)	46.7% (92/197)	53.1% (92/173)	54.1% (85/157)	57.9% (91/157)	53.9% (95/176)	45.2% (90/199)	39.7% (78/196)	34.7% (67/193)	36.5% (53/145)	32.7% (54/165)	24.6% (35/142)	41.5% (1127/2710)
Periodontal disease	18.1% (26/143)	23.0% (35/152)	20.1% (26/129)	37.2% (48/129)	25.9% (50/193)	30.4% (60/197)	25.8% (51/197)	31.2% (49/157)	34.3% (54/157)	31.8% (56/176)	27.1% (54/199)	27.0% (53/196)	24.3% (47/193)	21.3% (31/145)	21.2% (35/165)	21.1% (30/142)	26.0% (705/2710)
Ante-mortem tooth loss	39.1% (56/143)	46.7% (71/152)	75.1% (97/129)	19.6% (38/193)	11.3% (22/193)	3.5% (7/197)	6.3% (11/173)	13.3% (21/157)	10.1% (16/157)	7.3% (13/176)	4.5% (9/199)	8.6% (17/196)	18.6% (36/193)	60.6% (88/145)	38.7% (64/165)	38.7% (55/142)	22.9% (622/2710)
Caries	14.0% (21/143)	19.7% (30/152)	24.0% (31/129)	8.8% (17/193)	7.2% (14/193)	4.5% (9/197)	2.3% (4/173)	5/157 3.1%	2.5% (4/157)	6.8% (12/176)	5.0% (10/199)	8.6% (17/196)	11.3% (22/193)	20.6% (30/145)	17.5% (29/165)	15.4% (22/142)	10.2% (277/2710)
Dental enamel hypoplasia	2.7% (4/143)	3.9% (6/152)	8.5% (11/129)	9.3% (18/193)	17.6% (34/193)	30.9% (61/197)	19.0% (33/173)	17.8% (28/157)	15.2% (24/157)	17.0% (30/176)	33.1% (66/199)	16.3% (32/196)	10.8% (21/193)	6.2% (9/145)	1.2% (2/165)	1.4% (2/142)	13.6% (370/2710)
Abscess	1.3% (2/143)	3.2% (5/152)	5.4% (7/129)	- (0/193)	1.0% (2/193)	1.0% (2/197)	- (0/173)	2/157 1.2%	0.6% (1/157)	- (0/176)	1.0% (2/199)	3.0% (6/196)	3.1% (6/193)	6.8% (10/145)	5.4% (9/165)	- (0/142)	1.9% (54/2710)

Table 5.26 True prevalence rates of dental pathologies in the adult population according to teeth (n = number of teeth affected; N = number of teeth available for study; I = incisor; C = canine; P = premolar; M = molar)

recorded as present when a distance greater than 2mm was observed between the alveolar crest and the cemento-enamel junction (Ogden 2008), in the maxilla or mandible, regardless of whether the teeth were present or not – in other words, by looking at the alveolar morphology and the root exposure. Periodontal disease was present in 24.4% (149/609) of all individuals studied (Table 5.24) with females most severely affected and subadults the least affected.

As observed in Table 5.25, true prevalence rates suggested that periodontal disease was, after calculus, the second most common dental pathology observed in the adult population from the Savoy Chapel, present in 21.1% (1268/5992) of all teeth examined. These results are in accordance with Ortner's statement (2003) that oral health (dental plaque and calculus) is directly involved in the aetiology of periodontal disease. These results are unsurprising, given the levels of calculus recorded, although the influence of genetics and diet should not be ruled out.

Comparisons with other sites were not always possible because of differences in the methodological approaches used to record the condition and present the results. However, two contemporary sites from the London area are worth mentioning owing to their comparatively higher prevalence: the St Mary and St Michael's burial ground (Henderson et al 2013) and All Saints, Chelsea Old Church (Cowie et al 2008). In the former, periodontal disease affected 34.9% (2578/7397) of all permanent teeth compared with 48.1% (512/622) at the latter. Comparisons between the sexes at the Savoy suggested that, as seen in Table 5.25, females were more affected than males but this was not statistically significant (χ^2=0.129459, df=1, p<0.05).

The observation of periodontal disease by tooth (Table 5.26) indicated that, although variable, maxillary molars and the mandibular incisors were equally affected by calculus and periodontal disease. Statistical comparison between upper and lower teeth showed no significant difference (χ^2=2.7319, df=1, p<0.05) but a similar high prevalence in these teeth was noted in the population from All Saints, Chelsea Old Church (Cowie et al 2008).

Periodontal disease among subadults was, on the other hand, almost non-existent (Table 5.27), recorded only in five deciduous teeth (1.0%, 5/458) and no permanent teeth (0/498). As stated by Hillson (1996) and Lu et al (2011) children are very rarely affected by periodontal disease before puberty because the condition progresses with advanced age. Indeed, as calculus deposition advances with age, so will the progression of alveolar resorption of bone.

Dental condition	Deciduous teeth (n/N)	Permanent teeth (n/N)	Total (n/N)
Caries	5.2% (24/458)	4.6% (23/498)	4.9% (47/956)
Dental enamel hypoplasia	2.4% (11/458)	6.4% (32/498)	4.4% (43/956)
Calculus	0.4% (2/458)	6.8% (34/498)	3.7% (36/956)
Periodontal disease	1.0% (5/458)	- (0/498)	0.5% (5/956)
Ante-mortem tooth loss	- (0/458)	0.6% (3/498)	0.3% (3/956)
Abscess	0.2% (1/458)	- (0/498)	0.1% (1/956)

Table 5.27 True prevalence rates of dental pathologies in the subadult population (n = number of teeth affected; N = number of teeth available for study (maxillary + mandibular))

ANTE-MORTEM TOOTH LOSS

Teeth not present due to pathology were recorded as lost ante-mortem (AMTL). There are a number of factors involved in the aetiology, which include trauma, decay, infection and periodontal disease, but dental calculus is to be blamed for the majority of tooth loss (Hillson 1996). AMTL affected 27.2% (166/609) of all individuals studied (Table 5.24), with females the most severely affected. As observed in Table 5.25 true prevalence rates suggested that AMTL was present in 18.1% (1086/5992) of all teeth examined, making it the third most common condition affecting the dentition of the Savoy population, supporting the link between this AMTL and the previous conditions. Comparisons between the sexes suggested that females were more affected than the males and statistical analysis based on true prevalence rates showed that the comparison was significant (χ^2=739.4556, df=1, p<0.05).

The tooth most often lost ante-mortem was the M1 (Table 5.26). Mandibular molars were lost twice as often as maxillary molars and canines were the teeth least affected. The M1 was also the most commonly lost tooth among the adult population of All Saints, Chelsea Old Church and New Bunhill Fields (Cowie et al 2008; Miles 2012). In fact, M1 was the tooth most severely affected by the majority of dental conditions in the Savoy Chapel population, except for periodontal disease. This is probably because they are the first permanent teeth to erupt in the oral cavity and the longest to be exposed to dental wear and other pathologies. Three adults were edentulous (toothless): a possible female, a female and a male, all of whom were estimated to be over 45 years old at the time of death.

AMTL within the subadult population should not be confused with natural loss of teeth because of dental development as opposed to pathology. Table 5.27 shows that as expected, AMTL was almost non-existent in this group, recorded only in the permanent teeth of three individuals (0.6%, 3/498). Only three teeth were lost ante-mortem, one lower right P2 from a juvenile individual, one upper right P1 in individual [610], an infant 7–12 years of age, and one upper left I2 from an infant 12 months–6 years of age. The most likely cause of tooth loss within these individuals is trauma. In skeleton [610] the possibility of having lost the P1 secondary to scurvy cannot be ruled out as this skeleton showed other indications of having suffered from this condition. Boston et al (2008) also recognised that scurvy appears to have contributed to AMTL among the Royal Hospital Greenwich population.

Comparisons with other sites from the London area (Table 5.28) revealed that the Savoy adult population was among the least affected by AMTL. The reasons for this could be differences in preservation of dentition and in methodological procedures. As no radiography was possible for all the M3s it is not known if they were congenitally absent or lost ante-mortem. It is for this reason that a large percentage of them were recorded as 'not present' and therefore not included in the final count of teeth lost ante-mortem. Of course, teeth may also have been extracted; the accessibility of dental treatment to the Savoy population is unknown but dental extraction of painful teeth was a common practice at this time (Roberts & Cox 2003).

The highest prevalence of AMTL was found among the pensioners from the Royal Hospital Greenwich and given that it can be considered a condition of the aged, this resulted, according to Boston et al (2008), from the aged composition of the sample.

London-area cemeteries	Prevalence (n/N)
St Benet Sherehog	18.2% (486/2617)
Queen's Chapel Savoy	21.5% (1083/5036)
St Mary and St Michael's burial ground	23.5% (1740/7397)
New Bunhill Fields burial ground	29.1% (1317/4524)
City Bunhill burial ground	29.2% (928/3178)
Bow Baptist Church	32.4% (1843/5684)
All Saints, Chelsea Old Church	34.4% (682/1977)
St Marylebone Church burial ground	34.6% (1492/4316)
Sheen's burial ground	34.9% (1088/3114)
Royal Hospital Greenwich	44.6% (1172/2624)

Table 5.28 Comparison of ante-mortem tooth loss in cemeteries from the London area (all adult individuals are pooled; n = number of teeth affected; N = number of teeth available for study (maxillary + mandibular); for references see above, 5.1)

DENTAL ENAMEL HYPOPLASIA

Dental enamel hypoplasia (DEH) represents the interruption or disruption of enamel formation owing to nutritional deficiencies and other non-specific environmental factors, including disturbances to normal physiological balance and other systemic related conditions (Hillson 1996). Infectious diseases such as congenital syphilis and tuberculosis are also known for producing a disruption in the enamel formation (Ortner 2003). In this study, DEH was recorded as present when pitting, grooves or transverse lines were visible on the enamel or when more radical changes of the normal crown morphology were present. DEH was present in 19.3% (118/609) of all individuals studied (Table 5.24) and it was slightly higher among males than females. True prevalence rates, on the other hand, as seen in Table 5.25, revealed no significant difference between the sexes (χ^2=0.1222, df=1, p<0.05).

As shown in Table 5.26, the teeth most severely affected by DEH were the upper and lower canines and incisors. As the development of enamel occurs at specific times for each tooth, observations of enamel defects on teeth can help to trace the specific age at which the stress took place. It is known that the development of enamel in the maxillary and mandibular incisors and canines takes place between the ages of 4 and 6 years, which correlates with the formation of their crowns. Despite the multifactorial nature of DEH (Hillson 1996), it can be assumed that the adult population from the Savoy was exposed to stressful factors during childhood and were therefore more vulnerable and exposed to the aetiological factors contributing to the development of DEH.

In line with these results, Bow Baptist Church and Sheen's burial ground showed that most of the enamel defects in the adult population of the former (78.3%, 335/428) and the latter (83.5%, 111/133) also occurred on the anterior teeth and predominantly the canines (Henderson et al 2013). Similar findings were also reported from the St Benet Sherehog (Miles et al 2008a), suggesting that the Savoy population was exposed to the same nutritional deficiencies and other systemic diseases as other contemporaneous populations.

Although DEH and dental caries were the two most prevalent dental conditions observed within the subadults (Table 5.27), the former affected only 4.4% (43/956) of subadult dentition, which represents a lower prevalence than that obtained from Sheen's burial ground (5.2%, 37/714), St Mary and St Michael's burial ground (6.1%, 204/3357) and Bow Baptist Church (6.4%, 158/2459) (Henderson et al 2013). The permanent teeth were more affected than the deciduous dentition – 6.4% (32/498) compared with 2.4% (11/458) – and a similar trend was found at Bow Baptist Church, where 13.6% (135/990) of permanent teeth were affected compared to 1.6% (23/1469) of deciduous teeth.

Comparisons of DEH with other sites from the London area (Table 5.29) revealed that the true prevalence rate found at the Savoy was at midpoint between the reported ranges of

6.0% to 20.1% and close to that reported for the Royal Hospital Greenwich. The explanation for this may reside in the fact that, as reviewed in Chapter 3, there were strict guidelines surrounding recruitment of military staff requiring specific levels of health to be met. Any individuals showing visible signs of physical stress, such as short stature, systemic infections and nutritional deficiencies may well not have been selected for the service and consequently DEH was low when compared with other sites as shown in Table 5.29. On the other hand, it is also recorded that recruiting officers would sometimes favour out-of-work labourers and workers, as well as seeking recruits from the poor and homeless teenaged and adult male population (Bucholz & Ward 2012, 232).

London-area cemeteries	Prevalence (n/N)
New Bunhill Fields burial ground	6.0% (165/2743)
Sheen's burial ground	8.2% (133/1617)
City Bunhill burial ground	10.3% (82/796)
Queen's Chapel Savoy	**13.6% (686/5036)**
Royal Hospital Greenwich	14.3% (178/1239)
Bow Baptist Church	14.5% (428/2950)
St Mary and St Michael's burial ground	16.5% (807/4887)
All Saints, Chelsea Old Church	17.3% (232/1335)
St Marylebone Church burial ground	20.1% (444/2211)

Table 5.29 Comparison of dental enamel hypoplasia in cemeteries from the London area (all adult individuals are pooled; n = number of teeth affected; N = number of teeth available for study (maxillary + mandibular); for references see above, 5.1)

CARIES

Dental caries are destructive lesions that damage the enamel, dentine or cement of the teeth, producing the formation of a cavity in the crown or root surface and it is the acid production of bacteria living in dental plaque that is responsible for these lesions (Hillson 1996). In this study, caries was recorded as present when lytic lesions were observed in any tooth surface. In other words, no distinction was made where in the tooth the caries was located. Carious lesions were present in 30.2% (184/609) of all individuals studied (Table 5.24). Females were the most severely affected group of the population and this was statistically significant based on true prevalence rates (Table 5.25) (χ^2=64.7197, df=1, p<0.05).

Carious lesions affected 11.5% (584/5036) of all adult teeth from the Savoy population (Table 5.26), a similar prevalence to that found by Boston et al (2008) among the sailors of the Royal Hospital Greenwich (11.7%, 147/1247) but lower than those found in other post-medieval cemeteries, which ranged from 12.8% (207/1617) at Sheen's burial ground to 76.0% (3715/4887) at St Mary and St Michael's burial ground (Henderson et al 2013). The reason behind such disparity may lie in the amount of sugar consumed by soldiers and sailors during their lives. Although some information on food and beverages consumed by soldiers at the Savoy Barracks is known (see Chapter 3), sugar consumption is not detailed. A number of intrinsic and extrinsic causes including diet, biological factors (salivary flow) and behavioural factors (oral hygiene patterns and products used) would have certainly played a role and contributed to the variation observed. Another reason for the disparity could be that unlike calculus, periodontal disease, ante-mortem tooth loss and abscesses, which tend to increase their prevalence over time, dental caries decreases with age (Demirci et al 2010), probably because of an increase in ante-mortem tooth loss.

Carious lesions have been associated with triggering other dental conditions such as AMTL, but in this study the low prevalence of this condition may suggest that at the Savoy dental calculus might be more responsible for tooth loss than dental caries.

As shown in Table 5.26 caries were statistically less common in the mandibular teeth, of which 10.2% (277/2710) were affected compared with 13.1% (307/2326) of the maxillary (χ^2=10.8223, df=1, p<0.05). The highest distribution of carious lesions was observed in the maxillary M1s and the premolars. In the mandible, the molars were the most carious teeth of the adult population. The studies conducted by Connell and Miles (2010), Cowie et al (2008) and Henderson et al (2013) report that M1 and M2 were the most frequent teeth of the adult dentition affected by carious lesions in post-medieval London. However, contrary to the observations for DEH, the upper and lower canines along with the upper and lower incisors were the teeth least affected by caries in the Savoy population. This trend was also noted among the All Saints, Chelsea Old Church population (Cowie et al 2008).

Modern clinical studies such as that of Demirci et al (2010) have also shown that maxillary teeth are more affected by caries than the mandibular teeth. Mandibular central incisors are the teeth least affected by caries when compared with molars and the explanation for this phenomenon is, according to these authors, a combination of complicated molar surface morphology and difficult access for effective oral hygiene.

Caries was the dental condition with the highest prevalence rate in the subadult population (Table 5.27). Carious lesions were recorded on 4.9% (47/956) of subadult teeth observed and was slightly more prevalent in the deciduous teeth (5.2%, 24/458) than in the permanent dentition (4.6%, 23/498). This is likely to result from poor oral health and nutritional deficiencies and supports the idea of an undernourished subadult population, exposed to infection and other systemic and metabolic diseases and more likely to develop malformed, hypoplastic teeth prone to cavities and caries.

PERIAPICAL LESIONS (ABSCESS)

A periapical lesion or abscess refers to a destructive lesion that produces resorption of the bone around the maxilla, maxillary sinus, mandible or nasal cavity resulting from pus accumulation (Hillson 1996). In this study, the evidence for alveolar bone destruction was recorded as indicative of dental abscess and recorded as present for a particular tooth when found adjacent to its root (Ogden 2008). Periapical abscesses (for example skeleton [1518], Fig 5.35) were present in 11.3% (69/609) of all individuals studied (Table 5.24) and the females were the most severely affected group of the population.

Poor oral hygiene may have been the common underlying contributory factor of dental abscess among the Savoy population and other contemporary populations from the London area as on the basis of true prevalence rates (Table 5.25) it affected 2.3% (138/5992) of all teeth observed compared with 2.6% (194/7397) and 1.3% (72/5684) of the respective St Mary and St Michael's and the Bow Baptist Church populations (Henderson et al 2013). Comparisons between the sexes (Table 5.25) revealed that the females were significantly more affected by dental abscesses than the males (χ^2=32.1589, df=1, p<0.05), suggesting that in line with the results obtained for PD, AMTL and caries, females were the most severely affected adult group within the population. This phenomenon may be related to a combination of factors including an earlier dental eruption in females, changes in hormones, the adverse impact of pregnancy in the immune system, food cravings and aversions during pregnancy as well as the biochemical and flow composition of the saliva (Lukacs & Largaespada 2006). Although these authors studied sex differences in dental caries, it is known that dental caries are precursors of a number of other dental conditions including infection (abscess), AMTL and periodontal disease.

Dental abscesses were significantly higher in the maxillary teeth (3.5%, 83/2326) than the mandibular teeth (1.9%, 54/2710) (Table 5.26) (χ^2=11.7437, df=1, p<0.05) and both maxillary and mandibular molars and premolars were the teeth most severely affected. M1 (maxillary and mandibular) had the highest prevalence rates and anterior teeth such as incisors and canines exhibited the lowest prevalence rates.

Finally, as observed with other dental conditions among the subadults of the Savoy Chapel, the presence of dental abscesses was almost non-existent among this group with only one tooth affected in one individual (Tables 5.25 and 5.27),
which is consistent with results from other skeletal assemblages from the London area. Among the subadult deciduous and permanent teeth at St Mary and St Michael's burial ground the condition was present in 0.2% (16/7242), at Bow Baptist Church it was present in 0.3% (8/3010) and at Sheen's burial ground it was present in 0.7% (5/750).

DENTAL TRAUMA

Dental trauma was represented by specific and non-specific patterns of dental wear as well as vertical fissures in the enamel of the teeth. Unlike other dental conditions, dental trauma was not systematically recorded apart from that resulting from clenching clay pipes. It was recorded in 9.6% (59/609) of the population studied and is summarised in Table 5.30. Specific patterns of dental wear resulting from clenching the abrasive stems of clay tobacco pipes (CTP) are the most prevalent traumatic lesion seen in the teeth of the Savoy population. These lesions were present as circular or semicircular grooves on the incisors, canines and premolars. They were recorded in 24 adults, such as individual [1719] (Fig 5.39), but no subadults, supporting the idea that smoking tobacco was an activity practised primarily by adults.

When looking at the cultural practice of smoking tobacco, other cemeteries from the capital present a comparatively low prevalence (Table 5.31) with the exception of St Mary and St Michael's burial ground, which reported the highest prevalence of clay pipe facets (23.4%, 58/248) to date. However, some differences between these prevalence rates may result from different methods applied to calculate them. Smoking was a developing aspect of London society and particularly common within the working classes (Henderson et al 2013), an activity that soldiers such as those from the Savoy would have embraced, as confirmed by historical records. As discussed in Chapter 3, clay pipes were provided at the Savoy Hospital and once admitted, soldiers could use their pension to supplement their diet with beer or tobacco (Gruber-von-Arni 2007a, 139).

Dental trauma	M+M? (n/N)	F+F? (n/N)	? (n/N)	Subadults (n/N)	Total (n/N)
CTP wear	6.7% (22/325)	1.9% (2/105)	- (0/89)	- (0/90)	3.9% (24/609)
Vertical fissures	4.6% (15/325)	4.7% (5/105)	- (0/89)	0.1% (1/90)	3.4% (21/609)
Non-CTP wear	2.4% (8/325)	5.7% (6/105)	- (0/89)	- (0/90)	2.2% (14/609)
Total	13.8% (45/325)	12.3% (13/105)	- (0/89)	0.01% (1/90)	9.6% (59/609)

Table 5.30 Crude prevalence rates of dental trauma within the total population (CTP = clay tobacco pipe)

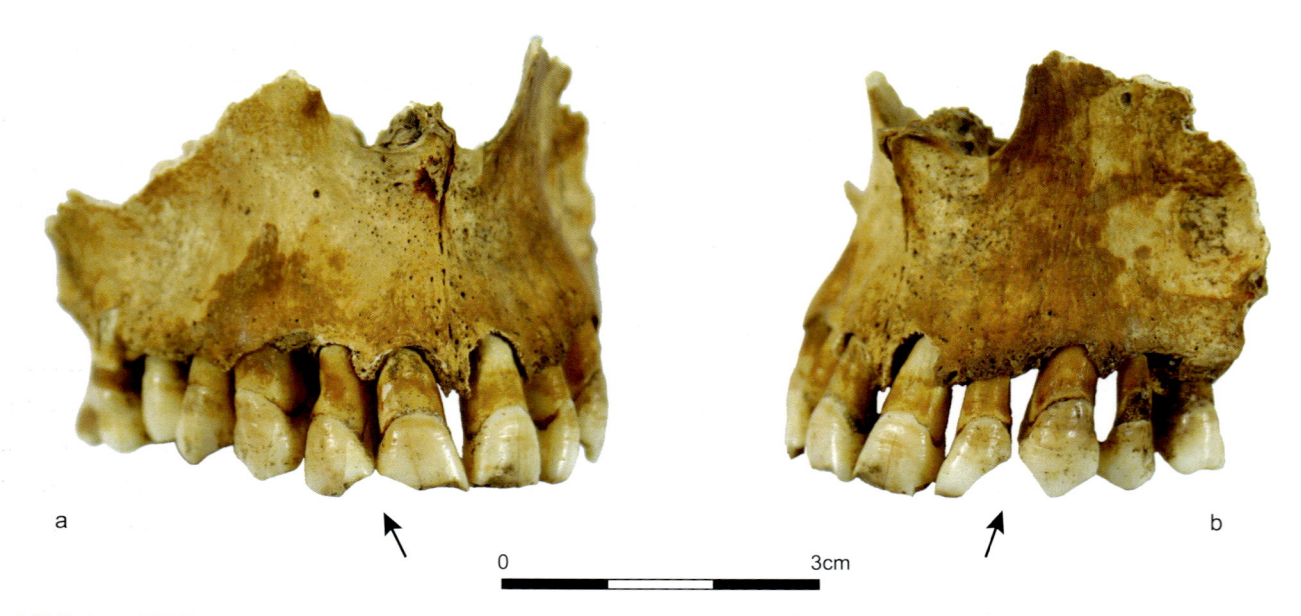

Fig 5.39 Skeleton [1719] showing maxillary teeth with circular and semicircular grooves, thought to result from clenching clay tobacco pipes: a – medial–lateral right; b – medial–lateral left

London-area cemeteries	Total (n/N)
St Marylebone Church burial ground	0.4% (1/223)
Bow Baptist Church	0.9% (2/214)
All Saints, Chelsea Old Church	1.2% (2/165)
Queen's Chapel Savoy	4.6% (24/519)
Royal Hospital Greenwich	13.4% (14/107)
St Mary and St Michael's burial ground	23.4% (58/248)

Table 5.31 Comparison of clay-pipe smokers within the adult population (all adult individuals are pooled; for references see above, 5.1)

Vertical fissures were the second most prevalent dental trauma observed, affecting 3.4% (21/609) of both adults and subadults. These fissures have not received a great deal of attention in the bioarchaeological literature and as they were not systematically recorded (as explained above) they may not represent the real number of cases affected. In modern dental practice they have been more widely studied and reported when incomplete enamel or dentine fractures progressing as deep as the pulp chamber, sometimes reaching the periodontal ligament, are seen in today's patients (Banerji et al 2010). Their aetiology is multifactorial. In other words, extrinsic factors such as mechanical stress resulting from excessive forces applied to a healthy tooth, grinding habits and masticatory accident and also intrinsic factors inherent to the health status of the teeth such as the thickness of the enamel, aged dentition, weak teeth and pathological teeth are all related to their onset (ibi). One particular example was adult female [1626] who, in addition to displaying vertical fissures on both upper central incisors, showed a number of palatine tori arising along the midline of the palate. These bony outgrowths or excrescences have been linked to activity-related and occupational stress (Brothwell 1981), which would give support to the mechanical stress aetiology of vertical fissures.

Also recorded were specific patterns of dental wear and trauma that resulted neither from the normal wear of teeth nor from smoking clay pipes. These were recorded as 'non-clay tobacco pipe wear' and were present on the occlusal and lingual aspects of the dentition of 14 skeletons, possibly representing the effects of bruxism, using teeth in occupational-related activities or an abrasive regime of dental hygiene. Both vertical fissures and non-CTP wear might be related as they would suggest that both males and females were engaged in practices that involved exerting mechanical stress in the masticatory system, although an underlying weakness of the dentition due to pre-existing dental pathology such as that resulting from caries or DEH cannot be ruled out.

CONGENITAL ANOMALIES

Congenital anomalies of the teeth included agenesis, retained teeth, rotated teeth, peg-shaped teeth and some other miscellaneous conditions. These groups of anomalies were present in both adults and subadults with a crude prevalence of 2.9% (18/609).

Agenesis

Dental agenesis, or the congenital absence of tooth development, was suspected in three adult males (Table 5.32). These individuals did not develop one of their incisors, which, according to Ortner (2003), are the teeth most commonly underdeveloped after M3. In one individual the upper right I2 failed to develop whereas in another it was the upper left I2. In the third individual, [208], it was both the upper and lower right

Dental anomalies	M+M? (n/N)	F+F? (n/N)	? (n/N)	Subadults (n/N)	Total (n/N)
Agenesis	0.9% (3/325)	- (0/105)	- (0/89)	- (0/90)	0.4% (3/609)
Retained teeth	0.6% (2/325)	- (0/105)	- (0/89)	2.2% (2/90)	0.6% (4/609)
Rotated teeth	0.9% (3/325)	0.9% (1/105)	- (0/89)	- (0/90)	0.6% (4/609)
Peg-shaped teeth	0.6% (2/325)	0.9% (1/105)	- (0/89)	- (0/90)	0.4% (3/609)
Fused teeth	0.3% (1/325)	- (0/105)	1.1% (1/89)	- (0/90)	0.3% (2/609)
Miscellaneous	0.3% (1/325)	- (0/105)	- (0/89)	1.1% (1/90)	0.3% (2/609)
Total	3.6% (12/325)	1.9% (2/105)	1.1% (1/89)	3.3% (3/90)	2.9% (18/609)

Table 5.32 Crude prevalence rates of dental anomalies within the total population

central incisors, but owing to the unusual occurrence of both of these underdeveloped teeth other possible aetiological factors such as absence resulting from trauma should be considered. As discussed above, without the aid of radiography it is difficult to confirm the congenital absence of the M3 and in other cases radiography examination may be unable to confirm whether the absence of a tooth is a result of trauma or of agenesis.

Retained teeth

Deciduous teeth retained into adulthood were present in two adult males and in two subadults aged 13–17 years (Table 5.32). In the adults, the teeth retained were the two upper canines and the lower right M1, and the upper right canine. The first of the subadults had retained the lower left M2, and the second had retained the upper right canine. As a consequence of this, the individual had a visible permanent upper right canine impacted.

Rotated teeth

Mal-aligned, rotated premolars were observed in three adult males and one female. The teeth involved and rotated 180° were the upper right P1 in one, the lower left P2 in another, the upper left P2 in a third and the lower left P2 in the female (Table 5.32).

Peg-shaped teeth

Peg-shaped teeth are smaller than normal (Ortner 2003). The condition can affect the whole or part of the tooth but the shape can also be abnormal. Peg-shaped teeth were found in one female and two males (Table 5.32). The teeth involved were the upper left I2 in the former case and the upper right I2 in the two males.

Fused teeth

Teeth can be fused through the crowns, the roots or both and this can affect the deciduous dentition more commonly than the permanent dentition (Ortner 2003). In the Savoy population, there was one individual with fused crowns and one with fused roots (Table 5.32). One adult male aged 30–45 years had two lower left premolars fused at the crown and an 18- to 30-year-old of unknown sex had two lower right central and lateral incisors fused into one crown.

Miscellaneous

Other unusual, congenital abnormalities included the fusion of the two roots of an upper right P1 in a subadult individual and a double rooted upper left I2 in one adult male, both observed by chance because they were loose. The crude prevalence rate of these miscellaneous conditions is presented in Table 5.32.

METABOLIC DISEASE

Metabolic disease is defined as any condition that produces a disruption to the process of bone formation and bone remodelling (Brickley & Ives 2008) mainly influenced by either insufficiency or excess of some food component of the diet and the physiological inability of the body to absorb those nutrients (Ortner 2003). In the extreme cases represented by individuals suffering chronically, metabolic diseases can be life-threatening conditions. In other situations they can be seriously detrimental to an individual's health status as several complications including bone tenderness, dental problems, muscle weakness, stiffness, risk of pathological fractures and the risk of long-term deformity of the limbs can all interfere with the normal performance of activities. The presence of metabolic disease within the population provides valuable information about their alimentary trends as well as their socioeconomic, cultural, environmental and nutritional conditions.

The metabolic conditions encountered in the population of the Savoy included cribra orbitalia, porotic hyperostosis, rickets, scurvy, osteoporosis and diffuse idiopathic skeletal hyperostosis (DISH). Both adults and subadults were affected. Of all skeletons analysed 19.3% (118/609) appear to have suffered from one of the above-listed metabolic conditions. As outlined below, dietary deficiency was visible in the Savoy population but with fairly low prevalence compared with contemporary populations, something that might be considered a surprise given the composition of the population. Henry VII's hospital catered for the poor, and the military was attractive to those in dire straits, often recruiting from the poor, criminal classes. With regard to the hospital poor, however, it is not certain how many were actually represented in the buried population (Chapter 6). As for the military hospital, barracks and prison, the limited evidence available from documentary sources suggests that the hospital and military diet, while not excessive, would have been adequate. It is also worth remembering that except in times of war, the military recruitment selection processes did include medical assessment (Chapter 3) so successful teenagers and young men should have started their military careers relatively fit and healthy.

Perhaps less surprising is the fact that diseases associated with rich and excessive diets were also comparatively uncommon among the population. The historical evidence suggests that the Savoy population was not primarily made up of what is known as 'the middling sort' but it did have its small share of more wealthy inhabitants. Up until the 17th century and the arrival of the soldiers, the precinct was partly occupied by the wealthy in society. Subsequently, in the later 17th century, lodgings within the hospital buildings were rented to nobles, and of course there were higher-ranking military officers within the precinct during the 18th century. It is also probable that wealthier individuals moved back into the precinct at the beginning of the 19th century once the areas had become residential and desirable again.

CRIBRA ORBITALIA

This has long been regarded as a condition that results from iron-deficiency anaemia and manifests as porous lesions in the roofs of the orbits (Roberts & Cox 2003). It is believed that these porous lesions result from thinning of the outer table of the skull, which in turn leads to the exposure of the underlying diploë in order to facilitate the influx of red blood cells in times of physical stress. However, the diagnosis of anaemia and the presence of cribra orbitalia in human skeletal remains cannot be interpreted solely as resulting from iron deficiency as other contributory factors such as parasitic infection, loss of blood and other metabolic conditions – inadequate diet, for example, as seen in scurvy and rickets – can also play a role (Brickley & Ives 2008).

The condition was recorded as present when observed affecting either one of the orbits or both of them. Crude prevalence rates of cribra orbitalia showed that these lesions were present in 3.7% (23/609) of the total cemetery population (Table 5.33). Males and females appeared to be similarly affected and the statistical analysis based on true prevalence rates (Table 5.33) confirmed this observation (χ^2=0.985812, df=1, p<0.05). A notable difference was observed between adults and subadults but the comparison failed to demonstrate a significant difference between both groups (χ^2=0.113734, df=1, p<0.05).

The pensioners from the Royal Hospital Greenwich (Boston et al 2008) recorded a higher percentage of individuals affected by cribra orbitalia. It was found in 33.3% (34/105) of all adults

	M+M? (n/N)	F+F? (n/N)	? (n/N)	Subadults (n/N)	Total (n/N)
Crude prevalence	3.3% (11/325)	3.8% (4/105)	- (0/89)	8.8% (8/90)	3.7% (23/609)
True prevalence	6.2% (11/175)	6.3% (4/63)	- (0/18)	102.1% (8/66)	7.1% (23/322)

Table 5.33 Crude and true prevalence rates of cribra orbitalia within the total population

analysed and was absent among subadults. As highlighted in the historical records (see Chapter 3) the Savoy prisoners as well as the soldiers in the barracks were provided with the same portions of bread, meat, cheese, potatoes and beer, 'all good of the kind'. This information suggests that at least sources of iron would have been available during this period of the history of the Savoy population. However, the absence of cribra orbitalia among subadults seems surprising, particularly at a time when changes in feeding practices, such as replacing milk with 'pap' or 'panada', a mixture of flour and water, would have been detrimental to the general health of children. These ingredients would not have nourished infants adequately, thus making them prone to a poorer immune system (Roberts & Cox 2003).

POROTIC HYPEROSTOSIS

Porotic hyperostosis appears to have a similar aetiology to that of cribra orbitalia. It manifests as an expansion of the diploë and results from increased demand for hematopoietic marrow associated with anaemia, but is located on the cranial vault (Ortner 2003). Porotic hyperostosis was present in 17 individuals (2.7%, 17/609) – two subadults (2.2%, 2/90) and 15 adults (2.8%, 15/519), with males more commonly affected (4.3%,14/325) than females (0.9%,1/105). One adult male aged 30–45 years and one subadult individual aged 1–6 years showed a combination of porotic hyperostosis and cribra orbitalia lesions. The combination of cranial vault and orbital lesions has been associated with prolonged iron-deficiency anaemia according to Roberts and Manchester (2005, 229).

RICKETS

Rickets is a condition that results from a deficiency in vitamin D, which is essential for the deposition of calcium and the mineralisation of bone. Its deficit produces softening and weakening of the bone and prolonged deprivation can lead to light, porous bones and osteopenia, which is a precursor of osteoporosis. Bending deformities, particularly those observed in long bones, usually occur in response to weight-bearing through crawling and walking, together with flaring of the metaphyseal endplates (Brickley & Ives 2008). The diagnosis of vitamin D deficiency rickets in the Savoy was based on the

medial view　　　　　　　　　anterior view　　　　　　　　　medial view

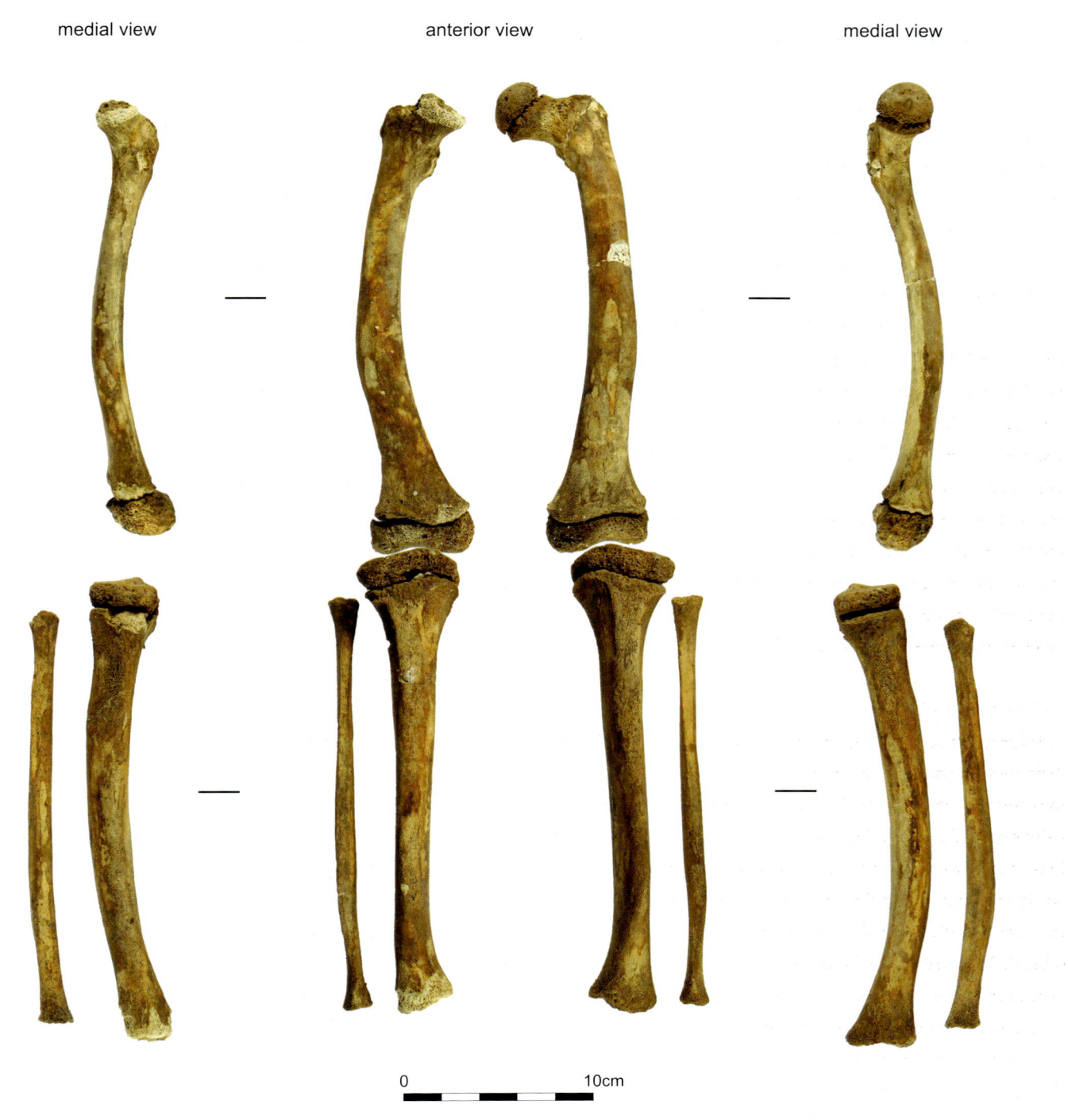

Fig 5.40 Skeleton [1770] showing anterior–posterior and medial–lateral bending of the lower limb bones, thought to relate to rickets

macroscopic observation of the bowing and bending of long bones as seen in skeleton [1770] (Fig 5.40).

As seen in Table 5.34, the condition was present in both adults and subadults with a total crude prevalence rate of 5.2% (32/609).

Within the subadult population, rickets affected individuals of all ages but the peak of the condition was observed among those of 1–6 years of age (Fig 5.41). This peak is coincidental with the age of weaning and other cultural and social trends adopted during the post-medieval period, such as the replacement of breast milk, rich in vitamin D, with adulterated milk and the introduction of artificial food such as 'pap' or 'panada', which lacked the necessary dietary requirements (above, 'Cribra orbitalia') (Roberts & Cox 2003; Brickley & Ives 2008). In the absence of vitamin D ingestion, the body can naturally synthesise it if exposed to solar radiation (Roberts & Manchester 2005). However, the cultural practices related to sunlight exposure and clothing fashion within an urbanised and,

M+M? (n/N)	F+F? (n/N)	? (n/N)	Subadults (n/N)	Total (n/N)
3.6% (12/325)	5.7% (6/105)	2.2% (2/89)	13.3% (12/90)	**5.2% (32/609)**

Table 5.34 Crude prevalence rates of rickets within the total population

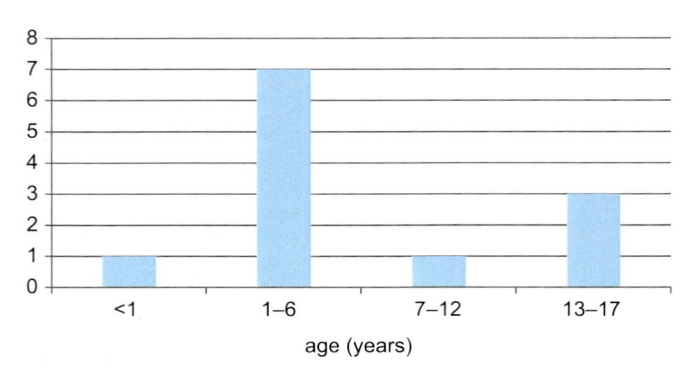

Fig 5.41 Distribution of rachitic subadults according to age

later, an industrialised and polluted capital like London, would certainly have had a detrimental role to play in the synthesis of vitamin D during children's vulnerable growing years.

Three subadult individuals, [220], [469] and [1716], in addition to suffering from rickets, displayed dental enamel hypoplasia in either their deciduous or their permanent teeth, which supports the idea of extended episodes of physical stress during childhood. The biomolecular analysis of the hair of [1716] (above, 5.5) also confirms the idea that the increasing nitrogen isotope values (Fig 5.7) relate to physiological stress such as malnutrition, chronic disease, breastfeeding and weaning (Nitsch et al 2011; Henderson et al 2014).

Adult individuals did not show signs of active rickets, only the distinctive bowing of the lower limb bones indicative of vitamin D deficiency during childhood. Bone changes resulting from residual rickets deformities were found in 20 individuals, giving a crude prevalence rate of 3.8% (20/519) for the adult population (Table 5.34). The evidence for residual rickets posed a unique opportunity to compare the sex-related basis of the condition, which otherwise, in the subadult population, would not be possible. A subgroup of six adults (30.0%, 6/20) also presented evidence of residual hypoplastic enamel defects and another 15 (75%, 15/20) showed cribra orbitalia while suffering from rickets, which would again support the idea of a stressful childhood as a result of an undernourished diet, among other extrinsic factors.

The crude prevalence of the condition at the Savoy Chapel fell at the midpoint of the range when compared with other contemporary sites from the London area (Table 5.35) and clearly exceeded that reported by Roberts and Cox (2003) of 3.6% for the post-medieval period, which included a large number of middle-class individuals.

SCURVY

Scurvy is a condition that results from a deficiency in vitamin C (ascorbic acid), essential for the synthesis of collagen, the main structural protein found in the skeleton. A deficit in its production leads to haemorrhage and contributes to the development of anaemia. Vitamin C also plays a role in maintaining the immune system and enables it to function normally and for this reason individuals with a deficit in ascorbic acid are more prone to infectious diseases. Scurvy can also inhibit osteoblasts from producing osteoid, which in turn leads to light and osteoporotic bones. Other bone changes indicative of scurvy are new bone formation and porosity, particularly in areas of rapid growth (Brickley & Ives 2008). The diagnosis of vitamin C deficiency scurvy in the Savoy Chapel population was based on the macroscopic observation of light porous bones (porosity on both the cranial and post-cranial skeleton), new bone formation secondary to haemorrhage and loosening of teeth (AMTL).

Scurvy was present among the subadult population with a crude prevalence of 8.8% (8/90) and 1.3% (8/609) of the total population. No distinctive bone changes relating to scurvy were noted among the adult population, which could be owing to the less straightforward identification of the condition in the adult skeleton. However, conditions such as cribra orbitalia, porotic hyperostosis and AMTL, found among the adults of the Savoy, can all be manifestations of scurvy. In line with the results observed for rickets, scurvy affected the subadult individuals from all ages, although the highest prevalence was observed among the youngest groups (Fig 5.42), suggesting that newborn babies and those of weaning age were at higher risk.

According to Brickley and Ives (2008) there are records of infants suffering from scurvy as young as the first month of life, their mothers being severely malnourished. The inability of the malnourished mother to produce adequate levels of vitamin C in the milk, added to cultural patterns of early weaning, might have contributed to the presence of the condition among the youngest

London-area cemeteries	Prevalence (n/N)
London Hospital	2.3% (15/636)
St Pancras burial ground	2.7% (20/715)
New Bunhill burial ground	3.9% (20/514)
St Benet Sherehog	3.9% (9/230)
Queen's Chapel Savoy	**5.2% (32/609)**
Sheen's burial ground	5.5% (14/254)
All Saints, Chelsea Old Church	5.6% (11/198)
City Bunhill burial ground	6.7% (16/239)
Bow Baptist Church	7.7% (32/416)
Royal Hospital Greenwich	9.3% (10/107)
St Marylebone Church burial ground	10.6% (32/301)
St Mary and St Michael's burial ground	11.1% (78/705)

Table 5.35 Comparison of rickets in cemeteries from the London area (all adult and subadult individuals are pooled; for references see above, 5.1)

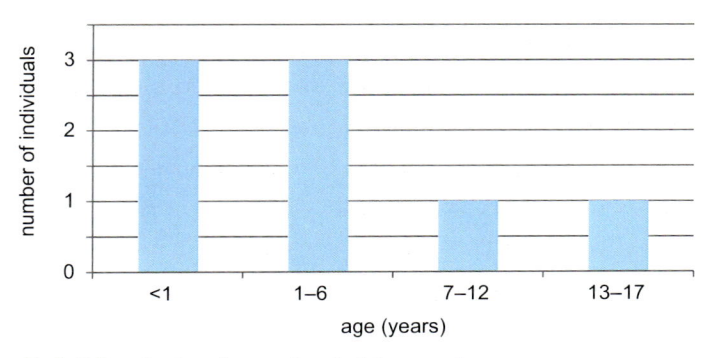

Fig 5.42 Distribution of scurvy in subadults according to age

individuals. Other predisposing factors to scurvy are premature births, infection and feeding with prepared infant foods.

Scurvy leads to loss of teeth through gum bleeding (Brickley & Ives 2008). One 7- to 12-year-old, [610], had suffered AMTL of the permanent upper right 1st premolar. The loss of this tooth could have resulted from trauma but in the light of other evidence such as porotic lesions in the cranium and the roof of both orbits, along with generalised new bone formation in the surviving bones of the upper limb and pelvis, the most probable causative origin was scurvy.

Crude prevalence of scurvy at the Savoy Chapel fits well with that obtained from other contemporary cemeteries from London (Table 5.36), mirroring the results obtained from rickets and the idea that metabolic conditions were not as severe in the subadult population from the Savoy as elsewhere.

London-area cemeteries	Prevalence (n/N)
Sheen's burial ground	0.4% (1/254)
All Saints, Chelsea Old Church	0.5% (1/198)
Queen's Chapel Savoy	**1.3% (8/609)**
St Marylebone Church burial ground	1.3% (4/301)
Bow Baptist Church	3.6% (15/416)
St Mary and St Michael's burial ground	6.0% (42/705)
Royal Hospital Greenwich	11.2% (12/107)

Table 5.36 Comparison of scurvy in cemeteries from the London area (all adult and subadult individuals are pooled; for references see above, 5.1)

OSTEOPOROSIS

Osteoporosis is the loss of bone mineral content and density, which leads to structural changes in the bone architecture and its incapacity to withstand load bearing (Brickley & Ives 2008). It is a multifactorial condition, in other words, its aetiology is linked with a number of variables, one of which is increasing age, as the condition does not manifest before the fifth decade. Furthermore, osteoporosis appears to be sex-biased as females are more frequently affected than males, particularly after menopause (Ortner 2003). Other contributory variables that can play a role are genetics, physical activity, nutrition and lifestyle (Brickley & Ives 2008).

Possible osteoporosis was diagnosed macroscopically by the reduction of weight in bones relative to other bones of the same size, which can admittedly be fairly subjective, in addition to the difficulty in differentiating between bone mineral loss as a result of osteoporosis or because of taphonomic processes. Osteoporosis secondary to underlying pathology, trauma, infection or other metabolic conditions was not counted here. Being a condition so closely associated with advancing age, it is not surprising that osteoporosis was present in the adult population of the Savoy. Crude prevalence rates suggested that it affected only 6.3% (33/519) adult individuals. Comparisons between the sexes suggested that, as anticipated, females had a higher prevalence (12.3%, 13/105) than males (5.2%, 17/325), with 3.3% (3/89) of adult individuals of unknown sex affected.

DIFFUSE IDIOPATHIC SKELETAL HYPEROSTOSIS (DISH)

This is a condition that affects spinal and extra-spinal joints of the skeleton, producing progressive ossification of tendons and ligaments at their attachment sites (Ortner 2003). The aetiology of DISH is unknown but, along with other B27 disorders such as psoriatic arthritis and ankylosing spondylitis, it is associated with the presence of abundant new bone formation, suggesting that the B27 gene is linked to functions of bone production (Resnick et al 1978). DISH is a condition of the aged, with its onset between 40 and 50 years of age, increasing its prevalence particularly after the age of 65. A variable associated with accelerated ageing is late-onset diabetes. Obesity and a sedentary way of life are other important variables that play a role in triggering the development of DISH. Thus in medieval times it was associated with a monastic way of life but in the post-medieval period it is associated with dietary excess in the middle classes (Roberts & Cox 2003).

The diagnosis of DISH varies depending on the number of vertebrae considered as bridging (Ponce 2004). In the population from the Savoy Chapel the condition was 'definite' in three cases where bridging occurred between three or more lower thoracic vertebrae and 'possible' or 'early' DISH in two cases when the union occurred between two contiguous vertebrae only along with the extra-spinal manifestations.

Male individuals are usually more affected by DISH than females in a 2:1 ratio. In agreement with this five adult males from the Savoy Chapel ([123], [731], [962], [1258] and [1912]) exhibited spinal and extra-spinal proliferative changes compatible with DISH, giving a crude prevalence of 1.5% (5/325) for the adult male population and 0.9% (5/519) for the general adult population. As the condition has been associated with high status, the upper classes and dietary excess, this gives an insight into the socioeconomic background of this population, reflecting the presence of the nobility in the 17th century, high-status military individuals or perhaps members of the 19th-century civilian population.

Male [123], aged over 45 years, had the anterior longitudinal ligament ossified on the right- and left-hand sides of T9 and T10. Extra-spinal manifestations included 'whiskering' on the iliac crests, ossification of the triceps on the left ulna and ossification of the patellar ligament on the left tibia. A number of ossified cartilages were also present, including the thyroid, cricoid, the first tracheal cartilage and a number of unsided costal cartilages.

Male [962], also aged over 45, displayed bridges of bones between T4 and T10 but ankylosis through the anterior longitudinal ligament took place only between T8 and T9. Extra-spinal manifestations of the condition were observed at the Achilles tendon of the left calcaneus. A third male over 45 years of age, [1258], presented the fusion of two segments of the thoracic spine. The anterior longitudinal ligament exhibited a flowing 'candle wax' appearance on the anterior–lateral side of T6 to T8 and on T10 to T11. Enthesophyte formation occurred on the iliac crests and ischia and a number of unsided ossified costal cartilages were also present.

A male of 30–45 years, [1912], showed ossification of the anterior longitudinal ligament and the supra-spinous ligament ankylosing T5 to T7. Well-developed enthesophytes were found bilaterally on the ischial tuberosities, acetabular rims, iliac crests, greater trochanters and linea aspera of both femora, proximal and distal muscle insertions on the tibiae and the patellae. The ossified thyroid and cricoid cartilages were also present along with numerous tracheal cartilages.

Finally, male [731], aged over 45 years, represented the most severe case of DISH found at the Savoy Chapel. Almost his entire thoracic spine was linked through bridges of bone formed across the anterior longitudinal ligament between T4 and T11 (Fig 5.43). Extra-spinal enthesophytes were present on the iliac crests and the acetabular margins of the os coxae. Along with the spinal and extra-spinal manifestations of DISH, the right tarsometatarsal bones of this individual were ankylosed, forming a unique bony mass, except for the right navicular, which remained separated from the rest. Early signs of ankylosis were also visible on the left tarsometatarsal bones. Furthermore, the right sacroiliac joint was fixed by an intra-articular bony union and although the left side was not ankylosed, early signs of fusion were evident.

Aufderheide and Rodríguez-Martín (1998, 98) suggest that sacroiliac intra-articular bony ankylosis is not compatible with DISH, so it is possible that this individual suffered from more than one condition. Some of the skeletal changes observed were compatible with some of the so-called seronegative spondyloarthropathies. This group of disorders of unknown aetiology characteristically affect the sacroiliac joints and the spine asymmetrically, but the joints of the lower limbs are less commonly affected. Enthesopathy formation is also a prominent characteristic of the spinal and extra-spinal joint involvement of these conditions (Ortner 2003). Finally, a number of sternal rib ends appeared to be ankylosed to the manubrium but poor preservation prevented confirmation of this. It is not known if this fusion resulted from joint degeneration (secondary to osteoarthritis) or from the manifestation of an underlying spondyloarthropathy condition, as DISH can occur with OA and with other erosive arthropathies, making differential diagnosis challenging in some cases (Ortner 2003, 559).

As previously discussed (above, 5.4) two individuals, skeleton [123] and skeleton [731], were analysed for nitrogen isotope values (Fig 5.4). The results are in accordance with studies of late medieval individuals with DISH who produced signatures indicative of a high-protein diet (Müldner & Richards 2007; Spencer 2009). In support of the biomolecular results, the burial records (as reviewed in Chapter 4) mention that high-ranking individuals were buried at the Savoy Chapel. As summarised by Bleasdale (2016) the military personnel buried in the churchyard would have consumed a relatively large amount of protein in comparison with prisoners and other working-class civilians. The differential diet of high-ranking generals and their wives could be represented by these DISH cases.

Finally, the prevalence of DISH at the Savoy Chapel was among the lowest observed among other contemporary cemeteries from the capital (Table 5.37), which could partly be due to the different ways in which DISH is diagnosed by different authors. On a wider scale, however, the Savoy Chapel population fits well within the expected crude prevalence rate of DISH in post-medieval England, which ranged from 0.9% to 5.8% (Roberts & Cox 2003).

CIRCULATORY DISEASE

Circulatory diseases are those affecting the arteries and veins that are responsible for the transport of oxygen, hormones, blood cells and a number of nutrients within the body. Three conditions found in the Savoy population that are not considered circulatory diseases per se are included within this category because cartilage, bone or joint were affected secondary to trauma to the circulatory system. These are Legg-Calvé-Perthes disease, slipped femoral epiphysis and

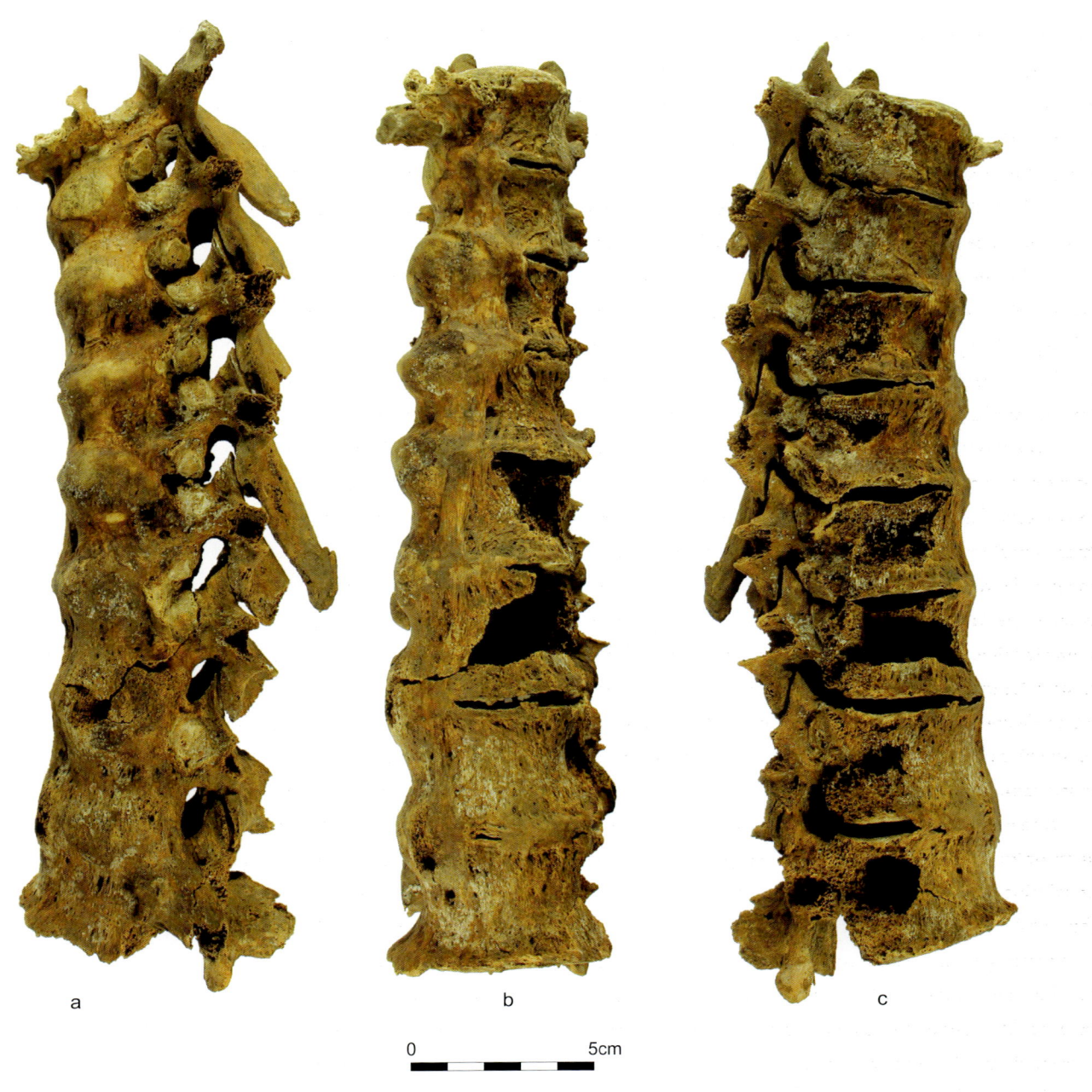

Fig 5.43 Skeleton [731] showing views of T4 to T11 with the so-called 'candle wax' flowing ossification of the anterior longitudinal ligament, thought to relate to DISH: a – left; b – anterior; c – right

London-area cemeteries	Prevalence (n/N)
St Mary and St Michael's burial ground	0.7% (2/268)
Queen's Chapel Savoy	**0.9% (5/519)**
St Pancras burial ground	1.1% (6/532)
St Benet Sherehog	1.2% (2/165)
Royal Hospital Greenwich	1.8% (2/107)
New Bunhill Fields burial ground	1.9% (3/157)
Sheen's burial ground	2.4% (4/166)
City Bunhill burial ground	2.6% (3/117)
St Marylebone Church burial ground	2.6% (6/223)
Bow Baptist Church	2.8% (6/214)
London Hospital	3.1% (5/603)
All Saints, Chelsea Old Church	6.0% (10/165)

Table 5.37 Comparison of DISH in cemeteries from the London area (all adult individuals are pooled; for references see above, 5.1)

osteochondritis dissecans. These conditions, although related to trauma and consistent with the physical demands of a military lifestyle, are also linked to the inherent health status and wellbeing of the individuals combined with extrinsic factors such as a disadvantaged socioeconomic background. Although circulatory diseases are not known for being life-threatening, they can result in some degree of disability if, as found in the Savoy Chapel population, they affect those joints of the body that are required for ambulatory activities, such as the hips, knees, ankles and feet. Although symptoms and prognosis might vary from person to person, osteoarthritis secondary to malalignment and joint incongruity would undoubtedly have been the outcome for those affected, as seen in some individuals. A total of 10.6% (65/609) of skeletons analysed showed evidence of having suffered from one of the above-listed circulatory diseases.

LEGG-CALVÉ-PERTHES DISEASE (LCPD)

LCPD is a very uncommon condition affecting 5.7 cases per 100,000 children aged 0–14 years per annum in the UK (Perry 2013). Examples described in the palaeopathological literature are scarce and for this reason the exceptional examples found in archaeological contexts are worthy of analysis, description and reporting (Ponce & Novellino 2014). The condition is triggered by trauma to the blood supply of the femoral epiphysis. This results in avascular necrosis of the trabeculae and the marrow, leading to structural failure of the femoral head. The weak weight-bearing limb, unable to withstand the mechanical stress, collapses and flattens, producing a permanent deformed femoral head that results in a 'mushroom-like' appearance (Aufderheide and Rodríguez-martín 1998; Ortner 2003; Solomon et al 2010).

One possible male, aged 18–30 years, [1090], showed pathological changes on the right femoral head consistent with LCPD (Fig 5.44). The superior portion of the femoral head showed extensive osteonecrosis, particularly around the fovea capitis that was no longer present. The neck of the affected femur was shorter when compared with the left side and the right femoral head was a flattened mushroom shape. In line with these changes, the right acetabulum was wider and shallower when compared with the left side and the affected femur showed a decrease of 70mm in length when compared to the left side.

LCPD is often associated with a number of biological and/or genetic factors and within this context socioeconomic factors are also believed to play a role, given that the condition is higher in underprivileged communities (Perry 2013). Therefore the short and often the smallest child of their class with delayed bone growth, and from low socioeconomic status, may be more susceptible (Bruce 2011; Perry 2013). Historical documents show that in its earliest days Henry VII's Savoy Hospital catered for the poor (see Chapter 3) and, although it is not certain how many of these individuals were actually represented in the buried population (Chapter 6), conditions such as LCPD do exemplify the less privileged among the population. Although 13- to 18-year-olds were being recruited into Foot regiments during the late 19th century, the able-bodied and those free from deformity would have been favoured, so, as LCPD would pose a higher degree of disability and impairment because of pain in the hip and restricted mobility of the leg (Joseph 2011), it seems unlikely [1090] would have been one of the recruited soldiers,

SLIPPED FEMORAL EPIPHYSIS

Slipped femoral epiphysis is a condition that results from a fracture or a series of minor traumatic events on the growth plate of the femoral head. It leads to a forward displacement of the femoral neck while the epiphysis remains within the acetabulum (Bullough 2010; Solomon et al 2010). As the condition progresses, a number of events may occur, including avascular necrosis owing to disruption of the blood supply to the femoral head, premature fusion of the epiphysis or early onset degenerative joint disease of the hip (Solomon et al 2010).

One adult individual aged over 45 years, [1436], appeared to represent a possible case of slipped femoral epiphysis on the left femur. Regrettably, the degree of preservation of this bone was poor, as was that of the right femur and both os coxae, which made it hard to confirm the diagnosis and to compare the condition with the opposite side. However, the abnormal location and marked displacement of the femoral neck in relation to the neck of the femur and the diaphyseal axis, which were all still visible, were suggestive of this condition along with the secondary formation of marginal osteophytes on the femoral head.

OSTEOCHONDRITIS DISSECANS

Osteochondritis dissecans (OD) is, along with Legg-Calvé-Perthes disease, an osteochondrosis, a group of disorders that affect the joints of children and adolescents, especially males. In

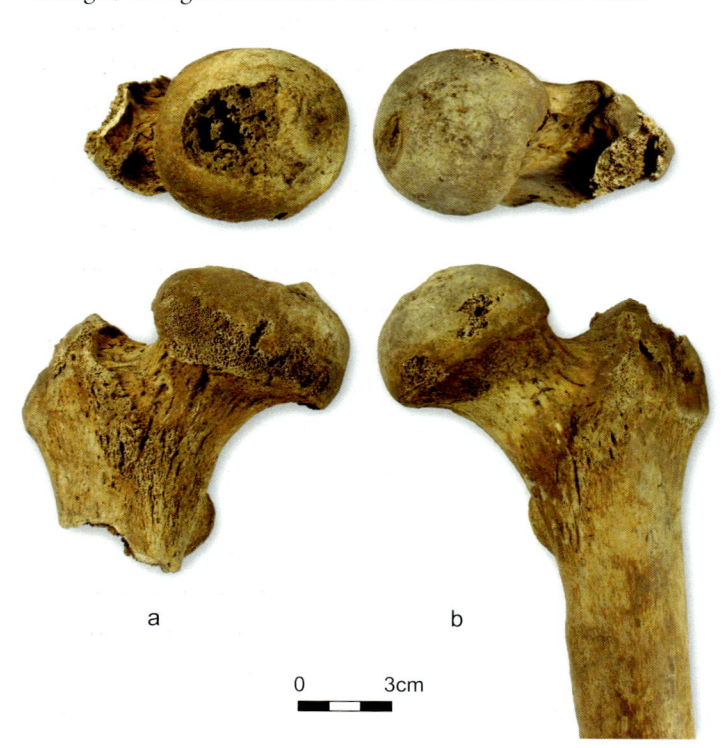

Fig 5.44 Skeleton [1090] showing: a – the flattened, mushroom-shaped, right femoral head; b – the normal left femoral head

OD a small piece of cartilage or bone detaches from its normal position at the joint after an interruption to the normal blood supply as a consequence of repetitive stress and microtrauma (Ortner 2003). The fragment can necrotise, remain loose within the joint cavity or reattach to the bone, but inevitable secondary osteoarthritis will develop in the affected area.

As seen in Table 5.38, OD was present in both sexes and all age categories of the Savoy population. There were 53 skeletons with at least one joint affected by OD, representing 8.7% (53/609) of the total population. Nine of these skeletons had OD in more than one joint, so 64 joints were affected in total.

The presence of OD within the Savoy population is not surprising given the underlying mechanical stress, microtrauma and physically active lifestyle experienced by soldiers. Indeed, as reviewed in Chapter 3, many of the recruits would have been teenagers (Bucholz & Ward 2012, 232), which concurs with the young age profile of the condition.

As observed in Table 5.38 and in line with observations carried out in the clinical field (Bullough 2010) the bones most commonly affected by OD were the humerus and talus. The capitulum of the humerus and the talar dome along with the posterior calcaneal articular facet of the talus (for example skeleton [1319], Fig 5.28) were the sites that presented the most examples of OD. In the femur, the affected areas were the femoral condyles and in the feet, the 1st metatarsal on both its proximal and distal articular joints along with the proximal articular facet of the 1st foot phalanx. In the tibia the condyles and the inferior articular facet were the sites most frequently observed with OD. In the spine, only the axis was affected. The lesion occurred on either side of the superior articular facets and was sometimes seen bilaterally. Other sites less frequently affected by OD were the glenoid cavity of the scapula, the articular surfaces of the patella and the navicular (proximal articular surface) and the semilunar notch of the ulna.

Examples of bilateralism were found in ten skeletons, for instance, in the tali of an adult male, 1st foot phalanges of two adult males and one female, both superior articular facets of the axis of an adult male, both femoral condyles of an adult male, both femoral condyles and tibial condyles of an adult male, both capitulums of the humeri of an adult male, both capitulums of the humeri and both femoral condyles of an adult male and both 1st metatarsals of an adult male.

NEOPLASTIC CONDITIONS

The term neoplasm refers to 'new tissue' or 'mass of new tissue' and is used to refer to cancer or tumour. Neoplastic tissue can be benign or malignant depending on whether its proliferation is capable of destroying surrounding cells or not (Aufderheide and Rodríguez-Martín 1998). This was the least prevalent pathology found among the Savoy Chapel population. Benign conditions included 'button' osteomas and a possible case of unifocal eosinophilic granuloma; within the malignant conditions was a possible case of multiple myeloma. The crude prevalence rate of neoplastic disease within the skeletal population was 0.9% (6/609). A total 0.9% (3/325) of males and 2.8% (3/105) of females displayed some form of neoplastic disease and according to the burial registers (Table 4.2) (see Chapter 4) only two deaths were recorded as resulting from cancer between 1754–6 and 1793–1813. These results support the information from the Bills of Mortality (Roberts & Cox 2003), where the osteological evidence of cancer and tumours during the post-medieval period is below 1%.

However, it should be borne in mind that cancer diagnosis in post-medieval patients would have been different from modern diagnosis and for this reason the extrapolation is not necessarily straightforward. In fact, since *Health and disease in Britain* was published (Roberts & Cox 2003) an increased number of new neoplastic cases have been reported. For instance, comparisons with other skeletal assemblages from the London area have shown that the prevalence rate found by others is higher than that found in this study: a crude prevalence rate of 5.6% (15/268) at St Mary and St Michael's burial ground, 4.2% (9/214) at Bow Baptist Church and 3.0% (5/166) at Sheen's burial ground (Henderson et al 2013).

Limb	Bone	M+M? (n/N)	F+F? (n/N)	? (n/N)	Subadults (n/N)	Total (n/N)
Upper	scapula	0.6% (2/325)	0.9% (1/105)	- (0/89)	- (0/90)	0.4% (3/609)
	humerus	1.8% (6/325)	1.9% (2/105)	1.1% (1/89)	1.1% (1/90)	1.6% (10/609)
	ulna	- (0/325)	0.9% (1/105)	- (0/89)	- (0/90)	0.1% (1/609)
Spine	axis	1.5% (5/325)	0.9% (1/105)	- (0/89)	2.2% (2/90)	1.3% (8/609)
Lower	femur	2.1% (7/325)	0.9% (1/105)	- (0/89)	- (0/90)	1.3% (8/609)
	patella	0.3% (1/325)	- (0/105)	- (0/89)	- (0/90)	0.1% (1/609)
	tibia	1.2% (4/325)	0.9% (1/105)	1.1% (1/89)	1.1% (1/90)	1.1% (7/609)
	talus	1.5% (5/325)	1.9% (2/105)	2.2% (2/89)	- (0/90)	1.4% (9/609)
	navicular	0.3% (1/325)	- (0/105)	- (0/89)	- (0/90)	0.1% (1/609)
	1st metatarsal	2.1% (7/325)	0.9% (1/105)	- (0/89)	- (0/90)	1.3% (8/609)
	1st foot phalanx	1.8% (6/325)	0.9% (1/105)	- (0/89)	- (0/90)	1.1% (7/609)
Total		13.5% (44/325)	10.4% (11/105)	4.4% (4/89)	4.4% (4/90)	10.3% (63/609)

Table 5.38 Crude prevalence rates of osteochondritis dissecans within the total population

BENIGN NEOPLASTIC CONDITIONS

Button osteoma

The most commonly found forms of cancer in archaeological populations are 'button' osteomas. These raised areas of dense bone, resembling a small mound or dome (Mann & Hunt 2012), are not known for producing adverse consequences to those that present them other than a lump on the outer table of the skull. They have been found in many post-medieval sites from the London area (Cowie et al 2008; Miles et al 2008a; 2008b; Henderson et al 2013). At the Savoy Chapel, button osteomas were found in the cranial vault of four adult individuals. One adult male exhibited a solitary osteoma located on the posterior aspect of the right parietal, measuring approximately 20 × 20mm. Another had an isolated button osteoma on the posterior aspect of the right frontal bone. This was round in shape and measured approximately 5mm diameter. One female presented a single osteoma in a fragment of one unsided parietal. Finally, a series of osteomas approximately 25mm long were located along the mid line of the sagittal suture of a female.

Unifocal eosinophilic granuloma

The right side of the mandible of adult male [1077], aged 30–45 years, presented a destructive 'punched-out' lesion of approximately 45mm extending from the lower right 1st molar to the lower left 1st incisor (Fig 5.45). The teeth from the affected area were recovered, indicating that they were *in situ* albeit in a soft-tissue lesion. A series of Cone Beam Computed Tomography (CBCT) images along with a panoramic radiograph were taken of the internal walls of the affected area of the mandible at Guy's Hospital Dental Radiology Department (London) thanks to Eric Whaites, Clinical Consultant, and Fiona Ball, Superintendent Radiographer. The images revealed how almost all the tooth-supporting periodontal bone had been destroyed.

Although this individual also presented skeletal lesions characteristic of tertiary syphilis (discussed above), infection can be ruled out as an aetiological factor of the anomaly of the mandible because there were no signs of sinus formation, no involucrum or reactive new bone formation around the necrotic margins of the mandible. The possibility that this was a malignant tumour, which emerged from the surrounding soft tissues of the mouth, tongue or throat, can also be rejected because the lesion appeared to be contained within a defined area. Instead, the condition may represent a rare unifocal eosinophilic granuloma, a tumour-like condition caused by the abnormal proliferation of autoimmune Lagerhans cells and eosinophic leucocytes (Whaites & Drage 2013). Clinical examples that resemble those observed in skeleton [1077] are described in Agarwal et al (2012).

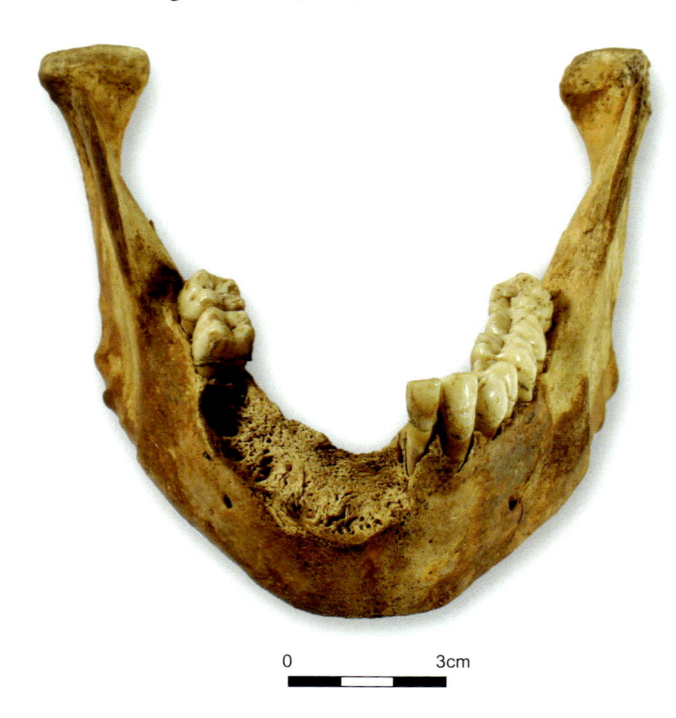

Fig 5.45 Skeleton [1077] showing a typical 'punched-out' lesion on the anterior right side of the mandible, extending from the right 1st mandible to the left 1st incisor

MALIGNANT NEOPLASTIC CONDITIONS

Multiple myeloma

Female [490], aged 30–45 years, exhibited perforating lytic lesions compatible with neoplastic disease in most parts of the skeleton. These lesions were present in the cranium, vertebrae, ribs, sternum, claviculae, scapulae, pelvis and epiphyses of long bones but not in the hands or feet. Only osteolytic lesions were present and these looked as if they had been produced inside the spongy bone and then expanded to emerge aggressively in the periosteum. Isolated roundish holes of irregular, sharp margins and varying sizes, ranging from approximately 0.5mm to 2mm, appear to have merged and coalesced into small clusters of lesions. These penetrated both outer and inner tables of flat bones such as the skull (Fig 5.46a), the scapula (Fig 5.46c) and the ilium (Fig 5.46b) sometimes producing complete perforations, sometimes affecting only the external or internal cortical bone. Diaphyseal and articular areas of most long bones also showed substantive necrosis. In the spine, the vertebral bodies and apophyseal joints appeared particularly badly affected, to the point of putting it at risk of collapse (Fig 5.46d). Furthermore, there were no signs of healing around the lesions.

Multiple myeloma could be responsible for the condition. This form of cancer represents the malignant growth of the

CHAPTER 5 THE HUMAN REMAINS

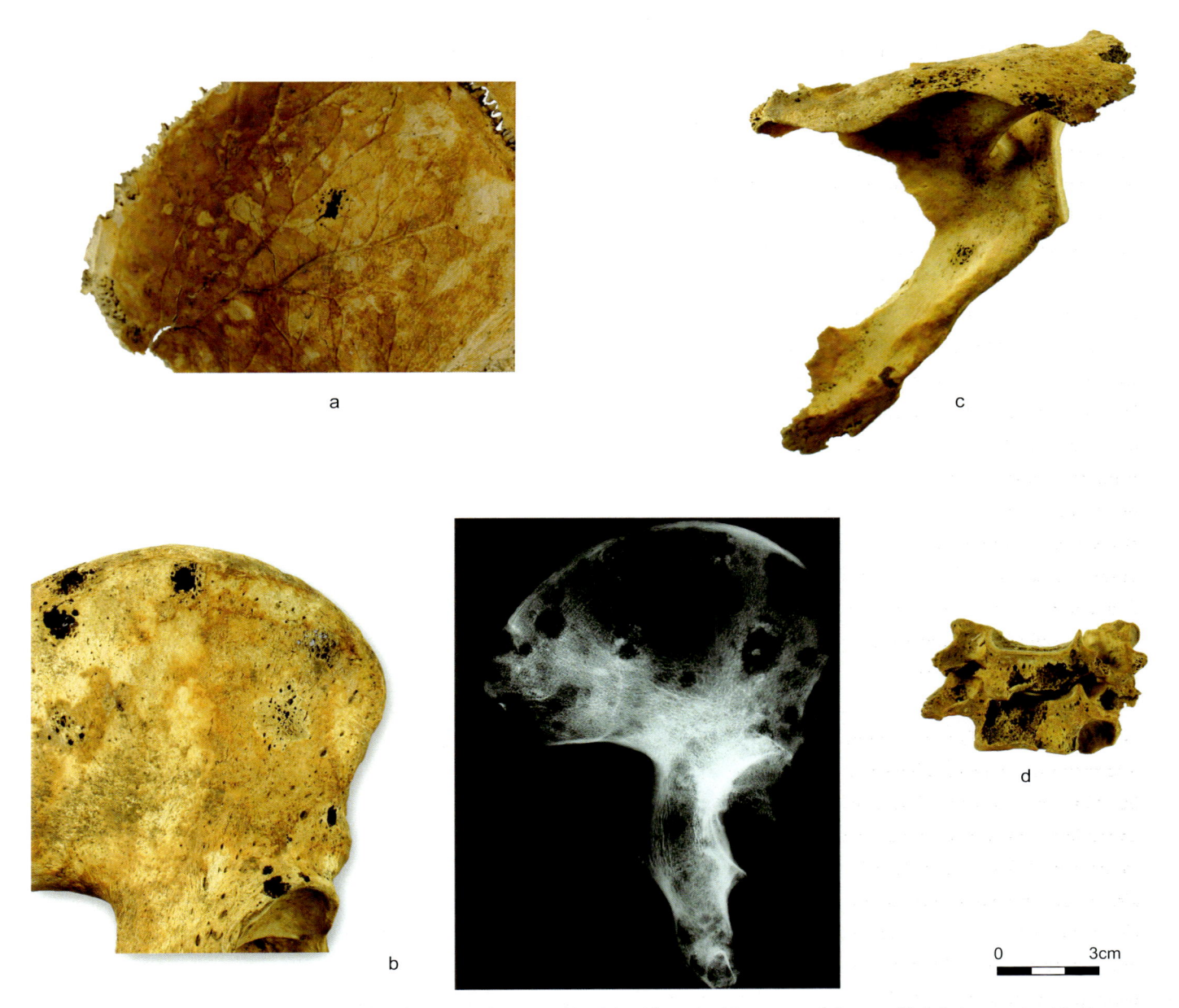

Fig 5.46 Skeleton [490] showing: a – a cluster of lytic lesions on the inner table of the right parietal; b – scattered clusters of lytic lesions on the right ilium; radiograph showing multiple 'punched-out' holes; c – lytic lesions penetrating the right scapula; d – destructive lytic lesions affecting the vertebral bodies and apophyseal joints of C4–C5

plasma cells of the bone marrow. The bones more frequently affected because of their content of blood-forming bone marrow are the spine, ribs, skull, pelvis, sternum, femora and humeri (Alt & Adler 1992). The totally lytic nature of myeloma lesions and the fact that there are multiple and generalised osteolytic destructions are indicative of this type of metastatic cancer (Aufderheide and Rodríguez-Martín 1998). Metastatic carcinoma, breast cancer in particular, is rejected as a possible differential diagnosis because this type of malignant cancer produces a combination of lytic and blastic lesions that were not present in skeleton [490]. The simple gross visual examination of any osteoblastic lesion should suffice to exclude it as aetiological factor (Aufderheide and Rodríguez-Martín 1998).

Multiple myeloma occurs in the fifth to seventh decades of life (Alt & Adler 1992) and at the time of her death skeleton [490] was between 30 and 45 years of age. The remains of a 26-week-old foetus, [491], were found in her grave between her ankles. It is not certain if this was her child but if it was, it is possible that the pregnancy might have deteriorated and weakened her health. These individuals are discussed further in Chapter 6. Her lower thoracic spine, particularly the vertebral bodies, were badly affected by lytic lesions and consequently very fragmented. A heavy pregnancy would have weakened this spinal area and put it at risk of collapse. It can also be suggested that her deteriorating health status might have contributed to an early end to her pregnancy.

MISCELLANEOUS CONDITIONS

Miscellaneous conditions include those that could not, because of their nature, be included under any of the pathological conditions discussed above. Two conditions, elongated styloid process and inferior turbinate hypertrophy, are discussed below. A total 0.8% (5/609) of all skeletons analysed displayed one of these miscellaneous conditions.

ELONGATED STYLOID PROCESS

It is generally accepted that the normal length of the styloid process of the temporal bone is between 25mm and 30mm (Mann & Hunt 2012). An elongated styloid process results eith from its natural elongation (primary cause) or as the consequence of the ossification, calcification or mineralisation of the styloid ligament (secondary cause). An elongated styloid process can lead to the so-called 'Eagle's syndrome' (Elimairi et al 2015), a symptomatic condition that produces head, neck and pharyngeal complications including pain on swallowing, partial atrophy of the tongue, dry mouth, loss of taste, altered speech, foreign body sensation in the throat, otalgia, tinnitus and ocular pain.

Three adult males and one female from the Savoy presented elongated styloid processes, giving a crude prevalence rate of 0.6% (4/609) of the total population. The only female of the group, aged more than 45 years, displayed the condition on the right styloid process, which measured 40mm in length. The left styloid process was broken and lost post-mortem and therefore it is not known if the condition was unilateral or bilateral. In the skeletons of two male individuals the condition was observed on the right styloid process but again the opposite side was broken post-mortem. In one case the styloid process presented a 60mm pseudoarthrosis (a segmental defect marking where the bony portion of the styloid process ended and the ossified stylohyoid ligament began); in the other the condition was mild, measuring only 38mm.

Lastly, a 30- to 45-year-old male presented the condition bilaterally with both styloid processes measuring 48mm. Numerous other cartilages were also ossified in this individual including the thyroid, the cricoid, numerous tracheal rings and costal cartilages, probably ossified secondary to DISH (above, 'Metabolic disease'). It can therefore be suggested that the elongated styloid process in this particular case was the result of this underlying metabolic condition, which produced an imbalance in the calcification and mineralisation metabolism.

The preservation of the styloid process is a rare occurrence in archaeological samples because of its fragility. It is therefore believed that the condition is more common than recorded and its prevalence is actually higher among the Savoy Chapel population than observed. Only one case was reported from a contemporary cemetery in the London area –an elderly male from St Marylebone Church burial ground, who was affected bilaterally (Miles et al 2008b).

INFERIOR TURBINATE HYPERTROPHY

Hypertrophied inferior turbinate is an abnormal enlargement of the inferior nasal concha. Although the aetiology of the condition can be multifactorial, it has been found that septal deviation may be related to a compensatory enlarged inferior turbinate (Mann & Hunt 2012; Dhulipalla 2015). The symptoms associated with this lesion are nasal blockage or obstruction, trouble breathing through the nose especially during exercise and trouble sleeping, along with allergic rhinitis, sneezing and watering from the nose. Inferior turbinate hypertrophy can affect individuals from all ages and males are more affected than the females, particularly between the ages of 20 and 29 years (ibid).

At the Savoy, one 18- to 30-year-old female, [1826], had the right inferior turbinate hypertrophied (Fig 5.47). The left inferior turbinate was broken post-mortem, hindering a bilateral assessment of the condition. The suggestion of a septal deviation cannot explain the aetiology of the condition here because in this case it appears to be normal.

This condition was also reported in the post-medieval skeletons buried at the St Pancras burial ground (Emery & Wooldridge 2011) where, similarly, the right turbinate was abnormally enlarged in the nasal cavity of one adult male.

CULTURAL MODIFICATION
CORSETRY EVIDENCE

Deformation of the rib cage secondary to the prolonged use of a corset was found in one adult female, [1525], aged more than 45 years, but the Savoy individuals were not systematically scrutinised for this kind of cultural evidence. Her mid lower thoracic ribs appeared bent inwards but also downwards giving the appearance of a narrow and constricted rib cage. The diaphyses of these ribs looked thinned and straightened from their angle to their sternal ends (Fig 5.48).

The evidence of corset use has been reported in females from other cemeteries in the London area, for example, at Bow Baptist Church (12.2%, 14/115), St Mary and St Michael's burial ground (11.9%, 32/268) (Henderson et al 2013) and St Marylebone Church burial ground (8.1%, 7/86) (Miles et al 2008b). The use of corsets has also been reported by Moore and Buckberry (2016) in a 19th-century male from Wolverhampton,

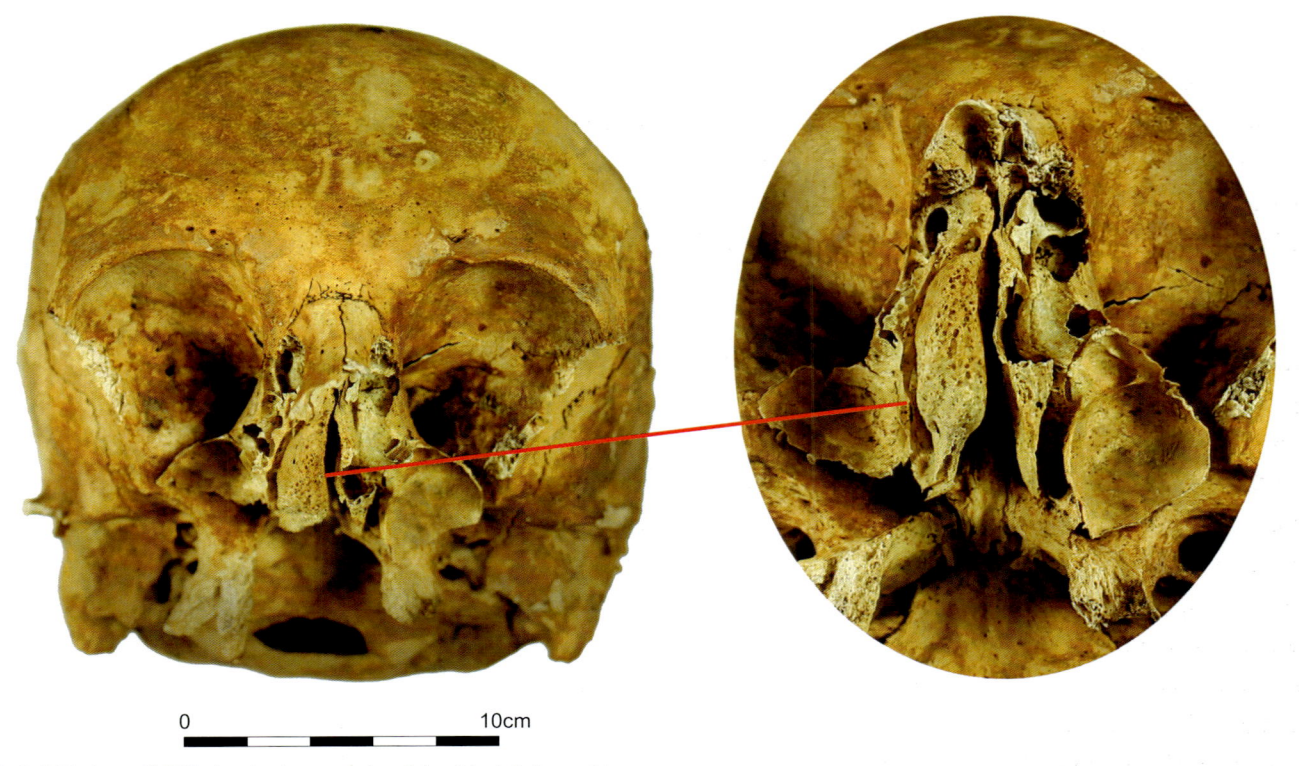

Fig 5.47 Skeleton [1826] showing hypertrophy of the right inferior turbinate

West Midlands – thought in this case to be worn for orthopaedic treatment of the kyphotic curvature of the spine resulting from tuberculosis. In the case of skeleton [1525] the absence of any obvious spinal condition that would have prompted the use of a corset for medical reasons may suggest that on this occasion the corset was used for fashionable purposes.

RESTRICTED FOOTWEAR EVIDENCE

Hallux valgus (or bunion) is a condition of the feet characterised by a medial–lateral deviation of the 1st metatarsophalangeal joint. A genetic predisposition has been suggested as a possible aetiological factor, but they are more likely to result from wearing restricted, pointed shoes (Trujillo-Mederos et al 2014). Although hallux valgus is not considered a joint disease per se it can lead to secondary osteoarthritis of the affected joints.

Four adult individuals, two females and two males, exhibited pathological changes in their metatarsal bones indicative of hallux valgus, giving a crude prevalence of 0.7% (4/519) of the total adult population. The condition was bilateral in two cases and unilateral, affecting the left foot, in the remaining two cases.

A female aged 30–45 years presented a lateral deviation of the left metatarsophalangeal joint and the presence of erosions or geodes of smooth margins on the para-articular margins of the 1st metatarsal head, particularly on its medial aspect. It can

Fig 5.48 Skeleton [1525] showing rib deformations thought to relate to the prolonged wearing of corsets

be surmised that these cavitations resulted from the intrusion of the bursal tissue overlying the bunion into the subchondral bone and no signs of osteoarthritis changes were observed. A male aged 30–45 years presented a medial–lateral displacement of the left metatarsophalangeal joint with concomitant eburnation and osteophytic lipping around the joint margins of both bones. Furthermore, two bony exostoses were present on the medial and lateral aspect of the plant surface of the 1st metatarsal bone.

Skeleton [1304], a possible female aged 18–30 years, presented bilateral subluxation of the 1st metatarsophalangeal joints (Fig 5.49). No sign of osteoarthritic change was present on either joint, but the head of the metatarsals had developed an ad hoc articular facet for the dislocated phalanges.

Fig 5.49 Skeleton [1304] showing abnormal lateral deviation of the big toes, thought to relate to the prolonged use of pointed shoes: a – left; b – right

Male [1654], aged more than 45 years, presented a slight dislocation of both metatarsophalangeal joints with para-articular subchondral cysts on both metatarsal heads, similar to those discussed above. This too could have resulted from soft-tissue bunion material invading the underlying subchondral bone.

Assuming that hallux valgus results from using restrictive footwear it can be suggested that both males and females were subjected to constrictive, pointed shoes. No evidence of footwear was present on site but, as observed by others (Trujillo-Mederos et al 2014), 18th-century high-status males would have worn high-heeled leather boots that placed constraint on the forefoot because they were appropriate for riding a horse and preventing a slip on the stirrup when mounting. Hallux valgus has been reported in other cemeteries from the London area, always with a higher prevalence than that found in the Savoy Chapel, possibly as the condition was not being systematically recorded. At St Marylebone church the condition was present in 3.8% (4/105) of males and 5.8% (5/86) of females (Miles et al 2008b), at St Mary and St Michael's burial ground it was found in 11.1% (16/143) of males and 15.2% (16/105) of females and at Bow Baptist Church it was recorded in 11.6% (10/86) of males and 12.1% (14/115) of females (Henderson et al 2013).

EVIDENCE FOR POST-MORTEM EXAMINATION AND SURGICAL INTERVENTION

Of particular interest when studying post-medieval England is the evidence for post-mortem examination, as there was significant progress in the study of anatomical science, medicine and dentistry during this period of 'Enlightenment' (Roberts & Cox 2003). Among the Savoy Chapel population the evidence for post-mortem examinations consisted of cut marks, drilled holes and six examples of craniotomies, the significance of which would have been greatly enhanced if it had been possible to date the burials more closely.

With individuals such as surgeon John French linked to the site it is possible that some of the autopsied individuals date to the mid 17th-century use of the buildings as a hospital – autopsies are documented as having taken place at the Savoy Hospital during this time (see Chapter 3). Alternatively, they may date to the later stages of the burial ground, after the Anatomy Act of 1832, which legalised the use of unclaimed bodies. Before the enactment of the Anatomy Act in 1832 the only legally available bodies to be used after death for furthering the understanding of the human body were those that belonged to executed criminals (Mitchell 2012b). As seen in Chapters 3 and 4 the Savoy burial registers record the presence of seven such individuals during the second half of the 18th century.

As the demand for bodies for anatomical teaching outnumbered those legally available, the so-called 'resurrectionists' came into existence. Their illegal activities consisted of digging up corpses from the graves while they were still fresh to be sold to doctors and physicists for dissection (ibid). After the enactment of the Anatomy Act of 1832 these clandestine activities disappeared as a result of the increase in the number of available bodies, sourced from the poor who died in workhouses and other charitable institutions but who were unclaimed by relatives (ibid). Another source of bodies for autopsy would be the wealthiest, educated part of the population, who would recognise the value of a post-mortem (Cherryson et al 2012, 137). Both these parts of the population are represented in the Savoy burial ground but it is not possible in most cases to work out which was which.

CUT MARKS AND DRILLED HOLES

Cut marks other than those described above were found also in the sternum of 18- to 30-year-old male [1172]. It displayed nine cut marks that crossed the manubrium in a fairly horizontal or parallel fashion. These cut marks appeared to have been produced with a sharp instrument such as knife or scalpel and were consistent with a thoracotomy. This surgical procedure was aimed at gaining access into the chest wall and the thoracic organs by removing the anterior portion of the ribs and the sternum (Mitchell et al 2011; Fowler & Powers 2012).

Skeleton [124] was that of an adult, possible female, aged 45+ years, displaying a circular cut of 15mm diameter on the iliac fossa of the left os coxa. The dimension of the circular pit and the sharpness of its margins are consistent with the use of a circular-bladed trepanning drill, commonly used in the 17th and 18th centuries to perform trepanations in the skull (Arnott et al 2003). The pressure to drill the hole was exerted on the ventral side of the bone, as its margins looked depressed. Consequently, two radiating fractures developed across the iliac fossa. On the posterior side of the bone there was considerable bevelling, which represented the exit of the perforation. No macroscopic evidence of healing was present, the procedure was probably carried out post-mortem, perhaps soon after death. There is no obvious reason for the drilling of this hole in the bone; this individual appeared to have suffered from osteoporosis and general degenerative joint disease, and it can be hypothesised that performing such a procedure was a part of surgical training.

Seventeen- to 20-year-old [1776] displayed a circular hole in the occipital bone, located 40mm below the intersection between the sagittal and the lambdoid sutures. As the skull in general, and the occipital in particular, was not well preserved, the hole was incomplete but its diameter was approximately 15mm. The sharp margins of the hole along with the absence of signs of bevelling endo-ectocranially are consistent with it being performed with a circular-bladed trepanning drill (Arnott et al 2003). The reason behind this procedure is not known but it is very unlikely to be related to the possible spina bifida, which was the only evidence of pathology observed. If the procedure was carried out while the individual was alive, it may have proved fatal as no macroscopic signs of healing were present. Some of the reasons for performing this procedure during the Enlightenment period of England were to relieve intracranial pressure and pain from haemorrhage and clot removal (Boston & Webb 2012). If performed post-mortem, it was probably in order to practise the techniques necessary to produce burr holes, drilled to relieve the above-mentioned ailments (Fowler & Powers 2012). As with the craniotomies described below, the same possibility exists for the post-cranial cut marks and drilled holes – that these individuals may have been executed criminals. In these cases, ages suggest that perhaps they could be James Collins or John Lewis, both aged 20, Henry Ives, aged 24, Patrick Keough, aged 25, or Thomas Davenport, aged 26.

CRANIOTOMIES

Jenna Dittmar, Paola Ponce and Lucy Sibun

The procedure of opening the skull to examine the brain is called craniotomy. These post-mortem procedures, aimed at determining the cause of death of an individual, were carried out by opening the skull to examine the brain. Five adults and one subadult showed evidence of cranial autopsy, giving a total prevalence of 0.9% (6/609). From the adult group, three were males, one was a possible male and one was assessed as a female. The subadult individual was of unknown sex but between the ages of 1.5 and 2.5 years.

The analysis of the craniotomies was conducted using a combination of macro- and microscopic techniques. Macroscopic techniques consisted of visually examining the location and orientation of the post-mortem cut marks observed in each skull in order to create a detailed map of all tool marks present. After this, silicone casts of the medically relevant post-mortem modification were made using a silicone, RTV Putty Silicone (Alec Tiranti Ltd, London) (Dittmar et al 2015). These impressions were then analysed to obtain the morphological characteristics of the tool marks using a Hitachi TM3000 tabletop scanning electron microscope located in the McDonald Institute at the University of Cambridge. As described below, the macroscopic and microscopic examination allowed for the reconstruction, orientation, sequence and direction of the cut marks identified as resulting from the use of knives and saws.

The skull of [205] displayed saw cut marks and both coronal- and axial-oriented knife marks. The coronal incision, located on the posterior aspect of the right parietal and inferior to the sagittal suture, indicated that a knife was used to sever the scalp along the coronal plane. Based on the trajectory of this knife mark, the incision extended coronally over the cranial vault from one mastoid process to the other.

The incisions along the axial plane were located on both the right and left parietal bones. There were several short knife marks on both bones but also long incisions that extended from the anterior portion of the right parietal to the lambdoid suture and on the left parietal the incision extended on to the occipital. These incisions were located above the craniotomy cut, immediately superior and inferior to the craniotomy incision, and provided clear evidence that a knife was used with the purpose of severing the temporalis on both the right and left parietals before the axial sawing. The saw marks opened the skull in two halves along the axial plane. The type of craniotomy carried out in the skull of this individual was excellently performed, with only a single false-start kerf located on the right aspect of the occipital. After the skull had been sawn, a chisel and mallet were used to pry apart the severed calvaria so that the brain could be examined.

The reasons behind the performance of a craniotomy in this individual are unknown as the only evidence of pathology recorded was the presence of conditions such as os acromiale in the right scapula and infection in the mandibular molars, neither of which would justify an autopsy of the skull.

Male [313], aged 30–45 years, presented a cranial dissection along with an additional procedure. A knife was used to sever the scalp with a coronal incision in order to perform the craniotomy. This incision began on the left parietal and extended over the skull and on to the right parietal, where it would have terminated. There were also several coronal knife marks present on the right and left parietal bones, and if the trajectory of these knife marks were extended they would pass on to the frontal bone. After the scalp was severed, to enlarge the amount of bone showing, the scalp would have been pulled away with one hand and the knife would have been used to sever the pericartium still adhering to the bone, as evidenced by several additional horizontal knife marks on the left parietal.

The sawing originated on the left aspect of the frontal bone, as determined from the striations on the sawn surface and the presence of two false-start kerfs located inferiorly to it. The sawing progressed clockwise until reaching the right aspect of the occipital suture where the saw was removed and restarted at the origin of sawing. The sawing was then continued in a counter-clockwise direction until reaching the right aspect of the occipital bone. There were several false-start kerfs present, both inferior and superior to the craniotomy incision on the left parietal and temporal. After the incision was complete, a chisel and mallet were probably used to pry apart the severed calvaria. Evidence in the form of pressure fractures and a breakaway spur was clearly seen on the posterior aspect of the right parietal.

The additional procedure was observed in the occipital condyles and the atlas. Both condyles were sawn along with the superior articular facets and neural arch of the atlas. The axis was not sectioned completely but a saw mark was present on the superior right articular facet and on its dens. Tool marks in these vertebrae were consistent with a craniotomy and an investigation of the spinal column. Although this investigation was consistent with autopsy, the explanations as to why this was performed on this individual are not known as the palaeopathological evidence showed only a broken clavicle and two broken ribs, which were well healed at the time of death. The only other evidence of pathological manifestations were Schmorl's nodes in the thoracic and lumbar spine and dental disease such as caries, abscess, ante-mortem tooth loss and dental enamel hypoplasia.

The cranium of 30- to 45-year-old possible male [445] (Fig 5.50) showed several knife marks present on the right temporal bone and right sphenoid located approximately 15–20mm inferior to the craniotomy incision. The location of these knife incisions suggested that a knife was used to remove the temporalis before performing the craniotomy. The presence of multiple false-start kerfs indicated that the origin of the craniotomy sawing was the left aspect of the frontal bone. From this point, the sawing extended circumferentially in a clockwise direction along the axial plane until reaching the lambdoid suture on the right aspect of the occipital. The saw was then removed and restarted at the sawing origin on the frontal bone. Sawing recommenced in an anti-clockwise direction along the axial plane until reaching the left aspect of the occipital bone. The saw was then removed again and restarted immediately superior to the sawn incision on the left parietal. The sawing continued in an anti-clockwise direction in a slight arc, which roughly followed the natural arch of the lambdoid suture until intersecting with the previously made incision on the right parietal.

The tool marks in the cranium of this individual were consistent with a craniotomy. No other tool marks were identified on the post-cranial elements, suggesting that this individual was autopsied rather than dissected. The reason behind this autopsy is not clear. Evident pathology was limited to a cranial–caudal shift, in which the coccyx was forced to unite to the sacrum, and dental disease, including caries and calculus. This individual is discussed further in Chapter 6, as the archaeological evidence has provided some possible identifications.

The only female who appeared to have undergone an autopsy was 30- to 45-year-old [1804]. Her skull displayed evidence of a craniotomy and knife incisions along the coronal and axial planes. This craniotomy was not executed as well as the others in this sample and the saw needed to be restarted several times to complete the circumferential cut. Although poorly executed, this craniotomy was consistent with an autopsy. The origin of sawing was still on the left aspect of the frontal, but it was more medially placed than in the other adult examples. The origin was also more superiorly placed. The sawing commenced clockwise at a dramatic angle, which extended through the temporal bone, where the sawing terminated. The saw was repositioned and restarted on the right aspect of the frontal, approximately 30mm superior to the zygomaticofrontal suture, and then progressed clockwise along the axial plane until reaching the occipital, where sawing terminated. The saw was restarted on the approximate midpoint of the skull and progressed anti-clockwise, again at an angle, which caused sawing to extend through the temporal bone. Taphonomic damage on the skull made it impossible to determine where the saw was repositioned but based on the sawing on the occipital it is likely that it was restarted superior to the squamous suture. A chisel was then used to pry open the severed calvarium, as seen on the frontal bone.

Although it is not certain, the autopsy on this individual might be linked to the presence of systemic infection that was active at the time of death. Her skeleton exhibited periostitis and woven bone deposits in diaphyseal areas of claviculae, humeri, radii, femora, tibiae, right fibula, right scapula and visceral aspects of right and left ribs. The skull also presented deposits of woven bone above the left orbit along with endocranial lesions on the frontal and parietals suggestive of a systemic active infection or perhaps early stages of syphilis.

When it came to burying an individual who had undergone an autopsy, every effort was usually made to restore the body to normal appearance, in other words to hide any signs of incision or dissection. Skull caps would usually be replaced in correct anatomical position, cavities might be stuffed with straw moss or grass and missing parts have been historically replaced with stone or wood in a coffin to make up the weight (Cherryson et al 2012, 144–6). Exceptions might be the burials of paupers or prisoners, for whom no such effort was deemed necessary. The individual that stood out at the Savoy was female [1804], who was found with three lumps of coal deliberately placed in the cranial cavity; no other examples have been found in the archaeological record thus far. The possibility that the coal was in some way symbolic was considered – coal is traditionally considered to be a lucky symbol, something known to have been believed in the 19th century (Webster 2008, 62). Through its connection with fuel and fire, it is thought to be linked in religious terms to cleansing and purification (Orr 1915; Becker 1994, 63). As with any other form of stuffing or weight replacement, the coal must have been inserted by the surgeon or undertaker, while the body was being prepared for the family. It seems more likely that any symbolic items would be placed by the family and positioned next to rather than inside the body. The most likely explanation in this case, therefore, however unusual, seems to be that the coal was simply there to replace the weight of the brain.

Skeleton [1508] was a subadult individual aged between 1.5 and 2.5 years (discussed further in Chapter 6). The craniotomy along the axial plane on the skull was conducted

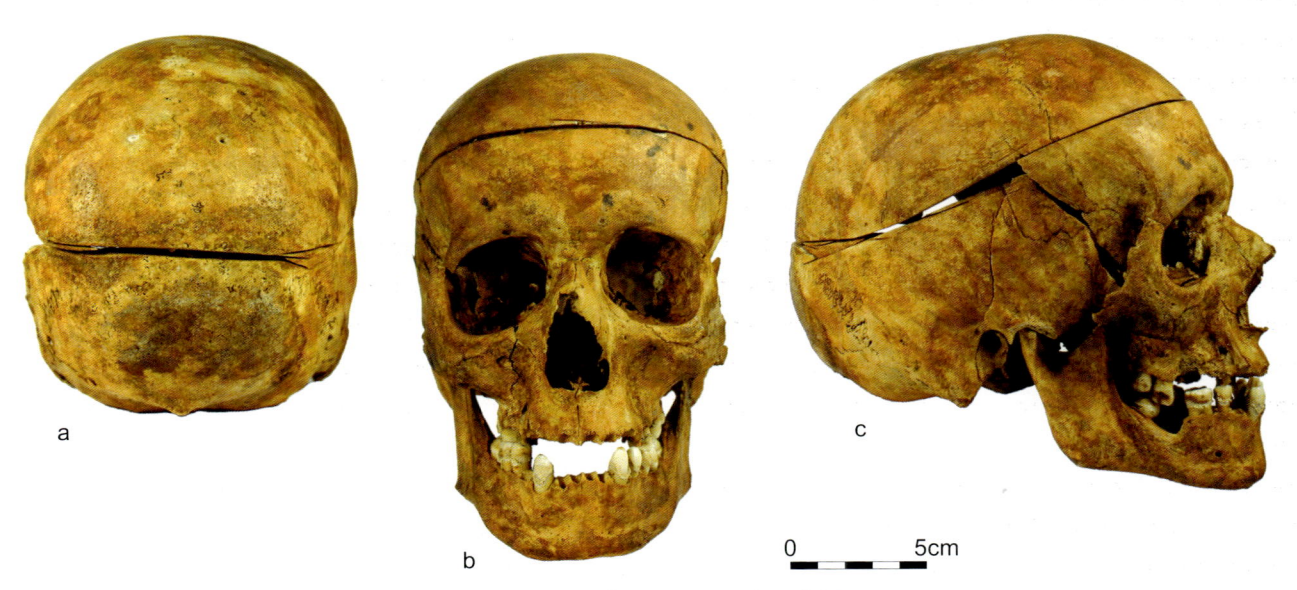

Fig 5.50 Skeleton [445] showing views of a dissected skull: a – posterior; b – anterior; c – lateral right

in a similar way to the adult craniotomies: two coronal knife incisions were located on the right side of the frontal, suggesting that the same method for opening the scalp was used. There were several other horizontal knife incisions on the frontal and the right parietal, very close to the sawn craniotomy incision. A series of knife marks were located on the midpoint on the frontal bone and located superiorly to the craniotomy incision, suggesting that the scalp needed to be removed further away from the origin of sawing before it could take place. One noted difference was the location of the origin of sawing, which was found on the midline of the frontal bone (Fig 5.51). The sawing progressed clockwise along the axial plane through the right parietal, but no further information is available as the occipital and both parietals were missing.

Once again, the absence of any evident pathology in the skeleton of this individual does not help to elucidate the purpose of carrying out this autopsy. This child represents the only possibly identified individual who underwent an autopsy: 3-year-old Agnes Mary Menzies, buried in 1830, before the Anatomy Act and before the introduction of death certificates (see Chapter 6). It is possible that Agnes underwent an autopsy at medical request but as she died seven years before the formal introduction of death certificates the reason for her death remains a mystery.

Lastly, one adult male skull from the disarticulated group presented a craniotomy but, as explained above (5.1, 'Disarticulated material'), this was not counted in the overall prevalence. Based on the knife marks observed, the scalp would have been severed in a very similar way as individual [313]. Only a single coronal knife incision was present on the right parietal. This knife mark was located approximately 60–70mm posteriorly from the coronal suture. Knife incisions along the axial plane were located on the left aspect of the frontal bone and two very short knife incisions were found on the occipital bone, immediately inferior to the sawn incision.

The origin of sawing was located on the left aspect of the frontal bone and progressed circumferentially in a clockwise direction until nearly reaching the lambdoid suture, where the saw was removed before being restarted at the sawing origin. Sawing then progressed anti-clockwise along the axial plane, around the left parietal and occipital until reaching the incision that terminated on the right parietal. There were several false-start kerfs and signs of saw slipping on the left parietal and the occipital. The craniotomy carried out along the axial plane of this individual was consistent with autopsy but it is not known if the presence of endocranial lesions on the frontal and parietal bones and any possible symptoms associated with them during life were the reason behind it.

To summarise, the analysis of the autopsied skulls suggested that knives and saws were used to perform cranial dissections. The tool pattern showed remarkable consistency in technique: a chisel was used to open the calvaria in three of four adult examples. No chisel mark was seen on the infant skull [1508], suggesting that a different approach was taken for children. However, the analysis showed that the same tools were used for the adults and for the child. The disarticulated skull was autopsied with a different cranial technique, which preserved the posterior aspect of the skull.

In general terms, this consistent pattern of autopsy and sectioning the skulls in the Savoy Chapel craniotomies may indicate that they were carried out by the same practitioner, but unfortunately it is not possible to determine when this might have been. The palaeopathological data do not provide sufficient evidence to justify the application of these procedures in these individuals. Perhaps the only exception is the skeleton of female [1804], which manifested a widespread systemic infection. There are, however, several conditions justifying an autopsy that do not leave traces in the bone. An alternative explanation is that the skulls belong to executed criminals as these, hung and dissected, are known to have been the among the first individuals to be buried in the cemetery (Somerville 1960, 124). However, the practice continued throughout the 18th century (Ward 2014, 158) so, without an obvious justification for the craniotomies, it is equally possible that some of the male skulls belonged to the executed criminals recorded in the registers (see Chapter 3). By looking at comparative ages it seems that Robert Damsell, aged 39, or James Whem, aged 33, are the most likely candidates.

Comparisons of craniotomies with other cemeteries from the London area revealed that the evidence of cranial dissections was not as highly prevalent at the Savoy Chapel as it was in elsewhere (Table 5.39). However, other post-medieval London sites report similar techniques and instruments used for both craniotomies and cut marks and drilled holes (discussed above).

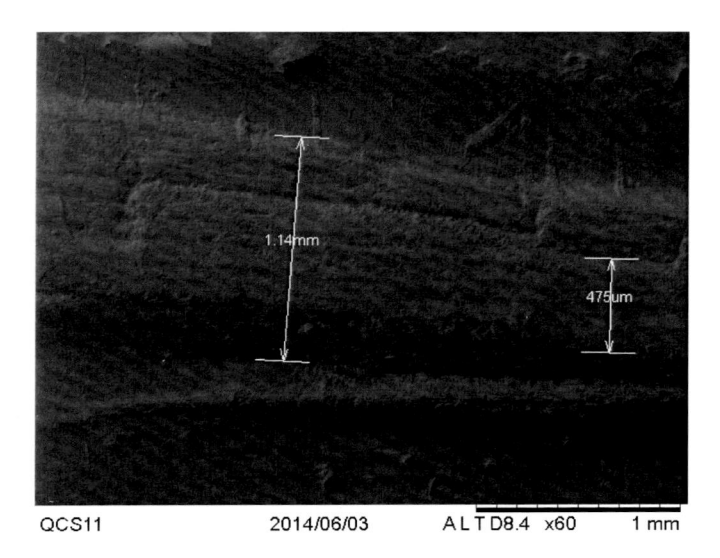

Fig 5.51 Skeleton [1508]: SEM image of a kerf mark showing the diameter of a single pass with the saw blade vs multiple passes

London-area cemeteries	Prevalence (n/N)
All Saints, Chelsea Old Church	0.4% (1/198)
St Mary and St Michael's burial ground	0.9% (6/705)
Queen's Chapel Savoy	**0.9% (6/609)**
Bow Baptist Church	1.2% (5/416)
Sheen's burial ground	1.2% (3/254)
New Bunhill Fields burial ground	1.6% (8/514)
St Pancras burial ground	1.6% (12/715)
St Marylebone Church burial ground	1.7% (5/301)
St Benet Sherehog	1.7% (1/230)
City Bunhill burial ground	2.9% (7/239)
Royal Hospital Greenwich	3.7% (4/107)

Table 5.39 Comparison of cranial dissections in cemeteries from the London area
(all adult and subadult individuals are pooled; for references see above, 5.1)

CHAPTER 6 ARCHAEOLOGICAL RESULTS

Lucy Sibun

> No subtle Serpents in the Grave betray,
> Worms on the Body there, not Soul do prey;
> No Vice there Tempts, no Terrors there afright,
> No Coz'ning Sin affords a false delight:
> No vain Contentions do that Peace annoy,
> No feirce Alarms break the lasting Joy.
>
> Ah since from thee so many Blessings flow,
> Such real Good as Life can never know;
> Come when thou wilt, in thy afrighting'st Dress,
> Thy Shape shall never make thy Welcome less.
> Thou mayst to Joy, but ne'er to Fear give Birth,
> Thou Best, as well as Certain'st thing on Earth.
> —Anne Killigrew, On Death (Extract)
> (Morton 1967, 14–15)

6.1 INTRODUCTION

This chapter examines all the archaeological data gathered during the excavations, both burial- and non-burial-related. By leaving the discussion of the archaeological results to this stage it has been possible to incorporate the information from previous chapters, which has helped to direct the analysis and to add meaning to the results and interpretations. Particular consideration has been given to the spatial distribution of the burials, possible phasing and burial ground development as well as the identification of named individuals; these studies have been greatly enhanced by the use of GIS and the survey data from the 1930s. Also included within the chapter are reports on artefacts specifically relevant to burials, such as coffin furniture and dress accessories.

During the excavations, 612 articulated skeletons were recorded (Fig 6.1). However, three of these were not lifted because they were located below the level needed for building construction. They were therefore recorded *in situ* and were not included in the demographic and palaeopathological analysis outlined in the previous chapter.

The excavation area measured approximately 24m north–south and 7.5m east–west, totalling approximately 180m^2 (Fig 6.2). When considered within the whole burial ground it is evident that the excavation area accounts only for a relatively small percentage of it (17%). The *in situ* burials recovered within this area (612) equate to only 5% of the total number of burials recorded in the burial registers, which do not include the earliest burials (pre-1680). Accordingly, with 17% of the area producing 5% of the burials it would seem that the excavated area was in fact less dense than the unexcavated remainder of the cemetery. However, the vast quantities of disarticulated bone recovered during the works do suggest that the area had been continually reused and it is likely that a good percentage of graves from the area had been obliterated over the years. The burial density for the Savoy (number of burials divided by area) equates to approximately 3.8 burials per square metre but this is not uncommon in London parishes, where burial densities frequently equate to 3 or more per square metre (Cherryson et al 2012, 16).

6.2 SPATIAL ANALYSIS

A stratigraphic matrix was completed on site during the excavation and all available dating evidence has subsequently been added to the individual graves on the matrix, with the hope that this would enable some phases to be applied to the excavation. Unfortunately, the majority of dating evidence was in the form of coffin furniture, which provides only a broad date range. Here, in common with most urban post-medieval burial grounds, the density of burials, the continual reuse of the burial soil and the resultant degree of truncation has meant that most spot dates derived from artefacts cannot be considered as contextually secure and as a result there were very few closely dated burials. However, it has been possible to assign burials to one of three phases: phase 1 burials dated from 1650 onwards; phase 2 from 1750 or later; phase 3, 1800 or later. It should be noted that these phases are not mutually exclusive: a phase 2 grave might actually have belonged to phase 3, but this cannot be ascertained (Fig 6.3).

Although the dating is useful at an individual level, the broad phases imposed on the plan do not shed any light on the development of the burial ground, with burials assigned to each of the phases scattered over the excavation area. Where concentrations were present, for example phase 1 graves towards the centre of the site, the majority of the skeletons included were phased by their stratigraphic position and could easily have belonged to phase 2 or 3. Of course, as a result of reuse of the burial ground over 300 years it is quite possible that the majority of the surviving graves did in fact date to the latter years of the burial ground's use and that the earliest graves were either heavily truncated or represented only by disarticulated bone, and it is certainly true that the lowest burials in the sequence appeared to be more truncated than those above (see below). Of the 612 burials recorded, 74% were disturbed or truncated (eg [147], Fig 6.4a), the remaining 26% recorded as complete (eg [1077], Fig 6.4b). The 'truncated' total, however, included those that extended beyond the limit of excavation, either at the edges of the excavation or within drain trenches, so the actual degree of survival for these

Fig 6.1 Plan of excavation area showing all recorded skeletons

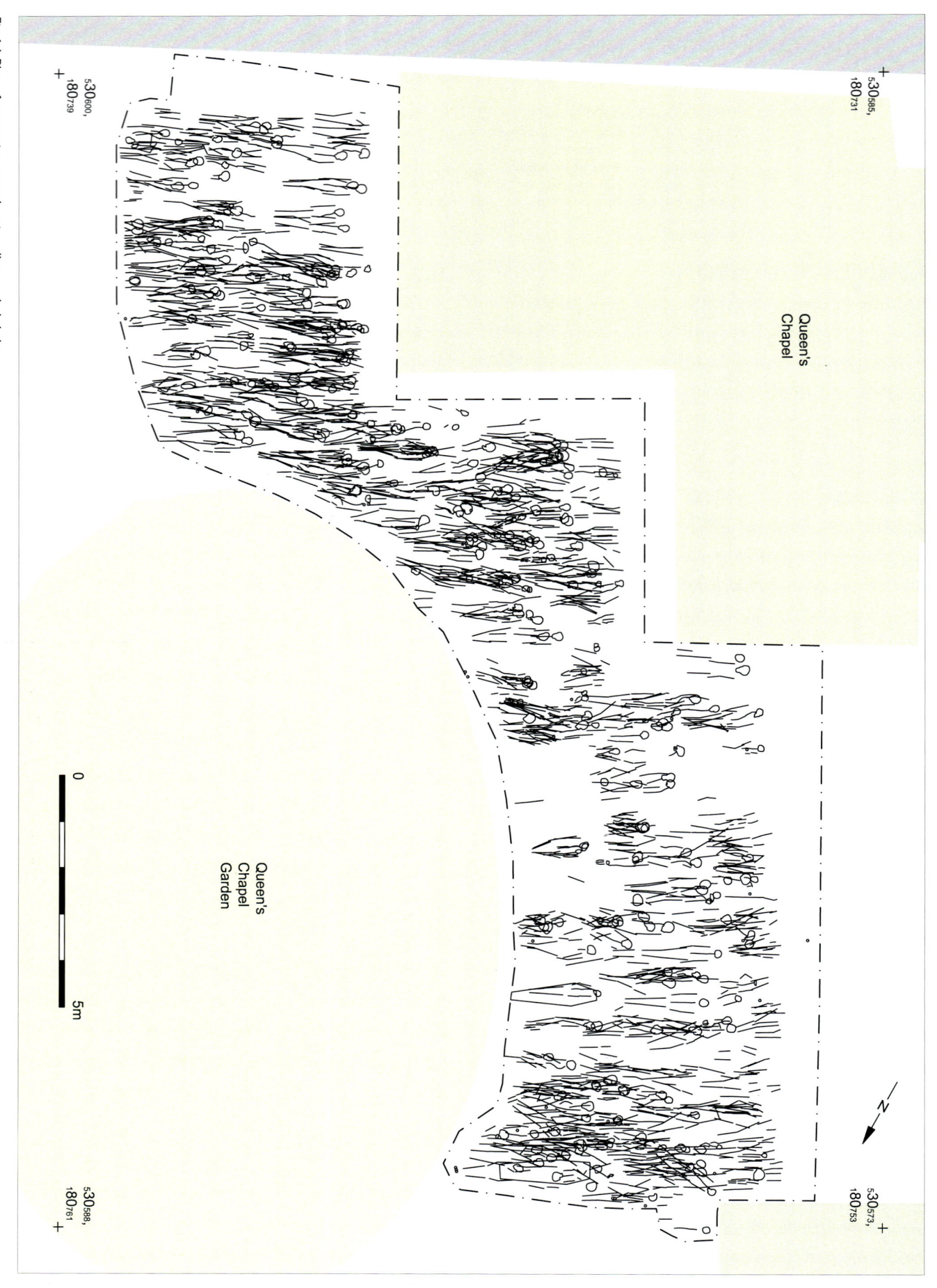

CHAPTER 6 ARCHAEOLOGICAL RESULTS

Fig 6.2 Excavation area within the burial ground

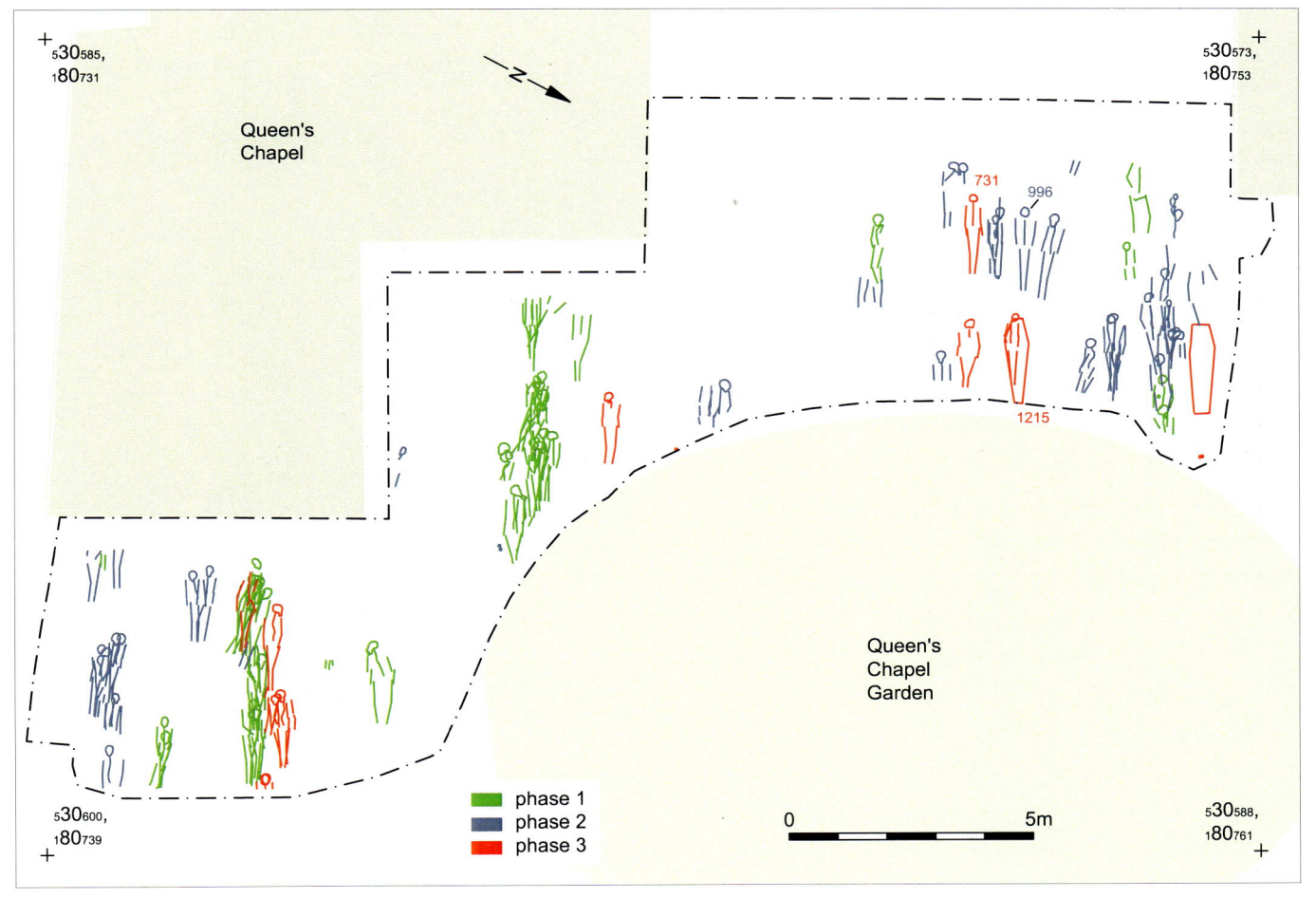

Fig 6.3 Phase plan

141

individuals could not be recorded. This percentage appears relatively high when compared to contemporary sites in London, many of which report limited intercutting (Connell & Miles 2010, 53; Powers & Miles 2011, 17; Henderson et al 2013, 15).

In among the truncated and layered burials were a number of graves that appeared to be isolated, undisturbed and without burials beneath them (eg [731] and [996], Fig 6.3). As there were unlikely to be any unused areas of the burial ground it seems probable that these were later graves and that they removed all traces of earlier burials.

Although burial depth cannot be considered as truly representative of burial date and in spite of an inevitable degree of variation, it would not be unreasonable to suggest that graves dug at a similar date would be dug to a similar depth. Also, within a burial ground used for over 300 years, there would have been a significant rise in ground level; documentary sources record the rise in the surface of the burial ground, which started level with the chapel floor but was by the 17th century already almost at the level of the chapel sills (Somerville 1960, 124). Consequently, the majority of the lowest burials might be considered as the earliest. However, at St Marylebone Church a possible explanation for the variation in depths noted was that gravediggers may have tried to fit new graves into visible spaces, rather than attempting to maintain existing rows (Miles et al 2008b, 35). Burials in the Savoy burial ground were located between 6.07m and 9.97m OD, equating to approximately 2.90m of burial soil. This compares well with contemporary sites, which report between 2.58m of burials (St Marylebone Church: Miles et al 2008b, 35) and 3.30m (St Mary and St Michael burial ground: Powers & Miles 2011, 27).

GIS was used to look for patterns in the burials divided according to depth, with the burials studied in 0.50m intervals. When discussing horizontal spatial patterns it is important to remember that this site is only a small percentage of the whole burial ground and sits in the central south-western portion of the site (Fig 6.2). Thus the northern end of the excavation would in fact be towards the central part of the whole burial ground.

The lowest burial was recorded at 6.07m OD, one of only 13 located below 6.49m OD (Fig 6.5a). Of these, two were left *in situ* as they were below formation depth and did not need to be disturbed. All but one of the lowest burials ([1981], Fig 6.15) were heavily truncated and those burials that survived were spread across the centre of the excavation area (Fig 6.5a). The next layer (6.50–6.99m OD) was much denser, with 138 burials spread over the entire excavated area (Fig 6.5b). This

Fig 6.4 Examples of skeletons: a – truncated skeleton [147]; b – complete skeleton [1077] (1.0m scales)

layer contained some of the latest burials recorded, for example, the lead coffin of John Bittleston dating to 1826 ([1215], Fig 6.3). The comparatively wealthy status of John Bittleston,

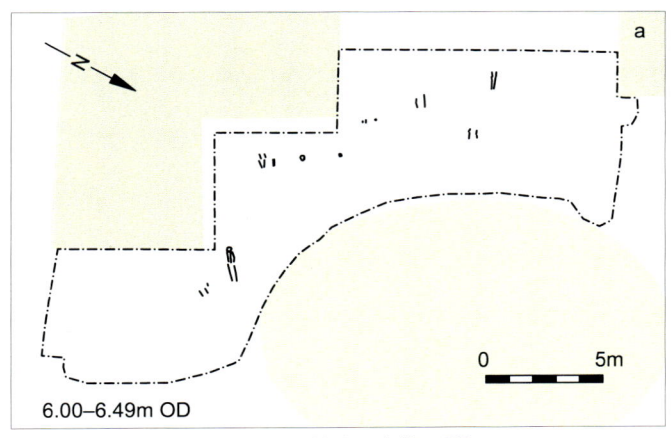

CHAPTER 6 ARCHAEOLOGICAL RESULTS

6.00–6.49m OD

Fig 6.5a Plan of adult burials located below 6.49m OD

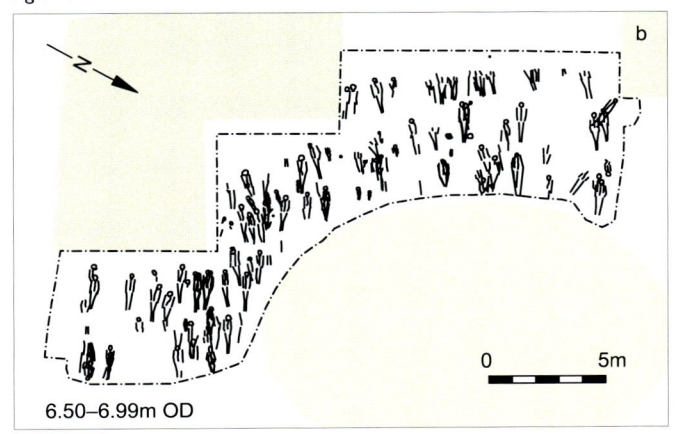

6.50–6.99m OD

Fig 6.5b Plan of adult burials located between 6.50m and 6.99m OD

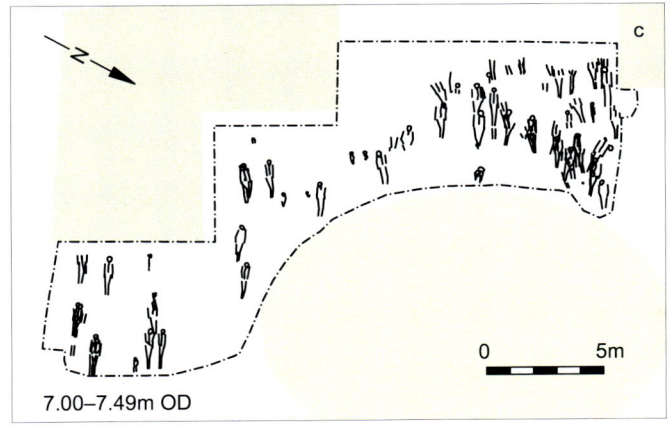

7.00–7.49m OD

Fig 6.5c Plan of adult burials located between 7.00m and 7.49m OD

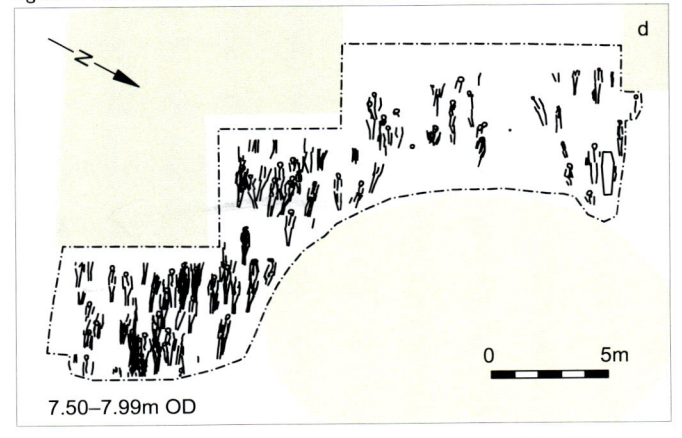

7.50–7.99m OD

Fig 6.5d Plan of adult burials located between 7.50m and 7.99m OD

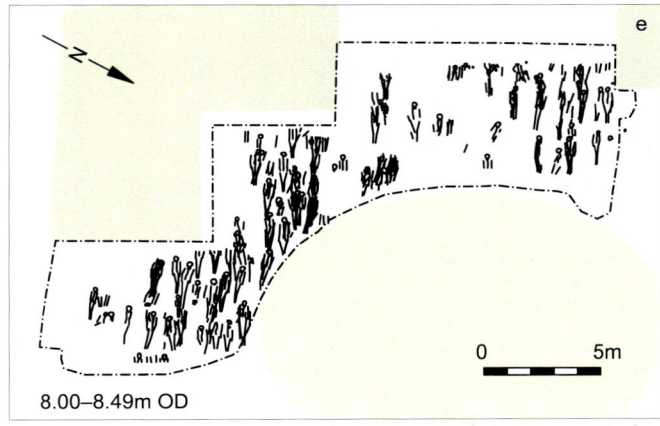

8.00–8.49m OD

Fig 6.5e Plan of adult burials located between 8.00m and 8.49m OD

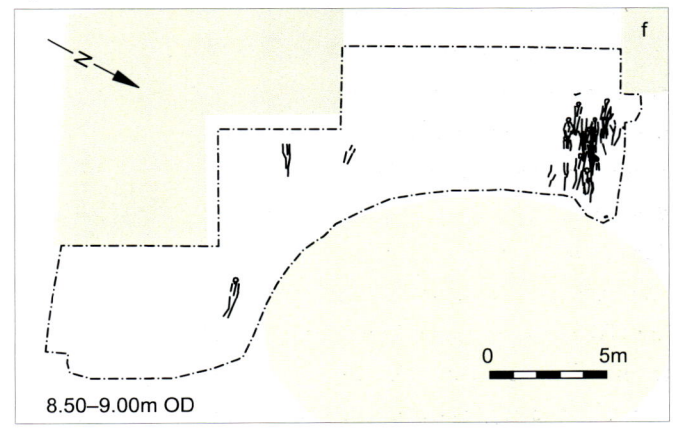

8.50–9.00m OD

Fig 6.5f Plan of adult burials located between 8.50m and 9.00m OD

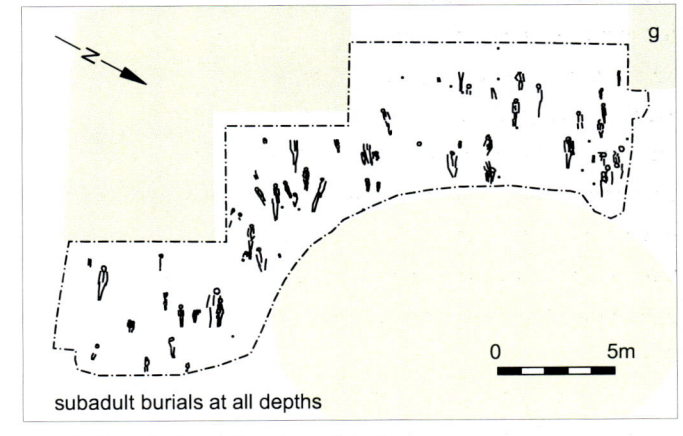

subadult burials at all depths

Fig 6.5g Plan of subadult burials at all depths

as exemplified by the lead coffin, which was one of only two recovered, might have resulted in more attention to the burial and a greater grave depth. The 83 burials between 7.00m OD and 7.49m OD were still spread throughout the excavation area but there appeared to be a slight concentration towards the north, towards the centre of the burial ground (Fig 6.5c). In the next two layers, 7.50–7.99m OD (176 burials) and 8.00–8.49m OD (172 burials) the densest area moved from the north of the site to the south (Fig 6.5d–e), a move which was reversed in the case of the highest 30 burials (located above 8.50m OD), which were concentrated in the north-western

143

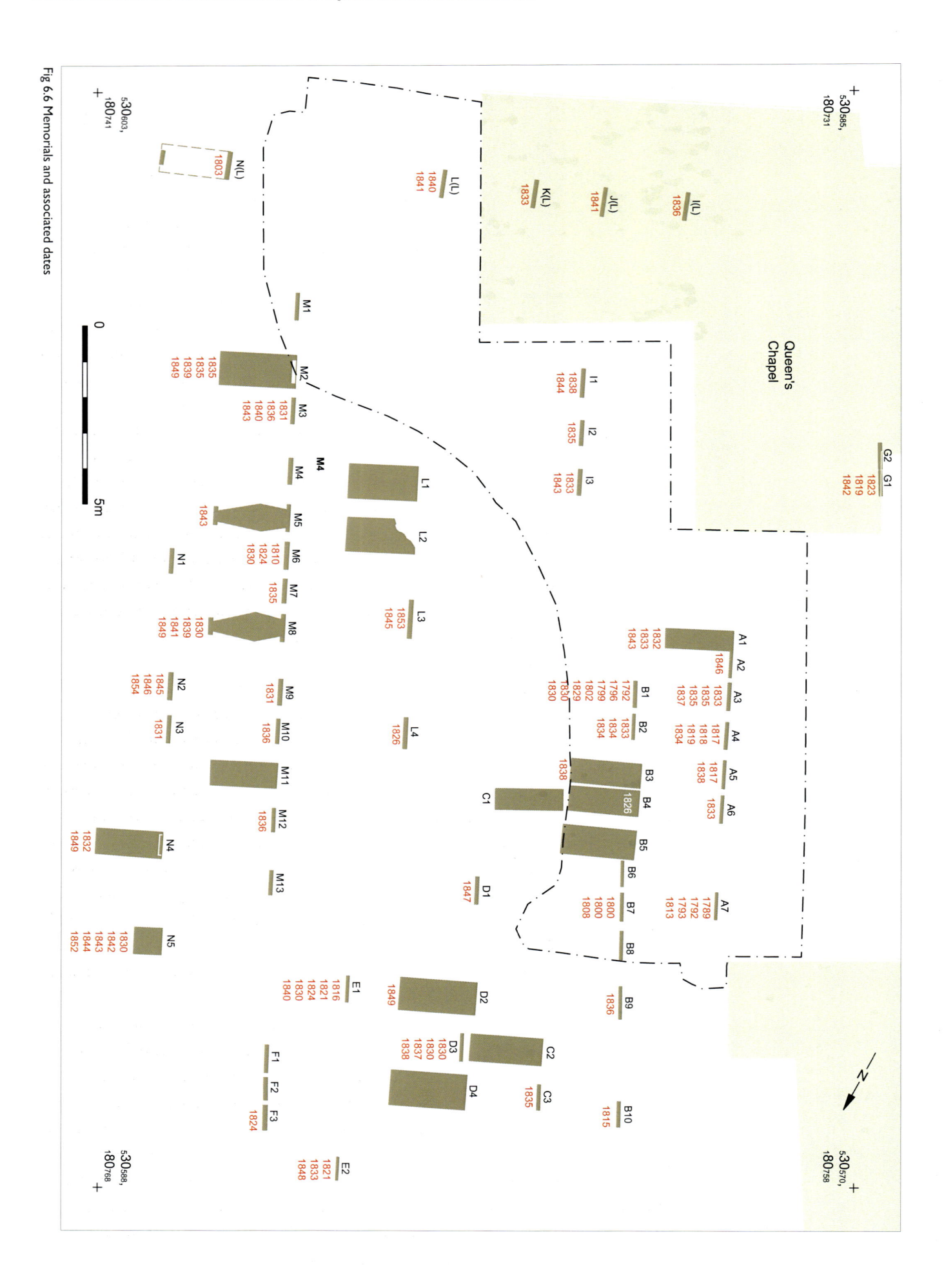

IN LIFE AND DEATH: ARCHAEOLOGICAL EXCAVATIONS AT THE QUEEN'S CHAPEL OF THE SAVOY, LONDON

Fig 6.6 Memorials and associated dates

corner of the excavation area (Fig 6.5f). The highest burial recorded, [185], was located at 8.97m OD.

Although the memorial data, discussed in detail below, indicate that burials continued across the excavation area up until 1844, this was not reflected in the pattern of highest graves (Fig 6.5f). It therefore appears that the latest graves were in fact dug to a greater depth. A similar situation was discovered during excavations at St Marylebone Church, where some of the deepest graves were associated with the latest burials (Miles et al 2008b, 45). As graveyards filled up it was not always possible to dig deep graves (see Chapter 2) and this would have been a particular problem at the busiest times, during the military occupation of the precinct, but once the area became primarily residential in the 19th century the burial rate slowed and it might once again have been possible to dig graves to a greater depth without disturbing fresh ones. Another consideration was the sloping ground, which fell away towards the south – while this might have been expected to affect the earliest graves, as the ground level rose quite quickly the effect would soon have been negated. Certainly, the sloping ground was not evident in the burials at the lowest levels as these were spread across the whole excavation area.

Rows were evident in all layers, suggesting that there was some degree of organisation and that grave markers may have been present throughout the use of the burial ground. The presence of an unstratified fragment of largely indecipherable gravestone recovered from the excavations dating to 1673 (below, 6.3) is testament to the fact that grave markers were in use before those of the late 18th and 19th century recorded in the surveys of the 1930s (see below).

Given the high proportion of male individuals recorded in both the burial registers and the skeletal assemblage (Chapters 4 and 5) the study was repeated, this time examining any patterns of sex distribution in the 0.5m-depth intervals described above. For the purposes of this study, the probable males and probable females were included in the male and female categories and subadults were included in the unknown sex category. The results are given in Table 6.1.

Depth (m OD)	Males (M+M?)	Females (F+F?)	Unknown sex (?+subadult)	Total
< 6.50	3	3	7	13
6.50–6.99	59	33	46	138
7.00–7.49	27	19	37	83
7.50–7.99	106	28	42	176
8.00–8.50	112	20	40	172
> 8.50	21	4	5	30

Table 6.1 Number of burials by depth and sex

The numbers indicate a strong predominance of males between 7.50m OD and 8.49m OD (Fig 6.5d–e). Studying the horizontal distribution of burials, males seemed to reflect the overall pattern, with a general spread evident in the lowest levels to concentrations at the southern end of the site, moving to the north at the highest level. When age categories were also taken into account the concentrations were still apparent, with males in young adult and prime adult age categories concentrated in the south. When considering females and those of unknown sex (either undetermined adult or subadult individuals) the same was not as apparent. With the exception of the clear move to the northern end of the site at the highest levels, there was a general spread at all depths. The subadults were considered in isolation (Fig 6.5g). Showing a general spread, these results do not suggest that any area within the burial ground was designated for infants or children. It is possible that such an area may not have been considered necessary given the composition of the population, based upon the burial ground's primary use for the poor men's hospital and then for the military. Certainly, distinct areas for children were noted at both St Mary and St Michael burial grouns and Bow Baptist Church (Powers & Miles 2011, 32, 69), and Bow Baptist Church produced an even smaller percentage of subadults (ibid, 17).

CHRONOLOGICAL DEVELOPMENT

The 1930s survey was used to see if any chronological development was evident in this part of the burial ground. Dates from the memorial stones were added to the survey plan to see if any patterns emerged (Fig 6.6). There are two obvious limitations to this study: the size of the sample, with the memorials present dating only to the latest phase of the burial ground (1789–1854), and the fact that the excavation was limited to a fraction of the overall burial ground. However, by using the entire survey area rather than just part encompassed by the excavation, the study was made more representative. Further dates were added where historical research was able to enhance the available information.

The burial ground did not seem to have developed chronologically. There were family plots that had been used repeatedly but, judging from the earliest dates on each memorial, they all – apart from the fact that the earliest graves recorded (dated 1789 and 1792) were along the western edge, closest to the chapel building – seemed to be scattered, rather than continuing rows that already existed. For example, the 1792 memorial (B1) was adjacent to one dating to 1833 (B2) and an 1810 memorial (M6) was located between memorials dating to 1835 (M7) and 1843 (M5).

ORIENTATION

It would be expected in a post-medieval burial ground that the vast majority of burials would be oriented east to west with the head at the west end. Here, however, the burials, although loosely east to west, appear to have been aligned with the burial ground boundaries, and were consequently in a north-east to south-west alignment. A number of exceptions were visible (Fig 6.7). Twelve burials ([257], [439], [486], [504], [748], [751], [760], [783], [792], [1191], [1325] and [1331]) were oriented east–west and three of these ([748], [751] and [783]) may have been lying within a family grave, located at 7.68m OD ([783]), 8.04m OD ([751]) and 8.09m OD ([748]). Six burials ([688], [1175], [1561], [1726], [1733] and [1823]) were oriented south-southwest to north-northeast. Three further exceptions were oriented north-east to south-west, with the head at the north-eastern end of the grave. Burial [1292] was an infant located in the northern corner of the site; burials [1957] and [1961] were located towards the southern end of the site and appeared to have been buried together.

The possibility that these variations were associated, perhaps contemporary, with each other was considered but there did not seem to be any evidence to support this. The north-west–south-east burials were located throughout the excavation area with depths ranging from 6.77m OD ([1325]) to 8.50m OD ([257]). Similarly, those oriented south-west to north-east were located through the northern and central parts of the burial ground with depths from 6.82m OD ([1823]) to 7.51m OD ([689]). Skeletons [1726] and [1733] were aligned south-west to north-east towards the southern end of the excavation and directly above one another. Skeleton [1733] was recorded osteologically as an infant and [1726] as a newborn infant. Their proximity and alignment suggests that they were buried at the same time in a single grave.

Three burials displayed a greater degree of variation, buried east to west with the head at the east end, but the reason for their orientation remains a mystery. One possibility considered was that the burials had been moved from elsewhere and perhaps reburied in a hurry. The fact that two of the burials ([1957] and [1961]) were apparently buried together in a single grave might support this argument. Historical documentation does record episodes of maintenance and repair work in the chapel and burial ground; ground disturbance is thought to have taken place in the 1930s and is recorded in the 1950s (See Chapter 1). However, if these burials were

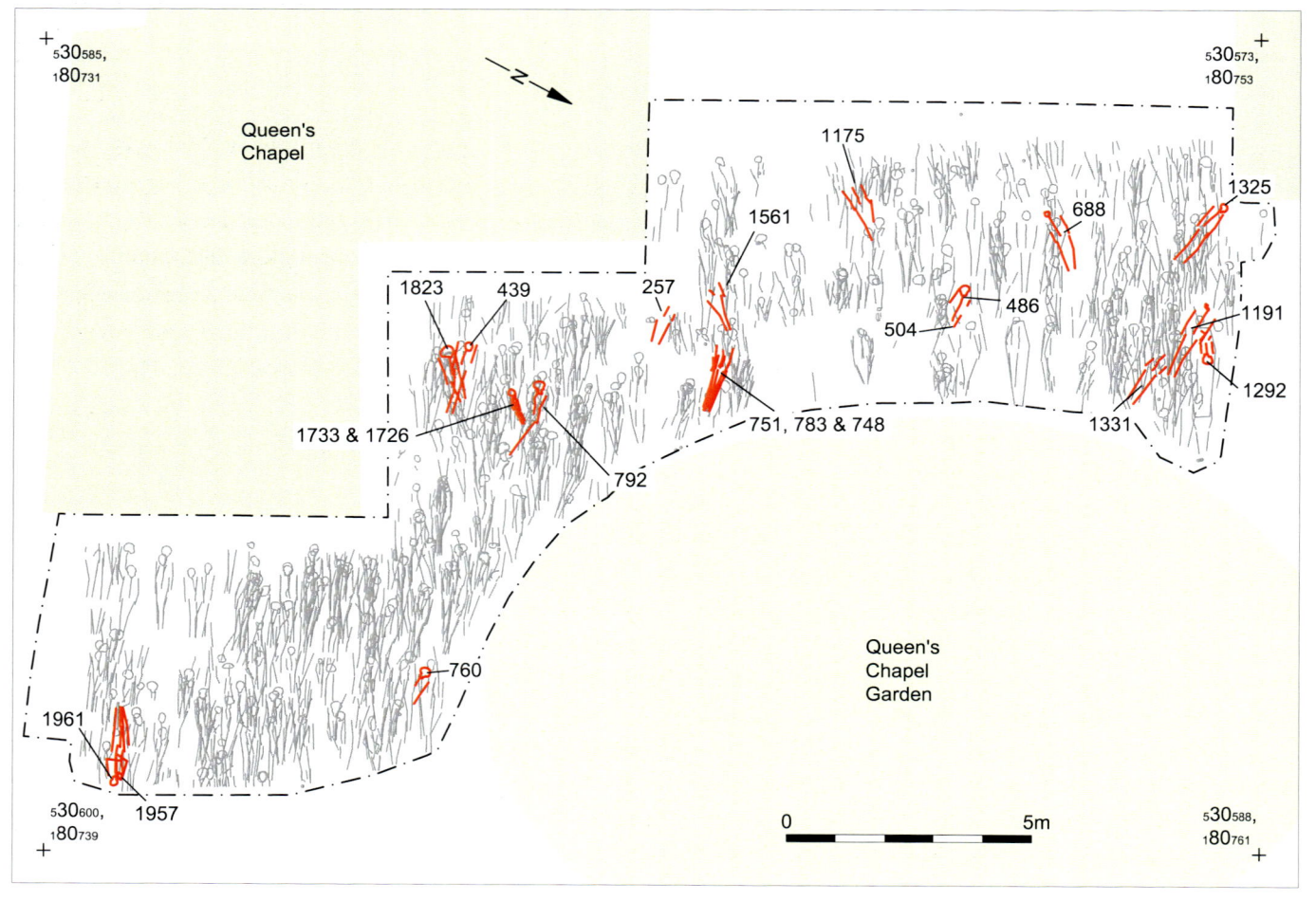

Fig 6.7 Variations in the orientation of burials

moved from their original burial site the move must have taken place soon after their deposition, in order for them to be complete and articulated, which means that both phases of 20th-century ground works can be discounted. Moreover, infant burial [1292], at least, pre-dates the 1839 burial [597] that truncated it. Other examples are known and are equally without explanation – the most likely cause remains human error (Powers & Miles 2011, 242). Where greater numbers have been recovered in this position, such as the 38% of burials at the New Bunhill Fields burial ground, it has been suggested that it was simply to make the best use of the available space (Miles 2012, 24). This seems an unlikely explanation at the Savoy, as these burials appeared randomly positioned. Priest burials have been recorded with their heads facing west, so that they would face their flock during resurrection (Daniel 1997, 149) and other misaligned examples uncovered close to gallows sites have been interpreted as hurriedly buried criminals (Cherryson et al 2012, 125). Is it possible that males [1957] and [1961] were execution victims buried hurriedly or perhaps even deliberately the wrong way? Certainly there are occurrences of double executions in the registers, for example soldiers, James Collins and James Whem in 1762, and Patrick Keough and Henry Ives in 1797 (Chapter 3).

6.3 TOMBS AND MEMORIAL STONES

Remnants of only three tombs were uncovered in the upper layers of the burial ground (Fig 6.8) A disturbed chest tomb [107] was located towards the centre of the site at 9.14m OD. The lower part of the structure, [109], was constructed from late 18th- to 19th-century bricks and measured 2.30 × 10.50m and 0.65 high. A cross-wall was present at the base of the structure towards the centre, [106]. This was constructed of bricks and brick fragments, two bricks wide, and survived for nine courses, with a levelling tile layer on top. Evidence suggests that this was contemporary with the construction of [109]. The upper part of the same structure consisted of Portland ashlar blocks, [107]. The surviving walls measured 0.92m at the eastern end, 1.00m on the south side and 1.25m on the northern side. With the cross-wall present to the base of the structure there is no evidence that it was built for the interment of individuals but rather for display (Fig 6.9).

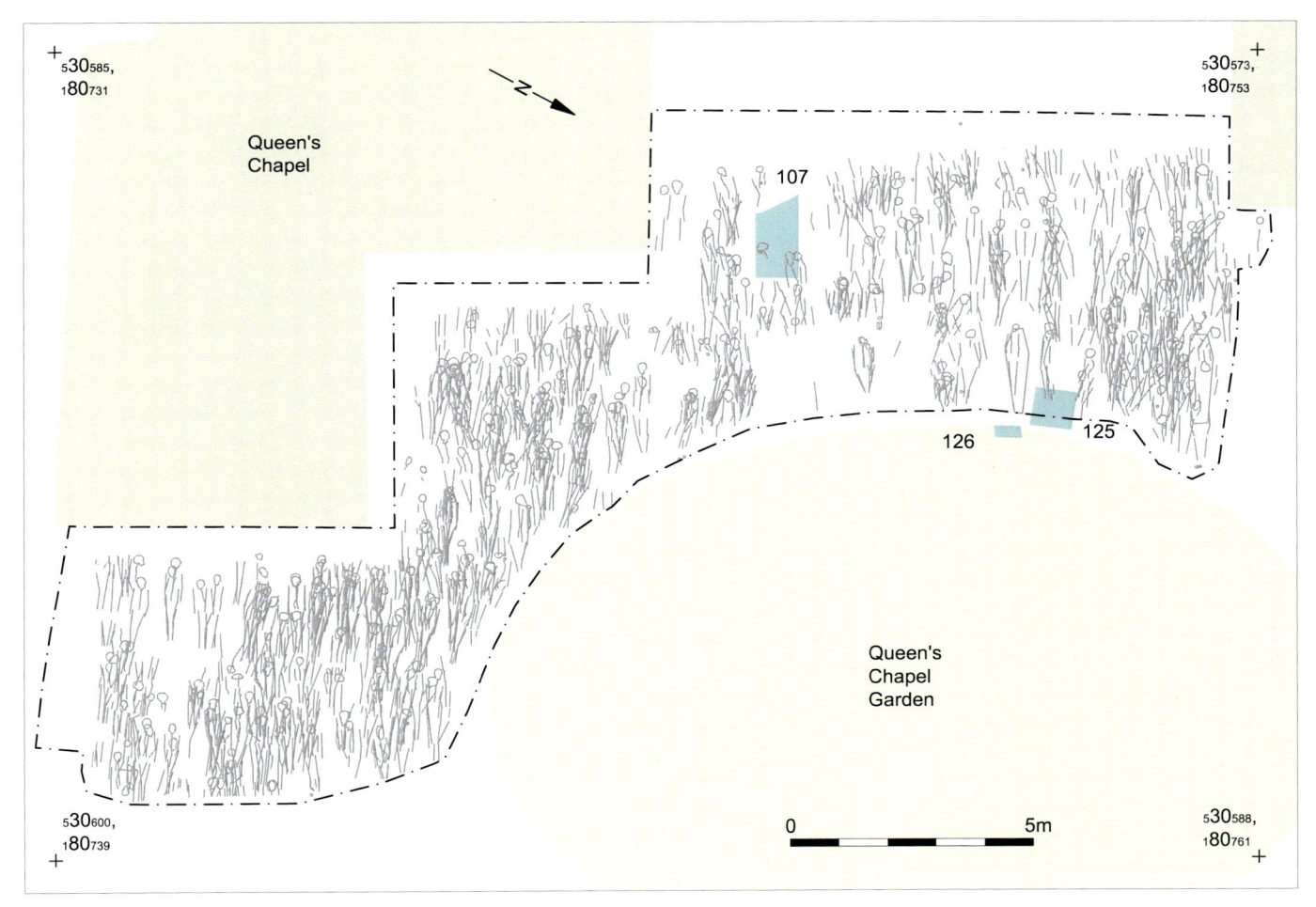

Fig 6.8 Plan showing the location of tombs

Fig 6.9 Photograph of tomb [107] (1.0m scale)

Mark Samuel carried out the analysis of retained ashlars and the following paragraph summarises his observations. Samuel points out that rather than continuing to construct the tomb structure out of the brick seen at lower levels, the family chose to pay for a very strong stone 'box' of Portland stone ashlars, all joints being positively attached with iron staples (Fig 6.10; Table 6.2, 'a'). The exterior surfaces were highly finished and it is probable that this tomb substructure was built freestanding and then backfilled. The fact that the structure had been buried allowed the tooling to survive with a fresh appearance. The ashlars retained clear marks of the pitcher and chisel on the joint surfaces and further mortar keying was provided on the bed, probably with a jadd pick or racer (Fig 6.11; Table 6.2, 'b'). The family grave probably dated to the early 19th century, when graverobbing to provide corpses for dissection was rife (Samuel 2015).

When the 1930s survey plan was overlaid on the excavation plan (see below) tomb [107] appeared to be approximately beneath the defaced flat stone, recorded as plot A1, the family grave of John Cochran, dating to 1832 (Fig 6.6). The slight misalignment of the slab and tomb could have resulted from the problems associated with matching the 1930s survey and the present data, discussed in more detail below. Attempts have been made to link upstanding memorials with skeletons (below, 'Identification of named individuals'; Fig 6.15; Table 6.3).

The other two tombs were located along the north-eastern boundary of the excavation area at approximately 9.90m OD. One of them, [126], proved to be outside the final reduced area (Fig 6.8). Tomb [125] was constructed from limestone blocks measuring 0.31m wide, 0.74m east–west and 0.19m thick. These blocks were sitting on a sandstone slab, which measured 0.91m wide and 0.08m thick. The structure was broken at the

Fig 6.10 Tomb ashlar with iron fittings

Fig 6.11 Mortar keying with jadd pick or racer

western end, where a quantity of broken slabs was recovered. The 1930s survey recorded a plan slab in this location (plot B5, Fig 6.6) but the memorial slab was indecipherable. To the south-east was the southern end of tomb [126]. This was of similar construction but visible only within the trench section. The overall width of the structure was 0.77m and the uppermost limestone slabs were narrower at 0.17m wide. Although this was beyond the limits of excavation it corresponds with plot C1 on the 1930s survey (Fig 6.6), which was described as a 'long flat slab, (raised a foot) with moulded edges'. The only biographical detail decipherable was the surname 'Little'. This was not seen in the burial registers after William Little was buried in 1752. As the earliest recorded memorial stone still standing when the surveys were undertaken dates to 1789, it seems unlikely that this is William's grave.

As might be expected in an excavation of this type, in addition to the *in situ* tombs, several fragments of stone from memorials and monuments were recovered from general grave soil; those retained are detailed in Table 6.2. The earliest appeared to date to 1673 and was cut from Purbeck marble (Samuel 2015). Several fragments of York stone were retained, some with legible descriptions. This stone derives from a number of quarries to the south of Leeds and Bradford and is more familiar as a paving material (Clifton-Taylor & Ireson 1983, 153). As it tends to laminate if used for standing gravestones it fares better as used for ledgers over family vaults (Samuel 2015). Plain ashlar and plinth blocks of Portland stone were also recovered as fragments of upstanding monuments. The weather-resistant close and even texture was popular in London from the mid 17th century until recent times (ibid).

ID	Building stone	Category	Function	Structure	Dimensions (mm)
a	Portland stone	ashlar	ashlar	walling	373 × 274 × 105
b	Portland stone	ashlar	ashlar	walling	373 × 360 × 105
	?York stone	monument	ledger	family vault	365 × 333 × 135
	?York stone	monument	ledger	family vault	310 × 180 × 134
	Portland stone	moulding	torus	plinth 2	171 × 245 × 286
	Portland stone	moulding	chamfer	plinth 1	260 × 148 × 305
	?Bath stone	moulding	chamfer	plinth 3	310 × 430 × 140
	Portland stone	moulding	torus	plinth 2	171 × 245 × 286
	Portland stone	moulding	chamfer	plinth 1	260 × 148 × 305
	Portland stone	moulding	chamfer	plinth 4	376 × 152 × 149
	?York stone	ashlar	quoining	walling	281 × 150 × 155

Table 6.2 Retained worked stones from memorials and monuments

Two fragments from the same York stone ledger were recovered from the grave soil. As recorded by Mark Samuel, one reads: 'Mrs Eliz (abeth…) Wife of …'. The other reads 'The F(amily…) o(f…)'. The chamfered margins were drafted with a pitcher, but the main field and reverse were highly finished. The slab was markedly weathered by the time of its destruction (ibid).

One further fragment of memorial slab belonged to the grave of Ann Elizabeth Finlay and kin (Fig 6.12). The reference to the African traveller makes this an interesting family group. The original location of this slab can be seen in Fig 6.6 (B2).

b SACRED

to the Memory of

M^{RS} ANN ELIZABETH FINLAY,

who died January 19th 1833,

Aged 26 Years

Also of RICHARD LANDER,

Son of MR RICHARD LANDER,

THE AFRICAN TRAVELLER,

and Nephew of the above,

who died January 29th 1834

Aged 13 Months and 4 Days.

Also of WILLIAM FINLAY,

Son of MR WILLIAM FINLAY,

and the above M^{RS} FINLAY,

who died February 4th 1834

Aged 15 Months and 4 Days.

Fig 6.12 Finlay and kin memorial stone:
a – photograph; b – transcription (1.0m scale)

RICHARD LEMON LANDER (1804–34) (FIG 6.13)

Fig 6.13 Richard Lemon Lander (NPG, D19755)

The story of Richard Lander has been summarised from information contained in the websites of the Encyclopaedia Britannica (Editors of Encyclopaedia Britannica 1998b) and of the Richard Lander Society (Dunstone nd). Born in Truro, Cornwall in 1804, Richard had travelled around the West Indies by the time he was 11 years old. He served Hugh Clapperton on his second expedition to Nigeria in 1825, returning to England in 1828 after Clapperton's death. Having carried Clapperton's journals home, he saw that they were published, along with his own. Richard tried to settle to a normal life, marrying and finding work with the Customs House at Truro but, unable to settle, he volunteered to return to Africa to trace the source of the River Niger.

He set out with his brother in 1830, arriving in Badagry, West Africa and travelling over 500 miles inland to the furthest point charted by the explorer Mungo Park. The brothers survived storms, close encounters with wildlife and being sold into slavery before finally making it home in 1831. Despite Richard becoming the first person to receive the Royal Geographical Society's Gold Medal, neither he nor his brother were given a reward or pension by the War and Colonial Office. On his final trip to Africa, Richard was leading a trade expedition when the canoes were ambushed by natives and he was shot. After three days he died on the Island of Fernando Po (now Bioko) on 6 February 1834.

The memorial in the Savoy and the burial of his son, sister and nephew in the Savoy burial ground suggest that his family had at some stage moved to London. The burial registers record St Martin-in-the-Fields as the parish for all three family members and the death of his wife Anne is recorded in the parish of Lambeth in 1884. A memorial window for Richard was inserted in the chapel in 1834 with the memorial beneath reading:

> In memory of Richard Lemon Lander, the discoverer of the source of the Niger, and the first Gold Medallist of the Royal Geographical Society. He was born at Truro in 1804, and died in the Island of Po in 1834, from wounds inflicted by the natives. This window is inserted, by her Majesty's permission, by some of his relations and friends, and by some of the Fellows of the Royal Geographical Society (Loftie 1878, 244).

It is interesting to note that he and his son and nephew died within 8 days of each other.

6.4 IDENTIFICATION OF NAMED INDIVIDUALS

It is possible to see evidence for at least five distinct rows of burials within the excavation plan (Fig 6.1). Unfortunately, at the time of the survey in 1934 the upstanding gravestones in this part of the burial ground were limited to burials from 1789 to 1846 and were not all legible. However, the 1930s plan has been superimposed on the digitised excavation plan (Fig 6.14) and it appears that the distinct rows evident in the survey plan do correspond to rows in the underlying skeletons.

Using GIS, an attempt was made to link specific individuals or groups of individuals to the overlying gravestones. Unfortunately, the superimposition of the plans was not straightforward. The 1930s survey, drawn to scale of '8 feet to the inch', was geo-referenced with the excavation plan using all common points, which included the site boundaries, the chapel buildings and surrounding roads. Although this resulted in a 'best fit' there was a degree of confidence that it was quite accurate. The data recorded in the graveyard survey were then compared to the data resulting from the skeletal analysis (Chapter 5) and any possible matches considered within the

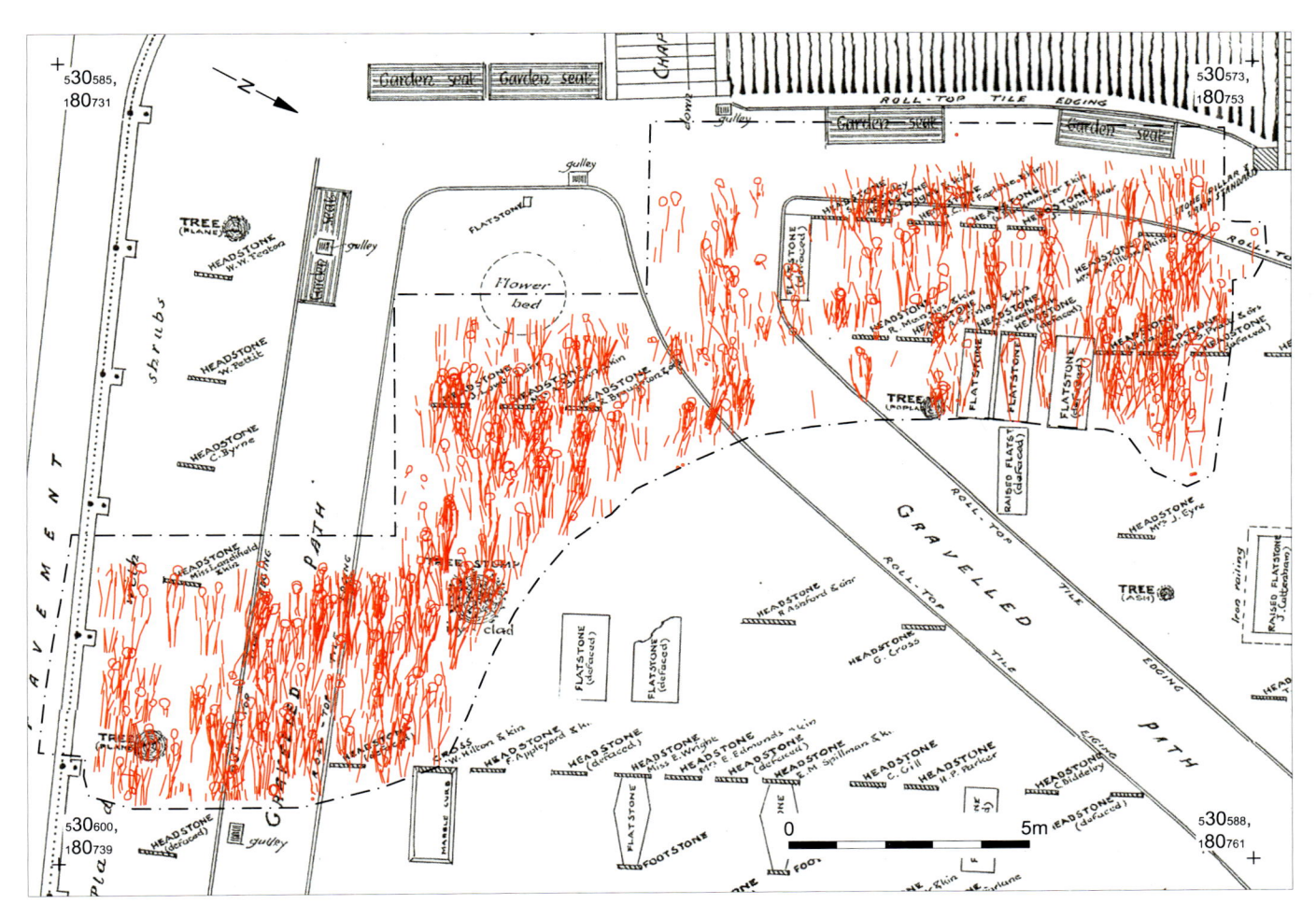

Fig 6.14 Excavation plan and superimposed 1930s burial ground survey

vicinity of each headstone. With such a densely packed burial ground this was not an easy task and in most cases there were either too many possibilities or no possible matches.

Nevertheless, there were two instantly noticeable cases ([1215], [1430]) in which individuals did appear to match overlying gravestones. The relative positions of the excavation and survey plans needed slight adjustment once individuals with excavated nameplates had been matched with overlying memorial stone data: both coffins were 1m south of their corresponding surface markers. Although a delay between the burial and the erection of the memorial could explain a discrepancy, it seems unlikely that they would be out by 1m. One further consideration is the accuracy of the 1930s survey. Although drawn to scale, it is possible that the larger features such as the site boundaries and buildings may be more accurate than the smaller internal features, such as grave markers. These may be more representative than accurate, perhaps indicative of their relative positions. As previously discussed, in a burial ground this crowded some flexibility between the location of grave marker and the underlying skeletons would be expected.

The complete absence of burials beneath some of the grave markers raises further questions. Assuming that later burials would remove or add to any pre-existing grave markers or inscriptions, these markers were probably indicating the latest graves in the area and should therefore have undisturbed burials beneath them. Of course, as natural deposits were not reached it is possible that more burials exist below the level of excavation. If this is the case, however, such burials, dating to the last decades of use of the burial ground, when the ground level would have been at its maximum height, would have to have been dug through an overlying 2.5–3.0m of burial soil, which seems unlikely. Alternatively, they may have been disturbed by an unrecorded episode of renovation works in the burial ground. With the exception of the levelling of the graveyard in 1723 (Somerville 1960, 124) and the ground works in the 1950s, the majority of renovations seem to have involved only the chapel building. The 1950s excavations refer to a large, brick drain running parallel to the east wall of the chapel and approximately 14 feet from it, at least 4 feet below the chapel floor. This places it beneath the 1950s vestry and therefore outside the current excavation area, but does highlight the depths to which the 1950s excavation went. Whatever the explanation, this apparent absence casts some doubt on to the accuracy of the location of grave markers.

Table 6.3 shows the details of this particular analysis, outlining the memorial survey data and the possible corresponding skeletons recovered during the excavation. In some instances, details from the burial registers have been used to fill in illegible details on the memorial stones. Ages at death are listed here as they were recorded in the burial registers, although data from additional historical sources have highlighted discrepancies of one or two years. In each case, given the fact that these marked burials were by their very nature likely to be the latest in the sequence, the completeness of skeletons and relative depths within stacks have been considered. The same information is illustrated in Fig 6.15, which visually highlights the problems encountered. Colour co-ordination has been used between the memorial stone and the corresponding skeletal matches. The problem is increased when more than one individual of the same sex and similar age have been buried in the same grave, as this has meant that any possible skeletal matches might in fact be a number of different individuals.

Of those listed in Table 6.3 there are few confidently identified individuals. In some cases this confidence is a result of indisputable, supporting archaeological evidence such as legible nameplates. In other cases, the degree of confidence is governed by a combination of factors: the location of the skeleton beneath the memorial stone, the similarities between the historical data and the results of osteological analysis and, in cases of multiple burials, the supporting stratigraphic information. However, for the majority of individuals this is not possible. For example, in the case of grave plot B2, commemorating Ann Finlay, her son William Finlay and her nephew Richard Lander there were in fact no skeletons directly beneath the memorial stone. Among the skeletons in close proximity to the stone were two possible sets of matching individuals. The first set included a female of juvenile or young adult age, [1099], and an infant, [1504]. While the demographic information provided a reasonable match, stratigraphically they could not both be correct: female [1099] was stratigraphically above the later burial [1504]

Grave no	Historical data			Archaeological data			
	Name	Age	Date of death	Skeleton no	Sex	Age category	Depth (m OD)
A1	Eliza Cochran	37	1833	[1446]	F	young adult	6.87
	John Cochran	52	1843	[594]	M	prime male	8.12
A2	Sarah Isabella Crowley	14	1846	[1699]	F	young adult	6.17
A3	Elizabeth (Mary) Jaggers	55	1833	[534]	F	mature adult	7.96
				[1150]	F	prime adult	7.10
				[1175]	F	prime adult	7.04
	Charlotte Matilda Jaggers	17	1835	[1188]	?	juvenile	7.10
	William Jaggers	21	1835	[1400]	M?	young adult	6.88
				[682]	?	young adult	8.07
	John Jaggers	60	1837	[1235]	M?	mature adult	6.91
				[179]	M	prime adult	8.16
				[1258]	M	mature adult	6.87
A4	Sarah Charlotte McFarlane	3	1817	[1169]	?	infant	7.06
	Thomas Robert McFarlane	2	1818	[157]	?	infant	7.30
	William Craig McFarlane	1	1819	[157]			
	Sarah McFarlane	45	1834	[462]	F?	?	7.66
				[1181]	F	mature adult	6.96
				[1138]	F	mature adult	7.15
A5	George Buckmaster	8	1817	[900]	?	infant	7.30
	Diane Buckmaster	58	1833	[200]	F	mature adult	8.23

Table 6.3 Identification of individuals by matching survey and archaeological data (highlighted entries indicate greatest degree of confidence)

CHAPTER 6 ARCHAEOLOGICAL RESULTS

Grave no	Historical data			Archaeological data			
	Name	Age	Date of death	Skeleton no	Sex	Age category	Depth (m OD)
A6	Joseph Whitaker	42	1833	[996]	M	prime adult	6.91
A7	Mary Martha	3	1789	[851]	?	infant	7.31
	Thomas Wilton	2	1792	[515]	?	infant	7.78
	George Wilton	1	1793	[515]	?	newborn/infant	7.78
B1	Thomas Burgess	63	1829	[1535]	M?	?	6.60
	Mrs Elizabeth Burgess	54	1830	[1507]	F	prime adult	6.70
	Agnes Mary Menzies	2	1830	[1508]	?	infant	6.77
B2	Mrs Ann Elizabeth Finlay	26	1833	[1099]	F	juvenile/young adult	7.12
				[1403]	F	young adult	6.81
	Mr Richard Lander	1	1834	[1504]	?	infant	6.90
	Mr William Finlay	1	1834	[1504]	?	infant	
				[942]	?	foetus and neonate	7.25
B3	Francis Wadbrook	54	1838	[1430]	M	mature adult	6.83
B4	John Bittleston	31	1826	[1215]	M	young adult	6.83
B7	Sarah Pratt	58	1800	[1331]	F	prime adult	6.84
	Catherine Susannah Pesey	54	1800	[566]	F	prime adult	7.63
	Mary Webb	72	1808	[162]	F	mature adult	8.70
I1	James Lowe	45	1838	[1820]	M	mature adult	6.65
	Marme T (Harriette) Philips	29 (33)	1844	[1801]	F?	mature adult	6.80
I2	Mrs Ann Brown	34	1834	[919]	F?	mature adult	7.97
	Miss Harriet Brown	62	1848	[816]	F	mature adult	8.16
I3	Richard Broughton	77	1833	[719]	M	mature adult	8.25
				[728]	M	prime adult	8.09
				[583]	M	prime adult	8.37
	Elizabeth Ellis	34	1843	[1157]	F?	mature adult	7.62
				[1610]	F	mature adult	6.81
L (L)	Susannah Landifield	92	1840	[1525]	F	mature adult	7.58
	Rebecca Summers	86	1841	[1810]	F	mature adult	7.24
	Elenor Kelly	46	1797	[490]	F	prime adult	8.08
	William Thompson		1738	[834]	M	prime adult	8.08
	Esther Thompson	?	1738	[836]	?	neonate	8.08
	Sarah Maries	47	1848	[1473]	F	young adult	7.34
	George Buckmaster	93	1850	[731]	M	mature adult	7.34

Table 6.3 continued

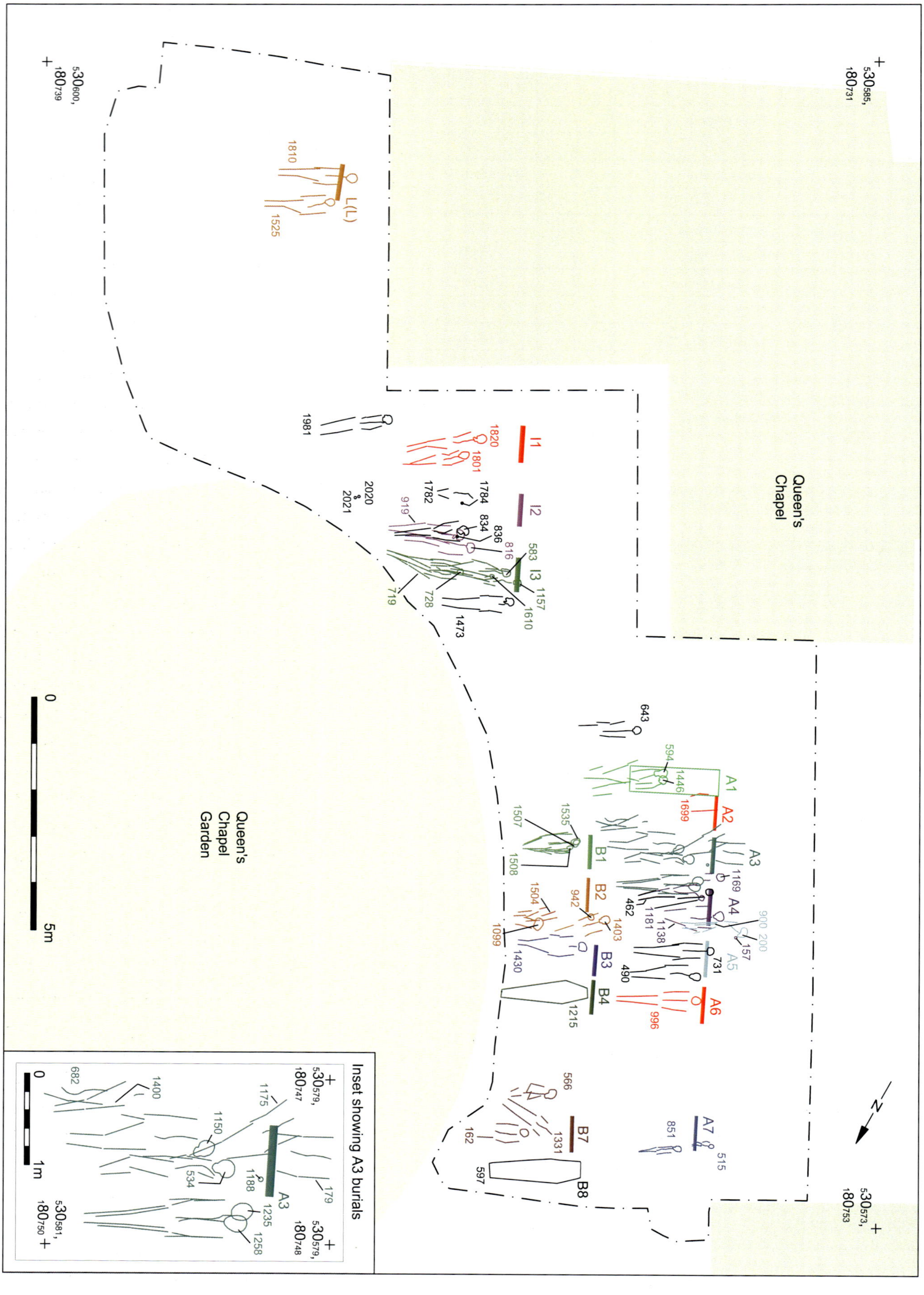

IN LIFE AND DEATH: ARCHAEOLOGICAL EXCAVATIONS AT THE QUEEN'S CHAPEL OF THE SAVOY, LONDON

Fig 6.15 Identification of individuals by matching survey, archaeological and osteological data. Colours indicate burials associated with grave plots

154

and apparently not truncated by it. A more likely match was young female [1403] to the west of the memorial stone and infant [942]. This pairing worked both stratigraphically and demographically but lacked a third individual – and the two cousins, William Finlay and Richard Lander, were buried on the same day. Similar considerations and difficulties were encountered in many of those listed.

Of interest was the possible identification of skeleton [1508] as 2-year-old Agnes Mary Menzies, buried in 1830, whose skull had undergone a craniotomy. Unfortunately, as death certificates were not introduced until seven years after her death, and in the absence of other supporting documentation, the reason for this autopsy cannot be ascertained.

Problems were encountered when trying to find individuals associated with plot A1 (Fig 6.6). The survey was able only to recover partial information: 'The family grave of John Cachran Mrs Mary --- mother-in-law/----- (J.C.) born July 28 1796 died May 4th 1832'. The burial registers were consulted in an attempt to fill in the gaps but no Cachran burials were recorded in 1832. However, an Eliza Cochran was buried on 12 May 1833, John Cochran on 10 March 1843, 'for many years chapel warden of this Parish', and Angelica Cochran, daughter of John, on 20 May 1846. Through further research it has been possible to link these individuals with those on the memorial stone. John Cochran (born 1793) married Eliza Imray on 6 June 1818. Eliza was born on 28 July 1796 and was buried on the 12 May 1833, aged 37 (actually 36). The birth dates correspond to those recorded on the memorial stone, and the date of death recorded as 4 May would fit with a burial on 12 May. The year of death was recorded as 1832 instead of 1833, an understandable mistake on a partially legible gravestone. One final link is that Eliza's mother is Mary, presumably 'Mrs Mary..., mother-in-law', as recorded on the stone ledger. A further search of the registers located Mary Imray, who was buried 17 June 1829, aged 71.

As well as being chapel warden, John Cochran was a bookseller and publisher, with a business located at 108 Strand. After the death of his wife Eliza in 1833 and his own in 1843 it seems that his daughter Angelica's life became troubled. According to the UK, Lunacy Patients Admission Registers 1846–1912, Angelica was admitted to Bedlam psychiatric hospital on 14 April 1846, recorded as a pauper. She died a month later on 15 May, and was buried in the Savoy burial ground on the 20 May. It is unclear whether she was laid in the family grave but it seems unlikely. First, there did not appear to be any likely skeletal matches in the vicinity of the grave. Second, there is no mention of her on the memorial stone, which records John as the latest burial in 1846. Last, this grave is believed to have been associated with the overlying tomb [107] (see above), whose presence would have made later interments impossible.

HISTORICAL RECORDS

In addition to the survey data, the Savoy site has the benefit of existing burial registers that can be used for comparison with the skeletal data. Moreover, as well as their use as a comparative data set (Chapter 4), it has been possible to attempt to match individuals based upon specific details contained within them.

They record the burial on 13 October 1738 of 'William Thompson and Esther his child in … same coffin'. For her to be buried in the same coffin it can be assumed that Esther was newborn or at least a very young infant. The excavations uncovered skeleton [834], a prime adult male, buried with a newborn infant at his shoulder (Fig 6.15). It seems possible that these individuals were indeed William and his daughter, though no evidence of a coffin survived. Another consideration to take into account is that it was not uncommon for infants to be buried in the grave of an unrelated individual for the sake of convenience; they did not always have their own grave (Cherryson et al 2012, 122; Woodward 2015). Without any surviving evidence for a coffin, it is possible that skeleton [834] and infant [836] were unrelated and just happened to die conveniently close together in date. Probable female [919] appeared to be in the same burial stack, beneath [834].

On 13 September 1797, Eleanor Kelly was buried, aged 46, the cause of death given as 'tumour in the womb'. The osteological analysis of skeleton [490] identified a prime adult female (30–45 years) who appeared to have been suffering from multiple myeloma, with the spine and pelvic region badly affected (Chapter 5.6, 'Neoplastic conditions'). It seems possible that skeleton [490], which dated to phase 2 (1750 or later), could be identified as Eleanor. Of added significance is the fact that lying between the feet of [490] was a 26-week-old foetus, [491]. If [490] was Eleanor, was she unknowingly pregnant? While alive it seems logical that any symptoms associated with cancer and a stomach growth could have been described as a tumour in the womb. The osteological analysis of [490] suggested that pregnancy would have exacerbated the condition and may have caused the premature birth of the foetus found at her feet. The questions remains, if [490] was Eleanor, does this explain why the cause of death was recorded as tumour in the womb rather than childbed? The burial registers record two individuals with 'cancer' as a cause of death: Finlay McCloud, buried on 21 January 1798, and

Thomas Clark, aged 50, buried on 2 July 1804. It is highly unlikely that either were osteological female [490].

Three individuals are recorded in the burial registers with gout as a cause of death: 49-year-old Catherine Dodd, buried in 1798, 60-year-old Penelope Fentham, buried on 10 June 1802, and 50-year-old Jane Stewart, buried on 13 October of the same year. It is immediately of interest that all three were female, as gout is generally more prolific in males (Chapter 5.6, 'Joint disease'). However, it is particularly interesting as one of the two individuals diagnosed with possible gout in the skeletal population was also female: [462]. It is possible that [462] was Catherine, Penelope or Jane, but it is not possible to be more precise. Skeleton [462] was located at a depth of 7.82m OD, suggesting a later date, but as all three women were buried within four years of each other this does not help clarify things. On a cautionary note, however, gout of the stomach was sometimes recorded as a cause of death, having nothing medically to do with arthritic gout as it is thought of today (N Powers, pers comm).

The excavations recovered the disarticulated skulls of three males, two of which contained gunshot wounds, the third a possible gunshot wound. Three individuals recorded in the registers were shot: soldier Samuel Jackson was buried in March 1752 having been shot for desertion; William Knox, aged 40, was 'shot by persons unknown' and buried in June 1755; and Adam McCoy, soldier (Chapter 3), was shot in the line of duty (although this is not given as a cause of death in the registers) and buried in October 1769. It is regrettable that all three skulls were disarticulated but perhaps, given that burials continued for almost another 100 years after the burial of the last gunshot victim in 1769, not surprising.

Towards the eastern boundary of the excavated area were two neonates, [2020] and [2021], buried together at a depth of approximately 7.94m OD (Fig 6.15). A fragment of clay pipe stem recovered from the fill implied a date of at least 1750 but could have been intrusive. They did not seem to be associated with an adult burial and were at the top of the stratigraphic sequence in this location, suggesting that they were more likely to be of a later date. According to a broadsheet article dating to 1800 (LMA, O/201/013) two infants, murdered and found in the Thames, were sent to Mrs Jones in the Savoy suttler's house. Apparently they were discovered in the water by soldiers, who rowed out to recover them. The infants, a boy and a girl and assumed at the time to be newborn twins, had been badly mutilated before having their feet tied with cloth and being dumped in the river. As well as other marks of violence, the boy's head had been nearly cut off and the girl's right hand removed altogether. Unfortunately, while it is probable that these infants, having been sent to the Savoy, would have been buried in the chapel burial ground, this is not proven. The burial registers do not contain any record of two infants buried on the same day around this time. However, as other searches have indicated, the burials registers are not complete. The two skeletons were examined microscopically for any signs of trauma but nothing conclusive was found. Both skeletons were missing the right hand. The lack of evidence is not a complete surprise, given the incomplete and fragmentary nature of the remains, but it does not help to determine whether these are the murdered twins or not.

Eighteen burials were recovered with traces of nameplates but most were illegible owing to the degree of degradation (below, 6.6, 'Coffin furniture'). It has, however, been possible to identify at least one individual from the archaeological results. Skeleton [1473] was located towards the centre of the site (Figs 6.15 and 6.16a) and osteologically recorded as a young adult female. A lead nameplate was recovered from the burial, identifying 'Sarah Maries', aged 4*, died 184*. The registers record the burial of 'Sarah Maries, aged 47 years' buried on '6th August 1848'. Sarah was located at a depth of 7.34m OD.

The lead coffin of Anne Hinton and her infant, [597], was located in the north-east corner of the excavation (Figs 6.15 and 6.16b, c). According to the coffin plate they died on 17 and 18 November 1839, respectively (Fig 6.16). Interestingly, however, these burials do not appear in the burial registers. Given the relatively late date of the burial it is not surprising that this was the latest in the stratigraphical sequence, at 7.86m OD. The burial overlay at least six others, including the reverse burial of infant [1292].

The lead coffin of John Bittleston, [1215], located in the north of the site at 6.83m OD was associated with a gravestone and overlying slab (Fig 6.15) but while the coffin plaque dated the death to 1 August 1826 (Fig 6.17), on the upstanding memorial stone only the name John Bill*ston was legible. A further burial, [962], lay immediately above the coffin, at a height of 6.91m OD. The spatial relationship of the two burials suggested that they were either very close together in date or perhaps that they were related. The osteological analysis assessed the later burial, [962], as a prime adult male. Although there are many other burials in the register that fit that demographic after the date of John's death, on 16 June 1848 the burial of a John William Bittleston, who died aged 27 years, is recorded. It is not possible to determine which burial is referred to on the memorial stone but it is very likely that the overlying flat slab was added after the second burial. If the upstanding memorial slab was erected at the same time then this must have replaced an earlier one, considering the accurate positioning of the second interment.

CHAPTER 6 ARCHAEOLOGICAL RESULTS

Mrs
Anne Hinton
Died 17th November
1839
Aged 36 Years
Also her Infant
Elizabeth
Died 18th Instant
Aged 6 Days

Fig 6.16 Named individuals: a – skeleton [1473] (1.0m scale); b – coffin plate for burial [597] (0.40m scale); c – transcription of coffin plate

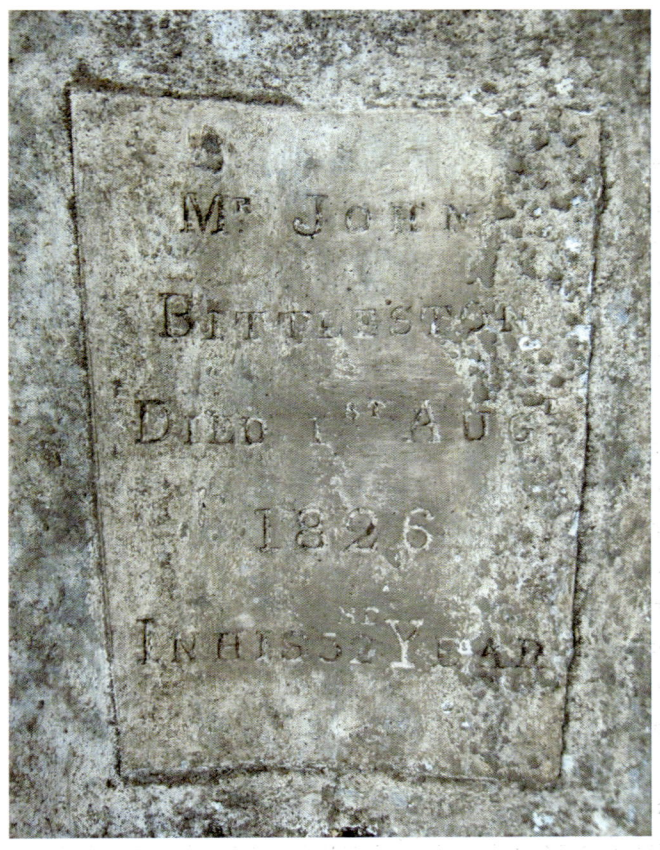

Fig 6.17 Coffin plaque for burial [1215] (0.24m across the top by 0.31m in height by 0.19m across the base)

Although coffin furniture usually provides only broad dates it has proven useful for one particular grave. A combination of the grips and plates recovered from burial [731] has provided a mid 19th-century date. Skeleton [731] was recorded osteologically as a mature adult male. This burial is located in the northern half of the site, apparently isolated, directly beneath the gravestone for G Buckmaster and kin (Fig 6.15, plot A5). As discussed above, the location of the gravestones is not necessarily accurate but the two individuals recorded on the memorial stone, George, aged 8, buried in 1817, and his mother Diane, aged 58, buried in 1833, have been cautiously identified as [900] and [200]. The registers also record the burial of a George Buckmaster, aged 93, on 20 May 1850. Looked at together, the location beneath the Buckmaster family grave, the mid 19th-century date and the osteological analysis results strongly suggest that individual [731] is George Buckmaster. Both Diane Buckmaster and George Buckmaster (senior) were residing in Covent Garden. Is it also interesting to note that skeleton [731] was suffering from a severe case of diffuse idiopathic skeletal hyperostosis (DISH), usually associated with dietary excesses, perhaps saying something about the status of the Buckmaster family.

157

CRANIAL VARIATION AND ANCESTRY

The crania from a sample of 50 skeletons were examined and analysed as part of an external study (MacKinnon 2013). It was concluded that approximately 68% of the population appeared to be Caucasian (ibid, ii, 43) with the remaining 32% being of non-British origin. This is considered a smaller majority of Caucasians than might be expected for the post-medieval period, despite the fact that trade and exploration was intensifying, resulting in increased immigration. MacKinnon concludes that while the results demonstrate the presence of different ancestries within the population, the numbers may be exaggerated as a result of problems inherent to the CRANID analysis program that was used to generate them. However, some particular results are of interest, for example the presence of a single individual of apparent African ancestry – skeleton [1981]. Although uncertain, the registers record the possible burial of a black servant on 15 August 1765. The entry is written between lines as a late addition to the registers, and reads 'A Black, Servant from …'. The placement of the apparent comma makes it hard to ascertain whether the name is 'A Black' or whether it is indeed referring to a black servant. Unfortunately, it is beyond the scope of this publication to examine the burial registers in great detail with regard to names and nationalities but it would make an interesting area for future research. It was noted, however, when studying the registers that several surnames suggest foreign origin, several are of French descent and at least one individual, John Anthony, buried on 14 October 1742, is recorded as 'Grecian'.

FAMILY GROUPS

A number of possible family stacks or pairs were identified within the excavation area (Fig 6.18). When looking at the biographical details of those located in the stacks it was noted that in most cases, according to the osteological analysis, all skeletons were male. This is not surprising given the 3:1 ratio of males to females overall in the burial ground, and the burial registers do contain matches for male family burials – for example, John Long, buried on 16 November 1792, and Robert Long, buried on 16 December 1792.

The burial registers record seven females who died in 'childbed'. These range in date from 1754 to 1812 with the women ranging in age from 22 (Mrs Grobie, 12 April 1812) to 39 (Rebecca Richards, 9 July 1799). The excavations recovered two individuals apparently buried with newborn infants. One of these women, [490] (with infant [491]), has been provisionally identified as Eleanor Kelly, aged 39, buried on 13 September 1797 (discussed above), although in her case the cause of death is given as cancer, not childbed. The other was adult [1782,] of unknown age and sex (although recorded as 'young adult' by an osteologist on site), buried with infant [1784] above the left ribs. The remains of both infant and adult were heavily truncated and located towards the base of the stratigraphic sequence (6.73m OD), which would suggest an earlier date. The earliest to die of 'childbed' in the registers is Mary Russell, buried in 1754 aged 23. Male [834] (discussed above) was also recovered with an infant, [836], at his left shoulder.

There are many instances of repeated family names in the registers, some appearing over decades, but there are also many records of two or more individuals with the same surname being buried within days of each other. If any of these are to be identified, the assumption is made that individuals with the same surname are indeed members of the same family, which seems quite likely given the small size of the Savoy; it is also assumed, given the density of burials within the burial ground, that when two or more graves were so closely linked and stacked, they were buried close together in date. For example, skeletons [427] and [445] were osteologically assessed as a prime adult female and male respectively and were located at the southern end of the site. Their relative positions suggest that the second burial ([427]) very quickly followed the first (Fig 6.19). The burials have been dated to 1750 or later and the lack of truncation and depth of the burials (7.97m OD and 8.01m OD respectively), located at the top of the stratigraphic sequence, suggests that they could be later rather than earlier in date. It is therefore possible that they were Francis and Jane Guy, recorded as husband and wife and buried on 3 February 1745. One further possible match was noted in the registers: Henry White, buried on 21 December, and his wife Susannah, buried on 30 December 1769, but the registers do not record ages at death during this time, or cause of death. It is of interest that skeleton [445] was one of the individuals that had undergone a craniotomy. The possibility that the individuals that underwent craniotomies were executed criminals was considered and discussed in Chapter 5, and while the burial of [445] and [427] together suggests a familial relationship it could simply be coincidence.

Three entries in the registers are sufficiently detailed to be able to look for possible matches from the skeletal assemblage. On 11 September 1749 three unnamed boys were buried on the same day, having drowned, presumably in a single accident. The burial of four individuals took place on 14 April 1763: two mothers and their sons, having been killed 'by the face of a knife'. Five individuals buried on the same day were simply recorded as 'kill'd'. Unfortunately, the only other useful data

CHAPTER 6 ARCHAEOLOGICAL RESULTS

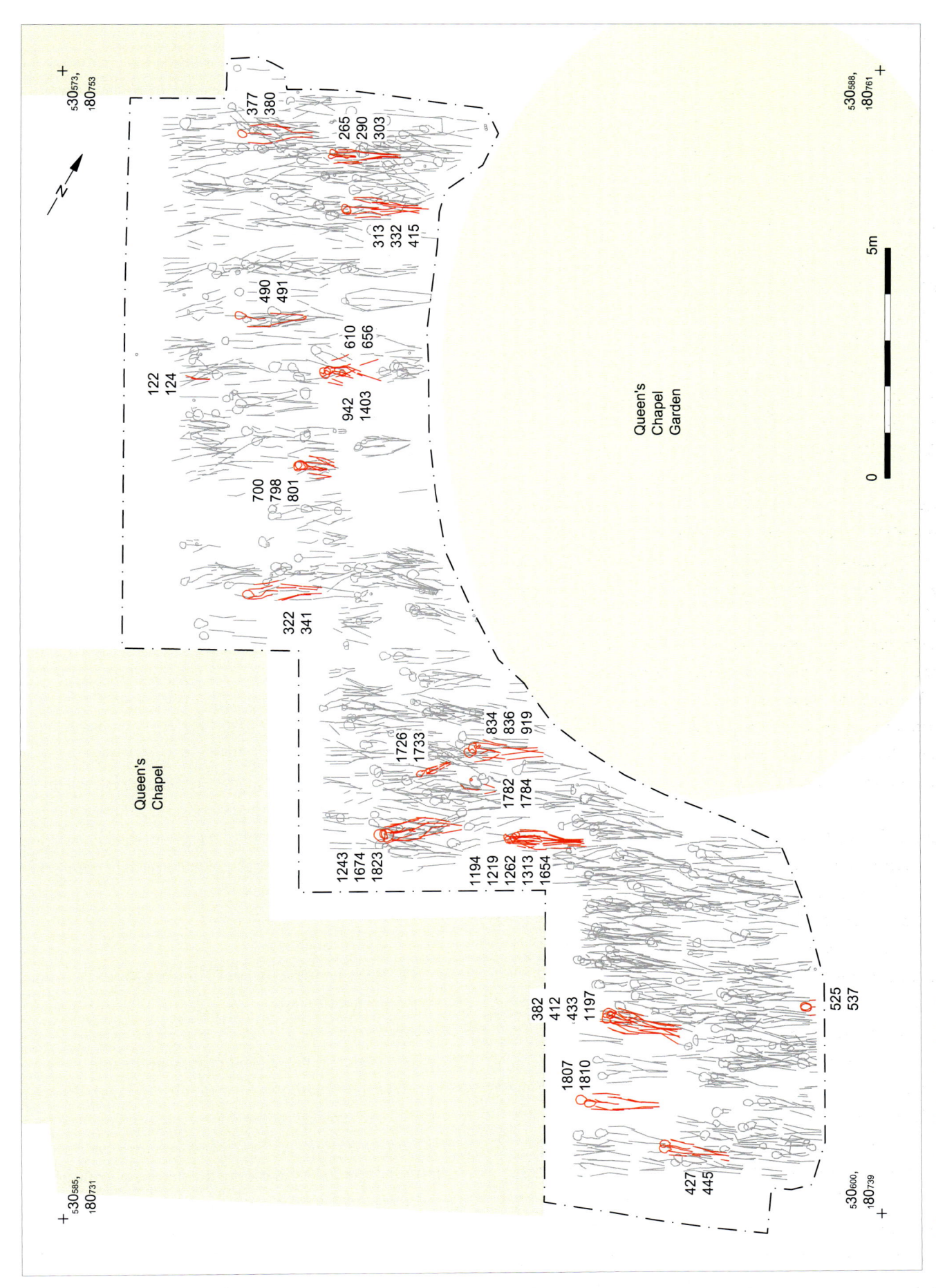

Fig 6.18 Location of possible burial stacks/family graves

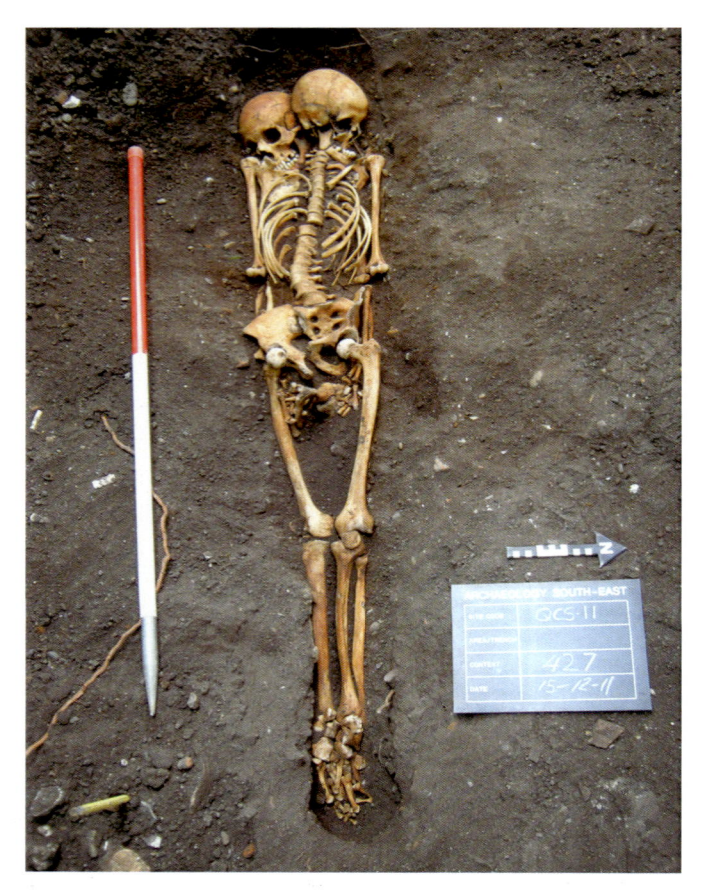

Fig 6.19 Photograph of burials [427] and [445] (1.0m scale)

recorded in these entries are names. In order to look for these individuals it was assumed that these burials were likely to be either in a single grave or at least close together. A GIS search for possible combinations of skeletons that could match the limited biographical data in the registers was carried out but with no success. It must, however, be remembered that the excavations encompassed only 17% of the total burial ground so there is every chance these individuals are located in the remaining 83%.

A final attempt to identify possible family groups was carried out using the data from the congenital pathologies recorded osteologically, as these abnormalities are often attributed to a hereditary factor (Chapter 5.6, 'Congenital abnormalites'). The locations of skeletons with congenital abnormalities were searched for in GIS to look for patterns. This search proved to be more productive and several possible related individuals were found within stacks. Burials [1674] and [1823] were identified as young females and buried beneath [1243]. Both had retained metopic sutures and also displayed spinal abnormalities. Other individuals with spinal abnormalities were males [1262] and [1654], both with extra lumbar vertebrae and buried in a larger stack towards the south of the site, and male [322], with a lumbarised sacral, and male [341], with an extra lumbar vertebra, buried towards the centre.

6.5 CHARNEL

Four charnel pits/deposits were uncovered within the burial ground (Fig 6.20). A small charnel deposit of skulls, [113], was located in the north-west corner of the site at 8.80m OD but no cut was visible. Charnel pit [714] was located centrally within the excavation area at a depth of 8.06m OD. It measured 0.55 × 0.51m and 0.25m deep, and contained a jumble of skulls and long bones. Charnel pit [1237] was located in the southern half of the site at a depth of 7.92m OD, measured 0.70 × 0.80m and 0.21m deep, and contained neatly aligned long bones (Fig 6.21). Just to the west of [1237], at a depth of 7.76m OD, was charnel pit [1277], measuring 0.40 × 0.40m and 0.06m deep.

Similar charnel pits have been recorded in many burial grounds (Cherryson et al 2012, 93) and they suggest a degree of consideration and care. A commonly used alternative was simple reinterment of the disturbed remains within the new grave fill. The quantity of bones recovered from each one suggests that they were generated from larger-scale groundworks in the burial ground, or that bone was being stored ready for reinterment. It is documented that by the 17th century the ground surface, which had been level with the chapel floor, had already risen to just below the chapel sills, and maintenance works in 1723 involved levelling the burial ground (Somerville 1960, 123–4). More recently, 20th-century groundworks resulted in the removal and reinterment of human remains, which included 78 skulls and over 200 large bones, reinterred in the south-east corner of the site in November 1957. Their location precludes them from being related to the charnel discovered in the recent excavations, which was probably of much earlier date, generated during the burial ground's active lifetime.

6.6 BURIAL-RELATED FINDS
COFFIN FURNITURE
Susan Chandler

As expected owing to the standard practice of the time for decorated coffins, a reasonably large quantity of coffin furnishings was collected during the excavations. Together, this material weighed 31.5kg and was collected from a minimum of 85 burials. It included all the expected fittings – coffin grips, grip plates, decorative plates or escutcheons, breast plates, upholstery nails and items used in the construction of the coffins, mainly nails but some screws. The majority of these items were made from iron or tinned iron and thus very poorly preserved because of the conditions of the soils. Where

CHAPTER 6 ARCHAEOLOGICAL RESULTS

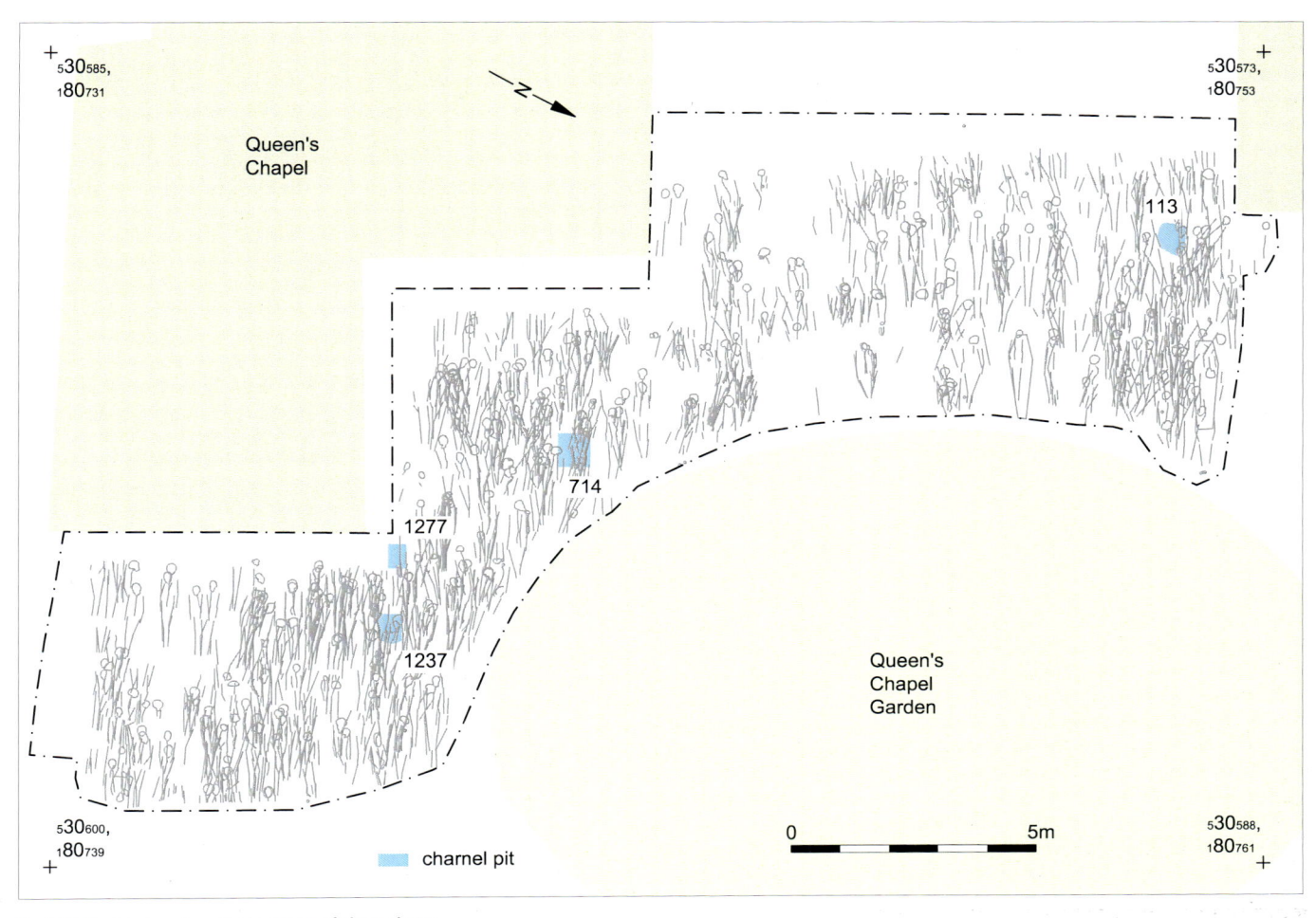

Fig 6.20 Burial plan showing location of charnel pits

Fig 6.21 Charnel pit [1237]

161

possible, the Spitalfields catalogue of coffin furnishings was used to identify types of fitting (Reeve & Adams 1993).

WOODEN COFFINS

As with the preservation of the fittings, the preservation of the coffins on site was poor. The majority of coffins were wooden and survived only as dark brown or rusty coloured organic deposits in each grave (Fig 6.22). However, some degraded wood was preserved by corrosion products from the metal coffin fittings, particularly with the brass upholstery nails. Although it has not been possible to get timber identifications for most of the coffin wood remains because of its poor condition, the most common timbers used in coffin construction at the time were elm or cheaper woods such as larch and pine (Miles et al 2008b, 50). In cases where identification was possible it was found that coffins [597] and [1226] were oak, and that [278] and [326] were elm (Fig 6.23); owing to poor preservation, however, the identifications for [278] and [597] were uncertain. Oak coffins were a later introduction as French polishing (still used today) became popular (Litten 1991, 117); oak takes the polishing well, in contrast to the other woods commonly used. This perhaps shows that [597] and [1226] may have been of a later date or for individuals of higher status.

Around 75 coffins were recorded on site, but poor preservation meant that no structural information was gathered about their construction. It is likely that they were made in the same way as examples excavated on contemporary sites. A standard timber coffin consisted of a kite shape with a flat lid and base, made from six planks of wood. Five or six sawn lines, known as 'kerfing', inside the coffins would allow the sides to be bent to create the shoulders of the coffins (Cowie et al 2008, 31; Miles et al 2008a, 59; 2008b, 50), permitting a degree of adjustment. The coffin would generally be nailed together but screws were occasionally used. Internally, the base of the coffin might be sealed with resin or pitch or lined with fabric. In some cases a layer of sawdust or similar material may have been used to provide a bed to lay the body as well as helping prevent any seepage (Miles et al 2008b, 50) particularly if there were a delay in interment. The sawdust would have been collected from woodworking businesses local to the area such as carpenters and cabinet makers. Packing material was noted in a few of the coffins from site, recorded in [300], [616], [1804], [1807] and [1817] (Fig 6.23). It is most likely that this material, though very degraded, was sawdust.

Herbal or highly scented plant material such as rosemary, balm (Miles et al 2008b, 50), wallflowers or roses (Miles 2012, 57–8) could be used to help combat smells though no evidence for such botanical matter was recovered on site or in the environmental sampling from site. However, given the large amount of evidence from similar sites such as Spitalfields and St Marylebone, it should not be concluded that it was not used, but rather that it did not survive because of the site conditions. In some cases, as seen in Fig 6.22, the base of the coffin appears

Fig 6.22 Example of poor survival of wooden coffins on site – skeleton [1810] (1.0m scale)

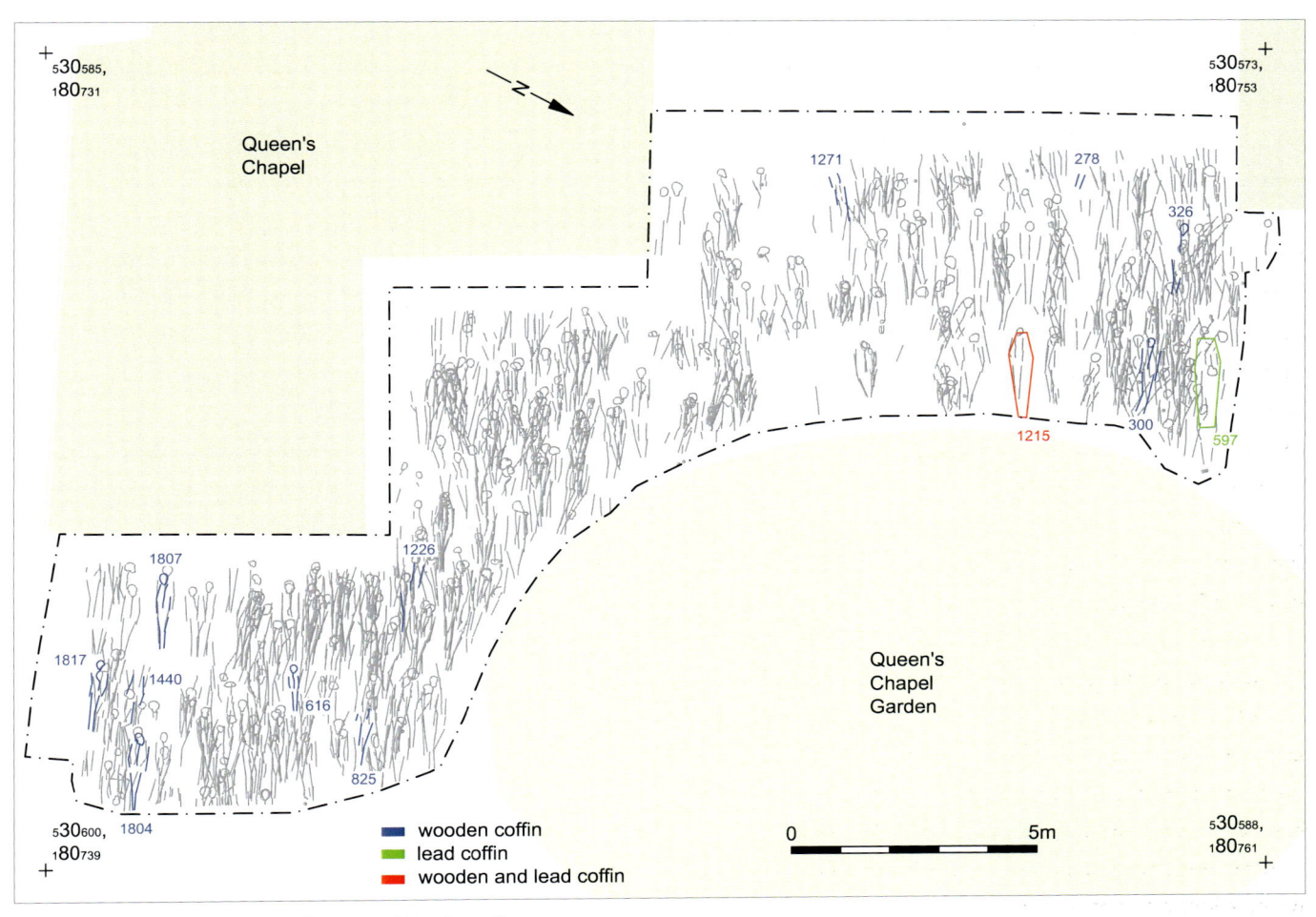

Fig 6.23 Location of burials with coffins or evidence for coffins

to have survived better than the lid and sides, which could perhaps be attributed to the use of pitch to waterproof the insides. Pitch was recovered from [1440] and [1807].

Externally, the coffins would first be covered or upholstered with a fabric such as wool, silk, velvet or felt (Cowie et al 2008, 35–6). This would be held in place by the upholstery nails, which in general were rather like oversized drawing pins, with domed heads between 10mm and 15mm in diameter and short pins (approximately 10mm). These nails would be made from iron or copper alloy and arranged in borders to the sides of the coffins (in up to three rows but more typically in single or double rows), as well as in decorative shapes such as diamonds, triangles or rosettes in spaces between the plates and grips. This added decoration to their function. They were often painted or enamelled black, particularly in the case of the iron examples (Miles et al 2008a, 59). In two of the burials, [825] and [1271], the copper-alloy upholstery nails had a white metal coating, giving a silvered finish. On top of this fabric covering the various grips (either six or eight depending on the coffin's size) and plates would be added, affixed with bolts for the grips and tacks for the plates. Owing to the poor preservation at the Savoy no fabric was recovered but it was possible to see some traces of weave in the corrosion of various fittings, especially on the backs of grip plates or with upholstery nails. It was not possible to identify any fabrics used.

UPHOLSTERY NAILS

Upholstery nails were recovered from 41 separate burials, made mostly from iron in 27 of the burials but with a number of copper-alloy examples from 12 graves (Fig 6.24a). Two graves contained a mix of both iron and copper-alloy upholstery nails, which may have been arranged in patterns taking advantage of the contrasting materials. A few examples of black-coated copper-alloy nails were found; it is probable that the iron examples were also coated but in general their condition was too poor to tell (Fig 6.24b). Linear arrangements of these nails were the most common pattern found in these burials. Some examples of triangular arrangements, similar to the Spitalfields types 3 or 4 added to lid borders, were seen and diamond-shaped arrangements were also recovered (Fig 6.24c). Upholstery nails on two surfaces of some of the surviving wood indicates a line along the external edge or lip of the lid as well as those on top (Fig 6.24d). It was noted during post-excavation recording that some examples of the upholstery nails seemed to be more ovoid or eye-shaped than their round counterparts, interspaced with round-headed examples to create a pattern of alternating shapes as shown in Fig 6.24e. No other examples of these ovoid nails have been found during research. It is possible that the shapes were due to corrosion rather than design.

LEAD COFFINS

Lead was also used to construct coffins, normally those for more well-to-do members of society. Lead coffins were used in a number of ways, depending on the requirements of the intended interment location (Litten 1991, 100–1). In some cases the lead coffin would be internal, with a wooden outer shell being used to host the ornamental elements. In others the opposite would happen, with the lead coffin being the external shell for a wooden coffin. Triple-shelled coffins of wood, lead and wood have also been recorded (Cowie et al 2008, 31).

Two lead coffins were recovered at the Savoy. Burial [597], at the northern end of the site near the northern limit of excavation, contained the remains of Anne Hinton and an infant (Fig 6.23). A simple breast plate was affixed to its lid, with flowing script giving the dates of 17 November for Anne's death in the year 1839 and of 18 November for the death of her daughter, Elizabeth (Fig 6.16b, c). To the south of [597], near the eastern limit of the excavation, burial [1215] contained the other lead coffin, for one John Bittleston (Fig 6.25). This coffin also featured a breast plate soldered to its lid, giving the information that John died on 1 August 1826, in his 32nd year. The inscription on John's breast plate is in a simple but firm, capitalised font (Fig 6.17).

Both these lead coffins were fairly simple in design. Their breast plates are of the common trapezoid shape and relatively plain. The plate on Anne's coffin features basic decorative elements such as a simple border and an inscribed floral motive at its base and it was soldered at its corners. The coffin lid itself has a single, simple border, suggesting that this was the external coffin. In contrast to this, the breast plate of John's coffin has no decorative elements, its plainness suggesting that

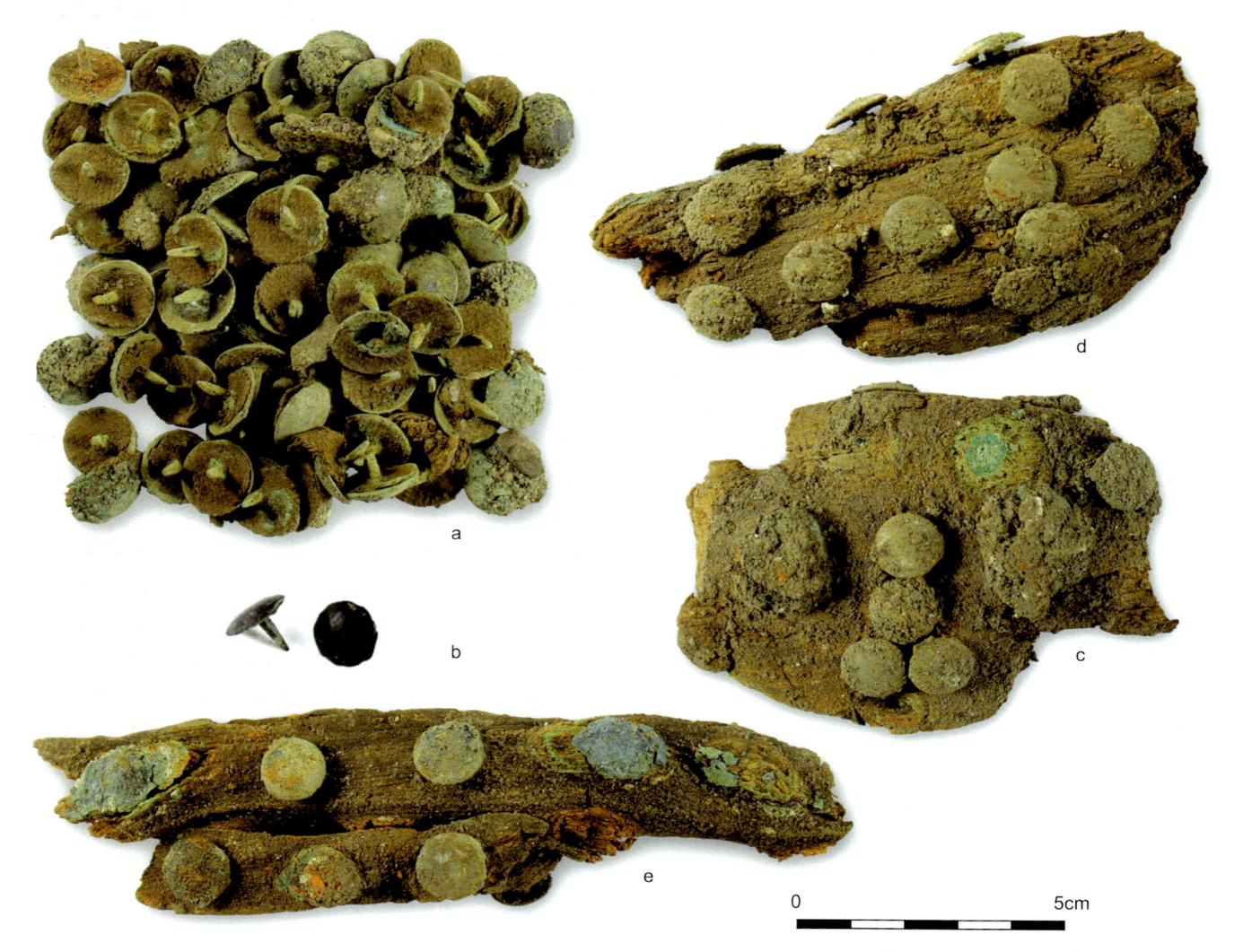

Fig 6.24 Copper-alloy upholstery nails: a – with fabric remains; b – with black coating; c – triangular patterns; d – nails on the lid and sides; e – possible ovoid/eye-shaped nails with round examples in coffin wood as found

Fig 6.25 Lead coffin [1215] showing staining remains from wooden outer coffin (1.0m scale)

this was an inner plate, while a more decorative one would have been used on the external skin of the coffin. The remains of a wooden external coffin were found as a brownish red stain on the outside of the lead coffin (Fig 6.25). Sadly no fittings were recovered from the external coffin. Both these lead coffins were reinterred on site.

BREAST PLATES AND OTHER DECORATIVE PLATES

Further to the breast plates attached to the two lead coffins, 16 burials were found to contain examples of lead breast plates. Of these, 12 were too degraded and did not survive excavation. Of the four that have survived, one is mostly intact, with the others being too damaged or fragmentary to a point where it is not possible to read the full inscriptions or make out details. Two are so degraded that all their information is lost. As with the plates from the lead coffins these are of the common trapezoid shape but with more decoration.

Comparison to the Spitalfields catalogue identified the lead breast plates that did survive excavation as mostly type 21 or 28, or similar. Unlike their pressed iron counterparts, it was difficult to establish a set typology for the lead plates because of slight variations in each design that became apparent only after close examination. The most common of these variations, apart from the inscriptions, is in the raised border of the plates, which would have been individually hand chased, perhaps at the direction of the relatives of the deceased. Other variations are found in the designs of shields, foliage, shells and similar (Miles et al 2008b 58).

The most complete of these plates, that belonging to Mr Francis Wadbrook, [1430] (Fig 6.26), is closest to Spitalfields type 21 but with variations in the border and foliage designs, as mentioned. It has been coated in order to leave it with a black finish, with either enamel or paint. This coating was carried out after the plate's inscription, but it is still possible to make out the tool marks created during the inscription and even some of the 'setting out' marks used to create its correct positioning. The inscription itself was written in a flowing script with flourishes on the capitalised letters. It provides standard information: Francis's name, age and date of death. The plate was attached to the coffin with ten iron nails, one in each corner with the addition along the sides of one central nail and two evenly spaced on either side of it. One of these nails partially survived in the top left corner of the plate. It has a domed head similar to that of the upholstery nails, but smaller.

Thin pressed iron plates were more common and it is highly likely that a number of the burials contained them, though because of poor preservation none survived in a condition to be fully recognised or recordable. The same can be said for the decorative lid motifs and escutcheons normally found on such sites. Fragmentary parts of decorative elements such as borders, foliage or shells were recorded but it is not possible to assign them to items.

Type 2a: the most common design, a simple undecorated curved design found in burials [157], [190], [200], [254], [265], [290], [332], [415], [454], [1347], [1369], [1415], [1473], [1817] and [1914].

Type 2b: very similar to type 2a, recovered from burials [547] and [589]. Dated burials containing grips of these types were interred between 1763 and 1837 at Spitalfields.

Type 1 variation: also undecorated but thicker than the type 2a and 2b designs, recovered from burial [326]. The date range for this type is 1747–1847.

Types 3a and 3b: possible grips of these types, a rectangular design with a central point, were recovered from [278], [789], [930], [1455] and [1855]. These were of early 18th- to early 19th-century date.

Type 4: the most elaborate grips found during the excavation; decoratively moulded grips found in burial [996]. These feature two cherubs flanked by elongated wings and foliage, with a

M^r

Francis Wadbrook

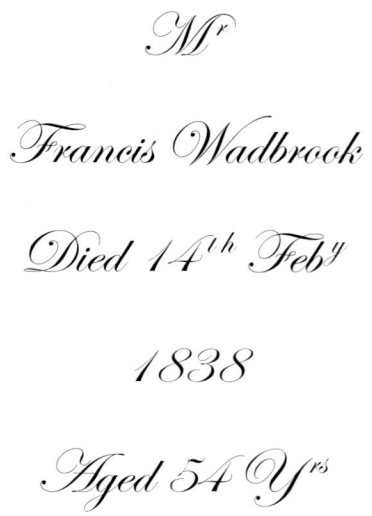

Died 14th Feb^y

1838

Aged 54 Y^{rs}

Fig 6.26 Inscription plate (0.36 × 0.24m) for Francis Wadbrook, [1430], and transcription

GRIPS AND GRIP PLATES

During the excavation 131 grips were collected, from 64 of the burials. Four further burials contained fragments of plate that may represent the remains of grip plates, although the grips themselves were not recovered. From this collection it has been possible to identify 71 grips of designs that match the Spitalfields collection (Figs 6.27 and 6.29).

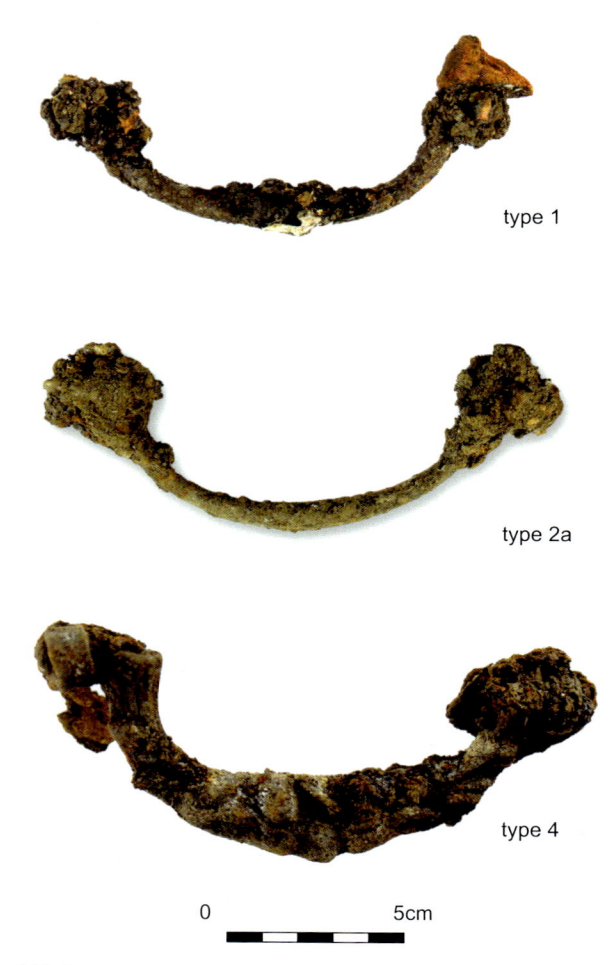

Fig 6.27 Grips: type 1, type 2a, type 4

CHAPTER 6 ARCHAEOLOGICAL RESULTS

similar date range to type 2. A single decorative grip of either type 4 or type 6 came from burial [439].

Most grips retained at least fragments of their plates, but these were more poorly preserved than the grips. Only one Spitalfields type was identifiable, type 14, featuring an urn surmounting a shield within a scrolled or foliate border over a radiating linear background. This came from burial [731] where it had been paired with type 6 grips, suggesting a mid 19th-century date for the burial (Fig 6.29). Burials [200], [332], [415], [462] and [589] contained grips and/or plates and other fittings with a black painted finish.

The remaining grips are of 17th- to 19th-century Kingston types I, IV, IVa, IVb and IVd, none of which feature moulded decoration. Burial [128] contained three grips of type I. Type IVa grips came from [1739]. Probable type IV grips were found in burials [845], [948], [962], [1036], [1150], [1671], [1801], [1895], [1925] and [2009] (Fig 6.29). Kingston-type plates, IVa and IVb, rectangular in shape with lobed ends and two heart- or arrow-shaped cutouts at the centre, were recovered from [303], [344], [418], [576], [1702] and [1739] (Figs 6.28 and 6.29).

A selection of the grips was X-rayed to see if this would aid identification. Owing to the heavy corrosion on most of

Fig 6.28 Kingston-type grip and plate

them it was not possible to gain detailed information about the decorative elements the grips may have had (such as cherubs or foliage) but it was possible to formalise a number of identifications based on the forms of the grips. Of these, grips from [1801], [197] and [406] were found to be Kingston

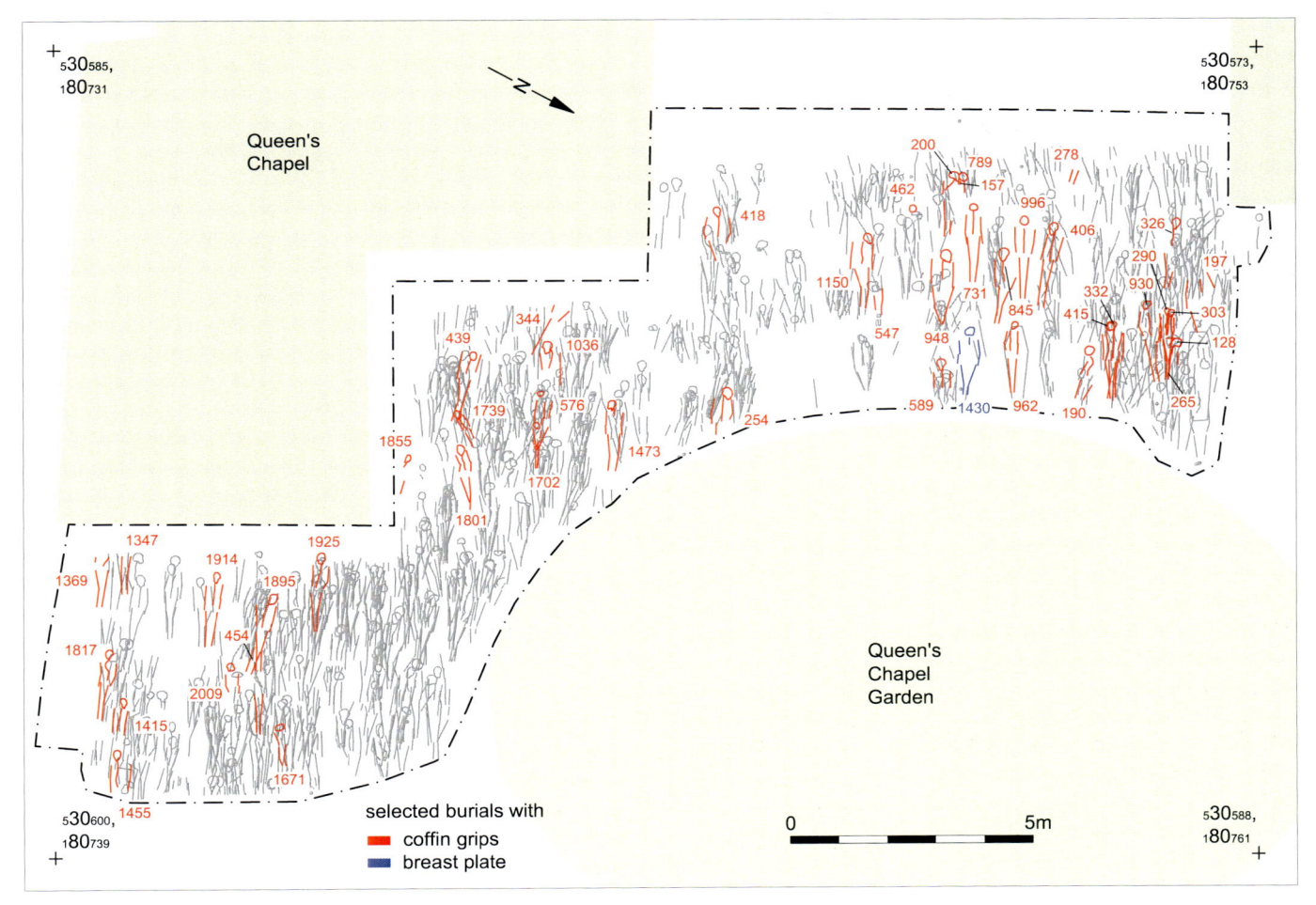

Fig 6.29 Location of grips, grip plates and breast plates mentioned in the text

type IVb. Spitalfields type 4 was identified in deposit [103]. On some of the X-rays it was possible to show that the grips had white metal or lead-based paint coatings which were not distinguishable in the corrosion. The prevalence of less decorative grip types may indicate that many of the individuals buried in the Savoy cemetery were of a lower social or economic standing.

INSECTS
Enid Allison

THE SAMPLES
Four bulk samples were taken from graves, three of which were found to contain abundant beetle remains: <3>, coffin [1907] associated with prime adult male [1807] (1.5 litres); <4>, coffin/packing [1908], from around mature adult female [1804] (2 litres); <5>, coffin/packing [1909], from around mature adult female [1817] (0.5 litres).

METHODS
The samples were processed using a flotation machine with residues and flots recovered on 500µ and 250µ meshes respectively. Both fractions were dried and submitted for examination of insect remains. The dry flots were scanned using a low-power stereoscopic microscope (× 10 to × 45). A brief inspection of the heavy residues indicated that much smaller numbers of insect remains were present in these than in the flots. The abundance of insects and other invertebrates was recorded semi-quantitatively as follows: + = 1–3 individuals; ++ = 4–10 individuals; +++ = 11–100 individuals; ++++ = >100 individuals. Nomenclature for Coleoptera follows Duff (2012). Authorities are given on the first mention of species below.

THE ASSEMBLAGES
There was no evidence that the deposits from which the samples were taken had ever been waterlogged so it is presumed that the insect remains had been preserved by desiccation (Lucy Allott, pers comm). Beetle sclerites (parts of the exoskeleton) were abundant in all three samples; it was estimated that over 100 individuals were represented in <3> and <4> and somewhat fewer in <5>, although this almost certainly related to the smaller size of that sample (see Table 6.4). Preservation of sclerites was reasonably good; cracking or fragmentation of sclerites was common but many were complete. Some sclerites showed a degree of surface erosion and colour loss. Occasional co-joined sclerites, some with dried-out body contents, were observed, particularly in <4>.

A similar range of beetle taxa was represented in all three samples with each assemblage dominated by large numbers of *Rhizophagus*. All of those examined closely were *R parallelocollis* Gyllenhal, commonly known as the graveyard beetle. This species is frequently found swarming in graves, graveyards and on 10- to 24-month-old corpses in coffins, often in association with fly (Diptera) larvae. It can also be found in other habitats, often subterranean, including mouldy substrates in basements, in deep layers of compost and animal burrows, on old bones, under bark and at sap (Peacock 1977, 8). In entirely natural situations it is probably a predator or mould feeder in dead rotten wood and has become adapted to artificial habitats created by human activity.

Other beetles noted during scanning (in approximate order of abundance) were *Triconyx sulcicollis* (Reichenbach), *Coprophilus striatulus* (Fabricius) and Aleocharinae spp, all of which are rove beetles (Staphylinidae), and *Clivina* and *Trechoblemus micros* (Herbst), both ground beetles (Carabidae). *T sulcicollis* is associated with rotten wood (Hackston 2013), *C striatulus* is a decomposer, *Clivina* is a burrowing species while *T micros* hides in cracks in the substrate; all are often found together in subterranean habitats (Kenward & Allison 1994; Kenward 2009, 393–4). Earthworm egg capsules, millipede body segments, pseudoscorpion chelicerae and occasional mites were also observed. No fly puparia were noted. Details from each sample are shown in Table 6.4.

DISCUSSION
Relatively little work on insect faunas associated with archaeological burials of either humans or animals has been carried out to date. Any that has been done has tended to focus on 'important' human burials, for example William Greenfield, Archbishop of York, who died in 1315 (Panagiotakopulu & Buckland 2012).

The large beetle assemblages from the three graves at the Savoy Chapel are of considerable interest since several species

Sample no	Context no	Sample volume (l)	Flot volume (ml)	Species noted during scanning
<3>	[1907]	1.5	10	earthworm egg capsules +, millipede segments +++, *Clivina* sp +, Aleocharinae spp +, *Coprophilus striatulus* ++, *Triconyx sulcicollis* ++, *Rhizophagus parallelocollis* ++++, pseudoscorpion chelicerae ++, mites +
<4>	[1908]	2.0	40	earthworm egg capsules +, millipede segments +++, *Clivina* sp +, *Trechoblemus micros* +, Aleocharinae sp +, *Coprophilus striatulus* +, *Triconyx sulcicollis* ++, *Rhizophagus parallelocollis* ++++, mites +, pseudoscorpion chelicerae +
<5>	[1909]	0.5	15	earthworm egg capsules +, *Coprophilus striatulus* +, *Triconyx sulcicollis* +, *Rhizophagus parallelocollis* +++, pseudoscorpion chelicerae +

Table 6.4 Insect sample details
(abundances estimated semi-quantitatively: + = 1–3 individuals; ++ = 4–10 individuals; +++ = 11–100 individuals; ++++ = >100 individuals)

are represented, enhancing the existing limited data on 'corpse faunas'. The taxa recorded accord particularly well with the group recovered from medieval graves on the Magistrates' Court site in Hull (Hall et al 2000), namely *Trechoblemus micros* (recorded as *Trechus micros*), *Coprophilus striatulus*, *Quedius mesomelinus* (Marsham), *Trichonyx sulcicollis*, possibly some small euplectines, and *Rhizophagus parallelocollis*. The most abundant beetles associated with Archbishop Greenfield's body were *R parallelocollis* and *Q mesomelinus*, with smaller numbers of Aleocharinae spp, *Phyllodrepa floralis* group, *Mycetaea subterranea* (Fabricius) and *Cryptophagus*. Poorly preserved Phoridae (scuttle fly) and Sphaeroceridae (lesser dung fly) puparia were also present. Archbishop Greenfield was buried in a lead-lined stone sarcophagus within York Minster, while the graves at the present site and in Hull were below ground in a cemetery. It is expected that the fauna of particular graves might vary somewhat depending on their location and also on how the corpse was contained, but there are currently not enough data to comment further on this.

It is almost certain that medieval and early post-medieval graveyards supported large populations of *Rhizophagus parallelocollis*, which would readily invade bodies after their interment (Girling 1981). As noted above it is characteristic of corpses that have been buried for 10–24 months that have undergone some decomposition. The other beetle species probably also entered the graves at some time after deposition of the body and the assemblages are therefore not informative about the original circumstances of the burials. They do probably indicate, however, that the buried organic matter was sufficiently well aerated to allow both decay of the contents of the graves and the development of substantial populations of beetles. *Triconyx sulcicollis* is associated with rotten wood and may have exploited decaying coffins.

BURIAL GOODS
Trista Clifford and Lucy Sibun

At the time when the burial ground was in use the majority of buried individuals would have worn burial clothes or shrouds, though day clothes were worn occasionally (Litten 1991, 57–83; Cherryson et al 2012, 24). Despite the number of burials excavated, very few artefacts that could be classed as dress accessories were recovered, suggesting that burial clothing was the favoured option at the Savoy. This is not a surprise considering that the cemetery was associated originally with the paupers' hospital and later with the military. Paupers would have had the simplest burials and as soldiers did not own their uniforms it is

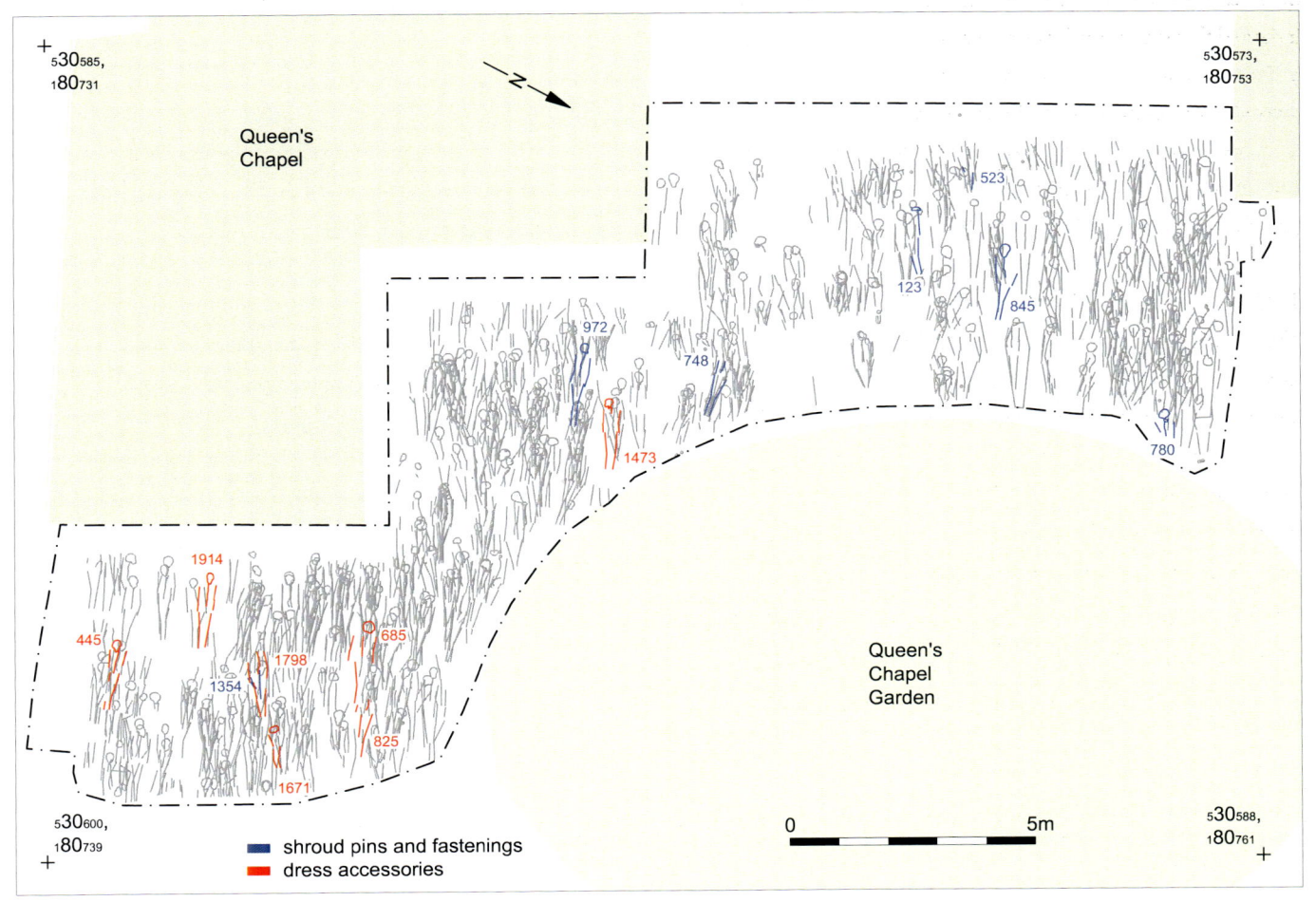

Fig 6.30 Location of burials containing burial goods

unlikely that they would be buried in them (Alistair Massie, pers comm). A similar situation was noted at the Royal Naval Hospital at Greenwich, where a lack of clothes fastenings suggested that shrouds were the preferred option for burial (Boston et al 2008, 27). For the location of burial goods, see Fig 6.30.

SHROUDS AND SHROUD PINS

With the rare survival of textiles (see below) evidence for shrouds can be inferred from the presence of shroud pins, or perhaps from body position. However, the frequent scarcity of shroud pins in many cemeteries suggests that pins were not necessarily the preferred way for securing shrouds, which could also be tied or sewn (Cherryson et al 2012, 24). Of the 612 burials recorded at the Savoy, shroud pins were recovered only from 25 while the body position of a similar number suggested that they may have been wrapped in shrouds at the time of burial.

The majority of pins are incomplete but there are complete examples of Caple type C (Caple 1991, 246): copper-alloy wire with spherical heads formed of two twists of wire tightly crimped to the top of the shaft; some also have a white metal coating. Complete lengths fall between 26mm and 40mm; head diameters range from 1.9mm to 2.8mm. Type C pins (Fig 6.31a) are the dominant form after 1700 (ibid).

One pin from burial [748] is significantly different from the rest. The length is 40.7mm, thickness of shaft 1.5mm and the spherical head has a diameter of 4.6mm. The head is cast in one piece and attached to the shaft through a central hole (Fig 6.31b). A similar pin from Colchester was recovered from a 17th-century posthole.

Other possible fastenings include copper-alloy rings of *c* 30mm diameter ([972], [845]), rings of *c* 17mm diameter ([1354], [123]), smaller copper-alloy 'eyelets' – possible fabric button frames – with the impressions of wound thread visible in the corrosion product ([445], [523]) and a twisted wire loop, [685], which may have held a small posy of flowers or been used as a fastener.

Fig 6.31 Shroud pins

In five cases, pins were recovered attached to part of the shroud or burial clothing. In burial [780] two pin fragments were attached to a piece of shroud fabric, braid and black hair. This may be the remains of a cap or bonnet and jaw cloth.

TEXTILES
Rob Janaway

Material examined

Seventeen samples submitted (recorded as Registered Finds) had cloth remains capable of analysis. The textiles appear to have survived only as small scraps; average dimensions are 56 × 34mm. Eleven of the fragments were either with a corroded copper-alloy object or exhibited copper corrosion staining (Table 6.5). Thus, we can assume that there was probably a high degree of preservation bias towards textiles in immediate contact with corroding copper alloy, especially pins.

Material

The woven cloth, where identification was possible, was very highly degraded wool, showing evidence of cuticular scale loss, fibrillation and insect damage. Some samples were too degraded to identify with confidence. One sample, RF<3038>, is very highly degraded but may be silk.

Textiles

The majority of the textiles are of a relatively open plain weave. This is consistent with the comparatively poor-quality woven textiles used for shrouds and body cloths for burial in the post-medieval period (Janaway 1998)

DRESS ACCESSORIES

Four buttons were recovered. General graveyard soil [117] contained two 17th- to 18th-century discoidal, slightly convex copper-alloy buttons with integral drilled loops, both measuring 23mm in diameter (RF<3026> and RF<3065>, Fig 6.32a, b). A similar button with three incised lines around the perimeter was recovered from infant burial [1671] and may have come from an item of clothing (RF<3033>, Fig 6.32c). This was the only *in situ* button recovered. It was hoped that conservation and X-rays might provide more detail, perhaps evidence of military insignia, but this did not prove to be the case. No decoration is apparent on any of the buttons, and certainly no regimental decorations. The grave of prime adult male [1914] produced a small mother-of-pearl button with four countersunk perforations at the centre (RF<1020>, Fig 6.32d). This is of 19th-century date, possibly from clothing or a burial gown purchased for the burial.

CHAPTER 6 ARCHAEOLOGICAL RESULTS

Registered Find no	Skeleton	Description	Weave	Counts per cm	System 1 ply/spin	System 2 ply/spin	Maximum length of fragment (mm)	Maximum width of fragment (mm)	Fibre type
<1006>	[523]	copper-alloy ring 11mm diameter; very degraded cloth	plain?	too small	1 S	1 S	11	6	impossible to identify
<3003>	[1873]	copper-alloy pin; very heavily degraded cloth fragment, heavily contaminated	plain	too degraded	too degraded	too degraded	25 20 12	10 20 30	no identification
<3005>	[1716]	mass of fibre and open-weave cloth fragments	plain	too small	1 Z	1 Z	40 80	50 40	wool
<3010>	[703]	cloth fragment with copper-alloy stain	plain	14/17	1 Z	1 Z	120	60	wool
<3011>	[780]	mass of open-weave cloth with copper-alloy staining	plain	15/16	1 Z	1 Z	60	30	wool
<3014>	[945]	copper-alloy pin, length 28mm; cloth in two fragments	plain	too small	1 Z	1 Z	20 29	5 8	wool
<3017>	[565]	multiple fragments of open-weave cloth with copper-alloy staining	plain	12/16	1 Z	1 Z	-	-	poor preservation – too difficult to identify
<3024>	[922]/[923]	copper-alloy pin; cloth	plain	15/15	1 Z	1 Z	40	20	wool
<3081>	[1990]	fragments of cloth with copper-alloy staining	plain	too small	1 Z	1 Z	15 22	10 18	wool
<3038>	[1452]	loose fibre, fragments of cloth with copper-alloy staining	plain	19/18	1 Z	1 Z	50	45	possible silk – very poor condition
<3039>	[2015]	two S-plied cords and mass fibre			1 S		60	40	wool
<3040>	[1922]	copper-alloy pin; cloth wool very degraded	plain	too degraded	1 Z	1 Z	45	20	wool
<3041>	[1686]	copper-alloy pin; cloth	plain	15/18	1 Z	1 Z	60	40	very degraded wool
<3042>	[771]	degraded cloth	plain	18/22	1 Z	1 Z	40	25	no identification
<3043>	[1702]	2 fragments of cloth	plain	18/14	1 Z	1 Z	60 70	26 40	very degraded wool
<3070>	[566]	2 fragments of cloth, highly degraded, copper-alloy staining	plain	too degraded	1 ?	1 ?	25 20	15 8	no identification
<3073>	[1925]	plain open-weave cloth with copper-alloy staining; hair	plain	14/11	1 Z	1 Z	70	55	no identification

Table 6.5 Catalogue of textile materials examined

While buttons might be used to secure a burial gown at the wrist or neck, evidence suggests that they are more likely to be associated with clothing. Certainly, copper-alloy buttons are unlikely to be associated with shrouds (Cherryson et al 2012, 28). Other evidence of fixings was found in the form of smaller copper-alloy 'eyelets' (possible fabric button frames) with the impressions of wound thread visible in the corrosion product, recovered from [445] and [523].

A small, rectangular, buckle frame was recovered from burial [445] (Fig 6.33a). This probable 18th- to 19th-century buckle is single-looped with two internal pins. While this is typical of a knee or shoe buckle, it appeared to be *in situ* at the

Fig 6.32 Buttons

Fig 6.33 Dress accessories: a – buckle; b – tortoiseshell comb

Fig 6.34 Jewellery: a – pale blue glass bead; b – gold fitting; c – colourless glass bead

waist and had a fragment of possible leather adhering to it. This individual also had a copper-alloy ring on their left shoulder (diameter 13mm). The presence of the buckle implies that this adult male, who was subjected to an autopsy (Chapter 5) and apparently buried with female [427] (above, 6.4, 'Family groups'), was buried in clothing rather than a shroud. This in turn implies that the copper-alloy ring on his left shoulder may have fastened clothing rather than a shroud. The same may therefore be true of the other copper-alloy and iron fixing rings discovered ([123], [845], [972] and [1354]). The only other dress accessory recovered was a copper-alloy rolled sheet lace-end, with the cut end of the lace still visible within it (not illustrated), recovered from [1798]. The form, which is consistent with clothing fastenings, is difficult to date since it changes little from the medieval period on, but it is probably post-medieval in date. It is tempting to try to link these items with military uniform, although burial in uniform was not common (see above). Uniform would have had both buckles and straps with several fixings and fastenings for carrying items such as a steel picker or small brush, which would be used for clearing the black debris that could build up in the musket touch hole and were usually attached by a chain to a coat button or cross belt (Holmes 2001, 299).

Dress accessories such as lace ends and buckles have been found in association with Civil War cemeteries, implying that funerary practices might have been more flexible in such times (Cherryson et al 2012, 24). Although the Savoy burial ground was not a war cemetery, exceptions might have been made for soldiers such as Adam McCoy, shot in 1769, whose funeral appears to have been an elaborate affair (Chapter 3).

Grave [1473], identified as that of 'Sarah' (above, 6.4, 'Historical records'), produced a decorative tortoiseshell comb (Fig 6.33b). The comb is a 19th-century example, which matches the 1848 date of the burial. As the presentation of the corpse for burial included suitable presentation of the hair it seems likely that the comb was used to style Sarah's hair and hold it in place. While funerary bonnets were popular, ladies' hairstyles were also becoming more elaborate and any attempt to re-create these in death might have required the use and inclusion of a comb. Similar examples have been found in contemporary cemeteries such as St Paul's Church, Hammersmith, City Bunhill burial ground and St Martin-in-the-Bull Ring in Birmingham (Cherryson et al 2012, 32).

The only evidence for jewellery was recovered from a single grave fill and general graveyard soil. The grave of prime adult male [825] contained a small opaque, pale blue, subcircular glass bead, measuring 3.5mm in diameter and 3.2mm in height (Fig 6.34a), and a biconical, faceted bead of transparent colourless glass was recovered from general graveyard soil [117] (Fig 6.34c). Both are of late post-medieval date. The graveyard soil also contained a gold jewellery fitting of 19th- to 20th-century date (Fig 6.34b). This is likely to be the backing from a small pendant. With the exception of finger rings, not evident at the Savoy, personal adornment was rare during the 18th and 19th centuries (Cherryson et al 2012, 36) so the lack of evidence from the Savoy is to be expected.

6.7 NON-BURIAL FEATURES

Several non-burial-related features were uncovered during the excavations: remnants of disused paths, surfaces and drains (Fig 6.35).

CHAPTER 6 ARCHAEOLOGICAL RESULTS

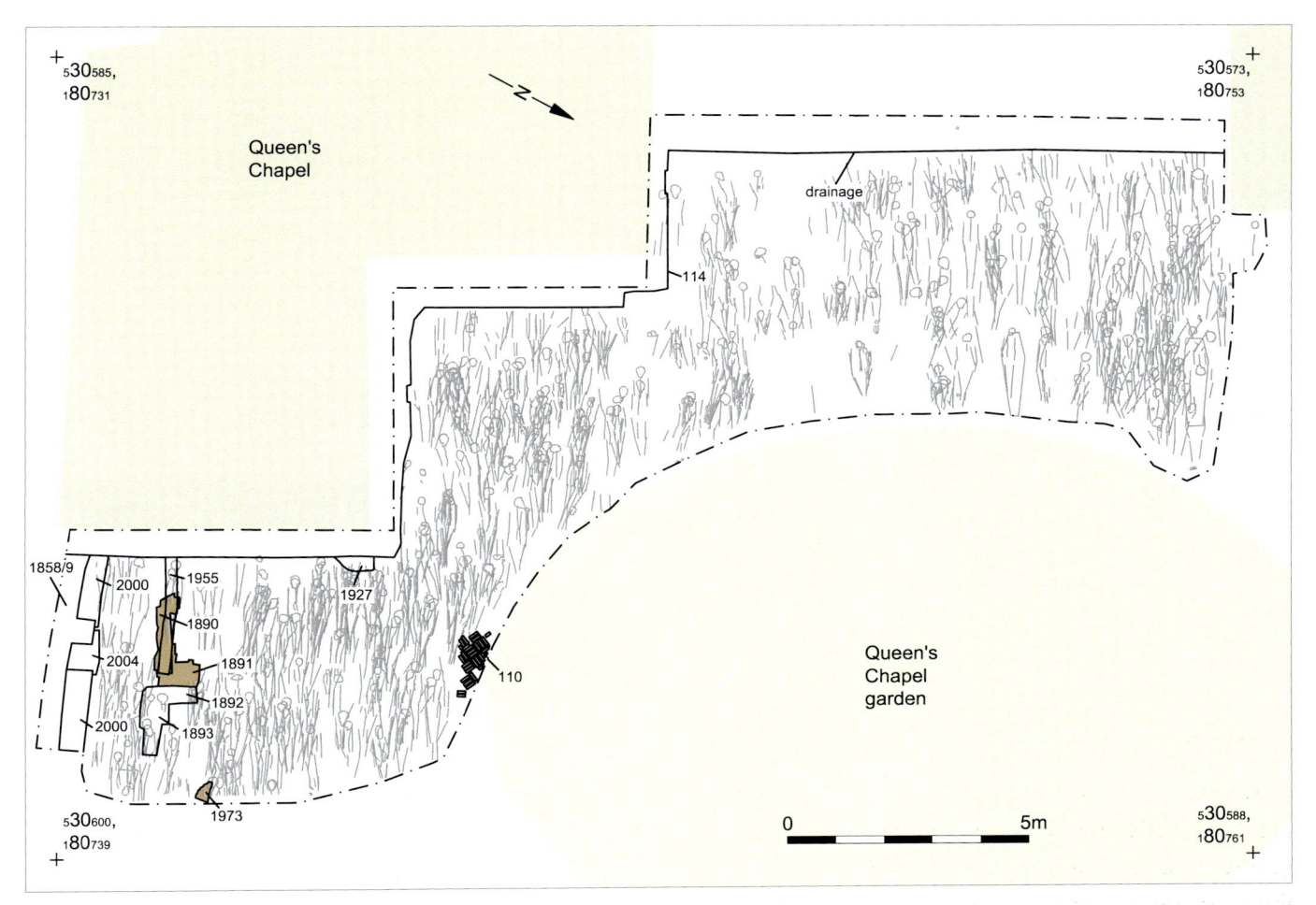

Fig 6.35 Non-burial-related features

One of the earliest features, uncovered at the base of the excavations, was a 2.50m length of box-drain, [1955], located at 6.87m OD (Fig 6.36). It was constructed from bricks of probable 17th-century date and was 2.5m in length, 0.23m wide and 0.16m high, terminating at the eastern end. The side was formed of a single course of bricks laid on edge with a single layer of bricks laid flat to form the drain cap. A large, arched brick drain was uncovered in the burial ground during works in the 1950s, running parallel to the eastern wall of the chapel at a distance of 14ft from it, and measuring 3ft wide and 4ft 6 in deep (Somerville 1960, 127). As it underlay the foundation of the early buildings it is thought to have been contemporary with the hospital. It may have been the drain described in 1669, running through the burial ground and 4ft below the chapel floor. Given its depth, dimensions and orientation, this was clearly not feature [1955] uncovered during the recent excavation works but does suggest a late 17th-century date for it.

The remains of several paths or surfaces were also uncovered during the excavations. As this area has been a burial ground since the hospital's foundation, these features were all probably external paths and walkways. At the base

Fig 6.36 Photograph of drain [1955] (1.0m scale)

173

of excavations (6.91m OD) and to the north of drain [1955] was a small section of path or floor, [1927], measuring 0.33 × 0.84m and 0.90m thick. It seems to have been constructed from crushed brick fragments, a sample of which has been dated from 1450 to 1700 AD (Fig 6.37a). Assuming that drain [1955] would have been beneath the ground surface, the fact that the path and drain were at approximately the same height suggests that the path pre-dated the drain and may have belonged to the earliest stages of the cemeteries use.

Also at the southern end of the site and partially overlying [1955] was surface [1890]–[1893] at a height of 7.10m OD. It was constructed from an irregular arrangement of bricks and half-bricks, [1891], edged by regularly aligned brick fragments, [1890]. Both layers were bedded on gravels and mortar [1892]/[1893] (Fig 6.37b). This path seems to have been constructed from reused bricks and tiles: the bricks were dated to 1600–1700 AD and the floor tiles to the 15th or early 16th century (Pringle 2014). Given the early date of the floor tiles, which were green-

Fig 6.37 Paths: a – of brick fragments, [1927] (0.40m scale); b – of reused brick and tile, [1890]–[1893] (1.0m scale); c – of reused tile and limestone fragments, [1973] (0.40m scale)

Fig 6.38 Paths: a – herringbone pattern, [110] (0.40m scale); b – photograph of burial ground showing perimeter path, taken in 1937 ©Duchy of Lancaster

or yellow-glazed and of typical Flemish design, it is possible that they originated in the hospital (Pringle 2014) but this association cannot be proved with the available contextual evidence.

On the eastern boundary of the excavation at the southern end of the site was evidence of one further surface, [1973], at a depth of 7.0m OD. This was also constructed of reused materials, including floor tiles dating to 1250–1550 AD and limestone fragments (Fig 6.37c). Although the remnants of all three floor/path surfaces at this end of the site ([1927], [1890]–[1893] and [1973]) were located at a very similar depth, which might suggest they were related, the construction methods and materials were different in each case. Unfortunately, given that the materials either had a broad date or were reused, they provided little dating evidence for the skeletons stratigraphically above or below them.

The most modern path was uncovered at the start of the excavations, [110], at 9.62m OD, constructed of 18th- to 19th-century bricks laid on edge in a herringbone pattern, bedded in sand. The surviving area measured 1.50m east–west and 0.90m north–south and was located along the eastern boundary of the site (Fig 6.35). This herringbone path is evident in a photograph from 1937, which shows the burial ground clear from any memorials (Fig 6.38a, b). The surveys carried out to record the memorials prior to their removal and repositioning were carried out in 1934, suggesting that path [110] may have post-dated these improvement works. However, a perimeter path is visible in both the 1930s survey and the 1937 photograph and given the dates assigned to the bricks used in the path's construction, it is possible that the same path remained in use for some time. This would imply that the 1930s improvements removed both the upstanding memorials and the diagonal section of path visible in the survey that crossed the burial ground from the north-east gate to the south-eastern entrance of the chapel, which dates to 1859–60 (Somerville 1960, 134). Although there had been a south-eastern entrance to the chapel before 1843 (Somerville 1960, 132), a painting of the fire in 1860 (Chapter 3, Fig 3.8) does not appear to show a diagonal path across the burial ground. Its absence may be due to artistic licence but it is equally possible that the path dated to the remedial works that followed.

The perimeter wall of the burial ground was recorded along the southern edge of the site as [1858] and [1859]. It was constructed from bricks laid in an English cross bond, with light yellowish-grey mortar. It was 0.40m wide and from the external road surface it stood between 2.00m and 2.70m high (Fig 6.39), with buttresses evident on the internal surface. An apparent earlier section of wall, [2000], was uncovered at

Fig 6.39 Walls: a – photograph of walls [1858]/[1859], [2000] and sandstone blocks [2004] (1.0m scale); b – watercolour of the Savoy Chapel, 1787 ©WCA J132 (03)

the base of [1858] (7.17m OD). This was also constructed in English bond, and measured 4.24m long, 0.26m wide and 0.07m high. A rough mortar surface on the top of [2000] perhaps suggested that it had been lowered or truncated at an earlier date. In the centre of the remaining section of wall [2000] were two large, shaped, sandstone blocks, [2004] (1.14 × 0.20 × 0.30+m, and 0.18 × 0.15 × 0.30+m).

The construction of northern and eastern perimeter walls is documented in 1723, before which time the burial ground seems to have been open (Somerville 1960, 123). Since the hospital's construction at the beginning of the 16th century, the western boundary of the burial ground had been the eastern wall of the chapel buildings, with the southern boundary formed by the northern wall of the main dormitory, which was later used as barracks. Despite several fires and periods of dilapidation, the east–west dormitory of the hospital/barracks seems to have remained in place until its final demolition at the beginning of the 19th century.

Walls [1858]/[1859] and [2000] are very similar: bricks of the same dimensions and constructed in English bond, held together with a yellowish-grey sandy mortar. Although the upstanding perimeter wall [1859] was not sampled, two bricks from [2000] were examined and given a likely date of 1600–1700. Despite the possible early date of these bricks, the construction methods and overall appearance of the walls suggest that they may all date to the early 19th century, when the hospital buildings were finally demolished and the large-scale improvement works took place in the Savoy. The apparent truncation or lowering of [2000] highlighted by its upper, irregular mortar surface, may instead be explained by a reinterpretation of the construction method employed, with [2000] built as a foundation with [1858]/[1859] (Michael Shapland, pers comm). It was noted in Chapter 3 that towards the end of the 18th century the dilapidated hospital buildings were being used as a quarry for brick and stone (Somerville 1960, 108). It seems quite probable that the 19th-century improvements would have made the most of the building materials available on site and that the earlier bricks were therefore reused.

Fig 6.39a shows that wall [2000] was in fact constructed around sandstone blocks [2004]. It has been suggested that the sandstone blocks are the remains of an *in situ* medieval buttress (M Samuel, pers comm). Fig 6.39b is a watercolour of the chapel and burial ground, dated to 1787.

The facing wall in the painting is the southern perimeter wall of the burial ground and buttresses can clearly be seen, equally spaced along it. Although it has not been possible to marry the two, by studying contemporary illustrations and taking measurements from the excavation plan using GIS, it can be concluded with reasonable confidence that the position of one of the medieval buttresses coincides with the location of the sandstone blocks.

Along the western edge of the excavation area was a modern drainage trench and the foundation cut for the 20th-century vestry ([114], (Fig 6.35). The cut had truncated a number of burials and presumably generated the large quantity of human remains that were subsequently redeposited in the south-east corner of the burial ground (above, 6.5). The base of the foundation trench was not reached during these excavations.

6.8 DISCUSSION

As discussed in the previous chapter, although the excavations covered only 17% of the area of the burial ground, the results do appear to be representative of the whole. The most significant difficulty encountered has been the inability to accurately phase the burial ground. However, the evidence seems to suggest that most burials related to the later stages of its use as a military hospital, barracks and prison, with few of the earliest hospital burials surviving. The demographics of the population are discussed in Chapter 5 but some aspects are of relevance here. One is the difference in the proportions of subadults recorded in both the historically recorded and excavated populations. The registers record a higher percentage of subadults – up to 27%, as opposed to only 15% of the excavated population. It is often asserted that the more fragile remains of subadults, particularly infants, are frequently under-represented in excavated populations because of their susceptibility to decomposition and destruction (Mays 2010, 28) and this may be partly responsible for the difference noted. However, the same is also true here for the females, with a higher proportion recorded in the registers: 32% of adult individuals, as opposed to only 25% of the excavated population. These results therefore seem to suggest that the unexcavated part of the burial ground contains a greater proportion of both subadults and females and perhaps that there was not a dedicated area for children as was recorded at contemporary sites such as St Mary and St Michael burial ground and Bow Baptist Church (Powers & Miles 2011, 32, 69). It is possible that such an area may not have been considered necessary at the Savoy Chapel given the composition of the population, based upon the burial ground's primary use for the poor men's hospital and then the military.

The only concentrations of particular demographic groups are the young or prime males buried towards the south of the excavation area, particularly between 7.50m OD and 8.50m OD. This, combined with the relative lack of subadults and females, suggests that the excavation area contains concentrations of soldiers. To go one step further, it could be hypothesised that the 1.0m depth might be linked to one or both of the peak decades when the numbers of burials were at their highest – the 1740s and 1790s.

The historical records suggest that large numbers in the burial ground died from jail fever or typhus, particularly in the 1740s. The cause of jail fever was thought to be a lack of cleanliness and fresh air, something familiar to the inhabitants at the Savoy, but has also been attributed to the sudden change in diet and environment to which new convicts were subjected. Prison convicts would generally be robust young men, used to exercise and free diet. When suddenly finding themselves with restricted diet, confined space and no fresh air they became worn down and more susceptible to illness (Howard 1791, 231). It was also noted that the problem became much worse in times of peace, such as 1783, when prisons became suddenly overcrowded (ibid, 232). Fevers in general seem to have been a problem across London, with further epidemics recorded in the 1790s (Creighton 1894, 88). Unfortunately, it is not easy to see evidence of either disease in the skeletal population so reliance then has to be placed on the archaeological record to pick up concentrations in burial patterns that may or may not be explained by a disease epidemic.

Through a combination of the 1930s survey data, archaeological evidence and historical research it has been possible to identify some individuals, although not as many as was hoped. Those identified confidently were either isolated beneath graves or found with a legible coffin plate. The overcrowded nature of the burial ground, a lack of dating evidence and possible inaccuracies associated with combining the survey and the excavation plan resulted in several possible, rather than positive, identifications. These include those whose identification is based upon osteological analysis and disease manifestations. The superimposing of the 1930s survey on the digitised excavation plan highlighted some other issues. For example, why do some of the latest memorial stones not appear to have a burial beneath them? It is unlikely that the bodies were removed by bodysnatchers since these post-date the Anatomy Act of 1832. Later 19th- or 20th-century ground disturbance is a possible explanation. Although some disturbances are documented, the details about locations, depths and so on are not always precise and it is likely that many more disturbances remain undocumented. Lastly, it is possible that the memorial stones themselves may be the problem – if their placement did not immediately follow the burial they may have been aligned with the adjacent stones, rather than directly over the grave. Other evidence also suggested that slight misalignment or positioning of stones was probable.

With regard to burial practice, there are some conclusions that can be drawn from the excavation results, although somewhat hindered by the poor preservation. It would seem that the majority of burials were simple shroud burials. Undoubtedly, there were more coffins present than were recorded but if they survived only as nails or stains, the constant truncation of graves would have removed some of this evidence. What is clear is that there were few tombs, lead coffins or lead breast plates, such as might normally be associated with more affluent burials, leading to the conclusion that most of the Savoy burials were not wealthy. The lack of burial or dress accessories, although these are not always expected during this period, leads to the same conclusion. This fits with the overall history of the site as a burial ground for paupers and soldiers, with only a small proportion dating to the later, civilian phase of the Savoy when more elaborate funerals might be expected. These results are also analogous to those from the comparable burials of sailors and marines at the Royal Hospital Greenwich, dating from 1749 to 1857 (Boston et al 2008, 7–8) and the London Hospital for the poor, although burials at the latter are of 19th-century date (Fowler & Powers 2012, 33). At both sites, evidence suggests that burials and coffins were simple and plain (Boston et al 2008, 73; Fowler & Powers 2012, 33), as might be anticipated.

The organisation of the burial ground may have been a response to fluctuating burial rates as much as any attempt at chronological development. Organised rows are evident and these are certainly apparent in the latest, civilian family burials but it may not have been possible to maintain clear rows during the busiest times and this may have resulted in the areas of concentration visible on the plans. To some extent the development of the burial ground was evidenced by the truncated sections of paths. These all appear to have reused earlier materials, some of which may have originated from the Savoy Palace or the early hospital. Three of the surfaces recorded were located towards the base of the excavations and were all within approximately 0.20m of each other. However, with differing construction materials there is no evidence that they were contemporary. At least one attempt to level the burial ground is documented in the early 18th century (Somerville 1960, 123) and this may explain the presence of differing paths at similar depths, with a later return to an earlier ground level. Alternatively, it is possible that the paths were contemporary and demonstrate the use of any available material, or areas of repair. The only other non-burial-related structural remains uncovered were the medieval buttress base, which could have formed part of the northern wall of the main hospital dormitory and barracks, and the probable 17th-century brick drain that ran beneath the burials.

CHAPTER 7 SPECIALIST REPORTS

> WE deem them moderate, but Enough implore,
> What barely will suffice, and ask no more:
> Who say, (O Jove) a competency give,
> Neither in Luxury, or Want we'd live.
> But what is that, which these Enough do call?
> If both the Indies unto some should fall,
> Such Wealth would yet Enough but onely be,
> And what they'd term not Want, or Luxury.
> Among the Suits, O Jove, my humbler take;
> A little give, I that Enough will make.
> —Anne Killigrew, First EPIGRAM.
> Upon being Contented with a Little
> (Morton 1967, 15)

In this chapter all finds recovered from grave fills have been numbered by grave (skeleton) for consistency and for ease of locating on the plan; it should be borne in mind, however, that these finds were from general grave fill and cannot be directly linked with the skeleton. Burials referenced in the text are located on Fig 7.1.

7.1 THE ARCHITECTURAL STONE
Mark Samuel

A number of fragments of architectural stone were recovered during the excavations. Most were recorded on site; some were partially recorded and retained for further analysis; some, owing to their large size and weight, were fully recorded on site and were not retained.

The majority of architectural fragments were recovered from the infill of the vestry foundation cut [114] and were therefore likely to have originated from the predecessor to the

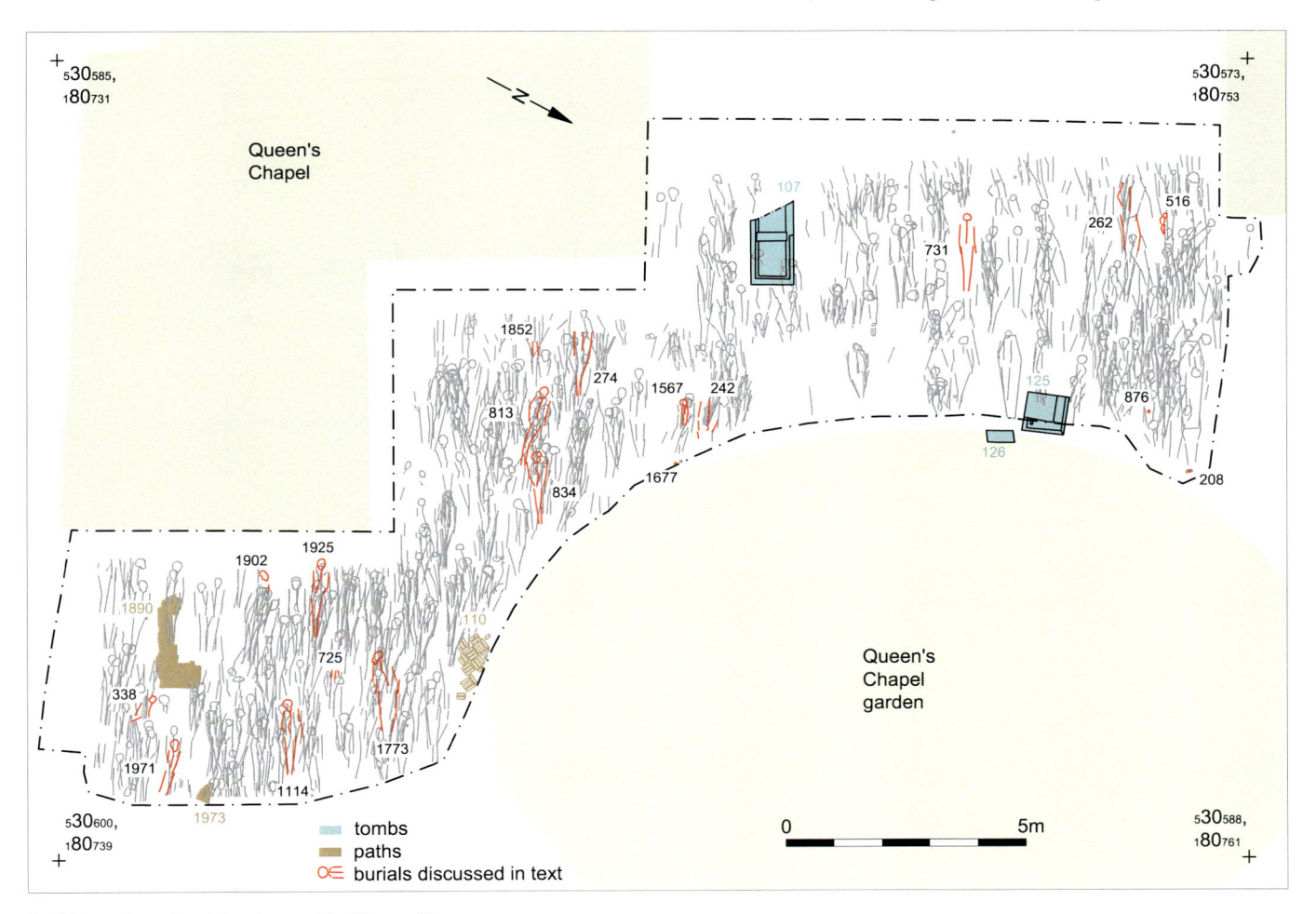

Fig 7.1 Location of burials referenced in Chapter 7

1950s vestry, constructed in 1877 (Somerville 1960, 135). Further fragments, including some derived from tombs, had been reused during the 20th century to form surfaces.

Eleven oolitic limestone (?Bath stone) items apparently derive from the same 19th-century building. All are severely weathered to a greater or lesser extent. The main physical characteristics of the retained items are listed in Table 7.1.

ID	Building stone	Category	Function	Structure	Dimensions (mm)
a	?Bath stone	moulding	jamb stone	window 1	174 × 227 × 306
b	?Bath stone	moulding	sill	window 1	230 × 205 × 360
c	?Bath stone	moulding	coping	parapet 1	291 × 276 × 272
d	?Bath stone	moulding	coping	parapet 1	340 × 242 × 305
e	?Bath stone	moulding	coping	parapet 2	299 × 231 × 225
f	?Bath stone	moulding	string	wall	155 × 161 × 536
g	?Coade stone	moulding	architrave	?door	143 × 110 × 300
	?Bath stone	moulding	drip	string 1	225 × 152 × 430
	?Bath stone	moulding	coping	parapet 2	231 × 205 × 365

Table 7.1 Retained 'worked stones'

GROUP 1

This group comprises two jamb stones, essentially identical, as well as most of a sill block (Fig 7.2). The midpoint of the sill is marked by a ?shutter pivot hole. The glass was carried on slender iron astragals, diagonally set. The glass hinged on iron pintles (traces of one survive). The light was 12.5in (32mm) wide and may have formed part of a single- or multiple-light window. The pattern of weathering illustrates that the window was weathered *in situ*, the interior-facing moulding being likewise weathered.

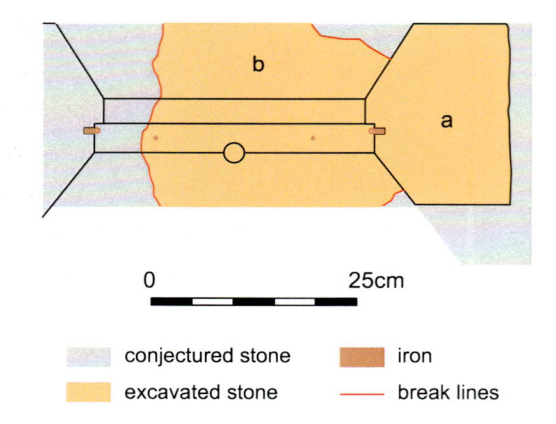

Fig 7.2 Window plan detail showing stones a and b

GROUP 2

Two fragments can be manipulated to create a 'composite reconstruction' of an elaborately moulded coping (Figs 7.3 and 7.4) that capped a wall 10in (0.254m) thick. One of the dressings has a lead 'plug' of unknown purpose set in the reverse weathering (Fig 7.4). The coping was very badly weathered *in situ* and protruding elements were completely destroyed. The cresting is therefore restored on the basis of stylistic probability.

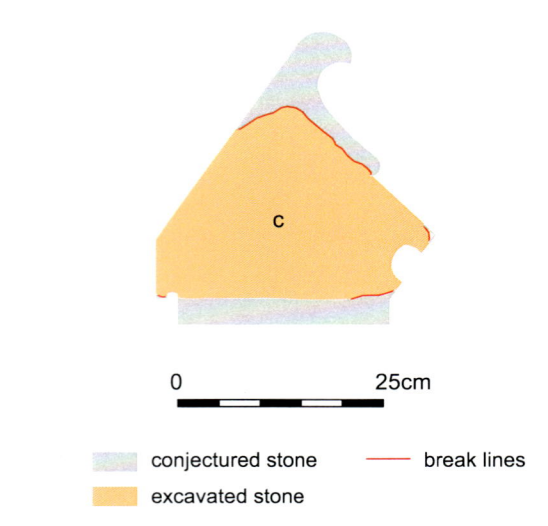

Fig 7.3 Coping stone c (composite reconstruction)

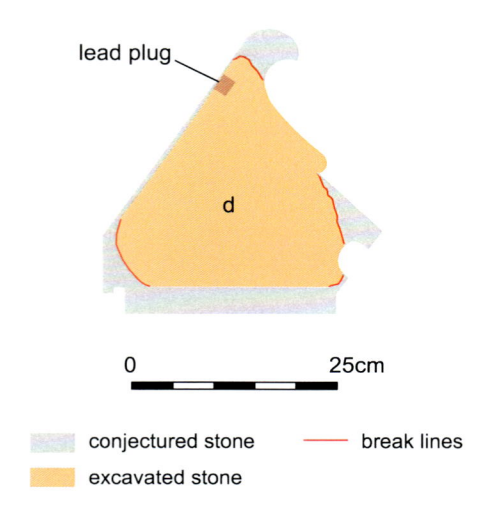

Fig 7.4 Coping stone d with lead plug (composite reconstruction)

GROUP 3

This pattern of coping stone is represented by three fragments, including a termination (now weathered beyond recognition). The coping was set against a wall and marked an offset. The reverse weathering has a deep groove cut into it, filled with very hard cement (Fig 7.5). This may have edged a flashing or gutter behind the coping. The degree of weathering is very severe. The moulding is notionally symmetrical, but has been 'adapted' for its special role. The underside of the drip has a hollow chamfer and the cresting is a simple roll. The copings were set on spacing blocks of very hard cement rather than a conventional mortar bed.

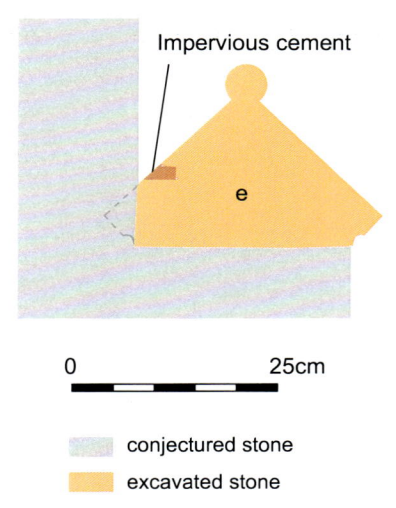

Fig 7.5 Coping stone e (wall-set)

GROUP 4

Four examples were found of an elaborate string-course moulding (Fig 7.6). This was cut in very long lengths which were attached at the ends by plugs or hard cement set in sockets. The mouldings were held in place by the same cement, which was freely applied to all jointing surfaces. The string course was probably set on an internal wall face, judging by its freshness.

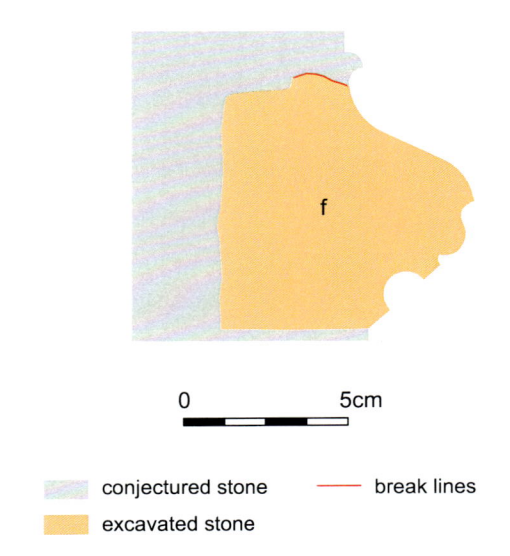

Fig 7.6 Drip mould f

DISCUSSION OF ?BATH MOULDINGS

The weathered ?Bath stone mouldings derive from a single building. The chief inspiration was a 'Late Decorated Style', but the windows were more 'Early English'. Various pattern books were probably used. The method of setting the stones was entirely 'Victorian', employing ?Portland cement as a 'glue' rather than the lime-mix mortars of pre-industrial England. The use of poor-quality Bath stone in inappropriate settings was a typical mistake of the late Victorian period. The degree of weathering is consonant with the recorded date of construction of the vestry in 1877 (Somerville 1960, 135) and final destruction in 1957.

GROUP 5

This isolated piece is cast from 'cement composition' around tiles embedded within (to conserve the expensive mix or deter shrinkage before firing?). The type of moulding allows it to be oriented; in pattern it most resembles a classical door architrave and it may have served such a purpose (Fig 7.7).

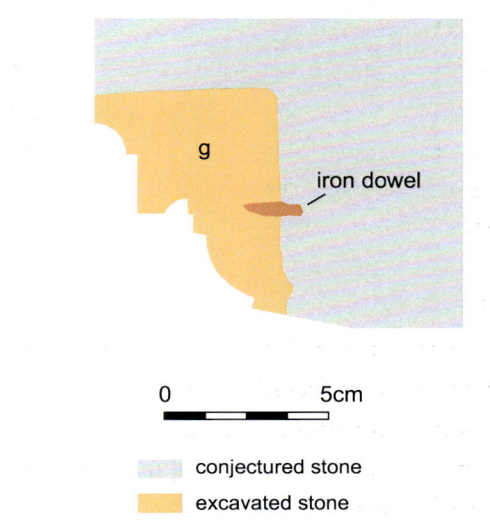

Fig 7.7 ?Coade architrave stone g

7.2 MISCELLANEOUS STONE

Susan Pringle

Two fragments of stone were recovered from graveyard soil [117]. One, a light grey shelly limestone slab, 26mm thick, with a flat, wear-polished surface and a slightly bevelled edge, was probably a floor tile. The other slab was of light grey or white marble streaked with dark grey, probably an imported stone. No worked edges were present, but a thickness of 23–24mm suggests that it was probably a fragment of marble veneer or floor tile.

7.3 THE POTTERY

Luke Barber

INTRODUCTION

The archaeological work produced 601 sherds of pottery, weighing a little over 18.5kg, from 59 individually numbered contexts. Some 387 different vessels are represented in the assemblage. The assemblage has been fully quantified (number, weight and estimated number of vessels (ENV)) for the archive using Museum of London codes for both fabric and form (http://www.mola.org.uk/medieval-and-post-medieval-pottery-codes). These data were input into an Excel spreadsheet, which forms part of the digital archive. Sherd sizes vary greatly. There are many small sherds (< 20mm across), particularly in association with burials, as well as numerous large sherds (> 50mm across). There is even the best part of a slipware bowl from grave [1971] though this is the exception rather than the rule. Sherd size tends to be largest for the mid 17th- to early 18th-century material with the earliest and later pottery generally being represented by smaller, often slightly abraded, sherds. Overall, however, a good proportion of the post-Roman pottery from the site shows moderate signs of abrasion, suggesting the majority of it has been subjected to some degree of reworking. For location of burials referenced, see Fig 7.1.

The assemblage spans a number of different periods. The earliest sherds are of probable later 12th-century date and the latest sherd dates to the middle of the 19th century (although this is an isolated example). By far the majority of the assemblage, including all the largest sherds, belongs to the early/mid 17th to the early/mid 18th century. A breakdown of the whole assemblage by period is given in Table 7.2. Although most of the contexts producing pottery can be considered stratified to a degree, virtually all were 'open' and had clearly received residual and/or intrusive material. This is hardly surprising considering the repeated digging for a constant stream of new burials throughout this period. The usually low numbers and small sherd sizes of pottery associated with the burials makes close dating impossible. Although the largest context assemblage consists of a notable group of 453 sherds (13,939g) from grave soil [117] only seven other contexts produced more than five sherds and none produced more than 20.

Period	Sherd count	Wt (g)	ENV
Early/high medieval (later 12th to late 14th/early 15th century)	10	81	9
Late medieval (late 14th/early 15th to early/mid 16th century)	2	93	2
Early post-medieval (mid 16th to mid 18th century)	580	18,317	368
Late post-medieval (mid/later 18th to 19th century)	9	74	8
Total	601	18,565	387

Table 7.2 Pottery assemblage by period

It was considered most appropriate, given the size and nature of the pottery assemblage, to give an overview by period rather than by dated context phases. The known history of the site, together with the nature of the assemblage, mean that the early post-medieval material is discussed in more detail.

THE ASSEMBLAGES

EARLY/HIGH MEDIEVAL (LATER 12TH TO LATE 14TH/EARLY 15TH CENTURY)

The small assemblage of medieval pottery was recovered as residual sherds from early post-medieval deposits (graveyard soil and grave fills). The single sherd of early medieval sand- and shell-tempered ware (EMSS) from grave [1567] is the earliest from the site and is probably of the mid/later 12th century. The rest of this small assemblage is dated between the late 12th/early 13th century and the 14th century, consisting of fragments from two different London-type ware (LOND) jugs, a single sherd of probable south Hertfordshire-type grey ware (SHER; uncertain form) and part of a green-glazed Kingston-type ware jug (KING).

LATE MEDIEVAL (LATE 14TH/EARLY 15TH TO EARLY/MID 16TH CENTURY)

There are just two sherds from this period, both obviously residual in their contexts (graveyard soil [117] and grave [731]). Both consist of London-area early post-medieval red ware (PMRE) of the 16th century. There is thus a notable hiatus in the ceramics between the mid/late 14th and the 16th century.

EARLY POST-MEDIEVAL (MID 16TH TO MID 18TH CENTURY)

The vast majority of the assemblage is of this period (Table 7.2) but although some contexts appeared to yield assemblages of purely 17th-century date, these are never large and are thus not reliable. Most of the larger groups contain some material that clearly belongs to the first part of the 18th century, even when they are dominated by 17th-century sherds. This is certainly the case with the large group from the grave soil [117]. Certainly the great majority of wares can comfortably be placed within the date range c 1640–1730. As such the bulk of the ceramics appear to relate to the period of the military hospital, with the latest material, always in the minority, probably deriving from the barracks or from some of the more wealthy lodgers in the precinct. The post-medieval assemblage in its entirety is summarised in Table 7.3, by both fabric and estimated number of different vessel forms; quantification of vessel type is given in Table 7.4.

Some vessels are represented by quite large pieces. Certainly many of the London-area post-medieval red ware (PMR), Surrey-Hampshire red border ware (RBOR) and metropolitan slipware (METS) sherds in [117] are both large

Code	Expansion	Date range	Sherd count/ Wt (g)	Vessels represented
AGAT	agate ware	1730–80	2/10	teapot × 1, cup × 1
BORDB	Surrey-Hampshire border white ware with brown glaze	1620–1700	3/36	jar × 1, cup × 1, uncertain × 1
BORDG	Surrey-Hampshire border white ware with green glaze	1550–1700	52/968	pipkins × 7, jug × 1, plates × 6, cups × 4, colander × 1, candlesticks × 2, chamber pots × 4, uncertain × 5
BORDO	Surrey-Hampshire border white ware with olive glaze	1550–1700	16/418	pipkins × 7, bowl × 1, plate × 1
BORDU	Surrey-Hampshire border white ware unglazed	1550–1700	1/54	lid × 1
BORDY	Surrey-Hampshire border white ware with clear (yellow) glaze	1550–1700	40/881	pipkins × 7, jar × 1, bowls × 5, plates × 2, chamber pots × 2, uncertain × 4
CHPO	Chinese porcelain	1590–1900	13/122	plates × 3, tea bowls × 3, saucers × 7
FREC	Frechen stoneware	1550–1700	30/820	bottles × 11, mug × 1, uncertain × 1
LONS	London stoneware	1670–1800+	23/630	bottles × 6, tankards × 9, uncertain × 1
LONS (WHITE)	white stoneware (London/Dwight)	1671–1703	1/6	tankard × 1
METS	metropolitan slipware	1630–1700	14/2102	bowl × 1, plates × 5, chamber pot × 1
MORAN	Midlands orange ware	1480–1820	2/22	butter pots × 2
MPUR	Midlands purple ware	1480–1750	13/753	butter pots × 8
NOTS/DERBS	Nottingham/Derby stoneware	1700–1800+	4/70	bowls × 2, tankard × 1
PMBL	Essex-type post-medieval black-glazed red ware	1580–1700	2/103	tyg × 1
PMFR	Essex-type post-medieval fine red ware	1580–1700	10/624	pipkin × 1 jars × 2, bowl × 1, dish × 1, chamber pot × 1, uncertain × 3
PMR	London-area post-medieval red ware	1580–1800+	127/5977	pipkins × 8, jars × 15, bowls × 34, colander × 1, dishes × 4, plates × 3, candlestick × 1, flowerpot × 1, uncertain × 12
PMSRG	London-area post-medieval slipped red ware with green glaze	1480–1650	11/236	dishes × 3, uncertain × 6
RBOR	Surrey-Hampshire border red ware	1550–1800+	56/1772	pipkins × 7, jars × 6, bowls × 6, lid × 1, dish × 1, plates × 2, jug × 1, cups × 2, chamber pot × 1, uncertain × 4
RBORG	Surrey-Hampshire border red ware with green glaze	1580–1800	15/483	jar × 1, bowls × 5, plate × 1, cup × 1, chamber pot × 1, uncertain × 1
RBORSL	Surrey-Hampshire border red ware with slip-trailed decoration	1580–1800	5/118	plates × 3
REFR	refined red earthenware	1740–1800	2/27	teapot × 1, cup × 1
REST	red stoneware	1765–80	2/19	teapot × 1
SAIPL	Saintonge ware with polychrome decoration	1480–1650	1/36	uncertain × 1
STMO	Staffordshire-type mottled brown-glazed ware	1650–1800	3/78	uncertain × 3
STSL	Staffordshire-type combed slipware	1660–1800+	20/284	dishes × 8, cups × 3, uncertain × 1
SWSG	white salt-glazed stoneware	1720–80	4/16	plate × 1, mugs × 2, saucer × 1
TGW	tin-glazed earthenware (undivided)	1570–1800+	2/12	ointment pot × 1, uncertain × 1
TGW BLUE	tin-glazed earthenware with pale blue glaze	1650–1800+	18/190	bowls × 3, plates × 2, uncertain × 1
TGW C	tin-glazed earthenware with plain white glaze	1630–1800+	19/362	bowls × 2, jars × 3, plate × 1, porringer × 1, ointment × 1, uncertain × 4
TGW D	tin-glazed earthenware with polychrome decoration	1630–1700+	62/940	bowls × 8, jars × 7, chargers × 8, plates × 15, salt? × 1, tea bowls × 2, uncertain × 7
TGW G	tin-glazed earthenware with 'Lambeth polychrome' decoration	1701–15	2/5	cup × 1
TGW M	tin-glazed earthenware with 'Persian blue' decoration	1680–1710	1/7	uncertain × 1
WEAL	Wealden buff ware	1480–1800+	2/126	uncertain × 2
WEST	Westerwald stoneware	1590–1800+	2/10	mug × 1, uncertain × 1
Total			580/18,317	

Table 7.3 Summary of the early post-medieval pottery assemblage

and fresh. The large proportion (3 sherds, 1505g) of METS bowl from grave [1971] is of significance. The design on this vessel can be paralleled from the Harlow kilns (Davey & Walker 2009: rim slip pattern 3.4 (reversed S), rim type E1B and slip wall pattern 9.3 (inverted) (wheat type)). The presence of these fresh sherds perhaps suggests that graves dug in preparation within the burial ground may unofficially have been used for the dumping of pieces of rubbish before the intended occupant was laid to rest.

The coarse earthenwares make up the majority of the assemblage and all the usual sources of supply for the period are represented, namely London itself, Essex and the Surrey-Hampshire border. To what extent the RBOR vessels extend into the 18th century is uncertain, but none need be much after 1730 and all could be before that date. The assemblage also contains a number of London stonewares and tin-glazed wares, among them a sherd of early Dwight white stoneware (LONS) from [117] and some cylindrical tankards of 18th-century type (probably procured by soldiers from the barracks). The tin-glazed wares show a range of decorative types. Most can be placed in the 17th century, but a number are clearly of the early 18th century, including the few pieces from tea bowls.

Wares from the Midlands/Staffordshire are less common but both 17th- and 18th- century types are present. The earliest consist of sherds of Midlands orange and purple wares (MORAN, MPUR), probably from 17th-century butter pots. The Nottingham/Derby stonewares (NOTS/DERBS), agate ware (AGAT), Staffordshire-type mottled brown-glazed ware (STMO) and white salt-glazed stoneware (SWSG) demonstrate their increasing numbers in early 18th-century London. Some of these, and the forms in which they appear, suggest a few more affluent households. Whether these relate to officers at the barracks or civilian lodgers in the precinct is uncertain.

Imported wares constitute only 7.9% of the early post-medieval assemblage by sherd count. Most include the standard German Frechen (FREC) and Westerwald (WEST) stonewares that were common at all levels of society. However, the single late Saintonge vessel (SAIN) hints at an affluent household of the later 16th to mid 17th century, just as the scatter of Chinese porcelain (CHPO) hints at one or more of the early/mid 18th century. The latter include plain blue painted as well as Imari-type plates, saucers and tea bowls, some of which are quite finely finished.

Taken together the wares and vessels are fairly typical of a domestic assemblage that includes the storage, preparation and consumption of food and drink, together with a scattering of household items (such as the candlesticks) and sanitary vessels.

Vessel type	ENV
Bottle	17
Bowl	68
Butter pot	10
Candlestick	3
Chamber pot	10
Charger	8
Colander	2
Cup	14
Dish	17
Flowerpot	1
Jar	36
Jug	2
Lid	2
Mug	4
Ointment pot	2
Pipkin	37
Plate	45
Porringer	1
Salt?	1
Saucer	8
Tankard	11
Tea bowl	5
Teapot	3
Tyg	1
Uncertain form	60
Total	**368**

Table 7.4 Summary of the early post-medieval pottery assemblage by vessel type

Most of the wares and forms are typical of households of all social standings but a small but gradually increasing element in the overall group is indicative of a household of somewhat higher status that may have been contributing to the waste by the early 18th century. Certainly the relatively common occurrence of early 18th-century tea wares would be in keeping with this.

LATE POST-MEDIEVAL (MID/LATER 18TH TO 19TH CENTURY)

The assemblage of this period is small (Table 7.2), strongly suggesting that domestic refuse was no longer being dumped on the area from perhaps c 1730/40 onwards. There are just four creamware sherds (CREA, 31g), including two plain plates and an industrially slipped jug, and only two sherds of transfer-printed pearlware (PEAR, 7g) both from bowls with Chinese-style decoration (all from [117]). The single English porcelain plate sherd (ENPO, 3g) is also likely to be of the later 18th or very early 19th century. The remaining sherds are all clearly of 19th-century date and include a fragment from a Seltzer bottle (BOT SELZ, 12g) and a handle from a refined white earthenware vessel (REFW, 21g). The latter is likely to be the latest sherd on the site, perhaps belonging to the middle of the 19th century.

7.4 CERAMIC BUILDING MATERIAL
Susan Pringle

The assemblage is predominantly post-medieval, although medieval building materials are also present; it is generally fairly abraded. The total weight and number of fragments from each functional category are set out in Table 7.5. For location of burials, see Fig 7.1.

The tile was quantified by fabric, form, weight and fragment count using the Museum of London (MOL) tile fabric type series (http://www.mola.org.uk/medieval-and-post-medieval-roof-tile-fabric-codes). The broad date range of the material in each context is summarised in Table 7.6. The dates for peg tiles and bricks are approximate; peg tiles in particular are hard to date precisely as the form changed very little between the 14th and the 18th century.

FABRICS AND FORMS
ROOF TILE

The roof tile assemblage consists of 16 fragments of peg tile, pantile and ridge tile weighing 1.568 kg. It is mainly post-medieval types that are present; only two small fragments of medieval tile have been identified (fabrics 2271 and 2586) in graves [242] and [731]. The tile in fabric 2586 was is splashed with glaze. Four pieces of pantile in fabrics 2275 and 3202 came from contexts associated with tomb [107] and [117]; this roof tile type, initially imported from the Low Countries, was first used in the 1630s. A decorated ridge tile dating from the late 19th or early 20th century was present in 20th-century layer [101].

	No of items	% Total count	Wt (kg)	% Total Wt
Post-medieval brick	44	51	42.086	83
Post-medieval roof tile	14	16	1.530	3
Medieval floor tile	11	13	1.922	4
Mortar and concrete	10	12	4.334	8
Post-medieval floor and wall tile	4	5	0.200	<1
Medieval/post-medieval roof tile	2	2	0.038	<1
Post-medieval garden furniture	1	1	0.782	1
Total	86	100	50.892	100

Table 7.5 Summary of building materials

Context no	Date range (approx)	Material
[101]	1850–1950	decorated ridge tile and garden edging tile
[102]	1950–2000	20th-century wall tile, late 18th- /19th-century brick
[103]	1480–1850	peg tile
[104] (tomb [107])	1750–1900	pantile, peg tile, brick
[106] (tomb [107])	1750–1850	bricks with shallow frog
[109] (tomb [107])	1750–1850	pantile, brick with shallow frog
[110]	1750–1850	brick
[117]	mixed: c 1650–1750; residual 14th- to 16th-century	pantile, peg tile, post-medieval brick, post-medieval tin-glazed floor and wall tiles, medieval glazed floor tiles
[125]	poorly dated: c 1830–1900?	concrete slab
[242]	1200–1800	tile flake
[375]	1480–1850	peg tile
[379]	poorly dated: c 1350–1550; residual Roman	unglazed floor tile, undated lime mortar
[762]	1200–1500	glazed peg tile
[1851]	1650–1800	unfrogged post-medieval brick
[1890]	1600–1700; residual 15th- /early 16th-century	post-medieval brick, residual 15th- /early 16th-century glazed floor tile
[1891]	1450–1700	post-medieval brick, some vitrified
[1892]	1480–1850	peg tile
[1901]	1600–1700	brick
[1927]	1450–1700	brick
[1955]	1600–1700	brick
[1973]	1250–1550	floor tile
[1993]	poorly dated: c 1450–1950	vitrified brick
[2000]	1600–1700	brick

Table 7.6 Broad date ranges of contexts containing ceramic building material

BRICK

Forty-four bricks or brick fragments make up the largest component of the assemblage. Almost all of them are made from the red-firing clays typical of the London area. Dimensions of complete bricks and larger fragments are set out in Table 7.7.

The earliest post-medieval brick type is represented by 18 bricks in fabric 3033. None of the bricks are complete, but surviving dimensions are in the range 103–108mm wide and 51–60mm thick. The bricks are unfrogged with indented margins and probably date to the middle part of their date range of 1450–1700 AD, c 1500–1650; most are from paving [1890] and [1891], and they were also present in [117] and brick path [1927]. A group of nine bricks, also unfrogged with indented margins, has a fairly clean, fine-grained fabric intermediate between fabrics 3033 and 3032; their likely date range is c 1600–1700 AD. They came from deposits [1890], grave [1902], box-drain [1955] and wall [2000]. Five unfrogged bricks with a probable date range of c 1650–1800 came from tomb [107] and grave [1852] (fabric 3032). Four bricks with shallow frogs are probably from the later 18th or 19th century; they came from tomb [107] and path [110] (fabric 3032). Of similar date is an unfrogged Kentish yellow brick in fabric 3035, from 20th-century layer [102]. The latest brick types are two 20th-century bricks from layer [102], including one with a V-shaped frog with part of a 'LBC' and 'PHORPRES' stamp which was made by the London Brick Company between 1910 and 1974.

FLOOR TILE

Eleven fragments of medieval floor tile were noted from soil layers as well as paving [1890] and [1973]. Unfortunately, none are suitable for illustration. The majority of tiles are green-glazed over a white slip with the corner nail holes and sandy fabrics typical of Flemish tile production; one tile from [1973] has a yellow glaze. No complete tiles are present, but the surviving dimensions and the variation in tile thickness between 20m and 34mm suggests that tiles of the 14th to 16th centuries are represented. Also present is a fragment of two-colour decorated tile from Penn in Buckinghamshire, probably design SBC9, dated to the second half of the 14th century (Betts 1997, 63, fig 72).

From the graveyard soil, [117], came two fragmentary 16th-century polychrome tin-glazed floor tiles. The earlier, 24mm thick with a design of a blue and yellow fleur-de-lis on a white background with a blue border, probably dates to between 1520 and 1550 (Betts & Weinstein 2010, 94, no 26).

Context no	Fabric	Length (mm)	Breadth (mm)	Thickness (mm)	Date range (approx)
[102]	3035	?	105	66	1750/1800–1950
[104] (tomb [107])	3032	227	103	69	1750–1900
[104] (tomb [107])	3032	?	102	0	1650–1800
[106] (tomb [107])	3032*	220	94	67	1650–1800
[106] (tomb [107])	3032	225	107	64	1750–1900
[109] (tomb [107])	3032	225	109	71	1750–1900
[109] (tomb [107])	3032	222	106	64	1650–1800
[1851]	3032	210	104	67	1650–1800
[1890]	3032/3033*	140+	105	55	1600–1700
[1890]	3032/3033*	?	108	67	1600–1700
[1890]	3033	?	107	51	1450–1700
[1890]	3033	?	106	56	1450–1700
[1890]	3033	?	104	52	1450–1700
[1890]	3033	?	108	52	1450–1700
[1890]	3033	?	108	60	1450–1700
[1891]	3033	?	103	57	1450–1700
[1891]	3033	?	104	56	1450–1700
[1901]	3032/3033	?	109	54	1600–1700
[1955]	3032/3033	147+	106	56	1600–1700
[1955]	3032/3033	226	109	61	1600–1700
[1955]	3032/3033	226	110	66	1600–1700
[2000]	3032/3033*	?	100	60	1600–1700
[2000]	3032/3033	225	103	64	1600–1700

Table 7.7 Brick dimensions by context and Museum of London fabric type

The other, 18mm thick, has a rather blurred flower vase design in blue and yellow on white and probably dates to the second half of the 16th century (ibid, 114, no 134). Both are worn from use.

WALL TILE

Two post-medieval wall tiles were noted. The earlier of these, from [117], is a Dutch tin-glazed tile with a purple and reddish-brown marbled glaze. A similar tile has been dated to the late 17th century (Betts & Weinstein 2010, 178–9, no 439). From layer [102] came a 20th-century glazed wall tile with a blue floral pattern on a white background.

MORTAR

A number of fragments of loose lime mortar were present in grave soil deposits, including a small fragment of lime mortar with tile chips, possibly of Roman date. Also present were fragments of yellow sandy mortar faced with a thin white ?plaster render and light brown sandy mortar with rose quartz and very coarse lumps of lime, the flat surface skimmed and painted or lime-washed white, from deposits. Sandy white roofing mortar with a curved profile was also noted. A fragment of modern concrete slab 16–21mm thick came from layer [102].

SUMMARY

The medieval assemblage is very small, consisting of two small pieces of roof tile and some fragmentary floor tiles. The glazed roof tile, the Penn tile and the thinner green-glazed floor tiles were all probably contemporary with the medieval palace but as they were residual in later deposits there was no firm evidence associating them with it. The thicker glazed tiles in [1890] and [1973] may have been contemporary with the early 16th-century hospital. The brick assemblage is likely to have come from the hospital although the majority of it appears to date from post-Tudor structural phases. The variations in brick fabrics and dimensions suggest that several different phases of construction were represented.

7.5 CLAY TOBACCO PIPE

Elke Raemen

Three hundred and sixty-four stem, bowl and mouthpiece fragments were recovered from the excavations. The majority of the 225 stem fragments can be dated only to the mid 17th–18th century but a few are slightly later in date: from the mid 18th to the 19th century. The assemblage also includes a single mouthpiece dated to 1660–1710, recovered from [725]. It comprises a straight cut end, which has been smoothed and crudely rounded off. For location of burials referenced, see Fig 7.1.

One hundred and thirty-eight bowls were recovered with a date range of the 17th to the 18th century. Bowls were principally classified according to the London 'Chronology of Bowl Types' (prefix AO) by Atkinson and Oswald (1969, 177–80). This was supplemented by the general pipe typology by Oswald (prefix OS; 1975, 39–41) for the 18th-century pipes. The earliest recovered are of type AO9 (*c* 1640–60). Others include a bowl of type AO17 (*c* 1680–1710) recovered from [876]. This particular type represents the West Country style with its typical overhanging bowl. A possible import was found in [338]. The bowl is close to type OS22 (*c* 1730–50) but the flaring mouth suggests a probable Bristol or Marlborough/Salisbury-area origin.

Makers' marks are found on 16 bowls (Table 7.8). The earliest examples, type AO13 (*c* 1660–80) and one recovered from graveyard soil [117], are stamped beneath the heel. The stamp on RF<3051> is illegible but the stamp beneath RF<3050> is shoeprint-shaped.

Bowl type	Count	Earliest date	Latest date
AO9	3	1640	1660
AO9/15	1	1640	1680
AO10/15	3	1640	1680
AO13	6	1660	1680
AO14	6	1660	1680
AO14/15	1	1660	1680
AO15	5	1660	1680
AO17	1	1680	1710
AO18	1	1660	1680
AO18/22	1	1660	1710
AO19	1	1690	1710
AO19-22	2	1680	1710
AO20	10	1680	1710
AO20/21	1	1680	1710
AO20/22	1	1680	1710
AO21	7	1680	1710
AO21/22	1	1680	1710
AO22	16	1680	1710
AO25	6	1700	1770
AO26	7	1740	1800
AO27	3	1780	1820
OS11	1	1730	1760
OS12	41	1730	1780
OS22	1	1730	1780
UND	12		
Total	138		

Table 7.8 Overview of makers' marks

None of the makers can be identified with certainty, and the vast majority of marks were used by multiple makers in the same period. Of interest are RF<1019> and RF<3060>, both of which have marks with older initials underneath (Fig 7.8). The bowls must therefore have been made with a modified mould, bought or inherited from another maker. This may imply that the mould was in use over a longer than usual period, and the pipes concerned (both types AO27) may have been manufactured when the type was already out of fashion. This practice has been seen elsewhere in London, for example in Southwark (Raemen 2010).

In addition to the marked pipes, there are a few decorated pieces, including an example with Prince of Wales feathers

(RF<3056>) and a bowl with rose and thistle design, a partial motto (DIEU (…) DROIT) and G. R. moulded on either side of the bowl (RF<3059>) (Fig 7.8). Both are type AO26 bowls and were recovered from general grave soil [117]. The latter pipe would have been manufactured in the reign of George III (1760–1800). Three of the marked pipes are fluted, and some of these contain leaf- or wheatsheaf-moulded decorated seams.

7.6 COINS

Trista Clifford and Lucy Sibun

Twelve coins and tokens were recovered. Those illustrated are shown in Fig 7.9. The earliest are two late 16th-century Nuremburg jettons from the general graveyard soil: RF<1012>, a jetton of the Rechen meister type dating AD 1550–80, and RF<1005>, a Hans Krawinkel type of similar date. This context also produced a 17th- to 18th-century halfpenny trade token (RF<1007>). The graveyard soil yielded two farthings of Charles II, one of which (RF<1016>) is dated to 1675, a halfpenny of George II (RF<3031>), a (possibly deliberately defaced) silver dollar (1792, Mexico 8 reales,

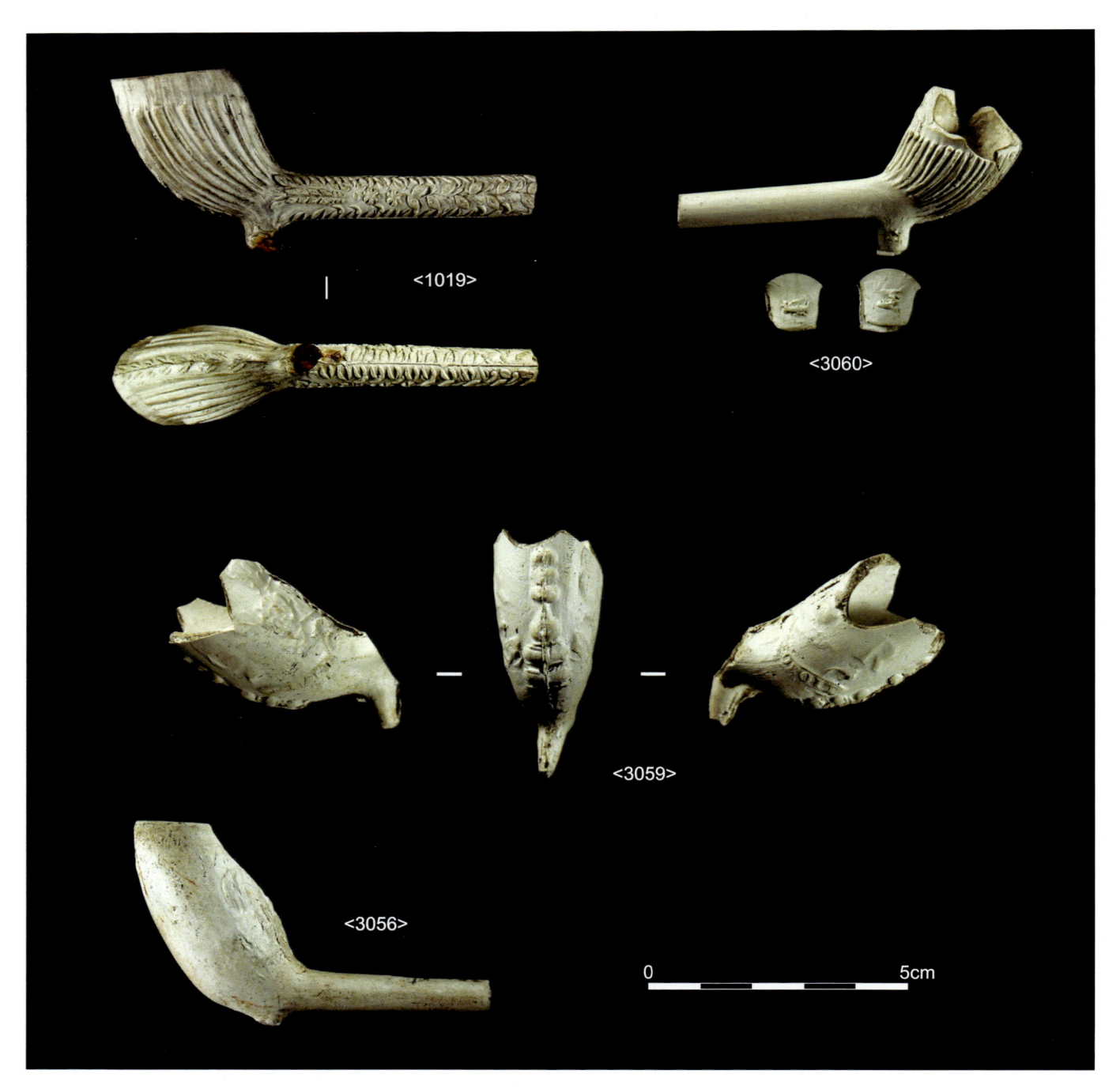

Fig 7.8 Decorated clay pipes

counterstamped George III (RF<3027>)) and a post-1660 farthing (RF<1013>).

Silver dollar RF<3027> is of particular interest. At the end of the 18th century Britain faced an economic crisis, owing to the drain on the country's finances as a result of their continuing involvement in wars, a run on the bank caused by invasion threats, and poor harvests (Manville 2000, 103–4). To combat the situation the Treasury authorised the counterstamping of foreign coins. These coins, the majority of which were 8 reales pieces originating in Spanish American mints, formed the Bank of England silver reserves at the time. They were stamped by the Royal Mint with a puncheon of the head of George III and then issued by the bank; vast quantities of these Spanish dollars circulated freely in England and worldwide (ibid, 104–5). The fluctuating price of silver made them a target for counterfeiters and many forged dollars and counterstamps were being made and circulated. It is also thought that there were even some forged dollars with genuine Royal Mint countermarks (ibid, 106). When the extent of the counterfeiting problem was realised the Bank recalled the dollars, agreeing to take genuine dollars with counterfeit marks taken honestly through trade.

The coin recovered from the Savoy is a Mexican 8 reales piece, with a hole punched through where the counterstamped head of George III should be, in a possibly deliberate attempt to deface the coin. However, with this part missing there is no way of knowing if this dollar had been counterstamped or not. The Savoy coin has gained a green discolouration (verdigris) through its time in the ground, typical of copper alloy but not of silver; genuine silver dollars were just that – silver. Furthermore, the hole punched through the middle displays what appears to be rust, not consistent with the corrosion of silver. This therefore implies that the Savoy dollar was in fact counterfeit. Fig 7.9 shows the Savoy coin next to a better-preserved example, also recorded as a counterfeit (IOW 01A6C2, Portable Antiquities Scheme). Although there is some silver still visible on the surface of the coin, this appears to be plate, which has rubbed off on areas of relief, with verdigris formed on the copper surface beneath. In 1797 genuine silver dollars averaged a weight of 416 grains (Manville 2000, 106) whereas the Savoy coin, although admittedly with a small hole, weighs only 318 grains.

Only four coins were recovered from grave fills (for locations see Fig 7.1). Burial [813] contained a silver sixpence of William III (RF<1010>, Fig 7.9) minted between AD 1689 and AD 1702, while burial [262] contained a post-medieval farthing (RF<1002>) of William III, George I or George II (minted AD

Fig 7.9 Selected coins

1689–1760). A much corroded post-1660 farthing (RF<3032>) was recovered from burial [834] and, lastly, an unidentified coin (RF<3028>) came from burial [1925].

The coins from the graveyard soil may result from casual losses or from disturbance of grave goods during subsequent gravedigging. The placement of coins within graves of this period may be deliberate; Cherryson et al (2012, 74) list a number of instances of coins recovered from post-medieval burials. Many of these have an obvious function, such as those placed over the eyelids to hold them closed (a practice not observed at the Savoy), but a few are interpreted as 'votive' offerings or continuation of folk traditions.

7.7 MUSKET BALL

Justin Russell

By the end of the 17th century the calibre of the military musket was fixed at 0.75in, to achieve standardisation throughout the British army. At the start of the 18th century, the diameter of musket shot was fixed at 0.71in. The ball, by necessity of the way it is loaded via the muzzle, must be of a smaller gauge for it to fit and be pushed into position near the flintlock mechanism. By 1752 the ball diameter was reduced to circa 0.690in, to accommodate the practice of loading balls wrapped in paper (part of the paper 'cartridge', which also included the gunpowder) (Harding 1999, 2). The paper provided a seal around the ball allowing less of the propelling gas, created on ignition of the gunpowder, to escape past it, thus ensuring a more powerful, consistent and accurate shot.

The lead ball from [516] weighs 524 grains (33.96g) and has a diameter of 0.715in (18.1mm) relating to a 13 gauge/large musket. It therefore fits well into the category of an early to mid 18th-century land pattern musket ball; balls cast prior to this date are hand-cast and often present in imperfect spherical shape. The ball also displays a visible seam with evidence of a snipped sprue and sprue scar. By the late 18th century military ball manufacturers clipped off the sprue and finished the balls by rolling them together in a mill to achieve smoothness and consistency in size (Harding 2012, 45). The fact that the ball from [516] still retains a sizeable sprue scar and a visible seam supports the early to mid 18th-century date. That is assuming the ball is of military origin; civilian shot would be hand-cast and show none of the refining factors mentioned above. Having been found in a cemetery with very strong military ties, the assumption of a military origin is not unreasonable.

The question of whether the ball has been loaded into a musket and fired or if indeed it is unfired, is not easy to answer. There are none of the distinctive marks on the ball that are generated in some instances from being loaded (ramrod marks, scratches on the ball from being forced down a dirty barrel), from being fired from a musket (setup or gas erosion) nor any of the effects one might expect from impact (distortion of the spherical shape or damage from contact with a hard surface) (ibid, 45–6). However, lead shot may well emerge from firing entirely intact and make a soft landing, retaining an unblemished spherical nature. The ball here does exhibit a number of tiny indents and scratches but none of them can be confirmed as having been generated as part of the firing process. Most likely, the scars upon the ball have been created by disturbance of the soil in which it was found, or from having been rolled on a hard surface prior to being buried.

In summary, the lead shot is likely to date to 1700–52, for use in a land pattern musket. Unfortunately, it is not clear whether it has been fired, nor is it possible to establish a connection between the musket ball and the gunshot victims recovered.

7.8 OTHER OBJECTS

Trista Clifford and Lucy Sibun

A number of other objects were recovered from the graveyard soil [117], including a domed circular lead weight (RF<3015>, Fig 7.10a) and a copper-alloy Nuremburg thimble dating to 17th century (RF<1014>, Fig 7.10b). The weight cannot be closely dated but its style is consistent with use on pan scales and there is no evidence that it was ever hung. It measures approximately 35mm in diameter and 9–10mm in depth and weighs 80.5g or 2.84oz. From the 17th century the Savoy Liberty employed four aleconners, who were responsible, among other things, for the inspection of weights and measures in all trades. The court, which had its own standard set of weights and measures, was perpetually in conflict with bakers over the selling of underweight loaves, victuallers for using defective measures and colliers for using non-statutory sacks. Schemes used in Savoy for cheating the customer included attaching pieces of metal beneath the pan, and wrapping farthings in paper and concealing them (Somerville 1960, 186). The fact that the lead weight recovered from the burial ground was plain, appeared to be roughly made and was without identifying markings suggests that it was not an official weight.

The graveyard soil also contained a fragment from a 17th- to 18th-century copper-alloy spoon handle with a white metal coating (RF<3023>) and a piece from a lathe-turned decorative bone knife handle (RF<1021>). The handle is very similar to two knives of *c* 1630 from London (Brown 2001, 87).

Fig 7.10 Finds from graveyard soil [117]:
a – lead weight; b – 17th-century thimble

The earliest object from [117] is a copper-alloy possible dagger chape formed of sheet metal with a decorative scalloped edge (RF<3018>) (Fig 7.11). Similar examples recorded on the Portable Antiquity Scheme database are of 14th- to 15th-century date (YORYM-2141F6; LON-6B44F5).

Fig 7.11 Dagger chape from [117]

Ceramic marbles dating to the 19th century were recovered from three grave fills: [208] (RF<1000>); [1114] (RF<3036>) and [1677] (RF<3037>). It is possible that the marble recovered from [1677] was deliberately placed since it was in an infant's grave, but the other two were recovered from the grave fills of adult males.

Three pipe clay wig curlers of 17th- to 18th-century date were also recovered (Fig 7.12). RF<3016>, from the grave of a probable male ([274]), was very similar to an example from Colchester (Crummy 1988, no 1871). RF<3000>, from [103], one of the upper layers, was probably used to produce a slightly different curled effect. The final example, RF<3062>, was recovered from soil deposit [379]. Although it was broken it did display an indistinguishable maker's mark. Wigs were fashionable in all parts of society at the time and would have been worn by both men, including soldiers, and women.

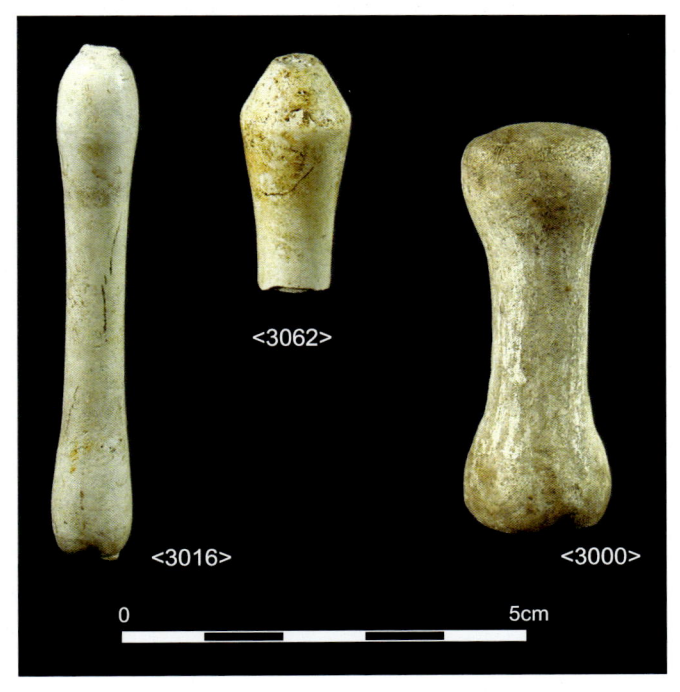

Fig 7.12 Wig curlers

7.9 GLASS
Elke Raemen

VESSELS
The earliest two fragments of vessel glass, both from graveyard soil [117], are an undiagnostic green body sherd from a cylindrical bottle (RF<3046>) of late medieval to early post-medieval date and a green neck fragment from a flask (RF<3045>) with mould- or optic-blown wrythen ribbing (Tyson 2000, type F4, 158–9), dating to *c* 1275–1500.

Green glass bottles of the mid 17th- to mid 18th-century bulbous type were the most common finds. Graveyard soil [117] produced 21 pieces representing five different bottles, but too little survived of each individual bottle to establish complete profiles and none of the green glass bulbous bottles could be dated more precisely. Four wine bottle fragments of mid 18th- to early 19th-century date were also recovered.

Two green glass case bottle fragments, a squat neck fragment and a base measuring 60 × 59mm, from two different bottles, were recovered from [117]. They can be dated to *c* 1675–1800. A green panelled bottle fragment and a green/aqua rectangular bottle fragment, both dating to the 18th century, were found in the same context and are also likely to represent spirit bottles.

Small cylindrical bottles and phials would probably have been used for pharmaceutical purposes. Fragments from these can be dated to the mid/later 17th century up to the 18th century. Diameters range between 17mm and 47mm, but none survive to their complete height. Most are colourless, although often green- or blue-tinged, and examples in both thin- and thick-walled glass were found. The majority again derive from graveyard soil [117], although a few fragments were recovered from grave fills. A late 19th- to mid 20th-century cylindrical bottle fragment was also recovered.

Two colourless/green-tinged cup or beaker fragments undiagnostic of type were recovered as well as a colourless stem fragment from a ribbed round-knop stem goblet (Willmott 2002, type 10.6) from burial [1773]. The type was in use between *c* 1550 and 1700, being most common in the second half of the 17th century. Other, higher-quality, glass includes a colourless handle from [117] that was probably from a posset or tankard, dating to the 17th century. Graveyard soil [117] also yielded a colourless solid stem fragment from a wine or spirit glass of 18th-century date.

WINDOW PANES
Twenty-one colourless, green- and blue-tinged, pieces of window glass were recovered. The earliest are three medieval fragments in green, devitrified glass (2.8mm thick) recovered from graveyard soil [117]. Later pieces are mostly of 17th- to 18th-century date, including two fragments of crown glass from [117].

7.10 DISCUSSION
Lucy Sibun

The finds assemblage recovered during the excavations is not vast but it does contain a selection of material and objects that help to tell the story of the site. The assemblage of ceramic building material provides a certain insight into the medieval Savoy

Palace, augmented by the findings of the Savoy Place excavations (Mackinder 2015). Although the medieval Savoy Palace did not survive in structural form, the quantities of medieval tiles recovered from the Savoy Place excavations suggested that a number of tiles had survived from the earlier Savoy Palace for reuse in the hospital buildings (ibid). The limited evidence from the chapel excavations would seem to support this, with tiles reused in burial ground paving. The only other evidence that may be linked, at least chronologically, to the Savoy Palace is a small quantity of contemporary pottery sherds.

The pottery assemblage confirms the lack of occupational activity in the area after the destruction of the palace in the 14th century until the 16th century, with very little recovered from this time. The majority of the assemblage dates from the 16th to the early 18th century, which would coincide with the use of the site as a hospital, both for paupers and the military, but after the dissolution of the hospital and its conversion into barracks the burial ground does not seem to have been used for dumping rubbish. This appears to be the only difference noted that can be linked to a change in use of the buildings. As noted above (7.3) the pottery assemblage would not be out of place in a domestic context, with little evidence of the strong medical or military history of the site. The same appears to be true for the glass vessel fragments, with only the pharmaceutical glass bottles and phials, which are not actually uncommon in domestic assemblages (Elke Raemen, pers comm), possibly hinting at the association with the hospital.

The variety and changing status of the precinct inhabitants is reflected both in this pottery assemblage and in that recovered from the nearby Savoy Place excavations (Mackinder 2015). Against a background that reflects all social standings, there is an apparent increase in the presence of wealthy inhabitants, be they nobles in lodgings or officers in the barracks. These wealthier inhabitants were also probably responsible for the higher-quality glass fragments recovered.

In among the domestic wares and household items, the presence of tankards hints at the notorious nature of military life, something that is also suggested by the clay pipe assemblage, which includes examples commonly procured from taverns. As early as the mid 17th century there was a 'Barre in the Savoy which they sell drinke at to the lame souldiers' (Loftie 1878, 151) and many more taverns could be found in the surrounding neighbourhood (Chapter 2). Smoking is known to have been allowed at the hospital in the 17th century (Chapter 3) and the habit became increasingly popular among soldiers, to the extent that when, at the beginning of the 19th century, an officer entered a barrack room 72ft long and 36ft wide he could not see any of the occupants through the smoke (Holmes 2011, 523).

The only archaeological finds that have possible military associations are the dagger chape and the musket ball. However, the dagger chape seems to pre-date the military associations of the site. Surrounded by barracks, the presence of a musket ball in the burial ground is not that surprising. Unfortunately, it has not been possible to determine whether the ball recovered has been fired or not. While the surface damage recorded could have resulted from its time in the ground, similar damage could have been inflicted by being kicked around under foot (Justin Russell, pers comm).

With regard to the history and development of the hospital buildings the archaeological evidence is limited to a few fragments of architectural stone – window mouldings and door architrave – all seeming to date to the vestry, which was constructed in the 1870s and taken down in the 1950s. The window glass fragments could come from any of the precinct buildings; the hospital buildings and the domestic ranges were all well glazed (Somerville 1960, 15) and included plain, clear and coloured glass as well as some heraldic designs. The chapel displayed many stained glass window designs over the centuries (Loftie 1878, 227–46), many of which had to be replaced, mostly as a result of the repeated fire damage in the mid 19th century. The early 19th-century demolition of the hospital buildings could have resulted in glass fragments being incorporated into the graveyard soil while the burial ground was still in use. The presence of reused burnt and heat-distorted bricks in a tomb, a path and the 19th-century boundary wall is a further reminder of the fires that plagued the site.

CHAPTER 8 CONCLUDING COMMENTS

Lucy Sibun

> As we by him have honoured been,
> Let us to him due honours give;
> Let us uprightness hide our sin,
> And let us worth from him receive.
> Yea, so let us by grace improve
> What thou by nature doth bestow,
> That to thy dwelling-place above
> We may be raised from below.
>
> —George Wither,
> 'Lord! When those glorious lights I see' (v4)
> (Carman 1904)

The site of the Savoy has been associated right from its beginnings with memorable events or people and the precinct has enjoyed a somewhat chequered history. The chapel itself, the one surviving element of the original hospital, was not free from controversy. Among its ministers were various colourful individuals such as Dr Killigrew and John Wilkinson. Several individuals of note were laid to rest within the chapel or burial ground, which was in active use from the time of the hospital's foundation until 1854.

The 14th century witnessed the destruction of the Palace of Savoy during the Peasants' Revolt. Then, following a period of inactivity, the site was established as the 'Hospital of Henry late King of England of the Savoy' at the beginning of the 16th century, becoming worthy of note in a more positive light as one of the 'sights' in London. Medieval hospitals in England had a bad reputation (Fowler & Powers 2012, 1) and the period after the dissolution and subsequent refounding of many hospitals after the English Reformation was seen as a time for change. In fact, the early 16th century was a time of considerable transformation in the hospital institution across Europe, with Italy leading the way and northern Europe adopting many of the ideas (Henderson 2006, 23). The Savoy Hospital was a prime example, basing its cruciform design and its statutes on a pre-existing example from the Santa Maria Nuova in Florence. These buildings were not alone in providing aesthetic beauty and it has been suggested that hospital design in the 16th century was primarily influenced by cultural rather than medical factors, aspiring to the 'grandiose concerns of patrons' and leaving it up to the architects and medical authorities to determine how to best use the space (ibid, 43). Like most hospitals at the time, at the Savoy the emphasis was on 'care not cure', offering clean surroundings and protection from the elements while aiming to treat the soul as well as the body (ibid, 41; Lindemann 2010, 160). Despite a promising start, however, the hospital soon attracted the wrong attention, being frequented by vagabonds and layabouts and with mismanagement causing untenable debts.

By the 17th century hospitals were becoming increasingly medicalised. Some larger, general hospitals such as St Thomas' and St Bartholomew's in London developed after their refounding, alongside institutions designed to cater for more specialised needs, such as lying in, mental illness and the military (Henderson 2006, 23). The Savoy was established as the first appointed military hospital, linked with influential characters such as surgeons Thomas Trapham and John French, and its formation shaped the future development of the precinct. Although set up to treat the parliamentary army during the Civil War, the hospital remained in service until 1702, accommodating seamen from the Dutch Wars alongside the few remaining poor and soldiers.

By the beginning of the 18th century the military had taken over completely, creating the barracks and prison that dominated the precinct for the next 100 years. They housed three regiments of Foot Guards, who were directly involved in several military campaigns as well as interacting in the lives of many Londoners – peace-keeping, quelling riots and indulging in many of the pastimes and pleasures that London had to offer. Finally, in the 19th century after the removal of the military, the burial ground was used for civilian burials until its closure.

There was little archaeological evidence that could be confidently linked to the earliest phase of the site's history as a hospital, either for paupers or soldiers. That is not to say that some of the individuals recovered were not associated with the hospital but rather that there was little supporting evidence. Issues associated with overcrowding and constant reuse of the burial ground undoubtedly contributed to the lack of dating evidence recovered. However, in this population most burials are likely to have been simple and without datable accessories.

Similarly, there was no archaeological evidence that provides strong links between the excavation results and the barracks and prison; the change in usage is not reflected by the artefactual evidence or style of burial. The material culture of the Savoy Chapel population has been hard to assess since most assemblages are limited by size. However, what is apparent is that the institutions associated with the burial ground did not provide assemblage signatures particularly distinctive from contemporary domestic sites. Perhaps there would have been more evidence of the original hospital had its fixtures and fittings not been stripped out and given to another institution when it was closed for the first time. On the other hand, it could be significant that the assemblages associated with the hospital and barracks do not vary greatly from domestic ones, revealing something about the way in which they were organised. As with all artefacts, they become more meaningful if considered in their historical context. One interesting aspect of this finds assemblage is that it has offered glimpses of the lifestyle in and around the Savoy as recorded historically, with tankards, clay pipes and occasional military accessories.

The 1930s surveys provided clues to identification of the 19th-century population, supported by some archaeological evidence. By this time the number of burials had greatly reduced and, according to the survey, spatially thinned out in this part of the burial ground. Problems encountered when trying to identify this part of the population have been discussed in previous chapters but the pre-existing density of burials in the ground made it a difficult task. Burial conditions that adversely affected the preservation of coffin furniture and nameplates also hindered the study. Consequently, with the exception of the few identifiable individuals, it has not been easy to separate the 19th-century civilian population from the military population that preceded them.

It is really due to the historic records that the nature of the excavated population can be understood and the rich and colourful history of the site fully appreciated. The records have facilitated a greater appreciation of the cultural environment in which the Savoy developed and thrived and have given life to those buried there. Undoubtedly, of most use were the burial registers. Despite the varying levels of detail recorded in them they have proved to be an invaluable resource. It has been possible to test the representativeness of the skeletal population against the buried population in terms of basic demographics and cause of death and in some cases the registers have enabled the identification of individuals. With this knowledge it has been possible to reinterpret the skeletal population based upon the osteological analysis and archaeological evidence, both of which strongly suggest that most of the individuals recovered relate to the military phase of the Savoy's history with the osteologically recorded young and prime adult males

employed as soldiers. Consequently, the records have also enabled characteristics of the population, whether demographic or pathological, to be explored further considering the lifestyle particular to this socioeconomic group.

Excavation results from a cemetery without detailed records might be interpreted against an understanding of the historical background and through comparisons with contemporary cemeteries. Undertaken here, the results of comparative studies indicate that life expectancy and many health issues were much the same for the soldier and the civilian, occupational hazards aside. Perhaps predictably, life in military barracks did not offer protection against some general health conditions. Indeed ailments such as fever and typhus would have been exacerbated by the cramped and confined conditions, spreading quickly through the poorly ventilated barracks and prison.

One of the most directly comparable excavation sites is the Royal Hospital Greenwich for sailors and marines. This was established in 1694 and its burial ground was in use from 1749 to 1857 (Boston et al 2008, 4, 7–8). Despite the obvious similarities between the sites, such as the military, male-dominated composition of the populations, the Royal Hospital was designed to care for retired seamen rather than those in active service, resulting in a preponderance of mature individuals (ibid, 34). However, while reflecting general health concerns being experienced by the wider populace, the osteological evidence from both populations also seems to reveal aspects of their specialised lifestyle, with diseases and traumas that could be linked to life on board or in barracks, the dangers associated with military activities and, in the case of the Savoy Chapel, interaction with London culture (Chapters 3 and 5; Boston et al 2008, 38).

The buried population recovered from excavations at the London Hospital (Fowler & Powers 2012) also offers a worthwhile comparison, although of 19th-century date, somewhat later than the Savoy Hospital. Despite the temporal differences, there are clear similarities between elements of the Savoy Chapel population and that of the London Hospital site (ibid, 33). Both hospitals were designed to serve the poor, the buried populations were male-dominated and the charitable nature of the institutions largely determined the simplicity of the burials. One significant difference stemmed from advancements within the medical discipline: whereas the 16th-century Savoy Hospital was aimed at care of the poor and infirm, 18th- and 19th-century hospitals such as the London Hospital aimed to treat and cure. The range of diseases evident in both populations was very similar, and comparable with those recorded at other contemporary London populations, suggesting that fundamental health issues in London remained the same over time and were felt by many parts of society. Poor housing with inadequate ventilation or sanitation persisted throughout the period and improvements were usually experienced only by the wealthiest (Roberts & Cox 2003, 297).

Perhaps one of the most surprising aspects of the results from the Savoy Chapel, given the site's history, is that there were no amputations and very few examples of possible surgical interventions; these were expected from the military phase of the hospital, considering the nature of the patients, the experimental medical practices and dissections associated with the hospital's surgeons as well as the historical evidence for the use of prosthetics. This was not the case at the Royal Hospital Greenwich, where six sailors and marines had undergone amputations, although unlike the Savoy, evidence for dissection was limited to four craniotomies (Boston et al 2008, 62–3). One possible reason for the lack of evidence for surgical intervention at the Savoy is that most hospital burials were in fact concentrated in another, unexcavated part of the burial ground. Certainly, one of the conclusions reached as a result of studying the archaeological and osteological data in combination is that the majority of the excavated population probably date from the later use of the site as a barracks and prison. Another possible explanation, given the density of burials and longevity of the burial ground, is that the earliest interments were disturbed and removed by later ones. Evidence for surgical intervention and dissection was, unsurprisingly, much more prevalent among the population from the London Hospital, which was also undertaking dissection and anatomical teaching (Fowler & Powers 2012, 151–99).

To conclude, even without detailed phasing the combination of the archaeological, osteological and historical evidence has made it possible to reach a level of understanding about this site that has brought its history to life. It has not been possible to identify confidently all the individuals highlighted in the preceding chapters and in many cases their remains may still lie underground in other, unexcavated parts of the burial ground. Nevertheless, the stories and histories that can be attributed to lifestyles and individuals associated with the Savoy Chapel have led to a greater understanding of the population that was uncovered and it is apparent that the significance of the site has not been lost over the years, still being summarised in publications such as Ward Lock & Co's illustrated London guide book of 1924. The excavations themselves have provided a valuable comparative data set for future studies of post-medieval London populations and have once more highlighted the value of combining archaeological and historical research.

Fig 8.1 Savoy Chapel and burial ground, c 1800 from Shepherd, T. H. & Elmes, J. 1831 London and its Environs in the Nineteenth Century: Illustrated by a series of views from original drawings. Jones & Co

The bustling lifestyle being played out in and around the precinct would have been mirrored by the constant disturbance to the individuals laid to rest in the burial ground. Once the military had moved on, life in the precinct would have become more sedate and less controversial, so much so that at the end of the 19th century it was described as 'years behind its age, hedged in and protected by its own laws and privileges' (Locking 1889, 656). A sketch by Thomas Shepherd dating to the early 19th century (Fig 8.1) gives an impression of tranquillity, with sheep and donkey grazing among the memorials. 'It is a peaceful place, and its well-trimmed grass and graceful trees come as an unexpected joy to those who chance to stroll down the street' (ibid). The ground was finally allowed to settle following the last burial in 1854.

> So run the sands of life through this quiet hourglass. So glides the Life away in the Old Precinct. At its base, a river runs for all the world; at its summit, is the brawling raging Strand; on either side, are darkness and poverty and vice; the gloomy Adelphi arches, the Bridge of Signs, that men call Waterloo. But the Precinct troubles itself little with the noise and tumult, and sleeps well through life, without its fitful fever
>
> —Dickens 1860, All the Year Round, Vol III (May 12th)120

BIBLIOGRAPHY

Places of publication are given where outside Britain

Agarwal, A, Agrawal, G, Alam, S, & Husain, B 2012 A case of unifocal eosinophilic granuloma of the mandible in an adult female: a case report, *Case Reports in Dentistry*, **2012**, article ID 521726, doi:10.1155/2012/521726

Alex, D, 2014 British land pattern musket (Brown Bess) muzzle-loading service musket, http://www.militaryfactory.com/smallarms/detail.asp?smallarms_id=361 (accessed 13 June 2017)

Alexander, M M, Gerrard, C M, Gutiérrez, A, & Millard, A R, 2015 Diet, society, and economy in late medieval Spain: stable isotope evidence from Muslims and Christians from Gandía, Valencia, *American J Physical Anthropol*, **156**(2), 263–73

Alsop, J D, 2007 Warfare and the creation of British imperial medicine, 1600–1800, in Hudson, 23–50

Alt, K, & Adler, C, 1992 Multiple myeloma in an early medieval skeleton, *Int J Osteoarchaeol*, **2**, 205–9

Andrianakos, A, Kontelis, L, Karamitsos, D, Aslanidis, S, Georountzos, A, Kaziolas, G, Pantelidou, K, Vafiadou, E, & Dantis, P, 2006 Prevalence of symptomatic knee, hand, and hip osteoarthritis in Greece. The ESORDIG study, *J Rheumatology*, **33**(12), 2507–13

Arnold, C, 2006 *Necropolis: London and its dead*

Arnott, R, Finger, S, & Smith, C, 2003 *Trepanation: history, discovery, theory*, Lisse

ASE 2011 Archaeology South-East, Queen's Chapel of the Savoy, Savoy Street, City of Westminster, London, unpub ASE rep

Atkinson, D R, & Oswald, A H, 1969 London clay tobacco pipes, *J Brit Archaeol Ass*, 3 ser, **32**, 171–227

Aufderheide, A, & Rodríguez-Martín, C, 1998 *The Cambridge encyclopedia of human paleopathology*

Banerji, S, Mehta, S, & Millar, B, 2010 Cracked tooth syndrome: Part 1, Aetiology and diagnosis, *Brit Dental J*, **208**, 459–63

Barash, C, 2001 *English women's poetry, 1649–1714*

Barber, M, & Thornton, B, 1755 *Poems by eminent ladies: Vol II*

Barnes, E, 2012 *Atlas of developmental field anomalies of the human skeleton: a paleopathology perspective*, Hoboken, NJ

Bashford, L, & Sibun, L, 2007 Excavations at the Quaker burial ground, Kingston-upon-Thames, London, *Post-Medieval Archaeol*, **41**(1), 100–54

Bass, W M, 2005 1971 *Human osteology: a laboratory and field manual*, 5th edn, Missouri Archaeol Soc Spec Pap, **2**, Columbia, Mo

Bates, B, 1992 *Bargaining for life: a social history of tuberculosis, 1876–1938*, Philadelphia, Pa

Beaumont, J, 2013 An isotopic and historical study of diet and migration during the great Irish potato famine (1845–52): high-resolution carbon and nitrogen isotope profiling of teeth to investigate migration and short-term dietary change at the Union workhouse, Kilkenny and Lukin Street, London, unpub PhD thesis, Univ Bradford

Beaumont, J, Montgomery, J, Buckberry, J, & Jay, M, 2015 Infant mortality and isotopic complexity: new approaches to stress, maternal health, and weaning, *American J Physical Anthropol*, **157**(3), 441–57

Becker, U, 1994 *The Continuum encyclopaedia of symbols*

Bédoyère, G de la, 2004 *The diary of John Evelyn (first person singular)*

Bennett, E H, 1882 Fractures of the metacarpal bones, *Dublin J Medical Sci*, **73**, 72–5

Bennett, K, 1993 *A field guide for human skeletal identification*, Springfield, Ill

Berridge, V, Gorsky, M, & Mold, A, 2011 *Public health in history*

Betts, I M, 1997 Ceramic building material, in *St Bride's church, London: archaeological research 1952–60 and 1992–5* (ed G Milne), 60–8

Betts, I M, & Weinstein, R, 2010 *Tin-glazed tiles from London*, London

BGS 2012 British Geological Survey, Geology of Britain viewer, http://mapapps.bgs.ac.uk/geologyofbritain/home.html (accessed 6 July 2017)

Bleasdale, A, 2016 The Queen's Chapel of the Savoy: a dietary reconstruction of a British post-medieval population using stable isotope analysis, unpub MSc dissertation, Univ York

Boston, C, & Webb, H, 2012 Early medical training and treatment in Oxford: a consideration of the archaeological and historical evidence, in Mitchell (ed), 43–67

Boston, C, Witkin, A, Boyle, A, & Wilkinson, D R P, 2008 *'Safe Moor'd in Greenwich Tier': a study of the skeletons of Royal Navy sailors and marines excavated at the Royal Hospital Greenwich*, Oxford Archaeology Monogr, **5**

Brackett, V, 2008 *The Facts on File companion to British poetry: 17th and 18th centuries*, New York

Brickley, M, & Ives, R, 2008 *The bioarchaeology of metabolic bone disease*

Brickley, M, & Smith, M, 2006 Culturally determined patterns of violence: biological anthropological investigations at a historic urban cemetery, *American Anthropologist*, **108**(1), 163–77

Brooks, S T, & Suchey, J M, 1990 Skeletal age determination based on the os pubis: comparison of the Acsádi–Nemeskéri and Suchey–Brooks methods, *J Hum Evol*, **5**, 227–38

Brothwell, D, 1981 *Digging up bones: the excavation, treatment and study of human skeletal remains*, 3rd edn

Brown, P (ed), 2001 *British cutlery: an illustrated history of design, evolution and use*

Browner, B, Jupiter, J, Krettek, C, & Anderson, P, 2014 *Skeletal trauma: basic science, management and reconstruction*, 5th edn

Bruce, C, 2011 Legg-Calvé-Perthes disease, in *Oxford textbook of trauma and orthopaedics* (ed C Bulstrode), 2nd edn, 1568–79

Bryant, C D, & Peck, D L (eds), 2009 *Encyclopedia of death and the human experience*, Los Angeles, Calif

Bucholz, R O, & Ward, J P, 2012 *London: a social and cultural history 1550–1750*

Buikstra, J E, & Ubelaker, D H, 1994 *Standards for data collection from human skeletal remains*, Arkansas Archaeol Survey Res Ser, **44**, Indianapolis, Ind

Bullough, P, 2010 *Orthopaedic pathology*, 5th edn, Maryland Heights, Mo

Burkhardt, M A, & Nagai-Jacobson, M G, 2002 *Spirituality: living our connectedness*, Albany, NY

Burnett, S, & Case, D, 2011 Bipartite medial cuneiform: new frequencies from skeletal collections and meta-analysis of previous cases, *Homo*, **62**, 109–25

Bynum, H, 2012 *Spitting blood: the history of tuberculosis*

Calvin, M, & Benson, A A, 1948 The path of carbon in photosynthesis, *Science*, **107**(2784), 476–80

Campbell, G, 2006 *The Grove encyclopedia of decorative arts: Vol 1, Aalto to Kyoto pottery*

Caple, C, 1991 The detection and definition of an industry: the English medieval and post-medieval pin industry, *Archaeol J*, **148**, 241–55

Carman, B (ed), 1904 *The world's best poetry: Vol 4*

Centre for Metropolitan History, 2011 Hearth tax: Middlesex 1666, Duchy of Lancaster Liberty, http://www.british-history.ac.uk/london-hearth-tax/london-mddx/1666/duchy-of-lancaster-liberty (accessed 14 June 2017)

Chambers, R, 1869 *History of the rebellion of 1745–6*

Cherryson, A, Crossland, Z, & Tarlow, S, 2012, *A fine and private place: the archaeology of death and burial in post-medieval Britain and Ireland*, Leicester Archaeology Monogr, **22**

Clark-Kennedy, A E, 1929 *Stephen Hales: an eighteenth-century biography*

Clifton-Taylor, A, & Ireson, A S, 1983 *English stone buildings*
Coldstream Guards, nd History, https://www.coldstreamguards.org.uk/histories-of-the-coldstream-guards.html (accessed 14 June 2017)
Connell, B, & Miles, A, 2010 *The City Bunhill burial ground, Golden Lane, London: excavations at South Islington schools, 2006*, MOLA Archaeol Stud Ser, **21**
Cook, H J, 1990 Practical medicine and the British armed forces after the 'Glorious Revolution', *Medical History*, **34**, 1–26
Copland, J, 1858 *A dictionary of practical medicine*
Coupland, A (ed), 1997 *Reclaiming the city: mixed use development*
Cowie, L W, 1974 The Savoy – palace and hospital, *History Today*, **24**(3), 173–9
Cowie, R, Bekvalac, J, & Kausmally, T, 2008 *Late 17th- to 19th-century burial and earlier occupation at All Saints, Chelsea Old Church, Royal Borough of Kensington and Chelsea*, MOLAS Archaeol Stud Ser, **18**
Creighton, C, 1894 *A history of epidemics in Britain: Vol II, From the extinction of plague to the present time*
Crist, T A, 2006 The good, the bad and the ugly: bioarchaeology and the modern gun culture debate, *Hist Archaeol*, **40**(3), 109–30
Crummy, N, 1988 *The post-Roman small finds from excavations in Colchester 1971–85*, Colchester Archaeol Rep, **5**
Daniel, C, 1997 *Death and burial in medieval England, 1066–1550*
Davey, W, & Walker, H, 2009 *The Harlow pottery industries*, Medieval Pottery Res Group Occas Pap, **3**
David, S, 2013 *All the king's men: the British redcoat in the era of sword and musket*
Davison, S, 2003 *The conservation and restoration of glass*, 2nd edn
Dawes, C, 2006 Why does supragingival calculus form preferentially on the lingual surface of the 6 lower anterior teeth? *J Canadian Dental Assoc*, **72**(10), 923–6
Defoort, S, Arnout, N, & Debeer, P, 2012 Myositis ossificans circumscripta of the triceps due to overuse in a female swimmer, *Int J Shoulder Surgery*, **6**(1), 19–22
Demetracopoulos, C, Kapadia, N, Herickhoff, P, Cosgarea, A, & McFarland, E, 2006 Surgical stabilization of os acromiale in a fast-pitch softball pitcher, *American J Sports Medicine*, **34**(11), 1855–9
Demirci, M, Tuncer, S, & Yuceokur, A, 2010 Prevalence of caries on individual tooth surfaces and its distribution by age and gender in university clinic patients, *European J Dentistry*, **4**(3), 270–9
Dhulipalla, S, 2015 Comparative study of response through reduction in the size of hypertrophied inferior turbinate causing nasal obstruction by different surgical modalities: a prospective study, *Indian J Otolaryngology and Head & Neck Surgery*, **67**(1), 56–9
Dickens, C, 1860 The Precinct, *All the year round*, **3**, 12 May, 115–20, http://www.djo.org.uk/all-the-year-round/volume-iii/page-115.html (accessed 14 June 2017)
Dittmar, J, Errickson, D, & Caffell, A, 2015 The comparison and application of silicone casting material for trauma analysis on well-preserved archaeological skeletal remains, *J Archaeol Sci: Reports*, **4**, 559–64. doi: 10.1016/j.jasrep.2015.10.008
Dodsworth, R, 2003 *Glass and glassmaking*
Donagan, B, 1998 The casualties of war: treatment of the dead and wounded in the English Civil War, in *Soldiers, writers and statesmen in the English Revolution* (eds M Gentles, J Morrill & B Worden), 114–32
D'Ortenzio, L, Brickley, M, Schwarcz, H, & Prowse, T, 2015 You are not what you eat during physiological stress: isotopic evaluation of human hair, *American J Physical Anthropol*, **157**(3), 374–88
Duff, A (ed), 2012 *Checklist of beetles of the British Isles*, 2nd edn
Dunstone, S, nd The Richard Lander story, http://www.richardlander.org.uk (accessed 14 June 2017)
Durston, G J, 2012 *Whores and highwaymen: crime and justice in the eighteenth-century metropolis*
Editors of Encyclopaedia Britannica, 1998a Ambroise Paré, http://www.britannica.com/biography/Ambroise-Pare (accessed 14 June 2017)
Editors of Encyclopaedia Britannica, 1998b Richard Lemon Lander, http://www.britannica.com/biography/Richard-Lemon-Lander (accessed 14 June 2017)
Education Scotland, nd Battle of Culloden, http://www.sath.org.uk/edscot/www.educationscotland.gov.uk/scotlandshistory/jacobitesenlightenmentclearances/culloden/index.html
Elimairi, I, Baur, D, Mehmet, A, Faisal, Q, & Amritha, M, 2015 Eagle's syndrome, *Head & Neck Pathology*, **9**(4), 492–5
Emery, P A, & Wooldridge, K, 2011 *St Pancras burial ground: excavations for St Pancras International, the London terminus of High Speed 1, 2002–3*, Gifford Monogr Ser
Farr, E, 1857 *Hallelujah, or Britain's second remembrance; bringing to remembrance (in praiseful and penitential hymns, spiritual songs, and moral odes), meditation, advancing the glory of God, in the practice of piety and virtue*
Fowler, L, & Powers, N, 2012 *Doctors, dissection and resurrection men: excavations in the 19th-century burial ground of the London Hospital, 2006*, MOLA Monogr Ser, **62**
Freeman, J, Cole, T, Jones, P, White, E, & Preece, M, 1990 Cross-sectional stature and weight reference curves for the UK, 1990, *Archives of Disease in Childhood*, **73**, 17–24
Fritze, R H, & Robison, W B (eds), 2002 *Historical dictionary of late medieval England, 1272–1485*, Westport, Conn
Fuller, B T, Fuller, J L, Sage, N E, Harris, D A, O'Connell, T C, & Hedges, R E M, 2005 Nitrogen balance and δ^{15}N: why you're not what you eat during nutritional stress, *Rapid Communications in Mass Spectrometry*, **19**(18), 2497–506
Gascoigne, B, 2001 (ongoing) The flintlock: 16th – 18th century, in History of arms and armour, *HistoryWorld*, http://www.historyworld.net/wrldhis/PlainTextHistories.asp?ParagraphID=kyf (accessed 14 June 2017)
Gearey, B R, Kirby, J, Dawes, O J, Hall, A, Kenward, H, & Carrott, J, 2002 Assessment of biological remains from excavations to the rear of 1 America Street, London Borough of Southwark (site code: AMA01), unpub Palaeoecology Research Services rep 2002/21
Girling, M A, 1981 Beetle remains, in The burial of John Dygon, abbot of St Augustine's (ed J C Thorn), in *Collectanea Historica: essays in memory of Stuart Rigold* (ed A Detsicas), 82–4
Goodrick-Clarke, N, 1999 *Paracelsus*, Berkeley, Calif
Gray, S, 2009 *The dictionary of British women artists*
Great Britain: Adjutant-General's Office, 1776 *The manual exercise, as ordered by His Majesty, in the year 1764: together with plans and explanations of the method generally practices at reviews and field-days; with copper plates*, Philadelphia, Pa
Great Britain Historical GIS Project, 2017 http://www.visionofbritain.org.uk/unit/10164394/cube/HOUSES; http://www.visionofbritain.org.uk/unit/10164394/cube/OCC_ORDER1881; http://www.visionofbritain.org.uk/unit/10164394/cube/GENDER (all accessed 10 July 2017)
Gregory, J, & Stevenson, J, 2007 *The Routledge companion to Britain in the eighteenth century 1688–1820*
Grotle, M, Hagen, K, Natvig, B, Dahl, F, & Kvien, T, 2008 Obesity and osteoarthritis in knee, hip and/or hand: an epidemiological study in the general population with 10 years follow-up, *Musculoskeletal Disorders*, **9**, 132–6
Gruber-von-Arni, E, 2006 *Hospital care and the British standing army 1660–1714*
Gruber-von-Arni, E, 2007a Who cares? Military nursing during the English Civil Wars and interregnum, 1642–60, in Hudson, 121–48
Gruber-von-Arni, E, 2007b 'Tempora mutantur et nos mutamur in illis': the experience of sick and wounded soldiers during the English Civil Wars and interregnum, 1642–60, in *The impact of hospitals: 300–2000* (eds J Henderson, P Horden & A Pastore), 317–40, Berne
Gustafson, G, & Koch, G, 1974 Age estimation up to 16 years of age based on dental development, *Odontologisk Revy*, 25, 297–306
Hackston, M, 2013 Family Staphylinidae, subfamily Pselaphinae:

key to British genera, https://docs.google.com/viewer?a=v&pid=sites&srcid=ZGVmYXVsdGRvbWFpbnxtaWtlc2luc2VjdGleXN8Z3g6NTkwMzhlMjkxNWM1MzY2Mg (accessed 14 June 2017)

Haeffner, M, 2004 *Dictionary of alchemy*

Hager, A (ed), 2004 *The age of Milton: an encyclopedia of major 17th-century British and American authors*, Westport, Conn

Hales, C, 1770 *A letter addressed to Cæsar Hawkins, Esq; serjeant surgeon to His Majesty, containing new thoughts and observations, on the cure of the venereal disease; the result of experience, in long and extensive practice. With a few extraordinary cases in that disease: particularly one of a servant, belonging to His Majesty's housbold; deemed entirely a lost case: authenticated by the officers of His Majesty's mews. By Charles Hales, late surgeon to the Savoy Hospital*, 2nd edn

Hall, A, Carrott, J, Jaques, D, Johnstone, C, Kenward, H, Large, F, & Usai, R, 2000 Technical report: studies on biological remains and sediments from medieval deposits at the Magistrates' Court site, Kingston-upon-Hull (site codes HMC94 and MCH99), unpub Environmental Archaeology Unit, York rep, **2000/25**

Hammond, P, & Hopkins, D, 2007 *Dryden: selected poems*

Harding, D F, 1999 *Small arms of the East India Company 1600–1856: Vol III, Ammunition and performance*

Harding D F, 2012 *Lead shot of the English Civil War: a radical study*

Harmsworth, A G, 2015 1745 Bonnie Prince Charlie, http://harmsworth.net/scottish-history-heritage/1745-bonnie-prince-charlie.html (accessed 14 June 2017)

Harris, F, 1916 Stephen Hales, the pioneer in the hygiene of ventilation, *Scientific Monthly*, **3**(5), 440–54; available online at http://www.jstor.org/stable/6053?seq=3#page_scan_tab_contents (accessed 14 June 2017)

Hays, J, 2005 *Epidemics and pandemics: their impacts on human history*, Santa Barbara, Calif

Hearth Tax Online, nd London and Middlesex, http://www.hearthtax.org.uk/communities/london/index.html (accessed 14 June 2017)

Hemer, K, Lamb, A, Chenery, C, & Evans, J, 2017 A multi-isotope investigation of diet and subsistence amongst island and mainland populations from early medieval western Britain, *American J Physical Anthropol*, **162**(3), 423–40

Hemstreet, C, & Hemstreet, M M, 1910 *Nooks and corners of old London*

Henderson, A, 1753 *Memoirs of Dr Archibald Cameron, brother to the famous Donald Cameron of Lochiel*

Henderson, J, 2006 *The Renaissance hospital: healing the body and healing the soul*, New Haven, Conn

Henderson, M, Miles, A, & Walker, D, 2013 *'He being dead yet speaketh': excavations at three post-medieval burial grounds in Tower Hamlets, East London, 2004–10*, MOLA Monogr Ser, **64**

Henderson, R C, Lee-Thorp, J, & Loe, L, 2014 Early life histories of the London poor using δ^{13}C and δ^{15}N stable isotope incremental dentine sampling, *American J Physical Anthropol*, **154**(4), 585–93

Hillen, R, Burger, B, Pöll, R, de Gast, A, & Robinson, M, 2010 Malunion after midshaft clavicle fractures in adults, *Acta Orthopaedica*, **81**(3), 273–9

Hillson, S, 1996, *Dental anthropology*

Hitchcock, T, Shoemaker, R, Howard, S, & McLaughlin, J, 2012 Bridewell prison and hospital, *London Lives, 1690–1800* (www.londonlives.org, version 1.1 April 2012), https://www.londonlives.org/static/Bridewell.jsp (accessed 14 June 2017)

Hobson, K A, Alisauskas, R T, & Clark, R G, 1993 Stable-nitrogen isotope enrichment in avian tissues due to fasting and nutritional stress: implications for isotopic analyses of diet, *Condor*, **95**(2), 388–94

Holland, E, 2004 *The nature of homosexuality: vindication for homosexual activists and the religious right*, New York

Holmes, B, 1896 *The London burial grounds: notes on their history from the earliest times to the present day*, New York

Holmes, R, 2001 *Redcoat: the British soldier in the age of horse and musket*

Holmes, R, 2011 *Soldier: army lives and loyalties from redcoats to dusty warriors*

Howard, J, 1777 *The state of the prisons in England and Wales*

Howard, J, 1791 *An account of the principal lazarettos in Europe*

Howard, J, 1792 *The state of the prisons in England and Wales*, 4th edn

Howard League, nd John Howard, http://howardleague.org/john-howard/ (accessed 12 July 2017)

Hudson, G L (ed), 2007 *British military and naval medicine, 1600–1830*, Clio Medica, **81**, Amsterdam

Hughson, D, 1817 *Walks through London, including Westminster and the borough of Southwark, with the surrounding suburbs; Describing every thing worthy of observation in the public buildings, places of entertainment, exhibitions, commercial and literary institutions, etc. down to the present period: forming a complete guide to the British metropolis*

Jackson, L, 2014 *Dirty old London: the Victorian fight against filth*, New Haven, Conn

Jackson, W, nd *New and Complete Newgate Calendar: or Villany Displayed in all its branches: Vol VI*

Janaway, R C, 1998 An introductory guide to textiles from 18th- and 19th-century burials, in *Grave concerns: death and burial in England 1700–1850* (ed M Cox), CBA Res Rep, **112**, 17–32

Jones, R, nd Gunshot wounds – rifled weapons, http://www.forensicmed.co.uk/wounds/firearms/gunshot-wounds-rifled-weapons/ (accessed 15 June 2017)

Joseph, B, 2011 Natural history of early onset and late-onset Legg-Calve-Perthes disease, *J Pediatric Orthopedics*, **31** (2 Suppl): S152–5

Jurmain, R, 1999 *Stories from the skeleton: behavioral reconstruction in human osteology*, New York

Kaneko, H, Kitoh, H, Mabuchi, A, Mishina, K, Matsushita, M, & Ishiguro, N, 2012 Isolated bifid rib: clinical and radiological findings in children, *Pediatrics International*, **54**, 820–3

Kenward, H, 2009 *Invertebrates in archaeology in the north of England*, Engl Heritage Res Rep, **12–2009**

Kenward, H K, & Allison, E P, 1994 Rural origins of the urban insect fauna, in *Urban–rural connexions: perspectives from environmental archaeology* (eds A R Hall & H K Kenward), Symposia of the Association for Environmental Archaeology, **12**, 55–77

Knapik, J, Reynolds, K, & Harman, E, 2004 Soldier load carriage: historical, physiological, biomechanical, and medical aspects, *Military Medicine*, **169**, 45–56

Knapp, A, & Baldwin, W, 1825 *The Newgate Calendar; comprising interesting memoirs of the most notorious characters who have been convicted of outrages on the laws of England since the commencement of the eighteenth century; with occasional anecdotes and observations, speeches, confessions, and last exclamations of sufferers: Vol II*

Lane Furdell, E, 2001 *The royal doctors 1485–1714: medical personnel at the Tudor and Stuart courts*, New York

Lewis, J E, 2010 *London: an autobiography*

Lindemann, M, 2010 *Medicine and society in early modern Europe*

Linden, S J, 2003 *The alchemy reader: from Hermes Trismegistus to Isaac Newton*

Litten, J, 1991 *The English way of death: the common funeral since 1450*

Lock, S, Last, J M, & Dunea, G, 2001 *The Oxford illustrated companion to medicine*

Locking, J E, 1889 The story of the Savoy, *The English Illustrated Magazine*, **6**, 656–65

Loftie, J, 1878 *Memorials of the Savoy: the palace: the hospital: the chapel*

Lovell, N, 1997 Trauma analysis in paleopathology, *American J Physical Anthropol*, **40**, 139–70

Lovejoy, C O, Meindl, R S, Mensforth, R P, & Barton, T J, 1985 Multifactorial determination of skeletal age at death: a method and blind tests of its accuracy, *American J Physical Anthropol*, **68**, 1–14

Lukacs, J R, & Largaespada, L L, 2006 Explaining sex differences in dental caries prevalence: saliva, hormones, and 'life-history' etiologies, *American J Physical Anthropol*, **18**, 540–55

Lu, H, Wong, M, Lo, E, & McGrath, C, 2011 Trends in oral health from childhood to early adulthood: a life course approach, *Community Dentistry and Oral Epidemiology*, **39**, 352–60

Luscombe, S, & Griffin, C, nd The First Regiment of Foot Guards, http://www.britishempire.co.uk/forces/armyunits/britishinfantry/1stfoot.

htm (accessed 19 June 2017); Third Regiment of Foot Guards, http://www.britishempire.co.uk/forces/armyunits/britishinfantry/scotsguards.htm (accessed 19 June 2017)

MacDonald, J, 2014 *Feeding Nelson's navy: the true story of food at sea in the Georgian era*

MacKenzie, C, 1953 *The Savoy of London*

Mackinder, T, 2015 Institution of Engineering and Technology, 2 Savoy Place, London WC2: post-excavation assessment and updated project design, unpub MOLA rep

MacKinnon, M, 2013 Cranial variation and its relation to ancestry: using the CRANID program to determine the ancestral diversity of two British skeletal collections, unpub MSc dissertation, University College London

McLynn, F, 2002 *Crime and punishment in eighteenth-century England*

Macpherson, E, 1995 Gentle Lochiel, http://www.lochiel.net/archives/arch184.html (accessed 15 June 2017)

Mann, R, & Hunt, D, 2012 *Photographic regional atlas of bone disease: a guide to pathological and normal variation in the human skeleton*, 3rd edn, Springfield, Ill

Manville, H E, 2000 The Bank of England countermarked dollars, 1797–1804, *Brit Numis J*, **70**, 103–17; available online at http://www.britnumsoc.org/publications/Digital%20BNJ/pdfs/2000_BNJ_70_11.pdf

Maresh, M, 1970 Measurements from roentgenograms, heart size, long bone lengths, bone muscles and fat widths, skeletal maturation, in *Human growth and development* (ed R McCammon), 155–200, Springfield, Ill

Maris, R W, Berman, A L, & Silverman, M, 2000 *Comprehensive textbook of suicidology*

Mason, T, & Riedi, E, 2010 Sport and the military: the British armed forces 1880–1960

Mays, S, 2010 *The archaeology of human bones*, 2nd edn

Mekota, A M, Grupe, G, Ufer, S, & Cuntz, U, 2006 Serial analysis of stable-nitrogen and carbon isotopes in hair: monitoring starvation and recovery phases of patients suffering from anorexia nervosa, *Rapid Communications in Mass Spectrometry* **20**(10), 1604–10

Miles, A, with Connell, B, 2012 *New Bunhill Fields burial ground, Southwark: excavations at Globe Academy, 2008*, MOLA Archaeol Stud Ser, **24**

Miles, A, White, W, & Tankard, D, 2008a Burial at the site of the parish church of St Benet Sherehog before and after the Great Fire, MOLAS Monogr Ser, **39**

Miles, A, Powers, N, Wroe-Brown, R, & Walker, D, 2008b St Marylebone church and burial ground in the 18th to 19th centuries: excavations at St Marylebone School, 1992 and 2004–6, MOLAS Monogr Ser, **46**

Mims, C A, Dimmock, N J, Nash, A, & Stephen, J, 2006 *Mims' pathogenesis of infectious disease*, 5th edn

Mitchell, P (ed), 2012a *Anatomical dissection in Enlightenment England and beyond: autopsy, pathology and display*

Mitchell, P, 2012b There's more to dissection than Burke and Hare: unknowns in the teaching of anatomy and pathology from the Enlightenment to the early twentieth century in England, in Mitchell (ed), 1–10

Mitchell, P, & Redfern, R, 2011 Brief communication: developmental dysplasia of the hip in medieval London, *American J Physical Anthropol*, **144**, 479–84

Mitchell, P, Boston, C, Chamberlain, A, Chaplin, S, Chauhan, V, Evans, J, Fowler, L, Powers, N, Walker, D, Webb, H, & Witkin, A, 2011 The study of anatomy in England from 1700 to the early 20th century, *J Anat*, **219**, 91–9

Molleson, T, & Cox, M, 1993 *The Spitalfields project: Vol 2, The anthropology: the middling sort*, CBA Res Rep, **86**

Molto, J, 2000 Humerus varus deformity in Roman period burials from Kellis 2, Dakhleh, Egypt, *American J Physical Anthropol*, **113**, 103–9

Moore, J, & Buckberry, J, 2016 The use of corsetry to treat Pott's disease of the spine from 19th-century Wolverhampton, England, *Int J Paleopathol*, **14**, 74–80

Moote, A L, & Moote, D C, 2004 *The great plague: the story of London's most deadly year*, Baltimore, Md

Moran, M E, 2014 *Urolithiasis: a comprehensive history*, New York

Morton, R (ed) 1967 *Poems (1686) by Mrs Anne Killigrew: a facsimile reproduction with an introduction*, Gainseville, Fla; poems online at http://digital.library.upenn.edu/women/killigrew/1686/1686-poems.html (accessed 6 July 2017)

Müldner, G, & Richards, M P, 2007 Diet and diversity at later medieval Fishergate: the isotopic evidence, *American J Physical Anthropol*, **134**(2), 162–74

New Annual Register (or General Repository of History, Politics and Literature), 1780–1825

Newman, G, & Brown, E, 1997 *Britain in the Hanoverian age, 1714–1837: an encyclopedia*, New York

Nitsch, E K, Humphrey, L T, & Hedges, R E M, 2011 Using stable isotope analysis to examine the effects of economic change on breastfeeding practices in Spitalfields, London, UK, American J Physical Anthropol, 146, 619–28

O'Connell, T C, Kneale, C J, Tasevska, N, & Kuhnle, G G C, 2012 The diet–body offset in human nitrogen isotopic values: a controlled dietary study, *American J Physical Anthropol*, **149**(3), 426–34

O'Dwyer, K, 1991 Proximal tibio-fibular synostosis: a rare congenital anomaly, *Acta Orthopaedica Belgica*, **57**(2), 204–8

Ogden, A, 2008 Advances in the paleopathology of teeth and jaws, in *Advances in human paleopathology* (eds S Mays & R Pinhasi), 283–307

Olsen, K, 1999 *Daily life in 18th-century England*, Westport, Conn

Orr, J, 1915 Coal, *International standard Bible encyclopedia*, http://www.biblestudytools.com/dictionary/coal/ (accessed 16 June 2017)

Ortner, D, 2003 *Identification of pathological conditions in human remains*, Amsterdam

Oswald, A, 1975 *Clay pipes for the archaeologist*, BAR Brit Ser, **14**

Oxford Archaeology, 2010 Queen's Chapel of the Savoy, London, WC2: archaeological watching brief, unpub OA South rep, **4896**

Packard, F R, 1921 *Life and times of Ambroise Paré 1510–1590; with a new translation of his apology and an account of his journey in divers places*, New York

Page, W, 1911a Table of population, 1801–1901, in *A history of the county of Middlesex: Vol 2, General; Ashford, East Bedfont with Hatton, Feltham, Hampton with Hampton Wick, Hanworth, Laleham, Littleton* (ed W Page), 112–20; available online at http://www.british-history.ac.uk/vch/middx/vol2/pp112-120 (accessed 7 July 2017)

Page, W, 1911b Industries: silk-weaving, in *A history of the county of Middlesex: Vol 2, General; Ashford, East Bedfont with Hatton, Feltham, Hampton with Hampton Wick, Hanworth, Laleham, Littleton* (ed W Page), 132–7; available online at http://www.british-history.ac.uk/vch/middx/vol2/pp132-137 (accessed 16 June 2017)

Panagiotakopulu, E, & Buckland, P C, 2012 Forensic archaeoentomology – an insect fauna from a burial in York Minster, *Forensic Sci Int*, **221**, 125–30

Parkin, J, 1859 *The causation and prevention of disease*

Park, K, & Henderson, J, 1991 'The first hospital among Christians': the Ospedale di Santa Maria Nuova in early sixteenth-century Florence, *Medical History*, **35**, 164–88

Partington, C F (ed), 1838 *The British cyclopaedia of biography: containing the lives of distinguished men of all ages and countries with portraits, autographs, and monuments: Vol II*

Peacock, E R, 1977 Coleoptera: Rhizophagidae, Handbooks for the Identification of British insects, **5**, Part 5(a)

Pećina, M, & Bojanić, I, 1993 *Overuse injuries of the musculoskeletal system*

Perry, D, 2013 Unravelling the enigma of Perthes disease, *Annals of the Royal College of Surgeons of England*, **95**, 311–16

Phillips, D L, 2001 Mixing models in analyses of diet using multiple stable isotopes: a critique, *Oecologia*, **127**, 166–70

Ponce, P, 2004 A study of diffuse idiopathic skeletal hyperostosis (DISH) in a medieval hospital from Chichester, Sussex, unpub MSc thesis, Univ Bradford

Ponce, P, 2010 A comparative study of activity-related skeletal changes in 3rd- to 2nd-millennium BC coastal fishers and 1st-millennium AD inland agriculturalists in Chile, South America, unpub PhD thesis, Durham Univ

Ponce, P, & Manchester, K, 2015 A diagnostic problem of paranasal sinus lesion in post-medieval London, poster presented at the 17th annual meeting of the British Association for Biological Anthropology and Osteoarchaeology, Sheffield, 18–20 September 2015

Ponce, P, & Novellino, P, 2014 A palaeopathological example of Legg-Calvé-Perthes disease from Argentina, *Int J Paleopathology*, **6**, 30–3

Ponce, P, Dittmar, J, & Grant, K, 2014 Cranial autopsies at the Queen's Chapel Savoy (London), poster presented at the 16th annual conference of the British Association for Biological Anthropology and Osteoarchaeology, Durham, 12–14 September 2014

Porter, N (ed), 1913 *Webster's revised unabridged dictionary of the English language*, Springfield, Mass

Porter, S, 2009a *The great plague*

Porter, S, 2009b *The great fire of London*

Postlethwayt, J, Graunt, J, Petty, W, Morris, C, & Heberden, W, 1759 *Collection of yearly bills of mortality, from 1657 to 1758 inclusive*; available online at https://archive.org/details/collectionyearl00hebegoog (accessed 16 June 2017)

Powers, N, 2006 Archaeological evidence for dental innovation: an eighteenth-century porcelain dental prosthesis belonging to Archbishop Arthur Richard Dillon, *Brit Dental J*, **201**, 459–63

Powers, N, & Miles, A, 2011 Nonconformist identities in 19th-century London: archaeological and osteological evidence from the burial grounds of Bow Baptist Church and the Catholic Mission of St Mary and St Michael, Tower Hamlets, in *The archaeology of post-medieval religion* (eds C King & D Sayer), 233–48

Prasad, B, Kejriwal, G, & Sahu, S, 2008 Case report: nasopharyngeal tuberculosis, *Indian J Radiology and Imaging*, **18**(1), 63–5

Pringle, S, 2014 The ceramic building material, in A post-excavation assessment and project design for Queen's Chapel of the Savoy, Savoy Street, City of Westminster, London, unpub ASE rep, **2014/259**

Probert, R, 2009 *Marriage law and practice in the long eighteenth century: a reassessment*

Proceedings of the Old Bailey, https://www.oldbaileyonline.org (accessed 16 June 2017)

Queen's Chapel of the Savoy, nd http://royalchapelsavoy org/who-we-are/; http://royalchapelsavoy org/history/renovations/ (accessed 16 June 2017)

Raemen, E, 2010 The clay tobacco pipe, in Clarke, C, The excavation of a Romano-British trackway and a post-medieval tannery at Spa Road, Bermondsey, unpub AOC Archaeology rep

Rappaport, S, 2002 *Worlds within worlds: structures of life in sixteenth-century London*

Raymond, S, 2014 *Tracing your ancestors' parish records: a guide for family and local historians*

Reid, S, 2002 *Redcoat officer: 1740–1815*

Reid, S, 2016 *The flintlock musket: Brown Bess and Charleville, 1715–1865*

Reid, S, & Hook, R, 1996 *British redcoat: 1740–1793*

Reitsema, L J, 2013 Beyond diet reconstruction: stable isotope applications to human physiology, health, and nutrition, *American J Hum Biol*, **25**(4), 445–56

Relationships: the law of marriage, nd http://www.parliament.uk/about/living-heritage/transformingsociety/private-lives/relationships/overview/lawofmarriage-/ (accessed 16 June 2017)

Resnick, D, Shapiro, R, Wiesner, K, Niwayama, G, Utsinger, P, & Shaul, S, 1978 Diffuse idiopathic skeletal hyperostosis (DISH) [ankylosing hyperostosis of Forestier and Rotes-Querol], *Seminars in Arthritis and Rheumatism*, **7**(3), 153–87

Richards, M, 2006 Palaeodietary reconstruction, in *St Martin's uncovered: investigations in the churchyard of St Martin's-in-the-Bull Ring, Birmingham, 2001* (eds M Brickley, S Buteaux, J Adams & R Cherrington), 147–151

Richardson, J, 2000 *The annals of London: a year-by-year record of a thousand years of history*

Rideal, R, 2016 *1666: plague, war and hellfire*

Roberts, C, & Cox, M, 2003 *Health and disease in Britain: from prehistory to the present day*

Roberts, C, & Manchester, K, 2005 *The archaeology of disease*

Rogers, J, & Waldron, T, 1995 *A field guide to joint disease in archaeology*

Ross, A H, 1995 Caliber estimation from cranial entrance defect measurements, Master's thesis, Univ Tennessee, http://trace.tennessee.edu/cgi/viewcontent.cgi?article=5598&context=utk_gradthes (accessed 7 July 2017)

Ross, S M, 2014 *Introduction to probability and statistics for engineers and scientists*

Rossignol, M, Leclerc, A, Allaert, F, Rozenberg, S, Valat, J, Avouac, B, Coste, P, Litvak, E, & Hilliquin, P, 2005 Primary osteoarthritis of hip, knee, and hand in relation to occupational exposure, *Occupational and Environmental Medicine*, **62**, 772–7

Rudy's List, nd A glossary of archaic medical terms, diseases and causes of death, http://www.archaicmedicalterms.com (accessed 19 June 2017)

Russell, M, 2014 *East End at war and peace*

Samuel, M, 2015 Architectural stone, in Archaeology South-East, A post-excavation assessment and project design for Queen's Chapel of the Savoy, Savoy Street, City of Westminster, London, unpub ASE rep, **2014259**

Sanders, R, Sanders, C, & Sanders Van der Heide, P, 2007 *Generations: a thousand-year family history*, [Philadelphia, Pa]

Scheuer, L, & Black, S, 2000 *Developmental juvenile osteology*

Scheuer, L, & Black, S, 2004 *The juvenile skeleton*

Scheuer, L, Musgrave, J, & Evans, E, 1980 The estimation of late fetal and perinatal age from limb bone length by linear and logarithmic regression, *Annals Hum Biol*, **7**, 257–65

Schwarcz, H P, & Schoeninger, M J, 2011 Stable isotopes of carbon and nitrogen as tracers for paleo-diet reconstruction, in *Handbook of environmental isotope geochemistry: Vol I* (ed M Baskaran), 725–42

Science Museum, nd a Ambroise Paré (1510–90), http://www.sciencemuseum.org.uk/broughttolife/people/ambroisepare (accessed 19 June 2017)

Science Museum, nd b Paracelsus (1493–1541), http://www.sciencemuseum.org.uk/broughttolife/people/paracelsus (accessed 19 June 2017)

Scott, S, & Duncan, C J, 2010 *Biology of plagues: evidence from historical populations*

Sharpe, K, 2000 *Remapping early modern England: the culture of seventeenth-century politics*

Siena, K P, 2004 *Venereal disease, hospitals, and the urban poor: London's 'foul wards,' 1600–1800*, Rochester, NY

Shoemaker, R, 2007 *The London mob: violence and disorder in eighteenth-century England*

Solomon, L, Ganz, R, Leunig, M, Monsell, F, & Learmonth, I, 2010 The hip, in *Apley's system of orthopaedics and fractures* (eds L Solomon, D Warwick & S Nayagam), 493–545

Somerville, R, 1960 *The Savoy: manor, hospital, chapel*

Spencer, R, 2009 Stable isotope analysis of DISH and diet, in *Food and drink in archaeology 2* (eds S Baker, A Gray, K Lakin, R Madgwick, K Poole & M Sandias), 90–9

Stewart, D, 1950 Some early military hospitals, *J Soc Army Historical*

Research, **28**, 174–9
Stewart, T, 1979 *Essentials of forensic anthropology: especially as developed in the United States*, Springfield, Ill
Stow, J, 1598 *A survey of the cities of London and Westminster*
Sugg, R, 2011, *Mummies, cannibals and vampires: the history of corpse medicine from the Rennaisance to the Victorians*
Swift, C, 2014 *Hospital chaplaincy in the twenty-first century: the crisis of spiritual care on the NHS*, 2nd edn
Tatchell, M, 1961 The accounts for the hospital of the Savoy for the year 17 to 18 Henry VIII, *Trans London Middlesex Archaeol Soc*, **20**(4), 151–9
The Twickenham Museum, nd Sir William Killigrew: courtier and playright 1606–1695, http://www.twickenham-museum.org.uk/detail.php?aid=301&cid=9&ctid=1 (accessed 19 June 2017)
Thomas, A J, 2015 *Cholera: the Victorian plague*
Thomas, R L, 1907 *The eclectic practice of medicine*, Cincinnati, Ohio
Thompson, A H, Wilson, A S, & Ehleringer, J R, 2014 Hair as a geochemical recorder: ancient to modern, in *Treatise on geochemistry*, 2nd edn (ed T E Cerling), 371–92, New York
Thornber, C, 2013 Glossary of medical terms used in the 18th and 19th centuries, http://thornber.net/medicine/html/medgloss.html
Topliss, G, nd 1745 Association: a day out in London 11 July 2007, http://www.1745association.org.uk/a_day_out_in_london.htm
Toulalan, S, 2013 Child sexual abuse in late seventeenth- and eighteenth-century London: rape, sexual assault and the denial of agency, in Goose, N, & Honeyman, K, *Childhood and child labour in industrial England: diversity and agency, 1750–1914*, 23–44
Trickett, M A, 2006 A tale of two cities: diet, health and migration in post-medieval Coventry and Chelsea through biographical reconstruction, osteoarchaeology and isotope biochemistry, unpub PhD thesis, Univ Durham
Trujillo-Mederos, A, Arnay-de-la-rosa, M, González-Reimers, E, & Ordóñez, A, 2014 Hallux valgus among an 18th-century population of the Canary Islands, *Int J Osteoarchaeol*, **24**, 590–601
Trumbach, R, 1999, London, in *Queer sites: gay urban histories since 1600* (ed D Higgs), 89–111
Tsutaya, T, & Yoneda, M, 2013 Quantitative reconstruction of weaning ages in archaeological human populations using bone collagen nitrogen isotope ratios and approximate Bayesian computation, *PloS One*, **8**(8), e72327
Tsutaya, T, & Yoneda, M, 2015 Reconstruction of breastfeeding and weaning practices using stable isotope and trace element analyses: a review, *American J Physical Anthropol*, **156**, Suppl 59, 2–21
Tyson, R, 2000 *Medieval glass vessels found in England c AD 1200–1500*, CBA Res Rep, **121**
Ubelaker, D, 1989 *Human skeletal remains*, 2nd edn, Washington, DC
UK Public General Acts, nd Burial Act 1853, http://www.legislation.gov.uk/ukpga/1853/134/pdfs/ukpga_18530134_en.pdf (accessed 7 July 2017)
Urban, S (ed), 1749 Ventilators in use, *The Gentleman's Magazine*, **19**, 282, https://babel.hathitrust.org/cgi/pt?id=inu.30000080774049;view=1up;seq=317 (accessed 19 June 2017)
Vincent, N, 2008 Savoy, Peter of, count of Savoy and de facto earl of Richmond (1203?–1268), in *Oxford dictionary of national biography* (eds H C G Matthews & B Harrison), online edn (ed D Cannadine), http://www.oxforddnb.com/view/article/22016 (accessed 19 June 2017)
Wadd, W, 1827 *Mems. Maxims, and Memoirs*
Waldron, T, 2007 *Palaeoepidemiology: the measure of disease in the human past*, Walnut Creek, Calif
Walker, G A, 1839 *Gatherings from grave yards; particularly those of London*
Ward, R M, 2014 *Print culture, crime and justice in 18th-century London*
Ward Lock & Co, 1924 *Illustrated guide books: London*
Wattanasirichaigoon, D, Prasad, C, Schneider, G, Evans, J, & Korf, B, 2003 Rib defects in patterns of multiple malformations: a retrospective review and phenotypic analysis of 47 cases, *American J Medical Genetics*, **122A**, 63–9

Webb, S, 2011 *Execution: a history of capital punishment in Britain*
Webster, C, 2002 *The great instauration: science, medicine and reform, 1626–1660*, 2nd edn, Studies in the History of Medicine, **3**, Berne
Webster, R, 2008 *The encyclopaedia of superstitions*, St Paul, Minn
Weinreb, B, Hibbert, C, Keay, J, & Keay, J, 2008 *The London encyclopaedia*
Whaites, E, & Drage, N, 2013 *Essentials of dental radiography and radiology*, 5th edn
White, J, 2012 *London in the eighteenth century: a great and monstrous thing*
Willetts, J, 2003–17 Free settler or felon: 19th century medical terms, http://www.jenwilletts.com/19thCenturyMedical.htm (accessed 21 June 2017)
Willmott, H, 2002 *Early post-medieval vessel glass in England, c 1500–1670*, CBA Res Rep, **132**
Willmott, R A, 1839 *Lives of the English sacred poets: Vol 1*, 2nd edn
Wilson, A S, 2008 The decomposition of hair in the buried environment, in *Soil analysis in forensic taphonomy: chemical and biological effects of buried human remains* (eds M Tibbett & D O Carter), 123–140, Boca Raton, Fla
Wilson, A S, Taylor, T, Ceruti, M C, Chavez, J A, Reinhard, J, Grimes, V, Meier-Augenstein, W, Cartmell, L, Stern, B, Richards, M P, Worobey, M, Barnes, I, & Gilbert, M T, 2007 Stable isotope and DNA evidence for ritual sequences in Inca child sacrifice, *Proc Nat Acad Sci USA*, **104**(42), 16456–61
Wood, J, Milner, G, Harpending, H, & Weiss, K, 1992 The osteological paradox: problems of inferring health from skeletal samples, *Current Anthropol*, **33**(4), 343–70
Woodward, G, 2015 A guide to church burials, http://www.gwoodward.co.uk/guides/burials.htm (accessed 21 June 2017)
Wrigley, E A, & Schofield, R S, 2002 *The population history of England 1541–1871: a reconstruction*
Yavuz, M, Aras, M, Büyükkurt, M, & Tozoglu, S, 2007 Impacted mandibular canines, *J Contemporary Dental Practice*, **8**(7), 78–85

INDEX

1930s survey, 3, 194
    excavation plan, comparison with, 150–51, *151ill*, 152-55, *152tab–53tab, 154ill*
        named individuals, identification of, 152–55, *152tab–53tab, 154ill*
    plan of, 148, 149

A

Agas, Ralph (The Strand, London, map of (1560), *6ill*
Anatomy Act (1832), 132
archaeological results
    1930s survey, comparison with, 150–51, *151ill*, 152–55, *152tab–53tab, 154ill*
    adult burials, plan of, *143ill*
    burial goods, 169-72
        combs and buckles, 171–72, *172ill*
        dress accessories, 170–72, *171ill, 172ill*
        shrouds and shroud pins, 170, *170ill*
        textiles, samples of, 170, *171tab*
    burial phases, 139, *141ill*, 142
        burial density, 139, 142–43
        and dating, 142
        disturbed or truncated burials, 139, *142ill, 143ill*
        reuse of burial ground, 139
    burial practices, 177
    burial-related finds, 160–68
        burial goods, 169–72, *169ill, 171ill, 171tab, 172ill*
        coffin furniture, 139, 156–57, *157ill*, 160–62
        lead coffins, *163ill*, 164
        upholstery nails, 163–64, *164ill*
        wooden and lead coffins, *163ill, 165ill*
        wooden coffins, 162–63, *162ill, 163ill*
    charnel pits/deposits, 160, *161ill*
    coffin furniture, 160–62
        as dating evidence, 139
        grips and grip plates, 166–68, *166ill, 167ill*
        nameplates (breastplates), 156–57, *157ill*, 165, *166ill*
    cranial variation and ancestry, 158
    excavation area, 139, *141ill*
    family group burials, 158–60, *159ill*
        Guy, Francis and Jane, 158
        White, Henry and Susannah, 158
    insects, 168–69
        Greenfield, William, comparison with burial of, 168–69
        Magistrates' Court site (Hull), comparison with, 169
        samples, and details of, 168, *168tab*
    introduction to, 139
    in situ investigations of burials, 139
    memorials and associated dates, *144ill*, 145
        and chronological development of burial ground, 145
        grave markers, use of, 145
    named individuals, identification of, 150–55
        1930s survey, comparison with, 152–55, *152tab–153tab, 154ill*

osteological analysis, comparison with, *154ill*
non-burial features, 172–76, *173ill*
    box-drain, 173, *173ill*
    paths, brick, 174–75, *174ill*, 177
    walls and sandstone blocks, 175–76, *175ill*
sex distribution of graves, 145, *145tab*
skeletons, position of, 139, *140ill*
spatial analysis, 139–45
    burial depths, 142–43, 145, *145tab*
    burial patterns, 142
    and topography of site, impact of, 145
subadult burials, plan of, *143ill*
tombs and memorial stones, 147–50, *147ill, 148ill* [107], 147, *148ill*
    Finlay, Ann Elizabeth, memorial of, 149, *149ill*
    fragments from, 149
    Lander, Richard, memorial of, *149ill*, 150
    stone used and origin of, 149
architectural stone finds, 179–81, *179ill, 180ill–81ill, 180tab*, 192
    bath mouldings (?), 181
    coade architrave stone (?), 181, *181ill*
    coping stone (Group 2 & 3), 180–81, *180ill–81ill*
    jamb stones (Group 1), 180, *180ill*
    string-course moulding stone (Group 4), 181, *181ill*

B

Ball, Fiona, 128
Bills of Mortality (London), 16-17, *16tab, 17ill*, 49
    age of death, figures for, 54
    cancer, deaths from, 127
    deaths recorded (1657-1758), *16tab*
    dental disease, as cause of death, 110
    infant mortality rates, 69
    record of diseases, 109
Bittleston, John
    burial of, *141ill*
        historical records associated with, 156
    death of, 164
    lead coffin, use of, 142–43, 156, 164–65
Bond, Kirk, 26
Bradford Royal Infirmary, 106
Bradley, William, 26
Bridewell Prison and Hospital, 23
Buckmaster family, grave of, 157
burial registers (Savoy Chapel), 17, 33, 35, 194
    burial records
        Cameron, Dr Archibald (of Lochiel), 43
        causes of death, 57–61, *57tab–58tab, 60tab, 61tab*, 177
        Clifton, Thomas, 59
        death and burial, time delay between, 61–65, *62tab–64tab*
        Guy, Francis and Jane, 158
        Harabin, Richard, 49
        Kelly, Eleanor, 158
        Killigrew, Anne, 43
        McCoy, Adam, 33
        military personnel, 50–51, 53–54, 57, *57tab*
        population, and place of residency, 65–66, *65tab, 66ill*
        women and 'childbed' deaths, 158
    burials per decade
        adults and soldiers, *55tab, 57tab*
        analysis of, 54–56
        infants, children and subadults, *56tab*
    causes of death, 57–61
        cancer, 155–56
        consumption, 59–60, *60tab*
        convulsions, 60–61, *61tab*
        fever, 60, *60tab*
        gout, 156
        medical terms used, *58tab*, 59
        military personnel, 58–59, *58tab*
        smallpox, 61, *61tab*
        suicide, and view of, 59
    census data, 52, *52tab*
    data analysis, 50–51
        deaths per decade, *50tab, 51tab*
        sex distribution of deaths, *51ill, 51tab*
        total number of deaths, 50
    death rates, analysis of, 52–54
        age of death, 54–56, *54ill, 55tab*
        military personnel, 50–51, 53–54
        peak decades (1740s and 1790s), 50, *51tab*, 52
        prison conditions, improvements in, 53
    information recorded in, 49–50, *49tab*
    jail fever, as cause of death, 177
    named individuals, identification of, 155

C

Cameron, Dr Archibald (of Lochiel)
    background and family of, 43–44
    Culloden, role in, 43
    execution of, 43, *44ill*
    memorial to, 43–44
    Queen's Chapel, buried at burial ground of, 40
Carden, George Frederick, 12
    General Cemetery Company, establishment of, 12–13
cemeteries (London), 12–14
    General Cemetery Company, establishment of, 12–13
    Kensall Green, 13
    overcrowding, 12
    Portugal Street, 13
    suburban cemeteries, proposals for, 12
ceramic building material finds, 185–87
    date ranges by context, *185tab*
    fabrics and forms, *179ill*, 185–87
        brick, 186, *186tab*
        floor tiles, 186
        mortar, 187
        roof tiles, 185
        wall tiles, 186
    summary of, *185tab*
Chelsea Waterworks Company, 7
clay tobacco pipe finds, *179ill*, 187–88, *188ill*
    makers' marks, overview, *187tab*
Clifton, Thomas, 59

Cochran, John, 148
  grave of, 155
  historical records associated with, 155
coin finds, 188–89, *189ill*
  silver dollar, 189, *189ill*
Collins, James, 36, 133, 147
Committee for Maimed Soldiers, 23, 29
Croll, Oswald, 27
Cruikshank, George, *10ill*

D
Daily Journal (newspaper), 31
Damsell, Robert, 35, 136
Davenport, Thomas, 36, 110, 133
Dickens, Charles
  All Year Round; A weekly Journal (Vol.III), 1860, v, 196
  Savoy Precinct, view of, 15–16
diseases, outbreaks of
  dental, 110-19, *110tab, 112tab*
  infectious diseases, 99–110
    cholera, 8
    plague, 6-7, *16tab*
    prison outbreaks and typhus, 37
    syphilis, 107-10, *108ill*, *110tab*
    tuberculosis, 105–07, *105ill, 106tab*
Duty, Maj.Gen. Alexander, 33

E
Ely House hospital, 24
  prosthetics, use of, 26
  spa treatments for patients at, 26
  state papers of, 28
Evelyn, Sir John, *25ill*
  Great Fire of London (1666), reports on, 7
  London, rebuilding plans for, 7, *8ill*, 12
  overcrowded cemeteries, concerns of, 12
  Savoy military hospital, request to reopen, 24

F
Finlay, Ann Elizabeth
  memorial stone of, 149, *149ill*
    and possible burial location, 152–55
Fleetwood, William, 22, 23
French, John (MD), 132
  Art of Distillation, The, 27, *27ill*
  Paracelsian physician, and beliefs of, 26–27
  surgical practices of, 26

G
Gin Shop, The (Cruikshank, G.)
glass finds, *179ill*, 191–92
  vessels, 191
  window panes, 191
Graunt, John, 109
graveyard soil finds, *179ill*, 190–91, *190ill, 191ill*
  ceramic marbles, 191
  dagger chape, 190, *190ill*, 192
  lead weight, 190, *191ill*
  thimble (17th C), 190, *190ill*
  wig curlers, 191, *191ill*
Great Britain Historical GIS Project, 14, 52
Greenfield, William, 168–69
Greville, Charles, 8
Guy's Hospital Dental Radiology Department, 128

H
Hales, Charles, 109
  medical career of, 28
  Savoy Hospital, surgeon at, 28
Hales, Stephen, 37, *37ill*, 53
  Savoy Prison, ventilation system, 37–38, *38ill*
Harabin, Richard, 49
Harvey, Gideon, 27
Hearth Tax records (Duchy of Lancaster/Savoy ward), 14–16, *15ill*
Henry VIII, King
  Savoy Hospital, proposal for, 19
  funding of, 22
Hinton, Anne
  coffin nameplate of, 156, *157ill*, 164
  lead coffin, burial in, 164–65
Holgill, William, 19, 22
Howard, John
  Howard's Report (1777), 39
  Savoy Prison, 37, 39, *39tab*
  prisons survey, 39
human remains
  bone collagen, isotopic analysis on, 71–72, *72tab*
  bone fractures, 74–75, *74tab*
    hands and feet, 77–79, *78tab, 79ill, 79tab*
    long-bones, 76–77, *76ill, 76tab, 78ill*
    multiple fractures and other locations, 79–80, *79ill*
    perimortem fractures, 80
    ribs, 75–76, *76tab*
    skull, 75, *75ill, 75tab*
  circulatory disease, 124–27
    Legg-Calvé-Perthes disease, 126, *126ill*
    osteochondritis dissecans, 126–27, *127tab*
    slipped femoral epiphysis, 126
  congenital anomalies, 91–98, *92tab*
    of the skull, 91–92
  cultural modification, 130–32
    corsetry evidence, 130–31, *131ill*
    restricted footwear evidence, 131–32, *132ill*
  demographic profile, 67
    age-at-death estimations, 67–69, *69tab*
    population distribution, comparison with, 69, *69tab*
    sex estimations, 70, *70tab*
    stature estimations, 70–71, *70tab, 71ill, 71tab*
  dental congenital anomalies, 118–19, *119tab*
    agenesis, 118–19
    fused teeth, 119
    peg-shaped teeth, 119
    retained teeth, 119
    rotated teeth, 119
  dental disease, 110–19, *110tab, 112tab*
    adult population, *113tab*
    ante-mortem tooth loss, 114–15, *115tab*
    calculus, 112
    caries, 116–17
    dental enamel hypoplasia, 115–16, *116tab*
    London area, comparative records for, 115–16, *115tab, 116tab*, 117
    periapical lesions (abscess), 117
    periodontal disease, 112–14
    sexes, comparisons between, 117
    subadult population, *114tab*
  dental trauma, 117–19, *117tab*
    clay-pipe use, 117, *117tab*
  disarticulated material, 67
  elongated styloid process, 130
  hair, isotopic analysis on, 72–73, *73tab*
    sample from skeleton [1716], 73, *73ill*
  infectious diseases, 99–110
    endocranial lesions, 103, *103ill*
    mastoiditis, 103
    maxillary sinusitis, 101–02, *101ill*
    non-specific infection, 100–04
    osteomyelitis, 103–04, *104ill*
    periostitis, 100, *100tab*
    rib lesions, 100–01, *101ill*
    skin ulcers, 102–03, *102ill*
    specific infection, 104–10
    syphilis, 107–10, *108ill, 110tab, 111ill*
    tuberculosis, 105–07, *105ill, 106tab*
  inferior turbinate hypertrophy, 130, *131ill*
  introduction to finds, 67
    comparative sites, 67, 70–71, *71ill, 71tab*
  joint diseases, 88–91
    ankylosis, 90
    extra-spinal joint disease, 89–90, *89tab*
    gout, 90
    osteoarthritis, 88
    rheumatoid arthritis, 90–91, *91ill*
    spinal joint disease, 88–89, *88ill, 88tab*
  location of skeletons, *68ill*
  London area (comparative records for)
    cancer, deaths from, 127
    corsetry evidence, 130–31
    dental disease and trauma, 115–16, *115tab, 116tab*, 117
    post-mortems and surgical interventions, evidence for, 136, *137tab*
    restricted footwear evidence, 132
    rickets, *122tab*
    scurvy, 123, *123ill, 123tab*
    smoking and clay-pipe use, *118tab*
    syphilis, 109–10, *110tab*
    tuberculosis, 106–07, *106tab*
  lower limbs, congenital anomalies, 96–98
    bipartite patella, 97
    coxa valga, 97
    os calcaneus, 97
    os cuneiform, 98, *99ill*
    os navicular, 98, *99ill*
    os trigonum, 97, *98ill*
    os vesalianum, 98
    tibiofibular synostosis, 97, *98ill*
  metabolic disease, 119–24
    cribra orbitalia, 120, *120tab*
    diffuse idiopathic skeletal hyperostosis, 123–24, *125ill, 125tab*
    osteoporosis, 123
    porotic hyperostosis, 120
    rickets, 120–22, *121ill, 121tab, 122ill, 122tab*
    scurvy, 122–23, *123ill, 123tab*
  neoplastic conditions, 127–29
    button osteoma (benign), 128
    multiple myeloma (malignant), 128–29, *128ill, 129ill*
    unifocal eosinophilic granuloma (benign), 128
  osteological analysis, 67
  palaeopathology, 73–74
    pathology quantification, 73–74, *74tab*
  pelvic girdle, congenital anomalies, 95
    congenital dislocation of the hip, 95, *96ill*
    sacroiliac coalition, 95
  post-mortems and surgical interventions,